Development, Democracy, and Welfare States

Development, Democracy and Welfare States

LATIN AMERICA, EAST ASIA, AND EASTERN EUROPE

Stephan Haggard
and Robert R. Kaufman

PRINCETON UNIVERSITY PRESS
PRINCETON AND OXFORD

Copyright © 2008 by Princeton University Press
Published by Princeton University Press, 41 William Street,
Princeton, New Jersey 08540
In the United Kingdom: Princeton University Press, 6 Oxford Street,
Woodstock, Oxfordshire OX20 1TW

Library of Congress Cataloging-in-Publication Data

Haggard, Stephan.
Development, democracy, and welfare states: Latin America, East
Asia, and Eastern Europe / Stephan Haggard and Robert R. Kaufman.
p.   cm.

Includes bibliographical references.
ISBN 978-0-691-13595-3 (hardcover: alk. Paper)
ISBN 978-0-691-13596-0 (pbk.: alk. Paper)
1. Welfare state—Latin America. 2. Welfare state—East Asia.
3. Welfare state—Europe, Eastern. I. Kaufman, Robert R. II. Title.
HN110.5.A8H33 2008   2007051791
330.12′6–dc22

British Library Cataloging-in-Publication Data is available

This book has been composed in Sabon

Printed on acid-free paper. ∞

press.princeton.edu

Printed in the United States of America

10 9 8 7 6 5 4 3 2

To Max Haggard, Noah Kaufman Brown,
and Leo Kaufman Brown

To allow the market mechanism to be the sole director of the fate of human beings and their natural environment . . . would result in the destruction of society. For the alleged commodity "labor power" cannot be shoved about, used indiscriminately, or even left unused, without affecting also the human individual who happens to be the bearer of this particular commodity.

—Karl Polanyi, *The Great Transformation*

Contents

Figures

Tables

Preface and Acknowledgments

The origins of this book go back to conversations we had in 2001 about the divergent nature of welfare systems in the developing world. These conversations were a natural outgrowth of our preoccupation with differences in the long-run political and economic development of Latin America and East Asia. Comparisons within and across these regions had motivated our separate and joint research on the political economy of growth, on the debt and financial crises of the 1980s and 1990s, and on democratization and economic reform. *The Political Economy of Democratic Transitions* (Princeton University Press, 1995) brought a number of these interests together.

The concerns that motivated this book followed logically from the earlier work. Like many others in the academic and policy community, we were both interested in and concerned about the social consequences of crises and economic reform. Having already explored how democratic transitions affected market reforms, it was a logical, if challenging, step to consider the effects of democratization and economic change on the nature of the social contract in the middle-income developing and former socialist countries. This effort also provided us an opportunity to extend the rich literature on the advanced welfare states into new contexts.

As in *The Political Economy of Democratic Transitions*, our initial intent was to focus primarily on the effects of democracy and variations in institutional design. Yet it immediately became apparent to us that neither regime type nor more fine-grained variations in institutions had straightforward effects on welfare-policy choices. For a number of reasons, the project proved to be considerably more complicated than we had originally thought.

First, social protections and services did not scale easily along a single dimension of "expansion versus retrenchment" or "neoliberal versus solidaristic." Nor were differences easily captured by a focus on spending or even on welfare outcomes. As the varieties of capitalism literature had underscored, the logic of policy choice in one area, such as social security, could not be separated easily from others, such as those affecting labor markets. Following the work of Gøsta Esping-Andersen, we came to see that welfare systems had to be considered as complexes of complementary policies that were most usefully viewed in their entirety. This complexity made it difficult, if not impossible, to frame hypotheses about the effects of regime type or political institutions in a linear way.

A related, and even more important, realization was that the focus on institutions was limiting. Contemporary political economy has come to view representative institutions as mechanisms for aggregating preferences; without an understanding of those interests, any institutional explanation is partial at best, misleading at worst. This recognition drove us in two complementary directions. First, we began to focus, as we did in *The Political Economy of Democratic Transitions*, on the economic determinants of public-policy choice. Growth and crises influenced the politics of welfare reform in important ways. We were also attracted to insights from the varieties of capitalism literature that emphasized the diversity in economic institutions. Different development models appeared to be associated with very different welfare-policy choices.

In thinking through how interests affected policy choice, we naturally gravitated toward models that had served well in understanding the advanced welfare state. How was the urban working class organized and represented? And in our cases, what role did the countryside play? These insights figure in our work, particularly with respect to our treatment of the origins of social policy. But we found that an attempt to reason a priori about the social-policy interests of different groups was problematic and that the reform of welfare commitments was heavily conditioned by prior policies. Democracies in Eastern Europe and Latin America, for example, faced similar social challenges stemming from economic crisis and the dislocations of market reform. But differences in social-policy legacies led to quite different policy approaches to these challenges.

In short, history mattered. What we had initially intended as a background chapter on the early development of social policy in the three regions grew to occupy nearly half the book. We believe the analysis of the effects of critical political realignments, development models, and political regimes on the origins of social policy is not only important for understanding contemporary efforts to recraft social contracts, but sheds light on a number of theoretical and empirical debates in the welfare-state literature as well.

Many people assisted us in various ways, but we should start with some collaborators who played particularly influential roles. We had the great good fortune of gaining our introduction to the political economy of Eastern Europe—an area of the world in which we trespass from our regional bases—from János Kornai. Professor Kornai convened a study group on the political economy of the transition at the Collegium Budapest in 1997-98 which brought together a number of other scholars from the region. The results of this collaboration were published as *Reforming the State: Fiscal and Welfare Reform in Post-Socialist Countries* (Cambridge University Press, 2000). This project not only introduced us to Eastern Europe, but focused our attention on the dilemmas associated with reforming social policy in particular. Matthew Shugart collaborated with us on our contribution to that volume on Hungarian fiscal and social policy; other contributors included Vladimir Gimpelson, Vito Tanzi, Bela Greskovits, Assar Lindbeck, Jerzy Hausner, and Joan M. Nelson. A subsequent invitation from Professor Kornai to return to the Collegium in the summer of 2005 permitted us to pursue our research in greater depth and provided introductions throughout the region that proved invaluable.

Haggard first began to explore contemporary social policy issues in East Asia in the course of writing *The Political Economy of the Asian Financial Crisis* (Institute for International Economics, 2000); Fred Bergsten is owed a particular debt of gratitude for encouraging that effort and orchestrating one of the Institute's demanding review sessions. Nancy Birdsall, a particularly astute observer of social policy issues, coauthored the chapter in that book on the social consequences of the crisis, later published in revised form as "After the Crisis: The Social Contract and the Middle Class in East Asia," in Ethan Kapstein and Branko Milanovic, eds., *When Markets Fail: Social Policy and Economic Reform* (Russell Sage Foundation, 2003).

In his contributions to the chapters on Latin America, Kaufman drew heavily on his collaboration with Joan M. Nelson in coediting *Crucial Needs, Weak Incentives: Social Sector Reform, Democratization, and Globalization in Latin America* (Woodrow Wilson Center Press and Johns Hopkins University Press, 2004), funded through the Latin American Program of the Woodrow Wilson Center for Scholars. The case-study chapters in that volume provided much of the foundation for the discussion of the contemporary politics of health and education reform in chapter 7. We are thankful to the authors of these chapters: Marta Arretche, Josefina Bruni Celli, Mary Clark, Javier Corrales, Sonia Draibe, Christina Ewig, Alec Ian Gershberg, Merilee S. Grindle, Alejandra González Rossetti, Peter Lloyd-Sherlock, Pamela S. Lowden, and Patricia Ramirez.

Collaborations between Haggard and Nita Rudra and Kaufman and Alex Segura-Ubiergo, published in *Comparative Political Studies* and *World Politics* respectively, introduced us to the complexities and frustrations of econometric work using social-spending data. Segura-Ubiergo has been a continuing source of assistance with data and technical advice.

Haggard also gained important insights into European social-policy debates through collaboration with Bob Deacon on a course on globalization and social policy.

A number of other people have been particularly generous with their time, commenting on large parts of the manuscript, sharing their own work, and providing us with leads of various sorts. Eric Wibbels and an anonymous reader for Princeton University Press offered particularly challenging and pointed criticisms. We also received extremely helpful comments and criticisms from Sarah Brooks, Javier Corrales, Linda Cook, Richard Feinberg, Tim Frye, Eduardo J. Gomez, Bela Greskovits, Evelyne Huber, Ethan Kapstein, Christine Lipsmeyer, Linda Low, Raul Madrid, Scott Mainwaring, Maria Victoria Murillo, Joan M. Nelson, Mitchell Orenstein, Michael Penfold-Becerra, Yves Tiberghien, Kurt Weyland, and Joseph Wong.

In addition to these people, a number of others have read particular chapters or provided assistance of various sorts. Our thanks go to Valerie Bunce, Rossana Castiglioni, Tun-jen Cheng, Jinhee Choung, Bill Clark, Noel de Dios, Rick Doner, Peter Egger, Christina Ewig, Rob Franzese, Peter Gourevitch, Allen Hicken, Paul Hutchcroft, Elena Iankova, Yuko Kasuya, Byung-kook Kim, Pil-Ho Kim, Wonik Kim, Vanya Kriekhaus, Yuen-wen Ku, Jan Kubik, Joohee Lee, Christine Lipsmeyer, Andrew MacIntyre, Isabela Mares, Jim McGuire, Claudia Maldonado, Amado "Bong" Mendoza, Gabriella Montinola, Woojin Moon, Katharina Müller, Ito Peng, Mike Pisa, Jonas Pontusson, Grigore Pop-Eleches, Kazimierz Poznanski, M. Ramesh, John Ravenhill, Bryan K. Ritchie, Kenneth Roberts, Richard Robison, Jon Rodden, Peter Rosendorff, Herman Schwartz, Dorotty Szikra, Dorothy Solinger, Orville Solon, Hokeun Song, David Soskice, Barbara Stallings, Bela Tomka, Tatiana Tomova, Peter Warr, Carol Wise, and Jae-jin Yang.

Research is not free, and we received support from a number of quarters. This work was supported by a generous grant from the National Science Foundation (Grant No. 0351439). The Chiang Ching-Kuo Foundation and Korea University supported a conference in September 2005 that brought together a number of people with an interest in varieties of capitalism in Asia. Haggard owes a particular debt to Lawrence and Sallye Krause. The endowed chair he holds in their name generously supported research and travel in connection with this project. Kaufman acknowledges institutional assistance from Instituto de Estudios Superiores de Administración (IESA), in Caracas Venezuela, arranged through Michael Penfold-Becerra, and at the Economic Commission on Latin America and the Caribbean (ECLAC) in Santiago, Chile, made available by Martin Hopenhayn.

We received tremendous research assistance on this project. We are particularly indebted to Barak Hoffman, and the extraordinary patience he showed for our endless questions and iterations; Barak was less like an RA and more like a tutor. We would also like to thank Jennifer Barret, Svetoslav Braykova, Jing Chen, Giselle Datz, Tanya Lloyd, WooChang Kang, Yeon Kyeong Kim, Renate Muenich, Noelia Paez, Michael Sitek, and Patricia Young.

Publication of preliminary versions of the book allowed us to test arguments. Haggard published reflections on East Asian social policy as "The

Political Economy of the Asian Welfare State," in Richard Boyd and Tak-win Ngo, eds., *Asian States: Beyond the Developmental Perspective* (Routledge, 2005), and "Globalization, Democracy and the Evolution of Social Contracts in East Asia," *Taiwan Journal of Democracy*, 1, 1 (2005). Kaufman published work related to Chapter Eight as "Market Reform and Social Protection: Lessons from the Czech Republic, Hungary, and Poland" in *East European Society and Politics*, 21, 1 (February 2007). Finally, Haggard and Kaufman published early versions of the statistical research in chapter 5 in "Revising Social Contracts: Social Spending in Latin America, East Asia, and the Former Socialist Countries, 1980–2000," *Revista de Politica*, 24, 1 (2004).

We have presented variants of this work at more American Political Science Association and International Studies Association conferences than we would care to admit. We are particularly thankful to colleagues who issued invitations for us to speak before engaged audiences of faculty and graduate students. These include Sarah Brooks at Ohio State University; Linda Cook at Brown University; Yun-han Chu at Taiwan National University; Anna Grzymala-Busse and Grzegorz Ekiert at the European Studies Center, Harvard; Yuen-wen Ku at National Chi Nan University; Andrew MacIntyre at Australian National University; Scott Mainwaring at the Kellogg Center at Notre Dame; Edward Mansfield at the University of Pennsylvania; Andrew Moravcsik at the Woodrow Wilson School, Princeton University; Maria Victoria Murillo at Columbia University; Ken Roberts at Cornell University; Richard Robison at the Institute of Social Studies, the Hague; Etel Solingen at the University of California, Irvine; Hokeun Song and Hak Pyo at Seoul National University; Carol Wise at the University of Southern California; and Meredith Woo-Cumings and Jim Morrow at the University of Michigan.

At Princeton University Press, we had the good fortune to work again with Chuck Myers. He has provided extraordinary support and encouragement for this project, and we are enormously grateful for his sage editorial judgment and advice.

Our wives, Sharon Crasnow and Laura Schoen, deserve our deepest gratitude for their endurance and support for this long and intense collaboration. We thank them for the good humor and forbearance with which they endured the early-morning phone calls, interrupted weekends, and professional trips. Of course, our debt to them extend very far beyond their support for this project; they both know that we love them, and why.

Despite all this help, we ultimately take responsibility for what follows. More than in our previous work, we are acutely aware of the unfinished nature of this book. Our hope, however, is that it will provide a useful step in moving the literature on the welfare state beyond the developed countries and in outlining an agenda for continuing research.

Our previous book was dedicated to our children, Kit Haggard and Lissa and Matthew Kaufman. Steph's son, Max, was born just after that book came out, and Bob's two grandchildren, Noah Kaufman Brown and Leo Kaufman Brown arrived later. We dedicate this book to the three of them, in the hope that they will grow up in a world more just than the current one.

Abbreviations

AD	Acción Democrática (Democratic Action Party, Venezuela)
ANSAL	Administración Nacional de Seguro de Salud (National Administration for Healthcare, Argentina)
APRA	Alianza Popular Revolucionaria Americana (American Popular Revolutionary Alliance, Peru)
ARENA	Aliança Renovadora Nacional (National Renewal Alliance Party, Brazil)
AWS	Akcja Wyborcza Solidarność (Solidarity Electoral Action, Poland)
BN	Barisan Nasional (Singapore)
CARP	Comprehensive Agrarian Reform Program (the Philippines)
CCSS	Caja Costarricense de Seguro Social (Costa Rican Social Security Fund)
CEDP	Community Agrarian Reform Program (the Philippines)
CIDSS	Comprehensive and Integrated Delivery of Social Services (the Philippines)
CLAS	Comités Locales de Administración en Salud (Local Health Administrative Committees, Peru)
CONTAG	Confederação Nacional dos Trabalhadores na Agriculture (National Confederation of Agricultural Workers, Brazil)
COPEI	Comité de Organización Política Electoral Independiente (Independent Political Electoral Organization Committee, or Social Christian Party, Venezuela)
COPLAMAR	Coordinación General del Plan Nacional de Zonas Deprimidas y Grupos Marginados (General Coordination of the National Plan for Deprived Zones and Marginal Groups, Mexico)
CPF	Central Provident Fund (Singapore)
CUT	Central Única dos Trabalhadores (Unified Labor Confederation, Brazil)
DPP	Democratic Progressive Party (Taiwan)
ECLAC	Economic Commission for Latin America and the Caribbean

EPF	Employment Provident Fund (Malaysia)
ESC	European Social Charter
EU	European Union
FIDESZ	Fidesz-Magyar Polgári Szövetség (Hungarian Civic Union)
FKTU	Federation of Korean Trade Unions (Korea)
FONCODES	Fondo de Cooperación para el Desarrollo Social (Fund for Cooperation for Social Development, Peru)
FOSIS	Fondo de Solidaridad e Inversión Social (Fund for Solidarity and Social Investment, Chile)
FUNDEF	Fundo de Mantenção e Desenvolvimento do Ensino Fundamental (Fund for the Maintenance and Development of Primary Instruction, Brazil)
FUNRURAL	Fundo de Assistência ao Trabalhador Rural (Rural Worker Assistance Fund, Brazil)
GDP	Gross National Product
GHIC	General Health Insurance Corporation (Czech Republic)
GSIS	Government Services Insurance System (the Philippines)
HDB	Housing and Development Board (Singapore)
HIF	Health Insurance Fund (Hungary)
HZDS	Hnutie za demokratické Slovensko (Movement for a Democratic Slovakia)
IFI	International Financial Institution
ILO	International Labor Organisation
IMF	International Monetary Fund
IMSS	Instituto Mexicano del Seguro Social (Mexican Institute of Social Security)
INAMPS	Instituto Nacional de Assistência Social (National Institute for Medical Assistance in Social Insurance, Brazil)
IPSS	Instituto Peruano del Seguro Social (Peruvian Institute of Social Security)
IRC	Interest Reconciliation Council (Poland)
ISAPRE	Instituciones de Salud Previsional (Health Provider Institutions, Chile)
ISI	Import-substitution industrialization
IVSS	Instituto Venezolano de Seguros Social (Venezuelan Institute of Social Security)
JCRR	Sino-American Joint Committee on Rural Reconstruction (Taiwan)
KCTU	Korean Confederation of Trade Unions
KDS	Křest'ansko demokratická strana (Christian Democratic Party, Czech Republic)

KMT	Kuomintang (Naitonalist Party, Taiwan)
LGC	Local Government Code (the Philippines)
LGU	Local Government Unit (the Philippines)
LICS	Low Income Card Scheme (Thailand)
MDF	Magyar Demokrata Fórum (Hungarian Democratic Forum)
NAFTA	North America Free Trade Agreement
NEM	New Economic Mechanism (Hungary)
NEP	New Economic Policy (Malaysia)
NGO	Non-governmental organization
NHIC	National Health Insurance Corporation (Korea)
NMSII	National Movement Simeon II (Bulgaria)
NSF	National Council of the Salvation Front (*Frontul Salvării Naționale,* Romania)
ODS	Občanská demokratická strana (Civic Democratic Party, Czech Republic)
OECD	Organisation for Economic Co-operation and Development
PAN	Partido Acción Nacional (National Action Party, Mexico)
PAP	People's Action Party (Singapore)
PBST	Programa de Salud Básica para Todos (Basic Health for All Program, Peru)
PDVSA	Petróleos de Venezuela S.A
PFL	Partido de Frente Liberal (Liberal Front Party, Brazil)
PIASS	Programa de Interiorização das Ações de Saúde e Saneamento(Program of Health and Hygiene in the Interior, Brazil)
PIT-CNT	Plenario Intersindical de Trabajadores–Convención Nacional de Trabajadores (Intersyndical Plenum of Workers–National Convention of Workers, Uruguay)
PLN	Partido Liberación Nacional (National Liberation Party)
PPP	purchasing power parity
PRD	Partido de la Revolución Democratica (Party of the Democratic Revolution)
PRI	Partido Revolucionario Institucional (Institutional Revolutionary Party, Mexico)
PROGRESA	Programa de Educación, Salud y Alimentación (Program for Education, Health, and Nutrition, Mexico)
PRONASOL	Programa Nacional de Solidaridad (The National Solidarity Program, Mexico)
PSD	Partido Social Democrático (Social Democratic Party, Brazil)

PSDB	Partido da Social Democracia Brasileira (Brazilian Social Democracy Party)
PSDR	Partidul Democrației Sociale din România (Party of Social Democracy in Romania)
PT	Partido dos Trabalhadores (Workers' Party, Brazil)
SNTV	Single nontransferable vote
PTB	Partido Trabalhista Brasileiro (Brazilian Labor Party)
SOCSO	Social Security Organisation (Malaysia)
SRA	Social Reform Agenda (the Philippines)
SSE	Seguro Social de Empleados (Employee Social Security Fund, Peru)
SSO	Seguro Social Obligatorio (Compulsory Social Security Fund, Peru)
SSS	Social Security System (the Philippines)
TRT	Thai Rak Thai (Thai Loves Thai party)
UDF	Union of Democratic Forces (Sajuz na Demokraticnite Sili, Bulgaria)
UMNO	United Malays National Organisation
UW	Unia Wolności (Freedom Union, Poland)
VHCS	Voluntary Health Card Scheme (Thailand)

Development, Democracy, and Welfare States

Toward a Political Economy of Social Policy

The comparative study of social policy in developing countries is of recent vintage.[1] Yet the middle-income countries of Latin America, East Asia, and Eastern Europe have welfare systems that originated in the early post-war period. The questions posed by these systems are the same as those that motivate the literature on the advanced welfare state: Why did governments undertake the provision of social insurance and services? How have welfare systems evolved over time, and how are benefits distributed?

The relevance of these questions has been heightened by epochal political and economic changes that occurred in the developing and formerly socialist world in the 1980s and 1990s. Most countries in the three regions democratized during this period, raising hopes that new governments would be more attentive to social issues. At the same time, most countries also experienced financial crises, recession, and associated fiscal constraints. These problems triggered wide-ranging reforms, including, but by no means limited to, liberalization and increased economic openness.

Economic crisis and market reforms entailed serious social dislocations and raised questions about the viability of existing welfare commitments. Could social spending be sustained in the face of severe fiscal constraints? Or would economic crises and reform force new democracies to limit, or retrench, social-policy commitments?

In this book, we analyze the development and reform of social policy among the middle-income countries of Latin America, East Asia, and Eastern Europe. By 1980, at the onset of the major economic and political changes of the late twentieth century, the three regions had developed distinctive social-welfare models. Eastern European welfare systems, though increasingly strained, provided comprehensive protections and services to almost all of their populations. East Asian welfare systems offered minimal social insurance, but a number placed a high priority on investment in education. In Latin America, the urban middle class and some blue-collar workers enjoyed access to relatively generous systems of public protection, but peasants and informal-sector workers were generally excluded or underserved.

---

[1] Comparative studies of the developing world that cut across regions and policy areas include Graham 1994, 1998; Esping-Andersen 1996; Huber 2002; Kapstein and Milanovic

These welfare legacies had a strong influence on both the politics and the economics of social policy as the countries of the three regions democratized. Past policies—or the absence of them—created constituencies and generated demands on incoming democratic governments. Prior welfare commitments also had important fiscal implications. In Eastern Europe and Latin America, entitlements placed heavy burdens on governments and generated strong pressures for reform and even retrenchment. In the high-growth Asian countries, by contrast, new democratic governments were relatively unencumbered by prior welfare commitments and had room to expand social insurance and services.

In exploring these distinctive welfare trajectories, we build on three lines of theoretical argument that have motivated the literature on the advanced welfare state. The first, and arguably the most basic, is the significance of distributive coalitions and economic interests. Following the power-resource approach, we consider the extent to which political elites incorporate or exclude organizations and political parties representing urban labor and the rural poor. We focus initially on critical political realignments that resulted in the long-term repression of these groups in some countries and allowed space for them to operate in others. Over time, as Pierson (1994) has argued with respect to advanced welfare states, the commitments established through these initial political choices created stakeholders and constituencies that influenced the subsequent course of social policy.

The second set of factors we consider are economic; this set includes both the performance of the economy and its organization. Economic performance exerts a crucial influence on social policy, particularly through its effect on the fiscal capacity of the state. High growth is at least a permissive condition for an expansion of entitlements and spending, slow growth, crises, and attendant fiscal constraints, by contrast, place political as well as economic limits on the ability to sustain welfare entitlements and services.

Our focus on the "organization" of the economy follows and modifies the varieties of capitalism literature.[2] We show how the development strategies of governments, and the resultant production strategies of firms, are complementary to particular social policies and labor-market institutions. Over time, the sustainability of these different economic models also had a crucial impact on the path of social policy. The crisis and transformation of Latin America's import-substitution model during the 1980s and the

---

2002; Gough and Wood 2004; McGuire 2001; Rudra 2007 and a number of cross-national quantitative studies that we review in more detail in appendix 1.

[2] Several pioneering works in this field are Schonfeld 1965; Katzenstein 1978; Gourevitch 1986; Hall 1986; Hall and Soskice 2001

rapid implosion of state socialism in the early 1990s undermined import-substituting firms and state-owned enterprises that had been central pillars of social policy in both regions. Privatization, restructuring, and greater exposure to international competition had important implications for the social contract.

Political institutions constitute the third cluster of factors that influence social policy. Given the political heterogeneity of the countries in our sample, and the "third wave" of democratization that began in the 1970s, we are particularly interested in the influence of regime type. To what extent did democracy and democratization affect the responsiveness of governments to the interests of low-income groups?

Regime type is an important component of any explanation of social policy. Dictatorship and democracy determine the extent to which competing parties can enter the electoral arena and the freedom interest groups enjoy in organizing and exercising influence. However, we also emphasize the limitations of a purely institutional approach. Institutional rules of the game—the supply side of the political market—are not sufficient to account for the character of social policy without consideration of underlying interests and their organization—the demand side of the political market—and the economic context in which governments operate.

THE SCOPE OF SOCIAL POLICIES AND VARIATIONS IN WELFARE SYSTEMS

What do we mean by social or welfare policy? An expansive view of the social contract between states and citizens would arguably begin with the capacity of governments to deliver economic growth. However, the question of growth is analytically distinct from the question of how governments choose to redistribute income, either through insurance schemes that mitigate risk or through spending on basic social services that are of particular significance to the poor. We focus on these two broad areas of social policy and on the particular way they are combined in broader policy complexes.

In principle, social insurance can offer protection against the full range of life-cycle and market risks, including sickness, work-related injury and disability, maternity and childbearing, unemployment, retirement, and death (through survivors' benefits). However, pensions and health insurance are the most significant forms of social insurance in the countries in our sample, and we pay particular attention to them. In our consideration of more recent reforms in part 2, we also examine antipoverty and labor market policies, which are relative latecomers to the social-policy mix.

The second area of social policy is the provision of basic social services. Access to high-quality education and primary health services is widely viewed as critical for expanding human freedom and capabilities (Nussbaum and Sen 1993; Sen 1999) and is an underlying determinant of life chances and arguably of growth itself.[3] Access to primary education and basic health care is especially important in labor-abundant economies, since it augments the human capital of the poor, their most basic resource (Lindert 2004).

Following Esping-Andersen (1990), we argue that specific social policies do not evolve in isolation but cluster together into identifiable complexes.[4] Table I.1 provides a stylized summary of these models across the three regions during the early post–World War II decades. In Eastern Europe, social policy was anchored by an overarching employment guarantee, but also by a strong commitment to education and training, universal health care and pensions, and family allowances. These commitments began as occupational ones but were transformed over the postwar period into universal citizenship rights. In Latin America, most states established occupationally based social insurance and health systems that favored formal-sector workers but typically excluded informal urban workers and the rural sector. The provision of basic social services also showed a marked inequity in distribution, reenforcing rather than mitigating long-standing patterns of inequality in the region. In Asia, social insurance was limited and, where it did exist, was provided through mandated individual savings programs that had little or no redistributive component. Nonetheless, governments attached a high priority to the provision of primary and secondary education and, somewhat more unevenly, to public health and basic health services.

Contrasts between these systems constitute the pivot around which we organize the core arguments of this book. In part 1 (chapters 1 through 4) we examine the initiation and expansion of welfare commitments in the three regions from the early postwar period through the late 1970s, and, in the socialist cases, through the 1980s. We trace the origins and evolution of these systems to political realignments that occurred during the early and mid-twentieth century and the subsequent adoption of distinctive development models. Part 2 focuses on the political conflicts over social policy during and after the "third wave" of democratization (c. 1980–2005). We show that economic conditions and welfare legacies strongly influenced how new democracies dealt with these conflicts.

---

[3] See, for example, Birdsall, Ross, and Sabot (1995) and Birdsall (1999), but also Easterly (2001) and Pritchet (2001, 2004) for skeptical views.

[4] Rudra (2007) makes the same case for the developing countries.

TABLE I.1
Regional Welfare Models, c. 1980

	Latin America	East Asia	Eastern Europe
Social insurance (primarily health insurance and pensions)	Defined benefit systems financed through payroll taxes and fiscal transfers. Coverage is partial and unequal in most countries.	Limited public provision of social insurance outside of state sector workers. Defined contribution systems in some countries for limited segments of the workforce.	Coverage initially based on employment in state enterprises, gradually universalized.
Basic health services	Unequal and incomplete public coverage; de facto reliance on private provision and financing.	Emphasis on public health and basic health services in some countries, but limited public provision and reliance on private provision and financing.	Universal government provision provided free at point of delivery.
Education	Access to primary education expands in 1960s and 1970s, but high drop-out and repetition rates and low quality. Significant regional inequalities. Biases toward tertiary education.	Early emphasis on expansion of access to primary education, followed by expansion of secondary education. Relatively high rates of completion and low drop-out rate.	Universal primary and secondary education, but with strong emphasis on vocational training and manpower planning.
Labor markets	Labor codes include extensive protections for formal sector workers, contributing to labor market rigidities and dualism.	Relatively flexible labor markets.	Centralized manpower planning and wage setting. Guaranteed employment, supplemented by unemployment insurance in "market socialist" experiments.
Political legacies and interests	Class of beneficiaries is relatively narrow but with generous benefits. Governments face simultaneous demands for maintenance of existing benefits and for inclusion of previously excluded groups.	Limited social insurance generates incentives for expansion.	Prior entitlements create wide class of beneficiaries with an interest in maintaining coverage.
Fiscal legacies	Social insurance systems supported by fiscal transfers, contributing to broader fiscal strains.	Public financing for schemes covering government employees only; limited fiscal constraints from existing programs.	Social insurance systems supported by fiscal transfers, contributing to broader fiscal strains.

These arguments are outlined briefly in the first two sections of this introduction. In the third section, we take up the issue of institutions and regime type in more detail. Section four considers some methodological issues that arise in the comparative historical analysis that forms the empirical core of the book. We close this introduction by locating our work in the broader literature on the welfare state, a task we revisit in the conclusion to the volume.

CRITICAL REALIGNMENTS, DEVELOPMENT STRATEGIES, AND THE ORIGIN AND EVOLUTION OF WELFARE SYSTEMS

In seeking to explain the origins and early development of welfare commitments, we must analyze why political elites have incentives to distribute and redistribute income in a particular way. But we must first make choices about the appropriate time frame for thinking about these issues. A number of recent studies of long-run growth have located the ultimate origins of key political and economic institutions in the colonial period (Kohli 2004; Acemoglu, Johnson, and Robinson 2001, 2005) or in wholly exogenous factors, such as resource endowments and geography (Engerman and Sokoloff 2000, 2002). These long-run constraints no doubt operate on social policy, and we consider the significance of colonial inheritance in particular. But this focus on very long-run forces seems misplaced for our purposes, given quite fundamental political discontinuities that occurred in the mid-twentieth century in the three regions, as well as important changes in the welfare policies we seek to explain.

A more plausible alternative is that the politics of social policy is determined by the more proximate processes of growth and structural economic change. The modernization approach to the welfare state traces the early origins of welfare commitments to the functional requirements of industrialization and the political demands unleashed by it.[5] The differences in welfare models that we have highlighted in table I.1 might result, not from distinctive political factors, but from variation in the level of development and the extent of structural change across countries.

Again, we are skeptical. Industrial growth and social modernization certainly contributed to the emergence of the modern welfare state. But these are highly general processes, and if we have learned one thing about modern capitalism it is the absence of a single model. Countries experiencing "modernization" end up with very different market institutions and social-policy complexes. In chapter 1, we provide some simple, cross-na-

---

[5] For example, Wilensky 1975. Collier and Messick (1975) provide an excellent summary of this early literature.

tional regressions to justify our skepticism. These models suggest that the relationship between level of development and social policy is by no means as robust as one might expect; even controlling for "modernization," important cross-regional differences persist. These results are consistent with our claim that the course of social policy depends on political and economic factors that cannot be reduced to the modernization process alone.

Critical Realignments and the International Setting

In contrast to these "deep" historical and modernization arguments, we focus on discontinuities in patterns of political domination that occurred in each of the three regions during the first half of the twentieth century.[6] We identify these discontinuities by the emergence of new ruling coalitions and political incorporation or exclusion of working-class and peasant organizations. The incorporation of urban working-class and rural-sector organizations influenced social policy through the basic mechanisms identified by the power-resource approach: by determining the constituencies to which politicians—whether democratic or authoritarian—responded. Exclusion of these groups gave elites greater leeway in pursuing their political and economic objectives.

In East Asia and Eastern Europe, critical realignments occurred in the aftermath of World War II and were strongly influenced by international political developments. In both regions, great powers provided crucial support for new political elites who brought with them novel political and economic projects. In both regions, these projects dramatically weakened organized labor, the left, and rural political movements.

However, they did so with fundamentally different aims. In Asia, the turbulent wave of decolonization set in train by the end of the Pacific War was followed quickly by the onset of the Cold War and the triumph of conservative, anti-Communist political leaderships. With external support, new governments beat back the challenge from the left in the cities and forestalled or defeated armed insurgencies in the countryside. But in varying degrees, and in contrast to Latin America, these new political elites also reached into the rural areas for political support.

---

[6] We are influenced by the literature on critical junctures but have opted for the term political realignment for two reasons. First, it is more descriptively accurate of the particular political factors—a change in the power of organized interests—that we believe to be causally important for understanding social policy. Second, the term *critical juncture* now carries particular theoretical implications with respect to the question of subsequent path dependence. Although we are sympathetic with path-dependence arguments, as will be seen in more detail in chapter 1, the enduring effect of any particular political realignment cannot be assumed.

In Eastern Europe, Soviet influence prevailed. As in East Asia, the postwar liberation initially unleashed a wide spectrum of new social forces. With the consolidation of power by Communist parties, however, came the destruction of independent social-democratic and peasant parties and the transformation of unions into arms of the party-state. The distinctive features of socialist social policy were not based on accommodation of labor and the left, as was the case in the European social democracies. Rather, labor and the peasantry were subordinated to the political, economic and organizational logic of the command economy.

In Latin America, we identify the critical realignments with reformist challenges to the oligarchic states of the nineteenth century. In contrast to Asia and Eastern Europe, these political changes predated the great-power rivalry of the Cold War era. New contenders for political power could not count on sustained support from powerful external patrons. Rather, they relied on the support of cross-class coalitions that offered legal status and influence to segments of organized labor and, in some instances, to popularly based parties. But antioligarchic coalitions also typically included some segments of the dominant landowning class itself, and urban-based political challengers found it difficult to penetrate the countryside to the same extent as in Eastern Europe and East Asia. Peasants and agricultural workers remained politically marginalized and the countryside relatively disadvantaged in the provision of social insurance and services.

The effects of these critical realignments cannot be reduced to differences in regime type. In Latin America, the incorporation of labor was accompanied by a widening of the franchise in some cases and various forms of authoritarian rule in others. In East Asia, decolonization was followed by democratic openings in some cases but not in others. In Eastern Europe, the shift to Stalinist political rule was uniform, but it is difficult to deduce the course of social policy from the nature of political institutions To the contrary, the socialist welfare state stands as a stark anomaly to the expectation that authoritarian regimes are likely to redistribute income in a more narrow way. In all three regions, critical realignments ran much deeper than formal institutions; they reflected fundamental shifts in the constellation of political interests.

Development Strategies

The middle of the twentieth century also marked the onset of industrialization and profound structural change in the countries of interest to us. Now, with the benefit of hindsight, we can see that the first three postwar decades were a period of unprecedented growth. The Eastern European countries were the first to take off, and they experienced rapid economic growth until the 1970s, when the constraints of the socialist model became manifest. The postwar period witnessed high growth across most of the middle-income countries of Latin America as well. Given subsequent crises, it is easy to forget that Brazil and Mexico were among the economic miracles of the period. The East Asian takeoff came somewhat later, but from the mid-1960s, the newly industrializing countries of Korea and Taiwan sustained unparalleled economic performance, followed by a number of Southeast Asian countries. Strong growth across the developing world did not necessarily lead to an expansion of social entitlements, as the East Asian cases show. However, it did provide the basis for increased social spending among those governments that chose to do so.

Growth occurred in the context of very different development strategies, however: import-substitution in Latin America and the early postwar period in East Asia, state socialism in Eastern Europe, and a more export-oriented model beginning in the 1960s in a number of the East Asian countries. In chapter 1, we extend the underlying logic of the varieties-of-capitalism approach by considering how differences in the development strategies of governments influenced labor-market and production strategies and the preferences of key groups with respect to social policy. We also show how the economic models adopted in the three regions reinforced and perpetuated the patterns of political incorporation and exclusion associated with the critical realignments we identify.

In the larger Latin American countries, the process of import-substitution industrialization (ISI) was accelerated by economic shocks that began as early as World War I in the larger countries and was subsequently pushed along by the Great Depression and World War II. The cross-class coalitions formed in the course of the critical realignments in the region were conducive to the adoption of ISI as a more self-conscious development strategy in the postwar period. ISI allowed state enterprises and private firms in the import-substituting sectors to accommodate welfare entitlements for the organized urban working class. However, such policies contributed to labor-market dualism and to well-known biases against agriculture and the rural sector. The social-insurance systems that developed in the region both reflected and reenforced these biases. Moreover, the structural characteristics of import-substituting economies also had adverse effects on the overall distribution of income and reduced incentives for governments, firms, and workers to invest in education.

In East Asia, the turn toward export-oriented growth occurred well after the conservative political realignments of the Cold War period. Nonetheless, outward-oriented strategies strongly influenced the incentives facing governments, firms, and workers with respect to social policy. On the one hand, strategies dependent on the export of labor-intensive manufactures put a premium on labor-market flexibility and made governments and firms highly resistant to social insurance schemes that would increase labor costs. The authoritarian regimes in the region, whether established early in the postwar period or after brief periods of semidemocratic rule, thus maintained far more limited systems of public protection than was the case in either Eastern Europe or Latin America. On the other hand, export-oriented growth strengthened incentives to expand access to primary, secondary, and vocational education. To a lesser extent, the policy emphasis on human capital as a core asset motivated the expansion of basic public health services as well.

In Eastern Europe, all Communist governments initiated centrally planned industrialization drives immediately after the consolidation of Communist power in the late 1940s. This strategy rested on high levels of investment in basic industry, the mobilization of labor, and a squeeze on the countryside. The commitment to full employment and government provision of social insurance and services emerged as side effects of the complete socialization of the economy. In the absence of any private sector, the government was perforce involved in both the financing and provision of health care, pensions, and even housing. Even though these entitlements originated in the state-owned enterprise sector, the collectivization of agriculture extended them into the countryside and provided the basis for the universalization of benefits. Similarly, government interest in the expansion of education, and its particular emphasis on vocational training, was a direct complement of the socialist system of manpower planning.

In sum, the welfare systems that had developed by the late 1970s and early 1980s in the three regions were deeply embedded in political interests and economic strategies that had evolved over decades. "Social contracts" were by no means the result of democratic politics, or even bargaining with affected interests; much more commonly, they were simply imposed from above. Nevertheless, distinctive social-policy complexes generated expectations about the benefits the state would provide. In turn, the interests, expectations, and even institutions formed through these earlier social-policy interventions strongly affected the political battles over social policy that unfolded in the new democracies that emerged in the 1980s and 1990s.

REVISING SOCIAL CONTRACTS, 1980–2005: ECONOMIC
  TRANSFORMATION, WELFARE LEGACIES, AND DEMOCRATIZATION

The 1980s and 1990s witnessed profound political and economic changes in the three regions of interest to us. Transitions to democratic rule strengthened incentives to expand public welfare commitments to vulnerable sectors of the population and to protect existing entitlements.

But the course of social policy was also deeply affected by economic developments and ideological trends that pushed in the direction of weakening the social responsibilities of the state.

In part 2, we show that responses to these cross-pressures varied substantially within and across geographic regions. Most countries instituted social-policy reforms, but the scope and direction of those changes depended on variations in economic performance and on the organizational and political legacy of past welfare entitlements.

Reversal of Fortune

The first three postwar decades can be considered a "golden era" of rapid growth. By contrast, economic performance since 1980 has shown much wider variance across regions and countries and much greater volatility within them. These changed economic circumstances not only directly affected the capacity of the government to maintain or expand existing entitlements but affected the *politics* of social policy as well. Good macroeconomic performance strengthened the hand of political actors arguing for an expansion of social commitments and weakened the force of technocratic arguments for reform or retrenchment. By contrast, crises—and particularly those accompanied by fiscal constraints and high inflation—increased the influence of technocrats and their allies in the international financial institutions. Liberal technocrats focused initially on macroeconomic stabilization and a variety of market-oriented reforms; but they came to press for liberalizing reforms of the social sector as well.

The Asian governments in our sample faced by far the most favorable economic environment. Growth remained robust in most of them until the financial crisis of 1997–98, providing the new democracies with the wherewithal to expand the state role in the provision of social insurance and services. The crisis of 1997–98 posed similar constraints to those seen in Latin America and Eastern Europe but did not pose the same fundamental challenge to the prior development model. Fiscal constraints were cyclical, rather than long-term and structural in nature, and as a result, new entitlements generally survived the crisis intact.

Latin America and Eastern Europe, by contrast, faced far more severe economic constraints. The Latin American economies experienced deep recessions during the debt crisis of the 1980s and a recurrence of financial crises in the 1990s and early 2000s. Eastern European countries faced a gradual slowdown in growth prior to the collapse of 1989, then deep "transitional" recessions in the first half of the 1990s.

Economic crises had contradictory implications for the politics of social policy. On the one hand, crises and the reforms that followed in their wake—liberalization of trade and capital markets, privatization, and a variety of other market-oriented reforms—were socially disruptive and exposed previously sheltered sectors to new market risks. These grievances provided the basis for electoral and interest-group mobilization.

On the other hand, crises increased the influence of technocrats, the international financial institutions, and domestic policy networks that favored short-term fiscal adjustments and restructuring of long-term fiscal commitments. Social spending was implicated in these adjustments. Sheer fiscal constraint limited the capacity of governments to spend on social programs. The social policy models of the ISI and state-socialist period were also vulnerable to the criticism that they had contributed to the fiscal crises of the 1980s and 1990s and that they were not well suited to the new, market-oriented policy environment.

Distributive Politics: Defense of Entitlements, Pressures for Expansion

In addition to economic conditions, the welfare legacy shaped the distributive demands placed on the state. Welfare entitlements created electoral and interest-group constituencies; in general, the wider the coverage and the more effective the services provided, the more difficult it was for liberal reformers to initiate changes in the social-policy status quo. Constraints on government did not operate solely through the electoral connection, moreover. Past welfare policies created not only beneficiaries but also complex institutional and interest group constraints on welfare reform: from civil servants and public service providers; to unions with an institutional stake in the welfare system; to an array of private actors, from the financial sector and pharmaceutical companies to socially-oriented nongovernmental organizations (NGOs).

Again, the Asian countries stand apart from those in Latin America and Eastern Europe. Relatively minimalist welfare states provided politicians and those favoring an expansion of public commitments with a political tabula rasa. Operating under highly favorable economic conditions, they could offer major new social programs to voter-beneficiaries while facing little organized resistance from existing stakeholders. As we discuss below, these incentives to expand entitlements and services were significantly strengthened by the advent of democracy.

Latin America and Eastern Europe resembled one another both in the economic adversity they faced and in the inheritance of much more extensive public commitments. However, the regions had quite distinct welfare legacies. Most Latin American welfare states were deep but not wide. They involved substantial public expenditures on social insurance, but access to these resources was typically highly unequal. Where coverage *was* wider, as in Uruguay and Costa Rica, efforts to reform the system of social insurance and services faced greater political difficulties. Where coverage had been narrow and unequal, market-oriented reformers gained greater traction over the social-policy agenda.

In the Eastern European cases, the transition to the market required a fundamental shift of resources out of the state sector. Yet the socialist welfare legacy had offsetting political consequences. Citizens had been incorporated into a dense network of social entitlements, and even where the value of these protections and the quality of services had deteriorated, scaling them back posed serious political risks. New democratic governments in Eastern Europe did undertake reforms. Yet they also strove to maintain universal coverage of a number of important life-cycle risks, most notably with respect to health and pensions. They also attached a relatively high priority to providing social safety nets for formal sector workers.

INTRODUCING INSTITUTIONS: THE EFFECTS OF REGIME TYPE

How do political institutions affect the political economy of welfare policy? More specifically, does the turn toward democracy result in more generous and progressive social contracts? The literature on the advanced welfare state has paid increasing attention to institutional differences within democratic systems, and these factors can be important to new developing-country democracies as well.[7] However, the tremendous heterogeneity in basic political institutions across the three regions in the postwar period and their more recent convergence on democratic forms of rule compel attention to the prior question of the effects of regime type. Does democracy result in a more generous and progressive social contract, *ceteris paribus*? Does authoritarian rule preclude or limit the scope of redistributive politics?

Democratic politics has long been associated with pressures for redistribution, through mechanisms that are basic, constitutive features of democratic rule itself. These include, most notably, the electoral connection and the freedom of association that allows interest groups to organize and press their claims on the state.[8] The coming of democracy is associ-

---

[7] These analyses have focused on the number of veto players (Birchfield and Crepaz 1998; Huber and Stephens 2001; Swank 2002; Crepaz and Moser 2004), presidentialism and parliamentarism (Milesi-Ferretti, Perotti, and Rostagno 2002; Persson and Tabellini 1999, 2000, chaps. 8 and 9, 2003; Alesina and Glaeser 2004), federalism (Swank 2002; Wibbels 2005), and electoral rules that affect the coherence or fragmentation of the party system (Cox and McCubbins 2001; Shugart 2006).

[8] Two alternative theoretical routes are worth noting. One that can be traced to Cox (1987) treats social policy as a public good (Lake and Baum 2001; Bueno de Mesquita et al. 2003). When the franchise is narrow, political leaders maintain support by providing

ated with an expansion of the franchise and competition for office. Politicians must appeal to broader constituencies in order to win and retain office. They do so by offering competing packages of public and private goods to voters, including those that redistribute income.[9] Similar expectations follow from an interest-group approach to the policy process (see Grossman and Helpman 2001 for an overview). Interest groups do many things: they mobilize votes; supply money and information to politicians; and engage in contentious politics (McAdam, Tarrow, and Tilly 2001). As Mancur Olson (1982) pointed out in *The Rise and Decline of Nations*, however, these various forms of collective political action are all undertaken with one fundamental aim: to redistribute resources toward the members of the given group.

Nondemocratic regimes also redistribute income, in some cases quite dramatically (Bueno de Mesquita et. al. 2003). Nevertheless, the presence of these two closely related mechanisms—electoral competition and independent interest-group activity—would lead us to expect democracies to be more generous in the provision of social insurance and services than their authoritarian counterparts.

The focus on these institutional differences finds justification in both the broader literature and in our own research. The relationship between the expansion of the franchise and the redistribution associated with the welfare state was noted by the early-twentieth-century European social democrats (Przeworski 1985), in the classic work of Marshall (1965) and more recently in Lindert's (2004) magisterial overview of the role of political "voice" in the expansion of social entitlements in the advanced industrial states. In appendix 1, we survey a broader range of empirical studies that test for the effects of regime type on social policy. A majority of these studies—but by no means all[10]—find that democracy has positive effects on government effort and on actual welfare outcomes, such as health.

---

predominantly private goods. As the franchise expands, leaders shift toward greater provision of public goods for efficiency reasons. A second theoretical strand linking democracy and welfare is Sen's (1984) emphasis on the role of information in mitigating social distress, which arose from his work on famines.

[9] Influential formal treatments include Romer (1975), Roberts (1977), and particularly Meltzer and Richard (1981), which shows most intuitively how differences between the mean and median income generate incentives for redistribution. See also Boix 2003. Persson and Tabellini (2000, chap. 6) and Drazen (2000, chap. 8) provide overviews. A crucial issue is whether social policy should be seen as a form of redistribution or insurance (Barr 2001; Wallerstein and Moene 2003). However, if we make the plausible assumption that the distribution of risk correlates with the distribution of income, we get similar results as with models that assume social policy is redistributive (see Przeworski 2003, 209–12).

[10] For example, a wide-ranging study by Mulligan, Gil, and Sala-i-Martin (2003) titled "Do Democracies Have Different Public Policies than Non-Democracies?" answers with a flat "no" after considering not only social spending but a variety of other tax and spending

We also find regime type consequential. In Latin America, welfare commitments in long-standing democracies such as Costa Rica, Uruguay, and Chile were more generous than in short-lived democracies and in those political systems that oscillated between authoritarian and democratic rule. The incidence of democracy in Asia prior to the 1980s was substantially less than in Latin America, but periods of democratic or semidemocratic rule were more likely to be accompanied by an expansion of social commitments than were periods of authoritarian governance. In all three regions, finally, the "third wave" transitions of the 1980s and 1990s saw renewed attention to the social question and pressures both to protect existing entitlements and to expand social insurance and services to new groups.

If electoral competition and freedom of interest groups to mobilize are the key mechanisms through which regime type operates on social policy, however, it is very clear that neither of these factors is strictly dichotomous. Some autocracies do not allow elections at all or completely monopolize the electoral process and interest-group activity. But a surprising number are "competitive autocracies" (Linz 2000, 34; Levitsky and Way 2002, 52). They subject themselves to controlled electoral tests and tolerate a degree of interest-group pluralism. Even controlled elections and limited ability to organize may create incentives for authoritarian rulers to seek support through redistribution.

We find vindication for the effort to distinguish among democratic and authoritarian regimes in a more nuanced way. Intermediate regimes—what we call semidemocratic and semiauthoritarian governments (chapter 1)—exhibit greater attention to social policy than do "hard" authoritarian regimes, at least in the nonsocialist cases.

Yet, as we have argued, it is unlikely that the institutional "rules of the game" that define regime type can fully explain the origins or reform of the particular complexes of social-welfare policies that are of interest to us. The analysis of institutional mechanisms provides insight into the supply side of the political market. But as formal models of redistribution show, the effects of institutions are conditional on the distribution of underlying preferences over the policy in question and the strength of contending social groups in the political process.[11] Purely institutional models are underspecified; the effects of democracy and authoritarianism depend

---

measures as well. James McGuire's (2002a) thorough work on infant mortality reached increasingly modest conclusions about the effects of democracy as well (see also Ross 2004). A small number of studies even yield the counterintuitive finding that authoritarian regimes—particularly socialist ones—perform better than democracies on at least some dimensions (Lott 1999; Gauri and Khalegian 2002; Ross 2004).

[11] For a formal treatment of this point, see the discussion of redistribution under democracy in Persson and Tabellini 2000, chap. 6.

on the underlying coalitional alignments and economic interests that we have outlined above.

This point is most evident in the wide array of social policies adopted by the authoritarian regimes that we examine in part 1—variations that proved highly consequential for subsequent reform efforts. Restrictions on the franchise allow rulers to censor the groups that can formally influence the political process through electoral or interest-group mechanisms. But even authoritarian rulers court support and vary in the extent to which they repress or coopt low-income groups. Examples of this variance in authoritarian strategies abound. In Latin America, military dictatorships were generally less inclined than democracies to extend coverage of social security to new sectors of the population, but most of them used existing schemes to deflect protest from workers. In Asia, authoritarian regimes expanded the provision of health and education services in the countryside both as a counterweight to urban political forces and to dampen insurgencies; indeed, they reached into the countryside more aggressively than most Latin American democracies.

The highly comprehensive socialist welfare states provide the most obvious anomaly. Despite the most rigid authoritarian rule in our sample, socialist governments committed to universal and quite extensive social protections. They did so not because of constraints operating through formal political institutions but as a component of a larger socialist economic project.

The distribution of social-policy interests is also important for understanding variation in the behavior of democratic regimes. In all three regions, democracy created a new politics of welfare reform. However, the policy outcomes were strongly affected by differences in economic conditions and in the distribution and organization of social-policy interests that had emerged in the earlier period.

The high-growth democracies of East Asia correspond most neatly to the expectation that democratization is associated with an expansion of social entitlements. Outside of education, these countries had the narrowest social-insurance coverage and had relied more extensively on government-mandated private savings, self-insurance, and private delivery. With democratization, NGOs, unions, and civil-society organizations burst onto the political scene and pressed for a broader public role in the provision of social insurance and services. Politicians saw significant opportunities to attract support through the extension of new social protections. By contrast, the two semiauthoritarian systems in the region—Singapore and Malaysia—show much greater continuity in social policy and even a bias toward a liberalizing agenda.

The effects of democracy were much more complex in Latin America's relatively costly but unequal welfare systems. The turn toward democracy expanded incentives for political entrepreneurs to appeal to marginalized voters but also provided opportunities for organized stakeholders to defend entitlements and institutional prerogatives. At the same time, the collapse of the old development model and deep recessions created especially severe fiscal constraints, and new governments faced strong pressures for liberalizing reforms of social insurance and even outright retrenchment of prior commitments. Given these economic conditions, expansion of the comprehensive social insurance initiatives visible in the East Asian democracies was largely off the table. Instead, reformist technocrats sought to combine far-reaching liberalization of existing social insurance schemes, compensation for some of the most powerful stakeholders, and targeted antipoverty programs aimed at the very poor.

In Eastern Europe, the socialist welfare state included broad segments of the population in a system of entitlements. With democratization, wide coverage created strong electoral and interest group constraints on liberalization and retrenchment, even in the face of strong fiscal pressures. Democracy also provided incentives for parties across the political spectrum to attend to the interests of labor and other groups disadvantaged by the transition to the market.

SOME METHODOLOGICAL ISSUES IN COMPARATIVE HISTORICAL ANALYSIS

Our analysis focuses on twenty-one middle-income countries drawn from three regions. In Latin America, we consider Argentina, Brazil, Chile, Colombia, Costa Rica, Mexico, Peru, Venezuela, and Uruguay. In Asia, we examine developments in Korea, Taiwan, Singapore, Malaysia, Thailand, and the Philippines. In Eastern Europe, we cover Hungary, Poland, Romania, Bulgaria, and Czechoslovakia with its successor states, the Czech and Slovak Republics. This choice of countries encompasses all or most of the middle-income countries of the three regions and allows us to consider not only differences across the regions but also variations within them.[12] The number of effective cases is much larger, however, because we con-

---

[12] It is worth outlining in somewhat more detail the logic behind the exclusion of certain cases. In Latin America, we do not consider the poorer South American or Central American countries, nor the small Caribbean ones. In East Asia, we excluded Indonesia, which fell below the middle-income threshold at the onset of the second period of interest to us. The complications of protracted conflict and the subsequent transition to socialism also seemed to justify the exclusion of Vietnam. In Eastern Europe, we excluded the Baltics. Although frequently compared with the other Eastern European cases, we excluded former Soviet republics. See Cook (2007). Finally, the complications of protracted conflict also seemed to justify exclusion of the successor states to Yugoslavia.

sider several policy areas within each country and exploit changes in the principal causal variables over time.

As we noted at the outset, our study was strongly motivated by quite striking cross-regional differences in the evolution of welfare systems; we outline these differences in more detail in chapter 1. Of course, there is an ample number of candidates for explaining this variation, and in both chapters 1 and 5 we introduce our comparative case studies with some cross-national statistical analysis. In chapter 1, this analysis considers some correlates of social spending and other measures of social-service delivery, controlling for a number of possible structural determinants. The purpose is to motivate our supposition that regionally distinct patterns of social policy do in fact exist. In chapter 5, we develop a more dynamic panel model that permits a consideration of political and economic changes on the path of social spending.

We believe, however, that the utility of cross-national statistical analysis faces much more severe limitations than is typically acknowledged.[13] Not only are the data on social policy characterized by fundamental limitations, but cross-national statistical designs also face a host of problems even when the data are of adequate quality. The tremendous heterogeneity that exists across developing countries places exacting demands on the modeling exercise; more cases can be a minus as well as a plus, because each dimension of heterogeneity must be correctly modeled. As these dimensions multiply, it becomes more and more difficult to arrive at the appropriate specification of the causal model, given a plethora of plausible models and the problem of modeling interactions among the covariates (Gerring 2006, 3). Identification problems, selection problems, and endogeneity are also serious constraints, although they are of concern to qualitative designs as well. Despite their increasing popularity, it is hard to solve these problems through instrumental variable techniques or selection models. Comparative case studies by no means resolve these difficulties, but they do provide a way to gauge the plausibility of contending conjectures.

Finally, comparative case studies provide the opportunity to demonstrate causal relationships in a way that statistical analysis cannot. The advantages of a larger sample and the ability to introduce controls in statistical work are offset by the difficulty of showing that the postulated mechanisms work as proposed—for example, that electoral competition or interest group pressures are the means through which democracy operates on policy outcomes.

Once we established that regionally distinct patterns of policy existed, we faced the question of how to choose cases for more detailed analysis.

---

[13] Gerring (2006) provides a useful overview.

One proposal from James Fearon and David Laitin (2005) is to randomly select cases from the larger sample. This method may be appropriate if the primary analytic objective is to test theories believed to have a general applicability and validity. As we will argue in more detail below, however, we are more concerned with issues of internal rather than external validity, and as a result, Fearon and Laitin's random sampling technique struck us as inappropriate. An alternative is to choose a representative or typical case from each region.[14] This method requires the identification of the distribution of cases within each regional subsample and the use of typical or modal cases or even ideal-typical analysis, to explore the differences across types (or regions, in our case); well-known studies by Esping-Andersen (1990) and Swank (2002) employ this strategy, as does the varieties-of-capitalism (VOC) literature (Hall and Soskice 2001). However, this method is always subject to the concern that the selected case may not be fully representative—even in the context of a broader statistical analysis—or that it may exhibit some idiosyncratic features.

We opted for a strategy of choosing virtually all the significant cases in the regions of interest to us. Despite the criticisms of such a "medium-n" strategy (including those of our earlier work; see Brady, Collier and Searight 2004, 92–94, 100), we believe that this approach is justified for at least three reasons. First, the comparative case analysis is nested in a wider cross-national statistical analysis that allows us to control for a range of other possible determinants of the observed variation. Second, the multiplication of cases increases the confidence that the findings with respect to interregional variations are not driven by unrepresentative or outlier cases and permits intraregional comparison; we return to this issue below.

The third justification for this approach requires somewhat more extended discussion. Our approach is unapologetically historical and configurative. We believe strongly that the phenomena that interest us are best explained as the result of long-run historical processes that vary across regions. We are struck by the fact that numerous cross-national statistical studies implicitly confirm this approach—although without adequate additional exploration—by finding that regional dummies prove to be statistically significant in cross-national models. We are therefore less interested than standard statistical analyses in questions of external validity and whether findings are portable to out-of-sample cases and time periods; to consider these questions, we believe, would require an extended historical consideration of how critical realignments, development strategies, and regime type interacted in altogether different regional set-

---

[14] A common criticism of such a method is that it selects on the dependent variable; see Geddes 2003. However, as Mahoney (2003) shows, such selection can be appropriate if identifying some necessary set of antecedent conditions.

tings. We are more preoccupied with questions of internal validity: whether the causal arguments we have outlined do in fact explain the cases in question.

Although we are interested in cross-regional variations, it is also clear that the cases within any given region also exhibit important variations as well, and that these differences provide additional opportunities for testing. Democracy provides an important example. We have already noted how we use differences between long- and short-lived democracies in Latin America to bolster our contention that regime type matters. Similarly, in part 2 we have a number of cases in which authoritarian rule persisted into the period of interest to us here, including Singapore, Malaysia, and Mexico, as well as cases that reverted to authoritarian rule following an initial transition, notably Peru and Venezuela. We also have differences in the political transition path. Although most countries in our sample moved relatively swiftly from authoritarian to democratic rule, we also have cases that passed through somewhat more prolonged semi-authoritarian or semidemocratic phases, including Mexico, Thailand, Taiwan, the Slovak Republic, and Romania. These variations all provide opportunities for testing conjectures about the effects of regime type.

Although we emphasize regional similarities in the economic environment facing new democracies in each region, there are variations, both across cases and over time, on this dimension as well. For example, in part 2 we exploit a comparison between three democracies that transited during periods of high growth—Korea, Taiwan, and Thailand—with the Philippines, which experienced a debt crisis similar to Latin America's. In Latin America, we sort cases on the basis of the severity of the crises they experienced in the 1980s as well as on regime type and legacies. Similarly in Eastern Europe, we consider differences between early reformers, which generally experienced more rapid recovery from the transitional recessions of the early 1990s, and late reformers that relapsed into crisis.

Narrative accounts also allow us to confirm the results of our cross-sectional time-series models by tracking the effect of changing economic conditions over time. Although we identify the East Asian cases as high-growth ones, all the countries of interest to us experienced the effects of the region-wide crisis of 1997–98. Conversely, the Latin American and Eastern European countries experienced severe crises at the outset of their transitions to democratic rule, but some experienced periods of relatively sustained recovery thereafter (such as Poland) and others fell back into crisis at some later point (Argentina, Brazil, Bulgaria, Romania). Again, these differences provide opportunities for more refined comparisons within the regions, and allow us to test some of our expectations regarding the effects of economic circumstances on the politics of reform.

TRESPASSING: THE ADVANCED WELFARE STATE
IN COMPARATIVE PERSPECTIVE

Our study is framed within the context of an extensive and rich literature on the origins, development, and reform of the advanced industrial welfare states.[15] This subfield has moved forward through intense theoretical debate, which has, in turn, spurred the collection of new data and outstanding empirical work across disciplines. We now have a much greater understanding of the evolution and distributive impact of social policy in the advanced welfare states (see Huber and Stephens 2005 for a compact review).

Despite ongoing controversy, the literature has converged around a relatively limited set of core metatheoretical preoccupations, including the role of distributive interests and their partisan representatives; the changing relationship between underlying economic structure, shorter-run economic performance, and welfare commitments; and the mediating role of political institutions. We, too, have framed our work in the context of these broad intellectual preoccupations, and on a number of issues we have come to conclusions that confirm consensus findings in the literature.

However, the literature on the advanced industrial states has been surprisingly insular, geographically confined to the advanced industrial states, and more particularly to an understanding of the European experience. An underlying motivation of this study is not only to extend and adapt this literature to new geographic and historical contexts, but also to place the advanced industrial-state experience in a broader comparative context.

We signal here a few of our findings that may be of particular interest to students of the advanced industrial states, revisiting them in more depth in the conclusion. These findings concern the merits of the power-resource approach; the effects of economic factors on welfare commitments, including both globalization and varieties of market coordination; and the effects of formal political institutions.

A central point of departure for the literature on the origins of the advanced welfare states is the observation that the balance of class power, and particularly the relative strength of encompassing unions and left parties, was an important determinant of welfare commitments. This power resource perspective has been challenged and modified in recent years. The effects of partisanship have been modified by a con-

[15] Among the comparative work on the advanced welfare states, we have relied on Korpi 1983; Baldwin 1990; Esping-Andersen 1990; Kitschelt 1994; Kitschelt et al. 1999; Garrett 1998; Iversen and Wren 1998; Hicks 1999; Huber and Stephens 2001; Pierson 2001a and b; Swank 2002; Iversen 2005; Pontusson 2005.

sideration of the effects of Christian Democratic and liberal traditions of welfare provision. Paul Pierson (1994) has argued that the importance of unions and left parties is likely to decline over time as welfare systems themselves generate broader constituencies of stakeholders and beneficiaries. And most recently, the focus on labor and the left has been supplemented, if not challenged outright, by research showing that private sector actors have their own distinctive social policy interests depending on their underlying production strategies (Estevez-Abe, Iversen, and Soskice 2001; Mares 2001, 2004). Despite these very important challenges and amendments, there is nonetheless ample quantitative and case study evidence that unions and left parties were, in fact, central determinants of the nature and scope of the welfare state (Huber and Stephens 2001, 113).

At the most general level, our study is anchored in an approach that emphasizes the causal significance of organized interests. Our explanation for early welfare commitments is rooted in the concept of critical political realignments, and we find some support for the general proposition that organized-labor and left parties are important actors in the extension of social insurance and services. We also follow Pierson in considering the subsequent influence of what we call the welfare legacy on the maintenance of welfare entitlements.

At the same time, we found ourselves pulled back to discussions of the origins of the European welfare state that emphasized not simply the urban working class but also the political position of the rural sector. Given the weight of this sector in the developing countries of interest to us, this emphasis should not be surprising. Both the comprehensive social entitlements of the socialist welfare state and the relatively egalitarian distribution of social services in a number of the East Asian cases ultimately hinged on the inclusion of the rural sector. This inclusion was not political in the same sense that we talk about the inclusion of the urban working class in Latin America. Nonetheless, the shape of the overall social contract could only be understood by grasping why governments had incentives to reach the countryside.

These considerations of the significance of the rural sector are not unrelated to how we think about the distributive consequences of partisanship and labor power. In Western Europe, the strength and scope of the labor movement seemed almost linearly related to the scope and progressivity of the welfare state. In the developing countries, by contrast, strong labor movements representing a narrow segment of the work force often had regressive implications. Benefits were financed not only by payroll taxes from workers and employers but also by general taxes and inflation levied primarily on low-income groups. Paradoxically, in Eastern Europe and East Asia, repression of the left and labor provided the conditions for policies that encouraged much more egalitarian distribution of social insurance and services and arguably more egalitarian distributions of income. These findings raise important comparative questions about the circumstances under which the interests of labor have progressive or regressive effects for social policy as a whole.

The structure and performance of the economy have also played a major role in the development of the welfare literature. We focus on two economic issues that have received particular attention: the potentially negative effects of globalization, and the consequences of different forms of market coordination on social-policy commitments.

Research on the contemporary effects of "globalization" has yielded highly mixed results. A number of studies have found that the impact of economic openness on the volatility of growth, income, or consumption is much less than thought and might work in the exactly opposite direction; more open economies may be better positioned to manage external shocks (Iversen 2001; Kim 2007). Moreover, this literature finds that the fate of the advanced welfare states has been affected much more substantially by technological and demographic changes or overall economic performance than by globalization, at least as narrowly conceived (Iversen and Cusack 2000).

We argue as well that a narrow focus on economic openness does not capture the most direct and significant economic determinants of social policy. In our sample, the sustainability of different development models, growth, and fiscal capacity all appear as much more important proximate causes of changes in social policy. Although these factors are no doubt influenced by the external environment, our results do not line up with common expectations about openness per se. The more closed economies of Eastern Europe and Latin America ultimately experienced the most profound shocks and the most severe crises, while the high-growth Asian cases combined high levels of economic openness with some of the more pronounced expansions of social entitlements in our entire sample. The effects of globalization on social policy are by no means resolved, but analysis along these lines should not squeeze out equally, if not more, promising lines of economic analysis, most importantly on the long-run fiscal capacity of developing-country governments and the effects of the tax base on the capacity to address the social question.

In addition to the effects of globalization, theories of the welfare state have increasingly focused on variations in the form of market capitalism (Hall and Soskice 2001). Our discussion of alternative development models is inspired by the VOC literature, but it is far from a simple extension of that perspective. The middle-income countries of the three regions pursued a far broader range of economic alternatives than captured in the typologies of the advanced industrial states. Such experiences indicate a need both for a broader understanding of the range of coordination mechanisms and a better understanding about how closed-economy models are being transformed.

The mediating effect of political institutions, finally, is a third important element in the theoretical scaffolding of the welfare-state literature. We have operated from the theoretical premise that democratic systems have institutional mechanisms that encourage redistribution and thus broader and more generous welfare systems. However, these expectations can be undercut both by economic constraints and by pressure from interest groups. Conversely, authoritarian regimes can, under specified circumstances, produce positive distributive effects. The research program on welfare and social policy needs to broaden its horizon beyond the democratic cases, to consider whether the benefits of democracy hold, if not why not, and under which conditions authoritarian regimes may be responsive to the interests of the poor. Such a research project would join the historical work on the European welfare state with the consideration of the developing and socialist systems we consider here.

PART ONE

The Historical Origins
of Welfare Systems, 1945–80

Social Policy in Latin America, East Asia, and Eastern Europe, 1945–80: An Overview

Our stylized discussion of welfare systems in the introduction emphasized cross-regional differences in the extent to which the state assumed responsibility in the provision of social insurance and services, in coverage, and in equity. In this chapter, we provide a more systematic analysis of the origins and evolution of these systems through the early 1980s. The first half of the chapter provides a detailed description of the systems in the three regions and examines a number of socioeconomic factors often used to explain differences among them. We show that cross-regional differences persist, even when controlling for factors such as level of development, growth, demography, ethnic fractionalization, and income distribution. In the second half of the chapter, we elaborate on an alternative set of explanatory factors for this variation that we sketched in the introduction: critical realignments in the early and mid-twentieth century, distinctive development strategies linked to these realignments, and differences in the incidence of democratic and authoritarian rule.

CROSS-REGIONAL DIFFERENCES AND SOCIOECONOMIC EXPLANATIONS

We turn first to a description of differences in welfare systems in the three regions. Our comparison and analysis provides a snapshot of these differences at the end of the first phase of their social policy regimes, the subject of part 1. At the same time, it outlines the starting point for an analysis of the politics of social-policy reform that we take up in part 2.

Welfare States Compared

Characterizing and comparing multidimensional welfare systems is not straightforward, and any effort at such an analysis must triangulate a number of different measures. We follow studies on the advanced industrial states by beginning with a consideration of spending on social security, health, and education. Although we are acutely aware of the limitations on social spending data, particularly with respect to its distributive impact (Kapstein and Milanovic 2002; Filmer and Pritchett 1999), these comparisons provide a first approximation of public commitments and the priorities attached to different areas of social policy.

Table 1.1 provides data on the overall size of the central government and of central government public welfare spending on social security, health, and education.[1] The data are expressed both as a share of GDP and as a share of total spending averaged over 1976–80 for Latin America and Asia. We do not have comparable data for the same time period in most Eastern European countries, but we show data for 1990 to provide an idea of the magnitude of social spending at the end of the socialist era.

The data on the size of the state and on social spending should not surprise. In 1990, government spending in Eastern Europe averaged over 40 percent of GDP. The more developed Central European countries— Poland, Hungary, and Czechoslovakia—devoted roughly 25 percent of GDP to welfare spending; these numbers equal or exceed European social spending. The share of public and social spending is also well above that of most Latin American and East Asian states.

In Latin America, there is considerably more intraregional variation. Even so, several of the older and more established welfare states (Uruguay, Costa Rica, and Chile) spend at levels comparable with those at the middle of the Organisation for Economic Co-operation and Development (OECD) range, and the regional average for social security expenditures is significantly higher than in Asia. The spending data do not capture the large mandated savings systems in Malaysia and Singapore. Nevertheless, almost all the Asian countries fall at or near the low end of the Latin American range.

The composition of social spending provides an insight into the priorities that the governments of the regions attach to different areas of social policy. Again, we see sharp differences between Latin America and East Asia. Notwithstanding wide intraregional differences, social security spending in Latin America dwarfs that of East Asia's minimalist welfare states, both as a percentage of GDP and as a share of government spending; these differences reach standard levels of statistical significance. The differences in health spending are not statistically significant, but as we will show, Latin American governments generally placed greater emphasis on social insurance and curative health than did Asian ones, which devoted greater effort to basic health care.

By contrast, despite a generally lower per-capita income, Asian countries spent more on education as a share of GDP than did the Eastern European countries, and a significantly higher share of government spending. The

---

[1] Appendix 2 addresses some of the complexities in the spending data that arise in federal systems, but consideration of this factor does not fundamentally change the results reported here.

TABLE 1.1
Government, Social-Security, Education, and Health Spending:
Latin America and East Asia, 1976–80; Eastern Europe, 1990

	Govt. spending/ GDP	Social-security spending/ GDP	Social-security spending/ total spending	Health spending/ GDP	Health spending/ total spending	Education spending/ GDP	Education spending/ total spending
Argentina	13.8	4.8	28.0	0.47	2.7	1.7 (2.7)[a]	9.9
Brazil	25.5	6.4	36.1	1.25	7.0	1.0 (3.6)[a]	5.8
Chile	29.0	8.0	25.6	2.26	7.1	4.2	13.6
Colombia	16.0 (1982)	3.0 (1982)	17.9	0.6 (1982)	3.6	3.1 (1982)	18.6
Costa Rica	23.7	4.5	21.9	2.16	9.5	5.7	27.5
Mexico	24.3	3.4	22.5	0.59	4.0	2.8	18.0
Peru	16.7	0.4	0.2	1.01	5.7	3.4	19.0
Uruguay	25.6	10.4	45.7	1.04	4.6	2.4	10.5
Venezuela	23.9	1.3	5.5	2.05	8.9	3.9	17.4
Latin America average	22.0	4.9	23.2	1.35	6.2	3.2 (3.6)[a]	15.2
Korea	16.3	0.8	3.2	0.2	1.3	2.5	15.9
Malaysia	30.4	0.3	2.1	1.58	6.5	5.3	21.8
Philippines	13.7	0.3	1.7	0.57	4.1	1.7	12.6
Singapore	25.1	0.6	3.8	1.5	7.9	3.0	16.4
Taiwan	22.8	<1.0[a]	n.a.	n.a.	n.a.	n.a.	15.5
Thailand	18.4	<0.5[a]	2.6	0.7	4.2	3.3	20.7
East Asia average	21.1	0.5	2.7	0.7	4.2	3.2	17.5
Bulgaria	42.4	12.1	4.0	0.9	n.a.	1.3	n.a.
Czechoslovakia	36.1	9.9	26.2	9.9	26.2	4.1	10.9
Hungary	49.8	14.9	37.2	4.1	5.2	1.7	7.8
Poland	39.7	20.7	29.8	4.0	9.6	3.5	8.3
Romania	33.5	10.6	26.5	2.9	9.2	0.9	10.0
Eastern Europe average	40.3	13.6	29.9	4.4	12.6	2.3	9.3
LA-EA (p-value)	0.62	0.00	0.00	0.34	0.45	0.60	0.55
LA-EE (p-value)	0.01	0.01	0.20	0.11	0.25	0.13	0.02
EA-EE (p-value)	0.01	0.00	0.00	0.08	0.19	0.35	0.00

Sources: See appendix 3.
Government spending is for all levels of government. For Taiwan, social spending aggregates "Education, Science and Culture" and "Social Security" and is therefore biased upward.
[a] Figures in parentheses are for 1980 and include state and local spending on education.
[b] Authors' estimates.

differences in educational spending between East Asia and Latin America are not significant. But we will show that the performance of the educational systems was vastly different for the money spent, with wider coverage and greater efficiency in the Asian cases. In contrast to both Eastern Europe and Latin America, in every Asian country, investment in education was also a higher priority than expenditure on social security and health.

The spending patterns in Eastern Europe reflect extensive public-welfare systems, although direct comparisons with Latin America and Asia are problematic. In 1990, the share of social security spending averaged close to 14 percent of GDP, and health spending reached 4.4 percent. Corresponding Latin American figures were 4.9 and 1.3 percent for the second half of the 1970s, a period that is comparable in terms of the evolution of the social contract. Spending on education in Eastern Europe was surprisingly low relative to the other regions and considerably more varied. However, the spending data do not reflect the expansion of access to education and training that took place under Communist rule.

Differences in spending do not fully capture underlying differences in the principles guiding the provision of social security and services in the three regions. These principles vary with respect to the role of public vs. private financing and both de jure and de facto coverage. Countries also vary not only in the generosity of benefits but in the quality and efficiency of services. These differences are best seen by considering in more detail the three major areas of social policy that constitute our focus in part 1: pensions, health care, and education.

PENSIONS

The evolution of pension systems in the three regions followed very different trajectories. In the Latin American cases, a small group of "pioneer" adopters established pension systems in the 1920s and 1930s, most notably Argentina, Brazil, Chile, and Uruguay; other countries followed in the 1940s and 1950s. All these welfare systems began covering the most powerful groups of public employees and organized formal-sector workers. Protections were then extended to a broader range of occupational categories. Mesa-Lago (1978, 15–16) refers to such expansion as the massification of privilege.

Not all systems expanded to the same extent, and at the onset of the 1980s, substantial differences existed across the cases. In Argentina, Uruguay, Chile, and Costa Rica, coverage of the economically active population ranged from 60 to over 80 percent. In most of the other cases, the range of coverage was from about 20 percent to just under one-half.[2]

---

[2] In Brazil, official coverage reached 90 percent of the workforce in the mid-1970s as a result of the extension of noncontributory social security to rural and informal-sector work-

Such variations in coverage in part followed the timing of initial adoption, which in turn depended on the level of development and the share of the population in "reachable" employ when these programs were initiated. As we suggest in chapter 2, however, electoral competition also played an important role in this expansion.

Despite these differences, the cases also show important commonalities. Governments established formal social-insurance systems that covered important sections of the urban working class while excluding or providing only minimal benefits to large informal and rural sectors. These systems were pay-as-you-go, defined benefit programs, and governments effectively assumed the role of covering any deficits they incurred. This commitment was reflected in very large welfare expenditures in a number of Latin American countries, most notably Uruguay, Chile, and Brazil. Generous commitments contributed to full-blown pension crises during the 1980s and 1990s in a number of countries in the region (chap. 7).

The history of pensions in Eastern Europe is of even longer standing than that same history in Latin America, with emulation of Germany playing a crucial role in their initial design in the interwar period (Müller 1999, 61). These schemes were taken over by the new Communist regimes. Favorable benefits for industrial workers in the state sector initially bore some resemblance to the occupationally based systems of Latin America. But the nationalization of the economy, the employment guarantees characteristic of socialist systems, and the collectivization of agriculture provided the basis for much wider coverage. Because of the nature of the socialist economy, the informal and self-employed sectors were highly limited in scope; all workers were effectively employees of the state. And in crucial contrast to the Latin American countries, state farms and cooperatives began to provide for the social security of peasants as early as the 1950s.

Pensions in Eastern Europe were financed out of social-consumption funds that also covered a wide variety of other social benefits, from family allowances to social assistance for the elderly. Work units made substantial contributions and administered funds at the enterprise or "work unit" level. However, despite residual social-insurance principles in several cases, these funds were ultimately financed by the government, and employees paid very low or no payroll taxes. Direct government control over the level of benefits—and indeed, over all consumption—meant that it could shirk on obligations. Nonetheless, by the time that the socialist systems collapsed, coverage was de facto universal in the countries of interest to us, creating a strong sense of entitlement.

---

ers. But actual coverage was as little as 30 percent of the economically active population (Weyland 2004).

In Asia as in Latin America, most countries developed special coverage for the military, for civil servants, and in some cases, for teachers as well. But coverage for private-sector workers in Asia was much narrower or involved a limited financial role for the government. As of 1980, Korea and Thailand had no publicly organized pension system for private-sector workers. In Taiwan, Singapore, and Malaysia, social-security systems followed a defined contribution model. Financial responsibility fell overwhelmingly on employers and employees, with the government's role limited to administration. The Philippines is the one exception; in 1954, the country adopted a social-insurance scheme that by 1980 covered over half the economically active population, but benefits were limited, and public employees received favorable treatment.

HEALTH SYSTEMS: INSURANCE AND BASIC HEALTHCARE

Healthcare systems mirrored pension systems to a substantial extent and, in some cases, were closely intertwined with them. The Eastern European countries established national-health systems with direct provision by government hospitals and clinics and services provided free at the point of delivery. By the 1980s, these national-health services were experiencing well-documented problems of undersupply, queuing, and under-the-table payments to healthcare providers. Though health indicators deteriorated in the 1970s and 1980s, all residents were nevertheless, entitled to public-health care, effectively as a citizenship right.

In most of the Latin American countries, health insurance for state and formal-sector workers was financed through payroll contributions and government transfers and administered through the same social-security funds that managed pensions.[3] Health expenditures were relatively high (table 1.2), but, as with pensions, were unequally distributed. The responsibility for uncovered sectors of the population was generally assigned to ministries of health, which remained underfunded and politically weak. By the late 1970s, coverage through social-security funds or government services had extended to most sectors of the population in Costa Rica, Uruguay, Chile, and Argentina. But biases toward the formal sector contributed to sharp inequalities in terms of quality and ease of access, and in most other countries, between 40 and 70 percent of the population fell outside the system entirely.

Once again, the mix between public and private commitments is very different in East Asia. Singapore and Malaysia, which inherited national-health systems from the British, had shares of public healthcare expenditures in gross domestic product (GDP) that approximated the Latin Amer-

---

[3] Partial exceptions were in Argentina, where unions directly controlled organizations (*obras sociales*) that financed healthcare for their members, and Uruguay, where semipublic mutual funds played a similar role.

TABLE 1.2
Basic Healthcare: Policy and Performance in Latin America, East Asia,
and Eastern Europe, c. 1980

	Percent of births attended by trained personnel	DPT immunization (percent of children under 1 year)	Hospital beds per 1000	Physicians per 1000
Argentina	93	41	5.59	2.68
Brazil	84	37	5.00	0.77
Chile	97	85	3.41	0.52
Colombia	61	16	1.56	0.76
Costa Rica	97	86	3.31	0.60
Mexico	69	44	0.70	0.96
Peru	57	16	2.50	0.72
Uruguay	n.a.	53	5.00	2.00
Venezuela	69	56	0.33	0.83
Latin America average	78	48	2.90	1.09
Korea	100	61	1.70	0.60
Malaysia	89	67	2.28	0.26
Singapore	100	84	3.96	0.85
Philippines	69	47	1.71	0.13
Taiwan			2.22	2.38
Thailand	52	49	1.54	0.15
East Asia average	82	62	2.24	0.73
Bulgaria	n.a.	97	8.85	2.46
Czechoslovakia	n.a.	95	11.30	2.30
Hungary	n.a.	99	9.10	2.30
Poland	n.a.	96	5.60	1.80
Romania	n.a.	95	8.78	1.48
Eastern Europe average	n.a.	97	8.73	2.07
LA-EA (p-value)	0.75	0.24	0.30	0.41
LA-EE (p-value)	n.a.	0.00	0.00	0.01
EA-EE (p-value)	n.a.	0.01	0.00	0.01

Source: World Development Indicators (World Bank 2007).

ican average. In all the other Asian countries, however, public-health spending was small and concentrated on public health rather than on social insurance. By 1980, Thailand provided no national medical insurance, Korea moved toward national-health insurance very late, and Taiwan provided only limited insurance as a component of a defined-contribution scheme.[4]

---

[4] The Philippines, again, represents a partial exception. However, social insurance was thin, with a substantial role for out-of-pocket expenditure and private provision.

The presence of health-insurance programs does not necessarily correlate with attention to basic health services; to the contrary, public-health-insurance expenditure and curative care can compete with the expansion of basic health services. Table 1.2 provides information on a number of indicators that capture different priorities across countries. We interpret hospital beds and the number of physicians as proxies for an emphasis on curative care, with more basic forms of healthcare indicated by government performance with respect to immunization and the availability of trained personnel to assist in births.[5]

The Eastern European countries had higher scores on measures of basic healthcare than did countries in the other two regions. Immunization rates were close to universal (Gauri and Kaleghian 2002). They also had significantly higher number of hospital beds and doctors per 1000 population, however, suggesting a strong emphasis on curative care as well. Despite this emphasis—and, arguably, because of it—actual health conditions for those who survived infancy did not continue to improve. In 1965, Eastern Europe had significantly higher life expectancies than Asia (for both men and women) and than Latin America (for women). But these differences narrowed and became insignificant by 1980 (Preker and Feachem 1994).

When we turn to Latin America, we see fairly substantial intraregional variance. Several Latin American cases, including Chile and Costa Rica, have high levels of immunization and birth attendance. In most countries, however, there is evidence of substantial inattention to basic care. In Venezuela and Uruguay, barely half the relevant cohorts were immunized, and the remaining countries fell under 50 percent. Poor performance in these indicators of basic health coexisted with high numbers of hospital beds and physicians per capita. Such discrepancies appear especially pronounced in Peru, Colombia, and Brazil.

Although Asian countries averaged somewhat higher rates of birth attendance and immunization than did Latin America, there was also considerable variation in that region. But even Thailand and the Philippines—the two poorest countries in the region—immunized children at rates close to the Latin American average and substantially more than Argentina, Brazil, Colombia, and Mexico—all much wealthier and more urbanized societies. Thailand and the Philippines had low rates of birth attendance, but Korea, Singapore, and Malaysia had scores comparable to or better than Costa Rica, Chile, and Argentina. Despite relatively low levels of healthcare spending in these countries, access to basic services contrib-

---

[5] Omitted from the table are standard measures of the effectiveness of health systems—for example, mortality rates (McGuire 2001a). These are influenced by a variety of factors such as economic growth and demography that are less directly related to social policy.

uted to reasonably strong performance with respect to infant mortality (McGuire 2001a).

EDUCATION

Cross-regional differences are once again marked when we consider education (table 1.3). East Asia and Latin America had quite similar levels of spending on education as a share of GDP. But when we look at other indicators, we see notable differences in priorities. First, the Latin American countries devoted a significantly higher share of total primary and secondary educational spending on the secondary grades. Korea, Taiwan, and Singapore achieved near-universal primary enrollment relatively early in the postwar period, and the remaining Asian countries quickly caught up. In the 1960s, Malaysia, the Philippines, and Thailand had levels of primary-educational achievement that were roughly half those of the Latin American countries; by 1980, they had surpassed them. Even in Chile, Uruguay, and Costa Rica, primary enrollments remained in the high eighties or low nineties. Overall, the difference in primary enrollments between the two regions is statistically significant (p-value 0.02).[6]

These differences in educational performance are confirmed by other cross-national work. Londoño (1995) calculates a simple correlation between the educational level of the population over the age of twenty-five and per capita income (purchasing power parity [PPP] adjusted). Running this regression on a cross-section of 173 countries using 1994 data, he finds that Asian countries and countries that were or had been socialist—including China and Eastern Europe—tended to have higher educational levels than expected for their level of development, while Latin America tended to have less. At the beginning of the postwar period, the labor force in Latin America had an average of 2.4 years of education, when its level of development would have predicted approximately 4 years.

These indicators of educational attainment measured by enrollments are mirrored even more strongly in two indicators of the *efficiency* of the educational system: the primary dropout rate and the share of each school-aged cohort reaching the fifth grade. Given missing data for Eastern Europe, we again focus on the contrast between Latin America and East Asia. Even if we exclude the extraordinarily high dropout rates in Brazil, the average dropout rate in Latin America is more than double

---

[6] The differences are less marked with respect to secondary education, but the performance is also more variable. In East Asia, Thailand has a notoriously weak record of secondary-school achievement. But a number of Latin American countries show net secondary-school enrollments below 50 percent in 1980, including Brazil (46 percent), Colombia (39 percent), and Venezuela (24 percent).

TABLE 1.3
Educational Spending, Enrollments, and Efficiency in Latin America, East Asia, and Eastern Europe, 1980

	Real government primary education expenditure per pupil (1985 PPP dollars) A	Real government secondary education expenditure per pupil (1985 PPP dollars) B	A/B	Net primary enrollment	Net secondary enrollment	Primary school drop-out rate	Percent of age group reaching 5th grade (M/F)
Latin America							
Argentina	413	778	.53	97	59	34.3	73/74
Brazil	191	569	.33	80	46	78.0	n.a.
Costa Rica	421	830	.51	93	70	25.1	82/81
Chile	331	567	.58	73	60	24.2	36/39
Colombia	140	205	.68	89	39	43.0	77/82
Mexico	210	495	.42	98	67	11.9	n.a.
Peru	n.a.	n.a.	n.a.	87	70	n.a.	78/74
Uruguay	442	678	.65	87	70	14.0	97/99
Venezuela	259	824	.31	83	24	31.5	n.a.
Latin America average	301	618	.50	87	56	33.0[a]	73/74
East Asia							
Korea	304	267	1.13	100	76	6.1	94/94
Malaysia	419	754	.55	92	48	1.0	97/97
Philippines	107	75	1.42	95	72	25.0	68/73
Singapore	474	878	.53	100	66	10.0	100/100
Taiwan	253	440	.57	97 (1983)	76 (1983)	<5.0[b]	96/94[b]
Thailand	180	200	.54	99[c]	29[c]	23.3	n.a.
East Asia average	289	435	.79	97	58.2	13.1	91/92
Eastern Europe							
Bulgaria	n.a.	4657	n.a.	95	73	n.a.	n.a.
Czechoslovakia	751	736	n.a.	n.a.	n.a.	n.a.	n.a.
Hungary	666	1235	n.a.	96	70	8.0	96/97
Poland	n.a.	n.a.	n.a.	98	n.a.	7.0	n.a.
Romania	165	308	n.a.	n.a.	n.a.	n.a.	n.a.
Eastern Europe average	527	1734	n.a.	96.3	72	8.0	n.a.
LA-EA (p-value)	0.88	0.26	0.13	0.01	0.60	0.03	0.13/0.11
LA-EE (p-value)	0.34	0.34	n.a.	0.01	0.02	0.01	n.a.
EA-EE (p-value)	0.32	0.28	n.a.	0.61	0.24	0.35	n.a.

Sources: Barro and Lee 2000.
[a] Excluding Brazil: 26.2.
[b] Authors' estimates based on net percentage of students entering secondary school (Republic of China 2004).
[c] Gross enrollment.

TABLE 1.4

Gini Coefficients for Education in Latin America, East Asia, and Eastern Europe, 1960 and 1980

	Education Gini 1960	Education Gini 1980	Absolute change
Latin America			
Argentina	.344	.325	−.019
Brazil	.628	.484	−.144
Chile	.413	.370	−.053
Colombia	.534	.472	−.062
Costa Rica	.390	.395	+.005
Mexico	.561	.497	−.064
Peru	.557	.414	−.143
Uruguay	.388	.357	−.031
Venezuela	.575	.426	−.149
Latin America average	.488	.412	−.076
East Asia			
Korea	.547	.333	−.214
Malaysia	.650	.471	−.179
Philippines	.470	.340	−.130
Singapore	.592	.510	−.082
Taiwan	.562	.333	−.229
Thailand	.465	.371	−.094
East Asia average	.548	.393	−.155
Eastern Europe			
Bulgaria	.322	.308	−.014
Czechoslovakia	.232	.211	−.021
Hungary	.224	.160	−.064
Poland	.271	.162	−.109
Romania	.354	.300	−.054
Eastern European average	.281	.228	−.053
LA-EA (p-value)	0.21	0.56	0.03
LA-EE (p-value)	0.00	0.00	0.43
EA-EE (p-value)	0.00	0.01	0.01

Source: Thomas, Wang, and Fan (2001, 2003, and communication with authors).

Note: Education Ginis are for entire population 15 and over, calculated using average years of schooling.

that of the five Asian countries for which there are data. These differences are significant at the .05 level for dropouts and the 0.1 level for the share of the cohort reaching fifth grade.

Thanks to the work of Thomas, Wang, and Fan (2001, 2003), we are able to provide an overview of the *distribution* of educational attainment as well. Table 1.4 shows these education Gini coefficients, calculated for both 1960 and 1980, using years of educational attainment for the entire population over the age of fifteen. Not surprisingly, the Eastern European countries have a significantly more egalitarian distribution of educational attainment than the other two regions. The East Asian cases in our sample had a more unequal distribution of education than the Latin American cases in 1960 (although not significantly so). By 1980, however, they had become more equal. While all three regions saw improvements in the distribution of education between 1960 and 1980, those improvements were significantly larger in East Asia than in either Latin America or Eastern Europe.

Socioeconomic Correlates

Our explanation for the cross-regional differences described above emphasizes political economy factors: critical realignments, the choice of development strategy, and regime type. However, the countries in our study also vary along a number of economic and social dimensions, any of which might influence the differences in welfare systems we have underlined. It is important to control for these other possible determinants.

The use of a panel approach to test for the impact of these factors over time is precluded by the paucity of data for the pre-1980 time period. We are, however, able to use simple cross-sectional regressions to frame our case analysis. We do not believe these regressions can be given a strong causal interpretation, but they are nonetheless highly suggestive. We consider four clusters of possible correlates of social spending and outcomes: the level of income and the speed and volatility of economic growth; economic structure and structural change; social stratification and inequality; and demographic factors. Appendix 3 provides descriptive statistics and a more detailed description of the models.

It is, first, important to take into account differences in level of development (Pampel and Williamson 1989). As of 1980, many Eastern European and Latin American countries were still wealthier and more urbanized than many of the Asian cases in our sample, which might account for higher welfare spending. Differences in the rate and volatility of growth might also affect welfare-state expansion. Countries in all three regions grew rapidly during most of the postwar period, but marked slowdowns in Latin America and Eastern Europe during the 1970s may have created weaker employment or wage growth, greater insecurity, and greater demand for formal social insurance. Conversely, in Asia, higher expected income growth may have dampened interest in redistributive policies (Benabou and Ok 2001; Haggard 2005). Differences in the *volatility* of growth can have a similar effect (Alesina, Glaeser, and Sacerdote 2001). In countries where growth is highly volatile, individuals and households may have a greater interest in public mechanisms for smoothing income.

In view of the debates over the possible consequences of exposure to international markets, we also consider the effects of trade openness. This variable is especially relevant for assessing differences between the relatively closed economies of Latin America and the more open East Asian cases.

There are also wide differences among the countries on various measures of heterogeneity, such as ethnic fractionalization and the distribution of income. Ethnic fractionalization has been associated with difficulties in providing public goods and can undermine redistribution as well (Alesina and Glaeser 2004). Predictions with respect to inequality are more indeterminate. A number of theoretical papers have argued that inequality generates greater political pressures for redistribution (Romer 1975; Roberts 1977; Meltzer and Richard 1981). However inequality in assets and income is likely to be closely related to inequality in political power, a condition that, in turn, might generate social policies that perpetuate existing patterns of social stratification.

Finally, we would expect demographic factors to influence the expansion of welfare commitments. As populations age, pension and healthcare expenditure can be expected to grow (see appendix 3 for basic demographic indicators). As populations age, the elderly also become more politically influential and thus able to command a larger share of public resources.[7]

Given our concern with the effects of regime type, we also include a "democracy" score, measured as the percentage of years in the postwar (or postindependence) period in which a country reaches a score of 6 or higher on the Polity IV index; in using this particular measure, we follow Gerring et. al. (2005) in conceptualizing democracy as a "stock" variable. To assess the possible impact of regionally specific factors that are not captured by these other variables, we add Asia and Latin America dummies for the countries of interest in this volume and dummies for the Eastern European countries where data are available.[8]

The dependent variables include real per-capita social-security and healthcare spending and per-pupil primary-education expenditure. Separate models also estimate variance in rates of immunization and adult illiteracy. The first is a useful proxy for basic healthcare efforts; the second reflects long-term efforts with respect to the educational system. Each

[7] See Brown and Hunter 1999 for a discussion of how to give demographic variables a political interpretation.

[8] We have dummied separately for Singapore, which is a large outlier in terms of openness, wealth, urbanization, and other key variables.

of these measures is averaged for 1976–80, the end of the historic period of interest to us here. The independent variables, with the exception of democracy, are averaged over the early part of the decade (1971–75). The sample sizes range from approximately 45 to over 90 developing countries.[9]

Eastern European countries cannot be included in most of the regressions because of data that is either missing or not comparable. However, we will show in chapter 4 that socioeconomic factors are unlikely to be significant. When welfare systems were imposed by the Communists in Eastern Europe, the countries of that region varied quite widely along many of the dimensions considered here, but then quickly converged on common models.

In constructing "base models"—those that do not include the regional dummies—we include controls that were relevant to the policy area in question and dropped others when they consistently failed to reach levels of standard significance. For the purposes of this volume, the regional dummies are of particular interest because they capture factors specific to each region that are not modeled by the other regressors. Inclusion of the regional dummies substantially increases the overall explanatory power of each regression and suggests significant cross-regional differences.

Contrary to the modernization approach, the models of social-security spending shown in table 1.5 display surprisingly weak results with respect to level of development, urbanization, and industrialization. Neither growth nor the volatility of growth proved significant. The age composition of the population is highly correlated with social-security spending. Ethnic fractionalization is negatively correlated with spending.[10] Coefficients for democracy are positive, although they fall below standard-significance levels once regional dummies are introduced; these results were not changed by using a selection model to account for democracy itself.

Even controlling for the effects of the level of development and other socioeconomic variables, the coefficients on the East Asia dummy suggests that social-security spending was significantly lower than that found in other countries in the sample. The Latin American dummy is not significant, but signs do go in a positive direction, opposite to those of the East Asian countries.

---

[9] In addition to the Latin American and Asian countries covered in this volume, these developing nations include African and Middle Eastern countries, poorer countries of Central America and the Caribbean, and Asian countries outside the East and Southeast regions.

[10] The Gini index is also negatively and significantly related to social-security spending, but interpretation of this result poses serious and obvious problems of endogeneity.

TABLE 1.5
Correlates of Social-Security Expenditure in Developing Countries (share of GDP, 1976–80)

Per capita GDP	0.000	−0.000					
	(0.80)	(0.62)					
Urban			0.020		0.020	0.022	0.019
			(1.05)		(1.06)	(1.06)	(0.99)
Industrialization				−0.022			
				(1.05)			
Yrs. democratic	2.354	1.908	1.966	0.969	1.966	1.718	1.970
	(2.00)*	(1.27)	(1.24)	(0.51)	(1.23)	(1.06)	(1.23)
Trade	0.002	0.013	0.003	0.012	0.003	0.009	0.003
	(0.34)	(2.03)**	(0.38)	(1.87)*	(0.38)	(1.15)	(0.32)
Population > 65	0.776	0.745	0.667	0.651	0.667	0.620	0.614
	(3.89)***	(3.63)***	(3.26)***	(3.67)***	(3.17)***	(2.74)***	(2.82)***
Log GDP	0.386	0.563	0.305	0.451	0.305	0.338	0.305
	(1.77)*	(2.42)**	(0.99)	(1.62)	(1.01)	(1.11)	(1.02)
Latin America		5.784	3.389	10.171	3.389	4.094	2.990
		(0.86)	(0.54)	(1.45)	(0.54)	(0.66)	(0.48)
East Asia		−2.361	−1.871	−1.824	−1.871	−2.157	−2.017
		(3.45)***	(2.35)**	(2.53)**	(2.27)**	(2.54)**	(2.42)**
Singapore	−3.446	−6.369	−4.572	−5.814	−4.572	−6.932	−4.519
	(1.72)*	(3.34)***	(2.58)**	(2.84)***	(2.54)**	(3.10)***	(2.44)**
Eastern Europe		Dropped	Dropped	Dropped	Dropped	Dropped	Dropped
Volatility of growth					0.000		
					(0.00)		
Growth						0.050	
						(0.74)	
ELF							−1.086
							(1.39)
Constant	−10.363	−14.735	−8.608	−11.283	−8.610	−9.881	−7.791
	(2.05)**	(2.69)**	(1.21)	(1.81)*	(1.24)	(1.40)	(1.10)
Observations	50	50	50	49	50	49	50
R-squared	0.62	0.68	0.69	0.65	0.69	0.70	0.70

Sources and definitions of variables: see appendix 3.
Robust t statistics in parentheses.
  * significant at 0.1 level
  ** significant at .05 level
  *** significant at .01 level.

In the area of education spending (table 1.6), the regional patterns are reversed. Latin American countries consistently underspend relative to the Asian countries and the rest of the sample, holding constant per-capita income, urbanization, and the school-age population. Regressions on adult illiteracy in table 1.7, which include Eastern Europe, show a similar

Table 1.6
Correlates of Spending per Primary-School Pupil in Developing Countries, c. 1980

Per capita GDP	0.063	0.090			0.076	0.090
	(2.45)**	(3.24)***			(2.65)**	(3.12)***
Industrialization			5.057			
			(1.05)			
Urban				6.921		
				(3.91)***		
Yrs. democratic	60.226	97.427	56.614	167.788	36.704	94.440
	(0.85)	(1.30)	(0.59)	(1.79)*	(0.38)	(1.22)
Trade	1.039	0.329	0.483	0.369	1.143	0.560
	(1.56)	(0.49)	(0.43)	(0.62)	(1.30)	(0.79)
Population < 15	−10.990	−10.155	−17.375	−13.001	−8.886	−12.057
	(2.32)**	(2.18)**	(5.37)***	(3.98)***	(1.68)*	(2.54)**
Log GDP	−21.078	−18.317	−16.511	−20.924	−5.687	−11.785
	(1.46)	(1.21)	(0.59)	(1.19)	(0.33)	(0.78)
Latin America	−253.050	−51.795	−269.866	−220.719	−257.373	
	(3.05)***	(0.60)	(2.71)***	(2.15)**	(3.04)***	
East Asia	−51.590	−63.074	−33.112	−82.585	−54.536	
	(0.91)	(0.94)	(0.53)	(1.18)	(1.11)	
Singapore	−566.277	−424.497	−256.436	−566.888	−674.235	−527.990
	(2.44)**	(1.99)*	(0.70)	(3.14)***	(2.32)**	(2.16)**
Eastern Europe		Dropped	Dropped	Dropped	Dropped	Dropped
Gini					−3.338	
					(0.76)	
ELF						133.711
						(1.56)
Constant	999.799	920.445	1,182.767	1,013.750	687.010	764.675
	(2.38)**	(2.37)**	(1.76)*	(2.08)**	(1.50)	(1.95)*
Observations	69	69	66	69	52	68
R-squared	0.54	0.62	0.42	0.59	0.64	0.63

Sources and definitions at variables: see appendix 3.
Robust t statistics in parentheses
  * significant at 0.1 level
  ** significant at .05 level
  *** significant at .01 level.

pattern. Countries in all three regions did better than the larger sample, which included Middle Eastern and African countries that still had huge educational deficits in the 1970s. But the differences in the size of the coefficients show that the magnitude of the regional effects were far larger in Asia and Eastern Europe than they were in Latin America. Latin American countries also lagged in reducing adult illiteracy. Coefficients for democracy in table 1.6 are positive but significant in only one of the models.

Table 1.7
Correlates of Adult Illiteracy in 1980 in Developing Countries

Urban	−0.577	−0.439
	(6.96)***	(4.54)***
Yrs. democratic	−19.691	−20.537
	(2.57)**	(2.77)***
Trade	−0.045	−0.085
	(0.81)	(1.32)
ELF	29.454	21.989
	(3.48)***	(2.69)***
Singapore	30.730	32.451
	(1.48)	(1.53)
Latin America		−14.365
		(2.42)**
East Asia		−28.349
		(3.28)***
Eastern Europe		−32.169
		(8.10)***
Constant	55.117	60.282
	(7.56)***	(8.84)***
Observations	89	89
R-squared	0.49	0.59

Sources and definitions of variables: see appendix 3.
Robust t statistics in parentheses.
  * significant at 0.1 level
  ** significant .05 level
  *** significant .01 level.

Democracy coefficients in table 1.7 (adult illiteracy) are negative and highly significant, but, the direction of causality remains far from clear.

Regressions on public-health spending (table 1.8) do not show consistent results, but results on immunization (table 1.9), suggest that spending is targeted in very different ways across the regions. Controlling for other factors, both East Asia and Eastern Europe devoted significantly greater effort to this aspect of basic health than did Latin America or other countries in the sample. Democracy and trade openness also have positive and significant impact in most of the models shown in tables 1.8 and 1.9.

We report these results with the appropriate degree of caution. These cross-section regressions do not capture the dynamics of the relationships between the changes in underlying social or demographic conditions and welfare policy; data limitations do not permit a more appropriately specified model or strong causal inferences. Two findings are noteworthy, however. First, many standard explanations for the development of welfare commitments do not appear to travel well to this group of countries. Sec-

TABLE 1.8
Correlates of Health Spending in Developing Countries (share of GDP, 1976–80)

Per capita GDP	0.000	−0.000	
	(0.76)	(0.34)	
Urban			0.007
			(0.92)
Yrs. democratic	1.132	0.935	0.918
	(2.19)**	(2.11)**	(2.08)**
Trade	0.009	0.013	0.010
	(2.39)**	(2.84)***	(1.95)*
Log GDP	−0.124	−0.105	−0.161
	(1.64)	(1.20)	(1.74)*
Latin America		2.818	1.731
		(1.69)*	(0.80)
East Asia		−0.417	−0.325
		(1.41)	(1.03)
Singapore	−2.973	−3.791	−3.339
	(2.46)**	(2.75)***	(2.48)**
Eastern Europe		Dropped	Dropped
Constant	3.534	2.953	4.213
	(1.88)*	(1.38)	(1.89)*
Observations	52	52	52
R-squared	0.43	0.48	0.49

Sources and definitions at variables: See appendix 3.
Robust t statistics in parentheses.
  * significant at 0.1 level
 ** significant at .05 level
*** significant at .01 level.

ond, the regional dummies consistently go in the expected direction and are significant in many of the models. Of course, the regional dummies do not tell us what it is about each group of countries that might account for the observed differences. Nonetheless, the results are generally consistent with our focus on divergent regional welfare trajectories.

THE ORIGINS AND EVOLUTION OF WELFARE REGIMES:
CRITICAL REALIGNMENTS, DEVELOPMENT STRATEGIES, AND DEMOCRACY

Our explanation for the observed differences in welfare systems rests on a more complex, historical configuration of political and economic developments than is fully captured by the variables examined above. We first examine the effects of the political realignments that occurred in the early

TABLE 1.9
Correlates of DPT Immunization in Developing Countries, c. 1980

Per capita GDP	0.003	0.002	
	(1.72)*	(0.84)	
Urban			0.207
			(1.04)
Yrs. democratic	20.316	22.852	23.972
	(1.65)	(2.01)*	(2.11)**
Trade	0.157	0.336	0.338
	(2.89)***	(2.10)**	(2.76)***
Latitude	−0.206	−0.275	−0.291
	(0.95)	(1.38)	(1.40)
Log GDP	1.039	0.701	1.154
	(0.38)	(0.18)	(0.37)
Latin America		13.980	10.121
		(1.13)	(0.69)
East Asia		22.078	22.735
		(2.11)**	(2.40)**
Singapore		−77.207	−84.790
		(1.36)	(1.98)*
Eastern Europe		72.459	73.930
		(8.61)***	(8.71)***
Constant	−8.148	−13.567	−29.235
	(0.13)	(0.14)	(0.39)
Observations	44	44	45
R-squared	0.34	0.58	0.58

Sources and definitions of variables: See appendix 3.
Robust t statistics in parentheses.
   * significant at 0.1 level
  ** significant at .05 level
*** significant at .01 level.

and mid-twentieth century. We then turn to the role played by development strategies and regime type.

Critical Realignments

Our explanation of the observed differences in welfare systems is historical and begins with critical political realignments that occurred in the early and mid-twentieth century. We define a critical realignment as a discontinuity in both the composition of the political elite and in the political and legal status of labor and peasant organizations and mass political parties. A critical realignment can involve the co-optation or inclusion of popularly based groups into the political arena through liberalizing changes in their political and legal status and appeals on the part of political elites for their support. In such settings, we would expect political elites to develop a new social contract by extending social insurance and services to these new groups. Alternately, a political realignment can entail restrictions on such groups, bans, or their outright repression. The predictions surrounding such a restrictive political realignment are much less straightforward, as the socialist cases show. In mixed-economy settings, however, we expect the control of labor and the left to limit social-policy concessions to the urban working class.

The idea of a political realignment captures our focus on the effects of underlying coalitional factors on policy choice. The importance we attach to the empowerment of left, labor, and peasant groups within these coalitions reflects our debt to the power-resource approach that has been pivotal to work on advanced welfare states. The outcomes of these critical realignments, however, reflect not only the initial strength of these groups but also the strategies of political elites and the resources available to either incorporate subaltern groups into the political system or exclude them from it. The influence of initially weak labor movements can be enhanced by elite attempts to attract them into governing coalitions; conversely, groups that are militant and relatively strong at the onset of a critical juncture can be crushed. What matters is the *subsequent* political and organizational capacity of the working class, the peasantry, and the parties that represent them.

In this section, we elaborate on the differences among the cross-class coalitions formed during critical realignments in Latin America and on the fiercely repressive Communist and right-wing governments that came to power during the Cold War era in Eastern Europe and East Asia respectively. We discuss the international context that shaped these realignments, and their long-term implications for the development of social policy.

LATIN AMERICA: THE CHALLENGE TO OLIGARCHIC RULE

Critical realignments in Latin America took the form of reformist challenges to the agroexport oligarchies that had dominated Latin American politics since at least the second half of the nineteenth century. Economically, oligarchic states generally embraced principles of free trade and capital movement and relied on the booming demand for primary products that accompanied industrialization in continental Europe and the United States. Politically, these governments offered some avenues of participation to portions of the middle class, but they remained closed to broader participation, and they reacted to emerging labor movements with a mixture of repression and ad-hoc concessions. The countryside was dominated by large landowners and conservative political bosses, and opportunities for peasant mobilization faced daunting constraints.

The political forces that challenged the old order encompassed a relatively wide cross-section of groups from the middle and even upper classes, including centrist politicians, intellectuals, military officers, and dissident factions of the oligarchy itself. However, as Ruth and David Collier (1991, 7) argue, political leaders also "began to pursue far more extensively than before the option of mobilizing unions as a base of support." Where reformers were able to break through and take power, they passed comprehensive labor codes. These codes imposed limits on organization and collective bargaining but also recognized unions as legitimate political actors.

At the time, international conditions were favorable to those realignments. All occurred at various points during the first half of the twentieth century, a period prior to the onset of the Cold War, in which American hegemony remained limited primarily to Central America and the Caribbean. Cold War pressures did become significant features of the Latin American political landscape in the 1950s, and particularly following the Cuban revolution. But at least until that time, new political leaderships could not count on foreign patrons to back, nor external threats to justify, sustained suppression of independent labor movements.

Table 1.10 draws on the seminal work of Ruth and David Collier (1991) to summarize the timing of these critical realignments, the strategy of new political elites toward labor and left parties, and the effects they had on subsequent partisan cleavages.[11] We also note the timing of important social-policy initiatives that occurred during these breakthroughs and the type of regime at the time they occurred. By the standards of the early- to mid-twentieth century, a number of Latin American governments were relatively democratic. However, most of them placed limitations on the extent of the franchise, on the freedom of groups to organize, or on parties to compete. In some cases, antioligarchic challenges were not associated with any changes in political regime.

The Colliers' study shows how different strategies of labor co-optation contributed to integrative or polarizing tendencies in party systems and class relations. For our purposes, however, the common features of these critical junctures are of greater interest than the differences. Unions were vulnerable to state control, but remained important actors in every country of interest to us. Even under authoritarian rule, there were no sustained efforts to demobilize and destroy the union movement as a whole until the advent of the neoliberal dictatorships of the 1970s. Even in these cases, only the Pinochet regime in Chile came close to succeeding.

[11] Costa Rica was not included in the Collier and Collier study.

TABLE 1.10
Critical Realignments in Latin America, c. 1900–1950

Government	Political strategy toward left parties, labor, and peasant groups	Regime type	Consequence for partisan cleavages and labor organization	Social-policy initiatives
Argentina	Military junta, 1943–45; Juan Perón, 1946–55.	Perón incorporates labor into populist movement.	Military authoritarian, 1943–45; semidemocracy, 1946–52.	Polarized conflict between Peronists and military elites.	1943. Health insurance and pensions significantly expanded under Perón.
Brazil	Getulio Vargas, 1930–45.	Conservative coalition establishes state-corporatist controls on labor and bans left parties.	Authoritarian. Rule by decree, 1930–37; *Estado Novo*, 1937–45.	Official unions penetrated periodically by radicalizing movements.	1934–36. Pension and health legislation.
Chile	Arturo Alessandri, 1920–24; Carlos Ibáñez, 1925–31.	Conservative coalitions establish state-corporatist controls on labor; left parties outlawed under Ibáñez.	Alessandri, semidemocracy; Ibáñez, military authoritarian.	Labor organizations dominated by left parties after collapse of Ibáñez regime.	1924; pension and health legislation under Alessandri, ratified under Ibáñez.
Colombia	Alfonso López, 1934–38, 1942–45.	Reformists in Liberal Party attempt to coopt labor.	Semidemocracy.	Continued electoral dominance of traditional parties; unions remain outside party framework.	1936; health-insurance legislation during first López term; 1943; pensions during second Lopez term.
Costa Rica	Calderón Guardia 1941–48, José Figueres, 1948–50.	Reformist faction of elite and Church allies with Communists.	Calderón, semidemocracy; Provisional government after brief civil war (1948).	Center-left PLN majorities in legislature; unions outside party system.	1941; Calderón establishes health and social-insurance fund, ratified under Figueres.

Populist and left parties had greater difficulty sustaining a foothold in Latin America and their power varied substantially from country to country. Yet even when military or right-wing civilian governments banned such parties from electoral competition, they were never fully eliminated. In Argentina and Peru, labor-based parties suffered the longest bouts of exclusion from electoral politics. Yet in Argentina, Peronist politicians maintained an organizational base in the powerful union movement that had been mobilized by Perón during the 1940s and 1950s, and the party

TABLE 1.10 (cont'd)
Critical Realignments in Latin America, c. 1900–1950

Government	Political strategy toward left parties, labor, and peasant groups	Regime type	Consequence for partisan cleavages labor organization	Social-policy initiatives
Mexico	Lázaro Cárdeñas, 1934–40; Manuel Ávila Camacho 1940–46.	Radical populist alliance with labor and peasant movements under Cárdeñas.	Dominant-party authoritarian.	Labor incorporated into dominant party as junior partner.	1943, pension and health funds established under Ávila Camacho.
Peru	José Luis Bustamante, 1945–48	Bustamante forms alliance with labor-based APRA coalition.	Semidemocracy.	Polarized conflict between APRA and military elites.	1936, pension and health funds established by conservative governments prior to "breakthrough."
Venezuela	Eleazar López Contreras, 1935–41; Isaias Medina, 1941–45; Romulo Betancourt 1945–48.	Democratic Action Party (AD); attempts radical populist alliance with labor and peasant movements.	López-Medina, military authoritarian; Betancourt, civil-military junta led by AD.	Centrist parties with close union ties alternate in presidency.	1936, pension and health legislation during "conservative modernizing" government of López-Contreras.
Uruguay	José Battle 1903–7; 1911–15.	Reformist faction of Colorado Party attempts sweeping democratic reforms.	Semidemocracy.	Continued electoral dominance by traditional parties; unions remain outside party framework.	1912, pension and health systems sponsored by Battle; universal and compulsory education during first Battle term.

returned to legality and political power in the early 1970s. Peru's Alianza Popular Revolucionaria Americana Party (APRA) also remained a significant political force, despite long periods of repression by the military establishment.[12]

In Brazil and Chile, the labor codes drafted during the period of critical juncture were intended to insulate unions from populist and Marxist movements (Collier and Collier 1991, 169–96). Neither of these projects succeeded, however. In Chile, after a brief period of repression under Carlos Ibáñez, the Socialist party was able to reestablish itself as a significant

[12] Prior to the election of Alan García in the mid-1980s, the high point of APRA's influence was greatest during the government of Manuel Prado y Ugarteche from 1956 to 1962 and as the dominant opposition party during the rest of the 1960s.

electoral contender and as a force in the union movement. The Communists were outlawed from 1946 to 1952, but they participated in governing coalitions during the 1930s and 1940s and emerged again as a powerful force during the 1950s and 1960s. In coalition with the Socialists, they formed a crucial component of Salvador Allende's Popular Unity government. In Brazil, the corporatist system established under Getúlio Vargas in the 1930s was more successful in undercutting the rapidly growing Communist Party, but populist politicians remained influential. Indeed, during the 1950s, Vargas himself resurfaced as a populist, and the labor movement became increasingly radicalized in the period prior to the military coup in 1964.

In Uruguay, Colombia, and Costa Rica, the major political parties did not establish strong organizational ties to the labor movement, but left and populist political movements were significant players on the political scene. Uruguay's Colorado Party was an outgrowth of the elite politics of the nineteenth century, but maintained a strong left-of-center ideological orientation from the early twentieth century to the 1950s. In Costa Rica, similarly, the dominant Partido Liberación Nacional (PLN) had little organizational support within the labor movement but was led throughout the postwar period by politicians who identified with European social democracy. The leaders of Colombia's Liberal Party remained more closely linked to the traditional oligarchy, yet even that party included highly influential factions on the left.

In Mexico and Venezuela, finally, labor-based parties came to dominate their respective governments for decades. The Institutional Revolutionary Party, or PRI, provided the foundation of Mexico's long-standing authoritarian regime. In Venezuela's more democratic system, the Democratic Action Party, or AD, was the leading party from the 1930s until almost the end of the twentieth century; crucial to its electoral and organizational capabilities was the incorporation of labor and peasant unions. The AD held the presidency for long periods of time, and continuously dominated the legislature. Over the course of the postwar period, both the PRI and AD became increasingly nonideological and patronage-oriented. But both parties retained strong corporatist ties to the union movement and relied on it for the mobilization of support.

The integration of unions and populist political movements into the political arena—even where they were subject to recurrent controls—does much to account for features of Latin American welfare systems described in the preceding section. The initiation of national pension and health-insurance schemes can be traced to this period, either as a consequence of reformist "breakthroughs" or as defensive measures undertaken by oligarchic incumbents. These systems initially covered relatively small fractions of the population, but marked important steps toward the expansion of occupationally- based systems of social protection and were subsequently scaled up to cover a wide range of middle-class employees and urban blue-collar workers.

Reform coalitions typically included rural bosses and some land-owners, as well as blue-collar unions and populist political movements. With the partial exceptions of Mexico and Venezuela, reformers did not challenge the dominant classes in the countryside, and even in these exceptional cases, agrarian radicalism eventually gave way to the establishment of more conventional, patronage-based electoral machines. As a result, access to formal mechanisms of social security and healthcare protection was generally biased heavily in favor of urban white- and blue-collar workers.

Inequalities in the education sectors were deeply rooted in concentrations of wealth and political power that dated back to the colonial period, and reform movements often emphasized the importance of expanding the educational franchise in order to modernize and integrate their societies. Reform initiatives were constrained, however, not only be opposition from the oligarchy and the church but also by the composition of the reform coalitions themselves. Rural elites included in these coalitions had little interest in such projects, and middle-class and working-class demands focused on universities and public schools in urban areas. Access to primary education did expand into rural areas during the 1950s and 1960s, but this progress was not accompanied by sustained efforts to improve quality or efficiency, and dropout and repetition rates remained high (Engerman, Mariscal, and Sokoloff 2002; Birdsall, Ross, and Satbot 1995).

DECOLONIZATION AND COLD WAR IN EAST ASIA

For most of the countries of East and Southeast Asia, the Pacific War marked the onset of fundamental political realignments associated with the end of colonial rule, the coming of political independence, and the ascent to power of nationalist movements (table 1.11). Japanese rule of Korea and Taiwan ended in 1945. The case of Taiwan is anomalous; rather than indigenous nationalist forces coming to power, the island reverted to the Kuomintang (KMT) government, which fled there in 1947–49 as Communist victory became more apparent. Korea acquired its formal independence in 1948, following a three-year occupation by the United States. The Philippines had achieved a modicum of self-rule in 1935 but did not become independent until 1946. Malaysia and Singapore achieved independence from Britain somewhat later, in 1957 and 1963 respectively. Only Thailand enjoyed an uninterrupted history of for-

TABLE 1.11
Critical Realignments in East Asia, c. 1945–60

Country, date of independence	Government	Political strategy toward left parties, labor, and peasant groups	Regime type	Consequences for partisan cleavages and labor organization	Early social-policy initiatives
Korea, 1948	Syngman Rhee (1948–60).	American occupation suppresses Communist and populist forces on the left; left parties and unions repressed.	Nominally democratic but increasingly authoritarian over time.	Absence of left parties; unions controlled by government.	Compulsory primary education (1949).
Malaysia, 1957	Tungku Abdul Rahman (1957–69).	British defeat rural insurgency and weaken labor movement prior to independence (the Emergency).	Semidemocratic.	Ethnic parties and cleavages dominate; weak left and labor subject to a variety of controls.	Universal primary education (1961); expansion of rural health scheme.
Singapore, 1963	Lee Kuan Yew (1959–90 [1959–63, self-rule]).	Initial strategy of co-opting labor and left. Electoral defeat of left followed by repression and new controls on unions.	Democratic, becoming single-party authoritarian.	Absence of meaningful opposition after 1963; unions controlled by government.	Universal primary education (1959); major housing initiative.
Philippines, 1946	[Quezon (1935–44), self-rule] Roxas (1946–48); Quirino. (1948–53).	Conservative governments target Communist left and Huks but permit space for union movement.	Semidemocratic.	Dominance of elite parties; no effective left parties; unions enjoy legal protection but are politically weak.	Universal primary education (1935).

mal political independence before that time, but the international and regional context had a defining influence on its politics after 1945 as well.

The nature of colonial rule differed quite substantially across the region, ranging from the harsh "developmental" authoritarianism of the Japanese in Korea and Taiwan to the semidemocracy of American tutelage in the Philippines and British colonial rule in Singapore and Malaysia. These legacies influenced the course of social policy, as we will see. However, in each case independence was preceded by a complex nationalist politics in which new political elites sought to mobilize groups into the political arena, both for the purpose of achieving independence and in

TABLE 1.11 (*cont'd*)
Critical Realignments in East Asia, c. 1945–60

Country, date of independence	Government	Political strategy toward left parties, labor, and peasant groups	Regime type	Consequences for partisan cleavages and labor organization	Early social-policy initiatives
Taiwan, 1949	Chiang Kai-shek (1949–75).	Independent political forces on Taiwan repressed in 1947.	Dominant-party authoritarian.	No opposition parties; unions controlled by government.	Compulsory primary education (1947 constitution); social insurance for military and certain workers (1950); rural public health and clinics
Thailand (continuously independent)	Phibun (1948–57).	Military-royalist alliance outlaws communists and purges unions.	Nominally semi-democratic, effectively military authoritarian.	Weak opposition, no left parties; unions in state-owned enterprise sector controlled by government; unions banned in 1958.	

order to defeat rivals for power within the respective nationalist movements (for example, Smith 1981).

In all cases, nationalist movements had left wings, typically anchored by Communist parties, which sought to operate in the countryside while at the same time pursuing united-front strategies in the cities. A distinctive feature of the Asian cases is thus the wider incidence of rural insurgency—in China, Malaya, the Philippines, Korea, and later, in Thailand—and the corresponding interest of conservative political elites both to defeat such movements and to assure that they did not recur. In the early postwar period, two countries in our sample—Korea and Taiwan—undertook quite extensive land reforms that dramatically reduced the power of landlords, and all conservative governments gave at least some attention to the rural sector as a counterweight to urban radicalism.[13]

However, in all cases of interest to us, the ultimate outcome of these nationalist struggles was the ascent of conservative political coalitions

[13] In Korea, this reform was begun under the Americans and pushed along by the example of land reforms in North Korea and by redistribution that occurred during the Korean War itself. As a foreign occupying force, the KMT had little or no dependence on the local landlord class.

dominated by anticommunist political elites, and the eclipse of communist, populist, and labor challengers. International factors were pivotal in
these critical realignments. In several countries, including the Philippines
and Malaya, nationalist movements that had mobilized against colonial
rule continued to operate during the war as anti-Japanese forces. To varying degrees, such movements received external support from the Soviet
Union and China and resurfaced in the immediate postwar period. At the
same time, however, American determination to resist Soviet expansion
gradually hardened. The progress and ultimate success of the Chinese and
Vietnamese revolutions in 1949 and 1950 respectively, reinforced American concerns. The Korean War had the effect of definitively extending the
Cold War to both Northeast and Southeast Asia (Jervis 1980).

Cold War conflicts played a decisive role in determining the outcome
of the conflicts that divided nationalist movements. Political movements—and, later, governments—aligned with the United States were
clearly less inclined to accommodate or co-opt political forces on the left.
Anticommunist politics took the harshest form in the "frontline" states
of Korea and Taiwan, which received massive assistance from the United
States. But similar arguments were deployed elsewhere in the region as
well. Singapore's Lee Kuan Yew justified his assault on the political opposition in terms of the Communist threat. Postindependence Malaysian
politics appears somewhat more removed from the rhetoric of the Cold
War, but this difference should not be exaggerated. The British defeated
a rural insurgency in Malaya prior to independence, and the first independence government maintained an Internal Security Act that remained an
enduring instrument of political control through the period covered by
this book.

The extent to which governments could pursue outright repression of
the left, labor, and rural social movements was to some extent a function
of regime type. But even in nominally democratic settings such as the
Philippines, the international context limited the options for labor, the
rural sector, and the left.

In Taiwan, the KMT liquidated key Formosan nationalists, Communists, and other independent political forces and quickly incorporated
labor into state- and party-controlled unions. Korea and Thailand experienced a brief period of democratic or semidemocratic rule in the early
postwar period but also moved in an authoritarian direction fairly early
in the postindependence period. In Korea, the American occupation government broke both the rural insurgency and the communist and independent unions prior to independence. The government of Syngman Rhee
was virulently anticommunist, as was his ultimate successor, Park Chung
Hee, who came to power following a brief democratic interlude in 1960.
In Thailand, a military coup in 1947 led to a purge of radical labor unions

and the use of anticommunist laws to jail left opposition. Following another coup in 1957, the government of Sarit Dhanarajata moved in a more explicitly authoritarian direction, declaring martial law, abrogating the parliament, reversing more liberal labor laws instituted briefly in 1956, and returning to state-corporatist forms of labor organization.

In the Philippines, Malaysia, and Singapore, politics was initially more democratic, and these differences in regime had some effects on social policy. But the parameters of political competition were delimited by Cold War politics. Manuel Quezon's presidency under the commonwealth (1935–44) established features of Philippine politics that were to persist following independence in 1946: not only strong presidential powers, corruption, and patronage politics but also anticommunism and the continued dominance of the oligarchy in the countryside (McCoy 1989). Initial U.S. policy in the Philippines appeared to favor a purge of the Japanese collaborators from the political elite. But the apparent strength of the Communist Party, urban labor, and above all, the rural insurgency of the Huks pushed Douglas MacArthur to support a restoration of conservative rule. The government of Manuel Roxas prevented progressive representatives from taking office in 1946, undermining the formation of a left party. The Communist Party was banned once and for all in 1957 as the Huk insurgency gained force.

In Malaysia, the British banned the radical Malay Nationalist Party in 1948, initiated a counterinsurgency campaign against the Communist Party of Malaysia, and encouraged conservative Malay nationalists (the United Malays National Organisation, UMNO) and a business-oriented Chinese party (the Malaysian Chinese Association) (Stubbs 1989; Jomo 1986). The Emergency had largely defeated the left and weakened independent labor unions by the time of independence in 1957. Subsequent "konfrontasi" with Indonesia provided a rationale for further repression of the Socialist Front (Crouch 1996, 89–91).

In Singapore, the first elected government under colonial rule (1955) was dominated by a labor party. Lee Kuan Yew's People's Action Party (PAP) managed electoral success in 1959 only by competing for the same urban constituency through promises of social reform (Barr 2000, 110–125). But Lee skillfully outmaneuvered the left in 1961–62 around the issue of merger with Malaysia and thereafter invoked threats to national security from the Communists to justify repressive measures against left politicians, labor leaders, and dissident unions. By the mid-1960s, the PAP dominated Singapore politics, the political opposition had been crippled, and the government-controlled National Trades Union Congress monopolized labor organization.

The conservative orientation of governments in the region and the relative weakness, if not outright repression, of left parties and unions help to explain a number of the contrasts we have seen with the welfare systems of Latin America. First, political elites had few incentives to court the support of urban workers through the extension of social protection. Incentives for public investment in occupationally based health insurance or curative care were also relatively weak. Some countries did undertake relatively ambitious preventive and primary healthcare measures; but with the exception of Singapore and Malaysia, which inherited British-style national-health systems, curative healthcare was largely financed by households and provided by private doctors and clinics.

As is the case with Latin America, explanations for the relative emphasis placed on primary education must include a variety of factors that operated independently of the critical realignments we have identified, including varied colonial legacies. In contrast to Latin America, the expansion of the educational franchise held appeal across the East Asian political spectrum as a component of nationalist politics and the desire to reverse colonial cultural policies. Independence constitutions typically enshrined an expansion of the educational franchise. In chapter 3 we take up the question of how democratic rule, even if short-lived, also contributed to the expansion of the educational franchise (Chen 2007).

The case of Taiwan shows that right-wing authoritarian governments also had an interest in education, albeit for different reasons; they saw it as a way to propagate particular conceptions of citizenship and distinctive political ideologies and to exercise social control. Even as democratic rule in the region gave way to authoritarianism, commitments to education established during the critical realignments of independence were maintained.

THE COMMUNIST SEIZURE OF POWER IN EASTERN EUROPE

During the interwar period, Eastern European countries appeared to be developing in ways that paralleled Latin America (Rothschild 1975; Chirot 1989). Large peasant populations remained under the control of landowners and were only weakly represented through peasant parties. Working-class movements and left parties, while weak, had begun to appear on the political scene, but politics was dominated by aristocratic elites, the military, the bureaucracy, and urban intelligentsia. With the exception of Hungary, the post–World War I landscape was nominally democratic but far from representative; with the Great Depression, the nominally democratic regimes gave way to a variety of different authoritarian regimes in all countries but Czechoslovakia, the most developed country in the region.

As in East Asia, these developments were radically altered by international events. German domination had weakened old ruling elites, and following liberation, a wide variety of political forces resurfaced and jockeyed for power, from communist and socialist parties on the left to labor unions, and revived peasant parties. These new political forces carried reformist ideas, and had an effect on social policy prior to the Communist seizure of power. However, the Soviet-backed Communist Parties put a swift end to this new pluralism and quickly retooled the political and economic systems.

The consolidation of Communist political authority consisted of two overlapping projects (Seton-Watson 1956, chaps. 8–11; Brzezinski 1967, chaps. 2–5; Hammond 1975; Rothschild 1989). The first was political and began with the elimination of competing political parties or their reduction to token forces. Communist Parties initially participated in interim coalition governments with social democrats and other political forces, typically against peasant parties that constituted the main political and ideological alternative to the left (Simons 1991, 63–65). The "Muscovites" sought to dominate these coalitions through control over key ministries, the military, and the police. The final seizure of power typically combined the manipulation of elections with intimidation and violence against opponents; table 1.12 provides the approximate timing of these turning points. In all cases, the international setting—support from the Soviet Union, in some cases, through military occupation, and the ultimate failure of the allies to act decisively—was crucial.

Communist political systems resemble "hard" authoritarian rule in some of the East Asian and Latin American cases, including the reduction of parliaments to a nominal role, a ban on some or all parties, and purges of the bureaucracy and other institutions. However, other elements of Communist rule were clearly distinctive, including the greater and more sustained use of terror, the thoroughness of organizational purges (including of the ruling parties themselves), and the use of the party to control all social organizations and economic units, down to the level of the factory or collective.

The details of how Communist elites seized power show a number of commonalities and can be summarized quickly.[14] The meetings of the Big Three at Yalta (February 4–11, 1945) and Potsdam (August 2) effectively acknowledged the reality of the Soviet military presence in Poland but provided face-saving for the alternative London government by insisting on a coalition government and elections. The Communist core of the coalition was able to control these elections, and by December 1948, it h forced a party merger that marked the effective seizure of power. Czec slovakia was also liberated by the Soviet army. The Czech Commr initially took a more moderate stance than did their counterparts land, but quickly came under Soviet pressure to control the key

[14] These summaries draw extensively on Rothschild 1989.

TABLE 1.12
Critical Realignments in Eastern Europe, c. 1945–50

Country	Final effective seizure of power by Communists, government	Political strategy toward left parties, labor	Regime type	Consequence for partisan cleavages and labor organization
Bulgaria	June 1947, Georgi Dimitrov, 1946–49.	Dominant Socialist Party banned, minority Socialists merged with Communists, unions brought under Communist control.	Single-party authoritarian.	No electoral competition, weak trade-union tradition.
Czechoslovakia	February 1948, Klement Gottwald, 1948–53.	Socialists merged with Communist Party in 1948, unions brought under Communist control.	Single-party authoritarian.	No electoral competition, strong tradition of socialist unions.
Hungary	November 1947, Lajos Dinnyés 1947–48; István Dobi 1948–52.	Socialists merged with Communist Party in 1948, unions brought under Communist control.	Single-party authoritarian.	No electoral competition, strong union tradition, divided between socialists and Communists.
Poland	December 1948, Bolesław Bierut, 1947–52.	Wide-ranging purges of socialists, forced merger with Communist Party in 1948, unions brought under Communist control.	Single-party authoritarian.	No electoral competition, strong union tradition but fragmented.
Romania	December 1947, Constantin Parhon, 1947–52.	Socialists merge with Communist Party, unions brought under Communist control.	Single-party authoritarian.	No electoral competition, weak trade-union tradition.

of violence and intimidation: the police, army, and "people's militias." By insisting that the parliamentary election of 1948 be turned into a plebiscite on the National Front government, the Communists provoked the resignation of ministers associated with the smaller nonleft coalition members, thereby providing their entry to power. As in Czechoslovakia, the initial aims of the interim government in Hungary also appeared moderate. Elections in November 1945 and August 1947, in which the Communists fared badly, were followed by reassessments in strategy and pressure on coalition parties to drop unsympathetic politicians. In late 1947, parliament was forced to delegate power to the government, and by the time of the third election in May 1949, all pretense of parliamentary procedure was dropped and the single government list secured 95 percent of the vote.

Romania and Bulgaria were even more rural than Czechoslovakia and Hungary, and their Communist parties and union movements were relatively weak. In Romania, a National Democratic Front formed in October 1944 was the multiparty instrument through which the Communists sought power. Elections pressed by the Americans and British were delayed until November 1946, when the Communists engineered an overwhelming National Democratic Front victory. Harassment and intimidation of the political opposition stepped up in 1947. The king finally abdicated at the end of the year, and by March 1948, the Communists had succeeded in merging all the major parties under their effective control. In Bulgaria, finally, Communist efforts to purge both the government and their opponents engendered a strong reaction from both socialist and peasant parties. However the United States effectively undercut any leverage it had by signing a peace treaty in June 1947. The consolidation of Communist power followed quickly as the Agrarian Union was dissolved and the Social Democrats forcibly merged.

Once in a dominant position, the consolidation phase included purges, bans, or mergers of other political parties, including most notably the Social Democratic parties, and shutting down of all independent civil-society organizations. The penetration and mobilization of unions was a common component of Communist strategy. Labor unions provided an additional source of leverage that could be brought to bear on fragile governments. Once in power, however, unions were purged and their function shifted; they became instruments for maximizing "primitive accumulation" and output (Pravda and Ruble 1986).

Of the three regions, the critical realignments in Eastern Europe are most easily identified; there can be little doubt that the Communist assumption of power marked the onset of an altogether different development path. Despite differences in national circumstances, the seizure of power by the Communists followed broadly similar political lines and was followed by broadly similar shifts toward the nationalization and socialization of the economy. These economic changes had immediate effects on social policy, as the provision of both social insurance and services fell of necessity to the state.

A THEORETICAL REPRISE: PATH DEPENDENCE AND THE PROBLEM OF CONTINUITY

The critical realignments we have identified marked fundamental changes in both the composition of ruling elites and in the political role played by labor, the countryside, and the left. However, a central contention of path-dependent approaches to historical change is that critical junctures have enduring consequences. Why might this be the case with respect to the political realignments we have identified in Latin America, East Asia, and Eastern Europe?

First, it is important to underline the ongoing significance of the international factors that contributed to these realignments in the first place. In both East Asia and Eastern Europe, the United States and the Soviet Union provided material and organizational support and even intervened militarily and politically to sustain their new political allies. The United States also expanded its influence in Latin America during the Cold War period. It actively worked to destabilize the Allende regime in Chile and supported right-wing military coups in Brazil, Argentina, and Uruguay. But the Communist threat was weaker in these societies than it was in the "front-line states" of Asia, and the aid provided by the United States to military governments was more limited and less decisive.

Path dependence can also be explained by institutional, social, and economic mechanisms that change the cost structure of political action. In all cases, critical realignments gave new political elites control over state resources, including the coercive apparatus.[15] New political elites also gained access to fiscal resources that could be used to consolidate their political authority and buttress bases of political support. Social policy was deployed for just this purpose. Welfare policies inaugurated following these critical realignments cemented bases of political support while also creating stakeholders in the status quo. Latin America provides an example. Occupationally based pension and health funds not only created a class of beneficiaries, but provided patronage for both politicians and labor leaders as well. Service providers were also major stakeholders in the system; these included both administrators and organized health-care workers and teachers. These political forces generated strong status-quo biases.

A third source of continuity has to do with the opportunity for collective action on the part of social forces. Unions, other interest groups, and parties that were permitted to operate gained strength over time through the building of organizations; through recruitment; through the formation of institutional links with both the state and their constituencies. Little in social life is utterly irreversible; such organizations could subsequently be suppressed, as they were for, example, in Latin America following the bureaucratic-authoritarian installations of the 1960s and 1970s. But they could be weakened only at a cost. Conversely, once the organizations and parties representing labor and the peasantry were penetrated or destroyed, they could not be resurrected on short notice. Excluded groups faced daunting collective action and organizational problems, even in the context of political openings.

---

[15] The extent to which repression could be used to maintain power depended to some extent on regime type, but control over the army and police was a crucial instrument of politics in weakly institutionalized democracies as well as authoritarian regimes.

Finally, the development strategies adopted during or subsequent to the critical juncture period reinforced initial political alignments. It is to this complex dynamic between economic strategy and welfare systems that we now turn.

Development Strategies

The critical realignments discussed in the preceding section unfolded in societies that were still predominantly rural and based economically in agriculture and mining. In subsequent decades, all were dramatically transformed by economic growth and corresponding processes of structural change, most notably the dramatic expansion of the industrial sectors.

The rapid growth of the postwar era marks a sharp contrast to the economic crises of the post–1980 period that we take up in part 2. High growth, however, was achieved through radically different development strategies that embodied different assumptions about the role of the state and the relationship between the domestic and international economy.

It is important to acknowledge that the term "strategy" implies a purposefulness that was often lacking. Socialist economic policies are the easiest to trace to planners working off common economic blueprints; the models pursued in Latin America and East Asia emerged in a more ad-hoc and evolutionary way. It is also important to acknowledge that such strategies varied within regions as well as across them in the mix of policies countries adopted, in their timing, and in their effectiveness. Nonetheless, there is ample evidence for a regional clustering of development strategies. Because of the way these development strategies structured the incentives facing firms and workers, they had an important influence on social policy.

LATIN AMERICA

An elaborated development strategy of import-substitution was not fully articulated in Latin America until the "Prebisch doctrine" of the late 1940s (Sikkink 1991). But as early as the Depression, and in the larger countries dating to the late nineteenth century (Haber 2005), import substituting firms developed endogenously, and Latin American governments responded with a variety of instruments that further encouraged their growth. ISI policies showed a number of similarities across the region, most obviously with respect to their trade and exchange-rate regimes.[16] Domestic manufacturing was protected through the extensive use of tariffs, quotas, and complex multiple-exchange-rate systems. In varying degrees, these were supplemented by industrial policies that included direct subsidies and the use of state-owned banks to support industrialization.

---

[16] Bruton 1998 provides a review of one debate on ISI.

ISI typically began with basic manufacturing activities such as textiles and apparel and food processing. Chile, Argentina, Brazil, Uruguay, and Mexico moved toward more self-conscious ISI strategies during the decade from the mid-1930s to the mid-1940s, spurred by the immediate effects of global depression and war and the diffusion and adaptation of Keynesian ideas. In the larger economies, the early stages of import-substitution were followed in the 1960s and 1970s by the adoption of "deepening" strategies that sought to extend the reach of domestic manufacturing into consumer durables, intermediates, and even capital goods (Kaufman 1979). Colombia, Venezuela, and Costa Rica adopted ISI policies in the 1950s. Peru was the partial exception, remaining a relatively open economy until the 1960s. But after that point, it too adopted a similar approach to development.

A substantial debate surrounds the macroeconomic implications of the ISI strategy. There is no reason why the pursuit of import-substitution—essentially a set of microeconomic policies—would necessarily be associated with inflationary monetary and fiscal policies (Rodrik 2003).[17] Nevertheless, subsidies and transfers to loss-making state-owned enterprises had adverse fiscal implications, and Latin America had a notoriously weak tax base. Especially in the countries with mature welfare systems—Chile, Brazil, Uruguay, and Argentina—revenue shortfalls and subsidies to the pension and healthcare system also weighed heavily on fiscal resources. However, monetary policy tended to accommodate fiscal policy and financial incentives extended through the banking system, in part because structuralist thinking was relatively tolerant of inflation.

The external implications of this strategy are somewhat less contested. The bias against exports and the reliance on both imports and foreign financing were "built-in" features of the model.[18] Throughout the region, countries faced recurrent balance-of-payments difficulties that only reinforced the biases toward protection and external controls. A concomitant of the inadequacy of exports was a growing reliance on external borrowing. By the 1970s, industrialization and overall growth had become increasingly dependent on external debt, setting the stage for the crises of the 1980s (Frieden 1992).

ISI, Labor Markets, and Social Insurance. Even before ISI became a self-conscious strategy, protectionist policies in Latin America had well-known effects on patterns of employment. Protection contributed to

---

[17] Colombia, for example, combined import-substitution with a relatively cautious macroeconomic policy and avoided recurrent episodes of inflation, balance of payments crises and stabilization that plagued many other countries in the region.

[18] Diaz-Alejandro 1965 provides an early analysis of the "import intensity" of ISI.

urban labor-market dualism and overt biases against agriculture and the rural sector.[19] The widespread use of an appreciated exchange-rate favored investment in more capital-intensive products and processes, inhibited the absorption of labor into the formal sector, and thus dampened employment growth.

Labor-market dualism was reinforced by the extension of labor market protections to the urban working class. These protections included limitations on the ability to fire workers in the formal sector and generous severance requirements. Such protections, to be sure, were frequently ignored, particularly during periods of authoritarian rule or economic crises. Nonetheless, studies that control for economic shocks find that job-security regulations had a substantial impact on the distribution of employment and turnover rates (Heckman and Pages 2004, 2).[20] Individual country studies point to similar conclusions.[21] Severance-pay requirements worked as "privately provided income insurance for workers in full-benefits contracts" (Heckman and Pages 2004, 251; see also Inter-American Development Bank 2004). The combination of trade, industrial, and labor-market policies was also complementary to the occupationally based social-security legislation we described in the first section of this chapter. Labor-market protections assured the formal-sector beneficiaries of pensions and health insurance that they could keep the jobs in which their benefits were anchored.

The costs of these protections were high. A study of 100 countries (Forteza and Rama 1999: 50–53) shows that the direct cost of complying with payroll taxes and other labor-protection legislation (as a percent of the average monthly wage) was at or above OECD levels in Argentina, Brazil, Colombia, Uruguay, and Peru and well above that of the East Asian countries. Among some business groups and international organizations such

[19] We refer here not to the "classic" dualism between agriculture and the modern sector (Lewis 1954; Fei and Ranis 1964; Fields 2004, for a review) but dualism in the urban labor markets between a formal sector, defined at least in part by formal sector wage and regulatory protections, and the informal sector. See Harris and Todaro 1970; Fields 1975; and Maloney 2004, for some current controversies.

[20] Maloney's (2001, 164) analysis of a limited sample of seventeen Latin American and OECD countries shows that informality and labor turnover were primarily influenced by formal-sector productivity, interest rates, and education but that job protections and payroll taxes had effects as well.

[21] Individual country studies of Colombia (Kugler 2004) and Peru (Saavedra and Torero 2004) show that turnover increased following the liberalization of labor markets in the early 1990s. Evidence on Brazil is more mixed. Paes de Barros and Corseuil (2004) show that short-term stability increased after the 1988 constitution increased employment protection but actually declined over the longer term. Heckman and Pages (2004, 60) speculate that this effect is attributable to incentives by more-senior workers to force firing (or to collude with employers) in order to capture penalties for "unjust" dismissals.

as the International Labor Organization (ILO), and even Economic Commission for Latin America (ECLA),[22] these costs provoked recurring expressions of concern about competitiveness, efficiency, and underemployment. However, trade protection allowed employers to pass the high payroll costs of social security on to consumers through mark-up pricing.[23] Similarly, employees in the state-owned enterprise sector—which formed a crucial component of national union movements—enjoyed extensive protections at public expense.

By the 1950s and 1960s, the "structuralist" arguments famously associated with Raul Prebisch, Celso Furtado, and others were influential not only among economists, intellectuals, and policy elites but also among politicians and the public at large. These structuralist ideas emphasized the stimulative effects of generous wage settlements, social entitlements, and labor-market protections. Welfare protections and job security were sustained not only because of the pressure of national-populist political coalitions but also because the ISI strategy made them tolerable to dominant segments of the business elite as well.

Adserá and Boix (2002) argue that closure of the economy through trade protection can act as a substitute for social-policy protections by insulating the domestic market from external volatility. But an alternative approach more solidly within the Keynesian tradition sees the closure of the economy as a necessary precondition for sustaining job protections, higher payroll taxes, and more expansive social spending. However, this political bargain had important social consequences. High payroll costs and the rigidities induced by job-security legislation reinforced labor-market dualism and the consequent marginalization of informal-sector workers and the rural sector from the welfare system.

Education: The Political Economy of Neglect. Import-substituting strategies also had a discernible impact on education policy and outcomes. Workers in the urban informal sector, and in the countryside that fed it, faced weak demand for unskilled or even semiskilled labor. As a result, these workers had limited incentives to acquire secondary educations, or even to complete the primary grades; as we have noted, dropout rates in the region are notoriously high.

The political-economy effects of the model also limited incentives for either government or business to address these problems. During the

---

[22] In an influential study on Colombia, the Inter-American Committee for the Alliance for Progress (CIAP) observed that "certain Latin American industries have to shoulder relatively heavy financial burdens in connection with wage and fringe benefits." Cited in Cordova 1972, 448.

[23] See Edwards and Lustig 1997; Heckman and Pages 2004, and Taylor 1990 for a succinct summary of structuralist ideas on the role of labor markets in a closed economy.

1960s and 1970s, educational spending and enrollments expanded quite dramatically across the region. But this expansion was driven not by economic concerns but by opportunities for politicians to distribute patronage and pork through the education budget and for teachers' unions to increase their access to resources. Missing from the coalition supporting the expansion of education were private-sector interests. Given the scarcity of skilled workers, both foreign and domestic firms preferred to diversify "horizontally" into new product markets rather than to innovate, improve production processes in existing product lines, or even adapt existing technologies (Schneider 2004, 16).

The political economy of education created a particularly debilitating gap at the secondary level, a critical stage in the development of semiskilled workers. Vocational training also received little support from government or business. At the onset of the industrialization process, business groups in some countries did back the establishment of vocational training programs,[24] but interest in such programs faded rapidly, and with the significant exception of Costa Rica, financing remained extremely low by both Asian and OECD standards (Schneider 2004, 12). In the absence of an effective infrastructure of public education, the training programs that did exist served primarily to provide remedial instruction rather than higher-level training geared to labor-market needs (Inter-American Development Bank 2004, 277).

ASIA

In the immediate postwar period, the East and Southeast Asian countries also pursued import-substituting policies, driven by a combination of external economic shocks and the demands of postwar reconstruction. New economic ideas (such as the appeal of Indian-style planning) and nationalist coalitions also played a role. However, at various points, countries in the region turned to strategies oriented to the production of labor-intensive manufactures for international markets.

The first to adopt export-oriented growth strategies were the four "newly industrializing countries" (Haggard 1990). Korea and Taiwan moved in this direction in the first half of the 1960s, partly in response to declining American aid. Singapore (like Hong Kong) had long been an open entrepôt, but sought to attract export-oriented foreign direct investment in the second half of the 1960s, following its separation from Malaysia. The larger Southeast Asian countries followed with a lag and with significant differences in approach (MacIntyre 1994). Malaysia always

---

[24] An influential model emulated elsewhere in the region was the Brazilian National Service of Industrial Training (SENAI) that was formed in the 1940s, financed by a 1 percent levy imposed by the government and managed by the national Federation of Industries.

had a relatively open economy, but the island of Penang and the state of Johore, immediately proximate to Singapore, began to attract export-oriented manufacturing from the late 1960s. Thailand adopted similar strategies later still, in the early- to mid-1980s.

The Philippines represents the one important exception to the regional pattern, exhibiting a number of similarities with the import-substituting approach described in connection with Latin America. Import-substitution had substantial support from both nationalist politicians and the domestic private sector in the 1950s and 1960s. Following his coup in 1972, President Ferdinand Marcos proclaimed an interest in emulating the East Asian newly industrializing countries, but these efforts were half-hearted, and the country experienced a debt crisis in the early 1980s similar to the crises in Latin America.

The defining policy elements of export-oriented growth have been even more contentious than ISI, and a number of studies have suggested that the differences should not be overdrawn (Wade 1990; Rodrik 1998). We concur strongly. Nonetheless, there are a number of contrasts with the policy regimes of the Latin American cases, beginning with trade and exchange-rate policies. Trade policies were by no means free, but protectionist biases were offset by a variety of policies to promote exports, such as granting access to imported inputs for exporters, drawback schemes, and other financial and fiscal incentives. Most importantly, the transition to export-oriented growth was typically signaled by substantial devaluations that shifted relative prices across the economy.

The links between macroeconomic policy and the export-oriented policy regime are, as in Latin America, somewhat ambiguous. However stabilizations and major adjustments in the conduct of fiscal and monetary policy typically preceded or accompanied the adoption of more outward-looking policies. The external implications of the export-oriented strategy were not common, either: Korea, for example, was a large debtor, while Taiwan was a capital exporter as early as the 1970s. Nonetheless, the rapid growth of exports made it easier for large borrowers such as Korea to maintain access to capital markets even in the face of shocks; although the fourth-largest developing-country debtor when the crises of the 1980s hit, it did not face the wrenching adjustments of the larger Latin American countries.

Export-led Growth, Labor Markets, and Social Insurance. The transition to export-oriented strategies in Korea, Taiwan, and Singapore took place in the context of conservative ruling coalitions that had already established a variety of controls over organized labor and the left. However, the incentives facing governments and firms were also shaped by the export-oriented strategy itself, and in ways that stand in sharp contrast to the import-substituting approach taken in Latin America.[25] The transition to a more outward-oriented strategy initially took place against the backdrop of a substantial "overhang" of low-productivity rural labor and stagnant real wages. Quite quickly, the success of the export-oriented approach led to the growth of manufacturing employment, the absorption of the labor surplus, a tightening of labor markets, and rising real wages (Fei and Ranis 1964; Fields 1994).

In the "first tier" of newly industrializing countries, and later in Malaysia and Thailand as well, these dynamics produced a recurring concern about the effects on competitiveness of rising labor costs. These concerns were reinforced by the heterogeneity of per capita incomes in Asia and the "flying geese" pattern of development that resulted.[26] The continuing entry of new countries into export-oriented manufacturing and the ability of export-oriented multinationals to shift their production operations within the region at relatively low cost meant that an outward-oriented development strategy was always being challenged "from below" by lower wage countries. The first tier of newly industrializing countries (NIC)—Korea, Taiwan, Singapore, and Hong Kong—began its industrialization by taking on sectors and manufacturing activities that were no longer cost-effective in Japan. The next tier—Malaysia, Thailand, the Philippines, and Indonesia—emulated the first generation of NICs in the 1970s. These countries were followed still later by a third tier, occupied by China and Vietnam.

Ex post, it is clear that this tiered pattern of development was highly conducive to the region's growth and served as a continuing spur to industrial upgrading. As labor costs rose and comparative advantage shifted out of light-labor intensive manufactures, companies in the "first tier" upgraded through increased investment in both physical and human capital.[27] Activities more demanding of capital and skilled labor subsequently stayed put and flourished, but other products and production processes migrated offshore to lower-cost sites.

However, the apparent seamlessness of this adjustment process viewed ex post does not provide a useful guide to its political economy at the time. Both domestic and foreign firms exporting into highly competitive, price-sensitive product markets had fairly clear and predictable prefer-

---

[25] Similar arguments can be found in Deyo 1989; Verma, Kochan, and Lansbury 1995; and most explicitly in Kuruvilla 1996.

[26] See Akamatsu (1962), Kojima (2000), and Bernard and Ravenhill (1995) for a critique.

[27] Foreign investment adjusted to shifting labor costs as well. Outward-processing investments located first in Hong Kong, Taiwan, Korea, and Singapore in the 1960s in sections such as textiles, apparel, and footwear manufacturing and simple electronic components and semiconductor packaging and testing. As costs rose, these activities shifted to Southeast Asia and later to China.

ences with respect to industrial relations, the wage-setting process, managerial flexibility at the shop-floor level, and any policy interventions that added to labor costs. If the private sector in Latin America could tolerate a certain degree of slack in its relations with labor, business associations and firms in East Asia had fewer degrees of freedom.

Governments were not only politically inclined to sympathize with these business concerns but were also heavily invested in the success of these growth strategies. In contrast to Latin America, economists, policy intellectuals, and senior economic bureaucrats, many of whom were trained in the United States, were generally sympathetic with arguments emphasizing the benefits of labor market flexibility.

Development Strategies and Education in Asia. We have already suggested how the critical junctures in East Asia were associated with an expansion of the educational franchise. Decolonization, the reassertion of national identities, and at least brief democratic openings provided strong political incentives for increased attention to education. However, the shift toward more export-oriented strategies also affected the incentives to provide and acquire education (Chen 2007).

As in Latin America, the story must be understood first at the level of the labor markets. The increasing demand for labor associated with the rapid growth of labor-intensive manufacturing offset the tendency for educational expansion to produce diminishing returns to investment in education and skills. As a result, the East Asian countries embarked on a growth path that was labor demanding and labor absorbing. On a variety of different measures of labor utilization—employment growth in manufacturing, real wages, even the labor share of total income—the East Asian countries outperformed their Latin American counterparts even when controlling for differences in the underlying growth rate (Birdsall, Ross, and Sabot 1995). They also showed a stronger record in total-factor productivity growth (deFerranti et al. 2003), a necessary condition for an increase in real wages over the long-run. The "virtuous cycles" among investment in education, the supply and demand for labor, and growth itself have become a staple of the literature on the East Asian experience (for example, Fields 1994).

Much less attention has been given to the political economy of the process. An aggregate social-welfare approach would argue that when the returns on educational investment are high, both politicians and households will invest accordingly. But despite the distortions we have noted, the returns on primary education were high in Latin America as well, without such a government response.

The political logic of different development strategies helps to provide an explanation. The early phases of export-led growth could rely on the absorption of relatively unskilled—although literate—labor coming from the countryside. Over time, however, the pursuit of such a strategy could not continue to rely on the initial "overhang" of labor or an earlier investments in primary education alone. Both government planners and export-oriented firms came to have an interest in upgrading labor quality to counteract the ineluctable pressures in the labor markets. Firms did this in part through internal labor market strategies and in-house training programs (Amsden 1989). But governments were equally cognizant of these needs and developed education and training strategies that complemented the demands of firms and households for a continuous upgrading of skills (Cheng and Townsend 2000).

EASTERN EUROPE

Because of the overwhelming influence of the Soviet Union, development models in Eastern Europe showed a greater uniformity across countries than in the other two regions. The nationalization of the economy and the shift toward central planning followed closely on the heels of the Communists' consolidation of political power in the late 1940s. The central objective of the new course was a forced march toward industrialization.

Socialist industrialization exhibited a number of well-known biases. The Stalinist approach to industrialization implied both autarchy with respect to foreign trade and investment and a tendency to replicate a similar industrial structure across countries. Domestically, state socialism emphasized industry, particularly heavy industry, and capital-goods production over light industry and consumer-goods production, agriculture, and services. Outside of Poland, the collectivization of agriculture was a central component of the development strategy. The purpose of collectivization was to capture the agricultural surplus, but control over the rural sector was an important precondition for the full universalization of social insurance and services as well.

As Stalinism receded and as the socialist economies began to experience difficulties of varying intensity, reforms of various sorts moderated "high" socialist principles. Some of these reform efforts sought to "perfect" the planning process (as was the case in Czechoslovakia and Bulgaria) while others moved in the direction of market socialism (Hungary from 1968 and Poland from 1981). Countries also differed in the extent to which they exploited the process of détente to open to greater trade, investment and borrowing with the West. Nevertheless, even in the reform-Communist cases, a number of basic principles of the command economy remained intact, including state ownership of all major economic sectors, reliance on central planning, and intensive regulation of the labor market.

The Socialist Welfare State. The early "big push" strategy of the Stalinist period rested on the forced mobilization of labor, but employment was also guaranteed. Labor was "decommodified" in the sense that administrative decisions determined job placements and wages, and workers were viewed primarily as instruments of the socialist planning process. The mobilization of rural labor into the industrial sector transformed large segments of the peasantry, provided upward mobility, and was accompanied by a dramatic narrowing of intersectoral wage differences. However, pay was initially low, in line with the overall objective of squeezing wages and consumption in order to maximize capital investment; real wages dropped sharply in the early plan periods and typically lagged productivity thereafter (Adam 1984, 21).[28]

A feature of the socialist employment system is the difficulty of disentangling the wage and nonwage components of total compensation; this point is crucial for understanding the nature of the social-welfare regime. The state took on the obligation not only for employment but for the provision of basic foodstuffs, typically at subsidized prices. Housing was also the responsibility of the state—although it was continually in short supply—and enterprises provided other social amenities as well, from childcare to group vacations. The precise nature of the social contract thus depended heavily on the enterprise and the priority it enjoyed within the overall planning process. As a result, total benefits were not simply a result of wage levels or social benefits but were closely tied to the availability and price of consumer goods, housing, and enterprise-level services.

In the absence of private markets for social insurance and services, the financing and provision of pensions, healthcare, and other social services of necessity fell to the state. At the outset of the socialist era, some occupationally based differentiation existed in the social-insurance systems, and agriculture was excluded from coverage. But the seeds of universalism were sewn by the socialist economic strategy itself. Benefits extended to urban workers necessarily covered a larger and larger share of the population as the industrial sector grew. Just as important, the social provision that accompanied the collectivization of agriculture effectively brought the peasantry into the socialist welfare state, a marked contrast with the marginalization of the countryside that persisted in Latin America.

Socialist Schooling. The relationship between development strategy and educational planning was most straightforward in the socialist economies. As in the authoritarian cases of East Asia, Communist leaderships had strong political motivations for expanding education.[29] When compared to Latin America and East Asia, however, the most distinctive fea-

---

[28] The pay structure was relatively compressed both across and within sectors, however. Favored branches received higher wages than others as well as benefits such as housing (Szelnyi 1983, 19–98).

[29] Following the seizure of power, governments purged the ranks of teachers, and overhauled curricula. The party maintained a separate apparatus for implementing and supervising political education in the regular school system (Heath 1981, 229). The political mission

ture of the early socialist educational effort was its complete subordination to the broader planning effort; development strategy and educational policy were joined at the hip. This socialist strategy entailed a shift in the general curriculum away from the humanities and arts and toward mathematics and the natural sciences and a rapid expansion of vocational education of all sorts: new technical, agricultural, and economic secondary schools; part-time, evening, and adult courses; and networks of apprentice training centers.

These changes were coupled with the diminution or complete elimination of student choice and the dominance of administrative means of channeling students. Once students completed compulsory education, they were channeled into secondary schools and vocational training and into particular types of vocational training on the basis of quotas linked ultimately to the plan. The same system applied to graduates of professional high schools and most university graduates (Spulber 1957, 395–401; Adam 1984, 107). Grant (1969, 84) summarizes neatly: "with all the variations [across countries], the new systems were alike in bringing in unification, comprehensive education, expansion at all levels, greater emphasis on technical schools. . . . In short, selective systems were converted into mass systems, and brought under complete control to make overall planning possible."

DEVELOPMENT STRATEGIES AND SOCIAL POLICY: A REPRISE

The development strategies adopted in the three regions are related in complex ways to the critical political realignments discussed in the preceding section. The political developments we traced in the previous section either preceded or accompanied the adoption of the strategies we describe here and arguably provided the political conditions that made them possible. At the same time, the choice of particular development strategies and their attendant social policies also had feedback effects on underlying political alignments. Social-policy choices served to reinforce the overall political equilibrium through the incentives they generated for politicians, private-sector actors, and even labor.

First, the welfare-policy instruments we have described served the objectives of political elites. This is most obvious in the Latin American cases, where the provision of social protections to the urban working class served to solidify crucial bases of political support in the cities. Yet it was true as well in the more restrictive political environments in East Asia. Asia's minimalist welfare states offered few formal protections to the urban working class, but access to education offered opportunities for employment, upward mobility, and the accumulation of personal savings

---

of the school system was also supplemented very early by the elaborate system of youth organizations (Grant 1969, 123–38).

that buffered risk. In the wake of de-Stalinization in the Soviet Union, Eastern European Communist parties moved toward a subtly different political approach that placed marginally greater emphasis on consumption and the expansion of social entitlements.[30] As we will argue in part 2 of the book, this approach generated strong expectations among voters and interest groups.

Development strategy and welfare-policy choices also generated patterns of support, or at least acquiescence, from managerial elites (a term we choose here for convenience to include the disparate cases of managers of state-owned enterprises). In Latin America, protection, subsidies, and other policy-induced barriers to entry reduced firms' costs of accepting occupationally based social protections. Similarly, in Eastern Europe, state ownership and soft-budget constraints allowed enterprise managers to assume an array of welfare responsibilities, even if it did produce a variety of perverse incentives that have been outlined most thoroughly by János Kornai (1992, 324–25, 417). In East Asia, both foreign and domestic firms benefited from the control of labor and the emphasis on skill development.

Finally, and most controversially, the development strategy and welfare complexes associated with them had an influence even on the behavior— if not the underlying allegiances—of labor. None of these regions was immune from outbursts of labor protest, and in some cases, peasant militancy. And in all three regions, states ultimately had recourse to coercive means for dealing with it, subject to the restraints of regime type. But overall economic strategy and attendant welfare policies mattered. Again, the point is most clear in Latin America, where unions in the core import-substituting and state-owned enterprise sector were incorporated into the political system and received substantial welfare benefits. In East Asia and Eastern Europe, rising incomes—and in the socialist cases, an expanding set of welfare commitments—undoubtedly played a role in containing if not altogether eliminating labor militancy.

Democracy, Authoritarianism, and the Nature of the Social Contract

We are now in a position to revisit the effects of regime type on social policy. We argued in the introduction that there are good theoretical reasons to believe that democracy would be associated with a greater redistribution of income and greater attention to the provision of social insurance and services, *ceteris paribus*. We have argued in this chapter that the *ceteris paribus* conditions are crucial and that the effects of regime type can vary substantially, depending on the nature of underlying political

[30] See in particular Cook 1993.

alignments and development strategies. In particular, we have noted the ways the socialist realignments in Eastern Europe led to dictatorial regimes that nonetheless pursued very comprehensive welfare entitlements.

Outside of the socialist context, however, we might expect regime type to influence the course of social policy. In the case studies that follow, we consider the effects of changes of regime within countries and comparisons across regimes of different types in order to test these propositions. This requires, however, that we enter the methodological thicket of how best to classify regime type.

Tradeoffs always exist in the choice of indicators. On the one hand, the simplicity of a dichotomous measure reflects our intuitive sense of a fundamental qualitative difference between democratic and authoritarian regimes. Przeworski et al. (2000) use such a measure to good effect. But regimes in many of the countries we cover are clearly mixed types, for which a dichotomous measure is an extremely blunt instrument. Efforts to create scales of the extent of democracy or authoritarianism also pose challenges, however. It is often difficult to discern the conceptual significance of the incremental differences in continuous scales and to have confidence that the intervals are of equal significance at all points (for example, that a change from 1 to 2 is equivalent to a change from 6 to 7 or 9 to 10).

In the following chapters, we modify a useful coding scheme developed by Mainwaring, Brinks, and Pérez-Liñán (2001, hereafter MBP-L) that establishes a middle ground between these alternatives. They code regimes along four dimensions that are directly germane to our theoretical interests: the integrity and competitiveness of national elections; the inclusiveness of the franchise (by the historical standards of the period); respect for civil liberties (which goes to the freedom of interest groups to organize); and whether elected governments actually exercise control over policy (a full description of the coding scheme is contained in appendix 4). Countries in which there are no significant "violations" of these standards are coded as democratic. Countries with "major" violations in one or more of these criteria are coded as authoritarian. MBP-L also introduce a third category of "semidemocratic" regimes for those countries in which there are "minor" violations in one or more of the four criteria.

Given our theoretical hunch that electoral competition plays a role in the expansion of social commitments, we supplement their scheme in several important ways. First, even though suffrage in some democracies may be inclusive "by the standards of the period," it is important to take into account significant restrictions on the franchise in some of the Latin American regimes which MBP-L code as "democratic" or "semidemocratic"; we note these restrictions in table 1.13.

TABLE 1.13
Measures of Regime Type

	Democratic years (1945 or independence to 1985) (N=369)	Semidemocratic years (1945 or independence to 1985) (N=369)	"Soft" authoritarian years (1945 or independence to 1985) (N=369)	"Hard" authoritarian years (1945 or independence to 1985) (N=369)	Polity IV: Number of democratic years (1945 or independence to 1985) (N=369)	Number of Przeworski et al. democratic years (1950–90) (N=325)	BDM W = 1 years (1945 or independence to 1985) (N=369)
			Latin America (from 1945)				
Argentina	5	13	8	15	5	18	0
Brazil	1	18[a]	21	1	5	21	0
Chile	29[a]	0	0	12	10	14	0
Colombia	12	19	0	10	29	23	2
Costa Rica	37	4	0	0	41	36	39
Mexico	0	0	41	0	0	0	0
Peru	11[a]	9[a]	0	21	6	17	0
Uruguay	28	0	0	13	21	24	20
Venezuela	29	1	0	11	27	27	17
Latin America, totals and shares	152 41.2% of all country years (N=369)	64 17.3% of all country years (N=369)	70 19.0% of all country years (N=369)	83 22.5% of all country years (N=369)	144 39.0% of all country years (N=369)	194 59.7% of all country years (N=325)	78 21.1% of all country years (N=369)

TABLE 1.13 (cont'd)
Measures of Regime Type

	Democratic years (1945 or independence to 1985)	Semidemocratic years (1945 or independence to 1985)	"Soft" authoritarian years (1945 or independence to 1985)	"Hard" authoritarian years (1945 or independence to 1985)	Polity IV: Number of democratic years (1945 or independence to 1985)	Number of Przeworski et al. democratic years (1950–90)	BDM W = 1 years (1945 or independence to 1985)
	East Asia (from 1945 or date of independence)						
Korea (from 1948)	1	0	21	16	1	1	0
Malaysia (from 1957)	0	12	15	2	12	0	12
Philippines	0	27	8	5	0	14	0
Singapore (from 1959)	4	5	18	0	4	0	0
							(from 1965)
Taiwan (from 1949)	0	0	0	37	0	0	0
Thailand	0	3	23	15	0	4	0
East Asia,	5	47	85	75	17	19	12
totals and shares	2.4% of all country years (N=213)	22.2% of all country years (N=213)	40.1% of all country years (N=213)	35.4% of all country years (N=213)	8.0% of all country years (N=213)	9.9% of all country years (N=194)	5.8% of all country years (N=205)

Sources: For Latin America, Mainwaring, Brinks, and Pérez-Liñán 2001. For Asia, authors' calculations.

Notes: Regimes are classified based on the characteristics of the government during the majority of the year. Thus a coup that overthrows a democratic regime before July 1 would result in that regime being coded authoritarian for the whole year; if the coup occurred after July 1, the regime would be coded democratic for the year.

a Mainwaring, Brinks, and Pérez-Liñán allow democracies to have restrictions on the franchise if they are typical of the historical period; see appendix 4. We nonetheless note these restrictions: in Chile, the absence of a secret ballot in the countryside until 1958; in Peru and Brazil, denial of the franchise to illiterates.

Second, following Levitsky and Way (2002), we distinguish between "competitive" and "hard" authoritarian regimes based on the presence of electoral competition. "Competitive" authoritarian governments have one or more major violations of the four criteria but permit electoral contests in which opposition parties are granted some leeway to mobilize voter support. Such contests are typically run on the basis of a censored opposition and without presumption that opponents will actually take office. But electoral contests do create incentives for incumbent authoritarian rulers to use social policy for electoral ends.

Table 1.13 summarizes the yearly scores on these indicators for the Latin American and Asian countries from 1945 to 1985.[31] (The Eastern European cases are not included, since all would fall into the category of authoritarian regimes by all measures reported here). We also report democracy scores from three other sources for comparative purposes: the Polity IV database (Marshall and Jaggers 2004), the Przeworski et al. (2000) dichotomous measure, and the Bueno de Mesquita et al. (2003) W measure that purports to capture the size of the "winning coalition." Each of these measures emphasizes a somewhat different mix of properties of democratic rule; although correlated, they are not perfectly analogous, as can be seen.[32] In conjunction, however, these four measures provide an overview of the incidence of democracy in Latin America and East Asia during the decades of interest to us in part 1 of this study.

---

[31] These regional differences are marginally affected by our choice of 1985 as a cutoff point, since Peru underwent a democratic transition in 1980 and Argentina became democratic in 1983. Yet these additional democratic years do not significantly affect the overall difference between the two regions.

[32] The Polity IV data reported in table 1.13 and elsewhere in the book is the widely used difference between the democracy and authoritarian scores, each measured on a 0–10 scale. We follow the convention of treating a score of 6 as the threshold for democratic rule. Gleditsch and Ward (1997) show convincingly that this measure is driven largely by the component of the index that captures decisional constraints on the executive. Bueno de Mesquita et al. (2003) purposely exclude the constraint component of the index in constructing their measure, which seeks to capture the size of the winning coalition (see Bueno de Mesquita et al. 2003, 51–55). W is constructed out of four other indices—the openness and competitiveness of recruitment, the competitiveness of participation, and the civilian character of the regime—and is measured on a five-point scale from 0 to 1 (0, .25, .50, .75, 1). A score of 1 would be considered the most encompassing democracy; a score of .75 would reflect some restrictions on the scope of the winning coalition and so on. Finally, the Przeworski et al. dichotomous measure requires democracies to have an elected executive, an elected legislature, and more than one party. A controversial feature of their coding is that a country is classified as democratic only if elected incumbents have been defeated for reelection at some later point. Countries in which incumbents are reelected for consecutive terms without eventually suffering defeat are not classified as democratic. The theoretical justification for this rule is that turnover is important to determine that the political system is in fact truly competitive. For a critique of dichotomous measures, see Elkins 2000.

Approximately 40 percent of all the years coded for Latin America using the MBP-L criteria were scored as democratic, and another 17 percent were coded as semidemocratic. Only about one-quarter of the years reach either democratic threshold in Asia, and all but a handful of those were semidemocratic. Even if we take into account the restrictions on the franchise noted in the table, these differences in the overall incidence of democratic and semidemocratic rule are significant. The regional differences are equally if not more apparent when we look at the Polity IV, measures utilized by Przeworski et. al., or Bueno de Mesquita et. al. Despite differences in the treatment of specific cases that we address in chapter 3, none of the four coding schemes find that more than 10 percent of relevant years are fully democratic in East Asia.

Of equal methodological significance is the variation in regime type *within* each region. Especially in Latin America, we see countries with little or no experience with full democracy (Mexico, Argentina, and Peru) as well as countries such as Costa Rica that experienced nearly four decades of democratic rule between 1945 and 1990. The array of semi-democracies and soft authoritarian regimes is also wide; Mexico was an electorally based autocracy throughout this period, and the Brazilian military dictatorship maintained some degree of electoral competition for almost two decades. Finally, as we will show in more detailed regional tables in chapters 2 and 3 (tables 2.1 and 3.1), there was also considerable variation within countries over time. These intraregional variations and changes over time allow us to explore whether democratization or its reversal are consequential, while controlling for region-specific effects.

Asia also exhibits intraregional variation. The Philippines had a sustained period of semidemocratic rule, with electoral competition from 1946 until the Marcos takeover in 1972, as did Malaysia in the immediate postindependence period. Singapore drifted fairly quickly from democratic competition to semidemocratic and finally to soft-authoritarian rule. Korea, Taiwan, and Thailand had a much greater incidence of hard authoritarian rule. Nevertheless, we show that even brief and incomplete openings produce initiatives to expand public protections and thus presaged the more dramatic welfare expansions that followed the third wave of democratization in the late 1980s.

The method we pursue in the following chapters is straightforward. In the Latin American and East Asian cases, we provide more detailed consideration of the influence of basic political realignments, development strategy, and regime type. In the Eastern European cases, there is no variation in regime type as we have defined it. However, there may be some variation in the extent or timing of the expansion of social-policy entitlements that is associated with functional equivalents to the political mechanisms we consider here, namely electoral competition and interest group pressures. In particular, we explore whether succession struggles or social protests from below might have generated pressures to build support through welfare concessions. Our conclusion is that these factors did not have an enduring significance. This region—more than either of the others—underscores the importance of situating institutional arguments within the context of the broader political realignments and development models discussed above.

CHAPTER TWO

The Expansion of Welfare Commitments in Latin America, 1945–80

As discussed in the preceding chapter, Latin America's stratified welfare systems reflected the urban biases of the political coalitions that challenged oligarchic rule. These biases were reenforced by the turn toward import-substituting development models. The size and coverage of the welfare state, however, varied widely across the region. More "advanced" welfare states such as Uruguay, Chile, Costa Rica, and Argentina provided more comprehensive, if still unequal, benefits than did others such as Peru, Colombia, or Mexico. In this chapter, we examine how regime type contributed to these differences. We find that the democracies, as well as some semidemocracies and competitive authoritarian regimes, exhibit a different approach from that of their hard authoritarian counterparts to the expansion of social-security and health coverage and to a lesser extent, access to education.

The mechanisms that drove this expansion are not straightforward. In the few long-standing democracies, as well as in Argentina, the expansion of the franchise and competition from popularly oriented political parties played an important role in the growth of social entitlements over time. The electoral connection and the sheer duration of democratic rule were consequential. With the partial exception of competitive authoritarian regimes in Mexico and Brazil, dictatorships were more inclined to retrench, to maintain the status quo, or to "deepen" benefits available to narrow but powerful groups already incorporated into the welfare system.

Democratic politics also expanded opportunities for labor unions to press their interests in the political arena, but this interest-group channel had ambiguous consequences. Latin American unions, unlike those in Europe, represented relatively narrow segments of the labor force and were generally unable to forge alliances with the peasantry or the urban informal sector. Although they pressed strongly for an expansion of welfare spending, their efforts were directed mainly toward social security and pension programs that were the least progressive, or even regressive, in terms of income distribution.

We begin with an overview of the diversity of political regimes in Latin America and the extent to which regime type appears to correlate with aspects of social policy. The next two sections look at the development of social policy in more detail, beginning with the democratic cases and then turning to the authoritarian regimes. The final section concludes with a discussion of intraregional differences in welfare legacies and their implications for the politics of welfare reform after 1980.

The Variety of Political Regimes in Latin America

During the period of interest to us here, Latin America exhibits a wider variation in regime type than either East Asia or Eastern Europe, running the gamut from relatively durable and inclusive democracies to "hard" dictatorships. Table 2.1 provides a coding of the Latin American countries from 1945 through 1985 using the MBP-L scheme outlined in chapter 1. The MBP-L coding of individual cases does not fully correspond with the other coding schemes presented in the table (the composite Polity IV DEM-AUTH score, Przeworski et al. [2000], and the Bueno de Mesquita et al [2003] measure), but we rely on it here because it provides a more nuanced, and more realistic, view of the differences among regimes than these other classifications.

Costa Rica and Uruguay (prior to the 1973 military coup) had the longest continuous histories of competitive politics. Until the advent of the Pinochet regime in 1973, Chile also experienced decades of constitutional government, although the lack of a secret ballot effectively disenfranchised the peasantry until the 1950s. Venezuela between 1958 and the late 1990s can also be classified as democratic. Most of the other countries experienced oscillation between military dictatorship and democracy or, as in Colombia, significant restrictions on party competition. Mexico's dominant party regime is the only continuously authoritarian system in the region.

To what extent do differences in the expansion of protection and services map onto these distinctions among regimes? In three of the four long-standing democracies (Chile, Uruguay, and Costa Rica) most of the population was covered by some form of health insurance and had access to public services by the early 1980s. Social-security coverage in these countries was among the highest in the region as well—between 60 and 80 percent of the economically active population (Mesa Lago 1989, 10). The percentage of the economically active population covered by social security was lower in Venezuela, which also experienced a long period of democratic rule. But this figure does not include a large segment of the population covered by funds outside the main social-security system.

Countries with intermittent experiences with democracy had more mixed records with respect to coverage. Argentina's welfare system, established during the Peronist era, matched those of Costa Rica, Chile, and

TABLE 2.1
Regime Type in Latin America, c. 1945–85

	Democratic years	Semi-democratic years	"Soft" authoritarian years	Hard authoritarian years	Polity IV: democratic years 1945–85	Przeworski democratic years 1950–85	BDM = 0.75 Years	BDM = 1 Years
Argentina								
No. of years	5	13	8	15	5	18	14	0
Periods	1973–74 1983–85	1946–50 1958–61 1963–65 1975	1945 1951–57	1962 1966–72 1976–82	1974–75 1983–85	1950–54 1958–61 1963–65 1973–75 1983–85	1958–65 1973–75 1983–85	
Brazil								
No. of years	1	18ᵃ	21	1	5	21	19	0
Periods	1985	1946–63	1964–84	1945	1946 1958–60 1985	1950–63 1979–85	1946–63	
Chile								
No. of years	29ᵃ	0	0	12	10	23	27	0
Periods	1945–73			1974–85	1964–73	1950–72	1946–72	
Colombia								
No. of years	12	19	0	10	29	28	29	2
Periods	1974–85	1945–47 1958–73		1948–57	1957–85	1958–85	1945 1948–1985	1946–47
Costa Rica								
No. of years	37	4	0	0	41	36	2	39
Periods	1949–85	1945–48			1945–85	1950–85	1945 1948	1946–47 1949–85

TABLE 2.1 (cont'd)
Regime Type in Latin America, c. 1945–85

	Democratic years	Semi-democratic years	"Soft" authoritarian years	Hard authoritarian years	Polity IV: democratic years 1945–85	Przeworski democratic years 1950–85	BDM = 0.75 Years	BDM = 1 Years
Mexico								
No. of years	0	0	41	0	0	0	0	0
Periods			1945–85					
Peru								
No. of years	11[a]	9[a]	0	21	6	17	19	0
Periods	1963–67 1980–85	1945–47 1956–61		1948–55 1962 1968–79	1980–85	1956–61 1963–67 1980–85	1946–47 1956–61 1963–67 1980–85	
Uruguay								
No. of years	28	0	0	12	21	24	6	20
Periods	1945–72			1973–84	1952–71 1985	1950–72 1985	1946–51	1952–70 1985
Venezuela								
No. of years	29	1	0	11	27	27	10	17
Periods	1947 1958–85	1946		1945 1948–57	1959–85	1959–85	1959–68	1969–85
Totals (N=369)	153	64	70	82	143 (N=369)	194 (N=325)	126 (N=369)	78 (N=369)
% country years	(41.5)	(17.3)	(19.0)	(22.2)	(38.8)	(59.7)	(34.1)	(21.1)

Sources: Mainwaring, Brinks, and Pérez-Liñán 2001; Przeworski et al. 2000; Bueno de Mesquita et al. 2003; Marshall and Jaggers 2004.

Notes: Regimes are classified based on the characteristics of the government during the majority of the year. Thus a coup that overthrows a democratic regime before July 1 would result in that regime being coded authoritarian for the whole year; if the coup occurred after July 1, the regime would be coded democratic for the year. The Polity IV democratic years are those in which the variable DEM-AUT is equal to or greater than 6.

[a] Major literacy restrictions on suffrage. Chile until reforms of 1950.

TABLE 2.2
Inequality, Urbanization, and Per Capita Income in Latin America, c. 1980

	Gini index c. 1980	Percent urban 1980	GDP per capita (PPP)
Argentina	41.0	83	9,200
Brazil	58.0	67	6,070
Chile	51.9	81	4,533
Colombia	51.5	63	4,706
Costa Rica	45.5	47	5,635
Mexico	53.9	66	7,130
Peru	48.0	65	4,496
Uruguay	45.0	85	5,872
Venezuela	44.4	79	5,326
Average Latin America	48.7	70.7	5,885

Sources: For Gini index, Deininger and Squire 1996; for urbanization and GDP per capita, World Development Indicators (World Bank 2007).

Uruguay. Coverage rates in Brazil were also high, because of the establishment of noncontributory pensions in the mid-1970s. But the distribution of benefits remained among the most unequal in the region. In Mexico, Peru, and Colombia, between 50 and 80 percent were excluded from core social security and health-insurance programs (Mesa-Lago 1989, 10).

As we showed in chapter 1, differences in the extent of public-welfare commitment in Latin America can be explained in part by social and demographic factors. Many of the countries with limited welfare systems were poorer and less urbanized than those with more extensive public commitments. Yet, as table 2.2 shows, it is doubtful that these differences tell the whole story. Mexico, with one of the most limited welfare systems, was wealthier than Costa Rica and Chile, and Peru was only slightly poorer. The correlation with urbanization is also quite imperfect. Although three of the large welfare states—Chile, Uruguay, and Argentina— all had relatively large urban populations, Costa Rica had the lowest level of urbanization of any of the countries in the sample. Although wealth and urbanization affected welfare commitments, other political factors were significant as well.

To provide a clearer understanding of how regime type affects social policy, we focus on the incidence of policy initiatives that either expand coverage to broader categories of blue-collar, informal-sector, or agricultural workers or add benefits to existing programs. We also discuss initiatives that sought to cut back on entitlements and funding or to rationalize the public financing or delivery of social insurance and services. Identifying these episodes is somewhat problematic, since many governments manipulated entitlements or other benefits in the short run to reward supporters or appease potential opponents (Ames 1987). We have tried, however, to identify those policy initiatives that go beyond short-run parametric adjustments and represent major shifts in the coverage, benefits, or administration of the social policy system.[1]

Table 2.3 aligns the timing of major initiatives in the provision of social insurance, health services, and education with the information on regime type presented in table 2.1. As expected, the table shows that democracies and semidemocracies were more likely than authoritarian governments to undertake a broadening of social insurance and services. In three of the countries that oscillated between democratic and authoritarian governments, the most significant initiatives to expand social insurance and health systems came from democratic or semidemocratic governments: during the Manuel Prado period in Peru, in Colombia after the establishment of the National Front, and in Argentina under Perón. In Venezuela, major social legislation was passed in the 1960s, after the overthrow of the Pérez Jiménez military regime, and in Chile and Uruguay, all of the major initiatives to expand social insurance and services came prior to the overthrow of democracy in 1973.

With the exception of Brazil and Mexico, authoritarian regimes did not generally expand social programs. Instead, their social-policy initiatives were directed either toward increasing benefits for privileged groups or toward the consolidation of existing programs. In the Andean countries, military coups cut short social-policy initiatives in Venezuela (1948), Colombia (1953), and in Peru (both 1948 and 1961). There was also surprisingly little expansion under the leftist dictatorship established in Peru under Velasco in the late 1960s, which concentrated primarily on unifying the social-security system (Mesa-Lago 1978, 120–25). Bureaucratic-authoritarian regimes of the southern cone focused primarily on the rationalization or retrenchment of the existing systems. We examine these experiences more closely in the following sections of the chapter.

WELFARE EXPANSION UNDER DEMOCRATIC RULE:
THE LONG-STANDING DEMOCRACIES

We begin with the countries with the longest experience of democratic rule prior to the 1980s: Uruguay, Chile, Costa Rica, and Venezuela. We argued

---

[1] Carmelo Mesa-Lago's (1978, 1989) pioneering studies identify landmark legislative initiatives for many of the countries in our sample.

TABLE 2.3
Regime Type and Social Insurance and Services Initiatives in Latin America

	Years (N=361)	Initiatives (administrations)
		Democracies (N=145)
Costa Rica	1949–80	1961. Constitutional amendment to universalize pensions and health insurance. 1971. Inclusion of self-employed and all rural workers in health and pension system; increased payroll taxes to expand benefits.
Uruguay	1945–73	1943. New entitlements for family-allowance and maternity benefits; coverage expanded to all workers in industry and commerce. 1954. Social security extended to rural workers. 1961. Social security extended to unemployed. 1970. Health insurance made mandatory for all public and private-sector employees. Ministry of Health increases services to poor.
Chile	1945–73	1952. Pensions expanded to new blue-collar categories. 1958–73. Expansion of primary education under Frei and Allende. 1964. Basic health program launched and expanded (Frei and Allende). 1970–73. Expansion of social-security coverage to self-employed; increase in blue-collar pensions
Argentina	1973–74	Plan to establish unified and universal social insurance and health systems aborted by interest-group resistence to standardization and by military coup.
Colombia	1974–80	Primary-school-building program, expansion of national public-education system, pushed by teachers' unions.
Peru	1963–67	Improved protection for covered groups, but also some expansion to some categories of noninsured peasants (selected Indian communities, peasants associated with agrarian reform and colonization). Expansion of hospital network into uncovered areas. Major expansion of health and social-security expenditures (by 66 percent and 250 percent respectively), but state does not pay contributions, and major deficits ensue.
Venezuela	1958–80	1961. New constitution guarantees free primary education, resulting in major expansion of access. 1966. New social-security entitlements to old-age pensions, integrated medical assistance, disability, and survivor benefits. Coverage extended to public employees and domestic workers.
		Semidemocracies (N=43)
Argentina	1946–50	Expansion of social-security and health-insurance coverage to most of the labor force. In 1954, health-insurance law established principle of defined health benefits, with progressive distribution.
	1958–61	1959. Frondizi increases benefits to covered workers.
	1963–65	No major initiatives.
Brazil	1946–63	New entitlements to covered sectors. In 1960, minimum age is eliminated as eligibility requirement for workers already covered by pension funds.

TABLE 2.3 (cont'd)
Regime Type and Social Insurance and Services Initiatives in Latin America

	Years (N=361)	Initiatives (administrations)
Colombia	1945–47	1946. Expansion of social security legislation.
	1958–73	1958. Plebiscite mandates at least 10% of government expenditures must go to education.
		1962. Establishment of Family Compensation Fund. Healthcare and education subsidies for affiliated white-collar workers.
Peru	1945–47	Initiatives to expand social-security coverage for white- and blue-collar workers cut short by military coup of General Manuel Odria.
	1956–61	APRA-Prado coalition expands social-security entitlements to blue-collar and public-sector workers. Financing for blue-collar funds increased, conditions for access were substantially eased, establishment of old-age pensions, disability and death benefits for blue-collar workers.
Venezuela	1945–47	1946. Law mandating primary education (reversed in 1948).
		1945. Establishment of Fund for Sickness and Maternity.
	Soft authoritarian regimes (N=77)	
Argentina	1945;	No major initiatives.
	1951–57	No major initiatives; *obras* expand, but public-health system allowed to erode.
Brazil	1964–84	1971. FUNRURAL extends limited social security entitlements to rural workers without a contribution requirement.
		1974. Pensions extended to old or disabled urban residents who had made partial but incomplete contributions to system.
		1976–77. Expansion of emergency health services through FUNRURAL.
		1977. PIASS: limited extension of clinics and sanitation programs for northeastern states.
Mexico	1945–90	1960. Expansion of pension coverage (Lopez Mateos).
		1973. Expansion of pensions and health coverage to rural areas (Echeverría).
	Hard authoritarian regimes (N=96)	
Argentina	1962	No major initiatives.
	1966–72	Partial consolidation of social-security funds, new restrictions on eligibility. After uprising of Córdoba unions, coverage expands as provincial employees are incorporated into system. *Obras* also expand coverage substantially after uprising, but government also encourages expansion of private providers.
	1976–83	Employer contributions eliminated, which increases financial strain on system.
		Primary education system decentralized to provinces, federal financing reduced.

TABLE 2.3 (cont'd)
Regime Type and Social Insurance and Services Initiatives in Latin America

	Years (N=361)	Initiatives (administrations)
		Hard authoritarian regimes (N=96)
Chile	1973–80	1975. Introduction of targeted work programs. Reduction of entitlements for blue- and white-collar workers. Partial consolidation of social security funds. 1980. Introduces mandatory private pension accounts for all entrants into the workforce. 1981. Establishes private health insurance funds (ISAPRES), and private schools to compete with public systems.
Peru	1948–55	No major expansion initiatives. Some benefits to white-collar workers.
	1962	Caretaker regime; no major initiatives.
	1968–80	Effort to consolidate blue- and white- collar social-security funds and standardize benefits, leading to slight improvement in access for blue-collar workers. Did not implement stated priority of extending coverage to rural and self-employed workers and left system underfunded.
Uruguay	1973–84	Partial consolidation of social-security funds, but increased retirement age and reduced benefits. 1981 law eliminated restrictions on affiliation to mutual funds of older persons and pregnant women but enacted significant cutbacks in expenditure. Efforts at greater control and centralization of education but no major changes. Expenditures lag behind increases in enrollment.
Colombia	1948–57	No major expansion initiatives.
Venezuela	1948–57	No major expansion initiatives.

in the introduction that the duration of democratic rule matters: long-standing democracies offer more-extended opportunities for the mobilization of parties and interest groups that appeal to low-income sectors and greater possibilities for the cumulative growth of social commitments over time. For this reason, they can be distinguished from countries in which democratic openings were either more partial or of shorter duration.

Uruguay

Both democracy and the origins of Uruguay's comprehensive social-welfare system date to the critical realignment of the early twentieth century. Under Colorado Party leader José Batlle y Ordóñez, the government pursued a broad reform project that included the establishment of mass suffrage, the provision of broad social protections, and even the beginning of a state-led effort to promote industrialization. During Batlle's first term

as president (1903–07), the labor movement was still very weak. Nevertheless, he believed that urban workers could tip the close political balance between his own Colorado Party and the Blanco opposition. (Collier
and Collier 1991, 279). Promotion of the organized-workers movement
and the extension of public welfare were thus an integral part of his larger
political project.

During his first term, Batlle focused mainly on fending off armed challenges and consolidating control over the Colorado Party itself (Collier
and Collier 1991, 273). Nevertheless, several important steps laid the
foundation for further welfare-state expansion in subsequent years. Most
important, voting rights were extended to most adult male citizens, and
by 1920, all restrictions on adult male suffrage were eliminated.[2] Efforts
to expand primary education went hand in hand with the expansion of
suffrage: new legislation passed during this period declared primary education to be free, secular, and compulsory and increased the share of education in the government budget (Engerman, Mariscal, and Sokoloff
2000). The creation of a civil service pension fund in 1904 marked an
important step in the creation of a broad system of social insurance
(Mesa-Lago 1978, 72).

By the time of Batlle's second term (1911–16), he had consolidated
control over the Colorado Party and secured the political hegemony of
the party itself, clearing the way for him and his successors to advance
the project of social reform. Additional social-security legislation, drafted
under Batlle, was passed in 1919 and 1920 by his immediate successor.
New funds were added for utility workers, providing protection against
old age, disability, death, and unemployment (Mesa-Lago 1978, 73), as
well as a noncontributory pension for indigents, a unique step for this
period. In 1920, the government added a maternal-healthcare program
and substantially expanded public hospitals (Filgueira 1995, 5). The
Batllista governments also continued to promote the cause of labor
unions, passing a labor code that established extensive rights to organize
and strike.

The shock of the Great Depression led to a tightening of political controls under Gabriel Terra (1933–38). But full democracy and unrestricted
party competition was restored in 1942, opening the way to a second
wave of social-security initiatives. Between 1941 and 1957, the dominant
factions of the Colorado Party, led by Batlle y Ordóñez's nephew Luis
Batlle, pursued an economic and social-reform agenda that included both
import-substitution industrialization and a major extension of social-security coverage. In 1943, family allowances were added to the social-
security program and extended to all workers in industry and commerce.

---

[2] The vote was extended to all female adults as early as 1932.

In 1954, the government incorporated rural workers into the system (Filgueira 1995, 21).

Electoral competition drove much of this expansion. In the run-up to the 1958 presidential election, for example, the incumbent Colorados extended family allowances to unemployed blue- and white-collar workers and approved paid maternity leaves for urban working women (Mesa-Lago 1978, 77). In the run-up to the 1965 election, an incumbent Blanco administration expanded coverage to its rural constituency, despite worsening economic conditions and high inflation (Mesa-Lago 1978, 79).

The health system was somewhat slower to expand and remained weighted toward curative medicine. But the ministry of health did establish low-cost public health services early in the century and began to shift some resources into preventive care beginning in the 1940s (Filgueira 1995, 5). As in Argentina, much of the blue-collar population was covered through semiautonomous health-insurance funds rather than through the social security system itself. In 1970, however, health insurance became compulsory for all public and private employees (about 60 percent of the population), and the urban and rural poor gained access to state and university hospitals and to rural clinics. As was the case almost everywhere in the region, the quality of services remained unequal. Nevertheless, by the early 1980s, most of the population had access to basic healthcare.

The Uruguayan welfare state came under increasing economic strain in the mid-1950s as revenues derived from meat and agricultural exports declined. By that time, however, it was politically costly for democratic governments to challenge established entitlements. Even the post-1973 authoritarian governments did not change the basic structure of the welfare system (Castiglioni 2005, 41–61).

Chile

As in Uruguay, the foundations of the Chilean social-insurance system were established during the decisive challenges to the oligarchic state in the mid- and late-1920s. In 1920, Arturo Alessandri Palma was elected to the presidency on a wave of popular protest in the northern mining camps and among the urban middle class. Social legislation was stalled for a period of years by a conservative congress, but in 1925, pressure from the military broke the stalemate and led to a series of legislative initiatives. These included the establishment of pension funds for miners, blue-collar workers, and white-collar employees and guarantees for blue-collar workers to medical attention.

Division of the system into special funds for different categories of white- and blue-collar workers reflected a deliberate strategy on the part of conservatives to co-opt and divide the workers' movement. This approach provided the institutional template for a multiplicity of new funds (over 160 different funds by the 1970s) and a system that was not only fragmented but highly stratified in terms of benefits and financial contributions (Borzutzky 2002, 49–50). Nevertheless, viewed as a whole, the system provided at least a partial safety net for a relatively broad share of the urban working class.

Throughout the 1930s and 1940s, both social security and covered health benefits expanded incrementally as competing center-left and center-right coalitions attempted to consolidate clienteles among segments of the union movement (Mesa-Lago 1978, 29–30). A major step in the development of the health system came in 1938. In that year, a newly elected center-left government, which included Salvador Allende as minister of health, launched a mother-and-infant health program for the families of workers covered in the social-security program (McGuire 2001a, 1683). The new healthcare program contributed to a substantial decline of infant mortality among the insured population (Borzutzky 2002, 61).

The big push across a range of welfare activities, however, occurred during the 1960s and early 1970s. The spur was a series of electoral reforms that dramatically increased the franchise, including the introduction of women's suffrage and a secret ballot in the countryside. These reforms opened the way to intensified competition for the rural vote between the reformist Christian Democrats and the Socialist-Communist coalition led by Allende (Valenzuela 1978, 26–39). Riding the expansion of the franchise, the Christian Democratic government under Eduardo Frei (1964–70) promised a "revolution in liberty" and undertook major social initiatives to build support among the peasantry and the urban informal sector. Fiscal constraints forced the government to retreat from its initial goals after its first three years in office, and an effort to unify and rationalize the disparate pension funds foundered on opposition from the left parties and allied union movement (Stallings 1990; Borzutzky 2002, 116–17). Health and education initiatives, however, were more successful. Education expenditure doubled during this period, and the primary enrollment rate increased from 67 percent to 100 percent of the school-age population. The Frei administration also expanded basic health services, building rural health clinics, training community health workers, and shifting financial and personnel resources from hospitals to community health centers. These efforts contributed to a steep decline in infant mortality during the 1960s and 1970s (McGuire 2001a, 10–13).

These programs accelerated during the brief and turbulent term of Salvador Allende (1970–73). Like Frei, Allende was unable to challenge the administrative interests and organized beneficiaries that controlled existing social-security funds. But he did increase blue-collar pension benefits and extended coverage to approximately 900,000 self-employed workers. These initiatives brought total social-security coverage to about 76 percent of the economically active population. (Borzutzky 2002, 140–41). Allende also widened and deepened the health and education programs launched under Frei.

These measures, however, were undertaken in a broader context of economic populism and increasing ideological polarization over land reform and nationalizations. Moreover, they placed serious strains on fiscal resources and thus contributed to the broader economic deterioration of the Allende period. A constitutional deadlock ensued when the government was unable to reach a compromise with the opposition Christian Democrats over stabilization or the pace of nationalization. In 1973 the government was overthrown in a bloody military coup (Valenzuela 1978, 93–8). The Pinochet dictatorship that emerged from this coup ushered in an entirely new phase of welfare policy; we discuss those developments in more detail below in our consideration of authoritarian regimes.

Costa Rica

In Costa Rica, the establishment of the first major social-security funds dates back to the critical realignment of the early 1940s. Rafael Calderón Fournier (1941–45), the leader of the reform coalition, was from an old family and was elected president in a system still dominated by the oligarchy. Nevertheless, an odd coalition of reformist Catholic clergy and Communist-dominated unions united behind his ambitious reform program. Conflicts deepened over the course of the 1940s, and in a dispute over the outcome of the 1948 election, the coalition that had backed Calderón was defeated by opposition forces in a brief civil war. Although conservatives were part of the opposition movement, however, the main winners were middle-class reformers. Staunchly anticommunist, they nevertheless identified broadly with the progressive goals pursued under Calderón. Under the leadership of their political party (the National Liberation Party, or PLN), democracy was quickly restored, and the welfare system, established during the 1940s, expanded in subsequent decades.

The Costa Rica Social Security Fund (Caja Costarricense de Seguro Social, CCSS), established initially during the Calderón era, was an important source of welfare proposals. Drawing on advice from the International Labor Organization (ILO), its officials pressed for a more unified administrative and financial framework than those introduced in Uruguay and Chile. The influence of the CCSS, however, depended on the support of politicians in the legislature, particularly within the left-of-center PLN. Broad social policies provided the PLN with an important resource against more conservative challengers in highly competitive presidential elections and allowed them to dominate the legislature.

Although social-security coverage expanded incrementally during the 1950s, the first big push came in 1961 with a constitutional amendment that mandated universal pension coverage and health protection within a ten-year period. The initiative came originally from the CCSS, which sought increased funding that would not be subject to legislative discretion. PLN legislators backed the request for earmarked funding but insisted on linking it to the progressive extension of coverage to the entire population. Although this goal was not reached on schedule, coverage did double from about 25 percent to over 50 percent of the economically active population (Rosenberg 1979, 127).

A second wave of expansion came during the 1970s under PLN presidents José Figueres Ferrer (1970–74) and Daniel Oduber Quirós (1974–78). The financial underpinnings of this effort were established by a series of measures that consolidated the financial base of the CCSS. Legislation raised salary caps on social-insurance contributions and increased employers' share of contributions. These reforms provided resources for new legislation that mandated obligatory pension coverage for self-employed workers and extended healthcare coverage and family assistance to all sectors of the population. The PLN administrations also established noncontributory old-age pensions for indigents, one of the first such programs in the region (Durán-Valverde 2002, 14). As in Chile during the 1960s and 1970s, the expansion included efforts to establish primary healthcare units in rural areas, beginning with a rural healthcare program in 1973. Over the course of the next five years, over 200 health centers served an additional 600,000 people, primarily in communities of fewer than five hundred people. In comparison to most other Latin American societies, these efforts to reach into rural areas and poor neighborhoods were distinctive and had a positive impact on inequality, poverty and infant mortality (McGuire 2001a, 7–10).

Venezuela

Unlike the situation in Uruguay, Chile, and Costa Rica, conservative military governments dominated Venezuela throughout the first half of the twentieth century. One of these, a new military government headed by Eleazar López-Contreras (1935–41), passed the first major pension and health legislation in 1940 to deflect popular discontent stirred by a movement of reformist intellectuals. Nevertheless, López-Contreras and his military successors were unwilling to share power with the reformists and had little interest in expanding social policy.

A coup led by military and civilian reformers opened the way for a brief period of democratization in 1945. Consistent with our expectations about the effects of democracy, the 1945–48 period—commonly known as the *trienio*—was marked by an ambitious agenda of social as well as political reforms. The civil-military coalition, led by the left-of-center Democratic Action (AD) party, drafted a constitution that eliminated major suffrage restrictions and mandated comprehensive social-security and health coverage. The coalition also placed substantial emphasis on public education, and funds allotted for this purpose tripled (Martz 1966, 81–89). Unlike what happened with most other populist movements in the region, moreover, this period also saw efforts to organize rural unions and initiate a program of land reform (Powell 1971).

These social initiatives, however, met with strong opposition. Military and business elites viewed plans for land reform with particular alarm, and the Catholic Church saw efforts to expand public schooling as a threat to its control of the educational system. In 1948, the reformist project was reversed by another military coup, backed by business leaders, the Church, and much of the middle class. For the next decade, Venezuela was again ruled by a conservative military dictatorship, headed by Marcos Pérez Jiménez (1948–58). The new regime presided over a period of high growth and lavished burgeoning petroleum revenues on the military and business cronies. At the same time, however, it reduced commitments to education and public health that had been made during the *trienio* (Martz 1966, 91) and repressed rural unions. Until the more enduring turn to democracy at the end of the 1950s, social protections remained limited to workers in Caracas and a few other large urban centers.

Following the overthrow of the Pérez dictatorship in 1958, Venezuela entered a more prolonged period of democratic rule. Democracy rested on a series of power-sharing agreements among the major parties and other organized interests. Chastened by a decade of repression or exile, leaders of the AD and supporters within the urban union movement were willing to abandon the rural radicalism of the *trienio* period and to scale back other plans for social reform. After a decade of corruption and cronyism under Pérez, conservative politicians, business elites, and Church leaders were also inclined to compromise. The broad coalitions formed during the early 1960s were essential for building informal norms of cooperation among political elites but were not conducive to major social-policy reforms.

In the mid-1960s, however, the two major parties—the AD and the COPEI (Comité de Organización Política Electoral Independiente), the main opposition party—began to compete more directly for votes. Radical attacks on the concentration of property remained off the table, but initiatives to expand more conventional forms of social insurance and services became a staple of the political debate. Formal-sector and state workers were the principal beneficiaries. In 1966, the government of AD president Raúl Leoni (1964–69) extended social-security coverage to a broader range of workers in the formal private sector and added a range of new benefits, including long-term disability and old-age and survivors' pensions (Márquez and Acedo 1994, 156–57). Competitive pressure from the AD, in turn, induced its main rival, COPEI, to reach out to unionized blue-collar workers as well. Employment-security legislation, sponsored by COPEI president Rafael Caldera (1969–74), helped the party to establish a significant base of support within the union movement.

Although social-security initiatives were restricted to formal-sector workers, the 1960s also saw substantial progress in the areas of health and education. Governments tended to overinvest in services for middle-class groups, such as hospitals and universities, but malaria was eradicated, and child mortality declined. Primary education also expanded, and adult illiteracy rates fell from over 10 percent of the fifteen-to-twenty-four age group in 1970 to under 6 percent in 1980 and to 4 percent by 1990 (UNESCO 2002).

The oil economy that financed these new initiatives also created well-known distortions and vulnerabilities. The massive influx of resources during the boom period of the 1970s financed the building of hospitals and the deepening of welfare benefits for middle-class and blue-collar workers at the expense of the unorganized (Márquez and Acedo 1994, 163–64). The close relations between the dominant parties and the unions may also have encouraged such priorities. With the end of the boom in the early 1980s, growth collapsed, leading to a disastrous decline in per-capita income and in social insurance and services. Through the mid-1980s, the government attempted to cushion the fall in oil prices with price controls and deficit spending. As part of this effort, the IVSS was compelled to accumulate nonnegotiable treasury bonds, with devastating effects on its finances. By the early 1990s, beneficiaries faced backlogs in the processing of payments and substantial erosion in the real value of benefits.

SHORT-LIVED DEMOCRACIES AND SEMIDEMOCRACIES

Compared to Uruguay, Chile, Costa Rica, and even Venezuela, experiences with democracy elsewhere in Latin America were much more limited in terms of their durability or competitiveness. Outside of these four cases, most of the governments we have classified as fully democratic in table 2.1 survived only a few years before being cut short by military coups. The opportunity for electoral or interest-group pressures to fundamentally change the shape of social policy in these cases was far more limited than in the longer-lived democracies. Semidemocratic regimes permitted electoral competition and interest-group organization, but the capacity of politicians and social groups to press distributive demands on the government was weakened by suffrage restrictions, military vetoes, or elite agreements that removed certain issues from effective political contention. Consequently, in most cases, coverage and benefits remained limited.

Argentina

Argentina is the exception to these generalizations: despite recurrent restrictions on democracy, the country ranks with Chile, Costa Rica, and Uruguay in the comprehensiveness of its welfare state. This development can be traced in part to the influx of literate and often highly militant immigrant workers in the early twentieth century and correspondingly high levels of urbanization.[3] Nevertheless, the major breakthrough did not occur until Juan Perón's rise to power in the late 1940s and early 1950s, a period of relatively open political competition and one that we have identified as marking the critical realignment in Argentine politics.

Our classification of this period as semidemocratic is open to debate. Perón often used harsh tactics in dealing with dissent and became increasingly repressive in the early 1950s. Nevertheless, from the mid-1940s to the early 1950s, important features of democratic politics were in place. In 1946, Perón ran for the presidency in a highly competitive electoral contest, defeating a broad and well-financed coalition of Communists, socialists, and the middle-class Radical Party. Throughout most of Perón's first term in office, moreover, he faced a vigorous opposition press and criticism from agrarian interests and other conservative groups. It was not until the early 1950s, and especially during his second term (1952–55), that Perón began to crack down on political challengers and to exercise increasingly authoritarian controls over his own base of support in the labor movement.

Until the advent of Perón, social-insurance protection was confined mainly to the military, white-collar workers, and a few strategically situated blue-collar unions. In his bid to establish a popular base, Perón initiated an aggressive program of import-substitution and used social security as a major instrument for consolidating support from, and control over the burgeoning labor movement. From the mid-1940s to the early 1950s, Perón expanded pension coverage to about 70 percent of the labor force. (Mesa-Lago 1978, 164-165). The government also sponsored the

---

[3] Literacy rates increased substantially in the late nineteenth century, from about a quarter of the population in 1869 to over 50 percent by 1900 (Engerman, Mariscal, and Sokoloff 2000, table 1). But this increase was attributable primarily to the massive influx of immigrants schooled in their home countries.

expansion of health insurance, run through union-owned funds (*obras*), and established a broad network of public hospitals that extended medical service to low-income sectors of the population (Collier and Collier 1991, 341; Rock, 1985, 263-265; Lloyd-Sherlock 2000: 146–48).

As Mesa-Lago (1978, 165) points out, Perón was also careful to add to the benefits of powerful groups that had already received coverage, including the military, civil servants, railroad workers, and the merchant marine. As happened in Chile and Uruguay, this fragmentation of funds and benefits created both inequities and financial strains that plagued the system in subsequent decades. Nevertheless, the rapid extension of benefits attracted the strong support of a powerful union movement and established a broad framework of entitlements that was not fundamentally challenged by successor military or democratic regimes until at least the mid-1970s.

Peru

The expansion of the Peruvian welfare system occurred in a very different sociopolitical context from that in Argentina, including a much larger rural population. Moreover, literacy and suffrage restrictions disenfranchised most of the indigenous population. Import-substitution began much later than it did in the other Latin American countries. Limited industrialization and the long-term exclusion of rural and indigenous populations from the political system help to account for the limited spread of welfare benefits and basic social services, including schooling. Periodic political openings, however, did provide opportunities for the popularly oriented APRA party to compete for power and helped urban workers gain access to social-security protection.

The framework of the major social-security fund for blue-collar workers, the Seguro Social Obligatorio (SSO), was established in 1936 under the conservative government of Marshal Óscar Benavides (1933–39). The initiative came in response to the Aprista challenges that marked the onset of the critical realignments in Peru (see table 1.9). Shortly afterward, however, Benavides cracked down again on dissent, and the SSO tightened eligibility requirements and restricted benefits to maternity care. In 1946–47, a second brief political opening under Manuel Prado also led to new initiatives (Mesa-Lago 1978, 117). These favored mainly white-collar workers but also allowed the SSO to expand hospitals and provide insurance for occupational diseases and injury. Again, however, the momentum toward expansion was halted by a military coup that installed General Manuel Odría (1948–56). The Odría government established a variety of new funds for the army, the police, the navy, the civil service, and white-collar workers. But SSO benefits remained restricted, and financing was cut substantially.

The most significant changes in the pre-1980 decades came during the semidemocratic and democratic periods that followed the end of the Odría dictatorship and the reentry of the Apristas into the political system. From 1956 to 1962, Manuel Prado returned to power in coalition with the Apristas. Mesa-Lago (1978, 118) characterizes the social-security legislation passed during this period as the "refounding" of the social-security system. As before, the government responded to substantial pressure from white-collar groups with new pension legislation for civil servants. But the inequities created by this legislation prompted public demonstrations and protests from APRA-led unions and generated strong pressure to provide an adequate pension system for urban workers (Mesa-Lago 1978, 118). In 1961, with the support of APRA congressmen, the government established a new Retirement Fund for Blue-Collar Workers, which substantially eased the conditions for access established in the 1936 legislation and quadrupled the old-age benefits provided to its participants (Mesa-Lago 1978, 158).

Another brief military intervention vetoed a likely victory for the Apristas in the 1962 presidential election. Electoral politics were restored the following year, however. The new president, Fernando Belaúnde Terry (1963–68), identified with the moderate reformist goals of the Alliance for Progress but faced both economic constraints and the structural inequalities of Peruvian society. Although the government continued to build schools, education in the rural areas remained badly underfunded. The Belaúnde government also established hospitals in areas not already covered by blue-collar (SSO) or white-collar (Seguro Social de Empleados, SSE) social-security funds; but the emphasis remained primarily on curative healthcare for the urban population (Mesa-Lago 1978, 134). Competitive pressure from opposition Aprista and Communist politicians did encourage an expansion of social security and health insurance coverage, from about 25 percent of the active population in 1961 to over one-third by 1969 (Mesa-Lago 1978,134). However, for most of this period, the government failed to meet its legal funding contributions, and by the end of the decade, the funds were in an increasingly precarious financial position (Mesa-Lago 1978, 145). By 1968, with Belaúnde's program stalled, this period of democratic politics was brought to an end by another military coup and the establishment of a military dictatorship.

Colombia

In Colombia, the basic social-security fund was established during the two presidential terms of the Liberal Party reformer Alfonso López Pumarejo

(1934–38, 1942–45) which marked Colombia's critical realignment. However, expansion halted during subsequent decades of interparty civil war and the military dictatorship of Gustavo Rojas-Pinilla (1953–57).

Civilian government returned to Colombia in 1958 with the initiation of the National Front. During the National Front period (1958–74), however, the form of rule is best considered semidemocratic. Until 1974, an elite power-sharing agreement divided all government offices between the dominant Liberal and Conservative Parties, precluding electoral challenges from new political forces.

Throughout this period, expansion of social-security and health coverage to the rural and urban remained modest. With respect to social security, a new initiative in 1962 provided family benefits for groups already incorporated into the social-security system, and new groups were gradually added during subsequent decades (Bushnell 1993, 226).

The National Front did expand public education, although with somewhat mixed results. Rojas, the military dictator ousted in 1957, had provided some lip service to public education, but most expansion occurred in the private educational sector (Arvone 1978, 3). During the 1960s and 1970s, by contrast, a series of legislative initiatives expanded public primary education. A new constitution mandated a minimum expenditure on education of at least 10 percent of the central-government budget (Bushnell 1993, 226). Between the early 1950s and 1980, illiteracy declined from 38 percent of the fifteen-to-twenty-four age cohort to only 7.5 percent (UNESCO 2002). Education-reform initiatives, however, encountered powerful headwinds from opponents in the Church, the private educational establishment, and politicians focused on the delivery of patronage. Consequently, the quality of the system remained extremely low, especially in the rural areas (Arvone 1978, 10). The high degree of centralization of education policy, moreover, contributed to the consolidation of a powerful teachers' union that became a serious impediment to reform initiatives designed to improve quality in the 1990s (Lowden 2004, 357–59).

Brazil

During the critical realignment of the 1930s and 1940s, the dictatorship of Getúlio Vargas implemented Brazil's first comprehensive effort to co-opt blue-collar workers into the political system.[4] As in Chile, corporatist institutions and accompanying social-security systems were implemented "from above," with the deliberate intention of segmenting workers along occupational lines. Unlike the situation in Chile, however, party

---

[4] Vargas modeled his measures after more-limited initiatives undertaken by conservative governments in the 1920s (Malloy 1979).

competition was entirely banned until the mid-1940s, eliminating both electoral challenges from below or incentives to compete for the votes of low-income groups. Consequently, the social-welfare system that evolved under Vargas was not only internally stratified but also very limited in overall coverage.

The reestablishment of constitutional government in 1946 might have been expected to lead to changes in this situation, but the new political order was also characterized by significant limitations on political contestation.[5] For most of the 1945–64 period, most presidents governed with the support of broad coalitions that included two outgrowths of the Vargas era: the Social Democratic Party (Partido Social Democrático, PSD), a party dominated by the rural oligarchy, and the Brazilian Labor Party (Partido Trabalhista Brasiliero, PTB), which appealed more to the urban popular sector. However, literacy requirements limited the size of the electorate, and unions remained shackled by corporatist controls established under the first Vargas regime. Moreover, competitively elected governments were subject to continuing threats of military coups or vetoes, and only two of the five presidents during the period succeeded in serving out their terms.

In these circumstances, the impulse to expand the social-security system remained weak. To sustain their heterogeneous coalitions, governments relied primarily on broad developmentalist and nationalist appeals rather than on social policy. Getúlio Vargas (1951–54), who returned to power as an elected president in 1951, focused primarily on a push toward import-substitution industrialization. There were also efforts to raise the minimum wage—a step that caused considerable controversy—but there were no major initiatives to expand or redesign the social-security or health systems. Juscelino Kubitschek de Oliveira (1956–61) succeeded Vargas after a brief military interregnum; he also pursued a developmentalist agenda that included the "deepening" of ISI and the construction of a new capital in Brasilia. However, the only significant social-policy initiative during this period, passed in 1960, increased benefits for groups already covered by eliminating minimum age requirements for pension eligibility and relying solely on years of service (Weyland 1996, 90).

Education policies also reflected the influence of a heterogeneous and elitist coalition of interests. Expansion of primary education provided an important means to sustain the support of the urban base of the ruling coalitions, but incentives to expand education into the rural areas were decisively weakened by suffrage restrictions and reliance on the rural bosses of the PSD. In urban areas, primary-school enrollments ap-

[5] MBP-L code Brazil as democratic from 1946 to early 1964, but they acknowledge that the regime could reasonably have been coded as a semidemocracy.

proached 90 percent by 1964 but remained below 50 percent in rural areas (Heimer 1975, 58–59). The quality of the rural schools also remained far below urban standards. Many were restricted to only one teacher and one classroom for all students enrolled, and dropout and repetition rates were about three times higher than those in the cities (Heimer 1975, 59).

Beginning in the late 1950s, militant unions and newly mobilized peasant movements began to protest against the basic inequalities of Brazilian society, and politics became increasingly polarized. As would later be the case in Allende's Chile, however, social-policy issues were overshadowed by severe macroeconomic instability and by deepening conflicts over land reform, foreign investment, and nationalization. As the incumbent government of João Goulart (1961–64) moved increasingly to the left, the shock waves of the Cuban Revolution hardened military and business opposition. In 1964, the Goulart government was ousted by an American-backed military coup. Ironically, as we shall see below, it was only after the military seized power that attempts were made to quell popular radicalism by extending the corporatist-based welfare system into the rural sector.

Authoritarian Regimes in Brazil and Mexico: Welfare Initiatives in Competitive Autocracies

In general, authoritarian regimes in Latin America were less inclined than more democratic ones to expand welfare protections and services, preferring instead to augment benefits for core constituencies within the government or powerful groups that already enjoyed coverage. Two competitive authoritarian regimes, however, were notable exceptions: the twenty-year military dictatorship in Brazil (1964–85) and Mexico's long-standing system of dominant-party government. Unlike the hard authoritarian regimes discussed in the following section, governments in Brazil and Mexico relied on managed electoral competition and other formalities of democratic government to legitimate their rule. During the 1970s, these semicompetitive institutional arrangements encouraged the expansion of coverage of the social welfare system, particularly into rural areas.

Brazil

Brazil's military dictatorship from 1964 to 1985 shared many features with the bureaucratic-authoritarian regimes that later came to power in the southern cone, including ambitious development programs and restrictive policies toward unions and the political left. The military's preservation of the outward formalities of constitutional government, however, constituted an important difference. Military elites never relinquished control of major policy decisions, and hard-line factions pressed continuously for crackdowns on any sign of dissent. But after a period of hard-line military rule during the late 1960s and early 1970s, the regime began to attach increasing importance to semicompetitive legislative elections and gradual political liberalization as a means of deflecting opposition. In the place of the political parties of the pre-1964 era, authorities established a "progovernment" party—National Renewal Alliance Party (Aliança Renovadora Nacional, ARENA), led by conservative supporters of the coup, and encouraged "safe" political leaders to form an official opposition party, the Democratic Movement of Brazil, or MDB.

Managing the opposition proved more difficult than expected as the MDB made a surprising show of strength in the 1974 congressional elections. The government responded to these electoral gains with changes in the electoral laws aimed at splintering the opposition into competing parties. But the MDB's successor, now called the PMDB (or Party of the Brazilian Democratic Movement), continued to build support, particularly in more developed parts of the country. The promilitary ARENA was dominated by political bosses based primarily in the less-developed northeast regions. As electoral challenges grew, the military relied increasingly on ARENA politicians to maintain control of the congress, the state legislatures and the electoral college, which was nominally responsible for the selection of the president.

The effects of the electoral connection on the military's social policy were significant but not entirely straightforward. One of the most important social initiatives of the military period, the extension of noncontributory old-age pensions to peasants and rural indigents in the Rural Worker Assistance Fund (Fundo de Assistencia an Trabalhador Rural, FUNRURAL), was launched in 1971, at a time when hard-line military factions were still ascendant. Though the initiative originated in the welfare bureaucracy (Schwarzer and Querino 2002, 8), it served the political purpose of preempting a resurgence of rural unrest and was guided by the corporatist principles of the Vargas era rather than electoral considerations. Unlike its semidemocratic predecessor, the military was also in a better position to override objections from urban-based unions that expressed concerns that resources would be diverted from their funds.

Electoral motivations, however, did become a major factor in the expansion of social-security programs during the mid-1970s as more moderate military factions regained control of the government and inaugurated a process of controlled political liberalization. A key feature of this strategy was to bolster the position of the civilian leaders of the ARENA party, particularly in the rural northeast. The FUNRURAL program quickly became a major source of patronage for both the ARENA politicians and the government-sponsored rural union (Weyland 1996, 100), and was followed by a number of additional initiatives that broadened access and benefits to the urban and rural poor. In 1979, the government launched a program to expand rural clinics in the impoverished northeast through the Program of Health and Hygiene in the Interior (Programa de Interiorizaçion das Açoes de Saúde e Saneamento, PIASS) and extended the right to emergency-healthcare services to all citizens.

By the end of the decade of the 1970s, over 90 percent of the population had acquired at least some formal entitlements to social-security and healthcare coverage. Although this change did have positive redistributive consequences, cash benefits to the rural and urban informal sectors— about one-half the minimum wage (Schwarzer and Querino 2002, 9)— remained minimal compared to those going to the civil service, other formal sector workers, and (of course) the military itself. As of the mid-1980s, approximately 80 percent of agricultural workers and one-third of the informal sector were not officially registered in the social security and pension system (Weyland 1996, 134–35). Those who did gain access, moreover, were required to apply for benefits through ARENA intermediaries, who provided the necessary documentation in exchange for votes (Schwarzer and Querino 2002, 9).

The alliance between the military and the patronage politicians of ARENA also tended to undercut the progressive impact of health and education programs in a variety of ways. Political connections linking the social-security bureaucracy to private hospitals drained resources away from efforts to expand the public-health system. The rural-health initiative aimed at the rural northeast (PIASS) reached only 25 percent of its target population (McGuire 2001b, 16).

In the education sector, the military did make some attempt to strengthen financing for primary schooling; a constitutional amendment passed in 1983 mandated that states spend at least 15 percent of federal transfers on primary education. The regime placed a much higher priority, however, on support for the universities, which were far more important to its middle-class supporters. Moreover, the effort to strengthen primary education was blunted by conservative political control of the ministry of education. The ministry became an important source of patronage for construction contracts and employment, with predictable consequences. In 1980, the illiteracy rate among young adults stood at 12 percent; although this was a decline of 7 percentage points since 1970, it was still by far the highest of any of the Latin American countries discussed in this volume—well above Peru and Mexico, as well as the more democratic countries of the region (see table 2.2). Only after the advent of democracy in the mid-1980s did Brazil see a significant acceleration of efforts to address inequalities in the educational system and to improve access to basic healthcare.

Mexico

Both the initial drive toward mass education and the origins of social-security protections in Mexico were closely linked to fundamental realignments in the political system. The federal government began to expand its jurisdiction over the education system in the 1920s, as the postrevolutionary elites began to consolidate power. Under Plutarco Calles, the strong man of that period, the regime created the first federal ministry of education and provided substantial increases in the education budget. In the words of Engerman, Mariscal, and Sokoloff (2000, 27), it marked "the first of the national campaigns to implant literacy nationwide." The first major social-security legislation was not instituted until later, under Manuel Ávila Camacho (1940–46). But the initiative followed the most radical phase of labor incorporation and the restructuring of the dominant Institutional Revolutionary Party (Partido Revolucionario Institucional, PRI) along corporatist lines; it was intended to isolate the more radical union leaders and to consolidate the links between the ruling elite in the PRI and their allies within the union movement.

The subsequent evolution of social policy during the early postwar era can be divided into two distinct periods. The first, roughly the decades of the 1950s and 1960s, has been called the period of stabilizing development. Politically, these decades were marked by the consolidation of the ruling party's control over the labor movement and the electoral arena and by sustained cooperation between the ruling elite and the import-substituting private sector. Welfare initiatives during this period were relatively limited. The second phase spanned the next two presidential terms of Luis Echeverría Álvarez (1970–76) and José López Portillo (1967–82). These administrations were buffeted by much greater economic turbulence—at least some of it of their own making—and by the emergence of serious political challenges to the stability of the regime itself. In response to these challenges, the government began to pay much more attention to social policy.

As noted, the social-security system and other social services expanded quite slowly during the "stabilizing development" period. As late as 1960, social security-coverage reached only 12 percent of the workforce (Mesa-Lago 1989, 150). By 1975 estimates of coverage still ranged from only 27 percent (Spalding 1980, 427) to about 35 percent (Mesa-Lago 1989, 151). This level of coverage fell well below that of the long-term democracies, including Venezuela. Demographic changes and industrialization were apparently the driving forces behind the expansion that did occur. Spalding (1980) shows that differences in urbanization and industrial production explain almost all the variance of coverage among Mexico's thirty-one states and the Federal District, while differences in unionization and electoral opposition had no significant effects.

This relatively passive approach to social policy reflected the political security of the regime, which rested on both its electoral dominance and the absence of meaningful organized social challenges. In the absence of such challenges, the regime's focus on the urban centers carried few significant political costs and offered a number of benefits. As Spalding (1980, 431) argues, concentration of beneficiaries in high-productivity urban-industrial centers simplified the administrative burden on the system and allowed the Mexican Institute of Social Security (Instituto Mexicano de Seguro Social, IMSS) to shift costs onto employers and workers. At the same time, the urban-based social-security system served the "long term purpose of forestalling the eruption of open political dissent," while avoiding risks to economic stability that might have come from extending social security to "disorganized and powerless sectors" that "rarely constituted a political threat." (Spalding 1980, 431–32).

Serious political challenges did emerge by the end of this period, however, and the calculus of the political elite changed accordingly. Electoral opposition carried less significance for social policy in Mexico than it did in Brazil because it came primarily from a party that stood to the right of the PRI, the National Action Party (Partido Acción Nacional, PAN). However, the eruption of student protests in the late 1960s and rural land invasions in the early 1970s prompted greater attention to the demands of the left and the rural sector. Rural unrest was especially worrisome because it threatened to undermine a key pillar of the PRI's electoral success: tight control of the peasant vote.

Under Echeverría Álvarez, the response of the government went well beyond welfare measures as we have defined them and included a highly controversial land-reform initiative, which contributed to political polarization and economic instability. New benefits did expand from about 35 to 44 percent of the economically active population, but the administration failed to achieve its stated goal of pushing coverage beyond the formal sector (Mesa-Lago 1989, 146–47). In 1973, new social-security legislation established the principle of covering rural and urban informal workers, but economic deterioration and political instability limited effective implementation.

More substantial advances were achieved under López Portillo, as the Mexican economy began to recover. The government undertook a series of electoral reforms aimed at encouraging leftist forces to shift from direct action to the electoral arena, where the PRI continued to enjoy overwhelming advantages. At the same time, the PRI moved to shore up its own electoral strength in the countryside with a variety of new social programs. In education, these included a rapid expansion of primary-school construction, pressed by the teachers' union allied with the PRI. Enrollments increased dramatically during this period, and illiteracy rates declined from about 13 to 8 percent among young adults (see table 1.3).

In healthcare, the government established the General Coordinated National Plan for Deprived Zones and Marginal Groups (Coordinación General del Plan Nacional de Zonas Deprimidas y Grupos Marginados, COPLAMAR). This program was the first major effort to expand healthcare to lower-income sectors and made significant progress in extending services into rural areas, adding approximately 10 percent of the total population to the 44 percent covered by the main social-security fund (Mesa-Lago 1989, 151). Though highly significant in terms of Mexico's previous record, however, these expansion initiatives fell short of the standards set by the long-standing democracies. Approximately half the total population lacked effective social-security or healthcare coverage, and these excluded groups were concentrated among the poorest sectors of the population and in the least developed regions of the country.

Hard Authoritarian Regimes

Hard authoritarian regimes varied widely in their formal political structure and ideological objectives, but in the absence of electoral incentives or meaningful interest-group organization, they only rarely undertook efforts to expand social insurance and services. Many of these regimes were personalist dictatorships that simply sought to establish "order" and gain access to wealth and power. The most durable of these were established during the 1940s and 1950s under Rojas-Pinilla, Pérez-Jiménez, and Manuel Odría in Colombia, Venezuela and, Peru respectively. These governments did distribute substantial fiscal largesse to cronies and white-collar groups, and in some instances, they deployed public works to build clientelist ties to sectors of the urban poor (Collier 1976). But none of these rulers had an interest in expanding coverage of existing social-security systems or in instituting new social programs.

In the populist military regime of Juan Velasco in Peru (1968–75), and in the exclusionary regimes established during the 1960s and 1970s in the southern cone, rulers pursued more coherent modernizing projects that included important social-policy components. But despite differences, these typically entailed either a halt to the expansion of entitlements and services or active efforts to consolidate or retrench them.

Inclusionary Authoritarian Rule: Peru 1968–80

The economic nationalism and populism that characterized the Peruvian military regime under Juan Velasco Alvarado (1968–75) differed markedly from exclusionary governments established around the same period in Argentina, Uruguay, and Chile. While these other regimes were undertaking macroeconomic stabilization and market-oriented reforms, Velasco veered left and initiated a crash program of import-substitution, nationalized the American-owned International Telephone and Telegraph, and launched an ambitious land reform. The government engaged in an intensive drive to mobilize workers and peasants into state-controlled corporatist institutions and pushed wage increases as a means of sustaining domestic demand. It also placed a high priority on redistributive wage policies and land reform.

For our purposes, however, the most significant aspect of this radical phase of the Peruvian military government was its continuing hostility to the APRA party and to its base in organized labor, and its suspension of the electoral process. The top-down approach precluded opportunities for politicians or interest groups to press for social insurance and services. Although the Velasco government did seek to consolidate existing programs, it did not expand them. Once economic crisis hit in the mid-1970s, moreover, Velasco's military successors imposed a significant retrenchment.

Planning for the consolidation of the social-insurance system began after the regime seized power in the late 1960s, but legislative steps in this direction were not undertaken until the early 1970s. In 1974, the Velasco government created a single health and social-security fund, the Peruvian Institute of Social Security (Instituto Peruano del Seguro Social, IPSS), and began a gradual unification of hospitals previously administered by the separate social-security funds and the ministry of health (Mesa-Lago 1989, 177–79; Cruz-Saco Oyague 1998, 167). But untangling the complex webs of patronage and political influence proved difficult. As was the case in the southern-cone countries, the impact of the consolidation was limited by the exemption of the armed forces and other privileged-sector groups whose pensions remained fully indexed to active salaries (Cruz-Saco Oyague 1998, 171). Nor did the reforms succeed in increasing efficiency or in achieving greater transparency in accounting and personnel. As of the late 1970s, the new Institute had still not managed to establish a unified registry of beneficiaries or to prepare actuarial studies and statistical series. Administrative costs, moreover, were estimated at about 11.5 percent of total social-security expenditures, almost 7 percentage points higher than in Argentina and about four percentage points higher than in Uruguay and Chile (Mesa-Lago 1989, 181, 195–96).

The unification of the system was intended to prepare the way for the incorporation of peasants and informal-sector workers, but plans to expand coverage failed to materialize. By 1975, the regime's expansionist economic policies had led to a major macroeconomic crisis, and control of the government was assumed by a more moderate military faction led by Francisco Morales Bermúdez. Faced with severe fiscal strains, Morales moved to contain public expenditures, but the government was reluctant to reduce military spending or to risk a debt default. Social spending, however, underwent a sharp decline. During Morales' time in power, public expenditures on social security, health, and education dropped from over 5 percent to less than 3 percent of GDP (Segura-Ubiergo 2007, 235). In 1977–79, the government stopped meeting its financial obligations to the IPSS, saddling the institute with a massive debt that plagued democratic governments during the 1980s (Mesa-Lago 1978, 178).

The Bureaucratic-Authoritarian Regimes: Chile, Argentina, and Uruguay

Unlike events in Peru, the formation of bureaucratic-authoritarian regimes in Chile, Argentina, and Uruguay during the 1960s and 1970s was motivated by the anti-Communist ideologies of the Cold War era, concerns over severe macroeconomic instability, and fears that labor unions and populist political movements threatened national security.[6] Although the severity of repression varied, all these regimes purged labor movements, outlawed strikes, arrested or exiled political opponents, and sought to destroy popularly based and even centrist party organizations. The crackdowns imposed by the regimes of the 1970s were especially harsh; in addition to political leaders and activists, thousands of ordinary citizens were imprisoned and often tortured or killed. Predictably, although these regimes differed in their approach to social policy, most responded to very high inflation and fiscal crises in ways that foreshadowed responses to the economic crises we will discuss in part 2. Considerable macroeconomic authority was delegated to liberal technocrats, and efforts were made to cut back or restructure social programs established in preceding decades.

The most radical changes in social policy were undertaken by the Pinochet government in Chile as one component of a much broader project of neoliberal reform and political transformation. In responding to the economic crisis inherited from the Allende period, Pinochet initially turned to moderate business leaders and economists, who advocated relatively gradual changes in the import-substitution model. But the macro-

---

[6] See also O'Donnell 1971; Collier 1979; Kaufman 1979; and Remmer 1989.

economic situation remained highly unstable, and in 1975, the moderates were replaced in key ministries by more radical technocrats, famously known as the Chicago boys. Inspired by the neoliberal doctrines of Milton Friedman and Arnold Harberger, these Chilean technocrats began to implement a radical project of market reforms and rollback of the scope and functions of the public sector. The project was intended not only to reinvigorate the economy but also to destroy the foundations of the existing party system and union movement by cutting them off from resources used to mobilize political support.

Scaling back and restructuring the welfare state was regarded as an essential step in this direction; it proceeded in two phases. Throughout the second half of the 1970s, opposition from corporatist-oriented officials in the social bureaucracy and in the military junta itself blocked the restructuring plans of liberals in the macroeconomic ministries (Borzutzky 2002). The latter were able, however, to impose a drastic reduction of social spending and a reallocation of funds toward the poorest sectors of the population (Segura-Ubiergo 2007, 177–91). Targeted antipoverty programs provided prenatal and infant care and succeeded in reducing infant mortality rates. But overall cuts in social spending meant substantial losses for families just above the poverty line, who depended on state-sponsored social protections to maintain their standard of living. As a consequence, inequality and poverty increased in Chile, despite high growth rates achieved in the late 1970s and again in the second half of the 1980s.

During the early 1980s, the Chicago boys consolidated their control of key social ministries, and the regime undertook a more radical reorganization of the institutional framework of the welfare state. Changes in the pension system began in 1979, with major cost-saving reforms that raised the retirement age and eliminated privileged pension funds for civil servants. In 1980, these preliminary steps were followed by the establishment of a defined-contribution pension plan, compulsory for all workers entering the workforce after May 1981 (Castiglioni 2001, 40). Innovations in the pension system were followed in the early 1980s by similar measures in the education and health sectors. The government introduced a school-voucher program that allowed private schools to compete with the public system for state funding. It also instituted a sweeping reform that allowed compulsory payroll contributions to be diverted to private healthcare providers that competed with the public-health service for clients.

The "Chilean model" became an important point of reference for social policy debates in Latin America in the 1990s. The reforms demonstrated to supporters that market-oriented policies could effectively and efficiently provide social insurance and services. The redistributive and welfare effects of the reforms were highly problematic, however. For the most part, low-income and self-employed workers remained outside the privatized pension system. Although initially popular among covered workers, the system lost support over time as a result of very high administrative costs and volatility in equity markets. The new health and education systems tended to reproduce or even exacerbate inequalities in the Chilean social structure. Middle-class families gravitated toward private schools and health plans, leaving the poorer ones in the public-sector facilities.

Whatever its overall effects, the liberalized welfare system marked a sharp change from the more state-centered programs that had evolved during the decades of democratic rule. It was a transformation that could have been engineered only by a dictatorship such as Pinochet's. Moreover, these social-policy reforms had enduring effects. Even following the transition to democratic rule in the 1990s, higher-income stakeholders made a full return to the principles of the previous system politically impossible.

None of the other southern-cone military regimes attempted such radical restructuring of their welfare systems. But liberal technocrats did gain considerable influence over social policy in these authoritarian settings, and all attempted to cut back significantly on existing public commitments. Argentina's first period of bureaucratic authoritarian rule (1966–73) was the most moderate, but welfare policies were far from generous. Although the government provided benefits to some favored unions, it cracked down hard on the labor movement as a whole. Notwithstanding robust growth from 1966 to 1970, social-security coverage declined from about 55 to 48 percent of the economically active population (Mesa-Lago 1978, 180).

In 1970, the eruption of Peronist-led strikes and social protests in the interior of the country led to the ouster of Juan Carlos Onganía and the ascent of more moderate military factions that sought accommodation with the Peronistas. This political decompression led to the only significant welfare state expansion undertaken by this group of military regimes. Among the steps taken by the new government was the assumption of federal responsibility for provincial pension funds, and as a consequence, national coverage rose from under one-half to almost 70 percent of the workforce (Mesa-Lago 1979, 180). The government also expanded access to medical insurance provided by the *obras sociales*. This step was a significant concession to the unions that controlled them, although it benefited private-sector contractors as well (Alonso 2000, 67).

The relative moderation of the "first round" of right-wing military rule in Argentina, however, was the exception in the southern cone. The successor regime in Argentina (1976–83) and the military dictatorship that assumed power in Uruguay (1973–85) pursued neoliberal projects that paralleled those of Chile and sought to crush rather than manipulate the union movement.

Military regimes in Argentina and Uruguay were less inclined than they were in Chile to undertake privatization of the social insurance and service provision that had developed over previous decades; these institutions were not dismantled as they were in Chile. But they were far more willing than their democratic predecessors to restrict funding and reduce the generosity of benefits. The Argentine regime made no major changes in the pay-as-you go pension system but squeezed the flow of funding by eliminating employer contributions to the payroll tax. In the education sector, the government sought to offload its fiscal burdens by shifting responsibility for primary education to the provinces, a move that was widely viewed as a blow to the quality of the system (Corrales 2002).

The Uruguayan regime made the fewest structural changes in the welfare system (Castiglioni 2005, 141–61). Although there were efforts to unify separate pension funds, the government made no attempt to roll back legal entitlements or coverage. On the other hand, it also allowed inflation to eat deeply into the real value of pensions, especially during the economic crisis of the early 1980s (Castiglioni 2005, 44–45).

In sum, military-welfare policies in Argentina and Uruguay were less radical than they were in Chile, but they also represented a turn away from the competitive expansion of benefits and the relative generosity of their democratic predecessors. As we will see in part 2, this combination of funding cutbacks and structural continuity in organization and entitlements had implications for politics after the return to democracy in the mid 1980s. More than it did in Chile, democratization opened the way for pensioners and other stakeholders of the old system to press legal and political claims for public-sector wage increases and improvements in the real value of benefits.

Conclusion: Regime Type and Welfare-State Expansion in Latin America

During the critical realignments discussed in chapter 1, authoritarian as well as democratic regimes in Latin America established social-security funds in their effort to co-opt established urban constituencies. The pursuit of inward-oriented development models accompanied or reinforced these initial efforts, providing the economic underpinnings for social insurance systems and social services favoring the urban middle and working classes. In subsequent decades, moreover, the cross-class bases of these models proved compatible with a wide variety of political regimes: democratic, authoritarian, and a number of points in between.

In this chapter, we have considered the effect of this variation on the provision of social insurance and services. We find that regime type did indeed appear to matter: the expansion of social insurance and services was related to electoral incentives and interest-group pressures to add new beneficiaries, increase benefits, and initiate new programs. These factors were strongest in the longer-standing democracies of Chile, Uruguay, and Costa Rica. Governments in these three cases were most likely to undertake reforms that went beyond the incremental expansion of occupationally based social security programs to encompass altogether new groups of people, including in the countryside.

Similar incentives also operated in shorter-lived democracies, semi-democracies, and even competitive authoritarian regimes. But in the shorter-lived democratic openings, opportunities for governments to expand welfare systems were more limited, and initiatives did not cumulate. Efforts to secure electoral support also influenced social-policy decisions in the competitive authoritarian regimes of Mexico and Brazil, but these effects were weakened by the limits on genuine electoral challenges. Finally, the "hard" authoritarian regimes that imposed the strictest limits on political contestation were also more likely to limit the expansion of social programs or to retrench and restructure them outright.

We found further evidence for the importance of electoral competition in the influence of the franchise on the politics of social policy. As we will see in the following chapter, independence brought a quite rapid expansion of the franchise in East Asia, even when democratic experiments were subsequently shut down; these democratic moments had important implications for the expansion of education in particular. By contrast the expansion of the franchise in Latin America was much more gradual, and in a number of countries in our sample, the rural vote in particular was constrained by lack of secrecy in balloting or wealth and literacy requirements. Table 2.4 provides information on the franchise at the outset of the period of interest to us, as well as data on the share of the population that actually voted.

Costa Rica and Uruguay, as well as Argentina, had fewer restrictions on the franchise and the highest share of the electorate voting at the outset of the period of interest to us. In Chile, the reform of rural voting procedures in the late 1950s was followed quite quickly by proposals from both the left and the Christian Democrats to extend primary healthcare and education into the countryside. Until that time, all the major parties, including the Communists and Socialists, focused primarily on their urban and mining constituencies. In Peru, on the other hand, literacy requirements continued to disenfranchise the indigenous population in the early postwar decades. The "mass of Indian peasants were not important to political groups such as APRA and Accion Popular."(Mesa-Lago 1978, 126). Despite reformist ideologies, neither party engaged in strong efforts to appeal to or incorporate these sectors even during periods of democratic and semidemocratic rule. Suffrage limitations maintained in Brazil

TABLE 2.4
Laws Governing the Franchise and the Effective Electorate, c. 1940

	Secrecy in balloting	Wealth requirement	Literacy requirement	Share of population voting (date)
Argentina	Yes	No	No	15.0 (1937)
Brazil	No	Yes	Yes	4.1 (1930)
Chile	No	No	Yes	6.5 (1931)
Colombia	Yes	No	No	11.1 (1930)
Costa Rica	Yes	No	No	17.6 (1940)
Mexico	Yes	No	No	11.8 (1940)
Peru	Yes	No	Yes	—
Uruguay	Yes	No	No	19.7 (1940)
Veneuzuela	Yes	Yes	Yes	—

Source: Engerman, Mariscal, and Sokoloff 2000, table 2, 226.

during the semidemocratic governments of the 1950s and 1960s also weakened incentives to change that country's highly stratified and exclusionary welfare system.

Democratic and semidemocratic regimes were also more likely than were "hard" authoritarian regimes to accede to union demands for an expansion of social insurance. However, yielding to (or anticipating) union demands was at best a mixed blessing in distributional terms. The incorporation of blue-collar workers did provide protection to groups that, while not among the very poor, were otherwise vulnerable to market risk. But the enlargement of the social-security system often had perverse effects on the overall distribution of income. The protections claimed by unions were typically limited to the specific occupational categories they represented, whereas costs were borne more generally through taxes and other channels, such as the higher prices charged by import-substituting industries. As we will argue in part 2, the unions' defense of these entitlements was often a major impediment to reforms aimed at reallocating resources toward the very poor.

Democracy also expanded opportunities for the emergence of left-of-center parties. These parties had a more positive impact on the design of social policy than did unions. This was again most evident in the long-standing democracies with the most limited barriers to participation. In Uruguay, the broad features of the welfare state were established during the 1940s and 1950s, at a time when the dominant Colorado Party maintained a progressive ideological orientation and had not yet evolved into the nonideological patronage party that it was to become in the 1960s. In Costa Rica, the PLN—a party loosely identified with social-democratic values—held legislative majorities continuously throughout the postwar period and supported the drive toward universalizing health services and other social protections during the 1960s and 1970s. In Chile from 1958 to 1973, competition between the Christian Democrats and a Socialist-Communist coalition contributed to an expansion of social services into the Chilean countryside.[7]

Significantly, only the Chilean left parties and, to a lesser extent, the Christian Democrats, had close organizational ties to the labor movement, and this fact may account in part for the especially extreme stratification that characterized that country's welfare system. In Costa Rica and Uruguay, unions were inclined to support rivals to the PLN and Colorados, and it is possible that the independence of these parties from the demands of organized labor mitigated the regressive effects of social security systems visible elsewhere in the region. Mesa-Lago (1978, 292) ranks Uruguay's system as less unequal than Chile's, despite internal stratification, and it is likely that the Costa Rican system—not included in Mesa-Lago's ranking—also had progressive effects on the distribution of income.

The pressure to expand social programs beyond the formal sector was far weaker where purely clientelistic parties dominated electoral competition. As we will see in chapter 3, the Philippines also fit this pattern. Arguably, the predominance of clientelistic parties can be accounted for in part by electoral laws and other institutional arrangements that encourage politicians to cultivate the personal vote through pork-barrel projects and political patronage; clientelism may be the result not of regime type but of particular features of democratic rule. However, the predominance of patronage parties was also a function of exclusionary practices that raised the barriers to entry for more progressive, popularly based parties or that excluded them entirely. In Peru, recurrent and prolonged repression of the APRA limited opportunities for low-income groups to press for more extensive social programs. The weakness of left parties in the semidemocracies of Colombia and Brazil also had much to do with elite power-sharing agreements, military vetoes, and suffrage restrictions that limited opportunities for political participation and popular organization. Parties that more explicitly espoused redistributive policies became much more important political actors only after such restrictions were removed with the democratization of the 1980s and 1990s.

[7] The Communist Party was banned from 1946 to 1953, but socialist parties participated in electoral politics and governing coalitions continuously from the late 1930s to the 1950s, and restrictions on the Communists were lifted in the early 1950s.

CHAPTER THREE

The Evolution of Social Contracts in East Asia, 1950–80

East Asian countries exhibit a very different pattern of social policy from that prevailing in Latin America.[1] Governments generally took a minimalist approach to the provision of social insurance along all the dimensions that we have highlighted: with respect to the extent of public commitment, the nature of financing, and the breadth and depth of coverage. Singapore and Malaysia are partial exceptions because they inherited both central provident funds and public-health systems from the British. But the provident-fund model involved minimal government fiscal commitment and virtually no redistribution, and the health systems also became more market-oriented over time.

At the same time, the role of human capital formation has been a leitmotif in the literature on the region's economic growth.[2] The extent of government commitment to the provision of basic healthcare remains an issue of debate, and there are important variations on this score across the region. McGuire (2001a) argues that the improvement in health outcomes in a number of East Asian countries owed as much to rapid income growth as to the extent and quality of public provision. But particularly in Korea, Taiwan, Singapore, and Malaysia, governments provided early and strong support for the expansion of primary education and, with the important exception of Thailand, a timely shift to support the expansion of secondary education as well.

Our point of departure for explaining these cross-regional differences was the conservative nature of the political realignments that accompanied independence and the early Cold War period. A party with a social-democratic orientation did hold office prior to independence in Singapore, and left or populist movements emerged during brief political openings in Korea (1960) and Thailand (1974–76). But the strategic context of Cold War Asia was not conducive to social democratic parties and

---

[1] On the nature of the East Asian welfare state, see Dixon and Kim 1985; Deyo 1989; Goodman and Peng 1996; Goodman, White, and Kwon 1998; Kwon 1999; Asher 2000; Ramesh 2004; Holliday 2000; Tang 2000; Gough 2002; Holliday and Wilding 2003.

[2] For examples: World Bank 1993; Birdsall, Ross, and Sabot 1995; although see Booth (1999) for a more skeptical view.

independent unions and social movements, particularly in the "frontline" states of Korea, Taiwan, and later, Thailand. We find nothing comparable in East Asia to the sustained political influence of Costa Rica's PLN, the Chilean left coalition, or even the Argentine Peronists or the Apristas in Peru. Even democratic periods were dominated on the whole by centrist or rightist parties.

Despite the conservative nature of the political realignments, democratic openings were accompanied by shifts in government priorities and the expansion of social insurance and services; regime type also played a role. But as we saw in chapter 1, the overall incidence of democracy in Asia was much less than in Latin America, and the duration of particular democracies was shorter (table 3.1).[3] Of the seven cases we code as democratic or semidemocratic, four lasted for five years or less. And with the possible exception of the Philippines and Malaysia, none of the Asian countries experienced the prolonged history of competitive politics visible in Uruguay, Costa Rica, and Chile. As we will see, these limitations had implications for the incidence and types of social policy initiatives; table 3.2 provides an overview.

As was the case in Latin America, authoritarian rule did not necessarily mean an inattention to social-welfare questions. However, conservative political alignments gave authoritarian social policy in East Asia a distinctive stamp. The military and civil servants typically enjoyed quite generous protections, but in the absence of pressure from independent left parties or unions, the share of the urban working class enjoying social insurance was small. Moreover, programs for private-sector workers were typically contributory in design and involved relatively limited public fiscal commitments or redistribution.

A major puzzle is why the strategy of these conservative governments— both authoritarian and democratic—were more forthcoming with respect to the provision of basic social services. Some of these commitments, most notably with respect to education, were initially enshrined in independence constitutions that reflected democratic expectations. Authoritarian regimes inherited these commitments but turned them to their own political purposes of political socialization and control.

Yet cross-regional differences with respect to education also reflect differences in early postwar political alignments, and the political role of the countryside in particular, as well as the effects of development strategy. In Latin America, the political realignments we have identified expanded the influence of urban political forces. Significant segments of

---

[3] The coding schemes differ in the treatment of the Philippines and Malaysia, but important restrictions on political competition and civil liberties led us to classify these countries as semi-democratic.

TABLE 3.1
Regime Type in East Asia, c. 1945–85

	Democratic years	Semidemocratic years	"Soft" authoritarian years	"Hard" authoritarian years	Polity IV: Number of democratic years (1945 or independence to 1985)	Number of Przeworski democratic years (1950–85)	BDM = 0.75 years	BDM = 1 year
Korea (from 1948; 38 years)	1 (1960)	0	21 (1948–59; 1964–71; 1985)	16 (1961–63; 1972–84)	1 (1960)	1 (1960)	10 (1960,1963–71)	0
Malaysia (from 1957; 29 years)	0	12 (1957–68)	15 (1971–85)	2 (1969–70)	12 (1957–68)	0	17 (1696–85)	12 (1957–68)
Philippines (41 years)	0	27 (1946–72)	8 (1978–85)	5 (1973–77)	0	14 (1950–64)	26 (1946–71)	0
Singapore (from 1959; 27 years)	4 (1959–62)	5 (1963–67)	18 (1968–85)	0	4 (1959–62)	0	21 (1965–85)	0
Taiwan (from 1949; 37 years)	0	0	0	37 (1949–85)	0	0	0	0
Thailand (41 years)	0	3 (1974–76)	23 (1945–56; 1969–71; 1978–85)	15 (1957–68; 1972–73; 1977)	0	4 (1975; 1983–85)	10 (1974–75; 1978–85)	0
East Asia (N=213) totals and shares	5 (2.4%)	47 (22.2%)	85 (40.1%)	75 (35.4%)	17 (8.0% of all years) (N=212)	19 (9.9% of all years) (N=191)	84 (40.2% of all years) (N=205)	12 (5.8% of all years) (N=205)
Latin America (N=369) totals and shares	152 (41.2%)	64 (17.3%)	70 (19.0%)	83 (22.5%)	144 (39% of all years) (N=369)	194 (59.7% of all years) (N=325)	126 (34.1% of all years) (N=369)	78 (21.1% of all years) (N=369)

Sources: See table 1.12.
Notes: From 1963 to 1965, Singapore was formally a part of Malaysia, but the Singapore government retained autonomy with respect to some internal political issues.

the countryside remained effectively under oligarchic domination well into the second half of the twentieth century. In East Asia, by contrast, landed elites were weaker outside of the Philippines, and histories of rural insurgency provided incentives for authoritarian leaders to provide basic services. Particularly where authoritarian leaders subjected themselves to controlled electoral contests, rural voters provided a conservative counterweight to urban oppositions.

Authoritarian regimes also showed an interest in education for reasons of economic strategy that are very different from those in Latin America. Particularly in the "first-tier" newly industrializing countries—Korea, Taiwan, and Singapore—education policy was linked to overall development strategy and manpower-planning efforts. These interests are visible in the development of strong vocational tracks and tight limits on student choice, features of educational systems that are even more marked in the Eastern European cases.

Our discussion is bounded at the starting point by either 1945 (for Thailand, which was politically independent at that time) or by the date of political independence. We end with the democratic transitions of the 1980s in the Philippines, Korea, Taiwan, and Thailand. For Singapore and Malaysia, which do not undergo substantial changes in regime, we extend the analysis of some developments into the 1980s, although for the most part, we consider the period from 1980 in more detail in chapter 6.

We begin our discussion with three cases—the Philippines, Malaysia, and Singapore—in which independence was initially accompanied by relatively competitive politics, albeit with important constraints posed by the Cold War setting. We then examine the welfare systems in these countries as they moved in a more authoritarian direction. Finally, we turn to the three countries in the region where authoritarian rule was more constant, even if unstable in form—Taiwan, Thailand, and Korea. In Thailand and Korea, we also consider the effects of brief windows of more open and competitive politics.

From Semidemocracy to Authoritarian Rule in the Philippines

The conservative restoration under American tutelage contributed to a number of enduring features of the Philippine political system: the oligarchic nature of the two dominant political machines; their resistance to taxes and orientation toward patronage and pork; and the weakness of any social-democratic or popularly oriented alternatives. Because of early restrictions on the scope of party competition, subsequent restrictions on the left, and the fact that whole regions of the country were dominated by what John Sidel (1999) calls "bossism"—in effect, local authoritarian rule—we code the country as semidemocratic from 1946 until the estab-

TABLE 3.2
Regime Type and the Expansion of Social Commitments in East Asia, c. 1950–85

	Years (N=213)	Initiatives
	Democratic (N=5)	
Korea	1960	No major initiatives.
Singapore	1959–63	Major school-building and teacher-training initiatives.
		Major housing-development initiative, coupled with extension of basic public-health services.
	Semidemocratic (N=47)	
Philippines	1946–72	1954. Social Security System (SSS) legislated.
		1955. Workman's Compensation introduced.
		1958–60. Expansion of social security to all private-sector workers
		1969. Medical Care Act legislates national health insurance.
Malaysia	1957–68	Expansion of Rural Health Services Scheme.
		1961. Education law followed by major school-building program.
		1969. Employees Social Security Act establishes insurance for work-related injury and invalidity.
Singapore	1963–67	No major initiatives.
Thailand	1974–76	Major educational and health initiatives proposed.
	Soft authoritarian (N=85)	
Korea	1948–59	1954–59. Major school-building program, targeted primarily at primary level.
	1964–71	1965. Pilot health-insurance program (noncompulsory)
		1965. Public Assistance Program.
		1968. Middle-school entrance examination abolished.
	1985	Major proposals for the expansion of health insurance and public pensions, legislated under subsequent democratic governments.
Malaysia	1971–85	1971. New Economic Policy favoring bumiputras, includes ethnic quotas in higher education and other redistributive measures.
Philippines	1978–85	1978. Maternity benefits extended to members of SSS
		1980. Extension of social security to self-employed.

TABLE 3.2 (cont'd)
Regime Type and the Expansion of Social Commitments in East Asia, c. 1950–85

	Years (N=213)	Initiatives
Singapore	1968–85	1979. Major educational reform establishes early "streaming." 1984. Compulsory medical-insurance program through Central Provident Fund. Ongoing incremental changes in CPF rules to allow wider use of funds and greater investment choice.
Thailand	1945–56 1969–71	1956. Workmen's compensation (employer liability model).
	1978–85	1978. Major education reform, including six years of compulsory primary education, elimination of entry exam for secondary schools, expansion of vocational education. 1983. Private provident-fund legislation. 1980–88. Variety of rural health and nutrition initiatives
	Hard authoritarian (N=75)	
Korea	1961–63	1963. Pension program for government workers. 1963. Industrial accident insurance.
	1972–84	1973. National pension plan (not implemented). 1974. High-school-entrance examination abolished. 1975. Pension plan for private-school teachers. 1977. National medical insurance, initially limited to workers in larger firms.
Malaysia	1969–70	Formulation of New Economic Policy.
Philippines	1973–77	1975. Reform of workmen's compensation system.
Taiwan	1949–85	[1947. Commitment to universal primary education, followed by school building program.] 1950. Labor Insurance Program. 1964. Beginning of manpower planning. 1968. Compulsory middle-school education. 1974. Labor Security and Health (pension scheme). 1972–75. Social-assistance legislation on vocational training, child welfare, and public housing.
Thailand	1957–68 1972–73 1977	1958. Educational reform. 1972. Workmen's Compensation Fund.

lishment of the Marcos dictatorship in 1972.[4] The nationalist turn in the 1950s toward an ISI strategy was accompanied by somewhat greater opportunities for union mobilization, and there are interesting parallels to be drawn with the Latin American experience. But the labor movement was weakened by the small size of the manufacturing sector, high unemployment, and organizational fragmentation (Ramos1990; Jimenez 1993). The political constraints outlined in chapter 1 also played a crucial role and ironically contributed to the country's recurrent history of insurgency.

Despite these constraints, the Philippines experienced the longest stretch of competitive politics in Asia during the period of interest to us here. Although the scope of electoral competition was bounded, parties did compete vigorously and alternated in office. Interest-group organization, both urban and rural, also affected the course of social policy.

Until the surge of urban radicalism during Marcos' second term (1969–72) and again toward the end of the authoritarian period after 1980, the primary political and social challenges in the Philippines were rural, including recurrent armed insurgencies. The first period of significant expansion of social services occurred in the early 1950s, during the presidency of Ramon Magsaysay (1954–57), and came in response to the growth of peasant unions and the spread of rural radicalism. As secretary of defense and under the infamous American advisor Edward Landsdale, Magsaysay had formulated a military-political strategy to counter the Huk rebellion. This strategy included improved provision of basic social services in areas affected by the insurgency (Kerkvliet 1977; Danguilan 1999). In 1953, during his presidential campaign, Magsaysay campaigned on a platform that included land reform, rural development, and the provision of social services (Starner 1961, 39). These themes were echoed in his bid for reelection in 1963. Buoyant growth, Magsaysay's populism, and the rural threat also allowed him to temporarily extract more resources from a fiscally conservative congress. Spending on health and education—the latter with extensive support from the United States—grew dramatically during his administration (Abueva 1971, 422–23).

Magsaysay's main policy initiatives were rural. But growing strike activity and a concern for deradicalizing the emerging union movement prompted initiatives with respect to urban labor that bear some resemblance to the Latin American pattern. The first steps at placating the urban working class were taken in 1953 under Magasayay's predecessor. The Quirino administration passed an Industrial Peace Act that overhauled the system of industrial relations, provided for collective bargaining, and created incentives for the formation of unions. Undertaken

---

[4] We are grateful to Allen Hicken, Paul Hutchcroft, and Gabriella Montinola for extensive discussions of these coding issues.

with American assistance, the measure was partly designed to channel union efforts away from politics toward bread-and-butter issues (Wurfel 1959) and to break a growing link between labor and radical forces in the countryside (Ramos 1990, 44–45). However, the reform was also a response to the growing strike activity that accompanied postwar importsubstitution. In a further parallel to the Latin American cases, in 1954 the Magsaysay administration legislated a relatively expansive defined-benefit pension system broadly modeled on the American system. Although the Social Security System (SSS) initially extended social insurance only to workers in firms with more than fifty employees, in 1958 benefits were extended to employees in firms with at least six employees, and in 1960 to all private enterprises with at least one employee. In 1955, the Magsaysay government passed a workers' compensation law as well.

Electoral competition was also a source of pressure for increases in government spending, although, as in Colombia and Brazil, the effects of social spending were diluted by electoral incentives favoring particularism, patronage, and pork. The political business cycle reached its apogee under the divided government of the first Marcos administration (1966–69), when the president used executive control of pork-barrel spending in rural areas, including an extensive school-building campaign, to bypass party elites in congress (Doronila 1992; Averich, Koehler, and Denton 1971, 98–102).

Just prior to the 1969 elections, the government passed a Medical Care Act (or Medicare, operative in 1972) that provided for national health insurance. The 1969 health-insurance program was initially limited to formal-sector workers covered by the social-insurance system (Roemer 1993, 300; Ramesh 2000, 94). Although the initial act envisioned future expansions, these were continually postponed under the Marcos dictatorship. Outside of a small number of isolated locations, the system did not run its own healthcare facilities, and provision was therefore dominated by the private sector. Reimbursement rates to private providers did not keep up with rising costs, and the government exercised no controls on private sector pricing (Lamberte 1986, 102–103). The real value of benefits thus eroded over time, falling from 70 percent of average hospital costs at the inception of the program to just over 30 percent in 1988 (World Bank 1994a).[5] The act also did nothing to increase public health spending, which remained among the lowest in the region.

The constitution committed the government to universal primary education, and the country has consistently had high primary enrollments for

[5] This falloff can be explained in part by the absence of cost controls on the rapidly expanding private healthcare sector (Gertler and Solon 2002).

its level of income (table 1.3). Yet despite American aid, overall spending on education remained low by regional standards, as did the efficiency of the educational system (table 1.3; Tan and Mingat 1992). The expansion of the physical infrastructure, which was useful for patronage purposes, was not matched by consistent attention to the more difficult task of improving educational quality.

The transition to authoritarian rule in 1972 took place against the backdrop of increasing urban and rural political mobilization, including left and labor groups. The government took a number of steps to demobilize the opposition, a move justified in part by technocratic proposals to mimic the export-oriented strategy of Korea and Taiwan. However, Marcos also sought to organize local representative counsels and initiated a new land-reform program to counter continuing rural unrest. The administration used the SSS as an instrument to extend new types of benefits and to include new workers. The separate workers' compensation system was folded into the SSS in 1975; the government granted maternity benefits to SSS participants in 1978 and extended social-security benefits to self-employed workers in 1980.

However, these new social-policy initiatives were shallow (Noble 1986, 100–101). With respect to social security, compliance (in the payment and collection of payroll taxes) and corruption (in the management of SSS funds) were problematic from the outset and only worsened during the Marcos years. The apparent inclusion of the self-employed was limited, as it was in Latin America, by the requirement that they shoulder both the employees' and the employers' contributions. The performance of the public-education and health systems remained poor. Only very late in Marcos' administration did the government expand support to primary healthcare on a pilot basis (Bautista 1999b, 29–30). Other social initiatives—such as urban-redevelopment programs under the direct control of Imelda Marcos—were notoriously mired in corruption and patronage. The more significant issues of rural development go far beyond the scope of this study, but the initial reformism of the administration gave way to crony-run monopolies in key sectors such as coconuts and sugar that had highly regressive effects. These policies contributed to a substantial deterioration in the distribution of income (Boyce 1993).

In sum, competitive politics in the Philippines periodically produced social-policy initiatives, both through the electoral mechanism and in response to rural and urban organization and radicalism. But these initiatives were bounded by the fundamentally conservative nature of the ruling elite, the catch-all nature of political parties, and the constraints on fully democratic rule, including the ongoing suppression and weakness of left parties and unions. These features of Philippine politics became much more marked under the Marcos dictatorship, which proved to be a period of regression in terms of social policy, poverty, and inequality. Nor did the Marcos dictatorship initiate a serious turn in the direction of an export-oriented strategy, which might have ignited growth and motivated government and business to collaborate around a project of upgrading human capital. Not until the return of democratic rule under Aquino, Ramos, Estrada, and Arroyo-Macapagal did the government again begin to address the social question.

FROM COMPETITIVE POLITICS TO DOMINANT PARTY RULE IN SINGAPORE AND MALAYSIA

As in the Philippines, both Singapore and Malaysia experienced periods of competitive politics following self-rule and independence. The left was initially a more substantial force in Singapore, and ethnic parties with redistributive objectives played a major role in Malaysia. As a result of these somewhat different early postwar political alignments, we would expect early democratic rule to be accompanied by more robust social initiatives than were visible in the Philippines; that expectation is in fact vindicated. Over time, however, politics in both countries became more restrictive, with observable implications for the conduct of social policy. These changes are particularly visible in Singapore, which combined authoritarian rule with single-minded pursuit of an export-oriented growth strategy focused on attracting foreign capital.

Singapore

Singapore's politics was initially among the most competitive in our sample. The first general elections under colonial auspices in 1955 were won by David Marshall's Labor Front. The more moderate People's Action Party (PAP) of Lee Kuan Yew garnered a large electoral majority in the self-rule elections of 1959, but it did so by competing for support with parties to its left and in a political setting with strong unions and well-organized ethnic associations. As with its rivals, the PAP aggressively took up social issues and adopted a redistributive stance.

Given crowded urban conditions, the PAP's early social agenda placed particular emphasis on public housing through the Housing and Development Board (HDB). Housing served Lee Kuan Yew's nation-building objectives by breaking down ethnic enclaves and his more narrow political objectives by building support for the PAP. Housing was also connected with the provision of basic social services through the inclusion of schools and clinics in government apartment complexes and the general improvement in public health associated with the building of new housing stock and the clearing of slums. Accounts of Singapore's social policy consistently refer to housing as a centerpiece of the PAP's early political as well as social strategy.[6]

The Central Provident Fund (CPF), the fully funded social-insurance scheme established by the British, played into the social-policy strategy of the government in unexpected ways. The British had introduced the CPF to buy off militant labor while minimizing the colonial government's financial responsibilities (Low and Aw 1997, 14–21). Once established, the CPF provided a vehicle for managing retirement needs without any fiscal commitments on the part of the government.[7] However, the government could also draw on the CPF to finance HDB construction. In 1964, the PAP launched a home-ownership program, and in 1968 individuals were able to draw on their CPF accounts to purchase HDB flats at highly subsidized prices, setting in train an explosion of apartment ownership.

The extension of the educational franchise was also an explicit component of the PAP's political strategy (Gopinathan 1974). After 1959, the Malay community questioned the PAP's commitment to Malay education, and the Barisan Nasional (BN) had similar doubts about Chinese-language instruction. Malay and Chinese teachers' unions reinforced these pressures, as did a mobilized student body in Chinese secondary schools. The government responded by reducing inequalities in the treatment of the four language streams and paying special attention to Malay needs. As Booth (1999 293–95) argues, the maintenance of multiple languages of instruction actually had an adverse effect on measures of achievement as parents pushed children into the desirable English-medium schools. Nonetheless, the government commitment was clear: the PAP rapidly expanded the number of schools, and total primary enrollments leaped between 1959 and 1965 from 261,000 to 360,000. At the same time, the government gradually centralized control over a diverse set of educational institutions, paving the way for the more top-down control of the educational system that became evident in the 1970s.

As democratic politics gave way to a dominant-party authoritarian regime, social-policy initiatives took a subtly different form. The redistributive component of social policy diminished as the left collapsed and labor was reined in through a corporatist union structure and new limits on the capacity to strike introduced in 1967. Labor control was transparently related to the new growth strategy that relied on attracting export-oriented multinationals (Deyo 1989; Rodan 1989). The Employment Act

---

[6] For example: Chua 1997; Low and Aw 1997, 39–53; Tremewan 1994.

[7] The early expansion of coverage came about through structural change in the economy and the growth of the formal sector rather than through policy initiatives that incorporated new segments of the workforce.

and Industrial Relations (Amendment) Act of 1968 marked a clear turning point in this regard. The bills established nonwage benefits to workers but also placed strict ceilings on them and prohibited unions from negotiating over managerial prerogatives with respect to all personnel functions: promotion, hiring, firing, and the allocation of tasks.

The basic organization of social insurance saw little change during the 1970s, but those changes that did occur tended to reduce rather than increase the government's role. In 1982, the government considered the introduction of public-health insurance but rejected the idea on moral-hazard grounds; it was feared that it would lead to oversupply by providers and overuse by beneficiaries (Ramesh 2004, 90). We have already noted how the government used the CPF to shift toward a private financing model with respect to housing, albeit with large implicit subsidies. In 1984, the government used the Central Provident Fund to establish a compulsory medical-savings scheme. At the same time, the government began to encourage the expansion of private provision and granted greater corporate autonomy to public hospitals. As we will see in chapter 6, these reforms changed the public sector's role in the financing and provision of health care, which had initially followed the model of the British national-health system (Ramesh 2000, 97). Except for the expansion of a small social assistance scheme run through voluntary agencies, the government also consistently resisted redistributive social insurance schemes (Ramesh 2000, 164).

Education policy also underwent a shift in emphasis during the authoritarian period, shaped strongly by the export-oriented industrialization strategy. As early as the first educational plan and following a commission of inquiry in 1961, the government revised the curriculum to place greater weight on mathematics and scientific and technical subjects and created vocational and technical commercial schools. The Economic Development Board also began its involvement in workforce training. But the shift in emphasis from academic to technical education accelerated following the transition to an export-oriented model dominated by multinational firms. In 1968, the ministry of education set up a technical-education department, and from 1969 all male lower-secondary students had to undertake technical subjects. Strict streaming was introduced into the upper-secondary grades; enrollment growth actually slowed in secondary schools in the 1970s (Booth 1999, 295).

A plethora of manpower initiatives followed (Tan 1997), as did closer public-private collaboration in the areas of education and training policy. In 1973, the government established the Industrial Training Board, which included representatives from the ministries of education, labor, and trade as well as representatives from labor and the private sector. In 1979, the mandate of the Industrial Training Board was modified to include vocational training, and the Council on Professional and Technical Education was created to focus on those already in the labor force (Ritchie 2001, 181).

The government attempted to force upgrading on multinationals through sharp upward wage adjustments in 1979–81—with mixed effects—but supplemented these measures with a wave of training initiatives designed to foster industry-specific skills. These included a Skills Development Fund to encourage on-the-job training and the creation of a number of specialized institutes with foreign partners, aimed at developing industry-specific skills. In 1979, the vocational emphasis became even more strongly etched in the core educational system through a reform that established very early streaming and expanded technical and commercial education. More effectively than in any other nonsocialist country in our sample, education policy in Singapore was tightly linked with labor-market needs and the dictates of broader economic strategy (Gopinathan 1991; Wong 1993; Tan 1997).

In sum, early political competition in Singapore did not change the inherited model of fully funded social insurance, but it did influence the provision of social services, particularly education and housing. During the more authoritarian period, the fully funded nature of Sinagpore's social-security system remained intact, and the central provident fund model was extended to support the financing of health care as well. But the government consistently and self-consciously resisted insurance schemes that pooled risk and transfer schemes that involved redistribution. Education continued to expand vigorously, but in a style that increasingly emphasized vocational training and the dictates of the country's export-oriented growth strategy.

Malaysia

Because of restrictions on the scope of political competition, we code the first decade of postindependence politics in Malaysia as semidemocratic. In contrast to Singapore, the Emergency under the British and the confrontation (Konfrontasi) with Indonesia in 1963 combined to virtually eliminate the left as an organized political force in Malaysia. Labor was more weakly organized than in Singapore or even in the Philippines, and it was subjected to various controls (Jomo 1986, 244). Nonetheless, formal-sector workers did enjoy the benefits of the contributory Employees Provident Fund (parallel to Singapore's CPF) and a Workman's Compensation Scheme also initiated under the British. Prior to the highly contested elections of 1969, the Alliance government also passed an Employees' Social Security Act (known as SOCSO) that established contributory Employment Injury and Invalidity Pension schemes for lower-income workers in the formal sector (Asher 1994, 23–25).

For the most part, however, political competition and the politics of social policy broke along ethnic rather than class lines. During the first decade of independence, Alliance governments dominated by the United Malays National Organisation (UMNO) focused their attention on the Malay base, which was overwhelmingly rural. They did this primarily through agricultural development programs, rural infrastructure, pricing policies, and land and credit schemes (Meerman 1979; Snodgrass 1980). But the delivery of basic social services was also an important part of UMNO's strategy toward the countryside. The government built schools and trained teachers who subsequently became an important pillar of the ruling party at the local level; primary enrollments increased dramatically, although from a lower base than in Taiwan and Korea (table 1.2).

As in Singapore, the independence government inherited a complex healthcare system dominated by public provision and financed by "varying levels of user charges in public hospitals, government grants, limited insurance, some compulsory savings and large out-of-pocket expenses" (Ramesh 2000, 91). Post-independence governments aggressively expanded the Rural Health Services Scheme, an interesting precursor to the primary-healthcare approach that was established by the British in response to the insurgency. The service provided free healthcare at the point of delivery. As a number of studies show (Meerman 1979; Snodgrass 1980), the pattern of public spending during the 1960s was both pro-Malay and pro-poor, and a number of basic social indicators, including rural-health outcomes, improved steadily (Heng and Hoey 1997).

Following the general elections of 1969, the country experienced a spasm of ethnic violence. Standard interpretations attribute both the gradual tightening of political controls and the launch of the New Economic Policy (NEP) to this event (for example, Jomo 1986). Not all the restrictions on political activity were new (Crouch 1996). The Internal Security Act, for example, was a British inheritance that was used effectively during the "hard authoritarian" interlude (1969–71) to detain opposition leaders and, in the mid-1970s, to consolidate power within the UMNO itself. After the return to parliamentary rule in 1971, a range of restrictions on political discourse and organization remained in place, and new ones were added (Hwang 2003, 91–134). Important among these were restrictions on labor unions' participation in politics, on the formation of general unions, and on the capacity to strike. Although these measures were largely political in their origins, they were extended over the 1970s in ways that reflected the new emphasis on export-oriented growth and foreign investment (Ayadurai 1996).

Despite these political constraints, competitive political pressures continued to operate both outside and inside the UMNO. The electoral setback to the UMNO and its Chinese partners in 1969 appeared to challenge Malay prerogatives. But the Alliance's losses came from Malays as well as from non-Malays, and shoring up the party's electoral base became a paramount objective of the government. The UMNO responded to the riots by forming a broader alliance—the Barisan Nasional—that provided the electoral vehicle for the consolidation of single-party rule during the Mahathir years (1981–2003; see chapter 6).

Analysis of the NEP typically focuses on its efforts at so-called "restructuring," or reducing inequalities between ethnic groups in the distribution of income and assets (Jomo 1986; Jesudason 1989). Most of these measures—including the controversial effort to achieve a target of Malay ownership of 30 percent of all assets—go beyond the scope of our study. In fact, however, the NEP was designed to have a second social prong of poverty reduction, regardless of ethnicity (Jomo 1994). The antipoverty component of the NEP consisted primarily of rural development schemes with a strong patronage component. But the government also continued the steady expansion of primary and secondary education—with Malay designated as the national language for educational instruction in 1971—and basic health services as well (See tables 1.2 and 1.3).

The transition to an export-oriented growth strategy came somewhat later in Malaysia than it did in Korea, Taiwan, and Singapore and therefore did not play the same central role in social policy during the period of interest to us here as it did in the three newly industrializing countries. Penang had begun to attract foreign direct investment from the late 1960s, but in 1975 the passage of the Industrial Coordination Act signaled a more forceful government effort to attract foreign investment. Ritchie (2001) details how national-level efforts at skill development were less effective than those at the local level, such as the Penang Skills Development Center. Nonetheless, he provides ample evidence of the link between a shift in strategy and increased efforts at vocational training, skills upgrading, and coordination with the private sector.

How did the early experience of competitive politics affect the course of social policy in Singapore, Malaysia, and the Philippines? Singapore was the one country in the region that combined relatively competitive democratic politics with a strong left and unions. The PAP clearly saw the provision of housing and basic social services as core to its political competition with the left. Early Malaysian governments did not face a similar challenge from the organized left, but the lessons of the Emergency and the rural base of the dominant Malay party focused government attention on the delivery of basic social services to the countryside. Thus, despite the more conservative political setting and the absence of strong left and labor-based parties or union movements, there is nonetheless evidence that regime type affected the course of social policy.

A similar argument can be made for the Philippines. Elite-dominated parties and the continuing dominance of the oligarchy in a number of rural areas dampened the effect of democratic rule. The well-documented tendency toward pork-barrel spending also influenced the nature of social policy. Nonetheless, parties did compete to some extent by using social-policy promises, and executives—most notably Ferdinand Marcos—used social expenditures to build personal support.

Democratization also influenced the course of education policy. Independence constitutions in all three countries included strong commitments to an expansion of education. In both Singapore and Malaysia, educational policy was a highly charged political issue that engaged well-organized ethnic constituencies. In the Philippines, educational policy was laced with patronage, and educational quality did not match its spread, but the commitments contained in the independence constitution cannot be dismissed. As table 1.3 shows, primary enrollments fell at the very top of the Latin American range, and secondary enrollments exceeded those in the entire Latin American sample and with comparable completion rates.

Evidence of the effects of regime type can also be seen in the shifts in social policy that occurred as governments became more authoritarian. In Singapore, social policy increasingly conformed to the perceived dictates of the export-oriented growth strategy: in the effort to control labor, to limit mandated benefits, and in the emphasis placed on technical education. Philippine authoritarianism did not exhibit the same singularity of strategic purpose, but the central comparative point remains; social policy shifted and redistribution became more regressive as political competition and interest-group organization were curtailed.

PROLONGED AUTHORITARIAN RULE: TAIWAN, KOREA, AND THAILAND

As our discussion of Singapore and the Philippines has already shown, authoritarianism in Asia has a variegated and changing face. Before we can draw firm conclusions about the effects of regime type, it is important to consider cases of prolonged dictatorship. Only in Taiwan do we have an example of sustained "hard" authoritarian rule, and even there the party allowed some highly controlled electoral competition at both the national and local level. As in most Latin American countries, authoritarian regimes in Korea and Thailand rested on the military rather than on a dominant party. Governments oscillated between periods of hard authoritarianism, "soft" authoritarian rule that permitted a degree of electoral competition, and at least two short periods of more genuine demo-cratic opening (Korea in 1960 and Thailand in 1974–76). While short-lived, these democratic experiments invite comparisons both with prior authoritarian rule in those countries and with democratic openings else-where in Latin America and East Asia.

The authoritarian regimes of these three countries were by no means immune to political challenge; indeed, the greater the political challenges prior to the authoritarian installation, the more responsive governments were with respect to social initiatives. However, these initiatives showed some similarities that we associate with authoritarian welfare politics elsewhere in the region. These characteristics include limited coverage with respect to social insurance and a reliance on fully funded or em-ployer-liability models. Where countries pursued export-oriented growth models, employer concerns about costs constituted a constraint on the generosity of such entitlements. Health systems focused on basic public health, eschewed social insurance, and relied heavily on private financing and provision.

Educational reforms were more diverse. Even more than in Singapore and Malaysia, education policy in the "frontline" states reflected political interests in social control and ideological indoctrination. However, the authoritarian "developmental states" of Korea and Taiwan also placed increasing emphasis over time on vocational education and integrated ed-ucation and manpower-planning efforts in line with their turn to export-led growth strategies (Cheng 1992, 93).

Taiwan

The KMT came to Taiwan in the wake of a crushing political defeat at the hands of the Communists that involved not only superior military organization but also the effective exploitation and organization of both urban and rural grievances. Despite its highly authoritarian structure, a leitmotif of the early history of the KMT on Taiwan was the determina-tion not to repeat the mistakes they had made on the mainland; social policy reflected both the regime's authoritarian form and perceived politi-cal challenges.

Taiwan is unique in the region in pursuing a social-insurance model, the so-called Labor Insurance scheme, that in principle offered protection against a range of risks, including old-age, disability, death and survivors' benefits, illness, injury, and maternity. Social insurance was initiated by the provincial government quite early, following the retrocession to Tai-wan (1950–51). However, it was initially limited to the military (under a separate, more generous scheme) and to workers in state enterprises and large private firms, and it expanded only slowly thereafter to various politically influential occupational categories.[8] By 1979, however, the year of a substantial amendment to the Labor Insurance Act, only about 15 percent of the population was covered (Chan 1987, 333; Ku 1997, 38).

A closer look at the scheme suggests that it bore little similarity to the Latin American model and was arguably not a social-insurance system at all. Even with its incremental expansion, a substantial share of those covered were government workers, perhaps as many as two-thirds. Moreover, the government's financial commitment was limited to the military and to civil servants, who enjoyed much more generous benefits. For private-sector workers, the system was purely contributory, although employers paid 75–80 percent of contributions.[9] As Kwon (1998, 44) concludes, "after the Labour Insurance Program was introduced in 1950, the welfare system stagnated until the 1980s." Social assistance for the poor was also extremely limited until the transition to democratic rule in the 1980s (Ku 1997, 38, 236–39).

By contrast, the commitment to human-capital development is widely recognized as a distinguishing feature of Taiwan's economic growth, and it is reflected in a relatively early and robust commitment to primary healthcare and particularly to education. Health insurance was limited to government employees and those workers in the formal sector covered by the Labor Insurance scheme. Moreover, provision was dominated by the private sector.[10] However, over the 1950s, as part of its broader emphasis on rural development, the Sino-American Joint Commission on Rural Reconstruction (JCRR) assisted in the expansion of basic health stations in the rural areas that focused on public health, vaccinations, health education, and family planning (Yager 1988, 195–209). As McGuire (2001a, 1688) shows, these interventions almost certainly contributed to the sharp drop in infant mortality over the 1950s.

Yeun-wen Ku (1997, 176–81) has shown how political and ideological motives played a major role in the early KMT strategy toward education. The KMT took over a highly centralized Japanese educational system and turned it to new political ends; the means included moral and civic education, tight political control over teachers and students, and the inculcation of Mandarin as a lingua franca and (attempted) source of national political identity. Although private provision was allowed, it was strictly regulated and subject to similar controls. Primary education expanded

[8] The insurance plan is part of the Labor Insurance scheme; see Chan 1987; Ku 1997, 31–34; Tang 2000, 72–78; Son 2001; Aspalter 2002, 51–58.

[9] For the entire period from 1950 through 1979, contributions actually exceeded benefits paid by over 40 percent (Aspalter 2002, 53 [table 3]).

[10] Wong (2004) shows that the share of beds in public hospitals declined to approximately one third of all hospital beds in the 1970s and that large private hospitals exercised substantial influence over pricing both for insured and uninsured services.

dramatically during the 1950s, and in 1968, the government extended compulsory and free education to the lower-secondary level.

Beginning in 1964, education development was increasingly integrated into overall economic planning. As Ashton et. al. (1999, 88) summarize, "the plans from the beginning made projections of growth by industrial sector, projections of the manpower requirements of various educational levels, employment (and employment levels) and distributions of enrollment (later quotas) in educational institutions." Moreover, these were backed by difficult policy decisions. Limits were placed on the expansion of general schools, which parents and students preferred, and tougher secondary-school entrance exams channeled students into the vocational track (Cheng 1992, 93). The late 1960s and 1970s also saw the initiation of government-business training partnerships financed through the creation of a Vocational Training Fund and levies on larger firms. Although it goes beyond the scope of our interests here, parallel initiatives were undertaken later in the 1970s to bring higher education into closer line with shifting industrial demands.

Thailand

Thailand's authoritarian system rivals Taiwan's in longevity, but has been subject to numerous swings between more and less closed periods, with the shift to hard authoritarian rule under Sarit Thanarat and his successors from 1958 to 1972 as a marked turning point. Yet even when the parliament was allowed to operate, the system was extremely restrictive in the range of political forces represented. The state was dominated by the armed forces, the police, and the bureaucracy. Parties were highly personalistic, Parliament typically included appointed members, and electoral rules allowed government officials to simultaneously sit as MPs. As we argued in chapter 1, the early postwar period was characterized by an effective purge of the urban opposition, the left, and labor, although the government later faced a stubborn rural insurgency in the 1960s and 1970s that shaped antipoverty initiatives. However, given the particular weakness of organized social forces in Thailand, our expectations about the effects of "soft" authoritarian rule are somewhat more modest than in other cases.

Until the political liberalization of the 1980s and 1990s, social insurance in Thailand was very narrowly based. In 1951, long-standing bureaucratic prerogatives were codified into a noncontributory Government Officials Pension Act. But the extension of social benefits beyond the state faced opposition that is highly revealing of welfare politics in an authoritarian setting (Pawadee 1986). In 1938 and 1946, Parliament rejected labor bills that included pensions and work-injury schemes, on the grounds that Chinese laborers stood to benefit more than Thais. In 1954, Parliament approved an ambitious government bill that covered maternity, sickness, invalidity, child care, old age, and death but insurance companies, public and private enterprises, and the mass media opposed it. Firms had liability for injuries and sickness of workers, and as a result, labor was also opposed because of the higher payroll taxes the reform would imply.

The hard authoritarian Sarit government (1958–63) moved to repress labor organization, but after some revision resubmitted the 1954 welfare bill to Parliament. The bill spent another seven years in revision and review by Parliament and other bodies, however, before officially being scrapped in 1965. Until the initiatives of the early 1980s that we discuss in chapter 6, the Thai government undertook only one significant social-insurance initiative and it fit the broader authoritarian pattern we have described here: a shift in workers compensation from the employer-liability model, which generated substantial labor dissatisfaction, to a Workmen's Compensation Fund in 1972. The fund was financed entirely by employers and limited initially to workers in larger firms in the Bangkok metropolitan area.

The distribution of basic social services—health and education—reflected the combination of authoritarian control and weak social organization and exhibited substantial inequalities. The royal family had a long interest in medicine and public health and as early as the 1930s, had built a number of rural health stations (McGuire 2002b). During the 1950s, the number of rural health facilities grew steadily, supported by American aid. By 1959, each of Thailand's districts (then about 500 in number) had at least one second-class health center (staffed by a paramedic and a midwife), and about one-quarter of them had first-class health centers (ideally staffed by a doctor and a nurse). In the 1950s and 1960s, the government also undertook a variety of public-health initiatives, such as an effective antimalaria campaign, a requirement as of 1967 that health-care professionals trained at government expense should work for a time in underserved rural areas, and a national family-planning program launched in 1970. However, most evaluations of the Thai health system reach the conclusion that the distribution of care was highly unequal, and public commitment showed strong biases toward curative care and the urban areas and limited financial commitment to basic healthcare (for example, Krongkaew 1982; Cohen 1989; McGuire 2002b). These biases were not seriously addressed until the 1970s.

A common feature of education policy in other Asian countries was an expansion of commitments associated with independence from colonial rule; this was true in the Philippines, Korea, Malaysia, and Singapore, and arguably in the move of the KMT to Taiwan as well. Thailand did not experience a similar political break. Not coincidentally, it also exhibited a much more incremental process of educational expansion and a much more unequal distribution of education spending and attainment. The first compulsory-education law was passed in 1921, but not until the coup of 1932 and the transition to a constitutional monarchy was primary education a serious objective of government. Even then, expenditure was concentrated around greater Bangkok and on tertiary education; private institutions were encouraged to pick up the slack, particularly at the secondary level (Nitungkorn 1988). Education was an issue in the unrest that preceded the Sarit coup in 1958, as rural areas felt they were being neglected by the government. The First National Economic Development Plan of 1961 included an education component. The new government expanded compulsory education from four to six years, and vocational education received greater emphasis than it had enjoyed in the past. But overall commitment remained weak; primary enrollments had reached 85 percent in 1970, but secondary enrollments were only 16 percent (Nitungkorn 1988, 28 [table 4]). It took the impetus of the democratic opening of the mid-1970s to generate more sustained attention to educational reform.

This "semidemocratic" opening from October 1973 to October 1976 proved short-lived. We would not expect such an opening to generate sustained initiatives, but it does suggest quite clearly the significance of more competitive politics and critical realignments for social-policy initiatives. Military and business elites and conservative politicians retained substantial influence during this period, but the rise of parties on the left and a groundswell of social demands from newly mobilized labor and farmer organizations—some with policy leadership from sympathetic academics and students—substantially affected social policy initiatives (Baker and Phongpaichit 2002, 314–24).

The political opening was marked by a plethora of proposals that sought not simply to pacify the countryside but also to mobilize the rural sector into politics in a more sustained way. Many of these measures such as land reform, agricultural subsidies, and increased spending on rural infrastructure are beyond the scope of this study. Others, however, established important social-policy precedents. The Low Income Card Scheme became the template for subsequent expansion of health insurance in the 1980s and 1990s (see chapter 6). Households meeting a means test were given cards that provided them access to a variety of health services at government clinics and hospitals, subject to a strict referral system. In 1978, this effort was supplemented by a Rural Primary Health Care Expansion Project that involved training more than half a million villagers as lay health workers.

The system was vulnerable to a number of criticisms, including the lack of effective communication, stigma, and the skewed nature of health spending; all of these factors limited uptake of the program. Nonetheless, nearly 70 percent of the population met the income cut-off at the time the program was launched even if actual coverage was as little as one-fifth of that much (Mills 1991). The democratic government also responded to pressure to equalize educational opportunities by expanding secondary schools in rural areas (Nitungkorn 1988). Early plans, formulated prior to the opening, contemplated a secondary school in every district. Under political pressure, the ministry of education was compelled to promise secondary schools at the village (*tambon*) level as well. Many of the re-form proposals of the democratic period were not brought to fruition and died with the authoritarian backlash of 1976. But the period saw several important initiatives that could be traced to the political opening.

Korea

As we argued in chapter 1, Korea had the most highly mobilized left in the region at the time of independence, including a communist party and highly mobilized worker and peasant organizations. These political forces were severely repressed during the American occupation and in the period between independence and the onset of the peninsular war, with enduring consequences for Korean politics.

Mapping the politics of subsequent social initiatives in Korea is compli-cated, however, by the volatility of the Korean political system and fre-quent changes of regime. The increasingly autocratic Rhee government fell to student protest and wider social disaffection in 1960. As in Thai-land, a brief political opening (the Second Republic of 1960–61) was char-acterized by wide-ranging social mobilization and the articulation of so-cial as well as political grievances. But the paralysis of government set the stage for a military coup of 1961 and a period of outright military rule from 1961 through 1963. Under American pressure, Park held elections for the presidency, in which he stood and won as a civilian, and undertook a transition to nominally democratic rule in 1964. This transition permit-ted some electoral competition (with presidential elections in 1963, 1967, and 1971) but in a highly controlled context and with pervasive abuses of executive power.

Even this semidemocratic system was shut down in 1972 with the initia-tion of the "hard" authoritarian rule of the Yushin period. The Yushin era came to a close with the assassination of President Park in 1979, and the brief "Seoul Spring" of 1980. But this brief political opening also fell quickly with the declaration of martial law in May 1980. Korea experi-enced yet another period of authoritarian rule, with controlled elections under Chun Doo Hwan from 1981 to 1987. Only with the election of Roh Tae Woo in 1987—where we end the story in this chapter—was the transition to democratic rule completed, and even then, it ended with president who had been a military officer and close associate of Chun Doo Hwan.

As this brief history suggests, although Korea's democratic experience was extremely limited throughout most of its postwar history, authoritarian elites faced serious political challenges. In 1961, 1972, and 1980, urban social mobilization and protest was a prelude to political closure and controls on labor and the left. Although these changes in regime were followed by new controls on labor, the government also had an interest in placating strategically significant portions of the urban working class and in maintaining the acquiescence, if not the support, of the rural sector. In contrast to the Latin American bureaucratic-authoritarian regimes, the Korean military exhibited a particularly strong populist streak following the coup in 1961, which had followed a period of slowing growth, stagnating employment, and even food shortages.

As elsewhere in the region, social insurance began with pension plans for civil servants and the military, initiated at the end of the Rhee period. Under these special systems, the government, contributed as employer, and the scope of benefits gradually expanded. Protections for private-sector workers were more minimalist. The new military government launched industrial accident insurance (under the military, prior to the presidential elections of 1963) and a pilot health-insurance program (in 1965). Both were fundamentally limited in their scope, the industrial-accident-insurance program by its initially restricted coverage (to firms with more than 500 workers), the health-insurance scheme by the fact that it was not compulsory. Over time, the employee-funded industrial-accident scheme provided a template for the expansion of coverage through a gradual reduction in the size of firms covered. The health-insurance scheme, by contrast, did not expand, since employers and employees who did not want to pay for coverage could simply opt out. The one significant innovation of the early Park period was a means-tested Public Assistance Program that provided transfers to several vulnerable categories, including the elderly poor, the homeless, and those with mental disability. Despite its extreme modesty, this initiative was one of the earliest social-assistance programs of its sort in the region (Kwon 1999a, 84–88).

The next round of welfare initiatives also followed a regime change: the installation of the authoritarian Yushin Constitution of 1972. Korea witnessed increasing political polarization in the late 1960s and early 1970s, and social issues played an important role in that process. Kim Dae Jung played to these issues during his presidential campaign of 1969, and labor and student militancy increased sharply. One response was to shore up the government's rural electoral base through a major rural pub-lic-works program, the Saemaul Undong or New Community Movement. Announced in 1970, this complex program of public-works spending be-came a major instrument of rural social policy during the Yushin period.

The Yushin announcement was accompanied by several other welfare initiatives that also conform broadly to a Bismarckian, or authoritarian, model. The government proposed a national pension system, partly as a way of mobilizing savings for Park's ambitious heavy industry drive. But it was postponed with the first oil shock and not revived until the very eve of the transition to democratic rule; we discuss this initiative in part 2.

However, national medical insurance was launched in 1977 along with a modest medical assistance or Medicaid program for the poor that cov-ered the medically indigent and low-income households on a means-tested basis. The initial insurance plan consisted of two components: a compul-sory scheme for workers in larger firms with more than 500 employees; and a voluntary, community-based plan providing medical insurance for all others. Government employees and private-school teachers gained cov-erage under a different, and somewhat more generous compulsory scheme in 1979. In combination, these schemes covered just over 10 percent of the population, with medical assistance covering another 6 percent (Kwon and Reich 2005 on the evolution of coverage).

Over the next decade, the program expanded fairly dramatically, but not as a result of increased public commitment; the scheme was financed entirely by employer and employee contributions. Growth took place rather by gradually reducing the size of firms required to participate, by the expansion of community-based funds, and by granting permission for occupational groups to establish quasi-public insurance societies (Kwon 2003; Kwon and Reich 2005). By 1987, the time of the democratic transi-tion, about 50 percent of the population was covered in a system that had grown increasingly fragmented by the proliferation of separate funds. Because risk was not pooled across funds, important inequities and fi-nancial difficulties arose, and farmers, the self-employed, and the urban informal sector were excluded altogether. As was the case in Taiwan, not until the transition to democratic rule did political incentives push in the direction of universalization of health insurance and serious consideration of a national pension plan.

With respect to provision, the Korean government did spend effectively with respect to certain elements of public health: the extension of services for disease prevention such as immunization, and environmental sanita-tion (McGuire 2002a). Prior to the initiation of public insurance, how-ever, overall health spending was dominated overwhelmingly by private spending. The predominant form of medical care was by physicians pro-viding services on a fee-for-service basis, with a strong bias, as in Thailand, toward the urban areas. The initiation of public insurance had the effect of further expanding the role of the private sector in the provision of health care. In 1975, 34.5 percent of all hospitals were public, but by 1994 that number had dropped to 5 percent (Yang 2001), with the remainder roughly split between private facilities, many owned by doctors, and not-for-profit foundations.

Thanks to the outstanding research of Michael Seth (2002), we have a particularly clear picture of the politics of education in Korea (see also McGinn et al. 1980; Cheng 1992, 93). The initial expansion of the system came under the American occupation, driven by the tremendous pent-up demand that had followed decades of the repressive cultural policy of Japanese rule. The American occupation authorities built cautiously on the centralized system inherited from the Japanese, but hundreds of private primary and secondary schools also jumped into the breach. As in the Philippines, Singapore, and Malaysia, the independence constitution promised universal primary education. With American support, a massive school-building program permitted a dramatic expansion of primary and lower-secondary enrollments in the 1950s. At the same time, the government held the line on the growth of private secondary and tertiary institutions and established a quota system for higher education.

The immediate postindependence period saw intense debates in the National Assembly about whether the new system should emulate the Japanese model, with greater centralization and tracking, or an American model with strong local control and a single general educational track. Although the latter model nominally won this protracted political fight, Seth (2002, 192–202) shows how the new system was quickly turned to Rhee's authoritarian political aims. The government purged leftist teachers, revised the curriculum to emphasize moral and civic education, and even organized students into a paramilitary Student Defense Corps—headed by the president himself—that could be mobilized to support various political aims. A similar pattern of purges, purification movements, and student mobilization for fundamentally political ends followed Park's seizure of power in 1961.

The Rhee administration showed little interest in coordinating education with broader development objectives. Almost immediately on coming to office, by contrast, the Park regime drafted a First Five-Year Educational Development Plan for 1962–66 that ran in conjunction with the First Five-Year Economic Development Plan. These new initiatives sought to universalize primary education, expand secondary education at a more rapid pace than high schools, and reduce university enrollments. They also shifted the emphasis from academic to technical and vocational education and brought the curriculum into closer alignment with private-sector demands. Despite substantial investment in vocational education,

Seth (2002, 120–25) and Cheng (1992, 93) both show how difficult it proved even in the semiauthoritarian setting to implement changes that appeared to shut the door on equal access to higher education or shifted the balance between vocational and academic education. Nonetheless, the period of the heavy-industry drive of the 1970s was accompanied by a number of new initiatives to increase skills, including the creation of vocational-training institutes and a Special Measures Law for Vocational Training that provided incentives (in the form of penalties) for larger firms to train workers in-house.

CONCLUSION: AN ASIAN WELFARE MODEL?

During the critical realignments in Latin America, political elites had strong incentives to appeal to urban working-class groups and used social insurance and services as a means of doing so, albeit at the cost of substantial inequality in their distribution. The international political context in East Asia contributed to quite different political realignments in the early postwar period. These influences were most obvious in Korea and Taiwan, the archetypal anti-Communist regimes, but they were increasingly visible in Thailand from the 1950s as well. A left-of-center party and strong unions initially influenced social-policy developments in Singapore, but the 1960s saw a fundamental political realignment and regime change in that country as well.

As in Latin America, the significance of underlying political alignments cut across regime type. Although at least semidemocratic, Philippine politics was powerfully shaped by the restoration of conservative political elites at the end of World War II and the corresponding marginalization of the left, labor, and the popular sector. An ethnically based party in Malaysia pursued a redistributive policy approach in that country under semidemocratic auspices, albeit focused on the rural sector rather than the urban working class. But even in Malaysia, politics was bounded by the experience with the insurgency and fundamental limits on the left and labor.

Development strategies also differed from those pursued in Latin America. The pursuit of ISI in Latin America increased the weight of the import-substituting and state-owned enterprise sector and provided the economic underpinnings for social-insurance systems favoring the urban working class. Development strategies in East Asia were by no means homogeneous, with respect either to the instruments used or to timing. The Korean and Taiwanese economies became increasingly export-oriented from the 1960s; similar structural changes did not occur in Thailand until the 1980s. Yet whenever these changes did occur, they exerted both a direct and indirect influence on social policy. On the one hand, the growing weight of a cost-sensitive private-export sector limited support for social-insurance initiatives that would increase payroll taxes. On the other hand, the export-oriented approach created some incentives for business-government cooperation with respect to education and training.

Within the bounds set by these underlying political and economic differences across the two regions, regime type did affect the core policy areas of interest to us: pensions, health, and education. These differences are most clear with respect to social insurance. Thailand and Korea, two of the long-standing authoritarian cases, eschewed social insurance almost entirely, limiting it to core constituents in the state itself: the military and civil servants. The KMT, with its troubled history on the mainland, took a more proactive stance toward the urban working class following its retrocession to Taiwan, but coverage was limited to the state sector and a very small set of formal sector workers in larger firms. Moreover, the system followed a pure defined-contribution model, and from its inception in the early-1950s through the end of the 1970s, it saw few innovations. In Singapore and Malaysia, social insurance was provided by inherited central-provident funds, and it was arguably this colonial legacy rather than politics that played the central role in limiting government expenditure and the extent of redistribution. But in both countries, the political forces that might have argued for a more redistributive model of social insurance were also weak. Innovations in the two central-provident funds were limited to parametric changes in how beneficiaries could use resources.

In the Philippines, competitive politics influenced the establishment of a pay-as-you-go pension system that bore a family resemblance to those seen in Latin America. But at the end of the period under review here, coverage extended to under half of the economically active population and benefits were both limited and heavily skewed toward public-sector workers. Nowhere in the region—with the possible exception of the early years of competitive politics in Singapore—do we see governments subject to genuine electoral competition and also constrained to reach out to labor as an important political constituency. And nowhere in the region do we see similar systems of social insurance to those that emerged in Argentina, Chile, Uruguay, or Costa Rica.

The influence of regime type is visible with respect to health insurance and spending as well. Health-insurance coverage in East Asia during this period was low, and health spending during the 1973–80 period was low by comparison to Latin America (table 1.1), even as the level of development between the two regions equalized. The two countries with the highest level of public health spending—Malaysia and Singapore—had inherited national-health systems from the British. In Malaysia, both the level and composition of health spending can be attributed in part to electoral calculations; in Malaysia's semidemocracy, the UMNO showed a strong concern with its rural electoral base. In Singapore, by contrast, the drift toward authoritarian rule was accompanied by efforts to privatize the health system and limit public commitments. Levels of spending in those two countries, although the highest in the Asian sample, only approximate the mean in a group of Latin American countries that include several with substantially lower levels of GNP per capita.

Elsewhere in the region, public-health spending was limited. Thailand and Korea—two of the three long-standing authoritarian regimes—took an extremely minimalist approach to healthcare; it was confined largely to a public-health approach. Not until the late 1970s did either government undertake any health-insurance initiatives, and in both cases they were fragmented: by occupation in Korea and by very narrow targeting in Thailand. The KMT took an active interest in basic public health in the 1950s and included some health benefits in a reform of the Labor Insurance system in the late 1960s. But coverage of this program was limited and benefits far from generous. That this lack of attention on the part of authoritarian regimes did not reflect public preferences was revealed strongly during the political opening of the mid-1970s in Thailand, when the expansion of rural public-health and nutrition programs became one of the major reforms of the short-lived democratic governments. However, as in other brief democratic openings in the region (for example, in Korea in 1960, and again in 1979–80), this opening was not durable enough to have marked consequences for social policy.

In the Philippines, with the longest history of competitive politics, the creation of a national health-insurance system was one of the last major social initiatives of the democratic period. But as was the case in the social-security system to which it was linked, benefits were minimal, and planned efforts to expand the system were postponed during the Marcos dictatorship; it took the return of democracy to revive the system and push it toward broader coverage (chapter 6).

As we saw in chapter 1, East Asia has a more impressive record than does Latin America, both in delivering basic services (as measured, for example, by immunization) and health outcomes (for example, in bringing infant mortality down). But as McGuire (2001a) has argued cogently with respect to infant mortality, health outcomes in Asia have as much to do with rising incomes, the relatively equal distribution of income, and corresponding improvements in nutrition as they do with public commitments. Even more than in Latin America, households relied on self-insurance, out of pocket expenditures, and private provision.

Perhaps the most striking interregional difference is in the commitment to education. Primary enrollment was not only higher in Asia than in

Latin America at the end of the period, but it was also higher earlier—that is, at much lower levels of GNP per capita. Moreover, the efficiency of the systems as measured by repetition rates, youth illiteracy, and dropout rates are also generally better.

Regime type has something to do with this difference, although by a complex route. The Asian countries experienced important political breaks with independence; these political openings generated strong political pressures for the expansion of educational entitlements. This situation held true in Singapore, Malaysia, the Philippines, and Korea. These political breaks—brief democratic moments—constitute a sharp contrast with Latin America where the extension of the franchise was much more gradual. Yet authoritarian governments also had strong political incentives—albeit of very different sorts—to maintain and expand the educational franchise. Expansion of the educational system served crucial ideological and socialization functions and was therefore less vulnerable to rollback following transitions to authoritarian rule. Developmental authoritarian governments, particularly in Korea, Taiwan, and Singapore, had an additional motive for expanding the educational franchise and investing in vocational and technical education that was lacking in Latin America: the interest in linking educational policy to overall development strategy.

In our discussion of the Latin American cases, we noted how the legacy of past entitlements posed challenges to new governments following the democratic transitions of the 1980s. Despite profound economic shocks, powerful stakeholders posed constraints on liberal reform of existing entitlements and the reallocation of spending toward the socially disenfranchised. Asia differed from Latin America in the first instance in its more favorable economic circumstances. The countries that transited to democratic rule in good times—Korea, Taiwan, and Thailand—had ample resources available to address social issues.

But the political legacy also differed. Rather than inheriting strong stakeholders in an existing system, these countries had legacies of weak public involvement in the provision of social insurance. In this setting, democratic rule, rapid growth, and ample fiscal resources combine to permit a rapid expansion of public commitments.

CHAPTER FOUR

Building the Socialist Welfare State: The Expansion of Welfare Commitments in Eastern Europe

Our analysis of welfare-state expansion in Latin America and East Asia showed that within the constraints set by underlying political alignments, democratic rule provided incentives for politicians to expand social insurance and services. The authoritarian regimes in Eastern Europe are an obvious reminder that neither political competition nor interest group organization are necessary conditions for such expansion. The communist systems of Eastern Europe were unquestionably "hard" authoritarian regimes. Yet despite the absence of an electoral connection or independent interest-group organization, welfare systems in Eastern European countries grew rapidly.

A number of characteristics of socialist social policy distinguish it sharply from the patterns we have observed in Latin America and East Asia. Despite the privileges enjoyed by the nomenklatura,[1] inequality in particular areas such as urban housing (Szelényi 1983, 73–79), and differences in some benefits across firms, the literature on socialist social policy generally finds that benefits were spread widely. Core benefits such as the employment guarantee, healthcare, pensions, and family allowances, all evolved into universal programs. Where benefits were tied to wages (as with pensions), the highly compressed nature of the wage structure meant that they were distributed relatively equally even when not explicitly redistributive in design. Benefits not tied to wages—education and, more importantly, health—had a strong equalizing effect because they were proportional to family size. Despite some debate on the point, social spending on the major entitlements that we focus on here appear to have contributed to the relatively egalitarian distribution of income in the region.[2]

What accounts for this quite distinctive welfare trajectory? The social-policy inheritance of the pre-Communist era did matter to some extent.

---

[1] On the benefits enjoyed by the nomenklatura see Lane 1982; Kende and Strmiska 1987; Atkinson and Micklewright 1992, 167–70.

[2] See, for example, Ferge 1979; Deacon 1983; Morrison 1984; Flakierski 1986; Kende and Strmiska 1987; Atkinson and Micklewright 1992; Milanovic 1994, 177–81; Milanovic 1998.

Limited subsets of the population were already covered by pension and sickness funds prior to the Communist takeover, particularly in the successor states and regions of the former Austro-Hungarian Empire, and the educational inheritance was relatively high at the time of the Communist takeovers. But there can be little doubt that the political realignments marked by the socialist seizures of power knocked Eastern Europe off its prior development path and were critical for subsequent developments.

Our central proposition, already sketched in chapter 1, is that core features of the socialist development strategy pushed the state toward quite comprehensive entitlements. The generosity of social spending was continually constrained by powerful ideological and bureaucratic pressures to prioritize investment over all forms of consumption, including services and transfers. Nevertheless, the drive to eliminate private property and markets left the state, by default, as the primary guarantor of employment, education, health, and protection against life-cycle risks for most of the population.

We discuss the evolution of Communist social policy during three overlapping historical periods. New governments first established basic social guarantees during the initial socialization of the economy in the late-Stalinist period through the remainder of the 1950s. Industrial and state workers were the initial beneficiaries of employment guarantees, pensions, and access to public health services and education. However, the collectivization of agriculture played a major role in the spread of the welfare state to still-sizeable rural populations. The contrast with Latin America in this regard is of particular interest. At the onset of the postwar period, the semi-industrialized countries of Latin America and Eastern Europe bore a number of similarities in their social policies. But while Latin America's subsequent development was characterized by the neglect of the rural sector, the Communist governments of Eastern Europe had extended basic healthcare, primary education and even pensions into the countryside by the early 1960s.

The second period—the 1960s and 1970s—witnessed an increase in the generosity of benefits and the innovation of new social programs such as family allowances and unemployment insurance. Post-Stalinist political and economic thinking attached greater emphasis to improving standards of living in order to win the acquiescence of the population. In some cases—particularly Poland—succession crises or protests from below also led rulers to increase the generosity of benefits, at least in the short run. These experiences fostered debates over whether and how authoritarian Communist regimes might be constrained by political competition (in the form of succession struggles) or interest group pressures (either from organized interests within the state or through "contentious politics" from below).

But despite cross-national differences in the frequency and intensity of such pressures, social policies evolved in a surprisingly uniform way throughout the region. While the path of social policy might have been affected by political constraints in the short run, the longer-run social-policy equilibrium reflected government responses to particular economic problems with respect to manpower planning, labor markets, and efforts to spur productivity. The establishment of family benefits programs, for example, was motivated by concerns about declining labor supply. But similar preoccupations were visible in debates over health and pension spending, education, and other labor market policies.

The 1980s, finally, constitute a third period characterized by economic stagnation and political decline. Fundamental problems in the social sector had surfaced well before this period; as in other sectors of the economy, these included problems of rationing, shortages, and the misallocation of resources. Beginning in the 1980s, however, governments entered a period of slow and erratic growth that fundamentally constrained their capacity to deliver on welfare promises. But these promises proved difficult if not impossible to retract except through reversion to wholesale repression, as occurred in Romania in the late Nicolae Ceaușescu years. By default, responsibility for comprehensive social entitlements remained a core feature of the socialist system even though benefits and the quality of services eroded.

We conclude with a summary of how these twin legacies of the socialist model—broadly based but underfunded and distorted entitlements—shaped the evolution of social policy during the transition of the 1990s.

THE STALINIST ERA: COLLECTIVIZATION, AND THE EXPANSION OF THE SOCIALIST WELFARE MODEL

The revolutionary restructuring of the Eastern European economies followed closely on the heels of the Communists' consolidation of political control. Five-year plans launched in the late 1940s and early 1950s emphasized accumulation and focused state investment on heavy industry and other strategic sectors such as transport and mining. The early plan periods were accompanied by a dramatic expansion of employment as labor shifted out of the countryside and households (through greater female participation) into the industrial sector. Consumption grew at a robust pace as well (United Nations Economic Commission for Europe 1967, 13–21).

In chapter 1 we outlined the implications of these revolutionary steps for the initial provision of social insurance and services. At the broadest level, new Communist governments quickly entrenched the principle of public responsibility for employment as well as all social insurance and services. As private enterprise and markets were suppressed, employment opportunities outside the state sector shrank. All insurance and services were monopolized by the state. Social spending reflected overall planning decisions about the allocation of resources between accumulation and consumption. Similarly, the provision of certain social services such as education was subordinated to the manpower-planning process.

Initial Expansion: Supporting the Heavy Industry Drive

By the early 1950s, almost all social insurance programs that had been established prior to the Communist takeover—in some cases, dating back to the late nineteenth century—were effectively absorbed directly into the state. In the pre-Communist era, these had functioned primarily along Bismarckian lines also characteristic of Latin America: separate, occupationally based pension funds financed through payroll taxes, with limited coverage and relatively generous benefits (Tomka 2004, 60; Müller 1999). Even where the fiction of social insurance was maintained through payroll taxes as in Czechoslovakia and Hungary, the burden of financing effectively fell on the central government, since all firms were state enterprises subject to allocation of resources through the central plan.

By the mid-1950s, the expansion of social insurance coverage was well under way, driven by the dramatic growth of the industrial workforce. In Hungary, for example, a highly fragmented pension system was unified in 1949, and between 1950 and 1955, coverage of the economically active population jumped from 37 percent to 52 percent (Müller 1999, 61–62). In 1954 in Poland, pensions were awarded to all workers in industry, retail, and services. Czechoslovakia saw a similar process of unification and expansion. Although pension benefits were generally pegged to earnings and thus higher in the privileged industrial branches, inequalities in entitlements were reduced by the compression of wage differentials across economic sectors (Milanovic 1998, 16–17). The pattern was similar even in the low-income countries; in Romania, for example, preexisting social-insurance schemes were integrated in 1949 and subsequently widened beyond the industrial core (Vasile and Zaman 2005, 6–7).

Communist governments also restructured the health and education systems during this period. The transition to nationalized healthcare— the so-called Semashko system, after the first Bolshevik minister of health affairs—was initiated in all the East European countries in the late 1940s and completed by the early 1950s. The independent medical associations that had regulated professional life were abolished and replaced by compulsory membership in official healthcare unions. Private practices were forced out of business by high taxes, extensive regulation, and fiat, and

TABLE 4.1
Net Primary School Enrollments in Eastern Europe 1935–40 and 1950

	1935–40	1950
Bulgaria	47.8	61.0
Czechoslovakia	65.4	88.0
Hungary	58.8	83.0
Poland	60.3	77.0
Romania	62.9	59.0

Source: Barro and Lee 2000.

the central government assumed full responsibility for providing and financing all health services. The allocation of resources to health occurred as in other sectors in direct, physical form. The central government set input and staffing quotas and material allocations to government-owned hospitals and polyclinics. These were supplemented by primary and secondary occupational-medical-health facilities attached to work units (Marée and Groenewegen 1997, 7–8). Patients had rights to services and did not pay for them at the point of delivery. But medical care was continually underfunded, with the continuing problems of moral hazard, inefficiency, and chronic shortages analyzed with such acuity by Kornai (1992, 228–301, 570–75; Kornai and Eggleston 2001, 135–40); we return to these problems in more detail below.

The educational system was also restructured during the early Stalinist period, both to reinforce political loyalties and to integrate it with overall manpower planning and the direct administrative allocation of labor.[3] Net primary-school enrollments in the immediate prewar period varied across the region but were relatively high when compared to educational attainment in both East Asia at independence or Latin America in 1945. Following the Communist seizure of power, new constitutions laid down the principle that basic education would be both compulsory and free. Realizing this objective took some time and was constrained both by resources and the challenge of building schools and training teachers. In Romania, for example, only four years of schooling could initially be made compulsory, and it was not until 1964 that eight years of education became mandatory for all (Grant 1969, 80–82). As table 4.1 demonstrates, however, the other countries in the region saw dramatic increases in enrollments as early as 1950. Illiteracy was largely eliminated by the

[3] Lott (1999, S127–31) argues that the relationship between democracy and education may not hold because totalitarian regimes invest heavily in education as a means of social control.

mid-1950s with the exception of Roma populations in Bulgaria and Romania. By the mid-1970s, Romania and Hungary required ten years of schooling, Czechoslovakia nine, and Poland and Bulgaria eight (Ganzeboom and Nieuwbeerta 1999, 346).

Preexisting educational systems, which drew on European models, were not altogether discarded, but curricula were reformed to emphasize natural sciences, technical and polytechnical education, and ideological indoctrination (Grant 1969, 90–122). Over time, the emphasis on secondary education shifted toward vocational training in response to the chronic labor shortages that were an endemic feature of the socialist economy (Adam 1984, 17–40). By the early 1970s, enrollments in vocational technical schools accounted for 67 percent of secondary-school enrollments in Czechoslovakia and Romania, 69 percent in Poland, 73 percent in Hungary and 75 percent in Bulgaria (Heath 1981, 240). Following the collapse of the Communist regimes in 1989–90, the narrow focus on vocational training came into conflict with the more generalized skill requirements of a market economy and citizen demand for educational choice. From the 1960s through the 1980s, however, the vocational track was a key instrument for channeling workers into the industrial sector, in line with shifting labor-market needs.

The Push to Universalism: Incorporating the Peasantry

Despite universalistic commitments, the early development of social insurance and services exhibited urban biases and excluded much of the agricultural population. Yet in most of Eastern Europe, as in the other regions of interest to us, peasants comprised large proportions of the total population. In 1950, the rural population was larger in Bulgaria and Romania (74 percent in both) and in the Slovak regions of Czechoslovakia (70 percent rural). But Poland and Hungary had large rural population as well (61.3 percent and 60.7 percent respectively) and even in the more industrialized Czech lands, 59 percent of the population lived in the countryside. The promise of universal coverage could not be realized without the incorporation of the peasantry.

The collectivization of agriculture played a vital role in the final push toward comprehensive coverage. The redistribution of land went through two phases in Eastern Europe in the fifteen years following the end of World War II. Even before the consolidation of Communist control, there was an unprecedented reshuffling of land ownership in favor of the peasantry. In Czechoslovakia, the seizure of German and Hungarian lands provided the basis for the initial redistribution, followed by the reform of Czech and Slovak holdings. In Poland, similarly, redistribution occurred both through breaking up existing holdings and mass colonization of newly acquired territories. In Hungary and Romania, the bulk of the redistribution came from the liquidation of latifundia (Spulber 1957, 227). Initial reforms in Bulgaria were relatively modest, but landholding was relatively egalitarian to begin with.

With the consolidation of political control in the late 1940s, the process of dislodging the upper strata of the peasantry ("kulaks") and socializing agriculture began in earnest. Politically, collectivization provided the means to fully penetrate the countryside, since the leadership of the cooperatives was, as with other productive units, controlled by the party (Kornai 1992, 82). From an economic perspective, the formation of cooperatives was intended to guarantee control over production and thus over the agricultural surplus that was key to primitive socialist accumulation.

Although the collectivization of agriculture was not completed until the early 1960s, the process unfolded fairly rapidly and by the mid-1950s had made considerable headway in most countries. As early as 1955, the socialist sector accounted for 64 percent of arable land in Bulgaria, 47 percent in Hungary, 43 percent in Czechoslovkia, and 26 percent in Romania (Spulber 1957, 261; *International Labour Review* 1960, 320). Even in Poland, where the government eventually abandoned efforts to collectivize a large class of small and medium peasant properties altogether, about 25 percent of the farmland had been collectivized by the mid-1950s (Jean-Charles Szurek 1987, 231).

One of the initial consequences of de-Stalinization was a reappraisal of agricultural policy, particularly in Czechoslovakia, Hungary, and Poland. One component of the "New Course" (1953–55) in Czechoslovakia was to moderate the excesses of collectivization. In Hungary and Poland, a temporary reversal of collectivization appeared to reflect a political strategy of granting concessions to the rural sector in the wake of urban protest (Ekiert 1996, 95–98). It quickly became evident, however, that these concessions were largely tactical. In all countries except Poland, collectivization resumed in the late 1950s and was pushed to completion by the early 1960s. In the mid-1980s, the socialist sector accounted for over 90 percent of arable land (although not of gross agricultural output) in Hungary, Czechoslovakia, Bulgaria, and Romania. Only in Poland did private smallholdings persist, accounting for 72 percent of arable land, even though most output passed through state channels.[4]

Collectivization entailed a massive dispossession of private property. The early stages of the process took such forms as progressive land taxes, an increase in obligatory deliveries, and the concentration of machinery in the hands of the state. However, positive incentives also played some role in the process. When large estates were converted into state farms,

[4] For succinct summaries, see Jeffries 1993, 85–87, 240–43, 250–52, 301–3, 312–14.

agricultural laborers were typically accorded rights available to other workers within the socialized sectors. The extension of basic social services, particularly healthcare, and entitlements such as pensions played an important role in getting farmers to join cooperatives. As Schöpflin (1993, 151) states: "The peasantry and agriculture were now included inside the political game and it became possible to argue in favor of agricultural investment without the risk of being howled down as a supporter of the reactionary peasantry. Collectivized peasants were politically and ideologically acceptable in a way that private peasants were not."

The nature of this bargain with the rural sector can be seen by tracing the expansion of core entitlements. Centralized social-security schemes for cooperative farm workers were instituted in Czechoslovakia in 1952, in Bulgaria in 1956, and in Hungary in 1957. These schemes were financed through contributions from the cooperatives and subsidies from the state, and they provided pensions for invalidity and old age, as well as maternity and child supplements. Benefits were generally lower than those of employees in industry and state farms, but as we have noted, pensions—by far the largest form of cash transfers—remained relatively egalitarian.[5]

Cooperative farmers were also incorporated both de facto and de jure into national health programs originally limited to government functionaries and employees in state-owned enterprises (*International Labour Review* 1960, 323–29). Although the official goal of full incorporation proceeded unevenly, the health authorities in all the countries in the region moved relatively quickly to build and staff clinics and public-health stations and to launch aggressive public-health campaigns in the rural areas. This advance was followed finally with universal access enshrined as a legal right (Kaser 1976, 12–15, 36).

In Hungary, for example, health-insurance coverage was 47.3 percent in 1950 but was effectively universal by 1963 as a result of incorporating the agricultural sector (Tomka 2004, 79). In 1972, access to healthcare was codified as a citizenship right, though this provision was not effected until 1975. In Czechoslovakia, healthcare was extended to almost all categories of rural and urban workers by the mid-1950s and declared a citizenship right in 1966. In Romania, the completion of farm collectivization in the early 1960s brought virtually all the peasantry except for a very small group of individual farmers under social-insurance cover. The government also expanded rural health services. Similar patterns are visible in Bulgaria, which codified universal medical insurance in 1971 (Kaser 1976, 93, 115–16, 167, 200, 237).

---

[5] Peasants were also compensated by their right to maintain ownership of houses and at least some land, which could be used to supplement income through the market.

Ample evidence suggests, moreover, that the relatively early commitment to universal healthcare had marked effects on health outcomes. In the decade starting in the early 1950s, infant mortality in Eastern Europe dropped by nearly half, and life expectancy at birth increased by around five years. These early achievements were not sustained, and after the mid-1960s, health conditions in Eastern Europe began to deteriorate in alarming ways. Yet even critics of the system admit its early achievements. As Preker and Feachem (1994, 289) summarize, "entitlement by the entire regional population to a full range of health services was one of the remarkable achievements of the socialist regime and its health care system. No other region in the world, not even Europe or China, has ever succeeded in providing such extensive coverage of comprehensive health care to a population of similar size."

In Poland, ironically, the extension of social insurance and free healthcare to farmers was slower precisely because collectivization stalled after the mid-1950s. Major initiatives to incorporate farmers were undertaken only after urban riots led to the replacement of Władysław Gomułka by Edward Gierek in 1971. Reforms instituted by Gierek authorized independent farmers and their dependants to use health facilities on the same terms as other employees, drawing the remaining one-third of the population that had been uncovered into gratis healthcare. Even after that point, farmers continued to complain of discriminatory treatment in terms of both investment and welfare. In 1980, as worker protests mounted, private farmers moved to establish their own rural unions and became allies of Solidarity.

Expansion in the education sector was less directly tied to collectivization than were access to social security and health. Indeed, the heavy industry drive relied on the forced drafting of agricultural workers into the urban proletariat. But educational policies reflected broader efforts to incorporate peasants as well as workers into a system consistent with a technically trained workforce. Children of manual workers and farmers obtained preferential treatment and quotas were imposed on the children of the bourgeois, equalizing educational attainment (Fischer-Galati 1990, 278).

In sum, by the beginning of the 1960s, most sectors of the population had access to core social insurance and services: pensions, basic healthcare, and primary and some specialized secondary education. Although this outcome was an inherent feature of the socialist system, the expansion of coverage hinged on the process of collectivization and the extension of benefits to rural populations. Party officials and state functionaries no doubt enjoyed special treatment, and firms in favored sectors were able to offer additional social services, such as vacations and childcare, that other units could not afford. Nonetheless, the breadth of coverage implied by the socialist model and the incorporation of peasants into it presented a marked contrast with the unequal Bismarckian systems that had evolved in Latin America, and with the heavy reliance on self-insurance and private provision in the Asian cases.

DESTALINIZATION AND THE POLITICS OF SOCIAL WELFARE

Although basic social entitlements were in place by the early 1960s, the next decade saw rising real wages, greater attention to the provision of consumer goods, including durables, and steady increases in real social spending.[6] There were also important new initiatives, particularly in family allowances and the creation of unemployment insurance in countries experimenting with market-oriented reforms of the central-planning system. To be sure, improvements in welfare—whether measured by wages, total income, or consumption—did not always keep pace with the growth of aggregate output because of the continuing emphasis central planners placed on accumulation.[7] And as we discuss in more detail below, declining investment in the social sectors became increasingly apparent over time in the declining quality of services. Nonetheless, the period of "mature" socialism was characterized by increasing real incomes, of which social spending constituted a significant part.

The political stage for the gradual expansion of the socialist welfare state was set by the fierce struggle for power within the Soviet leadership following the death of Stalin in 1953. The triumph of reformist factions led by Nikita Khrushchev—culminating in the "secret speech" to the 20th Congress of the Communist Party of the Soviet Union in February 1956—marked the onset of a new phase of Communist rule in the Soviet Union that had wide-ranging implications for Eastern Europe. The relaxation of external controls, signaled by Khrushchev's rapprochement with Tito in 1955, increased the space for Eastern European countries to pursue distinctive national economic and political strategies, albeit within boundaries set by continued fealty to Moscow and the maintenance of Communist Party dominance. In the economic sphere, post-Stalinist thinking recognized the limits on the "big push" approach to industrialization and the importance of more balanced strategies that included attention to agriculture, consumption goods, and social expenditure. Most governments experimented with new incentive mechanisms and even controlled marketization.

---

[6] Again, data is better for Hungary and Poland. See Ferge (1979) on Hungary; Flakierski (1986) on Poland and Hungary; and Atkinson and Micklewright (1992, chap. 6), on Hungary, Poland, and Czechoslovakia.

[7] The gap between consumption and GDP growth was particularly apparent in Romania (Lampe 1986, 191–92; Shafir 1985, 107–8).

The challenge to Stalinist orthodoxy also had a political component. Although the relaxation of political controls should not be confused with competitive authoritarian rule, it did open the way for internal political and ideological struggles within Communist Party leadership, greater play for contending forces within the state apparatus, and even protest from below (for example, Johnson 1970; Lowenthal 1976).

To what extent are these ideological, political, and economic changes relevant for an understanding of the evolution of social policy? Can leadership struggles, bureaucratic politics, and popular protest be viewed as functional equivalents of the political competition and interest-group activity in more democratic settings? To what extent might they lead to material concessions to mobilized groups or more generous benefits for the population at large?

Such a political consumption-cycle hypothesis was first postulated by Mieczkowski (1978) with respect to Poland and modified and generalized by Bunce (1980, 281; 1981, 230–42). Mieczkowski argued that lagging consumption in Poland was followed by political protest that ultimately resulted in leadership changes. New leaders expanded consumption to mollify protest and consolidate power but reverted to a less generous allocation to consumption once the political crisis passed. Looking at a wider sample of cases, Bunce (1980, 284–85) challenged the declining consumption-protest–leadership change portion of Mieczkowski's model, noting that mass protests were not consistently a causal factor in leadership changes in the region. However, she did find empirical evidence for a link between leadership change and the growth of aggregate consumption—including social consumption—for the Soviet Union, the German Democratic Republic, Poland, and Czechoslovakia, later expanded to include a wider sample of both socialist and nonsocialist countries (Bunce 1981, 42–46).

The absence of reliable and comparable data makes a convincing test of these propositions difficult, but the evidence we present below suggests that the political-consumption argument does not generalize to our sample of cases, either with respect to the timing of new social-policy initiatives or to changes in the funding of social entitlements.[8] Poland, the subject of Mieczkowski's (1978) initial study, does exhibit the behavior that he and Bunce describe, as do Hungary and Czechoslovakia to a lesser extent. On the other hand, in Bulgaria and Romania there appears to be no direct link between the expansion of the welfare state and either succession struggles or popular protest. Even in Hungary and Czechoslovakia, it is difficult to disentangle political and more purely economic sources of social-policy change.

[8] See also Bahry 1983.

TABLE 4.2
Economic Growth in Eastern Europe, 1950–80

	1950–55	1956–60	1961–65	1966–70	1971–75	1976–80
Bulgaria	15.6	11.7	7.7	10.4	9.1	6.9
Czech	9.6	7.9	1.6	7.9	6.1	3.9
Hungary	6.4	6.8	4.4	7.8	7.1	3.0
Poland	10.2	7.5	6.9	6.7	11.9	1.3
Romania	18.8	7.5	10.9	9.0	14.4	8.1
Average	12.1	8.3	6.3	8.4	9.7	4.6

Source: White 1986, 466.

Moreover, it is important for our purposes to underline a broader challenge to the political consumption-cycle approach. Governments in the region faced varying degrees of pressure from below and quite different patterns of leadership succession, from the high degree of political continuity in the Bulgarian case to the more tumultuous political histories of Hungary, Poland, and Czechoslovakia. Yet despite these political differences, the overall structure of welfare entitlements shows a striking similarity across the region. Moreover, countries not only converged to a quite similar *structure* of entitlements but also exhibited a common *expansion* of social spending and even a quite similar *level* of aggregate transfers. By 1988–89, social transfers equaled 25.4 percent of gross income in Czechoslovakia, 22.4 percent in Hungary, 21.2 percent in Bulgaria, and 20.7 percent in Poland, levels far in excess of any other developing country in our sample and even higher than the average of the advanced industrial states (Milanovic 1998, 13–14).

What accounts for this convergence on a quite similar social-policy model? An important permissive condition for the steady expansion of benefits in the 1960s and 1970s was relatively high rates of economic growth. With the exception of slowdowns in Czechoslovakia and Hungary during the early 1960s, growth rates were well over 6 percent in every country in our sample, and reached double digits during some periods in Romania, Bulgaria, and Poland (see table 4.2). Until the economic deterioration of the late 1970s, growth eased the tradeoff Communist regimes faced between investment and social consumption.

A complementary political explanation is that governments across the region converged on broadly similar political concerns and strategies. The post-Stalinist consensus reflected at least some recognition that repression and terror were inefficient ways to maintain political stability and promote economic growth. The workers' protests that erupted in East Germany in 1953 and in Poland, Hungary, and Czechoslovakia a few years later underlined the political risks of the Stalinist political model.

Through its actions in 1956 and again in 1968, the Soviet leadership signaled clearly that external intervention and repression remained crucial backups in the event of instability or direct challenges to political authority. Nonetheless, governments did seek to retain control through a social contract or compromise that traded material benefits for political acquiescence (Cook 1993, 207). Arguably, the new political strategy increased the leverage of the social ministries in the planning process and allowed them to press for increased social benefits.[9] Once governments pursued this course of action, it proved a self-reinforcing path; the social contract was extended to secure support but was then "locked in" by broad social expectations that proved difficult to reverse.

The idea of a socialist social contract is useful in underlining the increasing priority that post-Stalinist regimes attached to the distribution of material rewards. But it leaves unanswered the question of why, unlike other "hard" authoritarian regimes, they did so through a strategy that remained relatively egalitarian in the distribution of benefits. Given the absence of an electoral or interest-group connection and the ongoing ability to manage "contentious politics" with coercion, why distribute broadly? Why not focus benefits on strategically important groups?

To some extent, Communist leaders *did* reward key constituents, particularly in the Party itself. However, it is difficult to account for the puzzle of broad and largely equalizing entitlements without reference to the logic of the socialist economic system. Given the commitment to a socialist model that largely repressed alternative sources of income and eliminated private markets for insurance and services, governments were constrained to supply them. Even where governments began to experiment with the introduction of market forces, they remained directly responsible for employment in the case of market failure.

The evolution of family allowances provides an example of the close connection between the broader planning process and social policy, as well as the ongoing role of external influences. In the early postwar period, a number of social policies favored larger families.[10] Although high rates of population growth were seen as desirable, these policies also reflected social equity and productivist concerns (Berent 1970, 285). Communist Parties emphasized women's participation in the paid labor force, a sharp break from prewar norms, but they were also quite conventional in their support of the nuclear family and a traditional household division of labor (Fodor et al. 2002, 479–81). The general thrust of early family policy was thus to provide leave, lump-sum maternity payments, and family allowances that allowed women to withdraw from the workforce after

[9] We are indebted for this suggestion to Linda Cook.

[10] For example, housing priorities were in some cases linked to family size, as were other forms of consumer subsidies and family allowances.

the birth of children but with the expectation that they would return after some period of time.

In 1955, the Soviet Union liberalized its abortion laws, and all the Eastern European countries in our sample quickly followed suit. The result was a rapid falloff in fertility that is impossible to explain on the basis of standard demographic or economic factors alone. Given the centrality of labor input to the socialist model of accumulation, planners across the region began to rethink their population policy, and in the 1960s, they shifted toward an actively pronatalist stance. The range of these policies was wide and not altogether uniform across countries, but all of the Eastern European countries used positive incentives as well as controls to address the issue. Sharp increases in family allowances followed, though these were initially limited to industrial workers. Benefits were subsequently extended to rural areas, new benefits were added, and transfers, leaves, and subsidies adjusted in response to changing labor-market needs.

By the 1980s, the generous provision of family allowances had become one of the more important and distinctive social policy innovations of the post-Stalinist period. As a percentage of gross family income, transfers ranged from 17 percent in Poland to 25 percent in Hungary. These far exceeded levels in Western Europe and generally favored poorer families with large numbers of children (Milanovic 1998, 21).

Although family allowances demonstrate a particularly clear link between the planning process and social policy, they were by no means unique in this regard (Adam 1984, 17–40). As with employment, wage, and educational policy, other social benefits were continually adjusted in response to the recurrent disequilibria in the socialist labor market. Pension payments were adjusted to influence labor supply for those at pensionable age. Maternity leaves were developed to encourage reentry into the workforce. Benefits provided in kind at the level of the enterprise were similarly adjusted to manage labor supply and effort (Adam 1984, 70).

The following case studies consider both the political and economic determinants of social policy during the immediate post-Stalinist decades. Table 4.3 sets the stage by summarizing leadership changes from 1953 to 1989. We note whether Soviet pressure or intervention played a role in the succession process and if successions were accompanied by leadership struggles at the top and "contentious politics" from below—mass unrest, strikes, and protests. This political frame allows us to consider short-term constraints on social policy. However, we show that even where these short-run responses operated, they were nested in a more general trend toward greater generosity and a common structure of entitlements. We begin with Poland and Hungary, where ruling elites experienced especially severe political challenges.

TABLE 4.3
Leadership Change and Mass Protest in Eastern Europe, 1953–89

Country	Leadership	Cause of succession	Other mass protest
Bulgaria	Chervenkov, 1950–54	Death of Dimitrov, internal	
	Zhivkov, 1954–88	Death of Chervenkov, internal	1953: Riots following Stalin's death
Czechoslovakia	Novotný, 1953–68	Death of Gottwald, internal	1953: Riots following Stalin's death.
	Dubček, 1968–69	Growth of internal party reformist faction	1967: Student protests
	Husák, 1969–87	Mass unrest, Soviet intervention	1969: Mass demonstrations following Czech hockey victory over Soviet Union and on anniversary of invasion
	Jakes, 1987–88	Mass unrest	
Hungary	Rakosi, 1953–56	Soviet decision	
	Gero 1956; Kádár 1956–88	Mass unrest and Soviet intervention	
Poland	Bierut, 1948–56	Soviet decision	
	Ochab 1956	Death of Bierut, Soviet decision	1956: Poznań riots
	Gomułka, 1956–70	Mass unrest	1968: Student protests
	Gierek, 1970–80	Mass unrest	1976: Riots following food price increases 1979: Visit of Pope John Paul II
	Jaruzelski, 1981–89	Mass unrest	
Romania	Gheorghiu-Dej, 1948–65	Soviet decision	
	Ceauşescu, 1965–89	Death of Gheorghiu-Dej	1977: Miners' strike 1981: Miners' strike 1987: Riots in Brasov

Poland

In Poland, de-Stalinization opened the way both to divisions among the Party leadership and periodic social protest. The Poznań riots of June 28–29, 1956, led to a new leadership under Władysław Gomułka that adopted a more reformist stance, including greater emphasis on material benefits, a large increase in wages and consumption subsidies (Ekiert

1996, 216), and a hike in pension benefits to state workers. But these steps were quickly eroded by the government's continuing commitment to heavy industry and by increases in food prices. Moreover, the pause in collectivization after 1956, a step taken to avoid the spread of unrest to the peasantry, also meant that social insurance would not be extended into the countryside for almost another decade.

A much more reformist approach took root after 1970. Another round of food and fuel price increases in that year generated a wave of worker protest. Although brutally repressed, the episode led to the ouster of Gomułka and his replacement by Edward Gierek. The most direct channel through which the new government could improve welfare was through wage increases and efforts to increase the availability of food and other consumer goods. In the first half of the 1970s, Poland witnessed the most rapid real wage growth in our sample (Hirszowicz 1986, 89, table 4.1).

Gierek's program included not only wage increases but also the introduction of greater wage dispersion as well. The nomenklatura secured a variety of new social benefits, paralleling the pattern of particularistic rewards common to authoritarian regimes in other regions (Hirszowicz 1986, 95). Despite these particularistic benefits, however, the program also included ambitious proposals with respect to other social services that were more broadly distributed. These included the expansion of the secondary-school system and more money for housing, health and social-insurance entitlements, financed through the Institute of Social Insurance (Millard 1992, 121–22). Poland came to family policy somewhat later than the other Central European countries, in part because manpower-planning concerns were mixed with traditional Catholic values with respect to the family. As a result, policies were somewhat less generous, less favorable to working women, and slower to incorporate the rural sector. Nonetheless, by 1980, benefits were on a rough par with those of the other countries.

The incorporation of the peasantry was also a major objective of the new government. The first major initiative in this regard came in 1972, with the extension of free healthcare. In 1974, farmers gained access to pensions as well, although not on equal terms with the rest of the socialist sector.

Until the second half of the 1970s, the Gierek strategy appeared to have stabilized the political situation. But continued emphasis on consumption and improved social services ultimately depended on overall economic performance. Gierek's strategy looked to Western loans and technology to augment domestic investment and revive lagging productivity. But foreign borrowing was not accompanied by reforms of the rigid and inefficient central-planning system, and by the late 1970s, the economy began to slow significantly (see table 4.2). Nominal wage increases were undercut by ongoing shortages and inflation, and in the second half of the 1970s, real wage growth slowed sharply.

Inequality in both wages and the distribution of social benefits increased. Although Polish wages remained highly compressed by Western or Latin American standards, increasing income disparities became a source of discontent. The average level of transfers to total income remained relatively constant through the 1970s, but the ratio of social benefits enjoyed by the top and bottom income deciles widened (Bielasiak 1983, 232–33). Elites dominated a number of entitlements, including access to subsidized consumer goods, apartments, and cars as well as foreign exchange (Hirszowicz 1986, 101–108; 112–18). The share of education and health in total government spending also began to fall and the quality of services to deteriorate accordingly. Grievances over stalled or declining living standards, increasing inequality, and deteriorating social services provided an important spur to the emergence of the Solidarity movement at the end of the decade.

Of all the countries in the region, the Polish experience conforms most closely to the political-consumption-cycle hypothesis. In 1956, 1970, and again in 1980–81, governments responded to pressures from below with increased wages, social spending, and consumption. However, with the exception of the lag in the extension of social benefits to the rural sector, the overall structure of benefits appears quite similar to those found elsewhere in the region.

Hungary

In Hungary, the transition to a post-Stalinist leadership took place against the backdrop of the weakest growth performance in the region, declining real wages, and stagnation of social services (Ferge 1979, 64, 189). Deep divisions between conservatives and reformers in the party leadership led to the ouster of the orthodox Mátyás Rakosi in July 1956, a rapid unraveling of party and state control, and the emergence of independent workers councils and other social organizations. The near collapse of the party-state led eventually to the mobilization of Soviet troops in the country on October 23, 1956, and a subsequent intervention by outside military forces. The collapse of the revolution was followed by a prolonged and brutal repression that lasted well into the early 1960s.

As in Poland, certain aspects of the short-term response to the crisis reflected a political-consumption-cycle pattern. In the immediate aftermath of the revolution, János Kádár instituted wage increases, especially for strategic occupational groups (Adam 1984, 133) and placed greater emphasis on the production of consumer goods (Ekiert 1996, 111). But as soon as the government regained control, it moved in a more orthodox direction. The pace of real wage growth slowed substantially during the three-year plan unveiled in August 1958 and subsequent five-year plan (1961–65), which placed substantial emphasis on heavy industry.

Other aspects of welfare-state expansion appeared to reflect longer-term trends and more strategic-economic considerations. The collectivization process was temporarily halted in response to the crisis of 1956, but when it resumed in 1959, it was accompanied by increased investment in agriculture and a further extension of social insurance and services to rural areas. In 1961, cooperative farmers were fully integrated into the general pension scheme, bringing peasants closer to parity with urban workers in terms of eligibility and benefits. In 1966, the rural sector gained parity in family allowances. By the early 1960s, coverage of most health and life-cycle risks approached universality (Tomka 2004, 78), and thereafter, social benefits show a steady upward trend. Between 1960 and 1975, the value of all social benefits (in cash and kind) increased from 18.4 percent of total labor income to 27.3 percent (Ferge 1979, 190, table 5.10).

The evolution of the family-allowance system is instructive because it proceeded in a linear fashion that did not appear to have a direct relation to the 1956 crisis. Family allowances were sharply increased in 1959 for third-order births, then for second-order births in 1965. The government extended family allowances to the rural sector in 1966 and in 1967 added a new maternity-leave program that substituted almost completely for loss of income in lower-income families. After 1973, the government began to increase replacement rates for higher-income families as well, and in 1974 a new Social Security Act equalized family benefits to collective farmers. Further incremental changes followed, based on perceived manpower needs (Brown 2005, 225; Flakierski 1986, 98).[11]

Hungary introduced the New Economic Mechanism (NEM) in 1968. These "market-socialist" reforms, which included both incentive reforms in the socialist sector and official tolerance for the "second economy," distinguished Hungary from its more orthodox neighbors. The most notable social-policy innovation associated with the NEM was the introduction of limited unemployment insurance and active labor-market policies—policies "unnecessary" in systems that continued officially to guarantee employment. The incentive reforms associated with the NEM also had some effects on social policy at the level of the enterprise. Under new regulations promulgated in 1968, a higher share of profits remained with the work unit, which was also granted greater discretion in the use of welfare funds (Ferge 1979, 115–16).

---

[11] Despite the fact that family benefits were paid on a flat-rate basis, they had a progressive effect because of the relative poverty of larger families.

But, the extent of the changes arising from the NEM should not be exaggerated. The major entitlements remained national, and as Tomka (2004, 78) notes, already by the mid-1970s the degree of coverage in health and pension insurance was "equaled in Western Europe only by Scandinavian countries." The 1974 Social Security Act explicitly accommodated the second economy by extending family allowances to part-time and home workers. Firms' social plans did probably introduce somewhat greater differentiation in benefits across units, but all plans required central-government review and approval to avoid gross inequities. Detailed studies of the distributional effects of in-kind benefits find them less progressive than cash transfers. But the composition of aggregate social spending gradually shifted in favor of cash transfers over the late-socialist period, and the overall effects of in-kind benefits remained progressive as well (Ferge 1979, 250–61; Flakierski 1986, 98–100; Atkinson and Micklewright 1992, 152–54). The broad thrust of national social policy thus continued to push toward comprehensive decommodification of labor, citizenship rights, and an increasingly redistributive social policy.

Czechoslovakia

In Czechoslovakia, unlike the situation in Poland and Hungary, the thoroughness of the purges in the late 1940s initially forestalled both reformist tendencies within the party and the emergence of political pressures from below. The transition from Klement Gottwald to Antonín Novotný entailed few concessions, and throughout the 1950s, the country remained staunchly orthodox. Precisely because of the orthodox nature of early Communist rule, Czechoslovakia experienced a particularly radical and equalizing redistribution of income and a highly compressed wage structure (Stevens 1985, 51–57). As Teichova (1988, 110) summarizes, "Czechoslovakia had accomplished the most effective process of social leveling of all planned economies in Central and South-east Europe, including the Soviet Union."

Following a slowdown of growth in the early 1960s, the hard-line leadership came under pressure from reformist factions of intellectuals within the Party; a central concern was the slow growth of consumption associated with the biases toward heavy industry. A variety of commissions and working groups established after 1962 arrived at strongly reformist conclusions. These were reflected in a series of decentralizing reforms of both industrial enterprises and collectives after 1965, in the directives of the fourth Five Year Plan (1966–70) and ultimately, in a cautious series of price reforms from 1966.

As in Hungary, these reforms had implications for social policy. A new labor code promulgated in 1966 facilitated mobility by making it easier to transfer leave and welfare benefits. A number of other labor-market measures followed, including severance-pay requirements, retraining programs, and unemployment compensation (at a 60 percent replacement rate) if new positions could not be found. Clearly, these measures not only had an economic rationale but also reflected political concerns about how economic reforms would be received among the unions (Stevens 1985, 135, 151).

The economic reform movement in Czechoslovakia ultimately embodied a much broader challenge. In 1968, the struggle within the leadership was resolved in favor of the reformers and the highly orthodox Antonin Novotný was replaced by Alexander Dubček. At the high point of the reform movement in 1968, reformers were openly debating wide-ranging changes, engaging the National Assembly and effectively appealing to an increasingly mobilized public. A succession of social-policy initiatives followed (Skilling 1976, 421–22; Stevens 1985, 141). In May, the government approved guidelines for a five-day work week, albeit insisting that firms not compromise on production or increase wage payments. In early June, the government approved the principles for establishing enterprise councils, a measure that quickly gained widespread support. In late June, the National Assembly adopted three laws that improved sickness-insurance payments, maternity and children's allowances, and social insurance to cooperative farmers. The family-allowance legislation extended maternity leave, increased maternity benefits, and made payments progressive with the number of children. The government also announced a substantial increase in pension payments.

These measures seem to vindicate the political-consumption-cycle hypothesis, but some cautions are warranted. Unlike the situation in Hungary and Poland, broader social forces played a more limited role in the transition from Novotný to Dubček. The Prague Spring followed rather than led political developments within the Party and therefore had somewhat different characteristics than either the Hungarian revolution or the recurrent cycles of worker protest in Poland. Initially, Dubček's support came primarily from reformers within the party and the state. This support expanded as reformers liberalized and made more or less open appeals to the public. Nonetheless, support for the reforms among the working class was not altogether firm (Skilling 1976, 579–85) and the reformers were thoroughly isolated after Soviet and Warsaw Pact troops invaded in August 1968. Orthodox factions led by Gustáv Husák regained power and completely purged the Party, the state apparatus, and the unions. Institutional innovations such as enterprise councils gradually wound down. After the repression of two outbursts of mass protest in 1969, hard-liners remained in virtually unchallenged control until the late 1980s.

Yet despite the turn to economic orthodoxy (so-called normalization) and a short-term decline in consumption share, economic growth allowed the regime to increase consumption at respectable rates. Over the entire decade of the 1970s, the growth in social benefits consistently outstripped growth in real wages (Stevens 1985, 207 [table 6.11], 268 [table 7.24]) and the pattern of expansion viewed over the longer run paralleled that in Poland and Hungary. Despite rationing and hidden privilege—problems in all the socialist countries—by 1966, the healthcare system had formally shifted from an insurance scheme to a citizen entitlement (Kaser 1976, 115), offered wide access and treatment, and at least in terms of formal commitments, ranked among the top welfare states in the world (Castle-Kanerova 1992, 98).

Increases in the real value of old-age pensions lagged somewhat behind real wage growth, as they did in most socialist countries. Nevertheless, the Husák government also adjusted pensions upward in 1972 and again in 1976. As in Hungary, the Czech pension system saw a long-term trend toward equalization of benefits. The ratio of benefits paid to cooperative farmers and urban workers increased from just under 40 percent in 1960 to about 64 percent in 1975 (Porket 1979, 28), and in 1976, pension coverage was formally extended to collective farmers on the same basis as that applied to wage and salary earners. Differences among work categories within the urban sector narrowed as well.

Continuity is also visible in the continued expansion of maternity, childbirth, and family allowances, which were strongly augmented by a broad social program introduced in 1971. By the early 1980s, Czechoslovakia had family-support programs that were—according to the measure used—as generous as those in Hungary (Sipos 1994, 230). The return to orthodoxy was also accompanied by a reversion to more traditional manpower planning and central allocation, though coupled with a variety of active labor-market policies.

As Castle-Kanerova (1992) argues, Czech social policy masked de facto inequalities favoring state elites and privileged sectors, paternalism, and failures to protect vulnerable groups: indigents, minorities, single mothers. Yet these criticisms were common features of the posttransition period and should not detract from the central point. Reformers did initiate a number of social-policy innovations leading up to the Prague Spring. But even the crackdown of the early normalization period was not associated with fundamental changes in the nature of social entitlements. Czech social policy quickly reverted to a long-term trend that left it broadly similar in structure and level of entitlement to policies followed in Poland and Hungary.

Bulgaria and Romania

Bulgaria and Romania provide a number of important economic as well as political differences to the three foregoing cases. Both had much lower per-capita incomes at the onset of the transition and were more rural. Both subsequently sustained growth rates well above the regional average (see table 4.2). Between 1960 and the late 1970s, per-capita personal consumption increased faster in Bulgaria than in any of the other Eastern European countries (Troxel 1995, 236), driven by rapid growth of the industrial sector. After an economic slowdown in the late 1950s, Romania also experienced very rapid growth in the 1960s and 1970s. However, in contrast to Bulgaria, wages and consumption lagged as both the Gheorghiu-Dej and Ceaușescu governments placed a particularly high priority on maintaining a rapid pace of accumulation. By the end of the 1960s, the share of industry in Romania's national income exceeded that in Bulgaria or Hungary and was closing in on that of Poland and Czechoslovakia (Chirot 1978, 471).

The two cases also show some political differences that are theoretically germane. In contrast to Poland and Hungary, de-Stalinization in the two countries was not associated with the emergence of pressures from below. And in contrast to Czechoslovakia, Bulgaria and Romania did not have a "liberal moment"; instead, they showed a high level of political continuity. In Bulgaria, Vulko Chervenkov's ascent marked the triumph of the Soviet faction over local Communists. Although he was eased out by the Soviets in 1954, he was succeeded by Todor Zhivkov, who continued to dominate the country's politics until the late 1980s. Differences within the leadership emerged periodically, but they were far less severe than conflicts in the Central European countries (Schöpflin 1993, 114–16; Rothschild 1989, 116).

In Romania, the incumbent nationalist-Stalinist leadership under Gheorghiu-Dej consolidated power vis-à-vis the Khrushchevist reformers, stayed in office, and launched Romania on its more independent political and economic course. Yet despite the country's independent foreign-policy path, the tools for consolidating domestic support were broadly similar to those used in other countries. As Fischer-Galati (1998, 454) summarizes, the new course was accompanied by the decision to "satisfy the economic requirements of the population at large by providing the masses with higher salaries, better prices for their produce, improved housing and above all, a sense of participation in the construction of socialism in their own fatherland."

The transition to Ceauşescu in 1965 was also managed smoothly, although it took six years for him to fully consolidate his power. Ceauşescu later faced down strikes by miners with a combination of repression and targeted concessions that enshrined several differential benefits in the welfare system. But the strikes did not lead to "the kind of worker-intelligentsia alliance pressing for socioeconomic as well as political reforms that was forged in Poland between 1976 and 1980" (Rothschild 1989, 164), and the regime increasingly turned in a politically Stalinist and personalist direction.

In the other regions, these differences in the level of development and the nature of the political system might be consequential for patterns of social policy; in particular, we might expect a less generous social welfare system in lower-income countries with more rigidly authoritarian political orders. But the pattern of social policy in Bulgaria and Romania is broadly similar to the pattern in the Central European cases.

Bulgaria's rapid industrialization and early completion of collectivization combined relatively early to expand the socialist welfare state. Management reforms undertaken in the mid-1960s in the industrial sector were partly reversed, but a set of farm statutes introduced in 1967 extended pensions, health benefits, and other social services to the peasantry ahead of other Eastern European regimes (Lampe 1986, 203–204). The expansion of the Bulgarian healthcare system followed the Semashko pattern, and by 1971, universal healthcare was enshrined as a universal right. By 1975, peasants were fully integrated into the general pension system. Bulgaria took a more restrictive posture toward abortion, but coupled these restrictions with an increase in family allowances in 1968 and again in 1975 (Kaser 1976, 95–96). By the late 1980s, family support transfers averaged about 20 percent of income for a two-child family, roughly the same level as Czechoslovakia (Sipos 1994, 230). Replacement rates of old-age pensions in Bulgaria were high relative to most other countries in the region, and generally kept pace with the rise in wages during the 1960s and 1970s (Porket 1979, 258).

The particularly strong emphasis on heavy industry under both the Gheorghiu-Dej and Ceauşescu regimes influenced Romanian social policy in distinctive ways. In addition to low real-wage growth and ongoing problems in the agricultural sector, we have already noted the secular decline in social-sector investment in the country. Although directly comparable data is not available, Romania appears to have experienced particular imbalances in the housing sector through the 1960s (Gilberg 1975, 201–2; Chirot 1978, 474). However, Romania's peculiar emphasis on regional and urban planning—aimed at consolidating rural settlements, building up intermediate-sized regional cities, and limiting migration into larger cities—guaranteed the spread of social services. Most notably, Ro-

TABLE 4.4
State Employment as a Proportion of the Labor Force, 1988

Bulgaria	91.5
Czechoslovakia	98.8
Hungary	93.9
Poland	70.4
Romania	95.2

Source: Milanovic 1998, 12.

mania saw a rapid expansion of health services and a corresponding improvement in such indicators as the share of children born in medical facilities and infant mortality (Gilberg 1975, 203).

The pension system was somewhat slower to evolve than in the other Eastern European countries; even following a final reform in 1977, inequities remained between urban and rural workers (Vasile and Zaman 2005, 7). Nonetheless, the system was effectively universal in coverage. And although Romania adopted the most draconian controls on abortion (Kligman 1998, 52–59), it too coupled these measures with a variety of positive incentives after 1966, including sharply increased family allowances, expansion of child-care facilities, and part-time work opportunities for women. As Gilberg (1975, 199) summarizes, by the mid-1970s the Romanian government had "succeeded in providing the population with a comprehensive system of social and medical benefits, pensions, child and old age care centers, and other features of the welfare state."

As in the other countries, the generosity of social insurance and quality of social services in Bulgaria and Romania was not sustained in the 1980s. Particularly in Romania, living conditions became especially bleak following Ceaușescu's highly idiosyncratic decision to compress domestic consumption in order to liquidate external debts. But despite a lower level of per-capita income, urbanization, and industrialization at the outset of the period and the absence of protest from below or political crises, the overall structure of the Bulgarian and Romanian welfare systems resembled those in the other Eastern European countries.

A COMPARATIVE OVERVIEW

The foregoing sections have provided sketches of the evolution of socialist welfare systems through the first two post-Stalinist decades. Data on the welfare systems of these countries are neither altogether reliable nor strictly comparable across countries. But the comparisons provided below

TABLE 4.5
Pension Entitlements in Eastern Europe, 1960–78

	Pension as percent of monthly wage 1960	Pension as percent of monthly wage 1970	Pension as percent of monthly wage 1978	Increase in pension benefits 1960–1978
Bulgaria	49.0	45.8	49.4	91%
Czechoslovakia	51.6	49.6	44.0	57%
Hungary	47.1 (1965)	48.3	60.6 (1976)	120% (1965/76)
Poland	54.3 (1965)	65.3	52.5 (1976)	110% (1965/76)
Romania	n.a.	69.7	59.2	33% (1970/78)

Source: Porket 1982, 255–60.

attempt to provide somewhat more systematic evidence for our claim of convergence despite very different starting points, political histories, and varying degrees of experimentation with market-socialist reforms.

First, it is important to remember that the employment guarantee remained the centerpiece of the socialist system. As table 4.4 shows, at the time of the transition in 1990, employment in the state sector still exceeded 90 percent in all of the countries we consider here with the exception of Poland. Moreover, the Polish exception is not a result of the partial reform process of the Gierek administration but the consequence of the collectivization of agriculture, which did not follow the same path as was the case in the rest of the region. Until the very end of the socialist era, governments remained responsible for employment.

Table 4.5 shows the replacement rates of old-age and invalidity pensions and their relation to the average monthly wage. The increases in benefits were greatest in Hungary and Poland, the two regimes that encountered the most extensive pressures from civil society during the post-Stalinist period. Increases were lower in Czechoslovakia and Romania, a statistic that is also consistent with the "social pressure" hypothesis. But these differences should not be exaggerated. In Poland, the generosity of replacement rates (relative to current wages) was not sustained, and it declined markedly during the 1970s as the economy slowed. The Romanian data are reported over a shorter period, and the replacement rate is comparable to that in Hungary, despite the fact that fuller integration of the system came somewhat later, as we have seen. Bulgaria, which did not encounter serious political challenges in the 1960s and 1970s,

TABLE 4.6
Health Development in Eastern Europe and Selected Latin American and
East Asian Countries, 1965–85

	Infant mortality (1965)	Infant mortality (1985)	Immunization (DPT) 1985	Hospital beds (1985)	GDP per capita (1985)
Bulgaria	49 (1960)	20 (1980)	97	8.85	1,533
Czechoslovakia	22 (1960)	17 (1980)	95	11.30	5,269
Hungary	39	19	99	9.10	4,687
Poland	42	18	96	5.60	2,604
Romania	44	26	95	8.78	1,903
Argentina	58	33	41	5.59 (1970)	6,347
Chile	107	20	85	3.41	2,577
Costa Rica	72	18	86	3.31	2,716
Uruguay	48	28	53	3.25	4,373
Korea	63	25	61 (1981)	1.70	5,750
Taiwan	22	7 (1984)	n.a.	2.22	7,530

Source: World Development Indicators (World Bank 2007).
Note: Infant mortality per 1,000 live births; immunization, percent of one-year old children; hospital beds per 1,000 people.

had replacement rates and a growth of benefits that approximated those of Poland.

In all the countries, the achievement of de-facto universal coverage was followed by the codification of social rights as universal citizenship rights, a highly distinctive feature of the Eastern European countries and one that exercised tremendous influence over other welfare reforms. As we have seen, differences between urban and rural benefits gradually fell, and despite de-facto privileges accorded to political elites and strategic categories of workers, universalism guaranteed that differences across occupational categories were of necessity narrower than in Latin America.

Table 4.6 provides indicators for the health system. To provide a cross-regional perspective, we also include data from other countries that constitute interesting comparators: Korea and Taiwan, which outside of the city-state of Singapore, are the most affluent countries in East Asia in

1980; Argentina, the wealthiest Latin American country; and Chile, Costa Rica, and Uruguay, the three long-standing Latin American democracies. Again, the distinctive feature of the socialist systems is the universality of coverage. By the mid-1980s, immunization rates were close to universal in all five Communist countries and far higher than those in the other regions. Infant mortality also converged at low and roughly comparable levels. Romania lagged the other countries, but by the mid-1980s, infant mortality in that country was lower than in Argentina, a much wealthier society, and approximately the same as in Uruguay and Korea. Finally, by the mid-1980s, all the socialist countries had developed a relatively extensive network of hospitals when compared to the countries of the other regions. Although resources devoted to curative healthcare were arguably wasteful, indicators on immunization and infant mortality show that they did not initially cannibalize efforts to provide primary healthcare, as was the case in many Latin American countries.

Table 4.7 shows that all five socialist countries also achieved dramatic gains over the period in educational attainment. Primary-school enrollments were virtually universal by the early 1960s, and the average number of years that children spent in school was already higher than in the comparators from other regions. Nevertheless, years of schooling continued to expand over the next two decades. Average schooling was about nine years in Czechoslovakia, Poland, and Hungary. Children in Bulgaria and Romania stayed in school for just under eight years, but this period was longer than the years in Argentina or any of the long-standing Latin American democracies and was exceeded in Asia only by Korea. In contrast with these other countries, by the mid-1980s, adult illiteracy had also been virtually eliminated in all the Eastern European countries.

Finally, table 4.8 provides information on aggregate social transfers at the end of the socialist era for the four countries for which there is comparable data. These social transfers—dominated by pensions and family allowances—accounted for no less than 20 percent of average income, higher than that prevailing in the advanced industrial states. The table also shows the importance of family supports, which accounted for between 17 and 25 percent of the income of a two-child family. Despite its draconian abortion and divorce policies, the level of family allowances in Romania was comparable for a two-child family, equal to 19 percent of the average monthly wage of the head of household (Kligman 1998, 72).

In short, although we find some evidence of a political-consumption cycle for some countries, there are ample anomalies that do not fit the theory, and the long-run trends in social spending through the late-1970s appear broadly similar. Where we do see programmatic innovations, for example in the evolution of family allowances or passive and active labor-market policies, they arose from common problems in the socialist sys-

TABLE 4.7
Educational Achievement in Eastern Europe and Select Asian and Latin American
Countries, 1969–85

	Average years of school (15 years+)	Completion of secondary school (15 yrs +)	Illiteracy (15 years and above) 1985
Bulgaria			
1960	6.16	10.6	
1985	7.71	27.0	4
Czechoslovakia			
1960	7.47	20.0	
1985	9.22	44.9	—
Hungary			
1960	6.64	6.7	
1985	8.93	32.7	1
Poland			
1960	7.03	21.3	
1985	8.81	40.7	1
Romania			
1960	5.92	24.5	
1985	7.87	50.1	4
Argentina			
1960	5.25	14.8	
1985	7.09	25.6	5
Chile			
1960	5.21	24.6	
1985	6.69	33.6	7
Costa Rica			
1960	4.03	10.1	
1985	5.39	17.4	7
Uruguay			
1960	5.36	21.0	
1985	6.89	36.1	4
Korea			
1960	4.25	17.4	
1985	8.68	54.7	6
Taiwan			
1960	3.83	16.3	
1985	7.62	43.1	—

Source: Years in school and completion of secondary school: Barro and Lee 2000;
illiteracy: World Development Indicators (World Bank 2007).

TABLE 4.8
Social Transfers and Income, c. 1990

	Social Transfers as a share of gross income, 1988–89	Family allowances for two children as a share of average earnings, 1988
Bulgaria	21.2	20.0
Czechoslovakia	25.4	19.6
Hungary	22.4	24.9
Poland	20.7	17.0

Source: Milanovic 1998, 13 and 21.

tem, such as weak incentives for fertility or the emergence of unemployment following market-oriented reforms.

THE 1980S: ECONOMIC DECLINE AND THE DILEMMAS OF THE SOCIALIST WELFARE STATE

The ability of Communist regimes to continually improve living standards, including through transfers and services, depended on sustaining high rates of economic growth. By the late 1970s, however, the socialist model had begun to encounter serious limits, and in the 1980s, all of the economies in the region saw a sharp slowdown (table 4.9). By the early 1980s, the Polish economy had entered a deep recession from which it never fully recovered. Growth flattened in both Hungary and Czechoslovakia as well. In Romania, the economy continued to expand in the early part of the decade, but the mid-1980s saw a disastrous economic collapse induced by Ceauşescu's decision to liquidate the country's external debt. The partial exception to the gloomy overall picture was Bulgaria, which outperformed the other economies in the region and maintained positive growth until 1989. However, even in Bulgaria, average growth for the decade was less than 2 percent a year.

Perverse incentives built into the socialist model had long been a concern for economic planners, but these concerns became more acute as growth came to depend less on "extensive" mobilization of physical labor and capital and more on "intensive" increases in productivity. By the 1980s, productivity growth had fallen to very low levels. Approaches for dealing with these problems varied considerably across the cases. Czechoslovakia, Romania, and Bulgaria retained relatively centralized planning systems until fairly late. Hungary and to a lesser extent Poland delegated

TABLE 4.9
Economic Performance in Eastern Europe, 1981–90

	Output growth	Factor growth	Total factor productivity growth
Bulgaria	1.9	−0.2	2.1
Czech Republic	0.8	0.6	0.2
Hungary	1.1	−1.0	2.1
Poland	0.0	0.3	−0.3
Romania	0.4	−0.9	1.3
Slovakia	1.5	0.7	0.8
Average	1.0	−0.1	1.0

Source: Campos and Coricelli 2002, table 2, 798.

greater discretion over hiring and production to industrial managers and liberalized some prices. Both also borrowed heavily to relieve balance of payments constraints—as did Romania—and experimented with some liberalization of the external sector.

As Kornai (1992, 383–95) has argued with the greatest theoretical acuity, the misallocation of resources was a fundamental feature of the socialist system. Piecemeal reforms such as increased discretion for industrial managers might add flexibility to the system, but they could not eliminate core characteristics of the socialist system that generated inefficiencies: the soft budget constraint that undermined incentives for cost containment; the direct allocation of resources through the plan, which faced a myriad informational problems; the absence of functioning markets and meaningful prices; the moral hazard and incentive problems associated with a firm employment guarantee.

These problems with the broader socialist system had important ramifications for the socialist welfare state. The first of these dilemmas was fiscal. Public expectations with respect to entitlements had become a crucial fixture of the political landscape. But fiscal constraints limited both capital and current expenditure on social services and put pressure on transfers. Inflation also contributed to the deterioration of the real value of benefits. The marked decline in the capacity to deliver on the promises of the 1960s and early 1970s placed governments at odds both with particular sectors and groups on which adjustments fell and with the public at large.

But the problems in the social sector were not just financial; they mirrored the incentive problems in the socialist economy more generally. The healthcare sector provides the most telling examples. Because of the government's interest in limiting social expenditures—in making them residual to productive investment—healthcare was chronically underfunded. Yet despite low funding, universal benefits at no cost generated insatiable demand and recurrent problems of shortage—"crowding in clinics and hospitals, long queues in waiting rooms, and waiting lists for hospital beds, examinations, treatments, and long-postponed surgery" (Kornai and Eggleston 2001, 138–39). As early as the 1970s, Eastern European countries began to experience an alarming decline of health conditions, including rising morbidity, particularly among men, and a corresponding decline in life expectancy (Preker and Feachem 1994).

Doctors, who were underpaid for their skills, also faced a variety of perverse incentives. Medical personnel had a disciplinary role in socialist systems because of their control over sick leave, which was seen by planners as the result of malingering and lax medical practices. As a result, doctors were evaluated on quasi-political criteria that blatantly clashed with medical interests (Ferge 1991, 142). Moreover, by the 1980s low pay and underfunding of healthcare services had resulted in a complex and highly regularized system of gratuities that generated growing resentment.

The political consequences of these problems surfaced first in Poland. The second half of the 1970s marked the exhaustion of the reformist project begun under Edward Gierek and recurrent political conflicts over efforts to adjust the price of consumer goods that culminated in the showdown with Solidarity in 1980 (Poznanski 1997). The government responded with efforts to appease the organized working class; the Gdansk Accord of August 1980 included a host of social-policy proposals designed to reverse the increasing dispersion of wages and benefits. Many of these proposals were not immediately implemented (such as the establishment of a "social minimum" and the indexing of pensions). But others were put into practice, including most notably a change in the formula governing child allowances to make them more favorable to poorer families and an increase in the length of maternity leave.

The martial-law period, instituted following the Solidarity protests of 1979 and 1980, marked the last phase of Communist rule in Poland. The Jaruzelski government bore a number of parallels to the military dictatorships of Latin America. Very shortly after the new government was installed, wage dispersion once again increased as the government deployed particularistic benefits to sustain support and deflect opposition (Inglot 1994, 197). However, if this strategy could deter protest by the most organized and mobilized groups, it could not prevent a wider disaffection with the erosion of entitlements. During the steep economic downturn of the early 1980s, official estimates reported that 19 percent of Polish families had fallen below the "social minimum," with the burden falling especially hard on the elderly, single-parent families, and those with large numbers of children (Millard 1992, 128). Family-support policies, a major source of income for lower-income families, pension spending and overall social-security spending, all declined in the 1980s (Sipos 1994, 229; Inglot 1994, 111). In 1989, after a series of failed adjustment efforts, the Communist leadership agreed to roundtable negotiations with Solidarity, an event that marked the start of their withdrawal from power.

The deterioration of the party-state in Hungary was less dramatic, in part because the second economy allowed Hungarians to supplement wages and transfers with other sources of income. But this strategy also had its limits. As the economy stagnated, it also became increasingly difficult for the regime to deliver the consumption and welfare benefits that had been part of the social contract. Pensioners were hit, as in most other countries, by the failure of benefits to keep pace with inflation. Between 1980 and 1987, the real value of retirement payments declined between 25 and 30 percent (Szalai and Orosz 1992, 157). With social spending taking a roughly constant share of total spending over the 1980s, the shift to cash transfers meant a corresponding decline in funding for the health system, education, and social assistance. In an effort to compensate, the Hungarian government began to rely increasingly on political decompression to maintain the acquiescence of the population (White 1986, 473), a process that may eventually have facilitated a relatively smooth democratic transition.

Economic stagnation had similar effects on social insurance and services in Czechoslovakia. Serious consideration of reforms was delayed almost to the very end of the socialist era, and the 1980s were characterized by "a deteriorating health and education system, shortage of adequate housing, little free time because of families' need for two incomes, and a general lack of services" (Tomes 1991, 193). As elsewhere in the region, the combination of slowed growth, declining generosity, and creeping inflation resulted in a decline in the real value of old-age and disability pensions as well as family and maternity benefits. Despite the fact that incomes were higher in Czechoslovakia than in the other Eastern European countries and the Communist regime had formally maintained the most compressed wage structure in the region (Večernik 1991, 238–39), most observers believe that the fraying of the social safety net contributed to an increase in both inequality and poverty, particularly among groups such as pensioners and single-parent households (for example, Tomes 1991, 192–94).

Finally, as a consequence of the misguided planning efforts and devastating austerity policies of the Ceauşescu government during the late 1980s, the hardships suffered by the Romanian population reached extraordinary levels. The response of the regime to slowing growth was not to move toward reform but to tighten restrictions on emergent market forces through an even more egregiously centralized and distorted form of central planning. A highly controversial program of rural resettlement announced in 1988 would have destroyed 7,000 to 8,000 of 13,000 villages in the country altogether, concentrating populations in larger "agro-industrial centers" (Ronnas 1989, 546).

The Ceauşescu government pinned particular blame for the slowdown on foreign debt and in 1986 initiated a repayment program that imposed unparalleled hardships on the Romanian population. By 1989, on the eve of the transition, virtually all the hard currency debt had been liquidated, but consumption of goods and services had dropped by an estimated 40 percent (Nelson 1995, 204). The deterioration encompassed virtually all areas of Romanian life and was visible in declining real wages and a sharp erosion of social entitlements (Nelson 1995, 204–205). The education and health systems suffered a disastrous decline. By the 1980s, to save energy, hospitals were operating on a limited basis, with shortages of basic equipment, medical supplies, and even bandages (Gilberg 1990, 130). Similarly, schools were closed during the winter for months at a time. "Reforms" abolished government commitment to minimum incomes, and the regime introduced fees for certain services, including those charged in clinics and for childcare. As Gilberg (1990, 134) sums up, "the decade of the 1980s must be seen as a turning point in the history of communist Romania, when the trends of general achievement but occasional failures turned to general failure with occasional achievement."

Conclusion: The Legacy of the Socialist Welfare State

The Eastern European cases are an obvious reminder of the limitations of a purely institutionalist explanation of social policy. The Communist regimes of the region were unquestionably hard-authoritarian in form, yet they developed a generous system of welfare entitlements, albeit one subject to deterioration over time. In part, this development can be attributed to a long-run political equilibrium captured by the concept of a socialist social contract (Cook 1993, 19). In the absence of political representation and accountability, the maintenance of Communist political control required increasing material payoffs. However, this interpretation does not explain why governments with the capacity to restrict the scope of redistribution by targeting benefits to core groups chose to extend social insurance and services widely. Even if we take the privileges of the nomenklatura into account, both income and social benefits were distributed on a relatively egalitarian basis. Indeed, with the exception of Poland, the dispersion of benefits probably narrowed during the 1970s and early 1980s as a result of a more explicitly redistributive approach to social policy, anchored in the increasing generosity of family allowances (Ferge 1979, 241; Wolchik 1983, 262–166; Flakierski 1986, 126–127; Tomka 2004).

We also considered the possibility that political factors might have operated through functional equivalents of the mechanisms we have emphasized in the democratic cases—electoral and interest-group pressures. In particular, we considered whether the rivalries surrounding leadership changes or the emergence of contentious politics—strikes, riots, protests from below—might have resulted in an expansion of social entitlements. We found that these political factors had limited effect and that countries in the region converged around quite similar systems regardless of their somewhat different political histories.

In accounting for the expansion and breadth of benefits, we have emphasized the obvious: the central role of the Communist seizures of power in the region and the distinctive features of the socialist development model. Direct state control of the economy meant direct state control not only of employment and wages but also of aggregate consumption. Since insurance and social services were not available on private markets, the provision of employment, old-age and sickness support, and social services inevitably fell to the state. The basic contours of this social-policy system were laid down quite early. Once these entitlements were universalized by extending them to the rural areas, subsequent policy decisions tended to be incremental in nature and centered largely on the resources that would be devoted to existing entitlements.

The socialist regimes of Eastern Europe left behind a complex and somewhat contradictory welfare legacy that posed distinctive challenges for their democratic successors. On the one hand, citizens remained entitled to a broad array of protections and services, including the right to employment, free health care and education, and financial support in the event of invalidity, maternity, and retirement. Despite the hidden privileges of the party elite and other special sectors, these benefits were extended broadly and the commitment to egalitarian principles remained strong. On the other hand, the expansion of these entitlements was followed by a period of adjustment beginning in the late 1970s. Not only did beneficiaries experience declining real transfers, but features of the shortage economy became increasingly manifest in the delivery of social services.

Deacon (1992a, 3–5) provides a useful "balance sheet" that summarizes the positive and negative aspects of the socialist legacy and frames many of the political challenges faced by the new democratic governments in their efforts to refashion social policy.

- Formally, Communist states guaranteed citizens the right to work. Employment was high in Eastern Europe and was linked to a variety of paternalistic benefits, from cheap housing to paid vacations, day care, and cultural services. Yet labor productivity was low, and employment guarantees disguised hidden unemployment and second jobs in the gray economy required to supplement wages.
- The government provided comprehensive coverage for old-age and sickness benefits and extensive provisions for maternity leaves and family allowances. But replacement rates and transfers were not linked to inflation and tended to deteriorate substantially during the 1980s.
- Free curative health services were a highly valued feature of the welfare state. But the health system was inefficient and undercapitalized, and privileged users—or those facing desperate circumstances—could only secure quality service by paying gratuities. A variety of health indicators, most notably mortality and life expectancy, deteriorated during the 1980s as a result of the underprovision of preventive health services and environmental degradation.
- The socialist system offered free and comprehensive access to education. But students lacked choice as a rigid tracking system funneled young people directly into nonproductive jobs in the state-enterprise sector. Moreover, the educational systems suffered obvious disabilities with respect to curriculum and freedom of inquiry.

Deacon's balance sheet suggests two apparently contradictory conclusions. First, publics held positive views of the principles of comprehensive coverage and egalitarianism. He suggests (1992, 5) that, "if they existed in the context of the democratic, pluralist politics of . . . Western Europe, certain aspects of some social policies would be heralded by many as the progressive achievements of the social democratic regulation of market capitalism." But the general crisis of the socialist economies meant that governments could not deliver on these promises and that a widespread frustration with "actually existing socialism" extended powerfully to the social-policy sphere.

For the democratic governments of the 1990s and early 2000s, the legacy of low-quality but comprehensive welfare services presented a complex mixture of opportunities and constraints on social-policy reform. Particularly among younger and more skilled workers, deep frustrations with the shortcomings of the socialist system and doubts about the credibility of long-run social commitments created a constituency for reforms that shifted some welfare responsibilities out of the public sector in exchange for greater dependability of benefits and choice of services. Such attitudes provided some leverage for technocratic reformers to introduce contributory social-insurance principles into healthcare systems and to restructure pay-as-you-go pension systems.

Much more than was the case in the Latin American and East Asian countries, however, reformers' room for maneuver was limited by the very comprehensiveness of the socialist welfare system. Broad public support for the inclusive features of the system—despite dissatisfactions with its performance—stemmed from the fact that its services and protections extended to most of the population and in many cases, were guaranteed as constitutional rights. These conditions set the Eastern European countries apart from both the stratified social-policy systems in Latin America and the limited commitments to public social insurance in East Asia. Although democratic governments in Eastern Europe had some leeway for initiatives that changed the financing and organizational structure of the welfare state, challenging existing entitlements risked political and legal backlash.

PART TWO

Democratization, Economic Crisis, and Welfare Reform, 1980–2005

CHAPTER FIVE

The Political Economy of Welfare Reform

Between the 1980s and the early 2000s, transitions from authoritarian rule to competitively elected governments fundamentally altered the political landscape in Latin America, East Asia, and Eastern Europe. As was the case in the earlier period described in part 1, electoral competition and greater freedom for political organization opened the way to new social demands on governments. In all three regions, political entrepreneurs and newly organized interests pressed for the defense of existing social entitlements and the expansion of social insurance and services to previously excluded or underserved groups.

More than in the early postwar decades, however, democratic governments faced an international context that was much less propitious to the maintenance and expansion of publicly financed insurance and services. Just as new democracies were emerging in the developing and former socialist world, a complex of factors—economic, political, and ideological—were combining to call into question the principles that undergirded the advanced welfare state.

By the late 1980s, these factors had given rise to a new liberal social-policy framework that exercised substantial influence in debates about social-policy reforms in all three regions of interest to us. Diffused in part through the international financial institutions, these reforms sought to shift more of the costs of insurance and services onto individuals, to expand private provision, to increase competition and accountability within the public sector, and to target public spending more directly to the most needy. As in the advanced industrial states, this agenda raised concerns among defenders of the welfare state about the retrenchment of existing entitlements and the capacity of new democratic governments to address inherited problems of insecurity, poverty, and inequality.

In the face of these cross-cutting pressures, new democracies pursued quite divergent social policies. Contrary to fears of a liberal convergence, we see a continuing divergence in welfare strategies across the new democratic regimes (table 5.1). We argue that this variation can be explained by two main causal factors: economic and fiscal constraints on government; and the political legacy of prior social-policy commitments.

In this chapter, we elaborate these arguments and provide a comparative overview of social policy across the three regions. We begin by providing a stylized summary of the liberal social-policy alternative to models of

TABLE 5.1

Democracy, Economic Constraints, and Welfare Legacies in Latin America, East Asia, and Eastern Europe

	Latin America	East Asia	Eastern Europe
Democratization	Long-standing democracies: Costa Rica, Colombia, Venezuela. Democratic transitions: Argentina (1983), Brazil (1985), Chile (1990), Mexico (2000), Peru (1980), Uruguay (1985). Authoritarian reversions: Peru (1992), Venezuela (2000–2002).	Democratic transitions: Philippines (1986), Korea (1987), Taiwan and Thailand (gradual from mid-1980s). Long-standing authoritarian regimes: Singapore, Malaysia.	Democratic transitions (1989–90): Poland, Hungary, Czech and Slovak Republics (separated 1993), Bulgaria, Romania.
Economic crises and fiscal constraints	Severe debt crises in most counties in the first half of 1980s, followed by stabilization and wide-ranging reform of the ISI model. Recovery in 1990s, but recurrence of financial crises in a number of cases. Strong fiscal and financial constraints.	Generally rapid growth through the 1980s and 1990s until the region-wide financial crisis of 1997–98; Philippines is the exception. Relatively swift recovery from the crisis from 1999.	Severe transitional recessions at the outset of the 1990s, followed by stabilizations and wide-ranging market-oriented reforms. Recurrence of financial and fiscal crises in Bulgaria, Romania, and Czech Republic in mid-1990s.
Welfare legacies	Generous social insurance for relatively small class of urban middle- and working-class beneficiaries. Wide inequalities in the coverage and quality of basic social services. Strong stakeholders both inside the government (public sector unions) and outside it (particularly healthcare providers).	Very limited public social insurance, except through defined-contribution models (Singapore, Malaysia). Strong investment in education but weaker public commitment to health. Strong private-sector stakeholders in provision of healthcare	Effective employment guarantee and universal provision of basic social insurance and services through the state. Wide class of beneficiaries and strong stakeholders.
Policy outcomes	Strong pressure for liberalization of existing entitlements. Opportunities to gain support from marginalized low-income sectors provide incentives for expansion of targeted social assistance.	Strong incentives for expansion of basic social insurance, social assistance and unemployment policies.	Pressure for liberalization strongly tempered by wide class of beneficiaries and strong stakeholders. Maintenance of universalist norms with respect to social insurance and services.

social protection based on universal citizenship rights or social-insurance principles. We then consider how the politics of reform has been affected by economic circumstances and the social-policy inheritance. Our examination of economic circumstances focuses on differences in economic performance, structural change, and particularly fiscal constraints. In examining the social-policy inheritance, we consider how electoral and interest group politics were affected by past social policy choices, and how these political economy factors in turn influenced the reform of social insurance and services.

In the second half of the chapter, we provide an empirical overview of the cross-regional differences in social-policy outcomes. We first report the results of pooled-time series models of social spending in each of the three regions. Consistent with the arguments outlined above, these models suggest that the effects of democracy are stronger in the high-growth East Asian countries and in the broadly based Eastern European welfare systems than in the more narrowly based and fiscally constrained societies of Latin America. We close with an examination of cross-regional differences in the main policy areas of interest to us: pensions, health, education, and the establishment of social safety nets.

The Liberal Welfare Agenda

What we have called the liberal welfare agenda encompasses both a set of principles and particular policy reforms. As with the controversial "Washington consensus," any such characterization runs a substantial risk of caricature. Nonetheless, this agenda serves as a useful benchmark for considering the political economy of reform, particularly given fears (or hopes) that such a model would triumph.

The origins of liberal welfare ideas can be traced to a broader neoliberal approach to economic policy that gained momentum in the United Kingdom under the Thatcher government and the United States during the Reagan presidency; Chile's experience under Pinochet also exercised surprising influence. The presumed costs of a burdensome welfare state constituted an important motivating factor but the significance of ideological arguments should not be underestimated.[1] Advocates of welfare reform emphasized the moral-hazard problems associated with extensive social insurance and transfers as well as the economic (and moral) benefits of competition, private provision, and an ethic of personal responsibility. Over time, these ideas about social-policy reform gained influence within

---

[1] Important critiques of the welfare state from different perspectives include Gilder 1981; Murray 1984; Fukuyama 1995. For critical overviews, see Gilbert 2002; Hacker 2006.

international financial institutions, academic research centers, and public-policy networks as well as conservative critics of the welfare state.

A major component of this reform agenda—and by far the most controversial—was the effort to shift the balance between the public and private sectors in both the financing and provision of insurance and services. A core feature of financing reforms has been the effort to tighten the links between individual contributions and benefits. Examples of such reforms include the shift to defined-contribution pension systems, reforms in public health insurance that increase copayments, greater reliance on user fees for other social services, and the use of tax incentives to encourage individuals to save for retirement, health emergencies, or education.

Equally important were efforts to expand the role of private providers. Privatization was seen not only as a way of reducing the burden on governments but also as a means of improving the performance of the public sector by introducing greater competition. Examples include the privatization of pension-fund management, the deregulation or privatization of medical services, and the outsourcing of a variety of functions in the social-service sector. Even where the government maintained an important role in overseeing the provision of social insurance and services, reformers looked closely at mechanisms that expanded the scope of the private sector, such as combining public health insurance with increased private provision and the use of school vouchers to induce private entry into the provision of education.

Liberalizing reforms also sought to reorganize the public sector itself to address principal-agent problems that had emerged in welfare bureaucracies. These reforms imposed greater oversight of public spending through mechanisms such as global and performance-based budgeting, improved monitoring of public contracting, corporatization of service providers such as hospitals, and various other mechanisms of cost control. Decentralization also has played an important role across a number of social-policy areas, particularly in the provision of healthcare and education.[2] Advocated strongly by the World Bank and the Washington policy community, decentralization was seen as a way of improving accountability, avoiding moral-hazard problems associated with revenue transfers, and more closely matching the spending and taxing preferences of a given jurisdiction.

Finally, liberalizing reforms placed considerable emphasis on targeting social spending to the most vulnerable groups.[3] Advocates of such reforms argued, not implausibly, that comprehensive, publicly financed entitle-

---

[2] See for example Ahmad et al. 2005. For critical reviews, see Prud'homme 1995 and Bardhan 2002.

[3] John Williamson (1990) had even included such a reallocation of spending, including to primary healthcare and education as a component of the Washington Consensus.

ments were not only unsustainable but also inequitable, particularly in the context of developing countries. Focusing social spending on the poor was not only more efficient but fairer and more inclusive. Examples of these efforts include greater emphasis on basic social services and targeted antipoverty programs and safety nets.

The distributional implications of this agenda are enormously complex and remain the subject of ongoing debate. For our political-economy purposes, however, liberal reforms have important features that distinguish them from the expansion of social insurance and services that was the focus of our analysis in part 1. Expansion created new entitlements, added beneficiaries to existing programs, and increased social spending without directly challenging existing stakeholders. Liberal reforms, by contrast, sought to shift both spending and institutional prerogatives away from existing stakeholders, often well-organized ones; in this regard, they resembled many economic reforms.[4] Reformers faced opposition from beneficiaries adversely affected by the changes or simply uncertain about their effects (Fernandez and Rodrik 1991).

Efforts to expand basic social services and address poverty did, to be sure, offer opportunities for politicians to appeal to new constituencies. But these efforts typically proceeded within narrow political and economic limits, since those previously excluded from existing benefits were typically less well represented in the political system and weakly organized. As proponents of universalism have argued, moreover, the new emphasis on targeting implied greater vulnerability to fiscal cutbacks than did programs that appealed to a wider constituency (Nelson 1992, 231–61; Skocpol 2001, 22–24, 144–52).

THE ECONOMIC CONTEXT: GROWTH, STRUCTURAL REFORM, AND FISCAL CONSTRAINTS

The links between the liberal reform agenda and increasing economic openness have been a leitmotif of the literature on the political economy of the welfare state. A number of important early statements associated economic openness with an *increased* state role in the provision of social insurances and services.[5] Beginning in the 1980s, however, critics began to emphasize the potentially adverse effects of globalization on the social contract.[6] First, globalization directly exposed households and individu-

---

[4] For reviews, see Rodrik 1996; Haggard 2000b; Persson and Tabellini 2000.

[5] See Cameron 1978; Katzenstein 1985; and Rodrik 1997, 1998

[6] For reviews, see, for example, Huber and Stephens 2001; Swank 2002; Bardhan, Bowles, and Wallerstein 2006.

als to greater vulnerability and risk.[7] Yet at the same time, by strengthening the hand of mobile capital and weakening unions and labor-based parties, globalization undermined the capacity of exposed groups to protect themselves.[8] More ideational approaches in this vein emphasized the increasing diffusion of liberal ideologies through the international financial institutions, through bilateral aid programs, and through multilateral, regional, and bilateral trade agreements.[9]

We are mindful of the importance of "globalization" on the conduct of social policy. However, we believe that the emphasis on the effects of openness per se is overly restrictive and deflects attention from broader economic determinants of social policy: overall performance, development strategies, and fiscal resources.[10] Economic performance affects social policy through two channels. First, high growth encourages policy continuity or relatively incremental processes of economic reform. Economic crisis, by contrast, spurs more radical and socially disruptive reforms, with important implications for prior welfare models. Second, economic performance affects the fiscal capacity of the state directly. High growth allows the government to maintain existing commitments or expand them. Slow growth and crises, by contrast, limit governments' ability to spend and generate pressures for fiscal retrenchment. Given these possible economic effects, we begin with an overview of the growth record.

The Growth Record

Beginning with the breakdown of the Bretton Woods system and the oil shocks of the 1970s, economic performance across developing and socialist countries began to diverge dramatically. As table 5.2 shows, the Asian economies continued on a high growth trajectory throughout the 1980s and into the 1990s. By contrast, Latin America and Eastern Europe entered a period of low and volatile growth, punctuated in a number of countries by bursts of high inflation.

---

[7] For a contrary view, however, see Iversen 2001 and Kim 2007.

[8] On developing countries, see Rudra 2002; Kaufman and Segura-Ubiergo 2001; Wibbels and Arce 2003; and Wibbels 2006.

[9] For further discussion, see Deacon, Hulse, and Stubbs 1997; Deacon 2000; and Nooruddin and Simmons 2006.

[10] Not only are the arguments about economic openness vulnerable to theoretical ambiguity, but the empirical findings on its relationship to social policy have also proven mixed. See Garrett 1998, 2001; Iversen and Cusack 2000; Swank 1998, 2002; Brady, Beckfield, and Seeleib-Kaiser 2005; Bardhan, Bowles, and Wallerstein 2006. On developing countries see Kaufman and Segura-Ubiergo 2001; Rudra 2002; Wibbels and Arce 2003; Avelino, Brown, and Hunter 2005; Rudra and Haggard 2005. A fruitful line of inquiry is to distinguish the effects of openness per se from external shocks and other forms of volatility; see Wibbels 2006, and particularly Kim 2007.

TABLE 5.2
GDP Growth, Volatility of Growth, and Consumer Price Index: Latin America, East Asia, and Eastern Europe

	GDP growth 1960–80	GDP growth 1981–90	GDP growth 1991–2000	SD growth 1960–80	SD growth 1981–90	SD growth 1991–2000	CPI 1960–80	CPI 1981–90	CPI 1991–2000
Argentina	3.5	-1.4	5.6	4.8	5.3	5.8	81.6	787.0	21.4
Brazil	7.3	1.6	2.2	3.6	4.7	3.0		613.8	549.2
Chile	3.6	3.9	3.7	5.1	6.3	3.8	101.0	20.4	9.5
Colombia	5.4	3.6	2.9	1.6	1.7	3.1	16.4	23.7	20.2
Costa Rica	5.9	2.5	3.0	2.8	4.5	2.8	6.7	27.2	16.0
Mexico	6.7	1.9	3.7	2.4	4.0	3.6	9.8	69.1	18.7
Peru	4.5	-0.5	4.3	2.7	8.3	5.2	20.7	1223.6	60.1
Uruguay	2.2	0.2	3.8	2.8	6.2	3.6	55.9	62.5	38.1
Venezuela	3.9	0.9	4.7	3.6	4.9	4.9	4.8	24.9	45.0
Latin America Average	4.8	1.4	3.8	3.3	5.1	3.8	37.1	316.9	86.5
Korea	7.9	8.7	6.3	3.8	2.0	5.0	15.3	6.4	5.1
Malaysia	7.2	6.0	7.2	2.5	3.5	5.3	3.5	3.2	3.6
Philippines	5.4	1.8	3.1	1.4	5.0	2.6	10.3	13.7	8.6
Singapore	9.4	7.4	7.7	4.2	4.0	3.6	3.9	2.3	1.7
Taiwan	9.7	8.0	6.4	3.2	3.3	1.0	7.7	3.1	2.6
Thailand	7.5	7.9	4.6	2.3	3.3	6.2	6.1	4.4	4.5
East Asia Average	7.9	6.6	5.9	2.9	3.5	3.9	7.4	5.5	4.4
Bulgaria	4.4	2.5	-1.6	2.9	4.3	5.5	n.a.	7.6	187.2
Czechoslovakia[a]	2.8	1.1	0.2	1.7	1.6	4.8	n.a.	n.a.	7.6
Hungary	3.2	1.2	0.9	2.2	3.1	5.2	n.a.	10.9	20.3
Poland	3.9	n.a.	3.7	3.3	4.5	4.0	n.a.	107.7	28.4
Romania	5.1	-0.7	-1.6	3.2	3.9	6.4	n.a.	n.a.	121.0
Slovak Republic	—	—	0.6	—	—	6.8	n.a.	n.a.	9.2
Eastern Europe Average	3.7	1.0	0.4	2.5	3.2	5.5	—	—	62.3

Sources: See appendix 5.
[a] Includes Slovak lands, 1960–80, 1980–91.

The contours of the "Asian miracle" are well-known and need not be rehearsed here in detail (see World Bank 1993). From 1960 to 1980, East Asia was the fastest growing region in the developing world. Strong export sectors allowed most countries in the region to recover quickly from the oil shocks of the 1970s and debt crises of the early 1980s; the Philippines, as in so much else, is the clear exception. The financial crisis of 1997–98 was a major shock, but again the region returned relatively quickly to growth.

In Latin America, a sudden, regionwide reversal of capital flow following the Mexican default of August 1982 plunged the region into a decade of crisis, with slowed growth and painful stabilization and adjustment efforts. Despite wrenching policy reforms, most countries in the region fared only marginally better during the 1990s, and some—most notably Argentina—were hit by a new round of external shocks. Not until the mid-2000s did the region see a new phase of growth, fueled by a strong and unusually prolonged upsurge in international commodity markets.

As we showed in chapter 4, the Eastern European economies also began to slow in the late 1970s, and growth virtually ground to a halt during the 1980s. As was the case in Latin America, oil shocks and external debt played some part in these slowdowns. But the stagnation also reflected deep-seated structural problems in the socialist model. The transition to the market in the 1990s was even more disruptive. All countries in the region experienced deep recessions, and many experienced high inflation as well. Although the collapse of the Soviet Union and the socialist trading system played an important role in these transitional recessions, they also reflected the collapse of the planning process and of socialist economic institutions. Hungary, Poland, and Slovakia returned to vigorous growth in the second half of the 1990s, but Bulgaria and Romania experienced "second round" crises in 1997 and 1998, and the Czech Republic saw a marked slowdown as well.

Economic Restructuring

Crises in all three regions were followed by wide-ranging economic reforms. These reforms were particularly disruptive in Latin America and Eastern Europe and placed strong pressure on entitlements associated with earlier development models. One complex of reforms related to the external sector. The liberalization of trade and foreign investment exposed previously sheltered import-substituting industries to increased competition. These adjustments were compounded by crisis-driven changes in exchange-rate regimes that resulted in the abandonment of fixed or heavily managed rates and corresponding pressures to shift both capital and labor toward the tradable-goods sector. Crises also generated strong incentives to reduce barriers to foreign direct investment.

But policy reforms were by no means limited to the external sector. The state-owned enterprise sector also came under pressure, particularly in the Eastern European cases. Privatization was quite substantial in Latin America as well. Subsidies fell victim to fiscal constraints and international commitments through multilateral and regional trade agreements. The ability to use state-directed credit to shore up public and private enterprises was limited by deterioration in bank-balance sheets and reforms of the financial sector.

These reforms marked fundamental shifts in development strategies and thus affected the structural foundations of existing social-policy commitments. In the socialist cases, economic reforms put an end to the employment guarantee and immediately undercut the entire complex of benefits that had passed through the socialist enterprise. Although these problems were not of the same magnitude in the Latin American cases, they bore a strong family resemblance. Wage bargains, employment protections, and benefits in the state-owned enterprise and ISI sectors that had been sustained through protection, subsidies, and other rents immediately came under pressure.

Recessions and structural reforms also fundamentally transformed labor markets. Unemployment, which surged during the debt crisis of the 1980s in Latin America and the transitional recessions in Eastern Europe, continued at high levels even during periods of recovery and growth. Poland, Bulgaria, Slovakia, and Hungary experienced double-digit unemployment throughout much of the 1990s despite substantial growth in the latter part of the decade (table 5.3).[11] Unemployment in Latin America was also very high. Joblessness in Chile, Uruguay, and Colombia reached double digits in the early 1980s, and Venezuela and Costa Rica were also hit hard. During the second half of the 1990s—a period of renewed economic shocks—unemployment again surged to new highs in Brazil and reached double digits in Argentina, Colombia, Uruguay, and Venezuela.[12]

Unemployment in Asia was consistently lower than in the other two regions. The Asian financial crisis resulted in a substantial increase in formal-sector unemployment in the more industrialized countries in the region such as Korea and strong pressures on real wages across the region. But the relatively rapid resumption of growth reversed these trends.

[11] Unemployment rates in the Czech Republic were comparatively low in the early 1990s, but rose in the second half of the decade as governments accelerated the pace of privatization and structural reform.

[12] Unemployment remained relatively low only in Mexico, where unions were pressured to accept big wage reductions in exchange for sustained employment.

TABLE 5.3
Unemployment in Latin America, East Asia, and Eastern Europe, 1980–2003
(as percent of total labor force)

	1981–85	1986–90	1991–95	1996–2000	2001–2003
Argentina	4.5	6.1	8.3	14.8	17.5
Brazil	4.2	3.3	6.1	8.2	9.4
			(92–93 and 95)	(96–99)	
Chile	14.3	6.8	4.96	7.02	7.7
Costa Rica	7.8	5.0	4.5	5.7	6.4
Colombia	11.1	10.6	9.0	15.9	14.9
Mexico	n.a.	2.5 (88)	3.9	3.0	2.3
Peru	n.a.	8.6 (90)	8.2	7.6	9.3
Uruguay	12.2	9.0	9.1	11.6	16.3
Venezuela	9.9	9.6	8.6	12.6	15.3
Latin America average	9.1	6.8	7.0	9.6	11.0
Korea	4.2	2.9	2.5	4.4	3.4
Malaysia	6.4	6.8	3.3	2.9	3.5
	(84–85)		(92–93)		
Philippines	5.8	8.1	8.7	8.8	9.8 (01)
Singapore	3.2	3.9	2.5	3.5	4.7
Taiwan					
Thailand	2.7	3.2	1.6	2.2	2.0
East Asia average	4.5	5.0	3.7	4.4	4.7
Bulgaria	n.a.	n.a.	19.0	14	16.9
			(93–95)		
Czech Republic	n.a.	n.a.	4.2	6.5	7.7
			(93–95)		
Hungary	n.a.	n.a.	10.8	8.0	5.8
			(92–95)		
Poland	n.a.	n.a.	13.8	12.6	19.2
			(92–95)		
Slovak Republic	n.a.	n.a.	13.4	14.2	18.5
			(94–95)		
Romania	n.a.	n.a.	8.1	6.6	7.3
			(94–95)		
Eastern Europe average	n.a.	n.a.	11.6	10.3	12.6
LA-EE (p-value)	n.a.	n.a.	0.08	0.74	0.63
LA-EA (p-value)	0.02	0.22	0.06	0.02	0.01
EE-EA (p-value)	n.a.	n.a.	0.01	0.01	0.03

Source: International Labor Organization 1998.

Increasing informalization of labor markets was a related aspect of these structural changes. Particularly in Eastern Europe and Latin America, the growth of the informal sector reflected efforts by both employers and workers to avoid high payroll taxes, reducing both access to entitlements and the capacity of government to finance them. Informalization was evident as well in the more advanced countries of Asia, especially in Korea and Taiwan.

Fiscal Constraints

The underlying fiscal capacity of the state is ultimately a structural issue that depends on the political and institutional ability to extract resources through taxes. Nonetheless, the ability of governments to maintain existing spending or to undertake new commitments was affected in the short and medium run by revenue constraints. The fiscal indicators and measures of foreign debt presented in table 5.4 capture several important cross-regional differences in this regard.

With the exception of the Philippines and the somewhat misleading figures for Malaysia, the East Asian countries generally enjoyed strong fiscal and external financial positions.[13] Taiwan and Singapore had been net creditors for some time, and the other countries show low debt-service ratios. Moreover, none of the Asian countries discussed here experienced the very high inflation that constrained monetary and fiscal policy in so many Latin American governments. Decadal averages do hide important features of the Asian experience. The financial crisis of the late 1990s was followed by substantial increases in fiscal deficits as a result of costly corporate and financial restructuring. But Korea, Taiwan, and Thailand recovered quickly from the downturn, and neither fiscal problems nor inflationary pressures approached the severity visible in the other two regions (Green and Campos 2001, 310–12, table 1).

During the 1980s—the initial decade of democratization—Latin American deficits averaged close to 4 percent of GDP, as compared with only 2 percent in East Asia.[14] The stock of external debt in Latin America was also over one-third higher than in Asia as a percentage of GDP, and debt-service ratios were over twice as high. These differences in the stock of debt placed constraints on the ability to borrow and on the conduct of macroeconomic policies more generally. As with the performance indica-

---

[13] Malaysia also shows very high fiscal deficits, but these were financed at low cost by the pension system, and the government continued to enjoy access to domestic and external credit markets until the crisis of 1997–98.

[14] For further discussion of the fiscal situation in Latin America, see Gavin and Perotti 1997; Wibbels and Arce 2003; Singh et al. 2005; Wibbels 2006.

TABLE 5.4
Fiscal and Financial Constraints in Latin America, East Asia, and Eastern Europe
in the 1980s and 1990s

Country	1980–89: Decade average			1990–99: Decade average		
	Budget balance/GDP	Debt/ GDP	Debt service/export	Budget balance/GDP	Debt/ GDP	Debt service/export
Latin America						
Argentina	−3.8	56.1	56.4	−3.6	57.1	40.7
Brazil	−8.4	40.0	52.0	−8.8	39.5	45.7
Chile	0.3	93.6	47.2	−0.2	95.8	22.2
Colombia	−2.6	36.4	33.9	−2.0	38.8	36.5
Costa Rica	−2.5	117.8	31.1	−2.0	118.7	14.4
Mexico	−8.5	56.0	42.2	−8.4	57.0	27.8
Peru	−4.7	76.5	29.6	−5.2	79.6	26.9
Uruguay	−2.9	53.2	30.8	−2.8	56.4	22.9
Venezuela	−0.9	55.6	30.8	−0.9	58.4	22.7
Average	−3.8	65.0	39.3	−3.8	66.8	28.9
East Asia						
Korea	−1.0	40.4	22.3	−0.8	37.0	10.5
Malaysia	−7.5	56.2	16.4	−7.1	57.1	8.2
Philippines	−2.9	75.5	33	−3.1	77.0	18.2
Singapore	3.0	—	—	3.8	—	—
Taiwan	−0.1	—	—	−1.7	—	—
Thailand	−3.0	36.2	23.0	−2.1	36.9	15.0
Average	−1.9	52.1	23.7	−1.8	52.0	13.0
Eastern Europe						
Bulgaria	n.a.	n.a.	n.a.	−4.9	95.1	14.5
Czech Republic	n.a.	n.a.	n.a.	−0.1	34.2	11.5
Hungary	n.a.	n.a.	n.a.	−3.7	65.4	34.7
Poland	n.a.	n.a.	n.a.	−1.0	49.2	9.3
Romania	n.a.	n.a.	n.a.	−2.0	18.8	17.8
Slovak Republic	n.a.	n.a.	n.a.	−3.1	35.7	12.2
Average	n.a.	n.a.	n.a.	−2.4	49.7	16.7
LA-EA (p-value)	0.29	0.40	0.02	0.28	0.34	0.01
LA-EE (p-value)	n.a.	n.a.	n.a.	0.373	0.247	0.034
EA-EE (p-value)	n.a.	n.a.	n.a.	0.703	0.890	0.487

Sources: World Development Indicators (World Bank 2007): Global Development Finance (World Bank 2003).

tors in table 5.2, these averages do mask important intraregional differences. Governments in Chile, Costa Rica, and Colombia pursued relatively cautious fiscal policies through the 1980s, and Colombia's debt remained quite low by regional standards.[15] Nevertheless, external credit markets remained closed to all three of these countries until the end of the 1980s as a result of contagion from the regionwide crisis.

In Eastern Europe, fiscal imbalances were large in Bulgaria and Hungary but appear much more moderate in the other cases. But these deficits occurred against the backdrop of a massive reduction in the overall size of the state and a major reallocation of resources from the government to the private sector and households. Standard data on fiscal deficits also do not include substantial subsidies that flowed through the state-owned financial system to both public and private firms. Most countries also faced substantial debt burdens and were forced to reschedule their obligations over the 1990s. Overall, Eastern European states experienced financial and fiscal constraints that were equal if not greater in magnitude than those in Latin America.

THE ECONOMIC CONTEXT AND THE POLITICS OF WELFARE REFORM

What effect did these divergent economic paths have on the *politics* of social policy? We argue that favorable economic conditions strengthen the hand of "spenders": political actors—whether conceived as parties, individual politicians, ministries within a government, or interest groups—arguing for an expansion of social commitments. In particular, we expect robust growth to strengthen the hand of organized labor vis-à-vis employers and of the "social bureaucracy" vis-à-vis technocratic reformers. Countries undergoing rapid growth with moderate inflation also do not face pressures either to stabilize or to undertake major structural reforms, including those related to the provision of social-insurance and services. Even when existing or new social-insurance programs run into short-term financial difficulties, or are revealed to be financially unsustainable over the long run, high growth weakens the urgency of reform.

In many ways, the political logic of fiscal crisis presents the mirror image of the politics of good times. In the first instance, the fiscal constraints associated with crises and stabilization efforts immediately reduce the ability of the government to make credible commitments to expand, or even maintain, social-policy commitments. In principle, taxes could be

---

[15] Official fiscal deficits in Venezuela appear low, but these data disguise huge off-budget expenditures, particularly to or through state-owned enterprises and banks, which left the government virtually bankrupt by the end of the 1980s.

raised for this purpose, but such efforts face well-known political limits (Bird and Oldman 1990). In the short run, governments may attempt to evade such constraints through additional borrowing or the inflation tax. But given the underlying weakness of the tax base, shallow domestic capital markets, and a limited capacity to borrow abroad, the leeway for doing so is much more limited in developing and transitional economies than it is in developed ones (Wibbels 2006).

A substantial theoretical and empirical literature has explored why stabilizations are delayed, as groups struggle over the distribution of the costs of adjustment.[16] Yet as this literature also emphasizes, such delays have political as well as economic costs, and as these costs escalate, so does the pressure to adjust. The incentives to adjust are especially strong in countries experiencing high, or even hyper-, inflation (Drazen and Grilli 1993; Bruno and Easterly 1996), which erodes the real incomes of the middle- and working- classes and hits the poor and those on fixed incomes particularly hard. In such circumstances, the political gains from stabilization—even where it involves adjustments in social spending—can easily dominate concerns about the distributional consequences of reform (Rodrik 1994; Remmer 2002).

Regardless of partisan orientation, therefore, we would expect politicians in crisis settings to come under considerable pressure to stabilize and undertake structural reforms. Legislatures and parliaments are more willing to shift decision-making responsibility onto executives during crises. Executives in turn are likely to delegate policymaking to technocrats based in finance ministries and central banks, who in turn gain influence within the cabinet vis-à-vis spending ministries, including the social ministries.[17] The influence of the international financial institutions, most notably the IMF, is also likely to rise.[18]

These domestic and international technocratic actors typically placed the highest priority on stabilization, balance-of-payments adjustment and so-called first-round structural-adjustment measures such as trade liberalization. Beginning in the late 1980s, however, both international financial institutions and technocratic reformers became more engaged in efforts to reform social policy as well, influenced by the liberal policy agenda that we outlined above. Their attention naturally gravitated to the "big ticket" items in the welfare system, particularly pensions and healthcare

---

[16] See Alesina and Drazen 1991; Laban and Sturzenegger 1994; Tornell and Lane 1999; and Drazen 2000.

[17] See also Nelson 1990; Haggard and Kaufman 1992; Williamson and Haggard 1994; and Dominguez 1997.

[18] For a discussion, see Bird 2001; Stone 2002; Vreeland 2003; Dreher and Vaubel 2004; and Nooruddin and Simmons 2006.

(World Bank 1994b), but reform efforts typically expanded to include reform of the delivery of social services.

These reforms both attracted support from portions of the private sector and increased their bargaining leverage through the so-called threat effect (Freeman 1995; Choi 2006). In the first instance, a number of private actors have direct stakes in the rules governing the financing and provision of social insurance: doctors, nurses, and other healthcare workers; corporate providers of healthcare; pharmaceutical companies; the insurance industry; and segments of the financial sector. But market-oriented reforms also altered the preferences of "leading sectors" that had emerged in the course of market-oriented reforms. As these sectors became more exposed to international and domestic competitive pressures, they placed a high priority on reforms that would reduce labor costs and increase labor-market flexibility.

Of course, poor economic performance and the social distress that accompanies it also give rise to pressure for *more* social spending. Until at least the late 1990s, however, crisis and economic reform weakened unions, left parties, and other popular groups that historically had championed more extensive social protections. Organized working-class interests were hit hard by the decline in state and formal-sector employment, by the informalization of labor markets, and by the erosion of corporatist ties that had linked unions to the state and provided an institutional basis for their influence. Particularly in Latin America, the decline in unions also posed serious challenges to left parties with bases in the labor movement. Although these parties were sometimes able to maintain electoral strength by shifting their strategies toward broader, more catch-all appeals or more clientelistic ties to the electorate (Levitsky 2001; Roberts 2006), these adjustments necessarily weakened the voice of the organized working class and diluted their influence.

Alternatives to these traditional organizations and structures of representation did emerge, but their effectiveness in influencing the national policy debate remains questionable. NGOs proliferated during the 1980s and 1990s in all three regions, and a number of these organizations took up the social question or became directly involved in the provision of social services. But these organizations focused on quite disparate and localized interests. With precarious funding and limited personnel, they typically encountered serious difficulties in building broad alliances that could influence the debate in regard to core social-policy issues.

The vacuum left by the decline in established parties and unions was filled in some countries by electoral movements organized by populist leaders or by outbursts of "contentious politics" from below. The first trend was reflected, for example, in the electoral victories of self-proclaimed "left" leaders such as Hugo Chávez in Venezuela, in Argentina's turn to more populist economic policies under Nestor Kirchner, in the election of Joseph Estrada in the Philippines, in early nationalist-populist governments in Romania and the Slovak Republic, and in a post-2000 resurgence of right-wing populism in a number of Eastern European countries. Yet the ability of these movements to sustain social-policy promises was also highly contingent on overall economic and fiscal circumstances. Hugo Chávez could sustain an expansionist social-policy stance because of the flood of oil revenues; the Philippine and Romanian governments, by contrast, faced recurrent fiscal constraints.

Throughout the 1990s, the influence of contentious politics on the course of social policy reform proved much weaker than was initially anticipated. Bela Greskovits (1998) was among the first to note the surprising weakness and ineffectiveness of contentious politics in Eastern Europe, despite the wrenching depth of the transitional recessions and subsequent reforms (see also Vanhuysse 2006). Marcus Kurtz (2004) reached similar conclusions for Latin America, showing a substantial decline in strikes and other protest activities both during the economic-reform period and in the years following.[19]

In sum, we expect economic circumstances to have wide-ranging consequences for the political economy of welfare reform. Strong growth sustains existing welfare bargains and provides opportunities to expand them. Crises produce economic reforms which can undermine the institutional foundations of entitlements financed and administered through the firm. Crises and associated fiscal constraints also place pressure on government-funded entitlements and services and limit the credibility of future welfare promises. Economic downturns do generate new social demands on the state, to which we would expect new democracies to respond. But there are reasons to believe that these pressures will be muted, at least in the medium run, by the weakening of left and labor parties and unions and the inability of either NGOs or "contentious politics" to effectively substitute for them.

Welfare Legacies and Political Constraints

As we emphasized in part 1, we expect democracy to affect the conduct of social policy through two channels: electoral competition and interest-group organization. We have suggested how economic circumstances might affect both these channels. But the politics of welfare is also

---

[19] Ironically, the political success of populist leaders in the Latin American cases owes much to a favorable change in economic conditions—a commodity-led upswing in growth—which increased their capacity to deliver on their promises.

influenced by past social-policy choices. These policy choices do not magically persist; we suggest strong limits to arguments about path dependence. However, past policy choices do influence the preferences of voters, parties, and interest groups as well as the organizational capabilities of stakeholders.

The electoral effects of past policy are well captured by the scope of coverage: the share of the population with access to social insurance, services, and transfers of different sorts. Wide and generous coverage provides broad segments of the public with a stake in existing entitlements. Even when beneficiaries are not organized, their sheer electoral weight constrains politicians to be responsive to them (Pierson 1994). Moreover, where coverage is broad, competing parties are likely to converge in their defense of existing entitlements regardless of partisan identity.[20] Where coverage has historically been narrow, it is more difficult for beneficiaries to defend entitlements through electoral channels.

A second effect of the welfare legacy centers on the preferences and organization of interest groups. Welfare commitments, like any public policy, create vested interests. These can include organizations that directly represent beneficiaries, such as pensioner groups or private-sector unions, but also other stakeholders: public-sector unions; private contractors and suppliers; associations and informal networks of administrators, civil servants, and public service providers. These groups not only constitute a powerful constraint on social-policy reform, but they can play an important role in blocking the reallocation of social spending to the poor as well.

Groups embedded within the administrative apparatus of welfare systems constitute a particularly important set of stakeholders. Institutional reform typically requires the cooperation of groups that may be adversely affected by the reforms in question: middle-level bureaucrats; state and local politicians and health and education authorities; school, hospital, and clinic directors; teachers, doctors, and nurses. Such actors sometimes have only limited influence on legislation, but when implementation begins, they can use a variety of organizational resources to effectively block or modify the reform agenda or simply "wait out" the reformers.

How did welfare legacies affect the politics of reform in the three regions of interest to us? In the Asian cases, the modesty of the authoritarian social contract provided new democratic parties with strong incentives to compete for votes with social-policy promises. Even conservative parties used social programs to increase their popularity. Politicians naturally gravitated toward the expansion of social programs with wide electoral

[20] See Kitschelt (2001) for a discussion of electoral incentives with respect to welfare reform.

appeal, such as defined-benefit pension systems, comprehensive health-insurance programs, improvements in education, and protection against unemployment for formal-sector workers. Given the particular political history we traced in part 1, the involvement of unions in pressing for expansion was relatively limited. But new grassroots movements and NGOs flowered in the aftermath of the democratic transitions and provided an additional source of pressure for expansion.

Welfare legacies played a more complex role in Eastern Europe and Latin America, where economic circumstances gave liberal technocrats greater influence over the reform agenda. The central difference between the two regions was the scope of existing entitlements. Despite substantial economic and fiscal constraints, the broad scope of entitlements in Eastern Europe generated strong public expectations that the socialist social contract would not be abrogated altogether. The parties of the left—whether reformed Communists or social democrats—maintained important constituencies among older voters and state workers most directly threatened by market-oriented reforms (Kapstein and Milanovic 2002, 10–12). They typically campaigned on promises to moderate the pace of liberalization and expand social safety nets (Cook and Orenstein 1999; Lipsmeyer 2000, 2002; Vanhuysse 2006). When in government, they sometimes acquiesced to social-policy reforms, particularly in the area of pension privatization. But as we will show in chapter 8, they coupled such reforms with defense of wide public protections and ongoing attention to the effects of the reform process on formal-sector workers.

As we would predict under such circumstances, it was not only the left that defended such entitlements; other Eastern European parties—whether conservative, liberal, Christian Democratic, or peasant—also placed considerable emphasis on maintaining or even extending social protections. Governments dominated by nonleft parties were under strong pressure to maintain universalistic commitments, made substantial compromises with existing beneficiaries, and increased social spending as well.

Unions also played an important role in the politics of welfare policy in Eastern Europe. Prior to the transition, unions had been extensions of the party-state and lacked support or credibility with the rank and file. But they did occupy important positions as administrators of a variety of benefits and as the nominal representatives of large segments of the workforce. Following the transitions, unions were represented in tripartite bargaining structures established throughout the region. Although the importance of tripartite bargaining has been a subject of sharp controversy,[21] it provided a platform for unions to defend entitlements and to

---

[21] For further discussion, see Kubicek 1999; Ost 2000; Iankova 2002; and Avdagic 2003.

TABLE 5.5

Union Density: Latin America, East Asia, and Eastern Europe, 1990s.

Country	Density
Argentina	22.3
Brazil	23.8
Chile	13.1
Colombia	5.9
Mexico	22.3
Peru	5.7
Uruguay	12.0
Venezuela	13.5
Costa Rica	11.7
Average Latin America	14.5
Korea	12.7
Malaysia	13.4
Philippines	38.2
Singapore	15.9
Taiwan	33.1
Thailand	4.2
Average East Asia	19.6
Bulgaria	51.4
Czech Republic	36.3
Hungary	52.5
Poland	27.0
Romania	40.7
Slovakia	52.3
Average Eastern Europe	43.4
E. Europe–Latin America T-Test (P-value)	0.01
E. Europe–East Asia T-Test (P-value)	0.01
Latin America–East Asia T-Test (P-value)	0.34

Sources: Latin America: Roberts 2006, 168; Eastern Europe and East Asia: International Labor Organization 1998.

press for new social safety nets for formal-sector workers. Although membership declined during the 1990s, Eastern European unions continued to encompass a much larger segment of the workforce than those in Latin America or East Asia (see table 5.5). At least in some cases, they were also able to mobilize support for large-scale protests and even general strikes in defense of entitlements.

The extent of social-insurance coverage and the bureaucratic organization of the welfare system varied more widely in Latin America. In Uruguay and Costa Rica, the democratic governments of the 1980s and 1990s inherited fairly wide coverage of at least some social entitlements; the politics of social policy reform in these countries resembled Eastern Europe. Most other countries, however, inherited systems of social insurance that provided generous benefits to narrowly-defined occupational groups, much more limited benefits to others, and excluded large sectors of the population altogether. In these cases, limited or unequal coverage made it more difficult for organized beneficiaries to gain broad support for existing entitlements. Even left and populist parties distanced themselves from the traditional constituencies that had benefited from such systems in the past.[22]

Despite limited and unequal coverage, Latin America's relatively large and highly centralized public-welfare bureaucracies allowed insiders to gain access to the decision-making process and to influence implementation as well. Public-sector unions, particularly those with institutionalized influence over the management of social-security funds, were often able to extract important concessions in the course of pension reforms. The highly centralized health and education sectors also proved resistant to change. Liberal reformers sought to decentralize these services during the 1990s, in part precisely to dilute union power. But unions of teachers and public-health workers fought these initiatives and sought to retain their influence over wage setting, personnel assignments, and work routines.

As in Asia, narrow coverage also offered incentives for politicians to bid for the support of the urban and rural poor with promises of expansion. But long-standing fiscal constraints and economic crises limited the capacity of both incumbents and challengers to credibly promise an expansion of existing entitlements. Rather, targeted antipoverty programs were a favored policy instrument, popular with politicians across the political spectrum. Moreover, they often did have a measurable effect on poverty reduction. But, in most cases, public funding for these programs was only a very small share of total social expenditures, was vulnerable to retrenchment in the face of fiscal constraints, and had only marginal effects on the distribution of income.

REGIONAL PATTERNS OF WELFARE REFORM

In the remainder of this chapter, we provide an overview of how the core variables we have discussed in the preceding section—democracy, economic conditions, and welfare legacies—affected social-policy reform. We look first at trends in social expenditures during the 1980s and 1990s and then turn to a more detailed consideration of regional differences in the

---

[22] Gibson (1997), Levitsky (2001), and Roberts (2006b) offer insightful analyses.

organization, coverage, and financing of pensions, health, education, and antipoverty and labor-protection policies.

Democracy, Revenue, and Social Spending: A Pooled-Time-Series Analysis

As in part 1, an examination of spending provides a useful frame of reference for the more qualitative analysis that follows. A pooled-time-series design used in other studies of government spending in the advanced industrial states[23] allows us to explore the causal impact of a number of the economic and political factors discussed in the preceding sections. One advantage of the error-correction approach is that because it includes both the lagged level and lagged changes of the explanatory variables, it captures both their long-run and short-run or transitory effects (See appendix 5 for a detailed discussion of the model).

The dependent variables in these models are the changes in overall government spending and in three categories of social spending—social security, health, and education—expressed as a share of GDP. The two independent variables of particular interest are democracy, for which we use standard Polity IV measures, and fiscal constraints, measured by the change in revenue as a share of GDP.

We would expect these variables to have different effects across the three regions. Democracy should have a significant impact on spending in the regressions for Asia, where politicians had incentives to expand minimalist social insurance systems, and in Eastern Europe, which faced strong stakeholder pressures to maintain social commitments. It should be weaker in regressions for Latin America, where costly but unequal social-security systems were more vulnerable to retrenchment.

We use revenue as our indicator of fiscal constraints, but it is important to distinguish between the effects of the level and change in revenue, both of which are included on the right-hand side. The theoretical interpretation of the effect of the level of revenue is ambiguous, since taxes as well as expenditures can be adjusted over the long run. The *change* in revenue is of greater substantive interest, because short-run tax adjustments are generally difficult for developing countries to implement. A positive coefficient on the change in revenue can thus be interpreted as an indication that short-term fluctuations in available fiscal resources constrain spending. We would expect this constraint to be greatest in the Latin American countries, given the severity of the structural strains on the fiscal capacity of the state and the weakness of countervailing pressures to sustain or increase spending commitments.

---

[23] See particularly Iversen and Cusack 2000 and Iversen 2001.

We include controls for level of development, economic growth, "globalization" (measured by both trade openness and financial flows), country size (population) and relevant demographic characteristics. Real GDP growth is also included on the right-hand side of the equation to correct for the changes in the share of spending that might be attributable simply to growth. For ease of exposition, we do not report the coefficients for the wealth, demographic, and country-size variables, but they generally go in the expected direction and reach standard thresholds of significance. In separate models, also not shown, we test for the effects of a battery of other controls, including the presence of an IMF program, foreign direct investment, official net transfers, and inflation, as well as several political variables that have played a role in recent theoretical debates, including party fragmentation, the number of veto points, and the strength of left parties. The introduction of these variables did not alter our results for revenue change and democracy. The results were also robust to models which used purchasing power parity (PPP) adjusted values rather than constant U.S. dollars to measure trade openness and other economic variables.

Tables 5.6, 5.7, and 5.8 report these results.[24] As expected, democracy has different effects across the three regions. In East Asia, a country that experiences a permanent change to democracy (Polity) also experiences a permanent change in average social spending over the duration of the model. Although social spending as a share of GDP is very small (only 0.9 percent in the case of social security), increases over previous levels are quite large. For example, in a country that experiences a permanent change to democracy, the average share of social-security spending to GDP increases by about 23 percent.

Democratization (Polity change) also has a positive short-term effect on spending in education and health before these expenditures return to the trend average. These findings are consistent with our argument that the combination of a minimalist welfare legacy and favorable economic circumstances allowed East Asian democracies to increase social spending. The change to democracy also affected spending in postsocialist countries. The models show significant short-term effects of regime change on spending in health and strong and positive effects on long-term average shares of general expenditures and social security, which increase by 13 and 58 percent respectively.

---

[24] We also ran a model that pooled data from all three regions, not reported here. As would be expected from our emphasis on cross-regional differences, the inclusive model is subject to problems of panel heterogeneity. Although regional dummies are significant, findings for revenue and polity and other independent variables show no consistent results.

TABLE 5.6
Aggregate and Social Spending in Latin America, 1980–2000, PCSE Model

	Expenditure	Education	Health	Social Security
Lag DV level	−0.365	−0.184	−0.128	−0.230
	(4.44)***	(2.73)***	(2.57)**	(3.50)***
Polity	0.847	−0.028	−0.005	−0.436
	(1.49)	(0.24)	(0.06)	(1.97)**
Polity change	1.325	−0.198	−0.114	−0.419
	(1.31)	(1.07)	(0.78)	(1.00)
Revenue	0.359	0.002	0.019	0.098
	(4.13)***	(0.28)	(2.89)***	(2.90)***
Revenue change	0.349	0.010	0.029	0.108
	(3.04)***	(0.60)	(2.07)**	(2.86)***
Per capita GDP	0.000	−0.000	−0.000	0.000
	(1.01)	(0.70)	(0.43)	(0.64)
PCGDP change	0.000	−0.000	−0.000	0.001
	(0.28)	(0.63)	(0.09)	(1.33)
Trade	−0.031	0.005	0.003	−0.031
	(1.61)	(0.91)	(0.85)	(3.32)***
Trade change	−0.029	−0.016	0.002	−0.069
	(0.73)	(1.41)	(0.32)	(3.35)***
Transfers	−0.006	0.015	0.010	0.077
	(0.10)	(1.17)	(1.24)	(3.07)***
Transfers change	0.063	−0.010	−0.003	−0.005
	(1.29)	(0.94)	(0.50)	(0.19)
Recession	1.275	−0.302	−0.125	0.158
	(1.61)	(1.63)	(1.19)	(0.39)
Recession change	1.136	−0.094	−0.083	0.118
	(2.40)**	(1.00)	(1.38)	(0.58)
Constant	20.616	0.582	−1.136	11.110
	(1.57)	(0.41)	(0.59)	(1.72)*
Observations	163	123	122	117
R-Squared	0.29	0.17	0.22	0.33

Source: See appendix 5.
* Significant at 0.1 level;   ** significant at .05 level;   *** significant at .01 level.

In Latin America, on the other hand, democracy generally has no impact on social spending. This finding is also consistent with our hypothesis that new democratic governments in Latin America faced a number of political and economic constraints on social policy. Indeed, the only significant impact was a long-term *negative* relation between polity and social-security spending, which might reflect efforts to correct the profound inequities of the welfare legacy.

TABLE 5.7
Aggregate and Social Spending in Asia, 1980–2000, PCSE Model

	Expenditure	Education	Health	Social Security
Lag DV	−0.351	−0.572	−0.507	−1.007
	(4.47)***	(6.61)***	(3.92)***	(5.78)***
Polity	1.257	0.605	0.144	0.211
	(1.86)*	(4.36)***	(1.78)*	(1.66)*
Polity change	0.733	0.469	0.134	0.040
	(0.89)	(3.28)***	(1.90)*	(0.32)
Revenue	0.475	0.106	0.064	0.009
	(3.02)***	(2.56)**	(3.25)***	(0.42)
Revenue change	0.549	0.164	0.048	0.030
	(3.79)***	(5.51)***	(3.87)***	(1.40)
Per capita GDP	0.000	0.000	−0.000	0.000
	(0.44)	(3.44)***	(2.33)**	(4.18)***
PCGDP change	−0.004	−0.001	0.000	−0.001
	(2.05)**	(3.94)***	(1.21)	(2.76)***
Trade	−0.007	−0.001	0.001	0.005
	(0.68)	(0.68)	(1.12)	(3.03)***
Trade change	−0.046	−0.002	−0.001	−0.005
	(1.44)	(0.31)	(0.44)	(1.11)
Transfers	−0.035	0.005	−0.013	0.003
	(0.80)	(0.33)	(1.85)*	(0.43)
Transfers change	0.019	−0.002	0.010	−0.009
	(0.45)	(0.17)	(2.25)**	(1.26)
Recession	0.517	0.500	0.206	0.127
	(0.94)	(3.67)***	(3.19)***	(1.37)
Recession change	2.240	0.789	0.218	−0.002
	(2.58)***	(4.18)***	(2.41)**	(0.01)
Constant	−7.839	−13.997	−17.643	1.244
	(0.23)	(1.17)	(3.00)***	(0.25)
Observations	70	44	44	44
R-Squared	0.59	0.79	0.59	0.61

Source: See appendix 5.
* Signifiant at 0.1 level;   ** significant at .05 level;   *** significant at .01 level.

A number of studies have noted that Latin America appears especially prone to procyclical pattern of spending; contrary to Keynesian logic, spending increases during periods of growth but falls during downturns in the business cycle (Gavin and Perotti 1997; Wibbels 2006). We see similar patterns with respect to the effect of revenue on spending. The strongest effect is on overall expenditures, but we see significant fiscal constraint in health and social security as well. Substantive effects are modest but far from trivial. With respect to social security, a one-off per-

TABLE 5.8
Aggregate and Social Spending in the Former Socialist Countries, 1990–2000, PSCE Model

	Expenditure	Education	Health	Social Security
Lag DV	−0.728	−0.402	−0.388	−0.373
	(5.09)***	(4.04)***	(2.83)***	(4.31)***
Polity	3.163	0.248	0.139	2.579
	(2.74)***	(1.01)	(0.47)	(3.21)***
Polity change	2.326	0.200	1.064	−0.039
	(1.33)	(0.52)	(2.69)***	(0.05)
Level	0.591	−0.081	−0.052	0.134
	(3.40)***	(2.80)***	(1.89)*	(3.02)***
Revenue change	0.624	−0.005	−0.035	0.047
	(4.98)***	(0.18)	(1.20)	(0.85)
Per capita GDP	0.001	0.000	0.000	0.000
	(1.00)	(2.98)***	(1.77)*	(1.44)
PCGDP change	0.002	−0.001	0.001	−0.001
	(0.50)	(1.34)	(1.15)	(0.84)
Trade	−0.094	−0.022	0.009	−0.011
	(2.53)**	(2.73)***	(0.85)	(0.64)
Trade change	0.028	−0.011	0.006	−0.030
	(0.59)	(0.99)	(0.60)	(1.40)
Transfers	0.102	0.013	−0.019	0.051
	(0.75)	(0.43)	(0.54)	(0.79)
Transfers change	−0.242	−0.018	0.039	−0.100
	(2.34)**	(0.78)	(1.49)	(1.94)*
Recession	−0.375	0.095	0.365	0.245
	(0.43)	(0.50)	(1.60)	(0.60)
Recession change	1.095	−0.020	0.573	0.771
	(0.81)	(0.08)	(1.49)	(1.15)
Constant	43.398	18.979	4.949	−21.500
	(1.17)	(2.85)***	(0.52)	(1.59)
Observations	59	49	49	49
R-Squared	0.63	0.40	0.44	0.55

Source: See appendix 5.
* Significant at 0.1 level; ** significant at .05 level; *** significant at .01 level.

centage point decrease in revenue (revenue change) produces a cumulative five-year decrease in social-security expenditure of about 0.26 percent of GDP. To place this in perspective, the annual expenditures of major anti-poverty programs such as PROGRESA in Mexico or Bolsa Escola in Brazil range from 0.15 to 0.2 percent of GDP (Morley and Coady 2003, 21). These patterns appear to reflect long-term macroeconomic vulnerabilities and fiscal weaknesses that allowed very little room for countercyclical fiscal policy or the protection of social spending in the wake of crises.

In Eastern Europe, change in revenue has no significant effect on any of the social-spending categories; if anything, the signs on health and education indicate a tendency for spending to increase as revenues decline. Although we have no direct measure for the welfare legacy, this finding is at least consistent with our expectation that adjustments of social spending are constrained by the weight of stakeholders and beneficiaries inherited from the socialist system.[25]

Coefficients for revenue change in East Asia show that, as in Latin America, social spending is linked to short-term changes in revenue. However, it should be noted that this positive relationship occurred in the context of strong growth and a steady improvement in economic and fiscal conditions throughout the 1980s and most of the 1990s, rather than the highly volatile context faced throughout Latin America. In any case, the substantive effects of revenue changes were generally far smaller in Asia than in Latin America, never reaching more than about .05 percent of GDP in any of the spending categories. It should also be underlined that unlike the case in Latin America, spending on social security, the most important area of welfare expansion in the Asian democracies, was unaffected by changes in revenue.

Results for the control variables are mixed and take us beyond our core concerns. But they do raise questions about how "globalization," at least defined as openness, affects social spending. Consistent with earlier findings (Kaufman and Segura-Ubiergo 2001; Wibbels 2006), a permanent trade opening (Trade) has a negative impact on social-security spending in Latin America. Trade openness is associated with a decline in aggregate expenditure and education spending in Eastern Europe but an increase in East Asia. These results suggest strongly that the effects of trade are far from uniform across regions.

Changes in net transfers, a measure of external financial constraints, also fail to produce consistent results, either within or across the regions. Spending is most affected by capital flows in Latin America: the level of net transfers had a positive impact on social security, suggesting the adverse effects of capital outflows associated with the crisis. The level of transfers also had a positive impact on some categories of spending in the Asian cases (health and education), but it is much harder to interpret other findings for either that region or Eastern Europe. In several categories (aggregate spending in Eastern Europe and education in East Asia), spending and changes in net transfers moved in opposite directions: a falloff in transfers produced higher expenditures. It is possible that the negative signs indicate a determination to protect such spending from the volatility of capital flows, but it is equally plausible that short-term transfers inter-

---

[25] Even though we do not directly measure the welfare legacy, it is captured to some extent by the fixed-effects model.

act with revenues and other economic conditions that are not captured by the current models.

Our conclusions from these models with respect to the effects of economic openness are cautionary. First, it is important to underscore that the effects of openness are difficult to identify in an econometric sense; changes in openness to trade and in capital flows were but one component of larger policy, economic, and institutional changes associated with the transformation of existing development models. However, the results are by no means uniform or robust.

Beyond Spending: Regional Patterns of Welfare Reform

Our ultimate interest is not in spending per se but in changes in the principles and organization of social policy. In this section, we take up this issue through a closer consideration of the way countries in the three regions have addressed four policy areas: pensions, healthcare, education, and the creation of social safety nets and antipoverty programs. These modal patterns are summarized in table 5.9.

Each issue area posed its own specific set of policy challenges. Nevertheless, if our theoretical arguments regarding the conditioning effects of fiscal circumstances and welfare legacies have merit, we should see the broader cross-regional differences in each specific policy domain as well: an expansion of social protections and services in the high-growth Asian democracies; more targeted expansion and stronger pressures to liberalize in Latin America; and a greater continuity in entitlements in Eastern Europe.

PENSION REFORM

Pension commitments are typically among the most expensive social entitlements, and as a result, are the ones most likely to be targeted for reform. In Latin America and Eastern Europe, technocratic reformers pressed for either full privatization of pay-as-you-go systems along the lines of the Chilean model or less radical multipillar approaches that established contributory second (defined contribution) and third (strictly voluntary) pillars.

Whether fully substitutive or mixed, these reforms involved substantial transition costs as payroll taxes were shifted out of the pay-as-you-go systems into new accounts. For this reason, reform initiatives typically came only after short-term macroeconomic instability appeared to be under control.[26] Nevertheless, in the wake of crises, and particularly

[26] Perhaps for this reason, Raúl Madrid (2003) finds no correlation between economic crisis and pension reform. He does, however, show a link between reform and the size of the pension sector.

TABLE 5.9
The Reform of Social Contracts in Latin America, East Asia, and Eastern Europe

	Latin America	East Asia	Eastern Europe
Pensions	Full or partial privatization of pay-as-you-go pensions systems, along lines of Chilean or multipillar model. Attempts at parametric reforms of first pillar.	Expansion of defined-benefit public pension system in terms of both coverage and benefits. In central provident fund cases, greater flexibility in use of funds.	Partial privatization of pay-as-you-go pension systems, but more limited than in the Latin American countries. Attempts at parametric reforms of first pillar
Health	Increased role for private insurers and providers. Decentralization and increased competition among public insurers and providers. Some effort to expand basic healthcare services.	Expansion of public health insurance	Establishment of social-insurance health funds, but government effectively guarantees universal coverage.
Education	Administrative decentralization. Encouragement of local responsibility and community control. Tighter links between teacher pay and promotion and testing results.	Decentralization, depoliticization, increased accountability, and expanded student choice. Improved educational quality.	Shift away from vocational training toward more generalized skills. Decentralization, depoliticization, increased accountability, and expanded student choice.
Social safety nets	Severance pay for workers laid off in privatizations, but limited programs for unemployment. Expanded emphasis on targeted anti-poverty programs.	Expansion of social insurance and unemployment protection.	Establishment of unemployment-insurance program during initial transition. Early-retirements disability and family allowances used to cushion employment risks.

where public commitments were large, pension systems were viewed as a threat to fiscal stability. Most of the larger systems ran current deficits, and all faced substantial unfunded liabilities.[27] Over the longer term, reformers expected that full or partial privatization would strengthen the fiscal position of the government by deepening domestic capital markets

[27] Although only a few countries in our sample faced the severe demographic pressures of rapidly aging populations visible in a number of advanced industrial states, all suffered from declining contributions associated with shrinking formal-sector employment and outright evasion.

TABLE 5.10
Pension Coverage and Multipillar Reform in Latin America and Eastern Europe

	Type[a]	Projected benefits from 2nd pillar[b]	Share of payroll to 2nd pillar[c]	Share of workers in 2nd pillar[d]	Madrid index[e]	Contributors/ working-age population[f]
			Latin America			
Argentina	Mixed	54	.41	.67	.27	39.0
Brazil	None					31.0
Chile	Substitutive	100	1.00	.95	.95	43.0
Colombia	Parallel	100	.93	.38	.35	27.0
Costa Rica	Mixed	20	.36	1.00	.36	47.2
Mexico	Substitutive	91	.82	1.00	1.00	30.0
Peru	Parallel	100	1.00	.58	.58	20.0
Uruguay	Mixed	48	.37	.39	.15	78.0
Venezuela	Mixed	n.a.	n.a.	n.a.	n.a.	30.0
			Eastern Europe			
Bulgaria	Mixed	37	n.a.	n.a.	.17	63.0
Czech Rep.	None	—	—	—	—	67.2
Hungary	Mixed	43	n.a.	n.a.	.26	65.0
Poland	Mixed	49	n.a.	n.a.	.22	64.0
Romania	Mixed	n.a.	n.a.	n.a.	n.a.	48.0
Slovakia	Mixed	n.a.	n.a.	n.a.	n.a.	72.0

[a] Classification of reforms into replacement, mixed, and parallel systems by Mesa-Lago (2005, 49). Latin America, and Müller (2002a, 164) for Eastern Europe.

[b] Estimates of benefits from funded pillar for worker earning the average wage (Brooks 2007).

[c-e] The Madrid index is the product of the share of the payroll taxes to the 2nd pillar times the share of workers in the 2nd pillar (Madrid 2003, 16).

[f] Coverage from Palacios and Pallares-Miralles 2000.

and reducing contingent liabilities of the government. In the short run, they hoped to minimize transition costs by parametric changes such as raising the retirement age or adjusting benefit formulas.

During the 1990s, most Latin American and Eastern European governments instituted some type of structural pension reform. However, we would expect it to be more limited in Eastern Europe than in Latin America. Some of the differences between the two regions are captured in table 5.10. Although the majority of reforms in both regions involved the establishment of mixed or parallel systems, the only two fully privatized systems were in Chile and Mexico. More revealing are estimates of the extent of privatization developed independently by Sarah Brooks (2007) and Raúl Madrid (2003). Brooks simulates the returns accruing to a worker earning the average wage from a defined-contribution system.

Madrid calculates the percentage of payroll taxes going to the private pillar and the percentage of workers affiliated with it; his index is the multiplicative product of these percentages. With the exception of Uruguay and Costa Rica—two exceptionally large and popular pension systems—privatization went farther in Latin America than in Eastern Europe. Again, with the exception of Uruguay in Latin America and Romania in Eastern Europe, pension coverage remained wider in the Eastern European cases as well.

Some of these differences are consistent with an explanation based on regime type. The radical privatizations in Chile and Mexico were undertaken by authoritarian governments. Democracies vary in the extent of reform, however, and these differences can be attributed in part to welfare legacies. Eastern European democracies inherited pension systems that encompassed most of the old-age population and promised protections to almost all those still in the work force. Privatization was limited by pressures to provide guarantees to beneficiaries and workers approaching retirement age. Compromises with stakeholders also characterized pension reforms in Latin America. But outside of Uruguay and Costa Rica, narrower and less equal coverage weakened the capacity of pensioners, unions, and other stakeholders to exert political influence.

Pension policy in the new Asian democracies contrasts sharply with the focus on privatization found in Latin America and Eastern Europe. In Korea, Taiwan, and Thailand, pension coverage prior to the transition to democratic rule had been limited to generously funded plans for government employees and defined-contribution plans for small segments of the formal sector. Following the transition, Korea and Taiwan saw a dramatic increase in public-pension coverage, and Thailand witnessed important innovations as well. Similar pressures operated in the Philippines, which had developed a public-pension system in the 1950s, but these efforts were subject to recurrent fiscal constraints. By contrast, Singapore and Malaysia, which remained less democratic than the other Asian countries, exhibit greater continuity with the defined-contribution approach that limited public commitments and emphasized individual responsibility.

REFORMING THE HEALTH INSURANCE AND HEALTHCARE SYSTEMS

Inherited legacies and fiscal circumstances also play important causal roles in the politics of healthcare reform. With the exception of Malaysia and Singapore, the healthcare systems of East Asia had historically lacked any substantial social-insurance dimension outside of benefits provided to relatively narrow groups of core regime supporters. Individuals outside these privileged circles relied to a greater extent than did those in Latin

America and Eastern Europe on insurance provided through employers, private insurance, and particularly out-of-pocket expenditure. All four of the new democracies undertook major expansions of public health-insurance coverage, including the inauguration of national systems with broad coverage in Korea and Taiwan. By contrast, Singapore and Malaysia focused largely on liberalizing reforms: cutting costs, increasing the efficiency of public provision, encouraging competition, and shifting costs—and risks—onto households and individuals.

The politics of health reform in Latin America proved more complex. On the one hand, governments in the fiscally constrained countries of Latin America placed a higher priority than did the Asian democracies on financial and administrative reforms that untangled the complex cross-subsidies between the pension and health funds and increased the cost effectiveness of service delivery. In a number of cases, financial responsibilities were shifted to lower levels of government, where stakeholders were weaker. Reforms of the public-delivery system also included decentralization and cost-control measures such as per-capita budgeting for hospitals. In several countries, governments encouraged or acquiesced to a substantial expansion of the role of private-sector providers. These various reforms were often slowed by opposition from healthcare workers and public-sector unions, but the organization of most Latin American healthcare systems changed gradually over time.

Latin American governments also faced political pressure to improve on the highly unequal delivery of basic healthcare. Yet two features of this expansion are striking when compared with the high-growth Asian cases. First, we see few efforts to create a comprehensive and unified system of social insurance or public provision. Colombia and, to a more limited extent, Brazil, are the most notable exceptions. Elsewhere, efforts to improve public services were more incremental, taking the form of targeted human-development programs aimed at specific regions or subsets of the population. Second, these efforts were highly contingent on fiscal circumstances. When financial constraints eased, both democratic and semidemocratic governments expanded entitlements. However, these approaches to the expansion of healthcare were reversible and remained vulnerable to changing fiscal fortunes.

In contrast to East Asia and Latin America, both the financing and provision of healthcare had been dominated by the public sector in Eastern Europe. Following the transition to democratic rule, control over hospitals and clinics typically devolved to municipal governments, and doctors lobbied for a greater private-sector role in provision. Yet all the postsocialist cases showed continuing commitment to finance and to provide curative and basic services on a universal basis. Most governments opted to go "back to Bismarck" (Marée and Groenewegen 1997) by opting for national health-insurance systems. As a result, healthcare spending increased through the transition and remained high when compared to other regions.

Some of the cross-regional differences in health policy are captured in table 5.11, which shows the changes in public and private shares of total health spending between 1996 and 2005 and in the out-of-pocket and insurance shares of private spending. In East Asia, public-health spending rose substantially as a percentage of total health spending in two of the high-growth democracies, Korea and Thailand. Comparable data is not available from the WHO for Taiwan, but the creation of a national health-insurance system had similar effects there as well. In the Philippines, where fiscal problems posed particular constraints on government, the public share of health spending fell despite new social-insurance initiatives. In the two nondemocracies, public spending dropped in Singapore and rose only slightly in Malaysia, despite a long history of public-health provision. Although average spending remained somewhat below that of Latin America, the differences ceased to be statistically significant by the mid-2000s as public spending increased.

In Latin America, the share of public spending in total health expenditures increased slightly between 1996 and 2005, but it remained low relative to Eastern Europe and only slightly above East Asia. But the region exhibits substantial variation that confirms a number of our theoretical expectations. Public spending remained relatively low in Chile's partially privatized health system, a reflection of the Pinochet legacy. It declined over the decade in Argentina, Peru, and Venezuela, all countries experiencing severe fiscal pressures. In contrast, the public sector grew substantially in Colombia, which enjoyed exceptionally favorable fiscal conditions at the onset of the 1990s, and it remained high in Costa Rica, a long-standing democracy with a history of public financing and provision. Increases in Brazil and Mexico, both countries that experienced severe fiscal strain, run somewhat counter to expectations. But as we shall see in chapter 7, both countries faced substantial electoral pressure to redress extreme inequities in access to healthcare. It is also noteworthy that the average share of private health insurance was significantly different from that of both East Asia and Eastern Europe. Private health-insurance markets grew substantially over the decade in Argentina, Brazil, Chile, Colombia, and to a somewhat lesser extent, in Peru.

The ratio of public to private health spending declined in Eastern European countries from 1996 to 2005. Yet sixteen years after the transition, it remained far higher than in almost all the countries of the other two regions. Although the financing of the public sector shifted formally from the general treasury to social-insurance funds, principles of broad public responsibility remained intact. Unlike many of the Latin American and

TABLE 5.11

Public and Private Health Spending in Latin America, East Asia, and Eastern Europe, 1996 and 2005

	1996 Public/ total health[a]	2005 Public/ total health[a]	1996 Private/ total health[b]	2005 Private/ total health[b]	1996 Out of pocket/ private[c]	2005 Out of pocket/ private[c]	1996 Ins./ private[d]	2005 Ins./ private[d]
	Latin America							
Argentina	57.6	44.2	42.7	55.8	70.4	48.8	26.0	45.7
Brazil	40.4	53.7	59.6	46.3	68.6	64.4	31.4	35.6
Chile	47.4	47.1	52.6	52.9	51.5	46.1	48.4	53.8
Colombia	64.8	85.8	35.2	14.2	85.4	44.6	14.6	55.4
Costa Rica	76.2	77.1	23.8	22.9	87.5	88.7	2.7	2.1
Mexico	41.4	47.1	58.6	52.9	96.6	94.4	3.4	5.6
Peru	51.6	47.3	48.4	52.7	88.2	79.4	9.1	17.3
Uruguay								
Venezuela	50.8	42.9	49.2	57.1	89.1	88.2	4.6	3.8
Latin America average	53.8	55.6	46.3	44.4	79.7	69.3	17.5	27.6
	East Asia							
Korea	38.1	50.9	61.9	49.1	85.0	76.0	3.9	8.0
Malaysia	48.0	54.4	52.0	45.6	79.9	74.2	9.0	13.2
Philippines	41.0	38.3	59.0	51.7	81.8	77.3	6.6	12.8
Thailand	47.2	63.9	52.8	36.1	80.4	76.6	9.5	15.6
Taiwan								
Singapore	40.8	34.7	59.2	65.3	95.7	96.9	n.a.	n.a.
East Asia average	43.0	48.4	57.0	51.6	84.5	80.2	7.3	12.4
	Eastern Europe							
Bulgaria	69.1	57.5	30.9	42.5	100	98	0	0.3
Czech Republic	90.7	89.1	9.3	10.9	100	95.4	0	2.1
Hungary	80.8	72.6	19.2	22.4	95.1	93.0	n.a.	3.4
Poland	73.5	69.8	26.6	30.2	100	97.9	0	2.1
Romania	66.5	66.0	35.5	34.0	100	93.4	0	0.1
Slovak Republic	88.7	72.4	11.3	27.6	73.2	73.4	0	0
Eastern Europe average	78.2	71.4	22.1	28.8	94.7	9.2	0	1.3
LA-EE (p-value)	0.00	0.05	0.00	0.04	0.05	0.02	0.02	0.01
LA-EA (p-value)	0.05	0.38	0.05	0.50	0.43	0.23	0.12	0.11
EE-EA (p-value)	0.00	0.01	0.00	0.01	0.09	0.07	0.01	0.00

Source: WHO 2007.

[a] General government spending as a percent of total health spending.

[b] Private health spending as a percent of total health spending.

[c] Private households out-of-pocket payments as a percent of private health expenditure.

[d] Private insurance and risk pooling as a percent of private health expenditure.

East Asian countries, moreover, the increasing share of private spending was financed almost exclusively by households rather than private insurance markets, indicating significant holes in the healthcare safety net.

EDUCATION

Democratization has a number of immediate effects on public-education systems. In authoritarian regimes, education systems are instruments of political control and indoctrination. Democratization is typically followed by efforts to revise curricula to reflect democratic values, often unleashing bitter battles to reclaim and reinterpret the past. Democratization loosened political controls over faculty and curricula, changed patterns of recruitment into the teaching profession, and increased freedom of organization for teachers' unions; these unions came to play an important role in the other reforms that are of primary interest to us. Finally, democratization was typically followed by efforts to improve the responsiveness of schools to parents and to increase student choice.

At the onset of the period covered in part 1, substantial shares of the population remained outside the educational system altogether, and the expansion of enrollments was a useful gauge of public commitment. By the 1980s and 1990s, however, primary-school enrollments were no longer the main challenge facing most countries in the three regions. Debates about education shifted to quality and to other issues beyond the scope of this study, such as tertiary education and vocational training. However, access to secondary and even primary education remained a salient issue in several Asian and Eastern European countries, including the Philippines, Thailand, Romania, and Bulgaria. Moreover, in many Latin American countries, educational attainment was highly unequal and fell far short of what might be predicted on the basis of the region's level of development.

In our analysis of education, we place primary attention on these cases and show how our core theoretical arguments pertain. First, we expect the ability of governments to provide greater educational coverage and quality to depend on fiscal circumstances. We also expect fiscal constraints to drive reforms such as decentralization, efforts to control costs and increase efficiency, and the reallocation of resources to underprivileged regions and to primary and secondary education. However, we would also expect these efforts to be affected by the legacy of the existing system, including the distribution of spending across levels of education and regions and the political power of stakeholders, particularly of teachers' unions.

The more prosperous East Asian countries had already achieved universal or near-universal primary and secondary enrollments. In Thailand and the Philippines, by contrast, secondary coverage remained an ongoing issue. The two cases permit a virtual natural experiment on the effects of economic circumstances. In Thailand, fiscal conditions allowed a substantial expansion of secondary enrollments, while the Philippines faced ongoing fiscal constraints and fights over rationalization.[28]

Because of its weak educational inheritance and severe economic constraints, Latin America provides a particularly interesting set of cases with respect to educational reform. The reform of education did not face the same public opposition from beneficiaries as did pension and health-insurance reform, and it garnered support when it was linked to an expansion of services or improvements in quality. But teachers wielded organizational resources unavailable to pensioners, union representatives on pension fund boards, or even healthcare workers. Where public-sector unions were strong, they exercised substantial influence over both the formulation and implementation of educational reforms. A number of core reforms, from the implementation of standardized testing to merit pay and efforts to reduce teachers' unions' influence over assignments and promotions generated fierce resistance in both their adoption and implementation.

Even more than was the case in the authoritarian systems in Latin America and East Asia, the educational systems in socialist countries were instruments of both political indoctrination and manpower planning. Educational reform in the new East European democracies naturally reduced political interference, expanded academic freedom, and reversed excessive specialization and the almost complete lack of student choice. Perhaps because of the socialist legacy, we find greater tolerance, and even support, for reforms such as decentralization. The socialist countries also had broad primary and secondary coverage and were therefore much more equitable than the Latin American cases and even a number of the East Asian ones (table 1.14); outside of important educational deficits with respect to minority populations in Bulgaria and Romania, expansion at this level was not a central issue and we therefore do not pay equal attention to educational reform in the socialist cases. Nonetheless, we do see some parallels to the debate over education reform in Latin America, particularly in the very strong role played by teachers in resisting certain reform proposals.

[28] The design of vocational training and organization and financing of tertiary education took on increasing significance, particularly in countries that had achieved universal secondary education. But these efforts are largely beyond the scope of this study, which focuses on the provision of primary and secondary education.

Social Safety Nets: Addressing Poverty and Vulnerability

The transition to democratic rule also generated new political pressures to address both the new vulnerabilities associated with crises, economic reform, and longer-standing issues of poverty and inequality. Classifying such efforts is difficult, since governments can provide safety nets through a variety of means. Much of the literature on social protection nonetheless distinguishes between social-insurance programs designed to mitigate risk for broad sectors of the population and social assistance targeted to particular groups that fall outside traditional social-insurance systems (Lindert, Skoufias, and Shapiro 2006). The former approach includes both passive and active labor-market policies, disability insurance, family and maternity benefits, and child-support programs with broad eligibility criteria. Social-assistance and targeted antipoverty programs include most public employment programs, income supplements for poor families, subsidies to basic necessities or in-kind transfers such as food programs, social funds, and conditional transfer programs.

Social insurance and social assistance are not perfect substitutes, and countries in all three regions deployed a mix of these policy measures to address poverty and insecurity. Nonetheless, we find cross-regional differences in the timing and overall incidence of these different types of programs that reflect economic conditions, fiscal constraints, and welfare legacies.

Of particular interest is the comparison between the Latin American and Eastern European cases, both of which experienced profound crises but responded to them in quite different ways. The Latin American countries in our sample placed a greater emphasis on targeted antipoverty programs than did those in Eastern Europe. An important but controversial innovation of the crisis years in Latin America was the establishment of social funds that financed quick-disbursing public-works programs in poor communities. By the mid-1990s, such funds had been initiated in Chile, Peru, Mexico, Venezuela, Colombia, and Uruguay. In the late 1990s, a number of Latin American governments pioneered targeted human development or conditional cash transfer programs. These programs provided income supplements to poor families, but only on condition that they meet requirements with respect to the utilization of basic social services, such as attending clinics and keeping children in school.[29]

Several features of the Latin American approach to these safety nets are germane to the theoretical arguments outlined above. First, the targeted

---

[29] Mexico's Programa de Educación, Salud y Alimentación (PROGRESA) launched in 1997, was the first large-scale program of this sort, both in the region and globally, and it

approach to poverty reduction reflected the views of the World Bank, other international financial institutions, and domestic social-policy reformers that both chronic poverty and structural and cyclical unemployment would require greater efficiency in the use of scarce resources. Second, although leakage and clientelistic practices were common problems in these programs, benefits did appear to flow disproportionately to families and individuals in the poorest 40 percent of the population and often comprised a significant share of their income (Coady, Grosh, and Hoddinott 2004). Such targeted support was viewed as complementary to efforts to reallocate resources away from the core social-insurance programs that had dominated Latin American social spending.

Finally, both fiscal pressure and stakeholder entitlements placed significant constraints on the scope of such programs. Spending on these ranged from 0.5 to 1 percent of GDP and constituted only a small proportion of total social spending (generally between 5 and 7 percent in the early 2000s). Moreover, although benefits often comprised a substantial portion of income for recipient families, they were inversely related to coverage (Lindert, Skoufias, and Shapiro, 86–112). Thus, although these programs have generally had a measurable and quite positive effect on family income and human development, their overall impact on poverty has been relatively modest. As with social spending in the region more generally, they remained vulnerable to the recurrence of fiscal constraints (Snyder and Yackovlev 2000).

Arguably, Eastern Europe faced a much more daunting set of adjustments than did Latin America; however, contrary to expectations that the region would go a neoliberal or residualist route, new democratic governments tended to rely more heavily on universalistic or broadly targeted programs. Immediately following the transition, governments used existing instruments such as family allowances and disability pensions as tools for assisting workers dislocated by the transitional recessions of the early 1990s. During this period, they also adopted or expanded unemployment compensation and moved swiftly to implement active labor market policies. In Latin America, by contrast, only four countries (Argentina, Chile, Uruguay, and Venezuela) provided any unemployment compensation at all, and these programs were of very limited scope and duration.

Cornia (2002), Vanhuysse (2006), and others have argued that the social-security system inherited from the socialist era and the rapid establishment of unemployment insurance and social assistance dampened social conflict and thus contributed to the consolidation of democratic rule

---

was followed by Colombia's Familias en Acción program (FA), Chile's Subsidio Unitario Familiar, and the Bolsa Escola (later Bolsa Familia) program in Brazil.

itself. However, more detailed evidence on these programs that we present in chapter 8 indicates that they were by no means confined to the poorest or most vulnerable segments of the population. To the contrary, coverage was generally very broad, with the result that the distributive effects of programs were either neutral or even moderately regressive (for example, Coady, Grosh and Hoddinott 2004; Milanovic 1995).

In East Asia, the role of the government in providing social safety nets had been highly limited prior to the late 1980s. Robust economic circumstances in the three high-growth democracies—Korea, Taiwan, and Thailand—initially mitigated the demand for such programs; particularly in the two more industrialized cases, political attention focused on the expansion of core social-insurance programs. Nonetheless, all four of the new democracies developed new labor-market and social-safety-net programs following the transition to democratic rule. In Thailand and the Philippines, with their much larger rural populations, new democratic governments also experimented with a wide variety of rural antipoverty programs. Differences in fiscal constraints played a major role in the scope of these efforts, however; they received more sustained financial support in Thailand than they did in the Philippines. It is also noteworthy that regime type continued to be consequential; Malaysia and particularly Singapore hewed to a much more liberal model with respect to social safety nets (Ramesh 2004).

The financial crisis of the late 1990s in East Asia and accompanying structural reform efforts weakened protections once extended through the firm, increased the flexibility of labor markets, and reduced the defacto job security associated with sustained growth. Antipoverty responses, however, were wide-ranging. Korea expanded unemployment insurance and created a battery of new programs. Taiwan created an unemployment-insurance scheme, and the Thai government—after initially responding modestly to the crisis—was replaced by a more populist administration that introduced a variety of antipoverty measures. As we would predict, the crisis did strengthen the hand of technocratic actors. But in contrast to Latin America and Eastern Europe, the fiscal problems of the high-growth Asian democracies were more limited in both depth and duration and could not be credibly linked to long-standing social entitlements. As a result, the crisis produced a number of new social-policy initiatives to deal with vulnerability, and some of these initiatives were extended into more permanent entitlements. Again, the Philippines proved much more constrained in its ability to respond because of ongoing fiscal constraints. The absence of democratic rule resulted in a much more modest social-policy response to the crisis in Malaysia and particularly Singapore.

CONCLUSION

As in part 1, we have identified certain "modal" features of the reform process in each region that we believe can be traced to common causes: the nature of critical alignments and development strategies in the earlier period; economic circumstances and welfare legacies in the case studies that follow.[30] Yet the cases within any given region also exhibit important variations around these means. These differences provide opportunities for further testing of our initial expectations regarding the effects of democratization, economic circumstances, and welfare legacies.

In East Asia, we exploit the contrast between the high-growth democratic transitions—Korea, Taiwan, and Thailand—and the Philippines to demonstrate the role of fiscal constraints on social policy. The high-growth cases subsequently experienced financial crises as well, but their relatively short-lived nature and the absence of structural fiscal problems limited incentives for liberalizing reforms.

Two countries in Asia also remained authoritarian in important respects: Singapore and Malaysia. We show that the continuity of political rule was paralleled by continuity in the nature of social policy and a preference for liberalizing reforms.

The Latin American countries also exhibit variation on the three core causal variables of interest to us. Regime type had an important impact on the extent of liberalizing reforms, particularly in the pension sector; authoritarian and semidemocratic regimes had a greater ability to confront stakeholders and undertook more wide-ranging reforms than their democratic counterparts. But we find that both democratic and competitive authoritarian regimes had electoral incentives to expand antipoverty programs.

Differences in the severity of economic and fiscal constraints and in welfare legacies were also important. Technocratic influence was most extensive in democracies experiencing severe crises, such as Argentina, and more limited where fiscal and inflationary constraints were less severe; we find these fiscal constraints to operate in authoritarian settings as well. In most countries, finally, liberal reforms encountered significant opposition from stakehholders, despite the narrowness of coverage. Yet these legacy effects were greatest in countries such as Costa Rica and Uruguay that had the broadest and most generous welfare states.

Finally, in Eastern Europe, there is much greater commonality in the welfare legacy; we do not see the differences on that dimension that prove

---

[30] A common criticism of such a method is that it selects on the dependent variable; see Geddes 2003, 89–129. However, as Mahoney (2003, 351–52) argues, such a method of

important for explaining some of the variation within our Latin American sample. Nor do we see variations in regime type to the extent visible in East Asia and Latin America. We therefore focus our comparison around a commonly drawn distinction between early reformers such as Poland and late reformers such as Bulgaria and Romania. We show that these differences were associated with somewhat different approaches to social-policy reform in the early posttransition period. But the slow reformers ultimately faced renewed economic crises in the mid-1990s, and by 2005, when we end our narrative, the Eastern European countries showed substantial convergence with respect to their social-policy systems.

---

selection can be appropriate when it is designed to highlight some necessary set of antecedent conditions.

CHAPTER SIX

Democracy, Growth, and the Evolution of Social Contracts in East Asia, 1980–2005

The turn to democratic rule in the middle-income countries of Asia began in the Philippines with the "people power" uprising against the Marcos dictatorship in early 1986. Figure 6.1 tracks the subsequent process of political change in the region using Polity IV scores (with 6 typically considered the threshold for democratic rule). In Korea, the presidential elections of 1987 are typically considered the transition point, although an opposition candidate did not ascend to the office until 1993. Two other transitions occurred more gradually. In Thailand, the military slowly yielded its veto power over elected politicians during the 1980s before a brief military interlude in 1991–92. From 1992 to 2006, when the military again intervened, the country was continually democratic. In Taiwan, as in Mexico, the ruling KMT gradually introduced political competition at the national level from the mid-1980s. The presidency was not held by an opposition politician until 2000, but politics was solidly democratic by the early 1990s. As of 2005, Malaysia and Singapore remained less than fully democratic, although both systems had competitive elements.

Democratic transitions in Korea, Taiwan, and Thailand occurred in periods of vigorous economic expansion. Growth remained robust until the Asian financial crisis of 1997–98 (figure 6.2). Strong growth was associated with favorable fiscal circumstances (figure 6.3). In Taiwan, budget deficits averaged less than 1 percent a year from 1980 through 1988, before widening as a result of the political processes we will describe. In Korea, the fiscal position of the government remained broadly in balance through the democratic transition until the financial crisis hit in 1997. In Thailand, the 1980s began with fiscal deficits larger than those in the Philippines, but major adjustments in the early-1980s reversed them, and the transition to more democratic politics took place in the context of large fiscal surpluses.

This combination of economic, fiscal, and policy circumstances strengthened the hand of political actors arguing for an expansion of the state's social-policy role. Even when new social-insurance programs ran into financial difficulty, reformers inside and outside the government found it extremely difficult to roll them back.

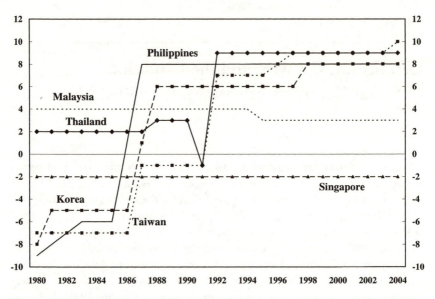

Figure 6.1. Democratic transitions in East Asia: 1980–2004. *Source*: Polity IV database (Marshall and Jaggers 2004).

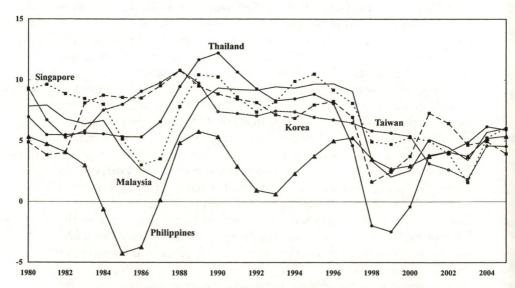

Figure 6.2. GDP growth in East Asia, 1982–2005 (three-year moving average). *Sources*: World Development Indicators (World Bank 2007); for Taiwan: Asian Development Bank 2005.

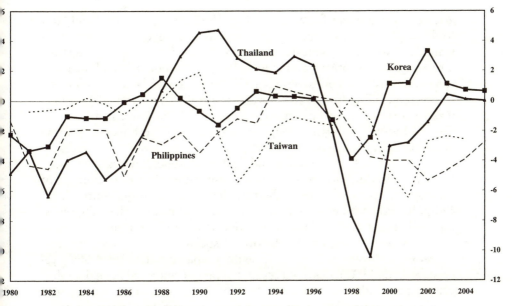

Figure 6.3. Budget Balance as a percent of GDP: Korea, Philippines, Taiwan, and Thailand 1980–2005. *Source*: World Development Indicators (World Bank 2007); for Taiwan, Asian Development Bank 2005.

The Philippines provides an important contrast to the three high-growth cases. The transition to democratic rule came on the heels of a debt crisis that resembled those in Latin America. Subsequent growth was erratic and the fiscal position of the state much less propitious. From the mid-1990s, the country experienced a secular deterioration in revenues. These circumstances limited social-policy initiatives and generated recurrent pressures for reform.

Singapore and Malaysia provide an opportunity to compare the evolution of social policy in the new democracies with semidemocratic and competitive authoritarian systems. Except for a short, sharp downturn in the mid-1980s, these two countries also experienced robust growth until the financial crisis of 1997–98. Political circumstances, however, differed markedly from the democracies. Electoral and other rules guaranteed the hegemony of dominant parties, and governments placed clear limits on the opposition, unions, and NGOs. Limited public commitments and a greater emphasis on liberal reform can plausibly be traced to these political circumstances.

As in Latin America and Eastern Europe, financial crises in Asia also generated sharply conflicting pressures on governments. We focus particular attention on the three countries in our sample that were most seriously affected by the Asian financial crisis of 1997–98: Korea, Thailand, and Malaysia. On the one hand, political leaders came under pressure to alleviate distress and to institutionalize more permanent protections against insecurity. On the other hand, crises placed both short-run and medium-run fiscal constraints on governments and spurred wide-ranging economic reforms, including further liberalization of trade and investment and extensive corporate and financial restructuring. As in Latin America and Central Europe, the crisis strengthened the hand of technocrats and the international financial institutions.

In contrast to Latin America and Eastern Europe, however, the Asian financial crisis did not generate significant reforms or retrenchment of social-policy commitments in the new democracies; to the contrary, social-policy commitments continued to expand. Outside of the Philippines, the crisis did not take place in the context of structural budget deficits or long-standing and highly elaborated social-insurance commitments. Moreover, recovery was relatively swift compared to the decade-long recessions in Latin America. As a result, liberal reformers did not gain political traction with respect to social policy in the new democracies. In a number of important cases, short-term ameliorative measures were broadened into more permanent commitments. This was much less the case in Malaysia, where restrictions on democratic politics continued through the crisis.

DEMOCRATIC TRANSITIONS AND SOCIAL POLICY: TAIWAN, KOREA, THAILAND, AND THE PHILIPPINES

Underlying structural and demographic factors influence the agenda of social policy reform and it is therefore important to control for them to the extent possible even in a qualitative design (table 6.1). The two "first-generation" newly industrializing countries, Taiwan and Korea, are broadly comparable. Although Taiwan had higher per-capita income in 1985, both countries had relatively large industrial sectors, still significant but rapidly declining agricultural sectors, and relatively egalitarian income distributions with low levels of absolute poverty. Thailand and the Philippines also share a number of features that make a paired comparison plausible. The two countries had a nearly identical share of employment in industry, and while Thailand had a much larger share of the workforce in agriculture (68 percent), nearly half of all employment in the Philippines was in agriculture in 1985 as well. Both countries fell at the more unequal end of the Asian cases and had comparable levels of $1-a-day poverty.

TABLE 6.1
East Asia: Development, Economic Structure, Inequality, and Poverty, 1985

	GDP per capita (constant)	GDP per capita (PPP)	Share of workforce in industry	Share of workforce in agriculture	Gini	$1 dollar a day poverty, 1985
Korea	5,322	5,750	29.5	24.9	34.5	< 5 (1984)
Malaysia	2,587	4,359	23.8	30.4	48.1	16 (1984)
Philippines	974	3,266	13.8	49.6	46.1	23 (1984)
Singapore	13,332	9,965	35.7	0.7	41.6	< 1 (est.)
Taiwan	7,530ª	8,000ᵇ	41.6	17.5	29.2	< 2 (est.)
					47.4	
Thailand	1,329	2,751	12.1	68.4	(1986)	25 (1988)

Sources: World Development Indicators (World Bank 2007); Gini coefficients: Deininger and Squire 1996; data for Taiwan: Republic of China 2004.
ª 1996 dollars.
ᵇ 1997 dollars.

An important determinant of the demand for both pensions and healthcare is the demographic profile (table 6.2). The more advanced countries in the region do show a more marked aging trend. But in the mid-1980s our standing point here, the share of the aged did not differ substantially across countries and therefore would not constitute an obvious explanation for policy differences with respect to pensions and health.

Taiwan

Taiwan shows clearly how electoral competition in a favorable economic setting can push even conservative parties to expand social commitments. Taiwan differed from the other East Asian cases in developing a social-insurance program, but as we saw in chapter 3, coverage and benefits were relatively limited. Prior to the political opening, the KMT's social insurance initiatives were directed primarily to expanding the benefits already enjoyed by core KMT constituents under separate, more generous schemes: civil servants, the military, private teachers and their dependents (Son 2001, 47; Aspalter 2002, 51–63).

TOWARD NATIONAL HEALTH INSURANCE

The period from 1985 to 1991 was a crucial one in Taiwan's transition; not coincidentally, social spending began to rise sharply (see figure A6.14).[1]

---

[1] Data on health spending (appendix 6) do not show the same increase as social-security and education spending because spending through the health-insurance system is not

TABLE 6.2
Aging in Asia: Share of Population over 65, 1985–2025

	1985	1995	2005	2015	2025
Korea	4.3	5.7	8.5	11.5	17.3
Philippines	3.4	3.5	4.0	4.9	6.7
Taiwan	5.1	7.2	8.9	10.3	15.9
Thailand	4.3	5.4	7.5	9.8	13.9
Malaysia	3.7	3.9	4.6	5.9	8.1
Singapore	5.3	6.3	8.1	11.4	19.5

Source: United Nations 2001.

The government allowed an opposition party to form and moved toward competitive elections at the national level. In anticipation of these developments, the KMT introduced a pilot program in 1985 to extend health insurance to farmers, an electorally important group excluded from the Labor Insurance scheme (Ku 1997, 82; Son 2001, 46–49). This program expanded dramatically in the following years. The government also formed an executive task force in 1988 to investigate the creation of a single-payer national-health-insurance system.[2]

In 1988 Lee Teng-hui lifted martial law and allowed electoral competition at the national level. In the 1991 National Assembly elections, the opposition Democratic Progressive Party (DPP) fared poorly by campaigning on a Taiwan independence platform (Rigger 2001, 125). Prior to the 1992 Legislative Yuan elections—the first direct elections for all its seats—more centrist factions of the party sought to rectify this mistake by advancing social-policy proposals. The 1993 DPP White Paper on social welfare promised an extensive array of entitlements, including universal health insurance and pensions, subsidized housing, government-guaranteed retirement income for the elderly, and expanded social assistance (Ku 2002, 159–60).[3]

The KMT drafted its own social-policy guidelines in 1994.[4] The guidelines struck a more conservative tone than the DPP White Paper (Ku 2002,

---

captured in Taiwan's fiscal data. On the course of aggregate health spending, see Wagstaff 2005.

[2] See Wong 2004, 77–79. On the history of the reform, see also Lin 1997 and Son 2001, 49–50.

[3] Fell (2002) traces the history of party platform change toward social issues over the 1990s.

[4] The KMT was pressured not only by the DPP but also by internal fissures that resulted in the formation of the New Party in 1993. The New Party (and later the People First Party,

161), but the KMT accelerated the introduction of its national-health program in anticipation of the 1995 legislative elections. Subsequent efforts to address emerging fiscal problems in the new system through the introduction of private insurers quickly fell victim to divisions within the bureaucracy, pressures from KMT legislators, and aggressive action by a broad social coalition of over 200 NGOs (Wong 2004 112, 133). Both the KMT government and its DPP successor delayed even minor adjustments in premiums until September 2002.

In a very short period of time following the transition to competitive electoral politics, the KMT had initiated a national-health-insurance system. This initiative expanded coverage from 57 percent of the population on the eve of its introduction to over 95 percent within two years, with a corresponding surge in both the government's share of total health expenditure and in overall health spending (Ramesh 2003, 367; Wagstaff 2005, 5).

PENSIONS AND OLD-AGE ALLOWANCES

The national debate over pensions unfolded more slowly. Coverage under the labor-insurance system increased gradually over the 1980s and 1990s, but the maximum payout was extremely modest.[5] Surveys of the elderly conducted in the mid-1990s found that only 18 percent of total income came from occupational pensions (Ku 2002, 156), and fully a quarter of all people over 65 had no pension (Chow 2002, 29).[6] In the 1993 elections for mayors and county commissioners, several DPP candidates promised old-age allowances—in effect, a noncontributory pension system. The KMT leadership berated the DPP proposal as blatant vote buying but responded with two "temporary" means-tested allowance schemes for elderly farmers and the low-income elderly. The party also promised to devise a national pension system (Ku 1998, 36–40; 2002, 160; Chiu 2004, 3-4). In 1997, the KMT's candidate for county commissioner of Taipei introduced an old-age allowance proposal backed publicly by President Lee Teng-hui. As Aspalter (2002, 99) argues, "Lee Teng-hui's proposal triggered a chain reaction in local politics. Other KMT candidates were forced by their voters to either propose similar plans . . . or to

---

formed in 2000) supported the KMT in the legislature; the "Pan-KMT" or "Pan-Blue" coalition enjoyed a relatively constant vote share and continued to dominate the legislature through 2004. Nonetheless, the relationship with these new parties was competitive and KMT leaders had to be attentive to coalitional dynamics and threats of defection.

[5] Core KMT constituents such as civil servants and the military were covered under separate and much more generous systems.

[6] The revised Labor Standards Law of 1984 created an additional compulsory occupational pension plan, the so-called Labor Pension, but it was neither vested nor portable; this problem was addressed in later reforms.

advocate a nation-wide old-age allowance system," which the president ultimately did.

In 2000, the DPP presidential candidate Chen Shui-bian ran successfully on a social-welfare platform (the "3-3-3 plan") that included elderly allowances (of NT$3000 a month), subsidized mortgages to first-time buyers (at 3 percent), and government-sponsored healthcare for children under three. The DPP also promised a national pension system after the KMT failed to legislate its own proposal.

Consideration of these initiatives took place under quite different political and economic circumstances, however. The new president faced a legislature controlled by a noncooperative opposition alliance (the so-called "pan-blues," led by the KMT) and the DPP was itself divided on the pension issue between more conservative and more progressive factions. Deadlock ensued.

Economic conditions also changed. Taiwan survived the Asian financial crisis relatively unscathed but experienced a sharp recession in 2001, a continual erosion of revenues, and widening budget deficits. These economic conditions empowered conservatives and technocrats to speak against further social spending, and the Chen government was forced to make overtures to the private sector. The administration backed away from its more ambitious national pension proposals, and sought hybrid formulas that would lessen the government's fiscal commitment.

Despite these setbacks, the Chen administration forwarded legislation for a nationwide monthly pension for those not covered under the existing system. The KMT derided the proposal as vote buying but proposed an even *more* generous plan of its own. In 2003, as elections approached, the law was amended again to expand benefits. In 2004, the government also succeeded in passing a reform that shifted from an employee-specific, nonportable defined-contribution benefit plan to a portable defined-contribution scheme monitored by the central government. Although without the redistributive elements in traditional pay-as-you-go systems, the reform constituted an important expansion of coverage.

LABOR-MARKET POLICIES

Reflecting their reliance on business support and the cross-class nature of their electoral base, both the DPP and KMT initially opposed unemployment insurance. But after 1996, unemployment started to increase steadily, jumping sharply in the recession of 2001 and not declining significantly thereafter. In 1998, the KMT instituted an unemployment-insurance scheme. In the wake of the 2001 recession, the DPP government expanded unemployment insurance to cover firms with as few as four workers as well as part-time employees. A battery of labor-market policies followed: short-run ameliorative measures such as public-works programs, limits on "large-scale" layoffs, subsidies to firms hiring unemployed workers, and a phased reduction of foreign workers in some sectors. Some of these efforts proved highly contentious with the private sector. Labor-intensive sectors such as textiles and apparel lobbied aggressively for labor-market flexibility and continued access to foreign labor; in 2003 the government initiated reforms that increased the ability of firms to use dispatched workers. These fights are a strong reminder that the expansion of social insurance by no means eliminates either political or economic pressures for labor market flexibility.[7]

Korea before the Crisis

Democracy and favorable economic circumstances also had identifiable effects on the expansion of social insurance in Korea. As in Taiwan, the social-insurance system inherited from the authoritarian era was a fragmented and highly unequal one. Although the initial expansion under the conservative governments of Roh Tae Woo and Kim Young Sam was dramatic (see appendix 6), remaining inequities in coverage set the stage for a second round of expansion under the Kim Dae Jung government; we take up in those initiatives in our consideration of the financial crisis.

BUILDING OUT THE NATIONAL HEALTH INSURANCE AND PENSION SYSTEMS

Outside of coverage for the military and government workers, the National Health Insurance, initiated in 1977, constituted the main social-insurance effort prior to the democratic transition. It was initially compulsory only for government employees, teachers, and workers in the very largest firms (500 employees or more). Chun Doo Hwan expanded the system incrementally by allowing the formation of quasi-public insurance societies or health funds, but farmers, the self-employed, and the urban informal sector remained outside the system, leaving total coverage at about 50 percent (Hwang 2006, 87–89). As the political battle was joined to define the nature of the transition from authoritarian rule in 1986, the Chun administration announced its intention to expand health-insurance coverage, as well as a national pension scheme and the introduction of a minimum wage. When the protests of 1987 forced direct elections of the president, Roh Tae Woo integrated these social-policy initiatives into his campaign platform.

---

[7] Dispatched workers reduce costs to the firm since pension, health-insurance, and severance-pay requirements are managed by the dispatching agency. Dispatched workers also fall outside the unemployment-insurance system because periods of unemployment are considered voluntary.

After winning a narrow plurality, the Roh administration extended health insurance to the rural and urban self-employed through an expansion and partial subsidization of existing health funds (Kwon 2003, 78).[8] A new pension law passed in 1988 extended coverage to all firms with ten or more workers (lowered to five workers in 1992) through a funded scheme with a mild redistributive component. The scheme required workers (and employers) to contribute for 20 years before qualifying and thus did not involve any immediate outlays. But benefits were set at a very high level—a replacement rate of 70 percent after 40 years—and bargaining among the government, business and labor yielded contribution rates that were too low for the benefits extended; as a result, the program had financial weaknesses from the outset (Hwang 2006, 73–76; Moon 2001).

Kim Young Sam (1993–98) made further expansion of the pension system part of his election campaign, and in 1995 he extended coverage to farmers, fishermen, and the self-employed in rural areas as compensation for Korean commitments to open the rice market (J. Yang 2000, 115). But an appointed pension-reform commission was divided between liberal reformers arguing that the new system was financially unsustainable and those arguing for more marginal changes or further expansion.[9] The final proposal from the commission sought to balance these contending views, but this reform effort came very late in the Kim Young Sam presidency and did not achieve consensus within the commission. Moreover, the liberal reform proposals were ignored by Kim Young Sam's successor, Kim Dae Jung, who opted for an expansion of the system.

UNEMPLOYMENT INSURANCE

The Chun administration was actively hostile to unemployment insurance on both cost and moral-hazard grounds. Nonetheless, policy entrepreneurs within the social policy bureaucracy developed and promoted a program designed to win support not only from labor but from business and the economic technocrats as well (Yoo et. al. 2002, 287–89; Hwang 2006, 117–22). Strategically renamed an "employment-insurance" system, the proposal combined a mandatory unemployment-insurance scheme with active labor-market programs designed to secure wider support, for example, by subsidizing private training. All three major political parties incorporated variants of the proposal into their party platforms

---

[8] The president vetoed efforts by the opposition in the National Assembly to integrate the financial structure of the health-insurance system to permit greater risk pooling (Kwon 1999a, 65–67); this exact reform was later undertaken by Kim Dae Jung.

[9] Throughout the democratic period, governments have faced strong resistance to any rationalization of the generously funded pension systems for government employees, private teachers, and the military, all of which experienced deterioration in their financial positions (Moon 2001).

prior to the 1992 presidential elections, and final legislation was passed easily in 1993.

Social Assistance and Education in Taiwan and Korea

Briefer mention can be made of two other policy areas that saw important reforms following the transition to democratic rule in Taiwan and Korea: social assistance and education. In Korea, the Roh administration did not seek fundamental changes in the country's minimalist social-assistance program, the Livelihood Protection Act. When the Kim Young Sam administration announced welfare reforms linked to his globalization (*segyehwa*) initiative late in his term, they were conservative and "productivist" in orientation, emphasizing private provision of social services through firms, NGOs, and local community groups (Lee 1999, 30–34; Hwang 2006, 33–34). These proposals did not find their way into legislation, however, and had to await the onset of the economic crisis and the coming of the Kim Dae Jung administration.

In Taiwan, by contrast, the reform of social assistance and services involved more fundamental changes in principles, organization, and funding. Social assistance in Taiwan was historically the responsibility of local governments. In 1979, the KMT government passed an Aged Welfare Law, a Handicapped Welfare Law, and a new Social Assistance Law. But these measures received limited funding and lacked administrative means for enforcement and monitoring; the country did not even have a ministry of social welfare (Chan 1987, 350–51; Ku 1997, 159; Aspalter 2002, 73–80). The reform of these laws became the focus of intense NGO activity, pioneered by particularly effective social movements for the disabled and elderly (Hsiao 2001). In 1997 the KMT government passed amended and more expansive versions of all three acts with further incremental expansion under the DPP government as well (Ho 2005, 408–14).

Korea and Taiwan had achieved universal primary education at the outset of the period and had made important reforms to universalize secondary education as well; as a result, the policy issues in the education sector go beyond our focus on basic social services. Nonetheless, there are parallel reforms in both countries that reflect the influence of democratization. Prior to the transition the educational systems in both countries were highly centralized instruments of political and ideological control and manpower planning. Both countries ultimately undertook sweeping educational reforms through the appointment of independent commissions with wide-ranging mandates.[10] In addition to curricular reforms,

---

[10] In Taiwan, the Council for Education Reform and Review (September 1994–November 1996); in Korea, the Presidential Commissions on Education Reform (February 1994–February 1996 and April 1996–February 1998).

initiatives in both countries included decentralization, greater autonomy for schools and teachers, and wider scope for private provision. In somewhat different ways, the reforms also raised the issue of school choice—a strongly contested issue in Korea—eliminated or reduced the emphasis on centralized examinations, and reduced tracking by changing the prescribed weight given to vocational education at the secondary level. These reforms were still very much in play in both countries at the time we end our account in 2005, but the reforms did reflect a decline in the "developmentalist" approach to educational and manpower planning characteristic of the authoritarian era.

This comparison of Taiwan and Korea brings out differences as well as similarities in the evolution of social policy. Taiwan moved more quickly toward universal healthcare than did Korea and moved more rapidly with respect to expanding social assistance. Governments in Taiwan moved more slowly in changing its pension system and showed a greater revealed preference for cash transfers for the elderly and a defined-contribution approach. Korea developed a national-pension scheme on social-insurance principles, but was slower to address the problem of the elderly who lacked pensions altogether. These differences are interesting ones, and have been the subject of useful comparative research (for example, Ramesh 2003, 2004; J. Wong 2004).

It should also be underscored that the informalization of labor markets opened an important wedge between de jure and de facto entitlements. Yang (2006, 222–26) has shown that both employers and workers in the informal sector evaded payments, with a corresponding loss of social-insurance coverage. As we have seen for Taiwan, and discuss in more detail with respect to Korea below, new labor-market protections were coupled with policy reforms to increase labor-market flexibility.

Despite these important caveats, democratization in the context of strong growth and public finances created high-powered incentives to expand social welfare commitments. Even conservative parties and politicians backed an extension of entitlements, and in a number of important instances, even spearheaded them.

Thailand

As we saw in chapter 3, the democratic interlude of 1973–76 in Thailand gave rise to a rush of social reform proposals including a new labor law, a workmen's-compensation scheme, healthcare schemes for the poor, and education reforms. But the short-lived nature of the democratic experiment blocked implementation of these initiatives.

Following the end of hard authoritarian rule, the military began to liberalize politics and use social-policy initiatives for its own political ends.

In 1976, the military considered social-security legislation as a means of preempting labor unrest, but no legislation was forwarded to parliament except medical insurance for civil servants.[11] But the military did initiate a number of antipoverty programs in response to the rural insurgency (Chai-Anan, Kusung, and Suchit 1990, 104–6). In addition to rural-development schemes, these included a Poverty Alleviation Plan targeting poor districts in the north, northeast, and southern provinces and several primary healthcare initiatives.

One instrument that proved important in subsequent policy developments was the 1983 Community Health Card program (1983, later the Voluntary Health Card Scheme [VHCS]): a voluntary, prepaid insurance program initially targeted at poor provinces and districts (Mills 1991, 1241–52; Donaldson, Supasit, and Viroj 1999, 38–39). The scheme did not receive sustained attention from the transitional governments in the second half of the 1980s, and coverage actually fell (Siripen 1997, 18). Nonetheless, the VHCS marked an important innovation that provided the basis for further expansion in the 1990s (Supasit et. al 2000, 303–11)

EARLY DEMOCRATIC INITIATIVES THROUGH THE 1991 COUP

The politics of social policy changed quite dramatically as politicians gained ground against the military beginning in the mid-1980s and as the economy took off into a period of sustained growth. In 1983, a coalition of political parties defeated efforts by the military to maintain a number of political prerogatives, and an influx of office-seeking provincial elites and businessmen transformed the political parties. The Prem government advanced a social-security bill to the legislature, but it did not pass. By contrast, the first popularly-elected prime minister, Chatichai Choonhavan (1988–91), endorsed a contributory social-insurance scheme almost immediately on coming to office. The proposal provided health insurance and maternity and death benefits for workers in firms with twenty or more employees. Parliamentary consideration of the legislation further expanded benefits, accelerated the timetable for introducing the plan, and mandated government contributions to the scheme. The parliamentary bill also promised to introduce pensions and family allowances within six years and called on the king to introduce an unemployment scheme. The bill set in train a constitutional conflict with the conservative senate, but the parliament unanimously overrode the senate in an important display of constitutional power in July 1990, and the program was implemented despite the coup of 1991.

---

[11] See Baker and Phongpaichit 2002, 210–11 and Reinecke 1993, 82. See also Brown and Frenkel (1993) on the labor movement.

It is important to underline the modesty of these early social-insurance initiatives when compared with Korea and Taiwan. In 1993, the new system covered only 2.5 percent of the population, overwhelmingly urban and therefore overwhelmingly in Bangkok. After the return to democracy in 1991, however, the scheme underwent incremental expansion by allowing the self-employed to join the system on a voluntary basis and by making contributions compulsory for firms with more than ten employees (Supasit al. 2000, table 8, 309).

FROM THE RETURN OF DEMOCRACY TO THE CRISIS (1992–97)

The health-card system underwent a much more dramatic expansion following the return to democratic rule. In 1993, near the height of the government's fiscal surpluses, the government moved to directly subsidize the purchase of health cards. A series of initiatives in the early 1990s also expanded the scope of the Low Income Card Scheme (LICS). Since the distribution of cards was in the hands of local officials and involved targeting, it was vulnerable to patronage (Kuhonta 2003, 100). Yet the expansion of the LICS also included the distribution of cards to those clearly in need, beginning with a Free Medical Care for the Elderly Scheme (initiated in 1992). Similar programs followed piecemeal for other disadvantaged groups, including low-income primary- and secondary-school students, infants, and the handicapped. On the eve of the financial crisis, the various targeted health-card schemes provided at least some coverage to about 70 percent of the population (Siripen 2000, table 1, p. 87).

As with health insurance, the pension system in Thailand was highly fragmented and expanded more slowly (Niwat 2004, 5–12). The defined-benefit pension scheme mandated by the 1990 Social Security Act covered only 22 percent of the private-sector workforce by 2004 and only 5 percent enjoyed the private provident funds to which the public effort was presumably supplementary (Niwat 2004, 7).[12] However, prior to the expansion of the 1980s, only the public sector enjoyed mandated coverage.[13]

As we saw in chapter 3, Thailand was a relative laggard with respect to education. Six years of primary education was not made compulsory until 1980. Despite a subsidy scheme to increase secondary enrollments in rural areas introduced in 1987, education did not receive sustained attention during the early period of political liberalization. Between 1980 and 1990, both the share of the population that had attended primary

---

[12] As in Korea, benefits only accrued after a stipulated payment period, and as a result, the Old Age Pension Fund was projected to accrue surpluses through 2014.

[13] Public-sector workers enjoyed a generous defined-benefit pension program financed directly out of the budget. As in several other Asian countries, teachers also operated under a preferential pension scheme. On the highly limited reforms of these systems, see Niwat 2004.

school or completed secondary schooling actually fell (Witte 2000, 225). Education policy changed dramatically following the return to democratic rule in 1991, however, when a confluence of political forces including politicians, the IFIs, technocrats and portions of the private sector combined to push a dramatic expansion of education spending.[14] Thailand's gross secondary enrollment ratio increased from 40 percent to nearly 75 percent between 1993 and 1998. Although increased enrollment undoubtedly reflected rising incomes and increasing returns, government spending increased as well. The 1997 constitution, described in more detail below, expanded compulsory education to twelve years.

Prior to the financial crisis, the gradual nature of Thailand's transition and structural features of the economy made for a more cautious expansion of social insurance when compared to Korea or even Taiwan. The piecemeal expansion of the system reflected distinctive institutional features of Thai democracy and implied inequality in coverage and financing, patronage, and leakage to politically significant constituencies (Warr and Isra 2004, 9–20). Nonetheless, the transition to democratic rule saw a renewed attention to rural poverty, expanded coverage of basic social services, and fundamental changes in principles with respect to the financing of social insurance, particularly with respect to health. Moreover, these initiatives provided the basis for a further expansion of coverage following the Asian financial crisis under the conservative-populist government of Thaksin Shinawatra; we discuss those initiatives in more detail below.

The Philippines

The transition to democratic rule generated strong political incentives to address the myriad social problems that had accumulated under the Marcos dictatorship. Each new administration—Corazon Aquino (1986–92), Fidel Ramos (1992–98), Joseph Estrada (1998–2001), and the first Gloria Macapagal-Arroyo government (2001–2004, when we stop our account)—came to office making social-policy promises (Reyes 2002, 37–40, 42). Throughout the new democratic period, we see a number of important social-policy initiatives. However, the Philippines underwent the transition to democracy in highly adverse economic circumstances and witnessed more erratic performance than the other new democracies. The Aquino administration enjoyed a degree of good will from the international financial institutions and donors, but the administration was also saddled with a highly controversial foreign and domestic debt burden

---

[14] The information is based in part on UNESCO 2000.

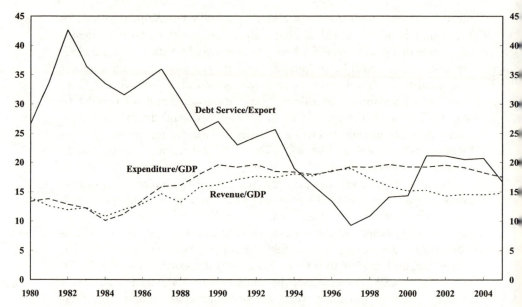

Figure 6.4. Philippines' expenditure, revenue, and debt service as a share of GDP, 1980–2005. *Source*: World Development Indicators (World Bank 2007).

(figure 6.4). Growth in the last two years of Aquino's term was interrupted by a political-economic crisis—rapidly increasing fiscal deficits and another stabilization episode (1990–92). The economic reforms and recovery of the Ramos years fell victim to the Asian financial crisis and a particularly severe El Niño shock. Estrada ran on a populist platform in the midst of these difficulties in 1998, but his initiatives were also interrupted by the political-cum-economic crisis of 2000–2001 that led to his ouster. Moreover, the country experienced a secular deterioration in revenues beginning in the late 1990s that continued into the Macapagal-Arroyo administration.

Successive Philippine governments thus faced recurrent fiscal constraints and pressures to stabilize—in 1990–91; at the time of the Asian financial crisis in 1997–98, and again in the early 2000s. We find evidence that social policy initiatives tracked the business cycle: recovery allowed new policy initiatives, most notably under Ramos, but downturns were followed by policy initiatives being put on hold, reversed, or funded at reduced levels (see also figure A6.12). We also see evidence that a number of Philippine social-policy initiatives were targeted and reversible rather than in the form of new entitlements, a pattern we see in the Latin American crisis cases as well.

THE AQUINO YEARS

Given the high incidence of rural poverty—as well as the rapid growth and spread of the armed insurgency in the mid-1980s (Kessler 1989)—it is not surprising that Aquino placed particular emphasis on the countryside. The government dismantled the agricultural monopolies that had such an adverse impact on small farmers and launched a controversial Comprehensive Agrarian Reform Program (CARP).[15] The administration's first major social initiative was a temporary antipoverty program, the Community Employment and Development Program (CEDP), that used local infrastructure spending to create jobs in rural areas. The new administration also sought to expand the provision of basic social services, and engaged the rapidly growing NGO sector in the policymaking process toward this end.[16] Dramatically increased external funding from international financial institutions supported a variety of basic health initiatives that carried over into subsequent administrations, such as renewed effort to achieve universal childhood immunization.

Education saw the most dramatic increases in spending (appendix 6). The constitution, drafted by Aquino appointees and ratified in 1987, stipulated that education should receive the largest share of the budget and made secondary education free. Primary enrollment increased steadily in the first decade following the transition, and secondary enrollments jumped sharply following the constitutional initiative in 1988 and the nationalization of secondary schools, most of which had previously been run by local governments and financed by fees. These expansion measures did not meet their underlying educational objectives, but the fault is not to be found solely or even primarily in fiscal constraints. Legislative biases toward school-building and salary increases reinforced a long-standing bias in favor of expansion over quality improvements (Mingat 1998, 707; Manasan 2000, 6–9). The nationalization of secondary schools, popular as a status and pork-barrel issue with legislators but opposed by education planners, actually shifted the allocation of basic education spending away from primary toward secondary education.

Nonetheless, fiscal constraints did play a role in the reversal of gains in education performance that occurred under the Aquino and Ramos administrations. A 2000 assessment concludes that a combination of underinvestment and misallocation of resources had resulted in continuing problems with respect to repeats and drop-outs in both elementary and

---

[15] On land reform see Putzel (1992), Reyes (2002), and particularly Riedinger (1995), who argues that in the absence of progressive political parties, democratic transitions will not result in redistributive reforms.

[16] For overviews, see Silliman and Noble (1998), Bennagen (2000), and Reyes (2002, 44–48), on changing institutional arrangements.

secondary schools, persistently low test scores, significant and extensive pockets of educational disadvantage and inequality across regions, and a mismatch between labor-market needs and the education and training system (Human Development Network and United Nations Development Program 2000, 1–17).

Beginning in late 1989, the Aquino administration was hit by a near-perfect storm of political crises (including a serious coup attempt in December 1989), a succession of natural disasters (from earthquake, to typhoons and the eruption of Mt. Pinatubo), and the spike in oil prices associated with the first Gulf War. In the face of low tax collections and a large debt-service overhang, the government could pursue a more expansive social agenda only at the cost of more borrowing, confrontation with lenders, or monetization of the deficits and inflation. Some in the Aquino government made the case that the government should take a more militant stance with respect to debt repayment in order to free resources for other priorities. But these alternative strategies became more risky in 1991–92, when the country experienced a major deterioration in government finances and strong external and internal pressure for fiscal consolidation. During its last two years, the Aquino administration generated new rural developments and targeted antipoverty programs, but these were not implemented for lack of funding (Balisacan 1993, 9–10).

One of the most consequential reforms of the Aquino administration for subsequent social policy was the legislation of the Local Government Code (LGC) in 1991. Decentralization was enshrined in the 1987 constitution. Although motivated primarily by the centralizing excesses of the Marcos period, short-run fiscal constraints also played a role in the passage of the LGC, as it did in a number of the Latin American crisis cases we take up in the next chapter.[17] The LGC gradually increased the transfer of resources (through the so-called Internal Revenue Allotment, or IRA) from 20 to 40 percent of collected taxes in return for a devolution of a number of functions including both health and social welfare services (although not initially education, which followed only in 2001).

Congress and the ministries diluted the extent of devolution, for example by initially excluding education. Pressures from highly mobilized ministry-of-health workers and local politicians also forced some recentralization under the Ramos administration. Nonetheless, the LGC granted substantial discretion to local-level governments and opened new arenas of electoral competition, NGO activity, and policy innovation. The effects of democratization were also visible at the local level: local government

---

[17] For an overview of the politics of decentralization, see Hutchcroft 2003. Capuno (1999) shows the role of fiscal constraints with respect to decentralization of health care in particular.

units (LGUs) paid greater attention to social issues—controlling for the effect of devolved functions—although with somewhat different emphases from those used by the national government. However, the fiscal constraints operating at the national level had consequences for local administrations. During the financial crisis of 1998, in particular, the president asserted his right to reduce mandated transfers in the face of fiscal exigency, a decision the local governments were unable to reverse until they were helped by a Supreme Court ruling in 2004.

RECOVERY UNDER RAMOS

With the presidential elections falling in the midst of an economic downturn, all candidates emphasized social-policy issues in their campaigns. In his inaugural speech, Ramos promised a "war on poverty," and one of his first acts as president was the appointment of presidential commissions to fight poverty and on countryside development. However, the new administration was initially forced to rectify the country's deteriorating fiscal position by restraining expenditures and focusing on a number of major economic-policy reforms. Not coincidentally, the early years of the Ramos administration were also taken up with institutional reforms designed to improve the efficiency of the social ministries.[18] Only as the country saw a gradual return to growth and easing of fiscal constraints, did a new round of social-policy initiatives follow.

Although NGOs pressured the government to maintain its commitment to CARP and asset distribution (Bennagen 2000), the administration placed primary emphasis on the delivery of basic social services and "empowerment." The main antipoverty program to come out of the "war on poverty" was the Social Reform Agenda (SRA), a complex, multisector program that included a variety of new initiatives. Several features of this initiative are salient for our comparative purposes. First, the conceptual core of the SRA was a "minimum basic needs" approach based on geographical targeting; as in Latin America, targeting reflected both political and ideological principles and fiscal constraints. The most important of the so-called "flagship" programs was the Comprehensive and Integrated Delivery of Social Services (CIDSS) based on geographic targeting of the so-called basic sectors[19] in poor barangays within poor municipalities (Bautista 1999a, for an overview). CIDSS workers would in effect act as

[18] These reforms included redefining the role of the departments of health and social welfare and development in the wake of decentralization and breaking up ("trifocalization") the sprawling department of education, culture and sports.

[19] The "basic sectors" included farmers-peasants, artisanal workers, fishers, workers in the formal sector and migrant workers, workers in the informal sector, indigenous peoples and cultural communities, women, the differently abled, senior citizens, victims of calamities and disasters, youth and students, children, and the urban poor.

policy entrepreneurs in mobilizing public and private support for targeted interventions, from daycare centers and nutrition-and-health interventions to livelihood programs and improved access to clean water and sanitary toilets. The program was supported both by a reallocation of the budgets of the line ministries and by new, dedicated sources of funding in the form of annual Poverty Alleviation Funds.[20] Not coincidentally, however, a second underlying principle of the program that reflected both Christian democratic ideas and ongoing fiscal concerns was the concept of "convergence": that social initiatives should not be limited to national or even local governments but should engage and mobilize resources from the churches, the private sector, NGOs, and households themselves.

The Ramos administration undertook some parametric reforms of the core social-security institutions—the Social Security System (SSS) and the Government Services Insurance System (GSIS)—that expanded benefits and coverage and allowed workers to borrow against their accumulations. More significant, however, was a major reform of the public-health-insurance system. As we saw in chapter 3, the Medicare system established during the Marcos years provided benefits for formal-sector workers and government employees enrolled in the SSS and GSIS, with a strong role for private provision; prior to the reform, Medicare covered approximately 40 percent of the population (Beringuela 1995, 9). As in Latin America, the crisis of 1990–91, the opaque cross-subsidization between the pension and health systems and the administrative inefficiencies in the SSS and GSIS constituted important motives for the reform. The reform would also provide some relief for both the national government and the local governments, which continued to provide a substantial share of all care through public hospitals and clinics. By shifting to social insurance, these costs would be borne to a greater extent by employers and employees.[21]

A major difference from a number of the Latin American cases, however, was that Medicare enjoyed a substantial surplus at the time of the reform that could be used to facilitate a transition to wider coverage; bringing the better-off self-employed into the system was also seen as a plus. The final law, passed in 1995, made coverage under the renamed PhilHealth universal and mandatory, albeit with a permissive fifteen-year timetable (later extended to 2012) for doing so. Although a contributory social-insurance system in principle, the legislation required the national and subnational governments to fully subsidize the contributions of the

[20] PAF-1 was appropriated in 1996; PAF-2 and PAF-3 received diminished funding in 1997–98.

[21] Decentralization of healthcare and the expansion of public health insurance also spurred reforms of the ministry of health under the Estrada administration, including measures such as corporatization of hospitals, more effective cost controls, and regulation of the health sector.

indigent. As the indigent were ultimately defined, they accounted for no less than 25 percent of the entire population. LGU capacity to meet this requirement clearly constituted a constraint on coverage, but Arroyo-Macapagal made the implementation of the commitment to universal coverage a political priority after her assumption of the presidency in 2001, with campaign promises in early 2004 that would lift enrollment to nearly 90 percent. This objective was to be met through publicity efforts, by shifting subsidies back to the national level, through lottery earnings, and through the highly controversial distribution of health cards during the 2004 electoral campaign.

Although the Philippines did not experience the degree of economic distress of the so-called most seriously affected countries, the regionwide crisis of 1997–98 nonetheless marked another swing in the policy cycle as the government was forced to make large cuts in appropriations. A World Bank review of the social sectors argued strongly that the crisis was an opportunity to rationalize the management of social spending; the World Bank's priorities included "inefficient procurement, poor deployment of teachers, severe underfunding of textbooks and school maintenance, public health programs, and welfare institutions, creeping renationalization of devolved hospitals, [and] proliferation of low quality universities and colleges" (World Bank 1998, ii). The government sought to reallocate at the margin in order to defend social spending and even to initiate new social-safety-net programs, such as an increase in food subsidies, a new public-employment program, and an expansion of existing microfinance programs (Economic and Social Commission for Asia and the Pacific 2001, 8–41). Nonetheless, core components of the SRA saw sharp declines in funding (Bautista 1999a, 40).

FROM ESTRADA TO ARROYO-MACAPAGAL

The 1998 elections came in the midst of the Asian financial crisis. Movie actor Joseph "Erap" Estrada ran on an openly populist platform that included a lavish propoor agenda (Balisacan 2001). His Caring for the Poor ("Lingap Para sa Mahirap," or simply Lingap) program marked a sharp departure from the Ramos administration. Rather than the wider targeting of disadvantaged regions, municipalities, and groups, the Lingap sought to identify the poorest hundred families in each province and city and to focus welfare efforts on them; by one estimate, this approach would reach only 16,000 families, or 0.4 percent of all poor families. Total funds devoted to the Lingap program were less than those devoted to the SRA, but a higher share of those funds were under the direct control of the president or delegated to legislators rather than passing through the LGUs. This change in design implied an even higher-than-normal diversion of social spending into pork-barrel activities.

But poverty policy was only emblematic of much deeper management problems that plagued the Estrada administration's social-policy efforts: the organizational disarray in the policymaking process; the weakening of various social policy institutions, including the use of social-security funds for personal gain and the corruption of the national housing program through the involvement of business associates and cronies; the weakening of already deficient program-evaluation mechanisms; and the steady deterioration of public revenues, which had fallen from 19 percent of GDP in 1995 to barely 14 percent of GDP at the time his ouster. In the end, even these problems were eclipsed by a sustained impeachment crisis and mass demonstrations that ultimately resulted in Estrada's ouster.[22]

As in Taiwan, Korea, and Thailand, the transition to democracy in the Philippines was accompanied by greater attention to social issues than had been the case under authoritarian rule. The change in regime was followed by a constitutional commitment to education spending, the initiation of a universal health insurance system, and a plethora of antipoverty efforts centered on improving social-service delivery. Evaluations of these programs are mixed, and their problems can by no means be attributed to fiscal constraints alone; distinctive institutional features of Philippine democracy were also consequential. However, when compared to the pre-Asian financial-crisis experience of Taiwan, Korea, and Thailand, it is clear that Philippine social policy was vulnerable to recurrent fiscal constraints: at the outset of the Aquino administration; at the end of her administration in 1990–91; during the Asian financial crisis in 1997–98; and yet again during and following the political crisis of 2000–2001.

THE DOMINANT-PARTY CASES: SINGAPORE AND MALAYSIA

As figure 6.1 suggests, the dominant-party systems in Singapore and Malaysia exhibit substantial political continuity; indeed, the two polities arguably became less competitive and open over time. To the extent that governments undertook social-policy reforms, they tended to reflect the liberal social-policy agenda outlined in chapter 5. Such initiatives were particularly visible in Singapore, which also continued to exhibit a strong "developmentalist" approach to social services such as education. In Malaysia, UMNO governments continued to focus on their core political base in the Malay community, but even these redistributive policies underwent shifts that made them less progressive in nature.

---

[22] For overviews of the administration, see Doronila 2001 and Laquian and Laquian 2002.

Singapore

In chapter 3, we argued that the redistributive purposes of social policy in the politically competitive independence period gradually gave way to a more liberal welfare model as the PAP achieved single-party dominance and adopted an export-oriented growth strategy after 1968. Particularly during economic downturns—the mid-1980s, 1997–98, and 2001—or periods of inflation, opposition parties and policy intellectuals raised social issues and the government responded with new initiatives. However, of all the Asian cases in our sample, Singapore unquestionably shows the greatest continuity with its earlier welfare model: generous publicly funded benefits for state employees and strong support for education and vocational training, coupled with minimal direct state involvement in financing of social insurance, the absence of risk pooling, strong resistance to unemployment insurance of any sort, and a residualist system of social assistance that relied heavily on NGOs and the family.

The Central Provident Fund (CPF), which operates on nearly pure defined-contribution principles, has remained the central social-policy institution in Singapore. The basic principles governing the CPF changed little between 1985 and 2005. The government continued to exercise discretion over the setting of contribution rates but made a concession to the growing middle class by gradually expanding investment options. In 1981, the government allowed individuals to make withdrawals to purchase non-HDB residential properties (the Residential Properties Scheme), to upgrade existing flats (1989), and even to buy nonresidential real estate (Non-Residential Properties Scheme, 1986). A similar process of incremental changes occurred with respect to financial-investment options, including allowing beneficiaries to invest in foreign equities (Low and Aw 1997, 70–84). These policies shifted risk quite dramatically and had particularly adverse consequences during the financial crisis when members pursuing these outside options experienced steep losses (Asher 2004, 12).

The high level of withdrawal for housing purchases raised concerns that retirees would be left "asset rich and cash poor" (McCarthy, Mitchell, and Piggott 2001, 10–20; Low and Aw 1997, 177–89). In 1977, the government created the Special Account to assure that a certain share of total contributions was reserved for retirement, and in 1987 it insisted that a certain minimum sum had to be used to buy a private annuity, left with the CPF, or deposited in approved banks.[23] Nonetheless, despite very high contribution rates—peaking at 40 percent, shared between employers and

---

[23] The government also encouraged additional private and family savings through a succession of "topping up" schemes that provided incentives for individuals to make additional contributions for themselves or their parents.

employees—a combination of a high rate of preretirement withdrawals, technical difficulties in reverse mortgages, modest returns, and an unequal wage structure combined to produce a relatively low average replacement rate, probably in the 25–35 percent range (McCarthy, Mitchell, and Piggott 2001, figure 3, 38; Asher 2004, table 5, 23; Ramesh 2004, 73–74).

In contrast to Korea and Taiwan, health policy took a decidedly liberal turn in Singapore beginning in the 1980s. In 1983, the government announced a National Health Plan that sought to reduce the share of total health expenditures borne by the government by increasing private financing and provision (Ramesh and Holliday 2001, 643–44; Ramesh 2003, 364–65). One component of this effort was the creation of a compulsory Medisave account within the CPF for hospital care, an innovation that sparked a sharp international debate over the pros and cons of this means of financing (Hsiao 1995, Hsiao 2001; Barr 2001; Pauly 2001; Lim 2004). Given that the average amount deposited was inadequate to insure against serious contingencies, the government supplemented Medisave with a publicly managed voluntary health-insurance scheme called Medishield in 1990 (Lim 2004, 3; Barr 2001, 712). By the early 2000s, however, the scheme accounted for only 10 percent of total healthcare financing.[24] Outside of continuing subsidies to government hospitals, the only redistributive component of the healthcare system was a means-tested social-assistance scheme introduced in 1993, Medifund, that financed full or partial waiver of expenses incurred at government hospitals and clinics.

By the mid-2000s, Singapore had the lowest share of total health spending to GDP among the Asian cases, the lowest share of government spending to total spending, and the highest dependence on out-of-pocket expenditures (Wagstaff 2005, 5–7; Ramesh 2007). The preference for efficiency and cost control was not coupled with blind devotion to market-oriented solutions, however. Rather, it was achieved in part through policy measures that have proven difficult if not impossible to introduce under more democratic auspices in which hospitals and doctors' associations are more powerful: price caps and cost controls on government hospitals, overall control of the share of specialists in the medical profession, and even a tightened control on the supply of doctors (Barr 2001, 714).

Singapore undertook a number of important educational and training innovations from the mid-1980s. From one perspective, these changes marked a departure in focus, as Sharpe and Gopinathan (2002, 154) put it, from an "efficiency-driven" system that was "highly centralized, stan-

---

[24] The remainder comes from employer benefits, out-of-pocket expenses, private insurance and subsidies which continue to operate through the capital expenditure of the ministry of health, and differential user fees at public hospitals.

dardized, hierarchical, competitive, and efficient" to an "ability-driven system" designed to position Singapore in a knowledge-based economy. But these reforms did not result from electoral pressures or demands from parents and students. Rather, reform was the result of a succession of government-led planning exercises and changing perceptions of labor-market needs. When compared with the situation in Taiwan and Korea, Singapore's educational system exhibited a number of important continuities with the "developmental state" period: tight government control over educational opportunity; an extraordinarily strong coupling between the education and training systems and labor-market needs; and greater experimentation with market- and efficiency-oriented reforms.[25]

Given Lee Kuan Yew's caustic views of the welfare state, only the briefest of words need be said about social assistance and support for the unemployed in Singapore. Government departments support job training, course-fee subsidization, counseling, and job-data-bank services for the unemployed, but Singapore does not provide any transfers to the unemployed per se. The unemployed can get short-term financial assistance from a number of public-assistance schemes, most notably the Public Assistance Scheme. But this scheme is limited to those "who by reason of age, illness, disability or unfavorable family circumstances, are unable to work and have no means of subsistence as well as no one to depend upon." Despite these limitations, only half of all applications are approved (Ramesh 2004, 74; Cheung 2000, 6). Moral hazard is repeatedly cited by Singapore officials as the reason for this limited approach to social assistance. As Asher and Nandy (2006, 12) summarize succinctly, "the fiscal constraint is not a factor . . . the main constraint is the current socio-political norms which do not regard provision of a floor level of income as an essential element of a good society."

Malaysia

As we saw in chapter 3, early Malaysian governments focused attention on the provision of basic social services to their Malay base. The New Economic Policy (NEP) sought to reduce poverty and interethnic inequalities through a program of affirmative action for the bumiputra. The ascent of Mahathir in 1981 and the economic downturn of the mid-1980s, however, produced a gradual shift in Malaysia's development strategy that had social-policy correlates (Jesudason 1989; Jomo 1994; Gomez and Jomo 1997). One component of this new approach was more direct support for the Malaysian private sector by various means, including through

---

[25] For discussions of the Singapore education model, see Wong 1993; Kuruvilla and Chua 2000; Ritchie 2001; Kuruvilla, Erickson, and Hwang 2002.

deregulation, restraint in the growth of state-owned enterprises, and outright privatization (albeit to favored firms). A second key component of the new strategy was greater openness to, and incentives for, direct foreign investment, renewed attention to exports, and renewed concern about direct and indirect labor costs; in short, changes that in some ways mirrored the earlier shifts in development strategy seen in the "first tier" of newly industrializing countries discussed in part 1. Although we see continuity in many components of Malaysia's social policy, there is also evidence of a shift away from the redistributive aims of the NEP that mirrors developments in Singapore. These differences with the democracies were also evident during the Asian financial crisis; we take up that comparison in the following section.

As in Singapore, the social-insurance system in Malaysia has been anchored by a central provident fund, the Employees Provident Fund (EPF). The EPF covers less of the workforce than does Singapore's CPF, roughly half of the economically active population in the mid-1990s. The self-employed, the informal sector, and farmers and fishermen fall outside the system. Moreover, the replacement rate almost certainly falls below the fund's target of 50 percent, and despite the absence of firm data on the question, is probably close to the Singapore range.[26]

As in Singapore, the EPF started out as a pure defined-contribution retirement-savings program. In 1995 members' accounts were divided into three to allow investment in housing (account 2, 30 percent) and medical care (account 3, 10 percent); as in Singapore, this innovation was related to broader efforts to reform healthcare financing and to control costs. In 1996, similar although more cautious changes allowed members to invest some portion of their core account in securities. As in Singapore, but with a delay (2004), the government also began to consider ways to guarantee income adequacy by deferring withdrawals.

Also as in Singapore, Malaysia inherited a British-style public-health-care sector. The UMNO initially pursued a public, equity-oriented approach to healthcare provision and financing as a component of the party's strategy of attending to its rural Malay base. Clinics in rural areas provided services free of charge at the point of delivery. Public hospitals, mostly in urban areas, maintained a much higher share of beds with nominal fees than in Singapore (Ramesh and Holliday 2001, 645–46).

Following a review of financing in 1983 and the economic downturn of the mid-1980s, the government began to move away from this model. Not all of Mahathir's liberalizing initiatives were implemented, in part because of effective lobbying by NGOs and doctors who remained in the

---

[26] See Asher (1994, 26–27), Ramesh (2000, 47), Thillainathan (2004), and Caraher (2000) for overviews of institutional issues related to the EPF.

public sector (Barraclough 1999, 61–64). Most notably, the outright privatization of hospitals was quietly dropped after being mentioned in the Seventh Malaysia Plan (1996–2000) and in 1998, the Private Healthcare and Facilities Service Act established a more expansive regulatory role for the government in insuring quality care. Efforts to shift toward a social-insurance model that separated healthcare financing from the budget (the National Health Security Fund) were also blocked by a coalition of civil-society groups fearful that such a reform would be a prelude to a further erosion of the public sector role (Hong 2006, 10–14).

Nonetheless, hospitals were gradually corporatized and encouraged to compete with private providers beginning in the 1990s, and the private share of total provision expanded rapidly, sparking intense debates in the early 2000s about the exodus of doctors from the public to the private sector. Medical services and the country's drug distribution system were also privatized. Government plans continued to allude to the private sector's attaining parity with the public sector in provision but without any parallel movement to expand social insurance or coverage as was the case in Korea, Taiwan, and Thailand.

Briefer words can be said about education and poverty reduction. The National Education Policy (1961) provided for universal free education for all Malays as well as automatic promotion through grade nine. The adoption of Malay as the medium of instruction (extended to secondary schools in 1982) and the aggressive school building in rural schools had the effect both of dramatically increasing enrollments, steadily narrowing inter-ethnic educational attainment (Pong 1993, 254–57), and favoring the poor (Meerman 1979, 616–20).[27] These entitlements constituted a powerful restraint on liberalizing reforms; any reconsideration of either preferences or language policy has effectively been off the table. UMNO governments increased support for Chinese and Indian-language primary and secondary schools for electoral reasons, and a 1996 reform expanded private tertiary education. In contrast to reform efforts in the democracies, however, reform did not reduce the high level of political control and centralization of the educational system; indeed, it extended it to the regulation of private schooling (Hwang 2003, 253–55). Reform was also motivated (if not always effectively) by an effort to meet labor-market needs for more skilled workers in line with the country's shift toward a more export-oriented policy approach (Ritchie 2005, 282–85).

There are intriguing parallels between Singapore's approach to social assistance and Malaysia's approach to poverty. In 1989, the Malaysian

---

[27] The NEP also introduced affirmative action into tertiary education by establishing quotas at the highly selective national universities and reserving scholarships for Malay students.

government acknowledged for the first time that it had reached the limits of employment generation as a strategy for poverty eradication and established the Development Program for the Hardcore Poor. The program did include direct financial assistance on a means-tested basis to poor households headed by the disabled or elderly as well as housing and training. The core of the program, however, were income-generating projects such as petty trading, cottage industries, and agricultural projects. As the government itself put it, "the main strategy for poverty eradication was providing employment opportunities in higher-paying jobs, while welfare handouts were reserved for the aged and disabled who could not find employment" (Government of Malaysia, Economic Planning Unit 2002, 3). In an Islamic version of subsidiarity, the government expected that these programs would be complemented by social welfare NGOs, private corporations, and the *zakat* system of charity managed by the religious councils of the states.

The continuities we see in the social policies of Singapore and Malaysia were undoubtedly affected by a particular British social-policy legacy that differed from those in the other four countries in our sample. The central provident funds established under the British created a pure defined-contribution mechanism that proved functional for subsequent political leadership, and the public-health systems inherited from the British constituted a social-policy legacy that constrained subsequent governments. Yet politics clearly mattered as well. New democratic governments in Korea and Taiwan also inherited pension systems and fundamentally modified and expanded them. Korea and Taiwan developed universal health-insurance schemes as Singapore and Malaysia were explicitly rejecting them and seeking efficiency improvements through privatization. At lower levels of income per capita than in Singapore, Korea, and Taiwan developed unemployment insurance and undertook both educational and antipoverty reforms that marked a sharp departure with past practice. Moreover, these reforms also occurred through political processes that differed quite fundamentally from the top-down approach to social-policy planning visible in Singapore in particular, with more active roles for electoral politics and the legislature, NGOs, and interest groups.

The Asian Financial Crisis

The Asian financial crisis was a singular event in the region's economic history and the literature on it and on the social dimensions of the crisis is voluminous. Sophisticated monitoring work has tracked the effect of the crisis on different income groups (for reviews, see Birdsall and Haggard 2003; Fallon and Lucas 2002), and we have a number of reviews of the short-term social-policy responses to the crisis (Economic and Social Commission for Asia and the Pacific 2001; Atinc 2003). More germane to our purposes is the debate on whether IMF prescriptions limited the ability of governments to respond to social distress through greater social expenditure (contrast, for example, Lane et al. 1999 and Stiglitz 2002). As we argued in chapter 5, we expect such fiscal constraints to limit spending directly but also to affect the politics of social policy.

However, the East Asian crisis countries exhibit a number of differences with the countries in Latin America and Eastern Europe. They did not inherit a legacy of costly social commitments, and those that had recently developed could not plausibly be linked to the fiscal problems governments faced in the short-run. Moreover, recovery across the region was relatively rapid. As a result, pressures for liberal reform were limited, and the longer-run process of extending entitlements in the high-growth democracies continued in the wake of the crisis, particularly as growth returned.

Korea

The presidential election that brought the Kim Dae Jung government to office in December 1997 occurred only a month following the onset of the financial crisis in Korea. The new administration faced an immediate dilemma with respect to labor. With a large share of the workforce in the formal sector, unemployment was higher than in the other countries, and there were fewer opportunities for the rural and informal sectors to absorb displaced workers. Although the overall level of unionization was low, the high degree of industrial concentration had resulted in fairly strong and militant unions in the larger enterprises (*chaebol*).

But the administration was also under intense pressure from the IMF, the United States, and creditors to increase the flexibility of labor markets in order to facilitate the corporate restructuring process. To secure agreement to greater labor-market flexibility, Kim Dae Jung resorted to a tripartite commission that allowed the government to bring representatives from both labor federations (Federation of Korean Trade Unions, FKTU, and Korean Confederation of Trade Unions, KCTU) to the table (Kim and Lim 1999; Song 2003; Hwang 2006, 128–38). After weeks of intense debate, the government extracted an agreement from labor to permit layoffs when "urgently" needed or in case of takeovers and to allow the formation of a manpower-leasing system for both specialized professions and laborers. In return, the government made a number of political concessions to labor, including the right of civil servants to form a labor consultative body, of teachers to unionize, and the reversal of a long-standing prohibition on labor involvement in political activities. More vaguely, "all parties" would work to minimize layoffs and seek alternative solutions such as work sharing. The two sides saw the agreement very differently, however. Management believed it had gained greater freedom to retrench; labor believed that the terms of the bargain were not enforced. Over the next year, the government intervened to break a number of strikes, leading the more independent KCTU to pull out of the second tripartite process in February 1999 and effectively bringing the tripartite experiment to a close.

Despite the ambiguous reviews of the tripartite experiment and the administration's stormy relations with labor, the government did honor its commitment to expand the social safety net. Some initiatives were temporary components of a gradual turn—with IMF acquiescence—to a countercyclical fiscal stance (Moon and Yang 2002, 8–10). In 1998, fully 10 percent of the national budget was allocated for short-run ameliorative measures of various sorts.[28]

But the Kim Dae Jung government's response to the crisis was not just for the short term. Rather, the government continued to expand all the major social-insurance programs—pensions, health insurance, and unemployment insurance—while fundamentally changing the principles guiding social assistance. These reforms were bundled into a "productive welfare" initiative in August 1999 that showed some continuity with the "productivist" approach of his predecessors (Moon and Yang 2002 188–97).[29] But Kim also spoke of social welfare and employment as citizenship rights.

With respect to pensions, the new government explicitly rejected the liberalizing proposals of Kim Young Sam's pension-reform commission and assigned the task of drawing up a new proposal to the ministry of health and welfare (Yang 2000, 135–45). The ministry proposals sought to put the pension system on a more sound financial footing through regularly scheduled increases in both premiums and the retirement age and a new benefit formula that lowered the average replacement rate (from 60 to 55 percent). Yet the plan rejected proposals to separate the redistributive from the earnings-related portion of the scheme. It also took the difficult step of extending coverage to the heterogeneous urban self-employed. This sector included professionals such as doctors and lawyers as well as informal sector workers who strongly opposed inclusion in the system and the contributions it required. Moreover, the political process diluted the government's efforts to rationalize the existing scheme. The national

[28] These included a public-works program that supported 437,000 workers by February 1999; labor subsidies for small and medium-sized firms; temporary extension of unemployment benefits; a temporary livelihood program that covered 750,000 people by 1999; and scholarships for children of the unemployed.

[29] On the concept of a productivist welfare system, see Holliday 2000.

assembly rejected the lowering of the replacement rate, and World Bank reform efforts did not come to fruition during Kim Dae Jung's term, in part because of pending presidential and legislative elections.

Reforms of the healthcare sector proved highly contentious. Efforts to control healthcare costs by separating the prescription and dispensing of drugs and reforming the payment system confronted stiff and effective resistance from providers, including a succession of crippling doctors' strikes (Kwon 2003, 529–38). As Ramesh (2007) argues, the inability to control costs has been an ongoing weakness of the social-insurance effort. Despite compromises with these interests, however, the government did consolidate the geographically based funds covering the rural areas and the self-employed. Market-oriented reformers wanted to use the funds to introduce more competition, but progressive academics, fund workers, and farmers' organizations pressed for a solidaristic approach based on integration of the funds and wider risk pooling (Kwon and Reich 2005, 1006). In October 1998, the regional insurance societies and administration of the funds for public employees and teachers were subsumed into a National Health Insurance Corporation (NHIC); the remaining company associations followed in July 2000. Subsequent healthcare policies shifted from the question of coverage to containing costs (Ramesh 2007).

In addition to short-run measures, the Kim Dae Jung government also permanently expanded eligibility and coverage of its unemployment-insurance scheme from firms with thirty or more employees to effectively all firms (Yoo et al. 2002, 293–95; Hwang 2006, 134–38). Perhaps most interesting in terms of the change in principles of the new administration was reform of social assistance (Hwang 2006, 41–52). The Livelihood Protection Law and Public Assistance Program that dated to 1965 provided nonpecuniary assistance for those unable to work. The legislation of a National Basic Livelihood Security Law in 1998 used an income test in order to target the poor and allowed for cash benefits in addition to noncash assistance, resulting in a dramatic increase in eligibility for assistance and spending.

It is important to underscore that these social-policy initiatives did not fully compensate for the adverse effects of the crisis, nor did they fully achieve their stated objectives with respect to coverage and generosity. Modest benefits and strict work-and-training requirements reflected concern with incentive effects and the risks of "welfare disease" (Moon and Yang 2002, 8–10). More importantly, these initiatives were instituted in the context of important changes in the law governing dismissal—which could now be undertaken for "managerial" reasons—and a sharp increase in the use of contract or "contingent" workers. Partly as a result of these legal changes, the post-crisis period saw growth in the share of the self-employed and workers in smaller firms where organization was extremely low, collective bargaining limited and payment of social insurance contributions routinely evaded (Yang 2006, 220–26). The changes in Korean social policy under Kim Dae Jung's administration are nonetheless striking. In the face of crisis, the government moved quickly to provide a social safety net, expanded social-insurance coverage, changed the terms of social assistance, and allowed greater labor participation in both government and management decision-making.

Thailand

As in Korea, the crisis had powerful political consequences in Thailand. Not only did the economic collapse of 1997 lead directly to the fall of the Chavalit Yongchaiyudh, but it also influenced the passage of a wide-ranging constitutional revision that had important implications for subsequent social policy. Much of the new constitution was devoted to political reform: strengthening the rule of law, reforming the electoral system, and instituting various mechanisms for citizen participation and accountability. But it also included important social initiatives enshrined as citizen rights: free education through the twelfth grade (section 43; legislated in 1999); an "equal right" to standard health services and free care for the indigent (section 52); assistance for the elderly without adequate income (section 54); as well as more vaguely worded commitments to maintain a public healthcare system and provide social security (for example, sections 82 and 86). A sweeping commitment to decentralization also had important, though as yet unclear, implications for social policy.[30]

Like the Kim Dae Jung government, the Democrat government under Chuan Leekpai faced a variety of social pressures on coming to office, including resistance from the stronghold of the opposition in the poor and rural northeast, organized labor, and grass-roots organizations (Missingham 2004, 201–13). Unlike Kim Dae Jung, the Chuan administration did not enjoy close ties with these groups. By the summer of 1998, however, the fourth letter of intent with the IMF codified a relaxation of fiscal policy. Some of the fiscal loosening was explicitly earmarked to protect social spending, and the government dramatically increased public-works spending as a means of addressing rising unemployment. The government also completed negotiations with the World Bank and the Asian Development Bank for large social loans, and further support followed from Japan through the Miyazawa initiative in 1999.

Given the weakness of the existing administrative machinery for managing social safety nets, the loans generally supported or expanded ex-

---

[30] On the politics of decentralization, see Nelson 2001. On the possible effects with respect to health, see Kuwajima 2003.

isting programs rather than launching altogether new ones (World Bank 2002a, 3–5).[31] For urban workers, the government provided health-insurance benefits to those losing their jobs and extended severance pay from six to ten months. Both urban and rural workers were to benefit from a large-scale public-works program. Despite these externally funded initiatives, Warr and Isra's (2004, 9–15) analysis of the FY1998 budget finds that the increase in spending on the poor was concentrated largely on the controversial education-loan program, which was not unambiguously pro-poor; expenditures on school lunches, housing assistance, and job creation actually contracted. Although the Chuan government did ultimately introduce the pension and child-allowance scheme contained in the 1990 social-security law, the administration was openly reluctant to expand the existing social-insurance system or to consider more permanent innovations such as the introduction of unemployment insurance. To the contrary, the policy response to the crisis included technocratic efforts to further deregulate the labor market (Voravidh 2000, 108–24, and 2002, 255–57).

This reluctance can be traced in part to fiscal constraints and the ascent of the technocrats under Chuan but also to the broader political orientation of the Democrat Party leadership. In the words of one government official referring to short-term assistance, "the reason behind giving them such a tiny amount of money is to create an incentive for them to look for jobs; otherwise they may want to live on social security for the rest of their lives and take advantage of others" (*Bangkok Post*, June 7, 1998). This orientation, in turn, sprang from the perception that safety nets would be monopolized by relatively privileged segments of the working class, such as workers in the state-owned enterprise sector, or used for patronage purposes.

The important point for our purposes is not the merits or demerits of the Chuan government's social policy but its political vulnerability. The Chuan government gradually became associated with the IMF and austerity and ultimately spawned a political alternative in Thaksin's Thai Loves Thai (Thai Rak Thai, TRT) Party (Hicken 2006). The TRT won a large plurality in the 2001 elections and an outright majority in the 2005 elections on a platform that combined support for domestic business with a

---

[31] These initiatives included increased funding for the low-income health-card scheme and a student-loan program to keep children in school; an increase in social assistance via cash transfers targeted to the poor and elderly and disabled without other means of support; increased funding for employment services and job training; and the creation of a Social Investment Fund (SIF) similar to those in Latin America in support of the decentralization process.

populist economic platform that opposed the IMF reforms and promised much greater attention to social welfare.[32] A debt-suspension program for farmers was introduced in 2001. A wide-ranging "Village Fund" program combined outright transfers to village governments with the microfinance approach popular in other developing-country settings. But initiatives were not limited to the countryside; in 2003, the government made the surprising announcement that it was considering the introduction of unemployment insurance.

The most important and contentious social initiative of the new administration was a dramatic expansion of health insurance in the Health Security for All program based on a 30-baht health card (Towse, Mills and Viroj 2004 103–5). As the name suggests, the new scheme involved a card that granted fixed, low-fee access to provider networks with which an individual had to register. The system faced a number of political as well as administrative problems in implementation.[33] Yet as in Korea, the new government had taken initiatives that greatly expanded the social-policy reach of the state with respect to health and education, unemployment and rural poverty and did so in a number of important areas on the basis of a rights-based approach that marked an important innovation in Thai social policy (see figure A6.15).

Malaysia

Malaysian social policy during the crisis is much less expansive than is the case in Korea and Thailand. In Malaysia, Deputy Prime Minister Anwar Ibrahim initially outlined a fiscally restrictive response to the regional crisis, an "IMF program without the IMF" (Haggard 2000a, 59–64). But this stance was relaxed in the spring of 1998 in order to defend social spending. Initial cuts in the education budget were quickly restored; as a result, the country experienced no significant problem with respect to school dropouts (Jomo and Lee 1999). Health expenditures were cut in 1998 but increased in 1999, as were expenditures by ministries involved in agriculture and rural development.[34]

One pillar of the government's approach was the creation of a variety of temporary special-loan funds designed to lift the income of targeted

[32] On the rise of Thaksin and Thai Rak Thai, see Hicken 2006.

[33] These included controversy over capitation rates and long-run financial viability of the system; resistance from doctors and nurses, who complained of increased workloads; a resulting exit to private practice; and concerns about creeping socialization from private-sector providers, who were almost entirely excluded from the program.

[34] Roughly one-half of Malaysia's poor are concentrated in three states—Kelantan, Terengganu, and Sabah—that are more predominantly rural and in the first two cases, highly susceptible to appeals from the Parh' Islam SeMalaysia (PAS) as well.

groups (Abdul-Rahman n.d.; Jomo and Lee 1999). As with Malaysia's approach to poverty reduction in the past, these efforts sought to encourage productive activity: food production through low-interest loans to farmers (the Fund for Food scheme) and microcredit programs for low-income urban entrepreneurs (the Small-Scale Entrepreneur Fund and the Economic Business Group Fund). The government also expanded its Hardcore Poverty Development Program for the rural poor.

A distinctive feature of Malaysia's approach to the crisis when compared to the fully democratic cases was a particularly strong emphasis on maintaining labor-market flexibility. Trade unions in Malaysia have never been influential political actors because of various legal restrictions and formal and informal government controls over their organization and activities. In August 1998, the government undertook a number of labor-market reforms that included closer links between wage settlements and productivity and encouraging management to use pay cuts, reduced working hours, and temporary and voluntary layoffs rather than outright retrenchment.[35]

A final feature of the government's approach to the social contract was the particularly strong resistance to the use of transfers. The Social Security Organization (SOCSO) covered injury and invalidity but not other labor-market risks. Other forms of transfers were strictly limited and took a highly residualist form: means-tested social assistance was unavailable to those with families capable of supporting the claimant. Referring to social safety nets in the form of unemployment benefits, Prime Minister Mahathir argued in 1999 that:

> this method will only wreck the economy. When the unemployed is [sic] paid an allowance, then many will choose not to work. The Government will need to allocate money for dole which can only be done through raising taxes on the employed ... Of course the production costs for goods will increase, so will the cost of living. So each time dole is raised, taxes follow suit and the cost for manufacturing goods will only reduce our competitiveness in the world market. (*New Straits Times*, June 11, 1999)

As Abdul-Rahman summarizes (n.d., 6), the government relied "on labour market flexibility and rapid adjustment combined with ad hoc public expenditures to minimize the impact of the crisis on the poor. Although this approach has generated growth it implies a greater reliance on the informal social safety net system during times of economic uncertainties."

---

[35] The Malaysian government was the first in the region to announce plans to repatriate large numbers of foreign workers, as many as 200,000 between January and August 1998 (Jomo and Lee 1999, 12, 15). However, foreign workers returned with the recovery.

Crisis, Expansion, and Liberalization

These brief reviews show some commonalities across the crisis cases. All, for example, moved quickly to reverse their initially restrictive fiscal stances in order to protect or increase social spending. All instituted a variety of short-run programs in order to absorb labor-market slack, even if each precise mix differed between temporary-employment programs, private income-generation programs, and training and active labor-market policies. In all cases, these initiatives were supported by the IFIs and external donors.

Two differences are striking between Korea and Thailand on the one hand and Malaysia on the other. First, in the two democracies, governments used direct transfers, even if modest, to reach vulnerable groups; Malaysia explicitly eschewed such measures. Second, in both of the democracies, the crisis resulted not only in an expansion of existing programs but also in more fundamental changes in principles of coverage; examples include the rights-based language of the Thai constitution and the press to universalize pension and health coverage in Korea and to change the principles undergirding social insurance. We see no similar changes in Malaysia through the end of the Mahathir years in 2003; the basic outlines of the social-insurance system showed surprising continuity from the early developments traced in part 1.

Conclusion: Democracy and the Expansion of Social Commitments in Asia

In all four of the new democracies, parties and politicians scrambled to position themselves with respect to pressing social policy issues, from pensions and health insurance to unemployment, social assistance and rural poverty. In all four cases, we find evidence of the extension of new entitlements and reforms that widened access to, and improved the quality of, social services (table 6.3). However, we do find evidence that the high-growth cases witnessed a more wide-ranging expansion of these entitlements and services than was the case in the Philippines, where successive administrations struggled against the stiff headwind of recurrent fiscal constraints.

Singapore and Malaysia did have distinctive social-policy legacies that influenced the subsequent course of policy: central provident funds, public hospital systems, and well-entrenched policies of affirmative action in Malaysia. Nonetheless, we see much less social-policy innovation, and particularly in Singapore, efforts to roll back public commitments and to initiate liberalizing reforms.

TABLE 6.3
Social Policy Developments in East Asia, 1980–2005

	Pensions	Health	Education	Social assistance and antipoverty programs	Labor-market policy
		High-Growth Democracies			
Taiwan	Gradual expansion. Elderly and farmer allowances; reforms to make pensions portable.	Expansion. National health insurance (1994).	Major institutional changes following reform commission (1994–96).	Expansion. New aged welfare, handicapped and social assistance laws.	Partial expansion.Unemployment insurance (1998) and new labor-market initiatives from 2001, but some deregulation.
Korea	Expansion. Incorporation of nearly all occupational groups into national pension system.	Expansion. Gradual expansion efforts followed by integration of separate funds into national health insurance.	Major institutional changes following two reform commissions (1994–98).	Expansion. Minor revisions of social assistance prior to crisis; substantial reforms and increase in spending thereafter.	Partial expansion. Unemployment insurance (1993), coupled measures to increase labor-market flexibility following crisis.
Thailand	Gradual expansion. Wide-ranging social-insurance law (1990), but low coverage.	Expansion. Gradual expansion of healthcare schemes in 1980s and 1990s. Dramatic increase under Thaksin.	Expansion. Dramatic expansion of secondary enrollments, 1997 constitution makes 12 years of education mandatory.	Expansion. Succession of rural antipoverty programs; dramatic expansion of social safety nets, rural schemes and transfers under Thaksin.	No change. Unemployment insurance proposed, but not implemented.

To what extent did democratization in Asia contribute to an expansion of social entitlements by allowing for a reversal of the historical weakness of the left and labor? It is extremely difficult to find the standard left-right policy and social cleavages that have defined politics in the advanced industrial states in Asia. If we define a social-democratic party by a social-

TABLE 6.3 (*cont'd*)
Social Policy Developments in East Asia, 1980–2005

	Pensions	Health	Education	Social assistance and antipoverty programs	Labor-market policy
			Low-Growth Democracy		
Philippines	Limited change. Parametric changes in SSS and GSIS.	Gradual expansion. Universal health insurance (Phil-Health, 1995), with 15-year timetable to fully implement.	Expansion. 1987 constitution mandates education receive largest share of total expenditure; secondary education made mandatory.	Expansion. Succession of targeted antipoverty programs, but with funding contingent on fiscal circumstances	No change. Limited labor protections.
			Nondemocracies		
Singapore	Limited change. Parametric changes in use of CPF funds.	Liberalizing reforms. Measures to rationalize public hospitals and encourage private financing (Medisave) and provision; means-tested assistance scheme (Medifund).	Ongoing innovations in vocational training programs.	Limited change. Residualist public-assistance scheme.	No change. No unemployment insurance.
Malaysia	Limited change. Parametric changes in use of EPF funds.	Liberalizing reforms. Measures to rationalize public hospitals and encourage private provision.	Efforts to develop vocational training.	Limited change. Short-term ameliorative measures during crisis but no major innovations.	Deregulation Measures to increase labor-market flexibility, no majo innovations in protections.

ist or social-democratic label, the policy commitments typical of social-democratic parties in the advanced industrial states, or in terms of parties that explicitly appeal to a labor or popular sector base, such parties are largely absent in the region. Perhaps the closest to a "left" party to occupy office is the party headed by Kim Dae Jung. But it is important to emphasize that Korean parties are cross-class in nature, relied in the first instance on a strong regional political base, and did not have direct organizational ties with labor; indeed, until the Kim Dae Jung administration, they were prohibited from doing so.

The absence of a left arguably did have some effect on the nature of the expansion that occurred in East Asia. In Korea and Taiwan, for example, politicians were attracted first and foremost to broad middle-class entitlements—pensions and particularly healthcare—and in Thailand a number of initiatives were less redistributive in design than they might have been. When governments either initiated unemployment insurance or expanded it (for example, during the Asian financial crisis in Korea in and following the 2001 recession in Taiwan), they did so in conjunction with initiatives designed to increase labor-market flexibility.

However, a more plausible interpretation is that partisanship did not have marked effects. Given favorable economic circumstances and a limited government role in the provision of social insurance, parties of all political stripes stood to gain by making social-policy promises. In both Korea and Taiwan, the first steps toward the expansion of welfare commitments were taken by conservative political leaders challenged not by social-democratic parties but by oppositions emphasizing political issues. In Thailand, early welfare initiatives were aimed at neutralizing a leftist insurgency, but the most significant welfare legislation was initiated by a former military leader facing competition from patronage-oriented parties. As Herbert Kitschelt (2001) has argued, these apparently anomalous results can arise when conservative parties seek to neutralize challenges on some other, more salient issue, for example, along a democratic-authoritarian dimension.

Similar conclusions can be drawn about the role of labor. Democratization resulted in fundamental changes in industrial relations, but it did not lead to a noticeable increase in union membership outside of the Philippines where the nonagricultural workforce was a relatively small share of total employment (table 5.5). Moreover, we found only mixed empirical evidence that labor unions were important actors in the initiation of new social commitments in Thailand, Taiwan, and Korea. During these transitional periods, labor was typically more concerned with political, organizational, shop-floor, and wage issues than with advancing a social-policy agenda. In some cases, most notably in Korea and Thailand, organized labor in larger firms actually resisted initiatives that would have diluted existing benefits or pooled risks with other groups.

These findings have important implications for the debate about globalization and social protection. Despite relatively open economies and relatively weak left parties and labor movements, the democracies of the region experienced a dramatic expansion of social entitlements. Moreover, these new social policies were sustained in the face of large external shocks.

However, we do see developments in labor markets and labor-market policies that suggest some caution looking forward. In the wake of the crisis of 1997–98, countries in the region privatized state-owned enterprises and initiated wide-ranging corporate and financial restructuring of distressed firms. Deregulation of labor markets eased dismissal and increased the legal scope for temporary, part-time, contract, and other forms of informal employment. These developments, which came on top of long-run structural shifts in comparative advantage and increasing competition from China, could well have a corrosive effect on the trend toward wider social-insurance coverage over the longer run. Informal-sector workers are less likely to make social insurance contributions and more likely to fall outside established corporate benefits. Without government intervention, such as matching or subsidized contributions, strict workplace enforcement or alternative safety-net mechanisms, the de jure and de facto social contracts could well diverge. In the absence of stronger labor movements or labor-based parties, the expansion of the social contract in East Asia could therefore hide growing inequality in the distribution of benefits and vindicate at least some fears of the constraints associated with an open, export-oriented economy.

An alternative explanation for the outcomes we have described here might reside not in parties or interest groups but in institutional factors. Analyses of policy reform have emphasized the difficulties posed by fragmented party systems (for example, Haggard and Kaufman 1995, 151–82) that are visible in several countries in our sample, most notably Thailand and the Philippines. Yet fragmentation is not likely to be a stumbling block to *expanding* social commitments. Incumbent executives, party leaders and politicians faced problems not in securing support but in limiting the costs of their initiatives.

Incentives for particularism, or outright corruption, constitute another institutional feature that may be germane for the politics of social policy. Examples of institutional characteristics that generate such incentives include the single nontransferable vote (Taiwan) or systems in which party leaders have limited control over party lists (open-list systems) or other political goods (both the Philippines and Thailand). In such systems, politicians have incentives to steer particularistic and easily identifiable benefits (for example, pork and patronage) toward electorally relevant constituencies. Although we do not consider these propositions systematically, we see strong evidence of particularism in the preferences of Taiwanese legislators for cash transfers, in the notorious Philippine pork-barrel system, which allocates portions of the social budget directly to legislators' control, and in the distribution of health cards in Thailand. But it is important to underline that these propositions are in no way inconsistent with our broader claims about the effects of democracy and fiscal circumstances on the expansion of social entitlements; rather, they are relevant for understanding variation across the new democracies.

As we showed in part 1, the welfare legacy in East Asia combined robust investment in education and basic health services with a minimalist approach to social insurance. Prior systems of coverage often served as the template for early efforts to expand entitlements. We see evidence of this, for example, in both Korea and Taiwan, where governments initially opted to expand existing systems of social insurance by adding new groups. Once this process started, however, it generated pressures to move toward more universalistic norms. The welfare legacy in East Asia was thus a permissive one.

These opportunities could be realized in Taiwan, Korea, and Thailand because of the highly favorable economic circumstances in which transitions occurred. We demonstrated this point in part by using the Philippines as a contrasting case. The administrations of Aquino, Ramos, and Estrada, all signaled a strong commitment to social-policy reforms, but the ability to carry through on those promises was adversely affected by macroeconomic shocks even prior to the regionwide crisis in 1997–98.

The regionwide meltdown of 1997–98 posed both long-run and short-run fiscal challenges to governments in the region, and there is some evidence of the liberalizing initiatives that are a central theme in debates over social policy in Latin America and Central Europe. But with the exception again of the Philippines, democratic governments in the region did not enter the crisis facing long-standing structural deficits or weak revenue bases. Nor did any of them inherit expansive social programs that were themselves a major source of fiscal drain. Recovery from the crisis was relatively rapid as well. Whatever the inadequacies of the short-run social-policy response to the Asian financial crisis, democratic governments— either immediately or in the aftermath of the crisis—were able to fundamentally rewrite the authoritarian social contract.

CHAPTER SEVEN

Democracy, Economic Crisis, and Social Policy in Latin America, 1980–2005

The "third wave" (Huntington 1991) of democratization spread to most Latin American countries in our sample during the debt crisis of the early 1980s. Between 1980 and 1985, military regimes gave way to democratic governments in Peru (1980), Argentina (1983), Uruguay and Brazil (1985). The Pinochet dictatorship yielded power in 1990, and Mexico's ruling party relinquished control of the presidency in 2000 after a decade of gradual political liberalization. Political changes were not uniformly in the direction of democracy. Peru reverted to authoritarian rule under Alberto Fujimori (1992–2000), and Venezuela moved in a similar direction after the election of Hugo Chávez in 1998. Nevertheless, the 1980s and 1990s were marked by a clear regionwide trend in the direction of more competitive and representative political systems.

Figures 7.1 and 7.2 show this trend, distinguishing between the five cases that experienced democratic transitions—Argentina, Brazil, Chile, Peru, and Uruguay—and those that show greater political continuity over this period—the older democracies of Costa Rica, Colombia, and Venezuela and Mexico's dominant-party system.

Social policy in Latin America unfolded in an economic context markedly different from that in East Asia. Devastating shocks battered the region during the first half of the 1980s, the worst years of the debt crisis; with the exception of Chile, growth remained flat or highly volatile for the rest of the decade (see figures 7.3 and 7.4). Argentina, Peru, Mexico, and Brazil faced the most severe problems, including not only deep recessions but high or hyperinflations that generated recurrent pressures for stabilization. Venezuela escaped hyperinflation, but it also experienced severe economic decline and fiscal constraints during the oil slumps of the 1980s and 1990s. Economic performance in Uruguay, Colombia and Costa Rica was somewhat more stable, but all three countries also experienced serious difficulties.

As we argued in chapter 5, these difficult economic conditions posed major policy dilemmas. Governments were pressed to address the inequities in the distribution of social insurance and services, while at the same time facing demands from stakeholders seeking to defend entitlements. Crises amplified the demands for relief from the social distress associated

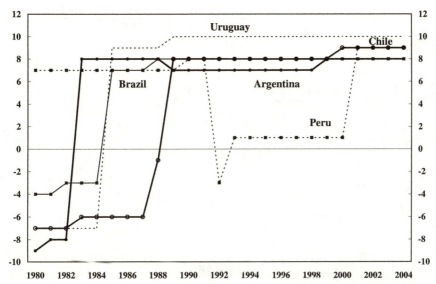

Figure 7.1. Democratic transitions in Latin America, 1980–2004. *Source*: Polity IV database (Marshall and Jaggers 2004).

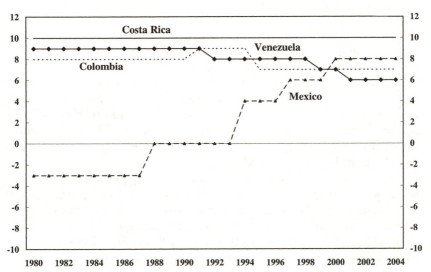

Figure 7.2. Latin American countries with continuous regimes, 1980–2004. *Source*: Polity IV database (Marshall and Jaggers 2004).

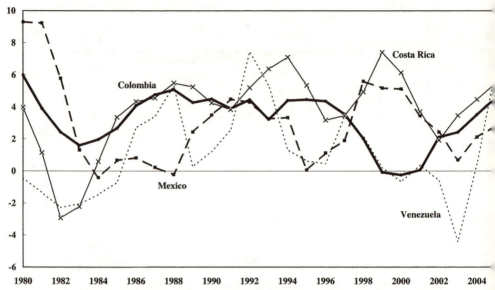

Figure 7.3. GDP growth in Colombia, Costa Rica, Mexico, and Venezuela. Three-year moving average, 1980–2005. *Source*: World Development Indicators (World Bank 2007).

with the collapse of the ISI model and market-oriented reforms, and candidates typically campaigned for office with promises to address the "social deficit." Yet fiscal pressures and ongoing concerns about macroeconomic stability placed severe constraints on the capacity of both democracies and authoritarian regimes to maintain existing social insurance and services or initiate new social programs. Indeed, social spending dropped sharply during the 1980s in most countries of the region, regardless of regime type (see appendix 6).

During the 1990s, economic circumstances improved, and governments were able to commit more fiscal resources to social programs. But with the exception of Chile, recoveries were fragile, and countries remained vulnerable to macroeconomic instability. The 1994–95 financial crisis in Mexico and the Russian crisis of 1998 both had regionwide effects, and in the early 2000s, another devastating debt crisis hit Argentina.

After 2002, fiscal constraints were greatly eased by the onset of a commodity boom, which increased the resources available to many Latin American governments. Until the onset of this boom, however, public-welfare commitments in most Latin American countries were constrained either by ongoing fiscal problems or by concerns that lax fiscal policy could result in a return of macroeconomic instability.

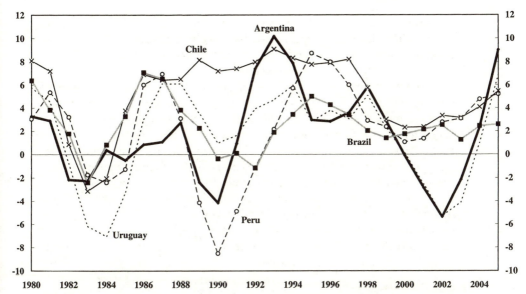

Figure 7.4. GDP growth in Argentina, Brazil, Chile, Peru, and Uruguay. Three-year moving average, 1980–2005. *Source*: World Development Indicators. (World Bank 2007).

In these circumstances, many politicians and technocrats viewed the "liberal agenda" as a way to reconcile demands for greater fiscal discipline with pressures to address the needs of previously excluded groups. On the one hand, reforms of costly social-insurance programs—particularly pensions and linked health entitlements—promised to relieve fiscal constraints by increasing efficiency and stabilizing public finances over the long run. At the same time, these could be supplemented by targeted antipoverty programs that reached new constituencies but were relatively cheap and often externally funded. Over the course of the 1990s and early 2000s, reforms of core social-insurance programs, efforts to expand basic social services, and the adoption of antipoverty programs constituted a "modal pattern" of social policy that was distinct from that of either East Asia or Eastern Europe.

There were, however, considerable differences among the Latin American countries in the priorities attached to different components of this social agenda. We would expect the influence of liberal technocrats over social policy to be most extensive in the countries experiencing the most severe economic shocks and to wane over time as the impact of these shocks diminish. We would also expect democratic regimes to expand social protections and services to new groups and to provide greater opportunities for organized stakeholders to blunt liberalizing welfare reforms. These defensive reactions to liberal welfare reforms should be most effective where coverage is relatively broad and/or where organized stakeholders are well represented in welfare bureaucracies.

In the following section, we begin our analysis with a discussion of competitive authoritarian regimes in Mexico, Peru, and Venezuela. In all three countries, the electoral connection encouraged leaders to deploy social assistance to marginalized sectors of the population. As we shall see, however, variation in economic conditions produced significant contrasts in the way these regimes dealt with reforms of core social-insurance programs. We then turn to a discussion of the five countries that experienced more continuous democratic rule during the 1980s and 1990s. We distinguish between Argentina, Brazil, and pre-Chávez Venezuela, which experienced the most severe macroeconomic problems of the democratic cases, and Uruguay, Costa Rica, Chile, and Colombia, which faced somewhat looser economic constraints.

Social Policy in Competitive Authoritarian and Semidemocratic Regimes: Peru, Mexico, and Venezuela.

Mexico, Peru, and Venezuela were the only countries in our Latin American sample to have either sustained authoritarian rule into the 1990s or to have reverted to significant restrictions on democratic politics. Although Mexico's competitive authoritarian regime began a process of gradual political liberalization in the 1990s (see figure 7.2), a powerful executive exercised substantial discretion over the allocation of resources until the presidential election of 2000. In Peru, Alberto Fujimori's *autogolpe* (literally, "self-coup") in 1992 marked the beginning of almost a decade of restrictions on civil and political liberties. Politics under Hugo Chávez in Venezuela remained somewhat more open until the early 2000s, but particularly after an aborted coup attempt in 2002, he began to dismantle legal and political checks on his personal dominance.

Peru and Mexico, as noted above, also suffered exceptionally severe fiscal constraints and, particularly in Peru, high inflation. As we would expect, these conditions encouraged a delegation of decision-making authority to market-oriented technocrats, who sought to restructure costly and inefficient social-security programs and the bureaucracies that administered them. Autocratic controls allowed executives to push sweeping pension reforms through compliant legislatures or simply to implement them by decree.

Because of the oil boom of the early 2000s, Chávez's increasingly autocratic regime faced much more favorable economic conditions. During the 1990s, severe fiscal and financial crises had forced a succession of democratic governments to undertake liberal reforms of the pension and healthcare systems and the labor market. The incoming Chávez government either failed to implement these reforms or abrogated them altogether. As the price of oil began to soar, it began a wholesale transformation of the welfare system through a dramatic expansion of new social programs.

Peru

Technocrats reached the height of their power in Peru under Fujimori, following a virtual collapse of the economy during the late 1980s and early 1990s. From 1980 to 1985, the new democratic government of Fernando Belaúnde Terry had initiated a tough stabilization program to cope with the debt crisis, but in 1985, a wave of protest against these measures carried Alan García, the populist head of the APRA party, into the presidency. In turn, García's expansionist macroeconomic policies led quickly to a devastating crisis and five-digit hyperinflation. In the course of this collapse, social spending dropped precipitously (see figure A6.7).

In 1990, Fujimori emerged as the surprise winner of a presidential election held at the height of the crisis. Although he ran as an economic moderate, he turned quickly toward a more radical reform agenda (Stokes 2001, 47–53). To reduce the enormous fiscal deficit, the government sharply reduced public subsidies for basic necessities. When this "Fujishock" proved insufficient to stabilize prices, the president delegated power to a new technocratic team under Carlos Bulaños and signed off on one of the most radical programs of privatization and trade liberalization in the region (Weyland 2002, 117–18). The decline of inflation to relatively moderate levels in 1992 and 1993 and the resumption of growth provided a substantial political payoff. Fujimori's approval ratings increased from under 40 percent in 1991 to over 82 percent by April 1992 (Weyland 2002, 129).

REFORMING THE PENSION SYSTEM

In the aftermath of the immediate macroeconomic emergency, privatization of the pension system became an important component of Bulaños's policy agenda. An important long-term objective of the reform was an increase in domestic savings, but the more immediate goal was to rein in the costly inefficiencies in the Peruvian Institute of Social Security (Instituto Peruano de Seguro Social, or IPSS). Despite Peru's relatively young population, the IPSS suffered from what Mesa-Lago (1989, 174) has termed a premature crisis stemming from widespread evasion of contributions and subsidies to the health and maternity funds. Administrative costs, directly related to patronage appointments, were among the highest in the region (Mesa-Lago 1989, 195–96).

The reform pressed by Bulaños eventually stopped short of fully privatizing the public system, but it ranked below only Chile and Mexico in terms of the percentage of workers enrolled in the second pillar and the benefits to be derived from it (Madrid 2003, 16). The reform also fundamentally reorganized institutions by shifting responsibilities from the IPSS to a new Office for Pension Normalization established under the auspices of the ministry of finance (Müller 2002a, 41).

There can be little question that the scope of these reforms was a function not simply of Fujimori's political popularity but of the *autogolpe* of April 1992. Congress had already delegated extensive emergency powers to the president, but Fujimori's party, Cambio 90, controlled only 15 percent of the congressional seats. The legislature therefore was not a reliable base of support for his program of radical economic reform. The *autogolpe* suspended the constitution, closed the congress, and created what we would consider a competitive authoritarian regime. Pension reform was authorized by decree in December 1992, prior to the swearing in of a new, unicameral legislature established under a new constitution.

In addition to the authoritarian controls imposed in 1992, Peru's social-welfare legacy also facilitated pension reform. Status quo interests were extraordinarily weak compared to other countries in the region. The economic crisis of the late 1980s had led to a virtual collapse of APRA and other established political parties, and union membership had shrunk to less than 6 percent of the workforce, by far the lowest among the Latin American countries we consider here (Roberts 2006, 169). Pension coverage was also among the lowest in the region, reaching only about 20 percent of the workforce during the 1990s (Palacios and Pallares-Miralles 2000, 41).

HEALTHCARE INITIATIVES

The devastation of unions and other stakeholder groups together with authoritarian controls also cleared the way for a series of healthcare initiatives. These initiatives expanded access to underserved groups, but were based on liberal reform principles with respect to labor relations and private participation. Two programs initiated in the mid-1990s targeted primary health services to the poorest Peruvian communities. The PBST, or Basic Healthcare for All, provided from 80 to 90 percent of all basic healthcare services. A distinctively liberal feature of this program was its reliance on flexible three-to-six-month labor contracts for healthcare workers, who were well paid but received no benefits and were subject to renewal on the basis of performance (Ewig 2004, 231). A second, smaller program (Local Health Administrative Committees, or CLAS) also relied on nonunion labor and operated through locally supervised NGOs (Ewig 2004, 238).

In 1997, Fujimori rammed through additional changes in the core health system that permitted private health-provider organizations to compete with clinics and hospitals of the Social Security Administration. Even more than with CLAS and PBST, this reform hit at prerogatives of unionized workers employed in the traditional system. Nevertheless, the weakened unions were unable to challenge the authority of the regime. Fujimori authorized the program by decree in 1996 and then pushed it through a compliant congress in 1997 (Ewig 2004, 238).

ANTIPOVERTY INITIATIVES

Despite restrictions on representative government, the electoral connection continued to play an important role in the framing of social policy. As the political impact of the disinflation began to fade, widespread abstentions posed a potential threat to Fujimori's legitimacy. Because of the elimination of literacy requirements in the 1979 constitution, moreover, the number of low-income voters had increased significantly, strengthening the incentives to use social assistance for political purposes.

Kenneth Roberts (1995) and Kurt Weyland (1998) have characterized such efforts as neoliberal populism. Anti-poverty social funds, and particularly the Fund for Cooperation for Social Development (Fondo de Cooperción para el Desarrollo, FONCODES), were the most important component of Fujimori's effort to expand social services. Although initiated in the early 1990s, the activities of FONCODES were ramped up dramatically in the year preceding Fujimori's bid for reelection in 1995, financed by revenue windfalls from privatization. As a political instrument of the president, FONCODES was characterized by patronage appointments to unqualified personnel, mistargeting, and corruption. Nevertheless, Falconi (2003, 18) estimates that over 60 percent of poor households received at least some benefits from the FONCODES programs and that food programs, the most urgently needed, reached almost 80 percent of the extremely poor households.

Mexico

Social-policy reforms in Mexico under Carlos Salinas (1988–94) and Ernesto Zedillo (1994–2000) were initiated in a dominant party system that faced growing electoral constraints. As figure 7.3 indicates, fiscal deficits during the 1980s were also the highest of any of the nine countries we examine. Inflation was lower than in Argentina, Peru, and Brazil; but it was very high by historical standards and a sharp acceleration of inflation in the late 1980s awakened serious concerns about the possibility of hyper-inflation (Kaufman, Bazdresch, and Heredia 1994, 371–77). During the 1980s, the share of social expenditures in GDP plunged (see figure A6.6).

As in Peru, the crisis led to an expansion of the influence of liberal technocrats. President Miguel de la Madrid (1982–88) provided strong backing to market-oriented economists in the finance and planning minis-tries and tapped Carlos Salinas, one of the key proponents of liberal re-form, as his successor. Under Salinas and Zedillo, technocrats consoli-dated their hold on the economic ministries and launched a sweeping program of trade liberalization and privatization. Beginning in the early 1990s, the government also began to focus more directly on social policy, and technocrats allied with the finance ministry assumed top positions in the social-security agency and the ministry of education.

REFORMING THE PENSION AND HEALTH SYSTEMS

Also as in Peru, the government succeeded in initiating one of the most extensive pension reforms in the region. The Mexican pension system, like Peru's, was not yet vulnerable to adverse demographic changes visible in Eastern Europe and some of the other Latin American countries. How-ever, technocrats saw the IMSS as a significant threat to the integrity of public finances.

As was the case in most other countries, the IMSS administered other social-security programs as well as pensions. The fiscal health of the agency suffered from cross-subsidies to the health system, and by the mid-1990s, the reserves of the pension fund had been depleted (Gonzalez-Rossetti 2004, 76). As we would predict, reformers were concerned not only with policy but also with institutional issues. The IMSS's control over health and social-security resources had provided it with a pivotal position within Mexico's corporatist system, a position the technocrats hoped to dismantle (González-Rossetti 2004, 72).

During Salinas's term, the government postponed efforts to restructure the IMSS and the pension system in order to focus on the politically charged effort to conclude agreement on the North American Free Trade Agreement (NAFTA). Following the signing of NAFTA and the onset of the second peso crisis in 1994–95, the Zedillo administration launched a radical reform initiative that, like the Chilean reform, involved a complete phasing out of the pay-as-you-go pension system. The government later offered significant compensation to corporatist stakeholders, including an exemption for the powerful social-security union and a provision that allowed the social-security administration to compete for affiliates with private pension funds. Nevertheless, its major elements survived intact (Madrid 2003, 89–97), and it passed through the PRI-controlled legisla-ture in a matter of months.

Zedillo also proposed a healthcare reform that envisioned, among other things, a substantial expansion of the role of the ministry of health in the provision of healthcare for uninsured sectors of the population. This measure, however, faced strong opposition from the IMSS. To avoid jeopardizing its pension proposals, the government dropped this reform from its legislative agenda. With the backing of the private sector, however, it did persist in the passage of a reform of financing that replaced revenues from payroll taxes with direct financing from the public treasury (González-Rossetti 2004, 79–80).

EDUCATION DECENTRALIZATION

In 1992, President Salinas also launched an initiative to transfer administrative authority over the school system to state governments (Grindle 2004, 290–312). In keeping with liberal prescriptions, the government viewed decentralization as a way to improve educational quality, but it was also motivated by the opportunity to weaken the powerful teachers' union which had opposed Salinas's bid for the presidency (Grindle 2004, 311–12). Negotiations over the reform were preceded by the arrest of the old-guard head of the union and his replacement by a more moderate leadership. Even after the purge of the old leadership, the teachers' union remained one of the most powerful in the country, and reforms were modest in comparison with those instituted in Argentina and Brazil, where teachers' unions were already relatively weak at the national level. Nevertheless, decentralization did strike a blow at the teachers' bargaining leverage and forced them to negotiate with governors as well as with the central government over pay, assignments, and budget allocations.

ANTIPOVERTY INITIATIVES

The government's conflicts with corporatist stakeholders in the social sectors coincided with growing electoral pressures from both right and left opposition parties. In the 1988 presidential election, the PRI had to engage in blatant fraud in order to stave off victory for the left opposition. Future elections threatened to bring recurrent social disruptions unless the PRI could make more credible appeals to voters.

The initiation of a major new anti-poverty program, Programa Nacional de Solidaridad (PRONASOL), was both a response to this challenge and an attempt by Salinas to develop an organizational counterweight to the power of corporatist opponents within the PRI. PRONASOL, like FONCODES in Peru, allowed the president to direct antipoverty resources to electorally important districts (Molinar and Weldon 1994, 123–41, Magaloni 2006). Although the popularity of both Salinas and the program collapsed after the 1994 crisis, until that time, PRONASOL served as a powerful electoral resource.

Under the Zedillo administration, a small group of policy experts within the social bureaucracy spearheaded a new type of antipoverty program—PROGRESA (Programa de Educación, Salud, y Alimentación),[1] later renamed OPORTUNIDADES under Vicente Fox. Unlike PRONASOL, PROGRESA transferred funds directly to families rather than to communities and tied disbursements to school attendance and visits to clinics. In 1999, PROGRESA covered 2.6 million families, and by 2005, the program had expanded to about 5 million (Diaz-Cayeros, Magaloni, and Estévez 2006, 15).

Unlike PRONASOL, PROGRESA remained relatively free of electoral clientelism. But the politics of establishing the new program were complex, and highlight the constraints placed by competing stakeholder claims on very limited fiscal resources. Policy specialists who designed the program based funding requests on the explicit premise that the program "could only be enacted if it maintained a relatively limited budget" (Diaz-Cayeros, Magaloni, and Estévez 2006, 56–57). At the same time, the government compensated PRI politicians for loss of control over antipoverty resources with a substantial shift of other resources into discretionary funds controlled by state governors.

Despite the limited budget, the program was a significant achievement. Along with Brazil's Bolsa Familia, to be discussed below, the initiative did in fact increase school attendance and add substantially to family incomes (Morley and Coady 2003, 35–40). Yet fiscal constraints and interest-group pressures also significantly limited the capacity of the program to reach all poor families or to reduce the country's overall poverty gap. Initially, only rural families were eligible for benefits. After the change of government in 2000, urban areas were also included, but as of 2005, transfers still remained unavailable to just under half of families in extreme poverty (Diaz-Cayeros, Estévez, and Magaloni, 2006: 26)[2]

Venezuela

Venezuela ranked among the long-standing democracies of Latin America from 1958 until the advent of Hugo Chávez in the late 1990s. Before turning directly to a discussion of the Chávez regime, therefore, it is important to trace the evolution of social policy under his democratic predecessors.

The stability of Venezuela's democracy rested on informal norms of cooperation among the leaders of the two major parties, the Acción Democrática (AD) and COPEI, and on an oil economy that permitted the

---

[1] Program of Education, Health, and Nutrition.
[2] Morley and Coady (2003, 52) estimate that they constituted only about 3 percent of Mexico's poverty gap.

distribution of rents to business elites, middle-class constituents, and allied blue-collar unions. The collapse of the oil market in the mid-1980s thus posed serious economic and social challenges and was accompanied by a sharp decline in the legitimacy of the established political parties (Karl 1997). By 1988, the year prior to the election of Carlos Andrés Pérez, fiscal deficits had reached 9 percent of GDP, spending on health and education had dropped precipitously (figure A6.9), and the poverty rate had climbed from about a third of the population in the early 1980s to over half (Naim 1993, 24).

As was the case in other countries experiencing such crises, presidents elected in the 1990s turned to liberal technocrats to oversee economic-reform efforts. The first attempt at structural reform under Carlos Andrés Pérez (1989–93) involved a sweeping package of measures that proved politically disastrous. Unlike most of the other crisis cases, the effects of Venezuela's huge fiscal deficit were obscured by price and exchange-rate controls that maintained the illusion of monetary stability. In the absence of a major inflation crisis, the Pérez government was forced to take the blame for the pain of adjustment without the offsetting political gains of restoring stability. Riots in Caracas (the so-called Caracazo) exploded over the liberalization of public transportation fares just a few weeks after Pérez's inauguration. In February 1992, the government was shaken further by an uprising of junior military officers led by Hugo Chávez, and a year later, Pérez was impelled to resign in the face of impeachment proceedings in the legislature.

After a brief transitional period, Pérez was succeeded by Rafael Caldera (1994–99). Caldera had campaigned as a vehement critic of neoliberal approaches, but his efforts to pursue an alternative strategy quickly ran into serious macroeconomic constraints. After a major financial crisis and a surge of inflation in 1996, the president was compelled to accept much more market-oriented approaches to both economic and social policy. To engineer this change of direction, Caldera appointed Teodoro Petkoff as minister of planning. Although a former leftist, Petkoff had become a staunch advocate of economic reform, and his program (Agenda Venezuela) included a tough fiscal adjustment, and an extensive deregulation of the economy.[3] This shift in policy was undertaken in an environment characterized by a sharp decline of support for the AD and COPEI and proliferation of new parties (Monaldi, et al. 2006; Penfold-Becerra 2004).[4] The president thus faced a legislature that lacked a stable majority.

[3] Key features were the elimination of exchange controls, a massive devaluation, expenditure cuts, and increases in public-sector prices (Weyland 2002, 226).

[4] Caldera himself had run as an independent, despite being one of the founding leaders of COPEI, and had won with only 30 percent of the vote.

In the rapidly deteriorating economic situation of the mid-1990s, however, fragmentation of the party system did not impede the turn toward economic orthodoxy. Both Caldera and most parties feared the political consequences of a major economic crisis, and Petkoff managed to maintain legislative acquiescence to the basic policy course he charted until the end of Caldera's term.

PENSION REFORM UNDER DEMOCRATIC RULE

Petkoff's program had a significant social-policy component. As in the other cases, pension privatization was a top priority, and it passed in 1997 after tripartite negotiations between the government, major business associations, and the established union elite. Technocrats sought to dismantle the Venezvelan Social Security Institute (Instituto Venezolano de Seguro Social, IVSS), which was essentially bankrupt and unable to meet commitments.[5] The legislation established a compulsory private pillar for all new workers and current workers under a given age and mandated phase-outs of special funds for powerful corporatist interests, including teachers, petroleum workers, and the military. Unions, which had been badly weakened by the crisis, acquiesced, and once agreements were forged within the tripartite committees, parties from across the spectrum accepted the legislation without significant debate.

HEALTHCARE AND EDUCATION INITIATIVES UNDER DEMOCRATIC RULE

Reform of the healthcare and education systems also reflected liberal principles. The government rejected proposals for a unified single-payer system advanced by health experts affiliated with the Ministry of Health in favor of a more complex plan that relied on private insurance and provision. The system was modeled after reforms introduced in Colombia several years earlier, but contained only weak guarantees of access to subsidized health-maintenance organizations.

The health and education ministries also negotiated a series of bilateral agreements that transferred social-sector responsibilities to state governors. Caldera, who had long advocated a strong central government, acquiesced only reluctantly to these steps. Nevertheless, by the end of his term, 11 of 23 Venezuelan states had signed transfer agreements with the federal government and had assumed significant responsibilities with respect to healthcare in particular (Penfold-Becerra 2004).

---

[5] By the mid-1990s, the fund was running deficits of 4 percent of GDP, payments were backlogged, and pensioners often had to resort to bribery or political connections to receive their entitlements.

ANTIPOVERTY PROGRAMS UNDER DEMOCRATIC GOVERNMENT

Finally, social protection for displaced workers and the poor combined compensatory policies and targeted programs. Social-fund programs, which had gotten off to a slow start under Pérez, were consolidated and expanded under the aegis of a new ministry of family. Responsibility for administering such programs was delegated to local officials and NGOs (Penfold-Becerra 2005). New labor-market legislation combined a cap on severance-pay requirements with a new program of unemployment insurance and lump-sum disbursement of benefits accrued by currently employed workers (Weyland 2002, 233).

A brief economic rebound in 1997 raised hopes that Petkoff's reforms had placed Venezuela on a road to recovery, but these hopes were dashed during the following year by a sharp drop in oil prices. These economic conditions paved the way for Hugo Chávez's landslide victory in the 1998 presidential elections.

SOCIAL POLICY UNDER CHAVEZ

Chávez interpreted his victory as a mandate for a sweeping overhaul of the political system, and during his first year in office, he focused primarily on the drafting of a new constitution that vastly expanded presidential powers. By 2000, Chávez had swept away most of the old institutional checks on executive authority, including those exercised by the established parties in the legislature, the courts, and the unions.

Economic and social policies were at first a lower priority, a situation that closely reflected changing fiscal fortunes. The new constitution abrogated the pension and health reforms legislated under Caldera and re-centralized social-fund programs (Penfold-Becerra 2005, 19). But with oil prices remaining low through 1999, Chávez allowed Maritza Izaguierre, the last finance minister under Caldera, to remain in her post and to continue a restrictive fiscal policy. Health and education expenditures actually declined in 1999, Chávez's first year in office (Penfold-Becerra 2005, 19).

Starting in the early 2000s, however, social policy took a more expansionist direction. Mounting opposition to the new regime provided the incentive for this change of course, and resurgent oil prices provided the means. Between 2001 and 2003, the regime faced down three general strikes, a crippling forty-five-day strike in the petroleum sector, and an attempted coup d'état. When direct action failed to topple the regime, the opposition sought to unseat Chávez in a recall referendum, held after a long political struggle in August 2004.

Fortunately for Chávez, the onset of the petroleum boom generated fiscal revenues that enabled him both to counter these challenges and to move the regime decisively to the left. Chávez and his loyalists assumed direct control of the state petroleum company (Petróleos de Venezuela S.A., PDVSA), and as dollars flooded into the system, expenditures on social services rose dramatically. Overall funding for these programs reached an estimated 3.5 percent of GDP in 2004, far higher than any of the other social-assistance programs discussed in this chapter (Ortega and Penfold-Becerra 2006, 8). The new oil-funded health and education programs were labeled "missions to save the people."

The health mission, Barrios Adentro, recruited approximately 10,000 Cuban health professionals to provide primary healthcare in poor communities, first in Caracas and then across the country, in exchange for the provision of subsidized petroleum exports to Cuba. Health workers lived as well as worked in the communities, providing residents with unprecedented access to preventive medicine and public-health services.

Within the education sector, the most popular program was Misión Ribas, which provided small stipends to students to finish high school through video courses monitored by activists and other students. Misión Mercal established a network of stores that sold food at highly subsidized prices. Identity cards needed to obtain access to these programs were issued by Misión Identidad, which also provided a mechanism for the regime to identify, register, and enlist the support of the beneficiaries (Ortega and Penfold Becerra 2006, 23).

As with FONCODES in Peru and PRONASOL in Mexico, minimal oversight and lack of fiscal accountability encouraged patronage and waste in the *misiones* (Ortega and Penfold-Becerra 2006). Nevertheless, even more than in Mexico and Peru, the *misiones* were a crucial pillar of Chávez's competitive authoritarian regime. The popularity of the mission programs and the access of the Chávez machine to a new pool of registered voters were key to a smashing victory for Chávez in the 2004 referendum campaign.

SOCIAL POLICY IN THE NEW DEMOCRACIES: THE CRISIS CASES OF ARGENTINA AND BRAZIL

The transition to democratic rule had important implications for the course of social policy in Latin America. The opening of the political system increased the leverage of interest groups and stakeholders and placed important political constraints on liberal reformers when compared to what occurred in Peru and Mexico. Yet, as we have already seen in the case of Venezuela, severe economic crises also influenced the politics of social policy. In both Argentina and Brazil, severe inflation and fiscal constraints had the countervailing effect of strengthening the hands of technocrats. Such was particularly the case in Argentina, where hyperinflation posed threats not only to the economy but to the political system as well. The political effects of crisis were mitigated in Brazil's new democracy by a stronger tax base and pervasive indexation but were nonetheless visible there as well.

Argentina

The technocrats who shaped the social policy reform agenda in Argentina came to power during the presidency of Carlos Saúl Menem (1989–98). Menem's predecessor, Raúl Alfonsín (1983–89), had been unable to halt the downward economic spiral inherited from the military government, and Menem therefore came to office in the midst of a crisis that in 1988–89 had veered into hyperinflation.

After several false starts, Economy Minister Domingo Cavallo engineered a major stabilization initiative, the controversial Convertibility Law of April 1991, which established a currency-board system with free convertibility of the peso. The Convertibility Law ended the hyperinflation virtually overnight, and as in Peru, generated a huge swell of support for the president. Cavallo not only consolidated control of the economy ministry but placed allies in many other cabinet positions as well.

REFORMING THE PENSION SYSTEM

Following the success of the Convertibility Law, reform of the pay-as-you-go pension system was the highest social-policy priority of the Cavallo team. Although pension coverage was relatively broad and generous in principle, inflation had severely eroded benefits, and payments to beneficiaries had dropped far below the official replacement rates guaranteed by law (Kay 2000, 11). Nevertheless, the system continued to run large deficits because of widespread evasion of contributions. By 1990, transfers from the treasury covered almost one-third of total pension expenditures (Madrid 2003, 103).

The reform initiative was formulated in consultation with Chilean experts under Walter Schulthess, the head of the social-security agency and a close Cavallo ally. The reformers knew that privatization would entail substantial transition costs. However, they believed that the reform would create the basis for sound public finances over the long run by increasing domestic savings and reducing the implicit debt of the existing system (Madrid 2003, 104–6; Brooks 2002, 498–99). In the meantime, they expected to reduce the costs of the transition by restrictions on eligibility and caps on entitlements (Kay 1999; 2000).

These restructuring proposals were generally supported by the private sector, but the initiative met widespread opposition from pensioners and the union movement. To gain passage of the initial reform legislation, reformers retreated from initial plans for full privatization to a multipillar system that gave workers greater choice. Unions also gained the right to create their own funds, an important side payment for several of the larger unions. Finally, the government backtracked on proposals for raising the retirement age and restricting minimum benefits in the pay-as-you-go pillar (Madrid 2003, 118–36).

Despite these compromises, the government retained political advantages that allowed it to shift policy back toward the preferences of the technocrats. In their accounts of the pension reform, both Madrid (2003) and Brooks (2002) highlight the importance of a unified government and strong legislative support. Peronists constituted a majority in the senate and strong plurality in the chamber of deputies. Yet these factors should not be overemphasized. The Peronist party had a long and well-known antipathy to neoliberal policies. Moreover, Menem had to share control of his party with powerful provincial governors—as well as with a swing group of congressmen aligned with the unions (Corrales 2002, 127–31; 2004, 326–33).

Menem's ability to manage these forces owed much to underlying economic and political circumstances. Because of the political gains from conquering inflation, both the president and his finance minister were at the peak of their popularity when the pension reform was launched. Success of stabilizing the economy gave the executive and the Cavallo team considerable leverage over politicians in the legislature, who had to weigh the risks of a return to macroeconomic instability. The structural changes associated with the collapse of the ISI model also had important consequences for the power of key stakeholders. Agreements with several of the most powerful unions were essential to gaining legislative support for the passage of the first pension-reform bill, but the union movement as a whole was clearly on the defensive (Roberts, 2006, 169; Levitsky 2001, 43–46). Despite the government's concessions, the initial pension legislation passed in 1993 made major changes in the system.[6]

Over the next several years, moreover, the government was also able to roll back a number of these concessions by arguing that they posed a threat to macroeconomic stability. In 1995, at the height of the Mexican

---

[6] Madrid (2003, 16) estimates that the second pillar enrolled approximately two-thirds of the workers, even though the share of payroll contributions was relatively limited (see also Mesa-Lago 2005, 49). Brooks's simulations predict that workers earning the average wage could expect to receive 54 percent of their pension benefits from that source (see table 5.10).

peso crisis, legislators agreed to a sharp reduction in the minimum pension guarantees after Cavallo warned that existing commitments in the public pillar would jeopardize the convertibility regime (Kay 2000, 13). The same legislation also officially abandoned the high guaranteed replacement rates, froze litigation over delayed payments, and established a maximum limit on benefits. In 1997, as budget pressures on the government continued to mount, Menem issued a further decree that deindexed basic minimum payments and left subsequent adjustments to the discretion of the executive. Finally, in 2000, in the midst of a new round of economic crisis, privileged pension funds were eliminated by the Radical Party president, Fernando de la Rúa, who succeeded Menem in 1999.

HEALTHCARE AND EDUCATION INITIATIVES

The Menem government also advanced ambitious proposals for the health and education systems that reflected the liberal orientation of its technocratic leadership. However, it proved harder for the technocrats to link reforms in healthcare and education to the maintenance of macroeconomic stability. Moreover, the proposed changes implied much higher costs for unions, which had reaped large financial benefits from their participation in the health sector in particular. Although outcomes fell short of the government's preferences, substantial changes were instituted in both sectors.

Reform initiatives in healthcare were crafted in close collaboration with World Bank advisors. One of the most controversial was an initiative to break the union monopoly of the approximately 300 union-owned health organizations (*obras sociales*) that provided insurance and medical services for most of Argentina's formal-sector workers (Lloyd-Sherlock 2004, 102–108). The payroll taxes flowing to the *obras* were both a major source of funding for the unions and a lucrative source of subcontracting opportunities for private hospitals and some private insurance groups. Breaking union control and introducing competition and choice into this system was part of a larger project to make the health sector more cost-effective and accountable (Lloyd-Sherlock 2004, 102–108).

Because changes in the system struck at interests so basic to the union movement, Menem instituted the reform through a series of decrees rather than subjecting them to legislative approval. He issued the first such decree, allowing union members to change affiliation, in 1993. The proposal garnered little support from private insurers, many of whom benefited from an unregulated system of subcontracting, and it faced fierce opposition from the CGT, which launched its first general strike against the Menem administration. In the face of this opposition, the government beat a tactical retreat. The administration assigned the new program to an agency controlled by the unions, the Administración Nacional de Seguro de Salud (ANSAL) and the decree was not implemented.

The government issued a second series of decrees in the wake of the Mexican peso crisis of the mid-1990s. Backed by a World Bank loan, the revised program reduced payroll taxes, centralized collection within the social-security administration, and offered financial assistance to unions seeking to upgrade the quality of their services. These measures gained support both from industrial and commercial sectors, which liked the payroll-tax reduction, and from some of the richer unions that saw opportunities to attract new members into their *obras*.

In the late 1990s, however, the *obra* reforms began to unravel. By that time, general support for the government had begun to fade. Concern about a return to inflation had subsided, unemployment had increased dramatically, and Cavallo had been forced to resign from the cabinet. The changing political tide was reflected in Peronist losses in the mid-term elections of 1997 that provided the unions with greater leverage. The anti-Peronist de la Rúa government reinstituted *obra* competition in 2000; but a vigorous union campaign against the "privatization" of healthcare impeded implementation, and the Peronists repealed the law altogether when they returned to power in 2002.

Education reform was a lower priority for the government, but also had strong fiscal motives. In 1991, Cavallo slipped a provision into budget legislation that abruptly decentralized responsibility for financing secondary education to the provinces and provided the federal government with wider discretion with respect to intergovernmental transfers. Teachers' unions led the opposition to the changes (Corrales 2004, 326–33). Compromises brokered in the chamber of deputies in the 1993 legislation included commitments for substantial increases in federal transfers, increases in the years of compulsory schooling, and maintenance of union control over assignments and promotions. Nevertheless, the law preserved the initial decentralization decision made under Cavallo. Although investment in education did increase in subsequent years, the government was unable to fully meet its funding commitments. Beginning in the late 1990s, the entire education system was profoundly disrupted by the resurgence of fiscal crises and provincial bankruptcies.

ANTIPOVERTY PROGRAMS

Until the crisis of the early 2000s, targeted social assistance remained relatively limited. The most widely known program was Trabajar, a public-employment program supported by the World Bank. Although this program was well targeted, it provided employment for only several hundred thousand workers a year in a context of double-digit unemployment. After the crisis of the early 2000s, social assistance to unemployed workers expanded substantially under the aegis of the more populist Peronist governments of Eduardo Duhalde and Néstor Kirchner. Even these governments, however, continued to pursue stringent fiscal policies. In the early 2000s, the programs reached only about 30 percent of the bottom income quintile (Lindert, Skoufias, and Shapiro 2006, 86). Moreover, their expansion came at the expense of cutbacks in health and education.[7] Severe fiscal constraints appeared to matter considerably.

Social policy in Argentina during the 1990s provides a stark contrast to the high-growth Asian democracies discussed in chapter 6. Economic crisis empowered technocrats who dominated the reform agenda for the better part of a decade. Their reform initiatives fell well short of the changes instituted in authoritarian regimes such as Chile; in every policy area, they were impelled to compromise with politicians, interest groups, and stakeholders. But the effects of crisis are clear: reforms were substantial and proved particularly wide-ranging in the case of pensions, where the technocratic team could link the reform effort to fiscal consolidation.

Brazil

Brazil, like Argentina, suffered exceptionally high inflation and high fiscal deficits during the 1980s and early 1990s. During the 1990s and early 2000s, these conditions encouraged governments to delegate extensive authority to technocrats in the finance ministry and central bank. In contrast to Argentina, however, the economic bureaucracy was unable to exercise direct control over the social ministries, and the government as a whole faced much greater pressure both to meet the demands of stakeholders and to address the notoriously unequal access to basic social services.

Much of the literature on policy reform in Brazil has focused on institutional impediments created by the country's famously fragmented political system: multiple veto points created by a multiplicity of parties, lack of discipline within the parties, and federalism (Ames 2001, Mainwaring 1999; but see also Figueiredo and Limongi 2000, 151–70). These factors did play an important role in several areas of social policy, most importantly in efforts at pension reform. But a consideration of institutions must be supplemented by an examination of both the economic context and the nature of underlying social-policy interests.

---

[7] Between 2000 and 2004, the share of social assistance in GDP rose by 0.3 percent (from 1.2 to 1.5), but the share of health and education fell from 10 percent to 8.7 percent in the same period. As shares of total social spending, social assistance rose from 5.7 percent to 7.1 percent, but health and education fell from 46.5 in 2000 to 43.9 in 2003 (Lindert et al. 2006, 86).

In part, the impetus to stabilization and economic liberalization was blunted by the timing of economic circumstances during the transition. The debt crisis hit in the last years of military rule, but the transition to democratic rule overlapped with a temporary upturn in the economy; annual average growth rates reached nearly 7 percent in 1984–86 before declining in 1987 and falling back into negative territory in 1988.

Several factors particular to Brazil also mitigated the political effects of high deficits and inflation on the power of the technocrats. In contrast to most other Latin American countries, Brazil had a relatively strong tax base (Economic Commission on Latin America and the Caribbean 1998, 67), a condition that made it easier to justify increased expenditures. The effects of very high inflation on middle-class and blue-collar incomes, moreover, were partially cushioned by the pervasive indexing of wages and financial instruments. As a result, inflation did not create the sense of urgency and tolerance for liberalizing reform visible in the other high-inflation settings.

Although the upswing of the mid-1980s was brief, it fueled strong expectations that democratic rule would result in an increase in social benefits. Formal and public sector unions affiliated with the Workers' Party (Partido dos Trabalhadores, PT) were particularly important players. Levels of unionization were roughly the same as in Argentina—about 25 percent of the workforce (Roberts 2006, 169). But whereas the Argentine movement had been weakened by decades of slow growth and deindustrialization, Brazil's dynamic industrialization and the expansion of the public sector during the 1960s and 1970s produced a radical labor movement outside the official structure of corporatist control. At the same time, pressure to address the needs of the poor was increased by suffrage reforms that eliminated literacy requirements and lowered the voting age and by increased opportunities for civil-society organizations to advocate pro-poor policies.

As we would expect, the confluence of democratization and favorable economic circumstances led in the mid-1980s to an expansion of social commitments. And by the time the economic boom faded, many of these commitments had been enshrined in a new constitution ratified in 1988 (Faria 2003, 10–11). The constitution guaranteed generous replacement rates for existing pensioners, as well as sick pay, employment guarantees, survivors' benefits, and other benefits already accruing to civil servants and formal-sector workers. It also promised social assistance to "whoever may need it, regardless of contribution to social security" (article 203). Further, all citizens were guaranteed "equal conditions for access to and remaining in school" (article 206), and health was declared to be "the right of all persons and the duty of the State" (article 196).

As the economy slowed and inflation surged in the late 1980s, governments focused primarily on stabilization, and it proved increasingly difficult to implement these mandates. An early stabilization effort in 1986–87 relied primarily on price controls and collapsed in less than a year. Under Fernando Collor (1990–92), the government imposed a harsh austerity plan that entailed sharp cuts on social spending (see figure A6.2). This, however, also failed to hold; inflation returned, and Collor was forced from office in a devastating corruption scandal.

In 1994, the then-finance minister, Fernando Henrique Cardoso, finally led a successful effort to tame the inflation. The "Real Plan" combined tight fiscal and monetary policies with gradual deindexation of price and wage contracts and the introduction of a new currency, the real (Bacha 1998). As in Argentina and Peru, the successful stabilization was immensely popular, and propelled Cardoso into the presidency in the 1994 election. Throughout Cardoso's two terms (1994–2002) and the presidency of his successor, Luiz Inácio Lula da Silva, known more simply as Lula, the Brazilian government attached the highest priority to maintaining economic stability. Powerful ministers of finance dominated the cabinet and set the budgetary parameters for social policy. Despite fractious legislative coalitions, the president maintained fiscal discipline through the use of decree powers and special authority delegated by the congress.

PENSION REFORM: GRADUAL AND PARAMETRIC

Although technocrats were able to set spending limits, their capacity to redesign welfare institutions faced ongoing constraints from the constitutional guarantees established in 1988 and from the powerful interests that had pressed for them. These constraints were most evident with respect to social-security entitlements, which required a supermajority of three-fifths of the legislature to change.

By the mid-1990s, deficits in the social security system (Instituto Nacional de Assistencia Social, or INAMPS) had grown to between 3.5 and 4 percent of GDP, and pensions to public-sector workers—about a third of all pensioners—accounted for approximately two-thirds of the total deficit (Bonturi 2002, 10; Medici 2004, 10). During the early 1990s, economic officials and the financial sector expressed support for the establishment of a fully funded pillar, but significant movement in this direction was halted by political scandals and the impeachment of Collor. In subsequent years, concern about high transition costs led government technocrats themselves to take privatization off the table and to focus instead on changes in eligibility and benefits (Pinheiro 2005). Legislation introduced by Cardoso in 1995 sought to limit early retirement, equalize eligibility between the public and private sectors, and gradually eliminate special concessions for specific categories of employees. (Madrid 2003, 150–51).

Predictably, these proposals were strongly opposed by the Unified Labor Confederation (the CUT) and its allies in the opposition Workers' Party, as well as specific interest groups (the military, civil servants, and the like) entrenched within the public bureaucracy. Negotiations with the unions and with pensioners' associations quickly collapsed, and the government was compelled to accept a succession of legislative amendments that drastically scaled back the initial proposal.

Continuing threats of macroeconomic instability did, however, allow the Cardoso and Lula governments to chip away at entitlements. In 1998, aftershocks from the Asian and Russian crises finally allowed the government to gain the three-fifths support necessary for passage of a constitutional-reform bill. The new legislation, however, dealt primarily with eligibility and benefits within the private-sector-workers' fund and left the much more costly public-sector pensions untouched.

Reform efforts continued under the Lula government. The prospect of a leftist victory had stoked concerns in financial markets, and to avert a panic, Lula pursued a surprisingly cautious macroeconomic policy that included a renewed effort at parametric pension reform. In December 2003, the government took on the highly sensitive issue of the benefits going to privileged public-sector workers.[8] Lula was able to use the risk of macroeconomic instability to gain support not only from the opposition but also from PT legislators, who had bitterly opposed the Cardoso legislation. Nevertheless, the final product to emerge from legislative bargaining was modest, and large expenditures in public-sector pensions continued to place heavy burdens on the treasury throughout Lula's term.

HEALTHCARE INITIATIVES

In the aftermath of the deep cuts imposed under Collor (see figure A6.2), Cardoso and Lula were able to increase spending in the social sectors. More important, appointments to top positions in the education and health ministries, previously controlled by politicians of the Liberal Front Party (Partido da Frente Liberal, PFL), went to policy experts who sought a more efficient and progressive allocation of federal transfers to states and municipalities (Arretche 2004, 155–89).

In the health sector, the Cardoso government built on constitutional reforms that had been pressed throughout the 1980s by a nationwide movement of healthcare professionals and left-wing activists (*sanitaristas*). The *sanitarista* campaign targeted the political and financial influence that private hospitals and curative health services exerted within

---

[8] The reforms, though modest, did include some important changes such as penalties for early retirement, equalization of public- and private-sector benefits for new entrants into the workforce, and a ceiling on nontaxable benefits.

INAMPS, the social security institute. The movement sought to break these ties by consolidating federal payroll revenues and regulatory authority within the ministry of health, reducing the power of INAMPS, and decentralizing responsibility for health administration to the municipalities (Weyland 1996, 162–63).

Both goals were incorporated into the 1988 constitution, and the congress passed ordinary legislation in 1990. But battles over resources and pressure from stakeholders delayed implementation for almost another decade. For a succession of health ministers, securing adequate resources remained a critical problem. Collor's stabilization initiative reduced funding for healthcare and exacerbated turf battles that continued into the Cardoso presidency.[9] Although per capita health spending did increase in the mid-1990s, it declined again as contagion from the Russian crisis hit Brazil in the last years of the decade.

The government did, however, take important steps toward administrative rationalization. A series of ministerial decrees increased federal transfers to municipalities willing to commit to public and preventive-health and home-care services and to accept stronger auditing and evaluation procedures. By 2002, almost all of Brazil's 5560 municipalities had met the regulatory standards for primary-care services, and about 560 of these received funding for all services in their jurisdiction (Arretche 2004, 178).

These reforms constituted a major reorganization of the Brazilian health system. The Brazilian health system continued to be plagued by serious regional and class inequalities.[10] Nevertheless, the policy changes indicated a substantial and somewhat surprising capacity of Brazil's democratic system to undertake reforms of significant scope and coherence, even in the face of institutional fragmentation, interest-group pressures, and budget constraints.

EDUCATION REFORM

In the education sector, we see similarly mixed results: progress in institutional reorganization and financing but within limits established by fiscal constraints and stakeholder pressures. A major issue in Brazilian education spending was the high share going to tertiary education, but this issue

[9] In 1993, for example, the welfare minister (*ministro de previdencia*), Antonio Britto, unilaterally withheld payroll tax revenues from the ministry of health on the grounds that they were needed to fund social-security benefits. The following year, the minister successfully promoted the legislation of a new tax earmarked for healthcare, only to have the finance ministry reduce allocations from general revenues in an effort to control spending (Arretche 2004, 175).

[10] Although there were some improvements in health indicators—most notably, a decline in infant mortality—these began during the military period and cannot easily be attributed to the reforms.

was taken off the table after strong protests against attempts to impose fees and cut salaries. Instead, the minister of education, Paulo Renato Souza, and his reform team focused mainly on reallocating resources within the primary-education sector and recasting the regulatory and oversight role of the ministry of education.

Financing for impoverished municipal schools in the rural northeast was bolstered significantly in 1996 by a new constitutional amendment known by its Portuguese acronym, FUNDEF (Fundo de Mantenção e Desenvolvimento do Ensino Fundamental). Expanding on legislation passed in the last years of the military regime (see chapter 2), FUNDEF mandated that at least 15 percent of federal transfers be devoted to primary education and that 60 percent of these funds be allocated to teachers' salaries. The reform also established a modest required minimum level of per-pupil expenditures at the primary level (Draibe 2004, 395–400). The poorer states that could not meet this were to receive additional federal transfers; but the minimum was deliberately set at a low level, and adjustment for inflation was left to the discretion of the legislature (Melo 2004, 34–36). The general expectation was that these funds would come primarily from a reallocation of existing federal transfers (Brown 2002, 137).

The legislation encountered opposition from PT legislators, who argued that it did not go far enough, and from teachers' unions in several of the wealthier states. Badly paid teachers in the poorer states stood to benefit considerably from salary guarantees, however, and the legislation had strong support from politicians representing the northeast and municipal systems throughout the country. The wide geographic appeal of the FUNDEF amendment allowed the government to overcome legislative and interest-group opposition and to gain the three-fifths majority required for passage; implementation began in 1998. As noted, the FUNDEF legislation had only limited redistributive effects across the federal system; the reallocation of funds occurred primarily *within* individual states (Brown 2002, 137). Nevertheless, its provisions provided a major boost to underpaid teachers of the northeast and to municipal school systems that had primary responsibility for basic education throughout the country.

ANTIPOVERTY INITIATIVES

The most visible innovation in the education sector occurred on the demand side, with the establishment in the late 1990s of a program that provided conditional income transfers to poor families with children in school. Electoral competition between the PT and Cardoso's Brazilian Social Democracy Party (Partido da Social Democracia Brasileira, PSDB) drove the expansion of this program, although within the context of tight fiscal constraints. During the mid-1990s, local governments established versions of this program in the city of Campinas, under a PSDB mayor, and in the state of Brasilia, under a PT governor. Proposals for a federal program were initially championed by leaders of the PT, but the idea quickly gained support among politicians in the government coalition as well (Melo 2004, 27–30).

Fiscal concerns led the Cardoso government to delay taking up the program until the run-up to the presidential election campaign of 1998. In December 1997, a law sponsored by the president provided for a multiyear phase-in of transfers to the poorest municipalities. Under pressure from the PT and a pending election campaign, Cardoso followed with a second law that extended the program to all municipalities (Melo 2004, 6).

The program, known as Bolsa Escola during the Cardoso years, reached 4.5 million families by 2002. It became the flagship antipoverty program (Bolsa Familia) of the Lula administration, reaching about 11 million families. Like PROGRESA, the limits of this assistance must be kept in perspective. Total resources devoted to the Bolsa programs were small: approximately 2.5 percent of total educational expenditures and only 0.15 percent of the GDP (Morley and Coady 2003, 21). Morley and Coady (2003, 53) also note that expenditures on the program constituted only about 3.9 percent of the amount required to close the "poverty gap." Nevertheless, the Bolsa program, like its counterpart in Mexico, had demonstrable effects in reducing dropout rates (Morley and Coady 2003, 44–45), and increased the family income of recipients (Morley and Coady 2003, 49). For these reasons, the program was enormously popular, and did much to account for Lula's sweep of the northeastern states in the presidential election of 2006.

What conclusions can be drawn from the Brazilian experience? It stands as something of an exception among the "crisis cases" (Argentina, Venezuela, Mexico, and Peru) in the sense that liberal technocrats were less able to dominate the social-policy agenda. Their efforts to reform the highly unequal pension system faced entrenched stakeholders and entitlements locked into the 1988 constitution at a time of robust growth. Nevertheless, successful stabilization did expand the influence of reformers, and Cardoso and Lula did succeed in deconstitutionalizing some entitlements and moderating benefits to public sector employees.

Health and education reforms were led by policy elites that were not directly allied with the finance ministry, and their policies placed much greater emphasis than in Argentina on correcting glaring distributional inequities. However, both the Cardoso and Lula governments prioritized fiscal discipline, and the finance ministry thus retained an effective veto over the allocation of resources. Financing expanded, but with a greater emphasis on targeting and a reduced role for the ministries as centers of patronage.

SOCIAL POLICY IN "LOW-CRISIS" DEMOCRACIES:
URUGUAY, COSTA RICA, COLOMBIA, AND CHILE

Economic conditions in the 1980s in Uruguay, Costa Rica, Colombia, and Chile were often difficult but less severe than in Argentina and Brazil. The Uruguayan economy was devastated in the early 1980s, while still under military rule; but democratic governments avoided the economic collapse experienced in the crisis cases. Costa Rica was hit hard by the debt crisis; but the economy rebounded after a tough fiscal adjustment and was bolstered throughout the 1980s by financial support from the United States. Chile's democratic government faced serious stabilization problems when it came to power in 1990, but it presided over the strongest economy in the region for the next fifteen years. Colombia, unlike any of the other countries, had enjoyed a long history of relative macroeconomic stability, although this began to deteriorate in the late 1990s. In short, although all experienced periodic economic difficulties, the severe fiscal constraints and inflationary pressures that drove reforms in the crisis cases were comparatively limited.

Substantial differences in the coverage of the welfare system and in stakeholder influences did, however, produce different social-policy trajectories. Social policy reform in Uruguay and Costa Rica was constrained by broad and popular welfare legacies. Colombia's system, by contrast, had relatively few beneficiaries, a situation that facilitated pension privatization but also encouraged an expansion of access to social services.

Chile constitutes an interesting comparator for our purposes because of the extensive liberalization of social policy that occurred under the Pinochet dictatorship. By the time of the transition, the new, more liberal system had generated its own bases of support, impeding radical changes in the privatized sectors of the system. But Pinochet's democratic successors also had strong electoral incentives to make improvements in the provision of public services and social assistance.

Uruguay

Changes in Uruguay's welfare system were considerably more limited than in Argentina or Brazil. Although the government did eventually pass a pension reform, it was the most modest in the region. Health and education policies maintained an emphasis on public provision and prioritized expansion of services over administrative reforms intended to increase efficiency.

The continuities in Uruguay's welfare system reflected two important differences with the systems in Argentina and Brazil. First, democratic governments in Uruguay did not experience financial crises or inflationary pressures comparable to those in Argentina and Brazil. Growth was flat or negative during the late 1980s and early 1990s, but relative success in containing inflation weakened incentives for either broader market reforms or major changes in existing welfare arrangements, despite a decline in effectiveness and generosity. Second, the existing welfare system had especially widespread political support. Politicians seeking to restructure entitlements and services confronted not only well-entrenched stakeholders but status quo preferences within the broader electorate.[11] In this respect, Uruguay bears a close resemblance to the Eastern European countries we discuss in chapter 8.

As was the case in Brazil, the fragmentation of political parties and multiple institutional veto points also worked strongly against major reform initiatives. Legislation required the negotiation of agreements among independent factions of the Colorado and Blanco Parties. Even more important, the constitution allowed popular referendums on social legislation (Castiglioni 2005, 78–82; Bergara et al. 2004, 27). But the importance of these institutional veto points as impediments to policy change depended in turn on a still more fundamental factor: the popularity of the broadly based welfare system among both the public at large and organized interests.

PENSION REFORM

From the onset of the democratic period, government leaders of both parties regarded Uruguay's large and generous pension system as a serious threat to fiscal stability, but efforts to contain pension spending proved unsuccessful. In 1985, the first Julio María Sanguinetti administration (1985–90) signed an IMF agreement that prioritized the reduction of pension spending. But parametric adjustments were beaten back by strong opposition from the Frente Amplio, the center-left opposition party, and pensioners, labor unions, and civic organizations.

In 1989, a broad coalition of these groups mobilized a referendum campaign to increase pension payments and index them to public-sector salaries. Opponents were able to exploit the direct-democracy provision in the constitution to press their interests; but they would not have succeeded without wide public and organizational support. Retired union leaders brought substantial organizational skills to the national pension organization, Organización Nacional de Asociaciones de Jubilados y Pensionistas

---

[11] During the 1990s, pension beneficiaries constituted 30 percent of the electorate, and public employees represented another 9 percent (Luna 2006, 17).

del Uruguay, which combined 120 retiree associations with branches throughout the country (Kay 1999, 409). The union movement was led by a unified and independent confederation, the Intersyndical Plenum of Workers-National Convention of Workers (Plenario Intersindical de Trabajadores–Convención Nacional de Trabajadores, PIT-CNT) (Kay 1999, 411). Left politicians were also among the main sponsors, but the issue was not strictly a partisan one. As Papadópoulos (1998, 156) notes, "other politicians, fearing the loss of the pensioners' vote either supported the reform or did not take a position on the issue." In the referendum, the provision was supported by over 80 percent of voters.

Fiscal strains escalated as pension expenditures soared from about 10 percent of GDP in the late 1980s to about 20 percent by 1994. President Luis Alberto Lacalle (1990–94), a Blanco leader inclined to market-oriented economic reforms, introduced four successive bills that sought to tighten eligibility and tie benefits more closely to contributions. All were blocked in the legislature. A fifth, relatively modest proposal passed with a broad coalition of Blancos and Colorados, but it was subsequently overturned in a plebiscite in 1994 by over 70 percent of the electorate (Kay 1999, 415).

A breakthrough of sorts was at last achieved during Sanguinetti's second term (1995–2000), after extensive negotiations among a wide range of social actors and political leaders. The Sanguinetti government passed a new pension law that provided for the establishment of a small second pillar.[12] But as noted, the scope of the reform was extremely modest. The private pillar, according to both the Brooks and Madrid indexes of privatization, was the smallest in the region. It was voluntary for all but a small fraction of the workforce earning over $800 a month and was the only capitalized pillar in the region required to provide an absolute minimum rate of return for its affiliates (Kay 2000, 17). As Filgueira and Filgueira (1997, 23) remark, "while this reform constitutes a clear departure from the old system, it is a far cry from the Chilean model, and also remains statist and committed to some redistributive goals that have been rather neglected in other countries' experiences."

HEALTHCARE AND EDUCATION INITIATIVES

Policies in the education and health sectors, even more than in pensions, either preserved or expanded the public universalistic features of the old welfare state. During the second Sanguinetti administration, the government instituted a series of measures aimed at expanding access to the public education system. With loans from the World Bank and the IDB,

---

[12] Indeed, concern over the limits of the private pillar and the continuing guarantees of the pay-as-you-go system caused the World Bank to withdraw support for the project early in the negotiations (Castiglioni 2005; Papadópolous 1998).

preschool was made universal for five-year-old children. Government spending on education increased from about 2.5 percent of GDP in 1995 to nearly 3.5 percent during the next three years (Castiglioni 2005, 71).

In contrast to developments in Argentina and Brazil, Uruguay saw considerably less emphasis on the reorganization of the existing system. In an effort to control costs, the Uruguayan reforms did reduce job-security protections for teachers in the new schools, a step that was strongly opposed by the Frente Amplio and allied factions of the teachers' unions. But the expansion of the system had strong popular support, and in contrast to the campaign against the pension legislation, the opposition was unable to exploit the "direct-democracy" provision in the constitution. A referendum to overturn the measure was defeated by almost three-quarters of the voters (Castiglioni 2005, 70–71).

Unlike the situation in Argentina and Brazil, there were no significant initiatives to change the health system, despite rising costs during the 1990s. Under the second Sanguinetti administration, Health Minister Alfredo Solari did attempt to reduce subsidies to the semipublic system of HMOs and to open healthcare provision in rural areas to private-sector competition. But these proved to be nonstarters in the legislature, where a number of influential politicians were themselves doctors with close ties to the main medical association.

Rosanna Castiglioni (2005, 82) sums up the course of Uruguayan social policy in all three areas: "In the context of Latin American nations that advanced pension reforms, Uruguay stands amongst the least radical reformers. In education, the reform expands the public system and it does not display any of the blueprints of the market-oriented reforms seen in the region. . . . Finally, in health care, an area that confronted a very powerful veto player, [reform] failed to get enough votes for approval."

Costa Rica

The broadly based Costa Rican welfare system also experienced relatively limited change during the 1980s and 1990s. In part, this stability was attributable to favorable economic circumstances. Costa Rica did not avoid painful adjustments and cuts in social expenditures during the debt crisis of the early 1980s, but relatively early stabilization efforts enabled the country to avoid the large deficits and high inflation that characterized Argentina, Brazil, Peru, and Mexico (see figure 7.1). United States aid during the Central American civil war also bolstered the economy; from 1982 to 1989, bilateral assistance averaged about 3.6 percent of GDP (Clark 2001, 47). Timely adjustments and strong external support made it possible for governments to introduce market reforms gradually, with less social disruption than occurred with the more rapid reformers of the region.

As in Uruguay, moreover, widespread entitlements and well-entrenched stakeholders also served to make major reorganization of the welfare system difficult. Costa Rica was one of the last countries in the region to adopt pension reform, and systemic changes were modest. In the health and education sectors, the government made some efforts to introduce greater accountability in financing, but organizational changes remained limited compared to either Argentina or Brazil. The main thrust of policy, particularly in the health sector, was on expanding services.

Pressures for economic and social reform did intensify in the 1990s as the Central American wars came to a close and United States assistance declined. But the response to these pressures also placed as much emphasis on plugging gaps in coverage as on liberalization. The Figueres government (1994–98) did sign on to a World Bank plan for decentralization of public hospitals and per-patient budgeting. It did so, however, in conjunction with funding commitments for the transfer of all primary health services to the CCSS and the expansion of clinics into rural areas. Predictably, this expansionary feature of the World Bank loan proceeded at a relatively rapid pace while implementation of the hospital reform stalled in the face of resistance from the healthcare administration. (Clark 2001, 89–95).

Initiatives to retrench the popular pension system met with an even stronger backlash throughout the 1990s. In 1995, the Figueres government succeeded in restructuring the nearly bankrupt teachers' fund by raising contributions and reducing benefits, but this reform came with a high political price tag: repeated twenty-four-hour work stoppages throughout the entire year and "the largest protest marches ever seen in Costa Rica" (Clark 2001, 86). The following year, the government launched a broader initiative to cut benefits and raise the retirement age but then withdrew it in the face of a new round of political protests.

As costs continued to mount, pension privatization was finally brought onto the political agenda in the late 1990s, under the right-of-center administration of Miguel Ángel Rodríguez. As in Uruguay, legislation proceeded only after extensive negotiations among a wide range of actors, including the major business and labor associations, civil society groups, administrators, and policy experts. The proposal that emerged from this process was passed into law with broad bipartisan support in early 2000 and went into effect in 2001. The legislation created a mixed multipillar system, but—predictably—the extent of structural change was modest. All new workers were required to join the mixed system, but mandatory contributions to the fully funded system were relatively small (Madrid 2003, 16). According to Brooks's simulation, the public pillar was likely to remain the primary source of protection for the average worker (See table 5.10).

Colombia: Permissive Fiscal Conditions and Welfare Expansion

The Colombian experience also contrasts with the crisis cases reviewed in the previous section. Throughout the 1970s, the country's elitist liberal and conservative governments pursued conservative macroeconomic policies and accumulated much less debt than did other countries in the region, a fact that in turn reduced the severity of the shocks that hit the rest of the region (Stallings 1990, 149–61). During the 1990s, successive administrations thus had more opportunity to expand coverage of the extremely limited social-insurance system.

The political incentives to address these problems were initially driven primarily by gueurilla violence and by drug trafficking, which had contributed to a significant loss of legitimacy for state institutions. In the 1990s, political elites attempted to address underlying popular discontent through comprehensive reforms aimed at redefining relations between the state and society, including a broad overhaul of the welfare system.

The convening of a new constituent assembly in 1991 marked an important milestone in this process. As it did in Brazil, the assembly provided a platform for popular and left-oriented groups previously marginalized from political power. The new constitution also incorporated broad commitments to the provision of universal health coverage, education, and other forms of social protection. Constitutional reform by no means insured that governments would authorize and implement these legal mandates. Unlike the situation in Brazil, however, Colombia's long history of fiscal caution left governments in a reasonably good position to follow through, and fewer excuses for not doing so. Social spending rose sharply throughout most of the 1990s (see figure A6.4).

PENSION AND HEALTHCARE REFORMS

The moderate, market-oriented government of César Gaviria (1990–94) took the lead in drafting implementing legislation for the new constitutional entitlements. Gaviria placed the highest priority on partial pension privatization and initially attempted to shelve implementation of constitutionally mandated healthcare reforms. He relented, however, at the urging of powerful allies in the legislature, who argued that pension reform was more likely to pass if it was bundled with more popular healthcare initiatives. The strategy worked. In December 1993, the congress established a modest second pillar that enrolled an estimated 38 percent of the covered workforce (Madrid 2003, 16), but the government also committed to a sweeping reorganization and expansion of access to health insurance and provision (Ramírez 2004, 130–39; Nelson 1998, 4–8).

The healthcare legislation had been guided through the congress by Juan Luis Londoño, an economist closely linked to the finance ministry, and it encompassed a complex mixture of liberalizing and expansionist components. The liberalizing components included substantial decentralization, an expanded role for private insurers, and the phasing in of performance-based budgeting for hospitals and clinics. The most popular feature of the reform, however, was a major expansion of coverage. The reform provided low-income families with an opportunity to enroll in a subsidized system of healthcare organizations, and after a transition period, promised a package of benefits identical to those offered in the contributory system.

Implemetation of the expansionary features of the program proceeded rapidly, while by contrast, bureaucratic resistance slowed cost-saving measures such as the rationalization of hospital financing. The proportion of the population with coverage increased from just over 20 percent in 1993 to 57 percent by 1997 and was especially rapid in rural areas and among the very poor.[13]

By the end of the decade, the rapid expansion of the system and delays in the cost-saving measures had become a matter of major concern.[14] One consequence was that coverage never reached the universality envisioned in the original reforms, and the package of services available in the subsidized system fell short of parity with the contributory regime. Nevertheless, health-system reform constituted a major expansion and was considered a model among advocates of wider coverage elsewhere in the region. Retrenchment, moreover, was impeded by the fact that the new arrangements had now created strong support, not only among politicians and private healthcare providers but also across a wider swath of beneficiaries. As in the East Asian cases, these beneficiaries quickly became a significant electoral constraint on subsequent efforts to rationalize the system even as its financial vulnerability became apparent.

DECENTRALIZATION OF EDUCATION

The influence of stakeholders was most evident in the area of education reform, which proved far less successful than reform in the health field (Lowden 2004, 350). As mandated by the constitution, legislative proposals provided for a substantial transfer of funding and responsibility to provincial and municipal governments in the expectation that decentralization would increase efficiency and accountability. The incentives for the Gaviria government to push these initiatives forward, however, were

---

[13] Coverage expanded in rural areas from 7 to almost 50 percent, and from 4 to 40 percent within the lowest income decile of the population (Ramírez 2004, 142).

[14] Decentralization of healthcare responsibilities had increased clientelism at the local level and ultimately added to, rather than reduced, the overall fiscal burden. Under Ernesto Samper (1994–98), Gaviria's successor as president, budgets were further strained by large pay increases to health workers.

weaker than in the case of healthcare reform. First, education was not, like healthcare, linked to the higher-priority goal of pension reform. Decentralization was also strongly opposed by the ministry of education and the powerful and highly centralized teachers' union. In the absence of executive leadership, the congress approved two bills with provisions that were unreconciled and contradictory: one advanced by the unions and its allies in the ministry of education, and the other by policy specialists with the National Planning Agency (Lowden 2004, 358–59).

Confusion and increasing fiscal strain were the predictable consequences. The laws mandated increasing transfers to provincial governments and large municipalities, regardless of performance or economic conditions. By 1998, virtually all these transfers were going to fund teachers' salaries. The Samper government established a fund to cover local educational deficits, but this only increased the incentives for politicians to extend their patronage networks by hiring more teachers. Absence of leadership, legislative compromises, and continuing pressure from teachers' unions and patronage-oriented politicians, all combined to produce the worst features of health reform without the benefits.

Chile

The moderate center-left governments that held power in Chile during the 1990s were constrained in their approach to social policy by commitments to accept the basic market reforms of the Pinochet era and to respect constitutional provisions that established an effective veto power for rightist parties in the senate. Throughout the 1990s and early 2000s, liberal technocrats remained in firm control of the economic ministries and of the independent central bank. With the acquiescence of most leaders of the new governing coalition (Castiglioni 2005, 116–18), social policies were thus subordinated to the principles of the broader economic strategy.

Despite these political constraints, however, at least two factors enabled the new government to both expand the public social-welfare system and to increase its effectiveness. First, incoming democratic governments inherited a strong economy. Although Pinochet had allowed fiscal deficits to grow in the run-up to the plebiscite of 1988, the new government stabilized relatively quickly, and high growth and a strong fiscal position were sustained to the end of the decade.

A second set of factors was related to the earlier restructuring of the welfare system itself; this circumstance shifted financing of social insurance and services from the public sector to households. The Pinochet reforms had their own legacy effects. Private pension funds and healthcare providers and insurers constituted powerful lobbies with strong ties to the larger business associations. The class of welfare beneficiaries had also changed fundamentally. Throughout the 1990s and early 2000s, approximately 25 percent of the population, mostly in the upper and middle class, were enrolled in private Health Provider Institutions (Instituciones de Salud Previsional, ISAPREs) and approximately 40 percent of school-age children were enrolled in publicly subsidized private schools (Raczynski 2000, 124). The creation of these new stakeholders substantially increased the difficulty of changing the basic principles of the Pinochet reforms.

At the same time, however, the Pinochet era saw a substantial weakening of groups that might otherwise have opposed public-sector reforms. The dramatic reduction of public employment hit hard at teachers' unions, health providers, and the general union movement. Between 1973 and the 1990s, union density declined from a peak of 35 percent to just over 13 percent of the workforce, the steepest decline in union density in the entire Latin American sample (Roberts 2006, 169). Thus, although the Concertación governments refrained from frontal challenges to the increasingly bifurcated welfare system, the way was relatively clear to focus on public anti-poverty programs and on improving performance within the social sectors.

PENSION POLICY

Reforms in the social-security and pension systems under the new democratic governments focused on three basic objectives. With respect to pensions, one of the first steps of Patricio Aylwin's administration (1990–94) was to restore the value of payments to retirees in the old system that had been allowed to deteriorate during the economic crisis of the mid-1980s (Castiglioni 2005, 194). Although there was no substantial modification of the system of fully capitalized individual accounts, both the Aylwin and Frei (1994–98) governments sought to increase the transparency and safety of the private pension funds.

ANTIPOVERTY PROGRAMS

The Concertación governments also upgraded and restructured the residualist safety-net funds initiated under Pinochet during the crisis of the 1980s. A new program—the Fund for Solidarity and Social Investment (Fondo de Solidaridad e Inversión Social, FOSIS)—shifted from an emphasis on emergency public works during the Pinochet years to a more integrated system of targeted income supplements and development projects in poor communities. FOSIS was widely acknowledged to be one of the most successful programs of its kind in the region.

EDUCATION POLICY

New democratic governments sought to improve the quality and efficiency of education through targeted reforms and rationalization of the
public sector. New revenues financed by earmarked taxes were used to
expand preschool enrollment and lengthen the primary-school day. Under
Frei, new regulations rationalized labor relations in the educational sector, increasing pay and improving working conditions for teachers, but
also placing greater emphasis on incentives through merit pay and job
flexibility. New targeted programs were an important part of these reform
efforts as well. None of these initiatives, however, challenged the government's subsidization of private schools or attempted to alter the decentralization of educational responsibilities that had occurred under Pinochet.
In the health sector, the Alywin and Frei administrations also focused
primarily on improvements in the organization and financing of public-
health services, for example by establishing new targeted healthcare services for the elderly, pregnant women, and other vulnerable sectors.

By the end of the 1990s, serious problems within both the privatized
pension and health sectors became the focus of increasing political debate.
Troubles in the pension system were evident as the first wave of workers
in the private pillar prepared to retire. Projected replacement rates fell
below initial expectations (as much as half, by some estimates). The savings of many workers were expected to fall well short of the minimum
public guarantees available to persons with at least twenty years of service. Many others did not meet even this eligibility requirement, and were
confronted with the need to rely on personal savings and means-tested
assistance (O'Neil 2005, 17–18). Concerns about the social and financial
fallout of these developments led parties across the spectrum to propose
systemic changes that involved greater public responsibilities. As of the
mid-2000s, however, legislation was still pending. While adjustments
were likely to continue, a broad restructuring of the system would require
resolution of major issues concerning financing, employer contributions,
the potential role of a restored public pillar, and the place of still-powerful
private funds.

HEALTHCARE INITIATIVES

Within the dualistic health system, problems of adverse selection also became increasingly evident. The private ISAPREs attracted healthier and
wealthier patients, leaving to the FONASA (the public sector) the burden
of caring for poorer- and higher-risk ones. As of the late 1990s, the private
sector, which managed about 26 percent of the population, was receiving
69 percent of mandatory contributions. The ISAPREs had grown into a
potent economic power, controlling a large network of private hospitals,

clinics, and laboratories (Borzutzky 2002, 234–38; Celedón and Oyarzo 2000, 322).

The administration of Ricardo Lagos (2000–2006) did attempt a comprehensive overhaul of the health system in the early 2000s but failed to pass a key redistributive measure that would have required ISAPREs to subsidize higher-risk patients treated in the public sector. Senate opponents, acting on behalf of stakeholders in the new system, argued that transfers from the ISAPREs into the Solidarity Fund would violate property rights by severing the links between mandatory health contributions and benefits.

The difficulties encountered by Chile's center-left governments in altering the basic structure of its inherited welfare system should not obscure the major social gains registered by the democratic governments of the 1990s and early 2000s. In the fifteen years that followed the democratic transition, poverty declined sharply, and welfare indicators such as infant mortality improved. These achievements were due in part to the country's strong growth record but at least in part to increased funding and improvement in the organization of public sector institutions.

The welfare system as a whole, however, continued to rest much more extensively than in any other country in the region on principles of private provision and individual responsibility established during the Pinochet dictatorship. Challenges to this system began to grow in the mid-2000s, but its durability reinforced many of the underlying inequalities in Chilean society (Borzutzky 2002, 203–41; Raczynski 2000, 127–29).

Conclusion

In this chapter, we examined intraregional differences in the extent to which Latin American countries shifted toward more liberal welfare models. Table 7.1 summarizes initiatives in pensions, health, and education discussed in the case studies and the extent to which they reflected principles of the liberal welfare agenda, and it shows how they are aligned with differences in regime type and economic circumstances.

The effect of regime type was most evident in the area of pension reform. Most democratic systems undertook some privatization of these systems, but reforms reflected substantial compromises with stakeholders and were generally moderate in terms of enrollments in and/or benefits from the private pillar. In contrast, Chile under Pinochet and Mexico were the only two countries in our sample to fully phase out the public pillar entirely, and although the Peruvian reforms stopped short of this step, it established a large private pillar that enrolled a large percentage of the covered workforce and provided a high percentage of total benefits.[15]

Liberal technocrats found it more difficult to transform the complex bureaucratic structures of the health and education sectors. Although Pinochet did impose radical changes in Chile, differences among the other countries did not appear strongly related to regime type per se. Still, authoritarian controls facilitated the imposition of a substantial rollback of the role that the social-security agency played in the provision of healthcare in Peru and a modest but consequential decentralization of education in Mexico.

The incentives facing ruling elites were also affected by economic circumstances. Among the authoritarian regimes, increasingly favorable economic circumstances played a crucial rule in facilitating Chávez's social radicalism. Liberal technocrats were, to be sure, blocked from influence well before the onset of the oil boom. Nevertheless, the flood of petrodollars into the treasury was crucial to the dramatic expansion of the mission programs.

Economic conditions also influenced incentives among the democratic regimes. In Argentina (under Menem) and Venezuela (under Caldera), severe macroeconomic crises provided leverage for technocrats to implement a comparatively broad agenda of liberal reforms. In addition to pension-reform initiatives, each country opened health funds to competing providers. Both also pressed for the decentralization of education, although these initiatives were slowed by stakeholder opposition.

The influence of liberal technocrats in Brazil was more circumscribed than we might have expected, given the severe inflation that the country experienced during the 1980s. Nevertheless, during the 1990s, macroeconomic policy placed important limits on social spending. The decision to shelve a pension-privatization initiative reflected technocrats' concern about the fiscal implications of the transition costs. Successive governments sought to improve the quality and equity of public education and healthcare, rather than shifting toward private provision. Still, the policies in these sectors also made efforts to break up the clientelistic networks that had penetrated the social ministries, to shift responsibilities toward municipal governments, and to reallocate limited funding toward poorer areas.

Countries facing less severe economic conditions were also generally more cautious in introducing liberal reforms. Pension privatization initiatives in Colombia, Costa Rica, and Uruguay preserved a large role for the

---

[15] It also received the highest score on Madrid's (2003) privatization index after Mexico and Chile. See table 5.10.

TABLE 7.1
The Reform of Social Policy in Latin America, 1980–2005

	Pension Reform	Health reform		Education
Policy reforms	Privatization.	Liberalizing reforms. Increase in private actors; decentralization of public services.	Expansion. Broader insurance coverage and basic provision.	Liberalizing Reforms. Decentralization initiatives.
		Authoritarian crisis cases		
Chile (1973–90)	Extensive. Fully substitutive private pillar; all new workers required to join (1981).	Extensive. Private health units financed through payroll taxes.	None. Targeted focus on infant mortality.	Extensive. Decentralization. Voucher funding for private schools.
Mexico (until 2000)	Extensive. Fully substitutive private pillar, all new workers required to join (1997).	Moderate. Decentralization of MoH but not of social-security services. Increase in private insurance.	Moderate. Basic healthcare package for those without access to public clinics.	Limited. Decentralization of primary schools but slowed by union opposition.
Peru (1990–2000)	Moderate/extensive. Mixed system, but most workers join private pillar (1992).	Extensive. Primary-care teams based on flexible labor contracts, private health units allowed to compete with social-security services. Increase in private insurance.	Moderate. Expansion of MoH services to poor communities (PBST and CLAS).	None. Major focus on construction of new schools.
		Authoritarian noncrisis case		
Venezuela (1999–2006)	None. Did not implement earlier privatization reform.	None. Recentralizes health provision.	Extensive. Expansion of access to clinics under Barrios Adentro.	None. Increases central control of system.
		Democratic crisis cases		
Argentina	Moderate. Mixed system, but substantial rollback of public pillar parameters (1994).	Extensive. Opens *obra* system to private competition. Big increase in private insurance.	None.	Extensive. Accompanied by funding guarantees but not fully met.

TABLE 7.1 (*cont'd*)
The Reform of Social Policy in Latin America, 1980–2005

	Pension Reform	*Health reform*		*Education*
Brazil	None. Modest parametric reforms (1998, 2002).	Mixed. Public sector unified and restructured. Muncipalization of healthcare responsibilities Limited increase in private insurance.	Substantial. Conditional fiscal transfers to poorer states for improvement in primary health services.	Extensive. Reallocates primary school spending to municipal systems and poorer states.
Venezuela (until 1999)	Moderate/Extensive. Fully substitutive private pillar. Elimination of special funds (1997).	Moderate. Transfer agreements with 11 of 23 states. Extensive privatization reforms in 1997 but not implemented.	None.	Limited. Decentralization slowed by funding disputes.
Peru 1980–90	None. Major cutbacks in social-security spending.	No major reforms, but major cuts in health and education spending	None.	None.
Democratic cases, limited crisis				
Costa Rica	Moderate. Mixed system. All workers receive modest benefits from private pillar (2000).	None. Centralization of control by social-security fund.	Moderate. Establishment of health teams in poor neighborhoods.	None.
Uruguay	Limited. Mixed system with very small private pillar (1996).	None.	None.	None. Expansion of preschools.
Colombia	Moderate. Mixed system with limited participation in private pillar (1994).	Extensive. Major responsibilities transferred to departments and muncipalities. Increase in private providers	Extensive. Large increase in coverage via subsidized insurance packages	Limited. Decentralization of responsibility but works poorly.
Chile (1990–2000)	None. Retains Pinochet privatization but increases regulation of investment funds and increase in minimum guarantees.	None. Retains Pinochet reforms but attempts to improve benefits of public system.	Extensive. Expands public care units.	None. Retains Pinochet-era reform but expands funding for public system.

public pillar in terms of both enrollments and benefits.[16] Compared to Argentina and Venezuela, noncrisis governments also placed less emphasis on cost-saving reforms in the health and education systems and attached greater priority to improving access for underserved sectors. In Costa Rica, the social-security fund consolidated its control of the health system and emphasized the expansion of primary-care units to rural areas. In Colombia, the government expanded the health market for private insurers and providers, but tied these changes closely to the expansion of access to a subsidized insurance sector. Democratic governments in Chile refrained during the 1990s from frontal challenges to the privatized systems established under Pinochet but worked to improve the quality and effectiveness of the health system and public schools. In Uruguay, there were substantial continuities in both social sectors.

Compared to the Eastern European cases we take up in the next chapter, the capacity of stakeholders to defend their interests in Latin America was generally limited by the narrowness and inequality of coverage. But again, there were interesting differences within the region. Maintenance of broadly based welfare systems in Uruguay and Costa Rica was facilitated by looser economic constraints than was the case in the high-crisis countries, but in both instances, the popularity of these programs also discouraged politicians from shifting costs out of the public sector.

Politicians in countries with narrower systems faced fewer electoral risks in attempting liberal reform. Even in these countries, however, groups entrenched within large welfare bureaucracies could pose significant impediments to liberal reform. Veto groups were especially strong in the education sector, which was the least closely tied to the macroeconomic concerns of the technocrats. With the partial exception of decentralization, stakeholder opposition successfully stalled most aspects of the liberal education agenda, including reform of pay and promotion standards, the promotion of voucher schools, and the use of standardized tests to determine school funding.

In summing up our findings with respect to pension and social-sector policies, it is important to acknowledge that the three causal variables we have emphasized can explain only part of the intraregional variation we have described. Differences in partisan competition and specific constitutional and electoral institutions were also important, and we have attempted to take these into account in the case studies presented in this chapter. However, the effects of these factors depended heavily on the specific national political and economic contexts in which they were embedded.

---

[16] The reform in Costa Rica did require new workers to enroll in the second pillar, but the public system was still to provide the lion's share of the benefits (see table 5.10).

Both as oppositions and as parts of governing coalitions, left parties faced substantial difficulties in adjusting to the collapse of the ISI model and strains on the financial foundations of the old welfare system, and their policy stances varied widely. In some instances, pressure from left oppositions spurred more conservative governments to expand access of welfare benefits to vulnerable groups; this response was particularly the case with respect to the expansion of social-assistance programs, discussed below. But left oppositions also frequently defended the claims of the existing stakeholders, as was the case with the Party of the Democratic Revolution (Partido de la Revolución Democrática, PRD) in Mexico and the PT in Brazil. When in government, left parties also varied in their approach to social policy. In Argentina, they sought to increase the role of the private sector in the provision of services; in Chile and Brazil, they sought to improve and expand the role of the public sector. On balance, strong left parties may have contributed to the evolution of more progressive social policies, but movement in that direction was uncertain and ambiguous.

Similarly, although particular features of political institutions were important in specific cases, it is difficult to tease out consistent patterns across countries or issue areas. The fragmentation of legislative parties provides an example. In Argentina and Mexico, solid ruling-party majorities facilitated passage of pension reforms but proved less reliable bases of support in the health and education sectors, where powerful unions constituted a constraint. In Venezuela, the Pérez administration gained little support from the AD's near majority in the legislature, while under Caldera, a heterogenous coalition of small legislative parties backed an ambitious package of rationalizing reforms. The Brazilian system is often cited as a paradigmatic case of gridlock caused by party fragmentation and particularistic incentives. But although these features of the political system impeded efforts to roll back pension entitlements, they did not prevent significant reforms in the health and education sectors. Constitutional design, party organization, and electoral institutions mattered, but their effects were contingent on underlying social preferences and organization.

Antipoverty Programs

Although antipoverty programs were typically components of the liberal reform agenda, they differed from the other initiatives because they offered relatively direct opportunities for politicians to build support among new constituencies. As discussed in chapter 5, and again in the case studies, funding allocated to these programs reflected the fiscal constraints felt throughout the region, as well as the competition for funding from established stakeholders. With the exception of the situation in Venezuela, spending on these programs was dwarfed by expenditures going to established stakeholders. Yet the distribution of benefits that were available was relatively progressive and constituted important income supplements for the families that received them.

If fiscal constraints were important in limiting their size, broad suffrage and electoral competition were spurs to their spread throughout the region. Suffrage reforms in the post-1980 period were most important in Peru and Brazil. The incentive to reach new voters through social assistance programs was substantially strengthened by the elimination of literacy restrictions and lowering of the voting age. Reforms that eased entry barriers for new parties played a similar role. In Colombia, Brazil, and Mexico, expansion of social-assistance transfers was closely linked to constitutional reforms that enhanced opportunities to challenge incumbent elites.

Does regime type matter in this regard? There is some evidence that the limitations on checks and balances may have influenced the design and effectiveness of anti-poverty programs. Although vote buying and clientelism was far from uncommon in the democratic systems, these practices appeared to be especially pronounced in Peru, Venezuela, and Mexico under Fujimori, Chávez, and Salinas respectively (Roberts 1995; Weyland 1998; Magaloni 2006). Yet rulers in both competitive autocracies and democratic regimes had strong electoral motivations to promote social-assistance programs for low-income voters entering the political arena. Despite the other important difference between these political regimes, the role played by the electoral connection in the promotion of these programs conforms with our general expectations about the effects of democratization.

CHAPTER EIGHT

The Legacy of the Socialist Welfare State, 1990–2005

In Eastern Europe, political transitions occurred nearly simultaneously and very rapidly in 1989–90 (figure 8.1). Poland held constrained elections in the spring of 1989, but by the end of that year democratic movements were on the ascent across the region. The overthrow of Ceauşescu did not initially result in the installation of a fully democratic regime, and Slovakia showed some departure from democratic norms in the early 1990s. But even in those two countries, political change was dramatic and by the end of the 1990s all of the countries in our sample had achieved a level of political competition that met standard thresholds of democratic rule.

The evolution of social policy in the new democratic regimes occurred in the context of extraordinarily deep economic crises and profound structural transformations. Figure 8.2 shows the path of GDP growth from the mid-1980s through the mid-2000s. All the countries in our sample suffered severe recessions during the early transition years. These bottomed out by 1992, and Hungary, Poland, and Slovakia witnessed fairly robust recoveries after that point. But Bulgaria and Romania experienced "relapses" in the mid- to late 1990s, and growth slowed substantially in the Czech Republic as well. Growth slowed again in the late 1990s across the region as a consequence of the fall-out from emerging-market crises in East Asia and Russia, but by the beginning of the 2000s, growth rates had converged around a more stable path.

All governments in the region faced severe fiscal constraints at some point in the 1990s (Afonso, Nickel, and Rother 2005). Standard data on deficits (figure 8.3) underestimate the extent of these problems, particularly those hidden in the balance sheets of the central bank and state-owned banking system. These fiscal crises came earlier and were deeper in Hungary and Bulgaria, but Poland, Romania, and the Czech and Slovak Republics also faced important adjustments, most undertaken in the context of IMF programs.

Except for the Czech and Slovak Republics, crises were also associated with bouts of high and even hyperinflation (figure 8.4). Hungary's inflation looks low by comparison to the other cases but the country undertook a serious stabilization effort in 1995. Poland had a very high transitional inflation that preceded its distinctive "shock therapy" approach to

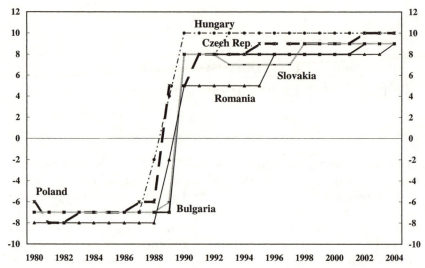

Figure 8.1. Polity values for Eastern Europe, 1980–2004. *Source*: Polity IV database (Marshall and Jaggers 2004).

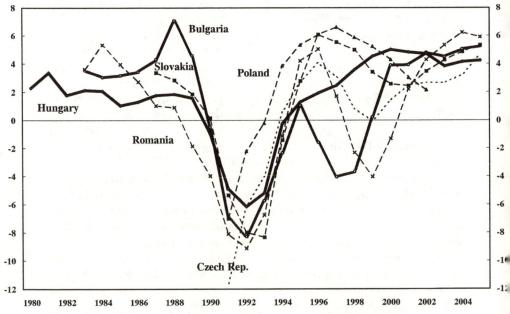

Figure 8.2. GDP growth (three-year moving average) for Eastern Europe, 1980–2005. *Source*: World Development Indicators. (World Bank 2007).

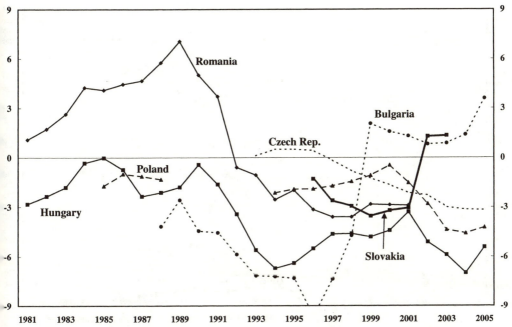

Figure 8.3. Budget balance as a percent of GDP (three-year moving average) for Eastern Europe, 1981–2005. *Source*: World Development Indicators (World Bank 2007).

reform. Romania and Bulgaria undertook early stabilization efforts but subsequently sought to maintain employment by slowing the pace of privatization and maintaining subsidies to both state-owned and private enterprises. Bulgaria had a bout of near-hyperinflation in the mid-1990s that triggered the adoption of a currency board system. Romania, by contrast, cycled through a succession of failed stabilization efforts.

Finally, all countries in the region underwent the shock of wide-ranging structural reforms associated with the transition to the market; figure 8.5 tracks this process using the average of the European Bank for Reconstruction and Development (EBRD) reform indices for eight discrete policy areas.[1] The figure shows considerable divergence between the early reformers, which exploited popular revulsion against the old order to institute wide-ranging reform programs, and Bulgaria and Romania, which took a more gradual approach to the transition. By the early 2000s, however, all six countries had undertaken extensive structural changes.

---

[1] The eight areas of reform are: large privatization, small privatization, corporate governance, foreign trade and currency liberalization, price liberalization, competition, bank reform and securities market reform.

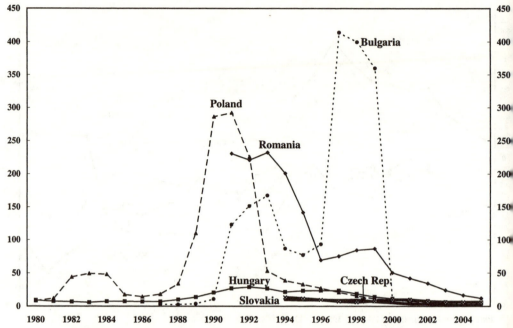

Figure 8.4. CPI change (three-year moving average) for Eastern Europe, 1980–2005. *Source*: World Development Indicators (World Bank 2007).

As in Latin America, crises enhanced the political influence of technocrats, who figured prominently in efforts to reform the socialist welfare state. Despite its shortcomings and the underfunding of entitlements, however, the inherited system of social protection and services had a profound influence on public expectations, and thus influenced the policy positions of parties across the ideological spectrum. The socialist welfare state also had defenders in organized stakeholders with an interest in the existing system of entitlements and services.

Table 8.1 provides insight into the depth of these political constraints by summarizing public opinion data from the mid-1990s on the government's social-policy responsibilities. Well after the transition, expectations about an expansive role for the state remained extremely high. The data show near unanimity of opinion with respect to health, education, and pensions. Publics not only affirmed a government responsibility but overwhelmingly called for "more" or "much more" spending on these entitlements. Lipsmeyer (2003, 550–55) notes the relatively weak preferences for spending on unemployment compensation, but this attitude comes in the context of widespread belief that the government should actually guarantee employment.

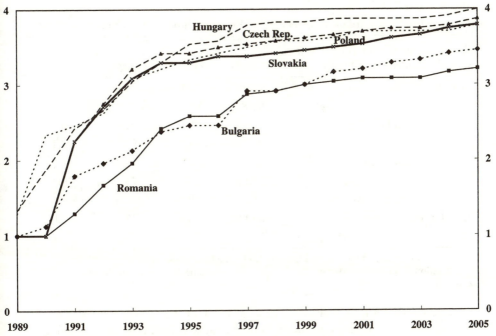

Figure 8.5. Overall reform index in Eastern Europe, 1989–2005.
Source: European Bank for Reconstruction and Development, various years.

We focus in particular on two important cross-regional differences in the politics of social policy. First, new democratic governments in Eastern Europe attached a much higher priority to the establishment of social safety nets aimed at compensating formal-sector workers displaced by economic reform. These safety-net programs were by no means uniform in their design or generosity, and initial commitments were not necessarily sustained. Nonetheless, the contrast remains noteworthy; compensation for unemployed formal-sector workers was a much lower priority in Latin America.

The second, and more striking, difference has to do with the approach to the reform of social insurance and services. In both Eastern Europe and Latin America, economic crises and fiscal constraints increased the power of technocrats and placed the reform of costly entitlements on the agenda. In Latin America, however, narrow coverage made social insurance more vulnerable to reform in the wake of crises. In Eastern Europe, by contrast, publics expected governments to maintain an array of protections on a universal basis at low, or even no, cost. When governments shifted from direct government financing and provision to social-insurance models, they nonetheless maintained principles of universalism de facto if not de

TABLE 8.1
Public Attitudes toward Government Social Responsibilities in Eastern Europe, 1996

Percent agreeing that government should definitely or probably:	Bulgaria	Czech Republic	Hungary	Poland
Provide jobs for everyone	79.2	74.9	85.4	86.4
Provide health care for the sick	95.8	95.7	97.7	95.2
Spend more on healthcare	92.2	80.9	91.6	90.6
Decent old-age living standard[a]	96.3	95.6	97.1	96.1
Spend more on retirement	77.1	64.6	82.9	79.0
Spend more on education	79.0	65.5	79.9	79.0
Support unemployed[a]	85.9	39.9	60.4	71.6
Spend more on unemployment	64.4	18.5	33.1	41.0
Reduce income differences	72.8	74.3	73.2	83.1

Source: ISSP 1996, adapted from Lipsmeyer 2003, 551 and 553.
[a] Question: "Should the government provide a decent standard of living for the old/unemployed?"

jure. Initial reforms were even cast in terms of *increasing* expenditures, and the public sector continued to play a large role in both the financing and provision of social insurance and services.

Moreover, those liberalizing reforms that were attempted were vulnerable not only to significant political compromises, as was also the case in Latin America, but to outright reversal by subsequent administrations. Governments found it extremely difficult to rationalize the finances or benefits of new social-insurance systems put in place during the transition, and as a result, programs operated on soft-budget constraints similar to those seen during the socialist era.

The Eastern European cases exhibit a somewhat greater homogeneity with respect to both their economic circumstances and social-policy legacies. As a result, we find much greater evidence of convergence on similar social-policy systems than is the case in Latin America. Nonetheless, there are differences in the timing of economic-reform efforts and recovery in Eastern Europe that proved consequential for the course of social policy. We begin our discussion with the early reformers, Poland and Hungary, followed by a consideration of the Czech and Slovak Republics, and closing with Bulgaria and Romania, which delayed social-policy reforms until the late 1990s. In each case, we begin with the policy challenges of the early posttransition period: crises, economic reforms, and the effort to forge new social safety nets. We then turn to conditions in the mid-1990s, as the first elected governments turned over and as economic and fiscal conditions led to the initiation of more institutionally-complex "second round" reforms of pensions and health care systems. In the conclusion we return to the debate over convergence and divergence in more detail, and address the possible effects of entry into the European Community and regional diffusion processes.

EARLY REFORMERS: POLAND AND HUNGARY

The political and economic transitions in Poland and Hungary exhibit a number of similarities. Both had experimented with political and economic liberalization prior to the end of Communist rule. In both cases, these reforms facilitated the transition to governments headed by opposition forces and the early initiation of market-oriented reforms. In both countries, subsequent stabilization efforts paved the way for improved relations with the IMF. Fiscal constraints, as well as the declining coverage of pensions and quality of healthcare, provided the opening for liberalizing reforms of core social-insurance functions. Yet as elsewhere in the region, these efforts were constrained by the policy legacy of socialist rule.

Poland

Poland was the first of the Eastern European Communist regimes to fall. Roundtable negotiations between the martial-law government of Wojciech Jaruzelski and the opposition Solidarity movement produced a transitional agreement that reserved two-thirds of the parliamentary seats for the Communists and their allies but allowed competitive elections for the remaining one-third of seats. After a smashing victory for Solidarity in June 1989, Tadeusz Mazowiecki, a Solidarity leader, became the first non-Communist to head an Eastern European government since the late 1940s. Full parliamentary elections were held in January 1990, and for the next fifteen years, coalitions led by Solidarity and Socialist governments alternated in power in roughly four-year cycles: Solidarity from 1990 to 1993; the Socialists from 1993 to 1997; a reconstituted alliance of Solidarity again from 1997 to 2002; and an alliance of Socialists and Liberals through 2005, when we end our account. These governments differed somewhat in their overall approach to reform, but we see some important continuities across governments with respect to social policy.

THE EARLY TRANSITION PERIOD: CREATING SOCIAL SAFETY NETS

By 1988, inflation in Poland had climbed close to 60 percent and threatened to veer into a full-blown hyperinflation. Partial reforms attempted under the last Socialist government had failed, and reformers within the Communist Party and leaders of the Mazowiecki government agreed on the need for a bolder approach (Johnson and Kowalska 1994, 193–96; Orenstein 2001, 30–32). The initial reform package was designed by a team of economists and foreign advisors led by Finance Minister Leszek Balcerowicz and featured rapid trade and price liberalization, the unification of the exchange rate, sharp cuts in subsidies to state enterprises, and a highly restrictive incomes policy (Orenstein 2001, 32). Parliament quickly ratified the program in January 1990, even though the Communists and their former allies still held a majority of seats. As the crisis deepened from 1990 to 1992, serious conflicts over the reforms and their social consequences emerged both within the heterogeneous Solidarity movement and from the reconstituted Communist Party. However, broad support for the transition, the rapid restructuring of the Polish economy, and the inability of the opposition to propose credible alternatives limited the influence of opposition forces (Johnson and Kowalska 1994, 230–31).

Solidarity had labor roots, and the new government committed itself quite early to the establishment of a social safety net for formal-sector workers. The government passed a comprehensive and generous package of unemployment benefits sponsored by Jacek Kuroń, the minister of labor in the first transition government and a towering figure in the Solidarity movement (Brown 2005, 113–16). This program was scaled back as it became clear that high levels of benefits were not fiscally sustainable. But the ad hoc use of early retirement and disability pensions and family allowances continued to provide a relatively broad safety net, and social spending increased sharply during the early transition (Surdej 2004, 7; see also figure A6.19).

This increase in social spending occurred in the context of a sharp decline in revenue, partly as a result of the rapid growth of the informal economy. Throughout the early 1990s, a succession of Solidarity governments tried unsuccessfully to reduce ballooning deficits. A suspension of IMF disbursements in 1991 marked the low point of this struggle. In 1992, a new government headed by Hanna Suchocka succeeded in regaining IMF support for a new stabilization initiative that brought the budget toward a more sustainable position. Parliamentary criticism of fiscal austerity came from within the governing coalition and from the opposition Socialist Party; it echoed criticism from unions and civil-society groups. Approval ratings for the Solidarity coalition plummeted, and the reformed Socialists, with the support of ex-Communist unions, gained substantial ground in the 1991 parliamentary elections. Although Suchocka's stabilization program held, her term in office did not. Following a decision to hold the line on wage increases in the health and education sectors, the government lost a vote of no confidence pressed by the Solidarity unions and was forced to resign.

With the return of robust growth, the pressure on social spending abated and the new Socialist government that came to office following the elections of 1993 could increase spending modestly. For example, although the Socialist government tightened eligibility requirements for unemployment insurance, it also increased benefits, extended concessions to miners, farmers, and railroad workers, and sought foreign support for active labor-market policies. Moreover, the government continued to use early retirement and other ad hoc assistance programs to manage structural unemployment (Cain and Surdej 1999, 159). Despite the shortcomings of this ad hoc social safety net (OECD 2004, 97–107; Brown 2005, 122–55), household surveys show that government interventions mitigated the effects of poverty among families headed by older workers and reduced the income inequality associated with the transition (Keane and Prasad 2002, 17–19) The programs had political effects as well. Transfers played a role in maintaining social stability and reducing political resistance to structural reform (Keane and Prasad 2002, 23).

SECOND-ROUND REFORMS I: THE PENSION SYSTEM

In part because of expenditures on early retirements, the pension system was in serious financial difficulty by the time the Socialists came to power (Müller 1999, 96). As in all the Eastern European countries, future benefit payments were projected to increase dramatically as the ratio of contributors to beneficiaries declined. Previous governments had attempted to relieve fiscal pressures by adjusting the indexation of benefits, but a Constitutional Court ruling argued that such caps on pension benefits violated the "acquired rights" of citizens (Inglot 1995, 369).

For the financial technocrats in the incoming government, a more systematic reform of the system was a high priority and was explicitly included as a priority in the standby agreement negotiated with the IMF in 1994 (Government of Poland 1994, 33). Proposals for the establishment of a fully funded second pillar were first advanced in 1994 by Finance Minister Grzegorz Kołodko, but passage was delayed for over three years by bureaucratic infighting with the ministry of labor and arduous negotiations with unions, pensioners, and party leaders (Hausner 2001, 215–16; Orenstein 2001).

Declining benefits and widespread public doubts about the sustainability of the existing system provided the political basis for a substantial reform. The reform provided for a fully funded second pillar that, according to Brooks's (2007) simulations, would pay almost half the benefits for workers entering the labor force. Moreover, the new law included a variety of parametric changes in the first pillar, including an increase in the retirement age.

To secure these reforms, the government had to accommodate both the electoral interests of the parties and the concerns of unions and pensioners. A widely publicized statement of principles, issued in 1997, guaranteed the acquired rights of current pensioners and pledged "full security" to all age groups (Hausner 2001, 217). The reform did not touch the beneficiaries of disability insurance or special funds for miners, railroad workers, and other branches that had been privileged under the old system nor the costly noncontributory pension system that served Poland's large rural population. In sum, despite strong pressures for liberalization of the pension system, the new system guaranteed protection of the elderly and left a number of costly entitlements from the socialist period intact.

SECOND-ROUND REFORMS II: THE HEALTHCARE SYSTEM

Poland came late to the reform of its health system. As happened in other Eastern European countries, doctors quickly gained the right to enter private practice, and larger cities were granted ownership of some public hospitals and outpatient centers. But internal divisions within the Solidarity coalition and the rapid turnover of governments delayed a more comprehensive financial and organizational reform (Bossert and Wlodarczyk 2000, 8–13; Nelson 2001, 253–61). Until the late 1990s, the basic features of the old system remained in place, despite widespread dissatisfaction with low quality of care, de facto rationing of access, and concerns over costs (Sitek 2005, 123).

After a lengthy period of debate, the Socialist government legislated a new system of financing and provision in 1997. The reform replaced financing through general taxation with a payroll tax at rates set annually by the Sejm. In an effort to control costs, the new legislation established regional insurance funds that were to negotiate contracts with both public and private providers. But newly established insurance funds remained within the public sector and retained monopsonistic bargaining power with respect to providers within their respective regions. Although the system was nominally contributory, the constitution passed by referendum in early 1997 enshrined a commitment to universal coverage. As Mihalyi (2000, 26) shows, the payroll-tax proposal was seen by the public as well as by doctors and healthcare providers as a way to *increase* funding by providing a dedicated and secure source of revenue.

The Solidarity coalition (Akcja Wyborcza Solidarność, AWS) that came to office in 1997 had sharply criticized the statist orientation of the Socialist reforms (Bossert and Wlodarczyk 2000, 14) and was allied with a small liberal party, the Freedom Union (Unia Wolności, UW). Moreover, the AWS also had links to groups that sought to limit the power of the insurance funds. Nonetheless, the new law that was passed in 1999 "did not mark a radical departure from the 1997 legislation with respect to coverage, benefits promised or even fundamental organization" (Sitek 2005, 134).

The fights over efforts to control costs and the organization of the insurance funds illustrate the political limits on liberalizing reforms. These fights pitted health workers linked to Solidarity against the finance ministry, which was controlled by the UW and headed again by Leszek Balcerowicz. Health workers pressed for higher payroll contributions and increased spending, and sought to increase their leverage in the negotiation of contracts by opening the insurance market to greater competition. However, Balcerowicz had observed the failure of the more liberal Czech reform, which had foundered on problems of information asymmetry, moral hazard, and the political difficulty of imposing hard budget constraints. He also argued that the reform should not be an excuse for an increase in public spending or payroll taxes. He prevailed on both points: the 1999 legislation retained the socialist framework of noncompeting regional funds, and payroll contributions in the 1999 legislation were lowered from 10 to 7.5 percent of earnings (Sitek 2000, 146).

The promise to maintain universal coverage and generous benefits in the face of relatively modest contributions made the question of cost control crucial. The new model assumed that competition for contracts would force a wide-ranging rationalization of provision. In fact, the quality of coverage and benefits began to diverge across regions, and opinion surveys showed that large and increasing majorities viewed the new system as worse than the one it replaced.[2] The government was forced to lend money to strapped regional funds, and it continued to subsidize hospitals.

The Socialist government elected in 2001 reacted by moving back toward a more centralized approach to healthcare financing and administration. Although the regional funds remained in operation, their powers were significantly curtailed. The national government reassumed responsibility for financing and defining the package of services available to the public. This recentralization preserved the principle of providing universal care but did little to address the underlying problems of financing and the quality of care that such a commitment entailed.

Hungary

The first free parliamentary elections in Hungary were held in January 1990, after several years of internal reform within the Communist Party and several months of so-called roundtable negotiations with the opposition. The largest party to emerge from the transitional election was the Hungarian Democratic Forum (MDF), a loose collection of antiregime

---

[2] Information taken from Public Opinion Research 2002.

notables with a conservative, nationalist orientation. In coalition with small Christian Democratic and Peasant Parties, the MDF formed the first transition government under József Antall.

Unlike Solidarity, the new governing coalition did not emerge from an upsurge of civil-society opposition, and the MDF disappeared from the political scene after losing to the reformed Hungarian Socialists in the general election of 1994. However, the political space they occupied was filled by FIDESZ, a party that drew support on nationalist and religious issues. The principal competitor to FIDESZ was a coalition of reformed socialists and liberals whose appeal to voters rested on their international-ist and secular orientation (Grzymala-Busse 2002, 171–73, 215–25). The posttransition period saw an alternation in power between these two blocs. The Socialists and their liberal allies held power from 1994 to 1998. FIDESZ followed in 1998–2002 and was in turn replaced by the socialist-liberal alliance in 2002.

As in Poland, these competing coalitions agreed on the need to move toward democracy and a market economy. But voters and organized inter-ests expected a continuation of the broad entitlements acquired under socialism, expectations that were also incorporated into the constitution as citizenship rights.[3] At the time of the transition, Hungary devoted about one-third of its GDP to spending on social programs, a share that exceeded that of any of the other Eastern European countries (Orenstein and Wilkens 2001, 4; see also figure A6.18). Governments of both parti-san orientations proved reluctant to liberalize the welfare system, even when faced with significant fiscal pressures. When they did, they paid a political price at the polls, and their initiatives were modified or reversed by their successors. This was particularly the case with aspects of the "Bokros package"—named for Finance Minister Lajos Bokros—of the mid-1990s to which we pay particular attention.

SOCIAL PROTECTION AND FISCAL POLICY IN THE EARLY TRANSITION

In contrast to Poland, the new Hungarian government was rhetorically committed to a gradualist approach to reform (Stark and Bruszt 1998, 149–53; Bartlett 1997). However, privatization, bankruptcy, and ac-counting legislation imposed hard budget constraints on firms and had radical consequences that were not fully anticipated at the time. Although

---

[3] "Citizens of the Republic of Hungary have the right to social security; they are entitled to the support required to live in old age, and in the case of sickness, disability, being widowed or orphaned and in the case of unemployment through no fault of their own," article 70D.

the government eventually bailed out some of the larger enterprises, unemployment increased rapidly.

As in Poland, the Antall administration viewed the establishment of a broad social safety net as a component of its overall approach to the transition. Unemployment insurance, introduced at the onset of the transition was even more generous than Poland's, and spending on it was sustained for a longer period of time (Orenstein and Wilkens 2001, 10). The government also placed greater emphasis than did Poland on active employment policies (Brown 2005, 161–66) and maintained an array of commitments from the socialist era. In addition to pension and healthcare commitments, family allowances and child support programs in Hungary were particularly generous and in the run up to the 1990 elections, were made a universal right (Szikra 2005, 9).

Both new social expenditures and existing entitlements resulted in high levels of social spending during the early transition period despite a sharp drop in revenue and the emergence of exceptionally large fiscal deficits (figure 8.3). A 1993 letter of intent to the IMF spelled out a number of specific actions related to social security, including targeting of family allowances and introducing copayments for some healthcare services (Bod and Szabo 1993, 7). However, in the absence of the kind of overt inflationary crisis that had spurred reform in Poland, the Antall government delayed fiscal adjustment, and only one disbursement from the standby was ultimately made (Haggard, Kaufman, and Shugart 2001, 79; Greskovits 2001, 119–30) .

Electoral and interest-group politics played a significant role in these delays. In 1993, an effort to reduce the deficit was greeted by a wave of hunger strikes organized by NGOs and strike threats by post-Communist unions in the strategically important steel, railroad, and mining sectors (Greskovits 1998, 157). To gain support for the stabilization package, the government offered the unions representation on new tripartite bargaining councils, yielded on proposed cutbacks in family allowances, and accepted increases in the minimum wage. Although civil society in Hungary was weak compared to that in Poland, the wave of social protest increased the risk of parliamentary defections from the government's coalition (Greskovits 1998, 166). Fiscal policy continued to drift through the end of Antall's term.

In 1994, a new government led by the Socialist Party came to office and assumed the political risks associated with undertaking a delayed stabilization. The 1995 program (the Bokros package) provides an important example of both the economic conditions in which technocrats acquire influence over social policy and the constraints placed on them by the socialist legacy.

The Hungarian Socialist Party, like its Polish counterpart, had thoroughly shifted course by the early 1990s. By the time it regained office, it had established an important constituency in the emerging private sector, and its leadership had come to include a small but influential liberal faction.[4] Nevertheless, the ex-Communist union movement remained a core constituency of the party, and the Socialists had campaigned promising greater attention to social issues.

Upon assuming office, the government initially sought a negotiated agreement on macroeconomic policy with representatives of the unions and business organizations in the tripartite Interest Reconciliation Council (IRC). After nine months of bargaining, however, negotiations remained at a standstill. At the end of 1994, the dangers posed by the growing fiscal deficit were compounded by contagion from the financial crisis in Mexico. Both the IFIs and the Western European governments signaled that financial assistance would not be forthcoming without a serious adjustment effort. With its back to the wall, the government abandoned negotiations through the IRC and turned to an internationally respected economist, Lajos Bokros, to craft a stabilization package (Haggard, Kaufman, and Shugart 2001, 196–200).

The ensuing eighteen months—first under Bokros and later under a new minister of finance, Péter Medgyessy—marked a high point of technocratic influence in Hungary. The Bokros package was unveiled in March 1995 without prior consultation with other ministers or party leaders. It closed the budget gap mainly by raising revenues with a temporary surcharge on imports and a large devaluation that had the effect of reducing real wages in the public sector. Although the package provoked bitter controversy, it was ratified by the government coalition.

In its original version, however, the package also tackled the political taboo of the country's generous welfare system, a reform effort supported by the IMF (Bokros and Suranyi 1996, 38). The most controversial steps concerned changes in the structure of family allowances: families with incomes in the top 10 percent were to be excluded from eligibility; paid maternity leaves were to be eliminated altogether. Although the government was able to push through the limits on family allowances, widespread protests erupted over the need to apply for benefits that had formerly been granted without a cumbersome administrative procedure (Szikra 2005, 9). The powerful constitutional court also ruled that an immediate suspension of maternity payments would violate the "acquired rights" of women who were already pregnant, and it removed the cuts from the stabilization initiative.

---

[4] The Socialists had also induced the Free Democrats—a small market-oriented party—to join the governing coalition.

The Bokros package contributed to a marked turnaround in the Hungarian economy, and in 1997, the country entered a period of vigorous growth. As growth returned, however, successive governments of both parties reversed many of the changes instituted during the Bokros period. Family benefits again provide an example. During 1998–2002, the FIDESZ government under Viktor Orbán fully reinstated the maternity- leave program. Inflation eroded the real value of family-support payments, but the government restored the principle of universal entitlement. The subsequent Socialist government, stung by its experience under Bokros, promised to raise expenditures and followed through in 2004 with a 40 percent increase in benefits and a "thirteen month" bonus (Szikra 2005, 9). Increasing budget constraints limited the capacity of governments to sustain the generosity of family transfers, but a strong defense of its basic principles was a recurrent feature of the political process.

PENSION PRIVATIZATION

By 1996, the short-term stabilization package had succeeded in staving off an immediate fiscal and balance-of-payments crisis and provided an opening for the economic team, together with World Bank advisors, to focus on pension reform (Haggard, Kaufman, and Shugart 2001, 160–63; Nelson 2001, 238–42). As in Poland, the declining real value of pension benefits had changed public opinion on the necessity of pension reform (Nelson 2001, 245). Predictably, however, pensioners conceived of "reform" as leading to an *increase* in benefits. Pension privatization also threatened stakeholders in the ministry of welfare and the ex-Communist unions, which held managerial positions on the boards governing the pension and health funds and emerged as intransigent opponents of the reform.

Negotiations leading up to the final legislation occurred principally within the government and the IRC. As in Poland, reforms such as an increase in the retirement age were made possible only by costly concessions to beneficiaries. The indexing of benefits was timed in a way that locked in large increases in payments to existing pensioners. Compulsory contributions to the new system applied only to new entrants into the labor market. The unions' opposition to the reforms was mitigated by new governing arrangements that strengthened their representation on the social-security and health funds.

As with family allowances, the terms of the pension reform have been subject to continuing adjustments as new governments have come to office. Concerned with restraining expenditures and reducing union control over payroll tax revenues, the FIDESZ government that succeeded the Socialists in 1998 reclaimed central government control over management of the funds. The government also undertook a variety of ad hoc measures such as a new indexing scheme to reduce the strain on the public pillar. But a planned increase of employee contributions to the private pillar was postponed (Tomka 2005, 9; Simonovits 2002, 16), and the Orbán government eliminated the requirement that made affiliation with the private pillar compulsory for new entrants into the labor market. The significance of the shift to a mixed multipillar system should not be under-estimated, but as Simonovits (2002, 17) has observed, the "lion's share of the contributions and probably most of the benefits will come to/from the public pillar."

REFORMING HEALTHCARE

Hungary moved much more quickly than Poland to shift the financing of both pensions and healthcare from general taxes to compulsory insur-ance. The separation of financing and provision was, in principle, ex-pected to reduce healthcare expenditures. In practice, however, the imple-mentation of hard budget constraints was impeded by an ongoing commitment to universal access, the failure to redefine the benefits pack-age, and the continuing ability of doctors and municipal governments to resist cuts in the public hospital sector.[5] As Mihalyi (2000, 13) summa-rizes, "In theory, health care is provided on an insurance basis. In reality, care is extended to all citizens irrespective of payments and the benefit package remains contractually and/or legislatively undefined." The gov-ernment was required to pay for the contributions of important groups such as pensioners and to cover deficits in the funds. Despite nominal social-insurance principles, the contribution of the central government to the HIF ranged from about 6 to 11 percent of total public expenditures during the first half of the 1990s (Gaal 2004, 39).

As we would predict, the onset of the fiscal crisis in 1994 was followed by efforts on the part of the Bokros team to rationalize both the financing and the provision of healthcare. Yet despite substantial increases in real health spending (Gaal 2004, 51), it proved difficult to raise taxes or even halt the slide in contributions, let alone redefine benefits or rein in provid-ers. Attempts to close underutilized hospitals met with local protests. New legislation in 1996 called for a reduction in hospital beds, but the task of deciding which ones to eliminate was given to county-level "consensus teams"; as a result, oversupply remained very high by OECD standards. A final effort at more comprehensive financial reform by the finance min-istry ran up against the electoral clock in 1997–98 (Mihalyi 2000, 10).

[5] The reform of 1992 separated healthcare financing under a nominally independent Health Insurance Fund (HIF) controlled by the ministry of health. Doctors gained the right to organize, and the Antall government legalized the private provision of primary care. But the control of polyclinics and private hospitals was devolved to local governments; outside of general practitioners, little was done to privatize provision.

Other attempts to trim benefits (for dental care, for example) were later reversed. Health spending declined as a share of GDP in the second half of the 1990s (figure A6.18), but HIF deficits peaked at almost 13 percent of total public-healthcare expenditures in 1998—well after the Bokros program—and remained at close to 10 percent in 2000 (Gaal 2004, 39).

The cycle of piecemeal reform continued under the next two governments. The center-right coalition of Victor Orbán (1988–2002) showed somewhat more interest in efforts to spur private insurance and provision than the socialist-liberal coalition under Medgyessey. The new government lowered payroll taxes and sought to exercise more direct control over spending by appointing its own nominees to the health fund and shifting control to the office of the prime minister (Gaal 2004, 107–10). But the Orbán government's proposal to create competing private funds was dropped. An OECD assessment in 2005 underscored structural problems similar to those outlined by critics over a decade before (OECD 2005, 4–5): perverse incentives with respect to treatment by both doctors and hospitals, waiting lists and effective rationing of care, and the persistence of under-the-table payments.[6]

The Czech and Slovak Republics

The collapse of the old regime occurred quite rapidly in Czechoslovakia. After demonstrations in December 1989, the conservative leadership of the Czech Communist Party abdicated, leaving a rump group to negotiate the transfer of power. The first "government of national understanding" was dominated by leaders of the two main opposition movements: the Civic Forum that had emerged in the Czech lands and its Slovak counterpart, Public Against Violence. Following the general election of June 1990, most of the top positions in the national government were held by leaders of the Civic Forum, which included both social democrats such as the new president, Václav Havel, and militant free-market liberals such as Finance Minister Václav Klaus (Orenstein 2001, 61–96). In the Slovak regions, more nationalist and conservative factions headed by Vladimir Mečiar's Public Against Violence predominated.

In contrast to Hungary and Poland, the purges of 1968 left the Communist Party without a strong reformist faction, and it was rapidly marginalized as a competitive electoral force (Grzymala-Busse 2002, 30–41). Although electoral support for the Social Democrats was also quite limited

---

[6] On the general persistence of these problems in the postsocialist healthcare system, see the analysis of Kornai and Eggleston 2001. On Hungary, see Osveiko 2002.

in the first half of the 1990s, the collapse of the Communist Party opened the way for them to quickly capture the leadership of the union movement.

With the parliamentary elections of June 1992, the political trajectories of the two regions began to diverge sharply. In the Czech lands, Klaus's liberal Civic Democratic Party (Občanská Democratická Strana, ODS) won a substantial plurality (34 percent) and formed a government with the Christian Democratic Party (Křest'ansko Democratická Strana, KDS). In Slovakia, Mečiar's nationalist Movement For a Democratic Slovakia (Hnutie za Democratické Slovensk, HZDS) won an even more decisive victory, setting the stage for the two rivals to negotiate the so-called "velvet divorce" of January 1993.

The Czech Republic

Klaus projected himself as the Thatcher of Eastern Europe. As finance minister of Czechoslovakia, he pressed for a radical reform strategy with a relentlessness and intellectual force that overwhelmed his more gradualist opponents. Klaus's initial social-policy agenda also focused on the goal of limiting the role of the government: privatization of pensions, a strengthening of the insurance principle and individual responsibility in the health sector, and a move toward means testing and tightened eligibility requirements in other areas of social policy (Večernik 2004, 4–5).

This aspect of Klaus's agenda encountered considerable opposition, however, forcing Klaus to sustain the broad framework of social protections (Potůček 2001, 88–98; Orenstein 2001).One reason for the relatively limited support for more liberal social reforms was that the fiscal pressures to liberalize were much more limited than in most of the other Eastern European countries. Although Czechoslovakia experienced a transitional recession as deep as those in the rest of the region, the post-transition government did not inherit the serious macroeconomic imbalances visible in Poland, Bulgaria, and Romania or even in Hungary. The budget remained in surplus for longer than the other countries in our sample and inflation was negligible (figures 8.3 and 8.4). Unlike the situation in Hungary and Poland, external debt contracted by the old regime was also modest. The absence of structural fiscal constraints, or even short-term fiscal problems, limited the ability of reformers—led in this instance by Klaus himself—to tackle the large social-welfare entitlements of the socialist era.

Equally if not more important were the political constraints on reform. Prior to the velvet divorce, Klaus's room for maneuver was limited by coalition partners and social forces that advocated a more gradualist and social-democratic approach to the transition: intellectuals with strong social-democratic orientations, such as Václav Havel; reformers who had been expelled from the Communist Party in 1968; Slovak nationalists such as Mečiar; and a relatively powerful union movement that benefited from tripartite structures.

The strong showing of the ODS in 1992 would appear to have weakened these constraints. However, social programs were popular with voters and important for sustaining the political base of the ODS and its two coalition partners. This was even more true following the 1996 elections, when the Social Democrats made significant gains on a platform of defending welfare, labor-protective legislation, and pensions and forced the ODS to rule as a minority government. Moreover, labor was organized in a peak union association that was relatively strong and able to institutionalize a meaningful tripartite structure early in the transition (Brown 2005, 58; Avdagic 2003, 9–13). As Večernik (2004, 7) summarizes, from the mid-1990s through 2004 "not much [went on] in the social sphere."

SOCIAL PROTECTION: THE SOCIAL-LIBERAL COMPROMISE UNDER KLAUS

A number of important comparative studies have noted the contrast between the "neoliberal" orientations of the early economic reform processes in Poland and Hungary and the "social liberal" compromises forged during the transition in Czechoslovakia (Stark and Bruszt 1998; Orenstein 2001, 61–96; Potůček 2001; Brown 2005, 157–261). The early social-policy components of the Klaus program—prior to the split—were framed mainly within the ministry of labor; they rested on an explicit quid pro quo negotiated between unions and the government within a tripartite framework. Wage restraint, the key concession on the labor side, contributed to the low-inflation, high-employment outcome we have already noted.

In exchange, the program presented by Klaus in 1990 granted temporary protection to viable enterprises, provided through credits from state-controlled banks, outright subsidies, and delays in implementing bankruptcy legislation (Stark and Bruszt 1998, 155; Orenstein 2001, 74). By the late 1990s, such policies had contributed to banking and financial scandals that led to Klaus's resignation and to the defeat of the ODS in the parliamentary elections of 1998. However, the gradual approach to reform was at least one factor in the lower level of transitional unemployment. In 1989–92, total employment fell by 13–16 percent in Poland, Hungary, and Slovakia, but only 9 percent in the Czech Republic.[7]

---

[7] There is substantial debate on the ultimate sources of the relatively low unemployment in the Czech Republic during the transition, including not only active labor-market policy but the effective move of labor into self-employment as a result of small-scale privatization and the slow pace of restructuring in privatized firms (Boeri, Burda, and Kollo 1998, 34 for data cited in text and 82–86; Ham, Svejnar, and Terrell 1998; Terrell and Sorm 1999).

Labor-market policy also played an important role in the Klaus strategy. Early in the transition, the government created a network of regional labor offices to administer very generous unemployment benefits and active labor-market policies. In early 1992, the priorities shifted; drawing on Western European practice and ILO advice, the government initiated subsidies for private-sector employment and cut unemployment benefits. In subsequent years, funding for active labor-market policies fell, but this change was possible in part because of the underlying compromise on corporate restructuring, the relative success of employment policies, and above all, the return to growth.

Pension reform moved far more slowly than it did in Poland and Hungary. Though the Klaus government set up a voluntary supplemental pension in 1994, technocratic efforts to shift the agenda to wider privatization goals were stymied by the ministry of labor and social affairs (Müller 2002b, 297–99). Because the system did not pose an immediate fiscal threat, the ministry of finance had little influence on the issue, and in the absence of serious external constraints on the government, neither did the IFIs (Potůček 2004, 259, 263). In the run-up and immediate aftermath of the 1996 election, the government faced mounting political resistance from both labor and the Social Democrats, who dramatically increased their share of votes and seats. The window for more wide-ranging reform quickly closed. Retirement ages remained relatively low, and minimum contribution periods in which to receive a full pension were short. In fact, the solidarity of the system actually increased under Klaus—and the link between contributions and benefits correspondingly weakened—as the result of generous new provisions for early retirees, families with children, the unemployed, students, and the self-employed.

Efforts to reform the healthcare system reflected a more radical market-oriented approach, but the reforms retained universal coverage and ultimately failed in spectacular fashion. Legislation passed in 1992 opened the social-insurance market to twenty-seven newly established private funds, on the assumption that such funds would provide greater choice for consumers and incentives to control medical costs. However, the government also established a General Health Insurance Corporation (GHIC), funded out of the general budget, to cover uninsured sectors of the population. In the absence of effective cost controls, the funds began to fail. By 2000, the GHIC covered approximately 75 percent of the population, including almost all nonwage earners. Moreover, survey evidence showed strong support for these arrangements.[8]

---

[8] In 1998 surveys cited in Večernik (2004, 6), 50.8 percent of respondents favored state healthcare "without limits" and another 44.8 percent favored it within "certain limits."

Other areas of social policy showed similar compromises with prevailing preferences for comprehensive public protection. Like Hungary, Czechoslovakia had a generous system of family allowances. In 1995, the Klaus government succeeded in introducing means testing of these benefits, but allowances were still granted to households earning up to three times the minimum income guarantees and continued to support dependent children up to the age of 26. Even broader protections were provided through cash transfers to families whose incomes fell below a minimum threshold (Brown 2005, 71). In combination, these benefits yielded one of the most generous safety nets in the OECD (Scheuer and Gitter 2001, 49).

SOCIAL POLICY AFTER KLAUS

By 1997, Klaus's ODS was not only subject to coalitional constraints, but was also forced to confront scandals, a series of bank failures, and a sharp economic downturn. This "second round" crisis forced the government to undertake a stabilization effort that included budget cuts and a devaluation (although it did not necessitate an IMF program). Following Klaus' resignation in November 1997, a caretaker government held office for six months before general elections brought the Social Democrats to power.

The Socialists had run for office against the "residualist" social policy of the ODS and on a platform of protecting social entitlements. Once in office, they adopted the European Social Charter and a National Employment Strategy designed to address rapidly rising unemployment through a revival of active labor-market policies. Like Klaus, however, the Social Democrats confronted competing pressures on social policy. On the one hand, they had to deal with a steady deterioration in the country's public finances, a situation that forced an abandonment of some of the core program of increasing social-welfare benefits. At the same time, their hold on office rested on a particularly fragile coalition that impeded efforts to address structural problems in the social sector (European Commission 2003, 4, 7). Through 2005, the Social Democrats had managed only the most marginal parametric changes in the welfare system.

Given the crisis, the Social Democrats initially focused their attention on a reform agenda to return to growth. The government resolved remaining issues surrounding accession to the EU, sought to attract FDI, and undertook a costly privatization of the banking system. But as noted, efforts at social-policy reform proved more difficult. In 1997, pension payments exceeded receipts for the first time in the posttransition period, but the parliament defeated two efforts to raise premiums in 1998. In 1999, the government formed a pension committee to try to forge a consensus among the parties on a wider reform, and in 2001 succeeded in passing measures to marginally reduce incentives to early retirement. But until 2005, the two major parties remained far apart on any fundamental reform of the system, and the Czech Republic remained the only case in our sample that had not undertaken at least some pension privatization.

Healthcare reform proved even more difficult. As the private funds failed, the task of financing healthcare reverted back to the central health-insurance fund. By 2003, no less than 91 percent of all health spending went through public channels. Yet a survey from that year also showed that 68.4 percent of respondents found the efficiency of the healthcare system either "very" or "quite" good (Večernik 2004, 14), making fundamental reform of the system politically difficult. The majority of hospitals remained in state or municipal government ownership, heavily dependent on subsidies and grants. Despite ballooning costs, the Social Democrats proved unable to introduce even minor parametric reforms.

With little room to raise contributions, given already high payroll taxes, cost containment would have to come through classic liberalization measures: consolidation of hospitals and improvements in management and efficiency; cost controls on private providers; and increased payments from beneficiaries. Yet in 2005, with doctors going on strike to protest late and inadequate payments from the insurance fund, the Social Democrat minister of health stated flatly that citizens would not pay one additional crown for services. Clearly, the system was fiscally unsustainable, and some reform initiative seemed likely to follow the 2006 elections. Yet it was equally certain that any reform would be constrained to maintain key features of the existing system.

Slovakia

Politics in Slovakia from independence through 1997 was dominated by Vladimir Mečiar and his party, the HZDS.[9] Although Slovakia was nominally democratic, Mečiar's government was characterized by the centralization of political and economic power, strong nationalist appeals, and intolerance toward the ideologically divided opposition and ethnic minorities. Studies of public opinion have detailed how Slovaks showed much greater reticence about the transition and more support for an extensive state role in the economy (Henderson 1994). Slovakia also inherited a strong peak union organization as well as the tripartite institutions established during the early transition period. Union membership fell dramatically over the course of the decade, but until 1997 the Mečiar government signed general social agreements with the social partners each year. The statist and populist orientation of the leadership and the constraints posed

[9] For an overview of the Mečiar years, see Krause 2001. For a comparison of the Czech and Slovak political systems, see Krause 2006.

both by voters' preferences and by the organization of stakeholders meant that the pressures to retain social protections were even greater than in the Czech Republic.

In July 1997, Slovak politics was jolted by the country's exclusion from negotiations on both NATO and EU membership, a joint American-European rebuke to Mečiar's autocratic tendencies. The parliamentary elections of September 1998 ousted Mečiar's HZDS and brought a broad four-party left-right coalition government to power; this government was united primarily in its opposition to Mečiar. Although the coalition was able to pass the constitutional changes and market reforms required for EU entry, it was internally divided on social-policy reform. Not until a decline of both the HZDS and the left in the 2002 elections did center-right, pro-European parties gain a mandate that permitted important social-policy reforms.

MANAGING THE TRANSITION: THE MEČIAR YEARS

As elsewhere, early Slovak social policy combined new social safety nets with the maintenance of existing commitments. In addition to unemployment insurance, the Slovak government developed an even more extensive array of active labor-market policies than did the Czech Republic, providing large subsidies for private-sector employment and the creation of public-sector jobs (Lubyova and van Ours 1997, 93–95).

As was the case in other countries in Eastern Europe, financing of social insurance was shifted to formally independent social-security agencies. But entitlements established during the socialist period were not reformed, and the government continued to finance the contributions of a number of stipulated groups. In the run-up to the 1998 election, the Mečiar government paid off key bases of support by creating noncontributory pensions for the police, customs, intelligence, and security forces. An early-retirement option played a politically important social-policy role in the transition, exercised by nearly 80 percent of all new claimants by 1994. Disability pensions also increased sharply.

Throughout the Mečiar years, Slovakia saw a number of efforts to initiate pension reform, driven by the eroding finances of the pension fund. None succeeded. Unions effectively vetoed even parametric adjustments in eligibility or benefits, and used their position to influence annual pension adjustments in the direction of greater generosity (Svorenova and Pretasova 2005, 123).

A broadly similar pattern of limited reform is visible with respect to health insurance (Svorenova and Pretasova 2005, 199–219; Hlavacka, Wágner, and Rieseberg 2004, 91–106). Early institutional reforms created autonomous healthcare facilities, privatized primary healthcare and pharmacies, and allowed private insurers to enter the healthcare market. But the constitution confirmed access to medical care as a citizenship right regardless of contributions, and implementing legislation offered generous packages of services. As of 2001, the state contributions covering such groups as children, pensioners, and students provided health insurance for no fewer than 3.1 million persons out of a total population of about 5 million people (Svorenova and Pretasova 2005, 111). Opposition to increases in the payroll tax, combined with evasion and company failures, caused contributions to lag well behind the payout of generous mandated benefits. As a result, approximately half the small number of private insurers either failed or were consolidated by the end of the decade. By the end of the Mečiar years, the healthcare system faced a standard set of "soft budget" problems: hospitals that were chronically underfinanced drug companies and pharmacies not fully reimbursed by insurance companies; and increasing lags in contributions.

Child allowances provide a final example of policy continuity with the socialist era. As in the Czech Republic, the government moved from a principle of universal fixed entitlements to means testing. This policy was relaxed, however, as the combination of means testing and failure to adjust entitlements in the face of inflation resulted in a decline in coverage and generosity of benefits. Parliamentary legislation in 1994 and 1997 restored coverage to fully 83 percent of all children in the country (Bednarik 1998, 12).

SECOND STAGE REFORMS: FROM DEADLOCK TO REFORM

The coalition government that came to office following the 1998 elections enjoyed a mandate to reverse the creeping authoritarianism and corruption of the Mečiar years. In May 1999, the coalition quickly outlined a major economic package that involved not only a current account and fiscal adjustment but dramatic price liberalization, banking reform, corporate restructuring, bankruptcy legislation, and efforts to jump-start the process of EU accession and attract foreign investment. Later in its term, the center-right parties in the coalition began to advocate radical tax cuts as a way of stimulating investment and growth.

Despite a steady increase in the operating deficit of both the pension and health funds, however, it proved much more difficult for the government to extend its reform program into the social sector. Unemployment remained high, but the country did not experience a full-blown crisis and was not dependent on the IMF. The resumption of growth initially made it difficult for reformers to gain traction.

After 2000, EU accession negotiations and the requirement to meet the Maastricht fiscal targets provided an important source of external pressure for social-policy reform: the government agreed to a World Bank loan that was linked to EU accession targets and monitored by the IMF.

In addition to a deepening of market reforms, the program also envisioned deregulation of the labor market, rationalization of healthcare provision, and overhaul of the pension system. Nevertheless, little action was taken on these social policy reforms until after the 2002 elections.

The main constraints were political. Not only was the ruling coalition fragmented, but it included the reformed Communist party. The government sought to secure social support for its reforms by reviving the tripartite mechanism that had lapsed in the late Mečiar years. Labor strength had waned considerably, but unions used the tripartite structure to voice concerns over a range of issues including social policy, tax benefits for low-income workers, and the minimum wage. Significant pension reforms also met strong political opposition,[10] and the government chose the softest of the three proposals under consideration; an increase in the retirement age favored by the trade-union confederation (Svorenova and Pretasova 2005, 126). Changes in the healthcare sector were similarly modest in scope.[11]

In the elections of September 2002, the path to more decisive social-policy reform was cleared by a sharp drop in support for the post-Communist left and by the continuing political isolation of Meciar's HZDS. The center-right and right parties quickly formed one of the most ideologically cohesive coalitions in our sample and moved quickly to undertake broad reforms of both the pension and the healthcare systems. Despite resistance from both labor and business in the tripartite council, the government passed a fundamental overhaul of the pay-as-you-go system in 2003, and an even more fundamental tax reform the following year.[12] The reform raised the retirement age, rewrote the benefits formula to give greater weight to actual contributions, and took indexation decisions out of the hands of parliament through a formula. Despite some side payments to secure support, there can be little question that the reform marked a departure from the more solidaristic approach of the prereform period. A second law passed in October 2003 established the second pillar, which was compulsory for new entrants into the workforce.

The reform of the healthcare system began with the introduction of copayments in 2003, a reform introduced over a presidential veto, strong criticism from both the opposition and labor, and an important constitu-

---

[10] The parliament rebuffed proposed rules that would have limited its capacity to spend and unilaterally voted substantial increases in pension benefits in 2000.

[11] In 1999, the government restated the commitment to universal access and high quality healthcare and promised to contain costs. But these parametric reforms "failed to address the essential issue of the future scope of the benefit catalogue covered by solidaristic financing" (Hlavacka, Wágner and Rieseberg 2004, 24).

[12] See Moore (2005) for an overview of these reforms.

tional-court challenge. The ministry of health also undertook a number of important internal, administrative reforms, including changes in the payment system and the network of public-provider institutions. The second phase of the reform sought to limit public responsibility by outlining a basic solidaristic benefits package and encouraging private insurance. The reform legislation included strong incentives for both employees and employers to enroll and to make contributions, including limiting public guarantees to urgent care and requiring that the unenrolled be forced to pay for services (Hlavacka, Wágner, and Rieseberg 2004, 24, 99–103).

The Slovak reforms of the early 2000s rank among the most decisive in our sample of East European cases. Why did Slovakia go as far as it did? A number of factors contributed: strong public support for integration with Europe following the isolation of the Mečiar years; the very particular external constraints on fiscal policy associated with accession; the ideological cohesion of the ruling coalition after 2002; and the fragmentation and isolation of the opposition.

The political costs of the reforms, however, were high. Despite a dramatic upturn in growth, the government experienced a sharp drop in public support and in the election of 2006 was soundly defeated by a left-leaning party that campaigned on promises to restore the "solidaristic" features of the social-safety-net and healthcare systems. Moreover, it is important to put Slovakia's liberalizing reforms in comparative perspective. The pension privatization retained the effective universalism of the pension system and was sold in part by arguing that replacement rates would rise. Healthcare reforms were similarly coupled with a restatement of the commitment to broad coverage, promises to improve the quality of care, and important concessions to low-income households. In these crucial respects, the system maintained important links to the commitments of the socialist era.

BULGARIA AND ROMANIA

Bulgaria and Romania share a number of features that differentiate them from the other Eastern European countries. The two countries had lower per capita incomes at the time of the transition, and more pressing problems of absolute poverty, particularly among minority Roma populations. Both were slow reformers that experienced lower overall growth during the first decade of the transition. Both were hit by a "second round" crisis in the mid-1990s. These crises forced a new round of stabilization programs, structural adjustments and negotiations with creditors, the international financial institutions, and the EU. Although Bulgaria undertook a more wide-ranging reform effort than Romania, both countries were late entrants into the EU and did not sign accession treaties until 2005.

This slower reform path can be traced to differences in the nature of the political transition. Although Romania did achieve a democratic breakthrough, the power of relatively unreformed post-Communists and the strength of the presidency under Ion Iliescu raised doubts about democratic rule that were even more serious than those raised by Mečiar's autocratic tendencies in Slovakia. Bulgaria's transition to democratic rule was cleaner, but post-transition politics was also dominated by a reformed Communist party.

These economic, policy and political differences mattered for both the timing and nature of social policy reforms. In Romania, features of the political landscape limited both the depth and coherence of reform initiatives well into the 2000s. In both cases, however, we also see early attention to creating social safety nets and continuity in the universal approach to core benefits. Moreover, we find a distinctive interest in both countries in addressing problems of structural poverty and inequality.

Bulgaria

The political transition in Bulgaria took place through the forced resignation of Todor Zhivkov in late 1989 and his replacement by a younger generation of party leaders. This first post-Communist government won a majority of seats in the June 1990 parliamentary elections but fell only five months later, following a wave of strikes by post-Communist and opposition unions. In the ensuing seven years, the country was ruled by a succession of fragile, short-lived governments: three left (1989–90, 1992, 1995–97), one right (1991–92), one transitional coalition (1990–91), and two interim governments appointed by the president (November 1994–January 1995 and February–April 1997).

The right-of-center Union of Democratic Forces (UDF) was the first government to complete its term (1997–2001). Coming to office in the wake of hyperinflation, it quickly stabilized the economy and initiated a new round of economic reform. Despite reasonable economic performance in the aggregate, the UDF fell to voter disaffection over continuing high unemployment and particularly perceptions of corruption (Valev 2004, 416–21). They were displaced not by the post-Communists, but by a conservative-populist party that emerged only shortly prior to the 2001 elections, the National Movement Simeon II (NMSII). Yet despite this somewhat more turbulent political history, we find very similar patterns to the other cases with respect to the evolution of social policy.

COPING WITH THE TRANSITION[13]

The succession of early Bulgarian governments had to deal with the largest drop in output in our sample of countries, the steepest decline in state sector employment, and the highest transitional inflation (Minassian 1998, 331–42). Although a newly emergent opposition-union confederation, Podkrepa, played a key role in bringing down the first socialist government, it cooperated with the stabilization effort undertaken by the UDF government under IMF auspices in 1991 (Iankova 2002, 52–91).[14]

Nonetheless, the weakness of successive governments meant that they were held hostage to consensus among the major parliamentary blocs; in the words of one prime minister, Lyuben Berov, "if just one group said no, the question was closed" (quoted in Stone 2002, 214). In return for concessions, labor effectively controlled key social policy ministries, including under the UDF government, and participated in a wide-ranging network of tripartite institutions that exercised strong influence over social policy (Iankova 2002, 52–91). Labor argued successfully for the introduction of social safety nets, the maintenance—at least initially—of centralized wage bargaining, and continuity or even expansion of established social transfers.[15]

In late 1989, unemployment insurance was introduced for the first time, initially to handle the displacement of Communist Party officials in the wake of the democratic transition. Benefits were modest at first and coverage was lower than in the other countries in the region, but by 1998 they were comparable to those in the Czech Republic and Hungary (Cazes and Nesporova 2003, 116–17). The absence of effective monitoring meant that the unemployed could collect benefits while working on informal contracts, which employers favored to avoid steep payroll taxes.

In addition to unemployment insurance, the government also revamped the social-assistance scheme inherited from the socialist period. The new scheme shifted from eligibility based on membership in defined categories, such as the disabled or single elderly, to an income formula and introduced a guaranteed basic minimum income (BMI). Several studies find that these safety nets ameliorated both poverty and inequality during the transition (Hassan and Peters 1996, 64; Orenstein and Wilkens 2001, 1–2), but benefits were in fact widely spread despite nominal efforts at targeting. In 1992, the middle 60 percent of the income distribution received 59 percent of unemployment benefits, 69 percent of children's al-

---

[13] For an overview of social policy during the transition see Sotiropoulos, Neamtu, and Stoyanova 2003.

[14] The collapse of state-sector employment also forced labor to back away from its initial desire to maintain an employment guarantee (Deacon and Vidinova 1992, 82).

[15] For overviews of the early political fights over social policy, see Deacon and Vidinova 1992; Shopov 1993; Shopov 2002.

lowances, and 57 percent of all social assistance, with significant shares also going to the top 20 percent of the income distribution (Hassan and Peters 1996, 642).

Pensions and disability payments became a further route for cushioning the transition.[16] Despite a low retirement age—sixty for men and fifty-five for women—strikes in 1990 secured even earlier retirement for a number of occupational categories, including fully 30 percent of all state employees.

In the 1994 elections, the socialists were returned with 43 percent of the vote and an absolute majority of seats on the populist ticket of "moderating the social costs of transition." The new government pushed through a package of policy measures based on the concept of "public correction" that included extensive price regulation, subsidies to energy, and increasing credit from state-owned banks to keep state-owned enterprises afloat. Prior to the 1994 elections, Bulgaria's relations with the IMF had been anything but smooth (Stone 2002, 210–17; Nicolov et al. 2004); following the elections, they soured badly. Fiscal policy was a major issue of contention. The contingent liabilities of the banking sector became an increasing point of technical concern, but entitlements also constituted a major fiscal drain. In principle, the socialist system had been organized on a social-insurance basis with a single unified fund covering a wide variety of risks. But earmarked taxes did not increase along with growing outlays, and as early as 1992, the government was forced to cover deficits in the social-insurance fund equal to nearly two percent of GDP (Hassan and Peters 1996, 641).

These strains reflected a variety of structural problems. The ratio of beneficiaries to contributors was high, and certain categories of individuals were exempted from contributions altogether. Private employers had strong incentives to evade payments. State-owned enterprises made payments but relied on subsidies provided through the banking system. The socialist government did create an independent National Social Security Institute that was managed on a tripartite basis. But the social partners could not reach consensus on a reform that would address the underlying structural problems (Shopov, Noncheva, and Tafradjiyski 2005, 9–14).

In 1994 and 1995, the economy showed positive growth, but by 1996, the banking system began to experience severe distress. Subsidies, the monetization of deficits, and declining confidence in the currency produced a full-blown balance-of-payments and financial crisis (Minassian 1998, 335–42; Stone 2002, 220–23). The economy contracted by 10 percent in 1996, and inflation peaked at around 2000 percent a month in March 1997.

---

[16] Orenstein and Wilkens (2001, 1–2) estimate that pensions accounted for 83 percent of total social-insurance spending during the 1991–95 period, the highest ratio in the countries of interest to us.

The economic crisis overlapped with a political crisis. In late 1996, the presidential election brought the UDF candidate Petar Stoyanov to office, and in December the Socialists relinquished sole control of the government in the face of political unrest that extended through the elections in April. The transitional government of Stefan Sofianski, in office the 90 days prior to the elections, initiated a number of significant reforms. But with the decisive victory of the UDF—which gained an absolute majority of both votes and seats—Bulgaria had its first opposition government, and one with a strong mandate, to accelerate the reform process.

SECOND-ROUND REFORMS

The first task of the UDF government was stabilization, which was achieved through the controversial mechanism of a currency board introduced on July 1, 1997. Inflation fell to near-zero levels by 1998. Structural reforms, including privatization, were equally dramatic. In November 1996, 67 percent of workers were still in the public sector; by December 2000, this number was down to just under 40 percent.

Somewhat more gradually, the UDF government also undertook reforms of social policy. The poor performance of the pay-as-you-go pension system provided a particularly important target for technocratic reformers. Thanks to the near-hyperinflation and lags in indexing, the average pension in 1998 was worth only about one-third of its value in 1989 (International Monetary Fund 2000, 45–46). The reform thus promised not only to increase the financial soundness of the system but to increase coverage and benefits as well (Shopov, Noncheva and Tafradjiyski 2005, 14–18).

As in the other cases we have reviewed, the reform was forged through a series of compromises that limited the costs for existing pensioners, maintained broad coverage, and left longer-term problems unaddressed (Noncheva 1999, 22–26). In 1992, the World Bank had held seminars on the Chilean experience, and a handful of liberal think tanks argued for a full-fledged defined contribution model. This option was quickly rejected in favor of a three-pillar approach. The reforms of the first pillar raised the retirement age, tightened the links between contributions and benefits, and gradually shifted the balance of contributions toward employees. However the first pillar remained large, and although there was no commitment to a particular replacement rate, the reforms were based on projections that it would finance between 40 and 50 percent of retirement earnings. Reforms were not paid for through substantially increased contributions or reduced benefits but a combination of borrowing, privatization receipts, transfers from the budget, and a slowing of the diversion of contributions from the first to the second pillar (International Monetary Fund 2000, 50).

A number of crucial categories of citizenry were also effectively exempted from contributions or gained access to noncontributory transfers. The agricultural sector was not formally excluded, as in Poland, but participation was extremely low. The loophole with respect to the self-employed and those not working on formal contracts remained open. At the same time, the government retained a variety of obligations that were ultimately funded directly from the treasury, such as disability pensions (16 percent of all pensioners) and additional social-assistance payments to low-income pensioners. Although income and property tested, in 2000, those qualifying for these additional benefits also equaled no fewer than 16 percent of the number of all pensioners (Tafradjiyski et. al. 2002, 15).

The healthcare reform followed a sequence similar to the other cases, including the decentralization of medical facilities, the establishment of private practices, and the formation of new medical associations. But the growth of private provision hit limits even more quickly; by 2000, only about 20 percent of doctors even offered services privately, and virtually all of them maintained their jobs in the state sector (Noncheva 1999, 27). With the coming of the economic crisis, the healthcare budget fell (Tragakes 2003, 35). Utilization fell, gratuities remained pervasive, and satisfaction with the status quo plummeted (Balabanova and McKee 2002, 379–84). Despite these problems, the Socialist government remained divided on a course of reform and failed to formulate a new approach.

As with the deterioration of the pension system, the deterioration of healthcare provided an opportunity for the UDF to reform the system. The most important healthcare initiative was the Health Insurance Law of 1998, which established a compulsory health-insurance system that guaranteed provision of a basic package of services. The inauguration of social insurance was seen both as a way to rationalize the system and as a means to increase dedicated resources in the context of fiscal constraints; doctors and other healthcare providers supported the social-insurance principle precisely on those grounds. The ultimate bargaining around the finalization of the bill hinged in large part on the level of the payroll-tax contribution. Bulgarian and foreign experts estimated that contributions of about 12 percent of income would be required to finance the services envisioned (Tragakes 2003, 26). In view of the difficult economic situation and the simultaneous introduction of the pension reform, however, the government opted instead for a 6 percent contribution rate.

The objective of shifting to a contribution-based system, strong political pressure to limit payroll taxes, and continuing expectations of universal coverage, all stood in quite obvious contradiction. Both central and local governments continued to cover a substantial share of the total healthcare bill; in 2000, the National Health Insurance Fund covered only 13 percent of all public healthcare expenditures. Contributions for large sectors of the population were still covered from general revenues: the unemployed and poor, pensioners, students, solders, civil servants, and some other vulnerable categories. Hospitals continued to rely on central government transfers and arrears to suppliers.

The final component of the UDF reforms was a rationalization of labor-market policy through the Protection against Unemployment and Promotion of Employment Act of 1997. In addition to restricting unemployment compensation, the new act moved toward more targeted forms of social assistance for the long-term unemployed. However, the new act also included expanded commitments in which European—as opposed to IFI—consultancies played a major role: job information and consultations; training; and support for entrepreneurship, as well as income support (Noncheva 1999, 22).

The fall of the UDF government in 2001 and the inauguration of the more conservative NMS II government might have presaged further liberalization of social-policy commitments. Although the new government took some administrative reforms and maintained a conservative fiscal policy, subsequent changes were largely parametric in nature. If anything, the onset of accession negotiations provided Bulgaria with new opportunities to tap EU resources to expand social-policy commitments, for example, through access to regional funds and the initiation of new anti-poverty programs.

Romania

The transition to democratic rule in Romania was the last and most difficult in Eastern Europe (December 1989). It was marred by violence against the opposition and doubts about the intentions of the National Council of the Salvation Front (NSF), a populist-nationalist party dominated by former Communists. Through 1996, political power was held by the Front, later the Party of Social Democracy in Romania (Partidul Democrației Sociale din România, PSDR), by its leader Ion Iliescu, who was elected to a relatively powerful presidency with an overwhelming mandate of 80 percent of the vote in May 1990.

The ruling coalition started to fray in late 1995, opening the way for a brief period of opposition rule. Between 1996 and 2000, power was held by a series of short-lived anti-Communist coalitions and then by two technocratic governments, one headed by Radu Vasile of the Peasant Party, which lasted barely a year before being replaced by a government under the national-bank governor, Mugur Isărescu. In the 2000 elections, Iliescu and the PSDR came back into power as the center of the political spectrum collapsed and right-wing nationalist candidates and parties showed major electoral gains.

The center-right did manage to reconstitute itself in subsequent years and in 2004, was returned to office in elections of questionable integrity (Pârvulescu 2004, 7–24). Yet for the period up through the 2004 elections—our focus here—Romania saw the longest period of rule by post-Communist parties (1989–96, 2000–2004). When anti-Communist forces did capture government, they faced ongoing conflict and deadlock with post-Communists and nationalists, intracoalitional rivalries, and high cabinet turnover.

These political circumstances were related as both cause and effect to the particularly inauspicious economic and social circumstances of the Romanian transition. The extreme depredations of the late Ceauşescu period made the posttransition electorate particularly vulnerable to populist appeals, and the NSF had close ties to the post-Communist unions. Technocrats had little political space in which to operate. Prime Minister Petre Roman's attempts at economic reform were blocked by the conservative wing of the party, and in September 1991, he was forced to resign after a second miner's uprising in Bucharest. Loss-making state enterprises were sustained by direct budgetary subsidies (up to 13 percent of GDP in 1992) and increasing reliance on both domestic and foreign debt. From 1995, the share of nonperforming loans in the banking system also started to rise. These adverse trends culminated in a balance-of-payment and financial crisis in 1997.

As in Bulgaria, it fell to the opposition government to introduce a difficult stabilization. The second transitional recession in Romania was even deeper than in Bulgaria, however; the economy contracted by 6.6 percent in 1997, 5.4 percent in 1998, and 3.2 percent in 1999. In May 2000, the technocratic government of Mugur Isărescu exploited negotiations with the EU to formulate a reform plan that was finally adopted by parliament. But both the National Front and the far right ran against the plan during the election campaign of that year, and subsequent relations with both the EU and the IMF were subject to ongoing conflict.

DEALING WITH THE TRANSITION

Although the posttransition governments in Romania sought to retain employment in the state-owned enterprise sector, they also sought to construct new social safety nets for those displaced by the transition. The reconstitution of tripartite structures served, at least initially, as a forum for negotiations over these policies (Iankova 2002, 5). The government introduced an unemployment scheme in 1991, and in 1995 it added a social-assistance scheme (the Social Aid Law) targeted at low-income sectors. In practice, severe fiscal constraints sharply limited the scope of such programs; during the crisis of the late 1990s, only 8 percent of poor families received assistance through the Social Aid Law (World Bank 2002b,

11–12). But even more than in other countries, the Iliescu government supplemented new safety nets with the expansion of existing entitlements from the socialist period. In 1990, a relaxation of restrictions on early retirement led to the most rapid increase of retirees of any Eastern European country; by the end of 1991, the number of beneficiaries had increased by 40 percent. Eligibility for disability pensions was also relaxed, leading to a 270 percent increase in such pensions during the period 1990–98.

As elsewhere in the region, the number of contributors to the system dropped as a result of increased unemployment and the migration of workers into the informal sector. An increase in the payroll tax in 1992—from 14 to over 25 percent of wages—had little effect on actual revenues. The relatively large rural sector posed a particular problem, given its electoral weight, the high share of the elderly in the rural population, and the effective bankruptcy of a number of the cooperative farms. The government created a special pension for retired agricultural workers, funded by a supplementary tax on food distributors, although benefits were small. Throughout the remainder of the NSF government, the main means of managing mounting pension obligations was through inflation. Prior to the elections of 1996, the real value of benefits was temporarily increased by changes in rules governing work histories and entitlements, but these populist measures fed directly into the broader macroeconomic problems and contributed to the crisis of 1997.

Among inherited entitlements, family allowances had played a particularly important role as part of Ceauşescu's pronatalist policies. In 1994, the government yielded to pressure to increase the child allowance and to make it a universal benefit. However, in contrast to Hungary's more encompassing benefits, parental leave and pay could only be claimed by women with an employment history; Romania is thus intermediate between Hungary and Poland in the generosity of these benefits (Fodor et al. 2002, 483–88).

SECOND-ROUND REFORMS

Accumulated imbalances and populist measures undertaken in the run-up to the November 1996 elections contributed both to a rapid deterioration in the financial integrity of the social-insurance fund and a wider fiscal and financial crisis. In a report on Romania's progress toward EU accession issued just before the 2000 elections, the European Commission found that Romania still did not have a "functioning market economy"—a requirement for entry—and specifically cited the relaxation of fiscal policy and the failure to undertake adequate reforms of the pension and healthcare systems. But fragmented and unstable coalition governments were unable to act in the face of labor militancy and severe problems of poverty. Indeed, the social portfolios were typically allocated to the parties most committed to retaining existing entitlements.

In the health sector, debate on comprehensive reforms accelerated after 1996, spurred on by the World Bank, the EU, and bilateral aid agencies. As in the other cases, however, reforms were constrained by broad public expectations and pressure from professional associations and unions. The 1997 Health Insurance Law shifted from a tax-based system to mandatory health insurance organized at the regional level. But central government transfers covered the noninsured and the reform explicitly sought to *increase* health spending (European Observatory on Health Care 2000, 67).

Pension reform was also a core objective of the new government and was incorporated as a condition of a World Bank adjustment loan that had been suspended under the old government. Initially conceived as a three-pillar reform, the effective insolvency of the pay-as-you-go system made reform of the first pillar a top priority. The legislation submitted to parliament in 1998 and passed in late 1999 gradually raised the retirement age, tightened eligibility for early retirement, and established a virtual link between contributions and benefits. However, the counterpart of the tighter provisions introduced in the new public law was a generous indexation formula and a massive "recorrelation" that effectively guaranteed to older retirees the additional benefits extended in the populist "reforms" of 1996 (de Menil and Sheshinski 2002).

Almost immediately on implementation, the new system ran into a firestorm of controversy as it appeared to dramatically lower the replacement rate for certain workers. This led the next administration to both raise the maximum pension allowed and make further adjustments in the equalization efforts. Legislation governing the creation of a second pillar had to be withdrawn by the Isărescu government and was not reintroduced.[17]

Probably the most important reform of the 1997–2000 period—and one affecting a number of other discrete policy areas—was the adoption of a new Law on Local Public Finance formulated under the Ciorbea government and adopted in October 1998. Decentralization expanded local financing and administrative responsibilities for many basic social services, including education, social assistance and services, and some health services. The incentives for such a change were multiple and included political reform. Nonetheless, as the World Bank (2002b, 6) notes, "the need to confront the budget shortfall provided an incentive for the

---

[17] Concern over the transition costs was one element, but the funded option was also opposed by unions. No further reform was undertaken during the Năstase government (Vasile and Uegaki 2003, 13–15).

government to shift increasing expenditure authority to lower levels of government." The reforms resulted in the emergence of major inequities in the level and quality of services across the country, as poorer jurisdictions found themselves overwhelmed by the demand for services and without the fiscal resources to respond effectively. These problems were particularly visible in the health sector (World Bank 2002c, 64–65) and ultimately resulted in strong political pressures for recentralization.

Despite efforts of the outgoing government to buy support through increased pension benefits and an increase in the minimum wage to public-sector workers, the November 2000 elections saw a complete rout of the center-right by the left and an upsurge of support for the extreme nationalist-populist Greater Romania Party. With near majorities in both the upper and lower houses, the PSDR formed a minority government in control of all ministries. The new government quickly faced the conflicting circumstances visible in the second-round crises in Bulgaria, including large budget deficits and increasing external pressures associated with EU accession negotiations and balance of payments problems. In the fall of 2001, the government reached a preliminary agreement with the IMF on a new program implicitly linked to accession. However in contrast to Bulgaria, these tasks fell to a leftist party with a core base of support that included industrial workers, pensioners, and the poor.

The PSDR did have certain political advantages in its ability to secure parliamentary support for its initiatives. However, the government inherited expansionary promises in the two largest social-insurance areas—health and pensions—and from the outset, spending in these two areas increased. Some of these increased costs reflected efforts to rationalize the system, such as changes in the calculation of benefits that encouraged early retirement. Yet other costs reflected political compromises and new social commitments: the quarterly indexation of pension benefits; a 40 percent increase in the minimum wage; an increase in transfers to the rural sector; and the creation of a minimum-income scheme that was anticipated at the time to cover nearly 600,000 households and cost nearly .5 percent of GDP (EIU 2001a).

Romania subsequently secured entry to the EU and moved toward a number of reforms that paralleled the social-insurance models seen elsewhere in the region. But progress remained very limited through the early 2000s. In the key area of pension reform, the government finally mandated the establishment of a second pillar in 2004. But negotiation of critical details continued to lag, and implementation was not projected to begin until at least 2007.

By way of conclusion, it is worth considering some of the salient differences between the course of social-policy reform in Bulgaria and Romania. Both experienced "second round" crises. But Bulgaria's very high inflation provided an opening for more dramatic reforms that reached into the social sector. In Romania, the second recession was more prolonged, but the absence of high inflation weakened support for a more radical reform effort. Partisanship and the fragmentation of government coalitions also played a role in the timing of reforms. In Romania, fragmented opposition coalitions were hamstrung in their ability to initiate virtually any social policy reforms. In Bulgaria, reform of the pension and health system was facilitated by a relatively unified government. Even there, however, liberal reformers accommodated citizen expectations regarding coverage and made new efforts to address labor-market insecurity, long-run unemployment, and poverty.

Conclusion

The transition to the market spelled the end of employment guarantees in Eastern Europe. Fiscal constraints and the ascent of market-oriented political forces also encouraged some movement in the direction of more liberal welfare policies, as a number of critics feared.[18] Yet despite rapid and wrenching transitions to the market, the principles of comprehensive protection that underlay the socialist welfare systems showed surprising resilience in Eastern Europe. Moreover, although governments certainly differed in their exact approach to social policy, the countries we consider showed a substantial convergence when compared with either Latin America or East Asia (table 8.2).

First, in most countries government financing of uninsured groups reflected de facto commitments to universalism, particularly in the area of healthcare and old-age protections. In some countries and policy areas, de jure commitments to universalism were enshrined in new constitutions. These commitments stood in contrast to the continuing fragmentation of Latin America's social-insurance systems and the ongoing deficit in access to even basic health and education that persisted in a number of countries in the region.

The Eastern European countries showed not only wide population coverage, but also commitment to insurance against a fairly wide range of risks, closer in principle to the broad European conception of social insurance enshrined in the ILO than more liberal models. Much more than was the case in Latin America, governments remained committed not only to public health insurance, but to active and passive labor market policies, disability insurance, and family allowances of various sorts. These com-

---

[18] For example, Deacon 1992; Standing 1996; Ferge 1997, 2001; Ferge and Tausz 2002; Brown 2005.

Table 8.2
Social-Policy Developments in Eastern Europe, 1980–2005

	Pensions	*Health*	*Social safety nets*
	Early reformers		
Poland	Moderate privatization establishes second pillar but retains broad coverage and large public pillar (1998); rural population covered under old noncontributory system.	Shift to social-insurance system (1997) but with guarantees of universal coverage.	Unemployment insurance supplemented with generous use of disability pensions, early retirement, and family allowances.
Hungary	Moderate privatization establishes second pillar but retains broad coverage and large public pillar (1997).	Early shift to social-insurance system (1992) but with guarantees of universal coverage.	Unemployment insurance, active labor market policies and generous use of family and child allowances. Strong opposition to rationalizing family allowances.
Czech Republic	No pension privatization through 2005.	Radical reform establishes private insurance funds (1992); reform fails, and system reverts to government social insurance.	Limited unemployment facilitated by government encouragement of employment guarantees and active labor market policies. Generous family allowances and minimum income guarantee.
	Late reformers		
Slovakia	Old pension system maintained until relatively extensive privatization in 2002.	Shift to social insurance but marginal changes until 2003 reforms including limiting benefit package and encouraging private insurance.	Limited unemployment facilitated by government encouragement of employment guarantees, active labor market policies and public employment schemes. Generous family allowances and minimum income guarantee.
Bulgaria	Moderate privatization establishes second pillar but retains broad coverage, large public pillar (1999). Large noncontributory disability pension and social assistance to low-income pensioners.	Shift to social-insurance system (1998) but with guarantees of universal coverage and substantial healthcare financing through general revenues.	Unemployment insurance supplemented with generous use of disability pensions and early retirement; some reform of these entitlements after 1997 with more active labor-market policies, broadly targeted minimum income scheme (1992).
Romania	Privatization effort in 1999 is withdrawn with only parametric changes. Moderate privatization establishes second pillar (2004).	Shift to social-insurance system (1997) but with guarantees of universal coverage and substantial healthcare financing through general revenues despite nominal decentralization.	Unemployment insurance supplemented with social assistance and particular reliance on early retirement, disability pensions, special measures for retired farmers, and broadly targeted minimum-income scheme (2001).

mitments were generally reflected in the continuing allocation of substantial fiscal resources for the social sector (figures A6.16–21).Recurrent fiscal constraints eroded entitlements and resulted in a deterioration in the quality of services, queuing for services and the persistence of under-the-table payments for services.

Despite their defects, however, principles of broad coverage persisted. Liberalizing reforms were not only slower to emerge than in Latin America, but were often reversed when they were tried. We have attributed these continuities to the influence of common welfare legacies. The organization and coverage of the old system produced strong and widely shared public expectations about the role of the government in providing protections and services, expectations that are repeatedly confirmed in the survey research literature (for example, Lipsmeyer 2003). This policy inheritance generated strong electoral and interest group pressures on governments (Vanhuysee 2006).

More than in the other regions, our analysis of the postsocialist transitions has relied on a relatively straightforward path-dependence argument. We are not alone; others have made similar arguments.[19] Yet this approach cannot be sustained without taking into account alternative explanations that might account for the convergence we see across the region.

The most important candidates are approaches that stress common external pressures and influences. One version of this argument, advanced most forcefully by Deacon (2000, 1997; Deacon and Stubbs 2005) and Orenstein (2006), is that the international financial institutions played a crucial role in defining social-policy options in the region, both directly by providing intellectual templates and indirectly by pressing for fiscal adjustments (see also Stone 2002).

The IFIs play a role in our account as well, but in a way that is somewhat different from that suggested by Deacon and Orenstein. We argue that the influence of the IFIs is not constant but rather contingent on economic circumstances. Crises and the emergence of pressing fiscal constraints are associated with an increase in the influence of both technocrats and of the international financial institutions. We also emphasize that external influence faced important domestic political limits. A substantial number of IMF programs were canceled or did not go to their conclusion (Stone 2002, 67–73). Similarly, welfare reforms accommodated the domestic political coalitions we have identified and were frequently modified or even reversed when fiscal conditions eased.

A second, quite different source of external influence is associated with the proximity of the European Union. Orenstein and Haas (2003), for example, argue that the "European" and "Eurasian" successor states had

[19] Examples include Kovacs 2002; Inglot 2003; Manning 2004; Cerami 2005.

similar social policy-regimes prior to the transition, but only the "European" ones have maintained broad social-insurance coverage and innovated new programs (see also Cook 2007). They explain this difference by what they call the "Europe effect."

On closer inspection, European influence on social policy is by no means clear, as Wade Jacoby (2004) has also argued in a thoughtful study of the influence of EU enlargement on Eastern Europe. After 1995, the EU gravitated toward the view that new members should conform closely to common EU standards from the outset rather than being allowed a lengthy transition process as had been the case in the Southern European applicants during the 1980s. The direct transposition of the 80,000-page *acquis communautaire* became the formal target for candidate members, organized through negotiations of 31 discrete "chapters." Moreover, there is ample evidence that—fears of rampant neoliberalism to the contrary—Eastern Europe borrowed widely from the diverse palette of Western European social policies.

But the direct European influence on social-policy outcomes was relatively limited in the core areas of interest to us. First, our case studies show that a number of key decisions on social protection came very early in the transition. These included both the promise to maintain certain commitments, such as healthcare, and the innovation of new ones, such as social safety nets. At that point, prospects for membership in the EU were highly uncertain even in the early reformers, let alone in Slovakia, Bulgaria, and Romania.

A closer look at the relevant sections of the *acquis communautaire* also suggests that the direct influence of the EU was fairly restricted (Wagener 2002, 167–70). The single market requires conformity with a number of health and safety restrictions; moreover, the amended European Social Charter (ESC), incorporated into the Treaty of Amsterdam, addresses a number of social issues including working time, equal opportunity, and "social dialogue." But the EU negotiations did not require the adoption of the social-security and health policies discussed in this chapter. The Social Charter stipulates basic rights of collective bargaining and enumerates rights to social security (ESC, arts. 12, 22); to protection of health (ESC, art. 11); to social assistance and services (ESC, arts. 13, 14); and to family protection (ESC, art. 17). But these are outlined as a statement of aims, not as specific requirements. More important, they are subject to the arguably contradictory pressure of meeting the strict fiscal requirements of entry, which by contrast are very precise. In the cases of Slovakia and Romania in particular, the indirect influence of the community probably pushed in the direction of the rationalization of social expenditure rather than convergence on Western European models.

As Jacoby (2004, 45–64) argues with respect to health care, finally, it is not clear what it means to speak of a "European" influence. Much of the literature on the European welfare state has been devoted to outlining and explaining its diversity, from pensions and healthcare to unemployment insurance, labor-market policies, and family policy. Although some protagonists such as Klaus might have looked longingly at Thatcherism, others sought policy advice from countries in the Community with quite different systems. In one interesting health-policy experiment in Bulgaria, the government self-consciously invited advisors from four different countries and even initiated pilot projects for the purpose of weighing the costs and benefits of different policy approaches.

We do not rule out the complex if important possibility that social-policy models owed some intellectual debt to borrowing from extant European ones. But this is a much more modest claim, and advocates of this diffusion approach have to explain why the borrowing took the particular form it did. Answers to that question can only come from some consideration of the political selection process.

Notwithstanding deep market reforms, broad entitlements were difficult to fundamentally amend because of both electoral constraints on politicians and pressure from organized stakeholders. Expectations with respect to the public sector's role in cushioning against risk contributed to the creation of new social safety nets and efforts to alleviate poverty and inequality. The relatively uniform nature of the socialist legacy that we outlined in chapter 5 is ultimately mirrored in important continuities in Eastern European social policy in the posttransition period. As in the other regions, the social-policy equilibrium that we identify as of 2005 is by no means immune from further revision. Yet by 2005, Eastern European social policy had "settled out" to a significant extent, revealing important contrasts with the Latin American cases in how new democracies respond to economic crises.

Latin America, East Asia, Eastern Europe, and the Theory of the Welfare State

Over the last two decades, welfare reforms in the new democracies of Latin America, East Asia, and Eastern Europe have moved along very different tracks. Some countries have expanded social insurance and services, others have attempted to liberalize existing commitments or even retrench them outright. We have argued that these current processes of reform are but the most recent phase in much longer social-policy histories. Far from being newcomers to the dilemmas of the welfare state, countries in all three regions developed quite distinctive welfare models over the postwar period.

These prior models exercised a strong influence over the course of social-policy reform in more recent decades. In the literature on the advanced welfare state, the concept of path dependence is invoked in such settings to explain why the status quo persists or changes only within narrow bounds. This book raises broadly similar questions about the contemporary politics of welfare reform in middle-income countries. How have the interests and institutions created by past policy choices affected current policy debates? To what extent do changes in social policy reflect not only contemporaneous variables but also the historical path through which the current state was reached?

Such questions pushed us to investigate the origins of these social-policy systems—how they developed in the first place. In our discussion of origins, we focused on fundamental political realignments: periods characterized by the rise to power of new political elites and fundamental changes in the political status of workers, peasants, and the organizations and political parties that represented them. We show that these realignments had a lasting influence on the subsequent course of policy. Where political elites sought to coopt these groups, they gained not only political representation but social-policy concessions as well. In Latin America, this process of accommodation resulted in the extension of social-insurance coverage to some portion of the organized urban working class, programs that became the template for further expansion of entitlements. However, critical realignments in Latin America were not associated with new political opportunities for the rural poor, and social policy in the region reflected their political exclusion.

Where lower-class organizations were controlled or repressed, social policy reflected the objectives—the projects—of ruling political elites. In the conservative, anti-Communist regimes of East Asia, governments sought to eliminate labor and the left as contenders for power. Coming to power in the wake of political independence, these political elites extended certain core social services widely, most notably basic education. However governments did not accommodate the social-policy interests of the organized urban working class as occurred in Western Europe and Latin America.

In Eastern Europe, repression of independent labor and peasant organizations was a necessary condition for a much broader socialist project that included the nationalization of the "commanding heights" of industry and finance and the collectivization of agriculture. The East European countries developed broad social entitlements, but these exhibited a number of features that differentiated them sharply from the advanced welfare states, including direct state control over the allocation of labor, complete absence of private financing and provision, and authoritarian control over the educational system.

Over time, these early patterns were reinforced by economic-policy choices. Development strategies did not "require" particular social policies; but major economic-policy choices structured the preferences and expectations of government, business, and labor over a wide array of other policies, including those involving social protections and services. In this sense, development strategies and social policy were complementary.

In Latin America, ISI accommodated the privileges extended to portions of the working class through protection, state ownership of certain industries, and subsidies and other industrial policies. East Asian countries also had an experience with import-substitution in the postwar period, albeit in a very different political context than in Latin America. But the pursuit of export-oriented strategies pushed governments and business to greater sensitivity about both the quality and cost of labor. In the Eastern European cases, the planning process and the monopoly on most economic activity by the state dictated both government and firm-level responsibilities with respect to social insurance and services.

The dramatic political and economic changes of the 1980s and 1990s—widespread democratization and economic crises—arguably marked a new critical juncture for all three regions. Democratization placed new demands on the state, but the capacity to respond was bounded by economic circumstance. Those countries hit with severe economic shocks faced concomitant pressures to rethink prior welfare commitments, readjust the scope of the state's role, and limit future social-policy commitments.

However, prior welfare commitments also influenced social-policy reforms. Welfare legacies created beneficiaries and organized stakeholders. Where coverage was initially narrow but growth was robust, the political logic of expanding social entitlements proved compelling; such were the circumstances in the East Asian cases. Where coverage was wide and economic circumstances adverse—as in Eastern Europe—electoral and interest-group forces combined to limit the scope of liberalizing reform or retrenchment. The unequal coverage and adverse economic circumstances in Latin America produced a more complex political economy of reform. Governments faced competing political pressures for both the expansion and reform of welfare systems, but they did so in the context of strong stakeholders with an interest in preserving the status quo. These factors combined to generate more extensive reform than occurred in Eastern Europe but with continuing inequalities in the distribution of insurance and services and a more targeted approach to welfare policy.

In this conclusion, we situate these arguments in the context of several ongoing debates about the future of the welfare state. We begin with the international constraints on social policy and the debate over globalization. Is there something about the current international political as well as economic context that might lead countries toward convergence on common social policies in the current period? We then revisit the economic issues in more detail, considering the political economy of growth and the longer-run fiscal capacity of the state. We close with the role of democracy in determining the nature of the social contract between governments and citizens.

THE INTERNATIONAL INFLUENCES I: THE GEOSTRATEGIC SETTING

No less than the objects of its study, comparative political economy has been transformed by globalization. The days when we could consider countries as isolated units are over; as in the fields of sociology and macroeconomics, comparative political economy is now open-economy in form (Bates 1998). Yet the precise way of modeling these external relationships is by no means straightforward. There is a plethora of ways that "the international" operates on states: war and security calculations; cleavages over economic openness; bargaining with external actors; the influence of international institutions; and the diffusion of policy ideas.

In considering the origins of different welfare systems, we argued that great powers had an important influence on domestic political realignments. In all three regions of interest to us, the capabilities of domestic political elites were dependent on external circumstances. Transnational alliances were most evident in East Asia and Eastern Europe, where conservative and Communist elites respectively gained or maintained power through international connections and support, if not outright diktat.

In more subtle ways, international political factors were germane in the Latin American cases as well. United States influence in the region was powerful and direct in Central America and the Caribbean, where it consistently supported staunchly antilabor military and oligarchic governments. Had we included these cases in our analysis, we would have expected these connections to be consequential for social policy. But from the onset of World War I through the late 1940s, U.S. influence over the larger countries of the region was circumscribed. The critical political junctures we have identified took place prior to the onset of the Cold War, at moments when Washington's attention was distracted by two World Wars and the Great Depression. United States intervention intensified with the onset of the Cold War in the late 1940s, and particularly after the Cuban revolution in 1959. But unlike the countries of Asia and Eastern Europe, Latin America was not a "front line" region of great power rivalry. Consequently, U.S. investment of military and economic resources was, comparatively speaking, more limited.

Should we be looking more closely at the current era through a similar geostrategic lens? Are international political factors once again affecting the political economy of social policy?

Several influential accounts have suggested the outlines of such an approach (Deacon 1997). The collapse of the Soviet Union—and the Soviet model—left the United States as a hegemonic political actor almost by default. The United States could not simply impose an Anglo-Saxon policy order, but it could change incentives in subtle and not so subtle ways. Channels for such influence included the international financial institutions, the WTO's trade-policy agenda (for example, the ongoing efforts to liberalize the service sector and to protect property rights in pharmaceuticals), and the ability to push similar issues through regional and bilateral trade arrangements.

We are skeptical of these arguments. As our discussion of cross-regional differences indicates, we are dubious about the starting premise: that social policy is converging in a neoliberal direction. But the presumption of America's hegemonic influence is also highly problematic. How swiftly the political landscape can change! Far from exercising an overweening influence, the United States has become entangled in a number of debilitating political challenges: conflicts across the Islamic world; a virtual collapse of support among the publics of most other developing countries; a rising, more assertive, and decidedly unliberal China; and a divided but nonetheless weighty agglomeration of economic and ideological influences emanating from the new Europe. Despite the talk of a unipolar international order, the ability of the United States to manipulate domestic politics abroad is in fact much more limited than it was at the height of the Cold War. Moreover, the triumphalist moment of post–Cold War American ideological influence has clearly waned; if anything, backlash against "neoliberalism" has become pervasive.

If there are international political factors that are relevant to our story, they probably lie at the regional level: in regional organization, diffusion, and emulation. A handful of interesting new studies are pursuing this line of thinking (Gleditsch 2002), although only some have extended to a consideration of social policy (Jacoby 2004; Weyland 2004; Brooks 2005; Orenstein 2006). The most obvious example is the pull of Western Europe on the former socialist countries. We argued in chapter 8 that the continuity in social protection in Eastern Europe could be explained largely by domestic political factors associated with the socialist welfare legacy rather than external influence or even emulation. Nonetheless, membership in the European Community, European aid and technology transfer, and intellectual influences have all operated in Eastern Europe and are likely to play an ongoing role in the future. These regional patterns do not operate in the same way in Latin America or East Asia, but both formal institutions, such as the regional development banks, and informal policy networks and emulation are undoubtedly at work there as well. Overall, however, we see very little evidence that international political forces, and particularly American influence, are leading to a homogenization of social policy.

INTERNATIONAL INFLUENCES II: THE GLOBALIZATION DEBATE

A broader debate in the literature on social policy concerns international economic, rather than political, influences. Among the landmarks of this literature are Cameron's (1978) demonstration of the correlation between economic openness and the size of the state and Katzenstein's (1985) work on the historical origins of European corporatism in the economic crises of the 1930s. According to this line of thinking, democratic governments had incentives to offset the increased vulnerability and insecurity associated with economic openness either through countercyclical Keynesian policies or by expanding the scope and depth of social insurance. In John Ruggie's (1982) felicitous phrase, the Bretton Woods era from the late 1940s to the early 1970s was grounded on a particular international and domestic social compact he called embedded liberalism. Leading governments, assisted by international institutions, sought to reconstruct the liberal international economic order that had collapsed in the interwar period. But the rules of the international economy allowed broadly liberal principles to be "embedded" within domestic social contracts that set limits on the scope of the market.

Research by Geoffrey Garrett, Dani Rodrik, and others found at least some empirical evidence for the embedded liberalism hypothesis. Garrett (1998) argued—somewhat modestly—that globalization did not negate the effect of partisanship on government spending in the OECD. He concluded that globalization therefore did not have uniform or consistent effects; countries diverged with respect to the overall size of the state and the nature of their welfare commitments. Rodrik (1998) found trade openness to be a significant determinant of both government consumption and spending, even when controlling for a variety of other possible economic determinants.

Beginning in the 1980s, however, a more skeptical view of globalization began to gain both popular and scholarly attention.[1] This literature argued that increasing trade and investment constrained government spending in the advanced industrial states, including spending on welfare. Capital mobility placed pressure on the capacity of individual jurisdictions to tax mobile assets. Greater reliance on exports and greater exposure to foreign competition in the domestic market had similar effects. Firms in the traded-goods sector saw taxes and other labor-market rigidities as constraints on the ability to compete.

What does our work show about this important debate? Do we see any parallel between the compromise of embedded liberalism in the advanced industrial states and the social policies of Latin America, East Asia, and Eastern Europe during the period covered in part 1 of the book, when a more selective approach to international economic integration prevailed? Did greater caution about openness permit a more expansive approach to social policy? Conversely, has the more recent period of liberalization of trade and capital flows lead to a rollback of previous entitlements?

We argued in part 1 that the import-substituting model did provide the space for a particular welfare approach in Latin America. Of course, the socialist model would have been impossible in an open-economy context. Even in the more outward-oriented East Asian cases, governments coupled export-oriented growth strategies with a variety of protective measures.

Although this period might have been one of high growth, however, it was by no means characterized by a liberal social compromise in the sense that Ruggie used the term. In Eastern Europe, entitlements were broad, but these were not the result of a democratic social contract but rather of a central planning process. In Latin America, some portions of the working class arguably gained from the closed economy, but the pattern of growth was associated with the continuation and even deepening of long-standing inequalities.

A consistent theme of the literature on the export-oriented East Asian newly industrializing countries is the limited attention these countries

---

[1] For a review, see Huber and Stephens 2001.

paid to the provision of social insurance. However, as we argued in chapter 3, these governments restricted social insurance prior to their turn toward an export-oriented approach to growth. Although we believe that an export-oriented strategy influenced social policy in the East Asian cases, the ultimate origin of these welfare choices must be traced back to critical political realignments that weakened labor and the left.

If the period covered in part 1 of this book was not a golden age of embedded liberalism, the entitlements developed during that period could nonetheless be vulnerable to the process of economic opening that subsequently followed. Some studies provide qualified support for the claim that economic openness has adverse consequences on social spending (Rudra 2002; Kaufman and Segura-Ubiergo 2001; Segura-Ubiergo, 2007). Yet our analysis finds only mixed support for the skeptical view. In the models we report in chapter 6, the effects of openness on social spending are modest, particularly when controlling for underlying fiscal circumstances, and vary across regions. In the regional case studies, we attempted to show that the effects of economic openness almost certainly paled by comparison to the broader economic circumstances in which new democracies found themselves.

These new economic circumstances were not limited to an increase in economic openness per se but included extraordinary volatility in international capital flows and other external shocks. We have argued, however, that in both Latin America and Eastern Europe, these external shocks were but one component of wider crises of prior development models. Similar arguments can be made about the Asian financial crisis, which exposed not only the resilience of the East Asian model but also the weakness of corporate governance and the regulation of the financial sector.

Moreover, both economic circumstances and the extent of openness were mediated by domestic political factors including democratization and prior welfare legacies. In East Asia, new democracies dramatically expanded welfare entitlements while also increasing international economic integration. In Eastern Europe, which probably experienced the most radical process of economic opening, governments managed to retain and even increase the scope of entitlements. Latin America is the region in which there has been somewhat more quantitative research suggesting that globalization has adverse consequences for social spending (for example, Kaufman and Segura-Ubiergo 2001; Wibbels 2006). But even there, the effects have been felt mainly in the area of social security rather than in health and education. Given that social-insurance systems were regressive to begin with, the distributional consequences of economic opening are far from clear (Nelson 1992).

We conclude as we did with the effects of international political alignments: that the effects of globalization are neither uniform nor are they likely on their face to be substantial when compared to the effects of crises and fiscal constraints. Those arguing that globalization puts a squeeze on social policy argue implicitly that political factors have little or no mediating effect on the relationship between globalization and social policy; governments facing very different types of political challenges are presumed to respond similarly to external constraints. Yet this assumption does not appear to hold; variety prevails. To understand why, we revisit our economic arguments about the effects of economic growth and the fiscal capacity of the state.

ECONOMIC GROWTH, WELFARE, AND SOCIAL POLICY

A range of government policies influences the welfare of citizens. Arguably, the most important is the bundle of policies that contribute to economic growth itself. What these policies are remains somewhat unclear, as suggested by the title of Elhanan Helpman's (2004) useful overview, *The Mystery of Economic Growth*. Although there is consensus on a handful of fundamentals—protection for property rights, the maintenance of macroeconomic stability, at least a modicum of economic openness and trade, and provision of an adequate array of public goods such as infrastructure and education—the scope within which these fundamentals operate is fairly broad. There appear to be a variety of policy packages that are capable of delivering robust economic performance.

Nonetheless, the significance of differences across countries in this regard cannot be denied, nor can the importance of apparently small differences in growth for variations in welfare over time. Consider the fate of a country beginning the postwar era in 1945 with a per-capita GDP of $1000, roughly equal to Malaysia's at that time. A yearly growth of 1 percent in real terms through 2005 would yield a per-capita income of $1,816. The same country growing at 4 percent a year over that period would have a per-capita income of $10,520; a 5 percent growth rate—admittedly an unusual feat over such an extended period—would yield an average income of $18,680.

Sadly, these differences are not merely hypothetical. Despite the crises we detailed in the second half of the book, all the middle-income countries we considered managed to achieve substantial growth over the postwar period. In all the countries we consider, with the exception of Peru and Venezuela, per capita incomes at least doubled, and in no case did per capita income actually fall, as it did in a number of African countries. Yet the differences across the countries in our sample are stark. Peru began the postwar period with a per-capita income of just over $2000 (in 1990 dollars); in 2000 this had risen to about $3700. South Korea, by contrast, began the postwar period with a per-capita income of under $700; by 2000, it had reached over $14,000.

For our purposes, however, the important point to explore is the influence of these differences on the nature of the social contract. East Asia's rapid and sustained growth was accompanied by a rapid rise in income across a large share of the population and a dramatic fall in poverty. In Eastern Europe, economic growth was high for most of the postwar period but slowed dramatically in the late socialist period, a prelude to the collapse of output during the transitional recessions of the early 1990s. Even prior to 1980, economic growth in Latin America was relatively volatile, and in contrast to the relatively egalitarian distribution of income in East Asia and Eastern Europe, expansion took place in the context of very skewed distributions of both income and assets. Latin American growth prior to the crises of the 1980s certainly had some effect on poverty, but these effects were dampened by continuing and in some cases increasing inequality.

How do these differences in the level of economic growth, its volatility, and the distribution of income across income classes affect the social policies of interest to us? Strong economic performance was at least a permissive condition for the expansion of social entitlements we described in part 1. In Latin America, the relative success of ISI policies prior to the financial collapse of the 1980s provided the basis for a gradual expansion of social entitlements, what Mesa-Lago (1978) has called the massification of privilege. This process was even more visible in Eastern Europe, where the high growth of the early Stalinist period produced profound changes in social structure through rapid industrialization, urbanization, and the extension of new social benefits to the growing urban working class. After the high Stalinist period, Communist parties across the region turned to a legitimating formula that put much more emphasis on consumption and social entitlements. When growth in Eastern Europe slowed in the 1980s, consumption and other benefits such as the funding of health care and pensions showed the strain, and in Poland this slowdown was an important source of political conflict.

Yet as the East Asian cases showed, high growth was only a permissive condition for an expansion of social entitlements in authoritarian settings. In these cases, rising incomes did not provide the foundation for an expansion of social insurance and redistributive transfers but quite the opposite; high growth was a substitute for them. In an authoritarian context, the benefits of growth could be widely distributed or "shared," as Campos and Root (1996, 44–49) put it, without a more expansive social contract in the sense we have used the term here.

If the relationship between growth and the expansion of social insurance and services is unclear under authoritarian rule, we might expect a somewhat closer connection in new democracies. In outlining this relationship, we focused largely on the fiscal connection. We argued that conditions of high growth not only directly weakened fiscal constraints on spending but also had political consequences; high growth and strong public finances provided incentives for politicians to expand entitlements. Periods of low growth and crises not only placed direct constraints on spending but also had political effects, weakening those political forces arguing for expansion and strengthening arguments for restraint and even retrenchment.

In his book *The Moral Consequences of Economic Growth*, Benjamin Friedman (2005) suggests a wider array of reasons why growth will influence the nature of the social contract. Drawing on social-psychological and behavioral approaches to economics, Friedman notes that "stagnant economies . . . do not breed support for economic mobility, or for openness of opportunity more generally" (86). In rapidly growing economies, people are more likely to benchmark their own well-being against the past, with a resulting sense of satisfaction. In slow-growing economies, by contrast, people are more likely to benchmark themselves against others and to see social spending—and even economic activity more generally—in zero-sum terms. Someone else's gain breeds resentment and a sense of unfairness and deprivation. As Friedman notes, "the resulting frustration generates intolerance, ungenerosity, and resistance to greater openness to individual opportunity. Slow growth also erodes people's willingness to trust one another, which in turn is a key prerequisite for a successful democracy" (92). Friedman shows that periods of high growth in the United States, France, Britain, and Germany are also periods of greater generosity in social policy. Periods of slowed growth are accompanied by a retreat from such generosity and the rise of social movements opposed to social fairness, including racist and nativist ones.

In sum, economic growth not only has direct effects on welfare but also structures the politics of welfare in democratic societies. Robust growth directly reduces poverty but also influences the way the disadvantaged are viewed and the way societies respond to their plight. Where growth is robust, the social contract is likely to be more expansive as well.

The Fiscal Foundations of the Welfare State

In part 2, we argued that the capacity for new democracies to maintain existing social commitments and expand social insurance and services was contingent not only on growth but on fiscal constraints as well. An expansion of revenue provided the basis for an expansion of social commitments; short-run fiscal shocks generated pressures for restraint. However, the point is not just germane in the short run. Much of the literature on the welfare state has focused on the spending side of the equation, but a handful of studies have started to investigate the fiscal foundations of the welfare state (for example, Steinmo 1993; Kato 2003). These studies underline the fact that social-policy initiatives depend ultimately on the ability to raise the taxes necessary to sustain such initiatives over time.

Put differently, a complete political economy of the welfare state should consider the joint determination of taxes and spending. This observation is congruent with an alternative theory of government accountability that looks not to the nature of political institutions but to the fiscal foundations of the state (Bates and Lien 1985; Levi 1988; Lake and Baum 2001). States can use coercion to raise revenue, but they are constrained in their ability to do so by the costs of extraction and monitoring and the ability of residents to resist, evade taxes, or migrate elsewhere. Governments not dependent on taxes—either because of income from natural resources, from state-owned enterprises, or from aid—will be less responsive to their citizenry and more corrupt than those that rely on taxation (Chaudhry 1997; Karl 1997; Ross 1999; Hoffman 2006; Smith 2007). Conversely, states that do rely on taxes are constrained to provide public goods to their constituents, including the basic social insurance and services that have been the subject of this book.

Holmes and Sunstein (1999) have developed this core insight into a broader normative theory of rights that is applicable to an understanding of the welfare state as well. In contrast to the distinction between negative and positive liberties, they argue, even negative liberties—most notably the protection of private property—hinge on the capacity of the state to enforce them. States provide such protection in return for taxes from the propertied classes. They continue:

> The delivery of welfare rights . . . is part of an ancillary exchange by which the government and the taxpaying citizens recompense the poor, or at least give them symbolic recognition, for their cooperative behavior in both war and peace. Most importantly, welfare rights compensate the indigent for receiving less value than the rich from the rights ostensibly guaranteed equally to all. (208)

How are such bargains forged? A dominant model of this process is majoritarian and focuses on redistribution: the poor, or alliances of the poor and the middle classes, use majority rule to impose redistribution on the wealthy or blackmail them with the threat of social disorder or even revolution. However, it may well be that social policy is less redistributive than it appears, and that stable welfare bargains work precisely when the incidence of benefits aligns most closely with the incidence of taxes—or put most simply, when people get what they are paying for. For the poor to be represented in the social-policy system, they must also be brought into the fiscal system, so that politicians will be made accountable to their interests.

Yet as Holmes and Sunstein suggest, we can imagine alternative routes to the fiscal bargain required to sustain the welfare state. Such bargains may be more likely when social insurance and services are understood not simply as mechanisms of redistribution, but also as public goods or solutions to genuine market failures (Barr 2001). For example, public health and education clearly have positive externalities for society as a whole; in addition, a number of forms of social insurance address problems, such as unemployment, retirement savings, and health insurance,that private markets and individual decision-making solve only imperfectly. In sum, shifting from a redistributive to a public-goods perspective has important political-economy implications that require further analysis.

THE EFFECTS OF REGIME TYPE

Does democracy lead to more inclusive and equitable social contracts? In summarizing our findings on this question, it is first important to take into account the wide political and institutional diversity we encountered among both authoritarian and democratic regimes.

The social policies pursued in nondemocratic regimes were by no means uniform; they varied profoundly depending on the extent to which they permitted semicompetitive elections, the types of social challenges they faced from below, and the development strategies pursued by ruling elites. In Latin America, even authoritarian reformers compromised with the urban working class to achieve their broader, antioligarchic objectives. In East Asia, authoritarian regimes in a number of countries, including most notably Korea and Taiwan, reached out to the rural sector through land reform and an expansion of basic social services in order to deter rural unrest and as a counterweight to urban opposition. Communist regimes radically redistributed resources not because of their responsiveness to underlying social pressures but because of political and ideological commitments to a socialist transformation. All of these cases provide an important reminder of the limits of purely institutionalist expectations.

Democratic regimes varied widely as well, and differences in electoral institutions and constitutional structure might have well been consequential. A full test of these ideas clearly goes far beyond the scope of this study, but it is useful to voice some words of caution about these approaches based on the more historical, economic, and interest-based approach we have pursued here.

One influential approach to come out of economics, developed by Persson and Tabbelini (1999; 2000; 2003), looks at differences in constitutional arrangements as a source of variation in the extent of redistribution. The authors argue that a separation of powers enables the voters to discipline politicians to limit waste and moderate the tax burden but that the conflict of interests between branches of government prevents politicians from providing an adequate level of public goods. By contrast, the legislative cohesion of a parliamentary system is associated with more taxation and more waste, but also greater spending on public goods and redistribution.

A cursory consideration might suggest that such an institutional argument finds some support among our cases; the parliamentary systems of Eastern Europe appear to have maintained a much more robust set of social protections than the presidential systems in Latin America. Yet such a conclusion would be a highly misleading one. The retention of social commitments from the socialist era may well have been affected by the PR nature of these systems and the coalition governments that typically ensued. But such electoral incentives would have operated even under very different institutional arrangements as a result of the social policy inheritance. It is doubtful that formal institutions were principal causal factors.

A similar set of reservations can be raised about a strand of literature to which we ourselves have contributed: the argument that multiple veto points, such as those that result from fragmented party systems or the existence of multiple institutional checks on decision making, are likely to stymie reform (Haggard and Kaufman 1995, 151–82; Haggard and McCubbins 2001; Tsebelis 2002). These arguments rest on the assumption that reforms are costly in the short-run or for some groups and that securing support for them is therefore difficult. In the absence of robust legislative coalitions or cohesive, even insulated, decision-making institutions (Haggard and Kaufman 1992), initiatives won't pass or are vulnerable to subsequent revision. Such arguments have recently been extended to the analysis of pension reform by Madrid (2003) and Brooks (2007).

Veto-point arguments are germane for understanding the political difficulties of liberalizing welfare entitlements, and a number of cases appear to vindicate them; we saw evidence of this in a number of the Eastern European cases and in Brazil with respect to pensions. But such arguments hinge quite fundamentally on the underlying preferences of the relevant nodes in the system. "Stickiness" depends on the presumption—often warranted—of differences in interests across veto points. Yet in many democratic settings, as we have shown, interests are structured by economic circumstances or welfare legacies that can force coherent action even on fractious legislatures.

In a similar vein, it is readily apparent that while a larger number of veto points may influence the ability of governments to pass and sustain liberalizing reforms or retrenchment, it is less likely to be a stumbling block to expanding social commitments. In these cases, the problems political leaders face are not in securing support and controlling potential veto players but in constraining bidding wars or choices that impose costs on future (unrepresented) generations.

Similar sets of reservations might be entered with respect to institutionalist work that focuses on incentives for particularism (Shugart 1992; Cox and McCubbins 2001). Party-centered electoral formulas, such as closed-list PR systems, encourage—or force—voters to emphasize their party preferences over their preferences for a particular candidate. Other types of systems, such as open-list systems or single nontransferable votes (SNTV), offer greater incentives for individual candidates to steer particularistic and easily identifiable benefits (e.g., pork and patronage) toward electorally relevant constituencies.

In a number of Latin American and Asian countries, it is possible to point to policies that reflected such incentives—for example, in well-known pork-barrel practices in the Philippines, Thailand, Brazil, and Colombia. As we have seen, however, several of these countries undertook quite ambitious and comprehensive social-policy initiatives. Taiwan's SNTV system, for example, generated a national health system as one of its first and most enduring social-policy reforms; it is hard to imagine a broader policy than that.

The institutionalist research program is an important one and has made important contributions to our understanding of the political economy of policymaking and reform; it will no doubt continue to make contributions to our understanding of social policymaking as well. However, we are concerned that these approaches risk neglecting some of the most central presuppositions of contemporary political economy, namely, the importance of beginning with a clear map of the distribution of preferences and their political organization.

Research that emphasizes differences in partisanship and the power of the left is much closer to the emphasis we have placed in this book on distributive interests and preferences (see, for example, Huber et al. 2004). Partisanship has been central to the literature on the advanced industrial states, where the strength of social democratic parties has influenced not only the level of spending but the nature of social-policy commitments. Drawing on this literature, we argued in part 1 that the incorporation or exclusion of labor shaped social policies in middle-income countries as well. Moreover, the presence or absence of left parties continued to make a difference within the Latin American and Asian democratic regimes examined during this early period.

In recent decades, however, fiscal constraint and the legacy of earlier welfare systems has made the role of strong left parties more ambiguous and varied. In Eastern Europe, ex-Communist and/or Social Democratic Parties were inclined to move more slowly with respect to both the overall reform effort and the reform of social policy. However, the significance of these differences—which appeared highly consequential at the time—seem to have faded over time. Slow reformers ended up experiencing "second round" crises that were typically accompanied by a new round of economic and social-policy reforms that converged with the early reformers.

Moreover, we argued that partisan differences with respect to social policy were likely to be muted in a setting characterized by wide entitlements and strong public expectations; rather than strong partisan differences on social-policy issues, we see a surprising degree of convergence across the political spectrum. Even where parties attempted to stake out neoliberal positions with respect to social policy, as in the Czech Republic under Klaus, they were pulled back to the center by powerful electoral and interest-group pressures.

Asia has been invoked as vindicating the partisan approach in a completely different way. The conservative critical realignments we have identified resulted in weak left parties and weak or controlled organization of labor and the peasantry. In part 1, we argued that this political configuration contributed strongly to a particular approach to social policy, albeit in a decidedly authoritarian context: strong emphasis on basic social services and particularly education, but only a weak commitment to the provision of social insurance designed to protect workers from the vicissitudes of the market.

However, one of the more striking findings with respect to the high-growth East Asian democracies was the extent to which they expanded a wide array of social entitlements. This result did not occur as a response to the sudden appearance of strong left parties in the wake of regime change; to the contrary, the historical legacy of earlier conservative critical junctures continued to operate in the region and the party systems in the region remain surprisingly nonideological to this day. Rather, the expansion of entitlements was a result of the fact that both centrist and even conservative parties also used social policy for political ends; this pattern was visible in Korea, Taiwan, and Thailand. As Herbert Kitschelt (2001) has argued, these apparently anomalous results can arise when conservative parties seek to neutralize challenges on some other, more salient issue—for example, along a democratic-authoritarian dimension.

Partisan cleavages varied more widely in Latin America, both across countries and over time. Left-of-center and labor-based parties that had their roots in the critical realignments of mid-century or during the heyday of ISI did generally press for an expansion of the social-security system.

Statistical work by Huber et al. (2004) shows that left parties that occupy office over the long term can have a positive social-welfare impact. As we have seen, however, these parties faced deep dilemmas about how to respond to the challenges of economic reform, fiscal constraints, and slowing growth. Consequently, it is hard to detect clear patterns across the region based on partisanship alone. Possibly the strongest vindication of a power-resource model is Chile, which had a strong tradition both before and after Pinochet of center-left coalitions acting to strengthen the public-sector role in the provision of protection and services. Yet the left in Chile faced strong impediments in transforming the conservative legacy of the Pinochet era.

Elsewhere in the region, the behavior of political parties seemed to hinge as much on fiscal circumstances and legacies as on partisan identity. In Argentina, the Peronists reluctantly accepted both market reforms and liberal approaches to social-policy reform. Although they made significant side payments to their old union base, they moved steadily toward an emphasis on clientelist links to low-income groups. During its time in opposition, the Brazilian left, led by Lula's PT, tended to defend the rights of public-sector workers and other interests linked to the old welfare system; in power, it pursued market-oriented economic policies and built incrementally on antipoverty programs initiated under Cardoso. In Mexico, there was considerable continuity between programs initiated under the old PRI governments and those pursued subsequently by the more conservative PAN party. Where fiscal constraints were loosened and coverage was narrow, both conservatives like Fujimori and radicals like Hugo Chávez responded to opportunities to extend welfare programs to low-income groups. In Costa Rica and Uruguay, broadly based welfare systems found defenders across the political spectrum.

In sum, the record with respect to partisanship is far from obvious to us. Looking across the regions, it seems clear that left and labor parties have very different interests, dictated as much by historical legacies and economic circumstances as by enduring social cleavages and ideologies. Equally important, we find opportunistic behavior among conservative parties as well; rather than a clear left-right split on social policy, we find strong evidence of parties across the political spectrum responding in relatively narrow ways to common economic circumstances and policy legacies.

Given these various qualifications, what conclusions can we in fact draw about the effects of democracy on the social contract? It is important to restate our priors. If we could conduct the necessary natural experiment—to compare the social contract in a given country under authoritarian rule with the social contract in the very same country under democratic rule, all else held constant—we do expect that the democratic regime would be more responsive to the interests of the poor and those most exposed to risk. However, the central point of this book is not simply that such natural experiments are difficult, but that the *ceteris paribus* conditions are crucially important for understanding the effects of regime type. The effects of democracy are conditional on economic and fiscal circumstances and the organization of social interests.

The fiscal foundation of social entitlements cannot be overemphasized. The promise of democracy is an empty one in the absence of the ability of the state to extract adequate resources to offset the risks of the market. Indeed, we have suggested that the tax bargain is critical to holding governments accountable to their citizenry, including with respect to policies that augment human capital and mitigate risk.

In closing, however, it is important to return to the significance of social and political organization. Almost by definition the poor and vulnerable are deprived not only of assets and income but of social and political connections and influence as well. Democratic rule provides incentives for politicians to reach such groups and opportunities for them to organize but by no means guarantees that these crucial steps in the political process will in fact occur. The fate of the poor and vulnerable is therefore never in their hands alone but will depend on the self-interest of other social groups and the formation of cross-class coalitions with an interest in equity and social justice.

Such cross-class coalitions have been a theme in the development of the welfare state for some time. Social democratic parties rested historically on coalitions that linked blue-collar workers to small farmers and later to white-collar groups. But these are not the only types of alliances that might conceivably incorporate the interests of the poor. John Ruggie's (1982) idea of "embedded liberalism"—a variant of Keynesianism—rests on the insight that support for economic openness is best sustained by complementary policies that mitigate risk. A central theme in a number of important works in the social policy literature[2] is that support for the poor is most likely to occur in the context of coalitions that include the middle classes—including particularly through universalist approaches— even if this action involves some "leakage" to the less deserving.

The ability to forge such coalitions is not guaranteed by democracy, but they are more likely under democratic than under authoritarian rule. Authoritarian rule may achieve a redistribution of income and assets more radical than anything achievable under democracy. But authoritarian rule deprives both rich and poor of liberties and freedoms that are necessary to hold governments accountable and are crucial to human dignity itself. In the absence of competitive checks, authoritarian rulers have few incen-

---

[2] In-depth discussion may be found in Nelson 1992 and Skocpol 2001.

tives to sustain egalitarian social contracts and ample incentives and opportunities to divert resources to themselves. The gradual decay and corruption of the socialist social contract in Eastern Europe provides the clearest example.

Simply listing the coalitional possibilities that democracies offer is not to conjure them; there are no blank slates in the social world. The social compromises that we have noted each came out of very distinctive historical circumstances. No single prescription—with respect to parties, interest groups or even social policies themselves—will provide a template for addressing the problems of injustice, inequality, and poverty that plague us. The opportunities to rectify past injustices are inevitably constrained by history. It is that history we have sought to tell, hopefully as a guide to future possibilities.

Cross-National Empirical Studies of the Effects of Democracy on Social Policy and Social Outcomes

Authors	Sample and Time Period	Findings
Social Spending and Policy Models		
Habibi (1994)	67 countries, 1984	Political rights (Gastil index) in prior period (12 years) positively influence budget shares for social spending
Lindert (1994)	21 countries, 1880–1930 (mostly European)	No effect of democracy on social spending
Brown and Hunter (1999)	17 Latin American countries, 1980–92	Democratic governments show more rapid increases in social spending in the face of economic constraints than authoritarian regimes, but differences diminish with level of income
Lott (1999)	99 countries, 1985–92 (cross-section for 1990 on health)	"Totalitarian" countries have higher education expenditures but lower health spending
Przeworski et al. (2000)	141 countries, 1950–90	Democracies have higher health spending
Kaufman and Segura-Ubiergo (2001)	14 Latin American countries, 1973–97	Democracy has a positive effect on health and education spending but negative effect on social security spending
Baqir (2002)	100 countries, 1985–98	Democracy is positively associated with the within-country variation in social-sector spending, but not with cross-sectional variation
Bueno de Mesquita et al. (2003)	Global sample, 1960–99	Coalition size is positively associated with education and health spending

Authors	Sample and Time Period	Findings
Social Spending and Policy Models		
Mulligan, Gil, and Sala-i-Martin (2004)	102 to 110 countries, 1980–90 (cross-section)	Average democracy scores (1960–90) have no influence on education spending, pensions, or non-pension social spending
Huber, Mustillo, and Stephens (2004)	22 Latin American countries, 1970–2000	Duration of democracy is significant with respect to health and education spending but conditional on the strength of left parties; democracy has no effect on social-security spending.
Dion (2004)	49 middle-income countries, 1980–1999	Democracies have higher levels of social-security, health, and education spending, but differences among democratic institutions (particularly the number of veto points) are also significant
Rudra and Haggard (2005)	59 developing countries, 1975–97	Democracies and authoritarian governments respond differently to economic openness, particularly trade; authoritarian governments are more likely to cut education, health, and social security spending and to see adverse trends in primary enrollments, and infant mortality
Avelino, Brown, and Hunter (2005)	19 Latin American countries, 1980–99	Democracy is positively associated with aggregate social spending, but through education spending only; democracy has no significant effect on social security or health spending
Brooks (2005)	59 countries, 1980–99	Democracy interacting with party fragmentation lowers probability of pension privatization
Stasavage (2005)	44 African countries, 1980–96	Democratization leads to greater spending on primary education
Nooruddin and Simmons (2006a)	137 countries, 1980–97	Trade openness is associated with more education spending in democracies than in authoritarian regimes; no such effects with respect to health care

AUTHORS	SAMPLE AND TIME PERIOD	FINDINGS
Social Spending and Policy Models		
Nooruddin and Simmons (2006b)	137 countries, 1980–97	Democracy is associated with higher education shares of budget in the absence of IMF programs but lower health and education shares in the presence of such programs
Outcome Models		
Moon and Dixon (1985)	116 countries, 1970–75 (cross section)	Democracy positively associated with PQLI
Williamson (1987)	80 developing countries, 1970	Democracy has no effect on PQLI
Shin (1989)	109 counties, 1960–80	Democracy positively associated with PQLI
Young (1990)	103 countries, 1985	Democracy positively associated with life expectancy
London and Williams (1990)	Global sample, 99–110 countries and subsamples of developing and "peripheral" countries, 1970	Democracy positively associated with PQLI and Net Social Progress Index in global, developing, and "peripheral" subsamples
Weede (1993)	Global sample (72–97 countries), 1987	Democracy has a modest positive effect on Human Development Index but not on life expectancy
Wickrama and Mulford (1996)	Global sample (82 countries, oil exporters excluded), 1988 and 1990	Democracy has a positive effect on life expectancy, infant mortality, primary education, and Human Development Index
Boone (1996)	96 developing countries, excluding OPEC, 1971–75, 1976–80, 1981–85, 1986–90	Liberal democracies have lower infant-mortality rates than emerging democracies, socialist, or authoritarian regimes.
Brown (1999)	94 developing countries, 1960–87	Democracy has a positive effect on primary-school enrollments, although diminishing with level of development
Frey and al-Roumi (1999)	87 developing countries, 1970, 1980, 1990	Democracy has positive effect on PQLI in 1970 and 1990 but not in 1980

Authors	Sample and Time Period	Findings
Outcome Models		
Zweifel and Navia (2000)	138 countries, 1950–90	Democracies have lower infant-mortality rates than do dictatorships
Lake and Baum (2001)	37 to 110 countries, 1970, 1975, 1985, 1987, 1990, 1992 depending on model	In cross-section tests, democracy has consistently positive effects on 17 indicators of education and basic health; the sole exception is immunization; democracy and transitions to democracy significant in pooled-time series on secondary enrollments, access to water, DPT and measles immunization, and infant mortality
Lake and Baum (2001)	Global (128 countries), 1967–97	Democracy positively associated with female life expectancy in poor countries and female secondary education in middle-income countries
Gauri and Khalegian (2002)	175 countries, 1980–97	Democracy associated with higher levels of immunization in poorer developing countries, but lower levels of immunization in middle-income countries
Gerring and Thacker (2002)	188 countries, 1995	Long-term experience with democracy associated with lower infant mortality
McGuire (2002a)	92 developing countries, 1990; 47 developing countries, 1995	Democracy (both long and short-run) has no effect on multiple measures of basic health care provision and under-five mortality.
Bueno de Mesquita et al. (2003)	Global sample, 1960–99	Coalition size is positively associated with a variety of outcome measures: cumulative years of schooling, literacy, and nine health measures, including infant mortality, immunization, and access to water
Ross (2004)	156–69 countries, 1970–2000	Democracy does not have positive effects on infant mortality using imputed data that corrects for systematic underrepresentation in existing data sets of high-performing authoritarian regimes

AUTHORS	SAMPLE AND TIME PERIOD	FINDINGS
Outcome Models		
Ghobarah, Huth, and Russett (2004)	179 countries, 2000	Democracy is positively correlated with World Health Organization's Health Adjusted Life Expectancy
Franco, Álvarez-Dardet, and Ruiz (2004)	140–62 countries, 1998	Freer countries (Freedom House measure) have higher life expectancy and lower infant and maternal mortality rates
Shandra et al. (2004)	59 developing countries, 1997	Democracy moderates adverse effects of various measures of globalization ("dependency")

PQLI refers to the Physical Quality of Life Index; HDI refers to Human Development Index. Unless otherwise indicated, studies with a single year reflect a cross-section design, while those showing a date range are panels.

Fiscal Federalism and Social Spending in Latin America, East Asia, and Eastern Europe

A consideration of central government spending creates two possible analytic problems. First, it could result in misspecification of the politics of social policy if subnational governments were independent of the center. Appendix table 2.1 provides information on formal constitutional arrangements in 1980 (1990 for Eastern Europe), whether countries were federal or not, as well as available data on the share of total revenue and spending by subnational governments and the share of subnational spending that goes to welfare and social security, health, and education.

As can be seen (following Watts 1999) Argentina, Brazil, Mexico, and Venezuela, as well as Malaysia are formally federal. Formal federalism does not necessarily imply decentralized control over spending, however. The political systems of all five federal countries were in fact highly centralized during this period; this was particularly true of Mexico and Malaysia. Similarly in the socialist systems, the assignment of spending, revenue, and responsibility for some social-policy issues to lower levels of government does not imply a delegation of political control but is largely an administrative matter.

A second analytic problem is more serious: a focus on central government spending could underestimate the relative size of both the public sector and social expenditure. A substantial share of total government spending in both Argentina and Brazil was lodged at the provincial and municipal level, as were some social-policy responsibilities. As can be seen from the "vertical imbalance" between spending and revenues in Brazil, transfers from the central government are significant; this was true in Colombia as well. Nonetheless, national level data does underestimate the share of total social spending even in this earlier period, and in these cases, some attention must be given to relations between the central and subnational governments. For most other countries, during this earlier period we are justified in focusing our attention on the central government. As we show in more detail in part 2, decentralization of social spending was one of the more important policy initiatives of the 1980s and 1990s. Moreover, the transition to democracy gave rise to strong pressures for political decentralization and the extension of democratic processes to the provincial and municipal levels.

APPENDIX TABLE A2.1
Federalism, Spending, and Revenue by Level of Government (1980 for Latin America and East Asia; 1990 for Eastern Europe)

	Constitutional design	Subnational government revenue/total revenue	Subnational government spending/ total spending	Social security and welfare spending/ total subnational spending	Health spending/ total subnational spending	Education spending/ total subnational spending
			Latin America			
Argentina	Federal	25.0	22.2	16.7 (1981)	16.7 (1981)	16.7 (1981)
Brazil	Federal	24.32 (1981)	32.4			
Chile	Unitary	2.5	3.7	10.6 (1981)	>0.1 (1981)	10.1 (1981)
Colombia	Unitary	17.9	29.9	4.4	19.0	42.0
Costa Rica	Unitary	4.3	4.0		25.4 (1987)	
Mexico	Federal	18.5	22.0			
Peru	Unitary					
Uruguay	Unitary	9.1	8.6			
Venezuela	Federal	1.2 (1979)	2.3 (1979)			
			East Asia			
Korea	Unitary	14.5	28.5	3.2 (1978)	3.1	45.6 (1978)
Malaysia	Unitary	15.3	18.3			
Philippines	Unitary	7.5	11.9			
Singapore	Unitary	—	—			
Taiwan	Unitary					
Thailand	Unitary	5.5	15.8	0.9 (1982)	4.2 (1982)	13.0 (1982)
			Eastern Europe			
Bulgaria	Unitary	18.1	18.3	5.1	23.9	29.7
Czechoslovakia	Unitary	20.2	29.3	5.3	24.6	19.4
Hungary	Unitary	11.0	19.1		19.1	41.8
Poland	Unitary	22.7 (1988)	26.5 (1988)			
Romania	Unitary	12.7	15.1	1.6	11.0	35.4

Source: World Bank Fiscal Decentralization Indicators (World Bank 2006).

A Cross-Section Model of Social Policy and Outcomes in Middle-Income Countries, 1973–80

In this appendix, we show and comment on socioeconomic variables used in the regressions discussed in chapter 1. As noted, the main causal factors of interest can be grouped into four categories: the level of income and the speed and volatility of growth; economic structure, including urbanization, industrialization, and openness to trade; social stratification and ethnic divisions; and demographic factors. At particular points, we have also examined the effects of other variables that might be expected to have an impact in particular policy areas—for example, proximity to the equator in the case of immunization, or female literacy in the case of birth attendance. In some regressions, these variables did have a significant impact, but generally, they did not affect the overall results including with respect to the regional dummies. Because of limited degrees of freedom and to maximize the clarity of presentation, we did not generally include the findings on such variables. There were also problems of multicollinearity with respect to the level of development and various indicators of structural change, and we have therefore run those models separately.

WEALTH, INCOME GROWTH, AND VOLATILITY (TABLE A3.1).

We tested the impact of the level of wealth using per capita GDP. With some dependent variables, we expect diminishing marginal returns from income growth; at higher levels of development, an additional dollar of GNP per capita is likely to have a weaker impact on welfare outcomes than it might at earlier stages of development (Moon and Dixon 1985). However, the results are not fundamentally different using a linear specification.

To capture the effects of growth episodes and volatility on social-security spending, we look at average real GNP growth rates for the period 1960–75 and the volatility of growth, measured as the standard deviation of growth rates over the same period. Volatility was not found to have a significant impact in any of our regressions. Table A3.1 displays the distribution of values across the countries of the three regions.

TABLE A3.1

Per Capita GDP (1980) and GDP Growth (1960–80): Latin America, East Asia, and Eastern Europe

	GDP per capita (constant 1990 dollars) 1980	GDP per capita (PPP) 1980	GDP growth, 1960–80	Standard deviation of growth
Argentina	6,347	9,200	3.5	4.9
Brazil	4,041	6,070	7.3	3.7
Chile	2,577	4,533	3.4	5.1
Colombia	1,875	4,706	5.5	1.6
Costa Rica	2,716	5,635	6.2	2.6
Mexico	3,235	7,130	6.6	2.4
Peru	2,320	4,496	4.6	2.7
Uruguay	4,373	5,872	2.0	2.7
Venezuela	3,354	5,326	4.4	3.1
Average Latin America	3,426	5,885	4.8	3.2
Korea	5,322	5,750	8.4	3.1
Malaysia	2,587	4,359	7.2	2.5
Philippines	974	3,266	5.4	1.5
Singapore	13,332	9,965	9.5	4.3
Taiwan	7,530	8,000	9.8	3.2
Thailand	1,329	2,751	7.7	2.3
Average Asia	5,179	6,504	7.7	2.8
Average Asia ex. Singapore	3,548	5,812	7.2	2.5
Bulgaria	6,044	n.a.	5.4	n.a.
Czechoslovakia	10,289	n.a.	3.7	n.a.
Hungary	6,306	n.a.	3.6	n.a.
Poland	5,740	n.a.	4.1	n.a.
Romania	4,135	n.a.	5.8	n.a.
Average Eastern Europe	6,503	n.a.	4.5	n.a.

Sources: Latin America, Korea, Malaysia, Philippines, Singapore, and Thailand: World Development Indicators (World Bank 2007); Taiwan: Asian Development Bank 2007; Eastern Europe GDP/capita: Maddison 2003. table HS-7, 225, using constant 1995 dollars; Eastern European growth is for 1950–79: Kornai 1992, table 9.2, 1968.

STRUCTURAL CHANGE

We consider the effects of three major indicators of structural change: urbanization, industrialization, and openness to international trade (table A3.2). Urbanization is measured as the share of population living in cities over one million and industrialization is captured by the share of industrial output in total output. To measure trade openness, we rely on the standard ratio between exports and imports and GDP. Table A3.2 also includes the percentage of the population in agriculture. Given the high correlation between these variables and per capita GNP, it is not possible to test for the effects of structural change controlling for level of development.

SOCIAL STRATIFICATION

Inequality, ethnic diversity, and poverty constitute a third possible cluster of theoretical candidates for explaining redistributive policies. Table A3.3 provides information on three measures of inequality. The first is the Gini coefficient (c. 1980) from the well-known Deininger and Squire (1996) data set. The second is a Theil index of industrial wage inequality for the 1980s. This index, constructed by University of Texas Inequality Project (2006), measures the dispersion of pay across industrial categories in the manufacturing sector, using data from the Industrial Statistics database of the United Nations Industrial Development Organization (UNIDO). The University of Texas Inequality Project (2006) has also developed a methodology to exploit the observable relationship between the overall household income inequality data in the Deininger and Squire data set and the industrial wage-inequality data from the UNIDO dataset to construct an alternative set of Gini coefficients (the Estimated Household Inequality Data Set, or EHII2).[1]

For ethnic fractionalization, we include the average of the widely used ethnic-fractionalization index (EFI) for the 1970s. The index measures the probability that two randomly selected people from a given country will belong to the same ethnolinguistic group; higher numbers suggest a higher degree of fractionalization.

The highly compressed patterns of social stratification in Eastern Europe are noteworthy, but they were almost certainly an effect, rather than a cause, of the welfare systems imposed in that region. Comparisons between Latin America and East Asia, however, show differences that are potentially of causal importance. The Gini coefficients from the Deininger

---

[1] We also added time and country dummies. The inclusion of time and country fixed effects did not charge the results of the model.

TABLE A3.2
Socioeconomic Structure in Latin America, East Asia, and Eastern Europe, 1980

	Share of workforce in industry	Share of workforce in agriculture	Urbanization
Argentina	17.5	3.0	83
Brazil	22.1	28.6	67
Chile	20.2	20.2	81
Colombia	24.0	39.0	63
Costa Rica	21.0	27.3	47
Mexico	23.9	15.4	66
Peru	13.0	23.7	65
Uruguay	21.8	3.9	85
Venezuela	24.9	16.2	79
Average Latin America	20.6	19.7	71
Korea	29.5	24.9	57
Malaysia	23.8	30.4	42
Philippines	13.8	49.6	37
Singapore	35.7	0.7	100
Taiwan	41.6	17.5	n.a.
Thailand	12.1	68.4	17
Average East Asia	26.3	31.9	51
Bulgaria	45.0	21.0	61
Czechoslovakia	47.7	12.1	75
Hungary	33.0	8.7	57
Poland	38.1	27.9	58
Romania	44.5	28.9	49
Average Eastern Europe	41.6	19.7	60

Sources: Taiwan: Republic of China 2000; Colombia: Economic Commission for Latin America and the Caribbean 2001; World Bank Development Indicators (World Bank 2007).

and Squire data set show especially sharp contrasts between Korea and Taiwan on the one hand and Brazil, Chile, and Colombia on the other, although these differences are much more muted using the alternative measures. It is important to underscore that the Philippines, Thailand, and even Malaysia still had significant rural poverty in 1980. The image of middle-income East Asian countries as low-inequality countries with

TABLE A3.3
Social Inequality and Ethnic Fractionalization

	Gini Index	Theil Index	EH1I2	ELF
Argentina	n.a.	0.038	37.8	31
Bolivia	42.0	0.047	40.6	68
Brazil	58.0	n.a.	n.a.	7
Chile	51.9	n.a.	39.4	14
Colombia	51.5	0.036	39.2	6
Costa Rica	45.5	0.07	39.3	7
Mexico	53.9	0.021	38.2	30
Peru	48.0	0.066	41.5	59
Uruguay	45.0	0.039	36.1	20
Venezuela	44.4	0.036	38.4	11
Average Latin America	48.7	0.044	39.1	26
Korea	34.4	0.033	36.6	0
Malaysia	50.4	0.032	37.8	72
Philippines	47.5	0.052	40.6	74
Singapore	42.0	0.07	34.5	42
Taiwan	29.6	0.016	30.3	42
Thailand	42.0	0.091	43.3	66
Average East Asia	40.5	0.049	37.2	49
Bulgaria	23.3	0.006	27.5	12
Czech Republic	21.8	0.006	20.9	27
Hungary	24.5	0.006	26.2	7
Poland	25.7	0.006	27.7	4
Romania	25.8	n.a.	n.a.	12
Slovak Republic	20.5	n.a.	n.a.	n.a.
Average Eastern Europe	23.6	0.006	25.6	12

Sources: Gini Index: Deininger and Squire 1996; Theil and EH1I2: University of Texas Inequality Project 2006; ELF: Roeder 2001.

limited poverty is based on the experience of a small number of countries or on much more recent experience.

Meaningful tests of the causal importance of economic inequality run up against serious endogeneity problems; even when the independent variables are lagged, it would be impossible to disconfirm the hypothesis that they are effects of the welfare outcomes on the left side of the equation. It is nonetheless interesting, that the statistical relationships between economic inequality and spending variables never reached standard levels of significance, nor did there appear to be a relation with immunization or adult literacy. Ethnolinguistic fractionalization, however, did show significant results in the expected direction with respect to social-security spending and adult illiteracy, and fell just short of standard significance levels in spending on primary education. Unlike the measures of economic inequality, these results to not pose serious problems of endogeneity, since it is less likely that spending or education efforts would impact basic ethnic or religious identities except over the very long run.

Demographic Factors

A fourth and final cluster of factors that might influence the expansion of welfare commitments is demographic. As the literature on entitlements has shown, public spending can increase quite dramatically even in the absence of new programmatic initiatives if certain classes of individuals are automatically eligible for some benefit and those classes are growing. Age distributions are shown in table A3.4. The sources of most of the data for the regressions described here are the World Bank (2004) World Development Indicators, including: per capita and total GDP, industrialization, urbanization, trade, population, growth, adult literacy, DPT immunizations, social security expenditures, and health expenditures. Data on per pupil expenditures are from Barro and Lee (2000); on inequality, from Deninger and Squire (1996); on democracy, from the Polity IV data set (Marshall and Jaggers 2004); on ethnolinguistic fractionalization, Roeder (2001). As with modernization theories, demographic approaches to welfare commitments can be given a political economy interpretation: as populations age, the elderly become more politically influential and are able to command a larger share of public resources.[2]

---

[2] See Brown and Hunter (1999) for a discussion of how to give demographic variables a political interpretation.

Table A3.4
Share of Population Over 65 and Under 15 in Latin America, East Asia, and Eastern Euro
1985–2005 (in percent)

	< 15 1985	> 65 1985	< 15 1995	> 65 1995	< 15 2005	> 6: 200:
Argentina	30.1	8.6	29.1	9.8	26.7	10.6
Brazil	37.0	3.7	35.5	4.7	28.1	6.0
Chile	30.9	5.7	29.6	6.6	25.5	8.0
Colombia	37.8	3.4	34.4	4.2	31.4	5.1
Costa Rica	35.9	4.5	34.5	4.8	29.0	5.6
Mexico	42.9	3.8	36.2	4.4	31.6	5.6
Peru	41.0	3.7	36.4	4.2	32.8	5.2
Uruguay	26.8	10.9	25.0	12.4	24.4	13.2
Venezuela	39.0	3.4	36.0	4.3	31.7	5.1
Average Latin America	35.7	5.3	3.0	6.2	29.0	7.2
Korea	30.0	4.3	23.4	5.7	19.0	8.5
Philippines	42.1	3.4	39.4	3.5	35.7	4.C
Taiwan	n.a.	5.1	n.a.	7.2	n.a.	8.9
Thailand	35.6	4.3	28.3	5.4	24.1	7.8
Malaysia	38.7	3.7	35.8	3.9	32.8	4.6
Singapore	24.3	5.3	22.3	6.3	20.2	8.1
Average East Asia	34.1	4.4	29.8	5.3	26.4	6.9
Bulgaria	21.3	11.3	18.0	15.2	14.0	17.2
Czech Republic	23.6	11.6	18.6	13.2	15.0	14.2
Hungary	21.5	12.4	18.1	14.1	16.0	15.1
Poland	25.5	9.4	22.8	11.2	16.8	13.0
Romania	24.7	9.5	20.5	12.0	15.9	14.6
Slovak Republic	26.7	8.9	22.6	10.9	17.2	11.9
Average Eastern Europe	23.9	10.5	20.1	12.8	15.8	14.2

Source: World Development Indicators (World Bank 2007).

Regime-Coding Rules

Mainwaring, Brinks, and Pérez-Liñán (2001) code regimes on the basis of four dimensions: whether legislatures and executives are elected; whether the franchise is inclusive; the extent to which civil liberties are respected; and the extent to which elected rulers can actually govern. Regimes are coded as "democratic" if there are no significant violations on any of these four dimensions, "semidemocratic" if they have one or more "minor" violations; and authoritarian if they have one or more "major" violations. We further distinguish between competitive and "hard" authoritarian regimes on the basis of their electoral system. Competitive authoritarian regimes allow national-level electoral contests that permit some degree of independent party organization. Hard authoritarian regimes do not allow national-level elections at all or do not permit opposition parties to contest them. Systems such as the Eastern European socialist regimes, in which the number of nominated candidates was sometimes allowed to exceed the number of contested seats, or Taiwan's system, where opposition candidates were allowed to run but parties were proscribed, are coded as hard authoritarian.

ELECTIONS FOR LEGISLATURE AND EXECUTIVE

In a democracy, the head of government and the legislature are chosen in free and fair elections. By "elected" we mean that he/she was chosen in fair direct elections or elected by a body that was itself mostly chosen in direct elections. In a similar vein, is there a legislative body in which the vast majority of the members have been fairly elected?

A major violation of this democratic principle occurs if:

1. the head of government or the legislature is not elected;
2. the government uses its resources (patronage, repression, or a combination of both) to ensure electoral victory—that is, there are systematic complaints of fraud or repression, and there is virtual certainty about the outcome of presidential elections.
3. through fraud, manipulation, or outright repression, the government makes it impossible for a wide gamut of parties to compete (or if they do compete, to take office).

A partial violation occurs if:

1. there are systematic complaints of rigged elections and/or harassment of the opposition, but there is still uncertainty about electoral outcomes, and the government fails to capture large majorities in the legislature; or
2. the military vetoed a few "unacceptable" but important presidential candidates; fraud affected but did not thoroughly skew the electoral results; or the elections were conducted under substantially unequal playing rules.

IS THE FRANCHISE INCLUSIVE?

In a democracy, the franchise is broad compared to other countries in the same historical period, and disenfranchised social categories, such as children, are not seen as politically excluded groups with distinctive electoral preferences.

A major violation of this democratic principle occurs if a large part of the adult population is disenfranchised on ethnic, class, gender, or educational grounds in ways that:

1. likely prevent very different electoral outcomes (or so it is widely believed); or
2. are unusually exclusionary for that historical period; or
3. trigger mass social protests.

A partial violation occurs if disenfranchisement of some social groups occurs in ways that are not likely to significantly shape electoral outcomes.

ARE CIVIL LIBERTIES RESPECTED?

In a democracy, violations of human rights are uncommon, parties are free to organize, and the government respects constitutional guarantees.

A major violation of democratic principles occurs if:

1. gross human rights violations or censorship against opposition media occur systematically; or
2. political parties are not free to organize-i.e., most major parties are banned, just a single party is allowed to exist, or a few parties are tightly controlled by the government.

A partial violation occurs if:

1. violations of human rights are less widespread but still affect the opposition's capacity to organize in some geographic areas or some social sectors; or
2. there is intermittent censorship of the media or regular prohibition of one major party or candidate.

Do the Elected Rulers Enjoy Real Governing Capacity?

In a democracy, military leaders and the military as an institution have negligible or minor influence in policies other than military policy, and their preferences do not substantively affect the chances of presidential candidates.

A major violation of this democratic principle occurs if:

1. military leaders or the military as an institution openly dominate major policy areas not strictly related to the armed forces; or
2. if the elected head of government is a puppet, such that the electoral process does not really determine who governs.

A partial violation occurs if military leaders or the military as an institution are able to veto important policies in a few areas not related to the armed forces (for example, Ecuador in 1961–62).

A Cross-Section, Time-Series Model of Social Spending in Latin America, East Asia, and Eastern Europe, 1980–2000

This appendix explains the properties of our model, how to interpret the model, and sources of our data.

MODEL

We estimate the regressions using an error-correction model (ECM) and correct for heteroskedasticity and serial correlation using panel-corrected standard errors (PCSE). ECMs reflect that the dependent and independent variables are in a long-run equilibrium but that there are also important short-term or temporary effects. ECMs have three central features. First, the dependent variable is always expressed as a first difference. Second, the lag level of the dependent variable must be an explanatory variable. Three, all explanatory variables must be expressed as both lagged-level and lagged changes.

An ECM with PCSE has a number of statistical and practical properties that make it useful for our analysis. First, and most important, the levels of our dependent variables have a high degree of serial correlation, typically about 0.9. In many cases, we are not able to reject the null hypothesis that the level of the dependent variable has a unit root. Using first differences makes these variables stationary and severely reduces the serial correlation. Second, using the lagged level of the dependent variable allows us to determine the rate of convergence following a change in one of our explanatory variables. Third, PCSEs correct for the cross-country heteroskedasticity and spatial correlation that may affect certain countries simultaneously, such as an oil supply shock or a financial crisis that spills across borders.[1]

Fourth, the model is useful because it allows us to examine short-term and long-term changes simultaneously (see below, "Interpreting Error Correction Models").

---

[1] We also added time and country dummies. The inclusion of time and country fixed effects did not charge the results of the model.

The basic specification of the model is:

$$\Delta Y_{i,t} = Y_{i,t-1} + \Delta X_{i,t-1} + X_{i,t-1} + e_{i,t}$$

Where the $\Delta Y_{i,t}$ is the change in spending in country i from time t−1 to time t, Y_{t-1} is the lagged level of spending, $\Delta X_{i,t-1}$ and $X_{i,t-1}$ are the lagged levels and lagged changes for all other explanatory variables, and $e_{i,t}$ is the residual.

The coefficient on the lagged-dependent variable is crucial to interpreting the results of ECMs, because the coefficient on the lagged-dependent variable shows how fast the dependent variable returns to its equilibrium after a shock. Thus, the coefficient on the lagged-dependent variable shows the long-term equilibrium relationship. The coefficient on the lagged dependent variable must be between 0 and −1 by definition, and the closer it is to 0, the longer a change will persist (for a formal treatment of the model, see Kaufman and Segura-Ubiergo 2001). The intuition behind this requires understanding the way that the lagged dependent variable relates to the dependent variable. In the most general form, the model states:

$$\Delta Y_t = Y_{t-1} + X_{t-1} + \varepsilon_t$$

which we can rewrite as

$$Y_t - Y_{t-1} = Y_{t-1} + X_{t-1} + \varepsilon_t$$

Focusing on the second equation can help to provide the intuition. If the coefficient on the lagged dependent variable is 0, that means the other variables in the model (X_{t-1}) are explaining the change in Y, and the lagged level of Y is irrelevant for predicting the change (in technical terms, a coefficient of 0 is a unit root). In practical terms, this means that there is no convergence from a shock. If, alternatively, the coefficient on the lagged-dependent variable is −1, then, as the second equation shows, X_{t-1} explains the level of Y, not the change in Y, because $-Y_{t-1} + Y_{t-1} = 0$. This means that the (negative) Y_{t-1} predicts perfectly the change in Y (ΔY_t), or that convergence is immediate.

Interpreting the effects of changes in the explanatory variables in ECMs is not as straightforward as interpreting an OLS coefficient, and we need to use different methods to calculate the effects of permanent and temporary shocks. Below, we describe these calculations using the first model in table 5.1, where the dependent variable is change in expenditure.[2]

---

[2] See Brown and Hunter (1999) for a discussion of how to give demographic variables a political interpretation.

TABLE A5.1
Effects of Shocks

Lag DV Level	−0.365 (4.44)***
Polity	0.847 (1.49)
Polity Change	1.325 (1.31)
Revenue	0.359 (4.13)***
Revenue Change	0.349 (3.04)***
Per Capita GDP	0.000 (1.01)
PCGDP Change	0.000 (0.28)
Trade	−0.031 (1.61)
Trade Change	−0.029 (0.73)
Transfers	−0.006 (0.10)
Net Transfers Change	0.063 (1.29)
Recession Change	1.136 (2.40)**
Recession	1.275 (1.61)
Constant	20.616 (1.57)
Observations	163
R-Squared	0.29

** Significant at .05 level; *** significant at .01 level.

Calculating the Effect of a Temporary Shock

Consider the effect of a one-time change in revenue on the change in expenditure that is offset subsequently by a reverse change in revenue of equal magnitude. The coefficient on the change in revenue is not sufficient information to understand how a change in revenue affects a change in expenditure because a change in expenditure in time t may lead to a higher level of expenditure in time t+1. Thus, the total impact of a change in expenditure at time t must take into account how the change in time t affects the level of the dependent variable in subsequent time periods, as well as the number of periods the change persists. The formula is:

$$\text{Coefficient of Interest} * (1 + \text{Coefficient on the Lagged-Dependent Variable})^t$$

To understand the intuition behind the formula, consider the situations where the coefficient on the lagged-dependent variable is 0 (no convergence) and −1 (immediate convergence). Using the coefficient on the lagged change in revenue (0.349), a coefficient of 0 on the lagged dependent variable would mean that the effect would be $0.349 * (1+0)^t$. In the

TABLE A5.2
Summary Statistics for Key Variables

	Observations	Mean	Std. Dev.	Minimum	Maximum
Expenditure	359	25.16	10.78	9.42	58.46
Education	278	2.99	1.39	0.57	6.71
Health	276	1.85	1.71	0.12	8.63
Social Security	271	6.46	5.59	0.14	21.08
Revenue	359	23.79	10.23	9.07	55.73
Revenue Change	337	−0.20	2.46	−14.14	11.81
Trade	393	78.20	76.36	11.55	439.03
Trade (PPP)	363	36.33	62.37	0.00	354.72
Polity Dummy	440	0.55	0.50	0	1

first period, the impact on the dependent variable would be would be 0.349; in the second period, the effect would be $0.349 + 0.349^2$, and so on. There would be no convergence. A coefficient of −1 would mean that the effect would be $0.349*(1+-1)^t$. In the first period, the impact on the dependent variable would be 0.349. In subsequent periods the impact would be zero.

In this case, the total effect of a change in revenue is the coefficient on the change (0.349) times one plus the coefficient on the lagged-dependent variable $(1+-0.365)^t$ where t is the number of periods the shock lasts. If the change is one-off (for example a one-time increase in privatization revenue), the effect is simply the coefficient on the variable of interest (in this case 0.349). If the change lasts for one-period, the total effect if $0.349*0.635$, or 0.22. If the change persists for two periods, the effect is the first period effect (0.22) plus $0.349*0.635^2$, or 0.36. A three period change would need to include 0.635 to the third power and so on.

Calculating the Effect of a Permanent Shock

The coefficient on the lagged dependent variable also is crucial for understanding the effect of a permanent shock to an explanatory variable as well. The formula is:

$$-1*\text{Coefficient of Interest/Coefficient on the}$$
$$\text{Lagged Dependent Variable}$$

To understand the intuition behind the formula, again consider the situations where the coefficient on the lagged dependent variable is 0 (no con-

TABLE A5.3
List of Countries

East Asia	Eastern Europe	Latin America
Korea	Bulgaria	Argentina
Malaysia	Czech Republic	Brazil
Philippines	Hungary	Chile
Singapore	Poland	Colombia
Taiwan	Romania	Costa Rica
Thailand	Slovak Republic	Mexico
		Peru
		Uruguay
		Venezuela

vergence) and −1 (immediate convergence). Using the coefficient on the lagged level of revenue, 0.359, a coefficient of 0 on the lagged dependent variable would mean that the effect would be −1*0.359/0, which is infinity, so the change in expenditure would persist until another exogenous shock occurred. A coefficient of −1 would mean that the effect on the change in expenditure would be −1*(0.359/−1), or 0.359, far less than infinity. Using the results from the above equation, a one-unit increase in revenue would lead to a −1*(0.359/0.365) or 0.98 increase in expenditure over the period covered in the model

DATA SOURCES

The main sources of our economic data are the IMF Government Finance Statistics (GFS), the World Bank's Global Development Finance (GDF), and the World Bank's World Development Indicators (WDI). Our measures of social-sector expenditures (education, health, and social security) come from the GFS. Net transfers come from the GDF. Government expenditure, per capita GDP, revenue, population, and trade as a share of GDP come from the WDI. Data on net transfers comes from the World Bank's Global Development Finance database. We define recession as negative GDP growth.

Our measure of democracy comes from the Polity IV database (Marshall and Jaggers 2004). Data for Taiwan (except for Polity) comes from the Asian Development Bank's Key Indicators (2007). Data on political variables other than Polity (veto points and left parties) comes from the World Bank (2005) Database on Political Institutions.

Social Security, Health, and Education Expenditure in East Asia, Latin America, and Eastern Europe, 1980–2005

Data for all figures in appendix 6 are from the International Monetary Fund's *Government Financial Statistics Yearbook* (2007) except for Taiwan, Malaysia, and the Philippines, which are from the Asian Development Bank's *Key Indicator Series* (2007).

LATIN AMERICA

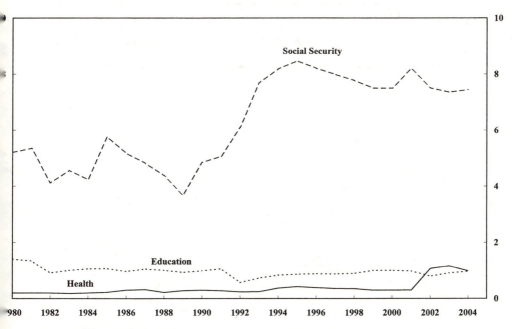

Figure A6.1. Argentina: Social security, health, and education spending / GDP.

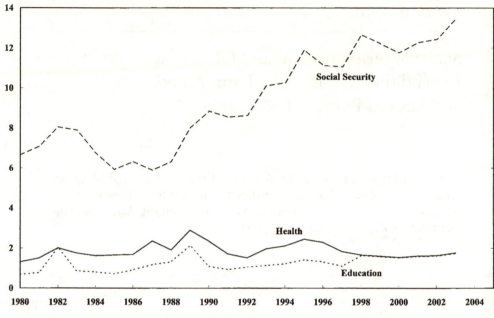

Figure A6.2. Brazil: Social security, health, and education spending / GDP.

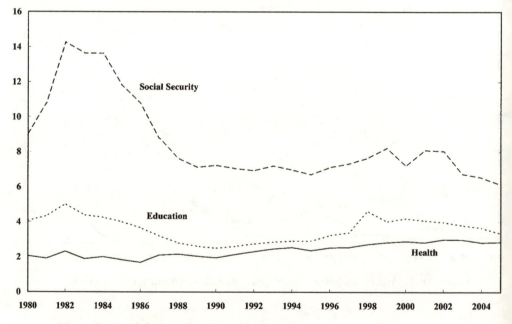

Figure A6.3. Chile: Social security, health, and education spending / GDP.

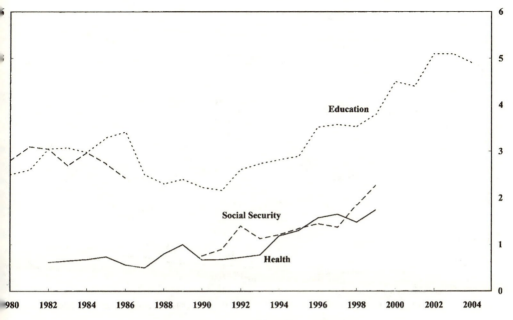

Figure A6.4. Colombia: Social security, health, and education spending / GDP.

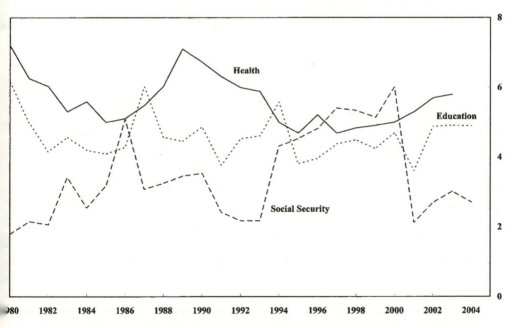

Figure A6.5. Costa Rica: Social security, health, and education spending / GDP.

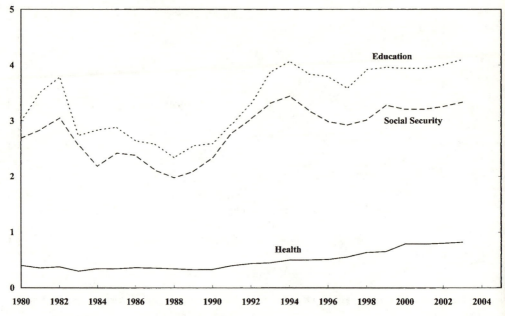

Figure A6.6. Mexico: Social security, health, and education spending / GDP.

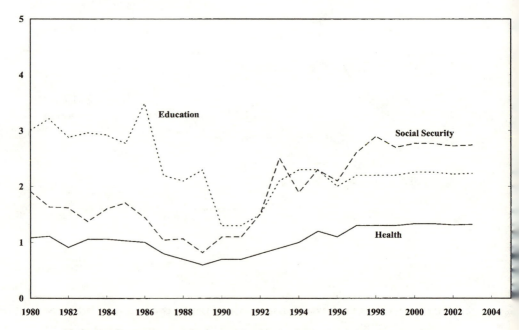

Figure A6.7. Peru: Social security, health, and education spending / GDP.

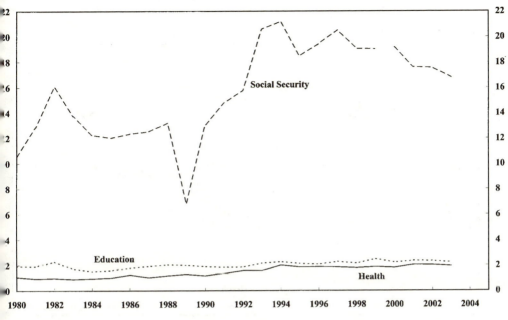

Figure A6.8. Uruguay: Social security, health, and education spending / GDP.

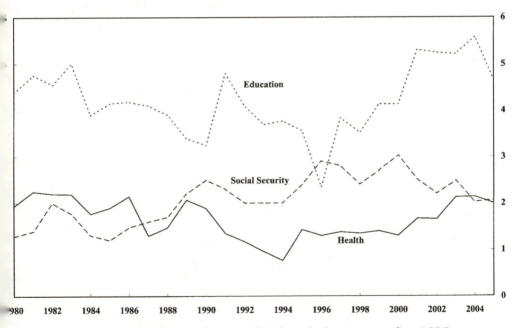

Figure A6.9. Venezuela: Social security, health, and education spending / GDP.

EAST ASIA

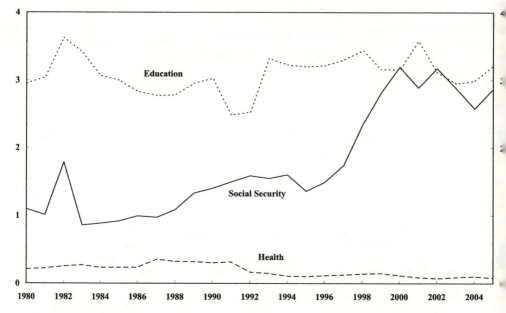

Figure A6.10. Korea: Social security, health, and education spending / GDP.

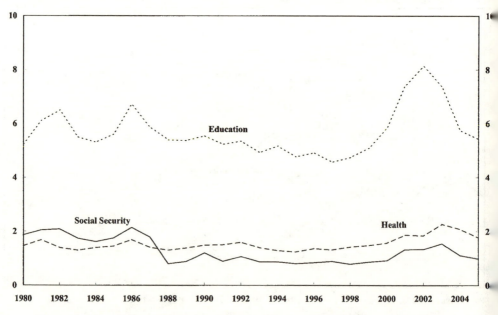

Figure A6.11. Malaysia: Social security, health, and education spending / GDP.

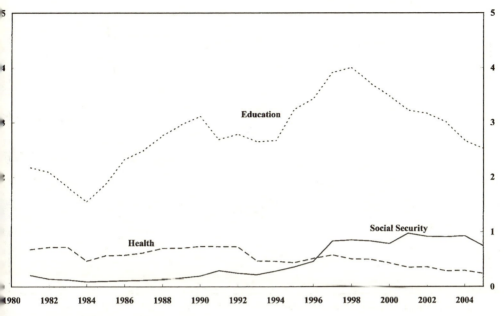

Figure A6.12. Philippines: Social security, health, and education spending / GDP.

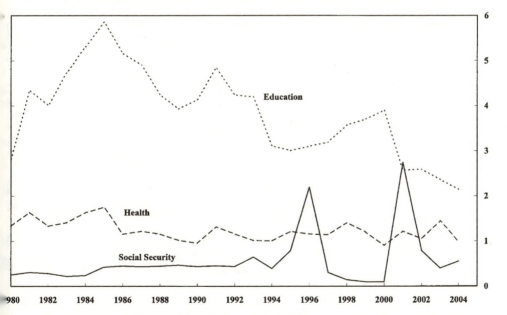

Figure A6.13. Singapore: Social security, health, and education spending / GDP.

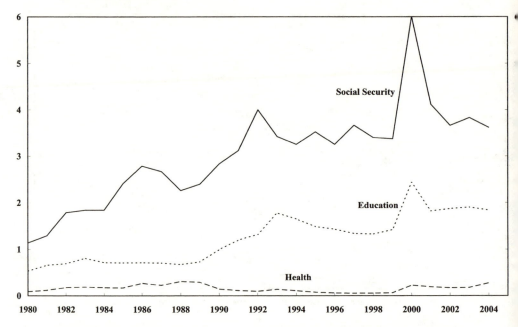

Figure A6.14. Taiwan: Social security, health, and education spending / GDP.

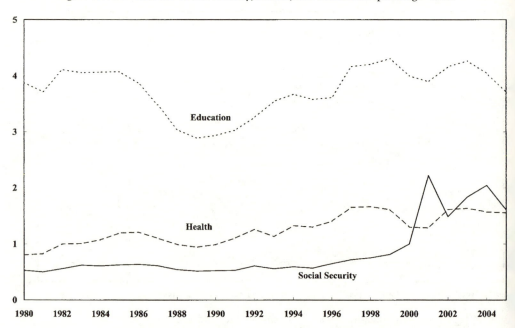

Figure A6.15. Thailand: Social security, health, and education spending / GDP.

EASTERN EUROPE

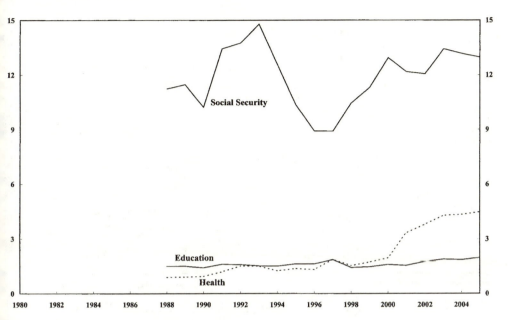

Figure A6.16. Bulgaria: Social security, health, and education spending / GDP.

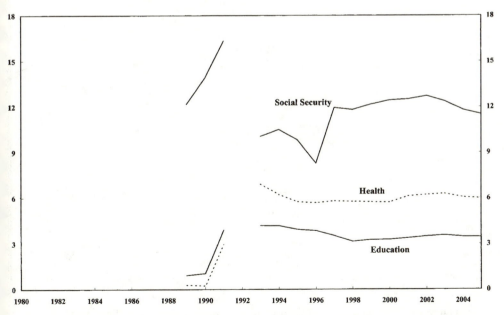

Figure A6.17. Czech Republic: Social security, health, and education spending / GDP.

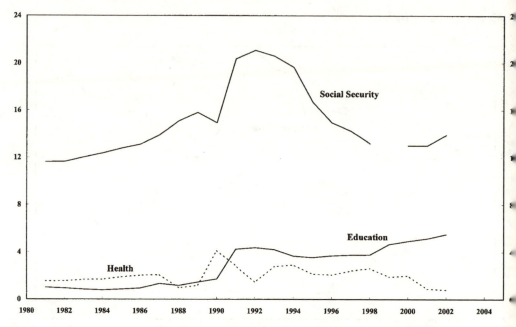

Figure A6.18. Hungary: Social security, health, and education spending / GDP.

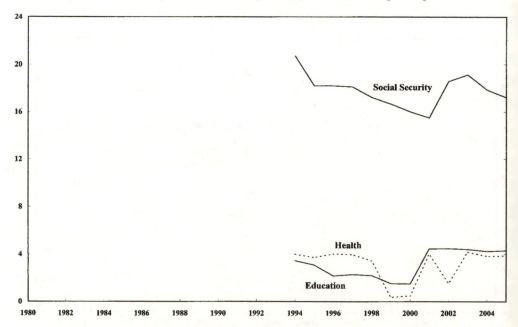

Figure A6.19. Poland: Social security, health, and education spending / GDP.

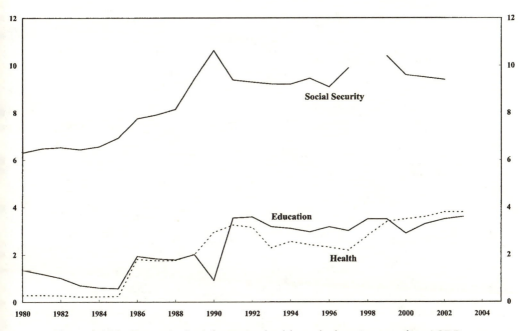

Figure A6.20. Romania: Social security, health, and education spending / GDP.

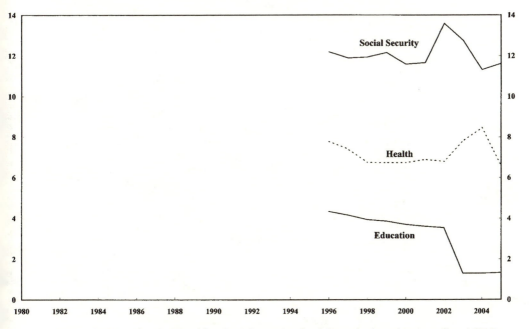

Figure A6.21. Slovak Republic: Social security, health, and education spending / GDP.

References

Abueva, Jose Veloso. 1971. *Ramon Magsaysay: A Political Biography*. Manila: Solidaridad Publishing.

Abdul-Rahman, Saaidah. N.d. "Malaysia: Policy Measures to Alleviate Poverty and Income Distribution Problems," unpublished manuscript. Kuala Lumpur: Faculty of Economics and Administration, University of Malaya.

Acemoglu, Daron, Simon Johnson, and James A. Robinson. 2001. "The Colonial Origins of Comparative Development: An Empirical Investigation," *American Economic Review*, 91, 5 (December): 1369–1401.

———. 2005. "Institutions as the Fundamental Cause of Long-Run Growth," in Philippe Aghion and Steven N. Durlauf, eds. *Handbook of Economic Growth*, vol. 1A. Amsterdam: North-Holland.

Acemoglu, Daron, and James A. Robinson. 2006. *Economic Origins of Dictatorship and Democracy*. New York: Cambridge University Press.

Adam, Jan. 1984. *Employment and Wage Policies in Poland, Czechoslovakia and Hungary Since 1950*. London: Macmillan.

Adserá, Alícia, and Carles Boix. 2002. "Trade, Democracy, and the Size of the Public Sector: The Political Underpinnings of Openness," *International Organization* 56, 2 (April): 229–62.

Afonso, António, Christiane Nickel, and Philipp Rother. 2005. "Fiscal Consolidations in the Central and Eastern European Countries." European Central Bank, Working Paper No. 473 (April). Frankfurt: European Central Bank.

Ahmad, Junaid, Shantayanan Devarajan, Stuti Kehmani, and Shekhar Shah. 2005. "Decentralization and Service Delivery." World Bank Policy Research Working Paper No. 3603 (May). Washington, DC: World Bank.

Akamatsu, Kaname. 1962. "A Historical Pattern of Economic Growth in Developing Countries," *Developing Economies* 1, 1: 3–25.

Alesina, Alberto, and Allan Drazen. 1991. "Why Are Stabilizations Delayed?" *American Economic Review* 81, 5 (December): 1170–88.

Alesina, Alberto, and Edward L. Glaeser. 2004. *Fighting Poverty in the US and Europe: A World of Difference*. New York: Oxford University Press.

Alesina, Alberto, Edward Glaeser, and Bruce Sacerdote. 2001. "Why Doesn't the U.S. Have a European-Style Welfare System?" National Bureau of Economic Research Working Paper #8524. Cambridge, MA: National Bureau of Economic Research.

Alonso, Guillermo V. 2000. *Política y seguridad social en la Argentina de los '90*. Buenos Aires: Mino y Davila Editores.

Ames, Barry. 1987. *Political Survival: Politicians and Public Policy in Latin America*. Berkeley: University of California Press.

———. 2001. *The Deadlock of Democracy in Brazil: Interests, Identities and Institutions*. Ann Arbor: University of Michigan Press.

Amsden, Alice. 1989. *Asia's Next Giant: South Korea and Late Industrialization*. New York: Oxford University Press.

———. 2001. *The Rise of the Rest: Challenges to the West from Late-Industrializing Economies*. New York: Oxford University Press.

Arretche, Marta. 2004. "Toward a Unified and More Equitable System: Health Reform in Brazil" in Robert R. Kaufman and Joan M. Nelson, eds. *Crucial Needs, Weak Incentives: Social Sector Reform, Democratization, and Globalization in Latin America*. Washington, DC: Woodrow Wilson Center Press; Baltimore, MD: Johns Hopkins University Press.

Arvone, Robert R. 1978. "Políticas educativas durante el Frente Nacional, 1958–1974," *Revista Colombiana de Educación*, No. 1 (primer semestre).

Asher, Mukul. 1994. *Social Security in Malaysia and Singapore: Practices, Issues and Reform Directions*. Kuala Lumpur: Institute of Strategic and International Studies.

———. 2004. "Retirement Financing Dilemmas Facing Singapore." Paper presented at the Seminar on Pensions in Asia: Incentives, Compliance and Their Role in Retirement, Hitotsubashi University, Tokyo, February 23–24.

Asher, Mukul, and Amarendu Nandy. 2006. "Social Security Policy in an Era of Globalization and Competition: Challenges for Southeast Asia." Unpublished ms., Lee Kuan Yew School of Public Policy, National University of Singapore.

Ashton, David, Francis Green, Donna James, and Johnny Sung. 1999. *Education and Training for Development in East Asia*. London: Routledge.

Asian Development Bank. 2007. "Key Indicators," Manila: Asian Development Bank, http://www.adb.org/Documents/Books/Key_Indicators/default.asp, accessed May 27, 2007.

Aspalter, Christian, ed. 2001. *Conservative Welfare Systems in East Asia*, Westport, CT: Praeger.

———. 2002. *Democratization and Welfare State Development in Taiwan*. Burlington, VT: Ashgate.

Atinc, Tamar Manuelyan. 2003. "How the East Asian Crisis Changed the Social Situation," in Katherine Marshall and Oliver Butzbach, eds. *New Social Policy Agendas for Europe and Asia: Challenges, Experience, and Lessons*. Washington, DC: World Bank.

Atkinson, Anthony, and John Micklewright. 1992. *Economic Transformation in Eastern Europe and the Distribution of Income*. Cambridge: Cambridge University Press.

Avdagic, Sabina. 2003. "Accounting for Variations in Trade Union Effectiveness: State-Labor Relations in East Central Europe." Max Planck Institute for Social Research Discussion Paper 03/6 (November).

Avelino Filho, George. 2000. "Economic Crisis, Democratization, and Social Expenditure in Latin America, 1980–1994." PhD dissertation, Stanford University.

Avelino, George, David S. Brown, and Wendy Hunter. 2005. "The Effects of Capital Mobility, Trade Openness, and Democracy on Social Spending in Latin America, 1980–1999," *American Journal of Political Science* 49, 3 (July): 625–41.

Averich, Harvey, John Koehler, and Frank H. Denton. 1971. *The Matrix of Policy in the Philippines: 1948–1969*. Princeton, NJ: Princeton University Press.

Ayadurai, Dunston. 1992. *Industrial Relations in Malaysia: Law and Practice*. Kuala Lumpur: Butterworths Asia.

Bacha, Edmar. 1998. "O Plano Real," in Aloizo Mercadante, ed. *O Brasil PosReal*. Campinas, SP: Universidade Estadual de Campinas, Instituto de Economía.

Bahry, Donna. 1983. "Politics, Succession, and Public Policy in Communist Systems: a Review Article," *Soviet Studies* 35, 2 (April), 240–49.

Baker, Chris, and Pasuk Phongpaichit. 2002. *Thailand: Economy and Politics,* 2nd ed. New York: Oxford University Press.

Baker, Dean, and Mark Weisbrot. 1999. *Social Security: the Phony Crisis.* Chicago: University of Chicago Press.

Balabanova, Dina, and Martin McKee. 2002. "Access to Health Care in a System Transition: the Case of Bulgaria," *International Journal of Public Health Planning and Management* 17, 4 (November): 377–95.

Balcerowicz, Leszek. 1994. "Understanding Postcommunist Transitions," *Journal of Democracy* 5, 4 (October): 75–89.

Baldwin, Peter. 1990. *The Politics of Social Solidarity: Class Bases of the European Welfare State, 1875–1975.* Cambridge: Cambridge University Press.

Balisacan, Arsenio. 1993. "Rural Development in the Philippines: Patterns, Constraints and Responses," in Arsenio Balisacan and Katsumi Nozawa, eds. *Structures and Reforms for Rural Development in the Philippines*, 1–24. Tokyo: Institute of Developing Economies.

——. 2001. "Did the Estrada Administration Benefit the Poor?" in Amando Doronila, ed. *Between Fires: Fifteen Perspectives on the Estrada Crisis.* Pasig City, Philippines: Anvil.

Bank of Korea, 1988. *Economic Statistical Yearbook.* Seoul: Bank of Korea.

Baqir, Reza. 2002. "Social Sector Spending in a Panel of Countries," International Monetary Fund Working Paper WP/02/35. Washington, DC International Monetary Fund.

Bardhan, Pranab. 2002. "Decentralization of Governance and Development," *Journal of Economic Perspectives* 16, 4 (Autumn): 185–205.

Bardhan, Pranab, Samuel Bowles, and Michael Wallerstein, eds. 2006. *Globalization and Egalitarian Distribution.* New York: Russell Sage Foundation; Princeton, NJ, Princeton University Press.

Barr, Michael D. 2000. "Lee Kuan Yew's Fabian Phase," *Australian Journal of Politics and History* 46, 1 (March): 110–25.

Barr, Nicholas. 2001. *The Welfare State as Piggy Bank.* Oxford: Oxford University Press.

Barraclough, Simon. 1999. "Constraints on the Retreat From a Welfare-Orientated Approach to Public Health Care in Malaysia," *Health Policy* 47, 1 (April): 53–67.

Barreto de Oliveira, Francisco E., ed. 1994. *Sistemas de Seguridad Social en La Region: Problemas y Alternativas de Solución.* Washington DC: Banco Interamericano de Desarrollo.

Barro, Robert J., and Jong-Wha Lee. 2000. "International Data on Educational Attainment: Updates and Implications." CID Working Paper No. 42 (April), www.cid.harvard.edu/ciddata/ciddata.html, accessed May 27, 2007.

Bartlett, David L. 1997. *The Political Economy of Dual Transformations: Market Reform and Democratization in Hungary.* Ann Arbor: University of Michigan Press.

Bates, Robert H. 1998. *Open-Economy Politics: The Political Economy of World Coffee Trade.* Princeton, NJ: Princeton University Press.

——. 1999. "Institutions and Economic Performance." Paper prepared for IMF Conference on "Second Generation Reforms" (September 22, 1999). Washington,

DC: International Monetary Fund, http://www.imf.org/external/pubs/ft/seminar/ 1999/reforms/bates.htm#V, accessed October 22, 2007.

Bates, Robert H., and Anne O. Krueger. 1993. "Generalizations Arising from the Case Studies," in Bates and Krueger, eds. *Political and Economic Interactions in Economic Policy Reform: Evidence from Eight Countries*. Cambridge: Blackwell.

Bates, Robert H., and Da Hsiang Donald Lien. 1985. "A Note on Taxation, Development, and Representative Government," *Politics and Society* 14, 1: 53–70.

Baum, Matthew, and David Lake. 2003. "The *Political* Economy of Growth: Democracy and Human Capital," *American Journal of Political Science* 47, 2 (April): 333–47.

Bautista, Victoria A. 1999a. *Combating Poverty through Comprehensive and Integrated Delivery of Social Services (CIDSS)*. Quezon City: National College of Public Administration and Governance, University of the Philippines.

———. 1999b. *A State-of-the-Art Review of Primary Health Care in the Philippines: Two Decades of Government Initiative*, 2nd ed. Quezon City: National College of Public Administration and Governance, University of the Philippines for the Department of Health.

———. 2002. *Readings in Governance of Poverty Alleviation*. Quezon City: Office of the Vice Chancellor for Research and Development, University of the Philippines.

———. ed. 2003. *Participatory Governance in Poverty Alleviation*. Quezon City: Center for Leadership, Citizenship and Democracy, National College of Public Administration and Governance, University of the Philippines.

Bautista, Victoria A., Perla E. Legaspi, Eden V. Santiago, Lilibeth J. Juan. 2002. *National and Local Government Roles in Public Health Under Devolution*. Quezon City: University of the Philippines Press.

Beck, Nathaniel, and Jonathan N. Katz. 1995. "What to Do (and Not to Do) with Time-Series Cross-Section Data," *American Political Science Review* 89, 3 (September): 634–47.

———. 1996. "Nuisance vs. Substance: Specifying and Estimating Time-Series-Cross-Section Models," *Political Analysis* 6, 1: 1–36.

Bednarik, Rastislav. 1998. "The Transformation of Social Security in Slovakia and Its Consequences for a Family." Paper prepared for the International Social Security Association Research Conference on Social Security, Jerusalem, (January), 25–28.

Bell, J. 2001. *The Political Economy of Reform in Post-Communist Poland*. London: Edward Elgar.

Benabou, R., and E. Ok. 2001. "Social Mobility and the Demand for Redistribution: The POUM Hypothesis," *Quarterly Journal of Economics* 116, 2 (May): 447–87.

Bennagen, Pia C. 2000. "Anti-Poverty Programs." Civil Society and Governance Program, Institute for Development Studies, http://www.eldis.org/static/DOC10898 .htm, accessed July 9, 2004.

Berent, Jerzy. 1970. "Causes of Fertility Decline in Eastern Europe and the Soviet Union II: Economic and Social Factors," *Population Studies* 24, 2 (July): 247–92.

Bergara, Mario, Andrés Pereyra, Ruben Tansini, Adolfo Garcé, Daniel Chasquetti, Daniel Buquet, and Juan Andrés Moraes. 2004. "Political Institutions, Policymaking Processes and Policy Outcomes: The Case of Uruguay." Paper prepared for the Latin American Research Network of the Inter-American Development Bank (April), http://www.iadb.org/res/pub_desc.cfm?pub_id=R-510, accessed January 15, 2007.

Beringuela, Ma. Luisa I. 1995. *The Performance of Medicare I: An Economic Evaluation* Discussion Paper Series No. 95–06. Manila: Philippine Institute for Development Studies.

Bernard, Mitchell, and John Ravenhill. 1995. "Beyond Product Cycles and Flying Geese: Regionalization, Hierarchy, and the Industrialization of East Asia," *World Politics*, 47, 2 (January): 171–209.

Bielasiak, Jack. 1983. "Inequalities and the Politicization of the Polish Working Class," in Daniel N. Nelson, ed. *Communism and the Politics of Inequality*, 221–49. Lexington, MA: Lexington Books.

Birch, Sarah, Frances Millard, Kieran Williams, and Marina Popescu. 2002. *Embodying Democracy: Electoral System Design in Post-Communist Europe*. Basingstoke: Palgrave-Macmillan.

Birchfield, V., and M.M.L. Crepaz. 1998. "The Impact of Constitutional Structures and Collective and Competitive Veto Points on Income Inequality in Industrialized Democracies," *European Journal of Political Research*. 34, 2 (October): 175–200.

Bird, Graham. 2001. "IMF Programmes: Is There a Conditionality Laffer Curve?" *World Economics* 2, 2 (April–June): 29–49.

Bird, Graham, and Thomas D. Willett. 2004. "IMF Conditionality and the New Political Economy of Ownership," *Comparative Economic Studies* 46, 3 (September): 423–50.

Bird, Richard, and Oliver Oldman, eds. 1990. *Taxation in Developing Countries*, 4th ed. Baltimore: Johns Hopkins University Press.

Birdsall, Nancy. 1999. "Education: the People's Asset," Brookings Institution Center on Social and Economic Dynamics Working Paper No. 5. Washington, DC: Brookings Institution.

Birdsall, Nancy, and Augusto de la Torre. 2001. *Washington Contentious: Economic Policies for Social Equity in Latin America*. Washington, DC: Center for Global Development.

Birdsall, Nancy, and Stephan Haggard. 2003. "After the Crisis: The Social Contract and the Middle Class in East Asia," in Ethan Kapstein and Brako Milanovic, eds. *When Markets Fail: Social Policy and Economic Reform*. New York: Russell Sage Foundation.

Birdsall, Nancy, David Ross, and Richard Sabot. 1995. "Inequality and Growth Reconsidered: Lessons from East Asia," *World Bank Economic Review* 9, 3: 477–508.

Bod, Peter A., and Ivan Szabo, 1993. "Letter to Michael Camdessus (August 19)," in International Monetary Fund, "Hungary: Stand-By Arrangement," EBS/93/138 Supplement 1 (September 20).

Boeri, T., M. Burda, and J. Kollo, 1998. "Mediating the Transition: Labour Markets in Central and Eastern Europe," in L. Ambrus-Lakatos and M. Schaffer, eds. *Mediating the Transition: Labour Markets in Central and Eastern Europe—Forum Report of the Economic Policy Initiative*. London: Centre for Economic Policy Research.

Boix, Carles. 1998. *Political Parties, Growth, and Equality. Conservative and Social Democratic Strategies in the World Economy.* New York: Cambridge University Press.

———. 2003. *Democracy and Redistribution*. New York: Cambridge University Press.

Bokros, Lajos, and Gyorgy Suranyi. 1996. "Letter to Michel Camdessus (February 2)," in International Monetary Fund, "Hungary: Request for Stand-By Arrangement," EBS/96/18 (February 5).

Bonturi, Marcos. 2002. "The Brazilian Pension System: Recent Reforms and Challenges Ahead," in OECD, Economics Department Working Papers, No. 340. Paris: Organisation for Economic Cooperation and Development.

Boone, Peter. 1996. "Politics and the Effectiveness of Foreign Aid," *European Economic Review* 40, 12 (February): 289–329.

Booth, Anne. 1999. "Education and Economic Development in Southeast Asia," *ASEAN Economic Bulletin* 16, 3 (December): 290–306.

Borzutzky, Silvia. 2002. *Vital Connections: Politics, Social Security and Inequality in Chile*. Notre Dame, IN: University of Notre Dame Press.

Bossert, Thomas, and Cesary Wlodarczyk. 2000. "Unpredictable Politics: Policy Process of Health Reform in Poland." Unpublished ms., Harvard School of Public Health and School of Public Health, Jagiellonian University (January).

Bowie, Alisdair. 1991. *Crossing the Industrial Divide: State, Society, and the Politics of Economic Transformation in Malaysia*. New York: Columbia University Press.

Boyce, James K. 1993. *The Political Economy of Growth and Impoverishment in the Marcos Era*. Manila: Ateneo de Manila University Press.

Brady, David, Jason Beckfield, and Martin Seeleib-Kaiser. 2005. "Economic Globalization and the Welfare State in Affluent Democracies, 1975–2001," *American Sociological Review*, 70, 6 (December): 921–48.

Brady, Henry, and David Collier, eds. 2004. *Rethinking Social Inquiry: Diverse Tools, Shared Standards*. Lanham, MD: Rowman and Littlefield.

Brady, Henry, David Collier, and Jason Searight. 2004. "Claiming Too Much: Warnings About Selection Bias," in Brady and Collier, eds. *Rethinking Social Inquiry: Diverse Tools, Shared Standards*. Lanham, MD: Rowman and Littlefield.

Brooks, Sarah. 2002. "Social Protection and Economic Integration: The Politics of Pension Reform in an Era of Capital Mobility," *Comparative Political Studies* 35, 5 (June): 491–523.

———. 2005. "Interdependent and Domestic Foundations of Policy Change: the Diffusion of Pension Privatization Around the World," *International Studies Quarterly* 49, 2 (June): 273–94.

———. 2007. *Social Protection and the Market: The Transformation of Social Security Institutions in Latin America*. Cambridge: Cambridge University Press.

Brown, Andrew, and Stephen Frenkel. 1993. "Union Unevenness and Insecurity in Thailand," in Stephen Frenkel, ed. *Organized Labor in the Asia-Pacific Region*. Ithaca, NY: Cornell University Press.

Brown, Dana L. 2005. "The New Politics of Welfare in Post-Socialist Central Eastern Europe." PhD dissertation, Massachusetts Institute of Technology.

Brown, David S. 1999. "Reading, Writing, and Regime Type," *Political Research Quarterly* 52, 4 (December): 681–707.

———. 2002. "Democracy, Authoritarianism and Education Finance in Brazil," *Journal of Latin American Studies* 34, 1 (February): 115–41.

Brown, David S., and Wendy Hunter. 1999. "Democracy and Social Spending in Latin America, 1980–92," *American Political Science Review* 93, 4 (December): 779–90.

Brown, James F. 1988. *Eastern Europe and Communist Rule.* Durham, NC: Duke University Press.

Browning, Edgar K. 1975. "Why the Social Insurance Budget is Too Large in a Democracy," *Economic Inquiry* 13, 3 (September): 373–88.

Bruhn, Kathleen. 1996. "Social Spending and Political Support: The 'Lessons' of the National Solidarity Program in Mexico," *Comparative Politics* 28, 2 (January): 151–77.

Bruni Celli, Josefina. 2004. "Innovation and Frustration: Education Reform in Venezuela," in Robert R. Kaufman and Joan M. Nelson, eds. *Crucial Needs, Weak Incentives: Social Sector Reform, Democratization, and Globalization in Latin America.* Washington, DC: Woodrow Wilson Center Press; Baltimore, MD: Johns Hopkins University Press.

Bruno, Michael, and William Easterly. 1996. "Inflation's Children: Tales of Crises that Beget Reforms," *American Economic Review* 86, 2 (May): 213–17.

Bruton, Henry J. 1998. "A Reconsideration of Import Substitution," *Journal of Economic Literature* 36, 2 (June): 903–36.

Brzezinski, Zbigniew K. 1967. *The Soviet Bloc: Unity and Conflict.* 2nd ed. Cambridge, MA: Harvard University Press.

Bueno de Mesquita, Bruce, Alastair Smith, Randolph M. Siverson, and James D. Morrow. 2001. "Political Competition and Economic Growth," *Journal of Democracy*, 12, 1 (January), 58–72.

———. 2003. *The Logic of Political Survival.* Cambridge, MA: MIT Press.

Bunce, Valerie. 1980. "The Political Consumption Cycle: A Comparative Analysis," *Soviet Studies* 32, 2 (April): 280–90.

———. 1981. *Do New Leaders Make a Difference? Executive Succession and Public Policy under Capitalism and Socialism.* Princeton, NJ: Princeton University Press.

Bushnell, David. 1993. *The Making of Modern Colombia.* Berkeley: University of California Press.

Cain, Michael J. G., and Aleksander Surdej. 1999. "Transitional Politics or Public Choice? Evaluating Stalled Pension Reform in Poland," in Linda J. Cook, Mitchell A. Orenstein, and Marilyn Rueschemeyer, eds. *Left Parties and Social Policy in Postcommunist Europe.* Boulder, CO: Westview Press.

Camacho, Luis A. N.d. "Evolución historica del sistema de seguridad social en Uruguay," Asesoria Económica y Actuarial del Banco de Provisión Social, www.bps .gub.uy/Informacion_general/T_Historia.htm.

Cameron, David. 1978. "The Expansion of the Public Sector: A Comparative Analysis," *American Political Science Review* 72, 4 (December): 1243–61.

Campos, Jose Edgardo, and Hilton Root. 1996. *The Key to the Asian Miracle: Making Shared Growth Credible.* Washington, DC: Brookings Institution Press.

Campos, Nauro, and Fabrizio Coricelli. 2002. "Growth in Transition: What We Know, What We Don't, and What We Should," *Journal of Economic Literature* 40, 3 (September): 793–836.

Capuno, Joseph J. 1999. "The Political Economy of Decentralization: Financing of Health Services in the Philippines." Discussion Paper No. 9910. Manila: University of the Philippines, School of Economics.

Caraher, Kevin. 2000. "Issues in Incomes Provision for the Elderly in Malaysia." Paper presented at the Year 2000 International Research Conference on Social Security, Helsinki, 25–27 September.

Carrothers, Thomas. 2002. "The End of the Transition Paradigm," *Journal of Democracy* 13, 1 (January): 5–21.

Castiglioni, Rossana. 2001. "The Politics of Retrenchment: The Quandaries of Social Protection Under Military Rule in Chile, 1973–1990," *Latin American Politics and Society* 43, 4 (November): 37–66.

———. 2005. *The Politics of Social Policy Change in Chile and Uruguay: Retrenchment versus Maintenance, 1973–1998.* New York: Routledge.

Castle-Kanerova, Mita. 1992. "Social Policy in Czechoslovakia," in Bob Deacon, ed. *The New Eastern Europe: Social Policy Past, Present and Future.* London: Sage Publications.

Cazes, Sandrine, and Alena Nesporova. 2003. *Labour Markets in Transition: Balancing Flexibility and Security in Central and Eastern Europe.* Geneva: International Labour Organization.

Celedon, Carmen, and Cesar Oyarza. 2000. "Los Desafíos en Salud," in Rene Cortuzar and Javier Vial, eds. *Construyendo propuestos económicas y sociales para el cambio de siglo.* Santiago, Chile: CIEPLAN-Dolmen Ediciones.

Centeno, Miguel Angel. 1997. *Democracy Within Reason.* University Park: Pennsylvania State University Press.

Cerami, Alfio. 2005. "Social Policy in Central and Eastern Europe: the Emergence of a New European Model of Solidarity?" PhD dissertation, University of Erfurt.

Chai-Anan Samudavanija, Kusuma Snitwongse, and Suchit Bunbongkarn. 1990. *From Armed Suppression to Political Offensive.* Bangkok, Thailand: Institute of Security and International Studies, Faculty of Political Science, Chulalongkorn University.

Chan, Gordon Hou-Sheng. 1987. "Taiwan," in J. Dixon and H. S. Kim, eds, *Social Welfare in Asia.* London: Croom Helm.

Chaudhry, Kiren. 1997. *The Price of Wealth: Economies and Institutions in the Middle East.* Ithaca, NY: Cornell University Press.

Chen, Chin-Shyan, Tsai-Ching Liu, and Li-Mei Chen. 2003. "National Health Insurance and the Antenatal Care Use: a Case in Taiwan," *Health Policy* 64, 1 (April): 99–112.

Chen, Hsiao-hung Nancy. 2004. "Universal Values vs. Political Ideology: Virtual Reform Experience of Taiwan's National Pension Plan (Draft)." Unpublished manuscript. Taipei: National Chengchi University.

Chen, Jing. 2007. "Globalization, Democratization and Government Education Provision in East Asia." PhD dissertation, Rutgers University.

Cheng, Tun-jen. 1992. "Dilemmas and Choices in Educational Policies: the Case of South Korea and Taiwan," *Studies in Comparative International Development* 27, 4 (Winter): 54–79.

Cheng, Tun-jen, and Stephan Haggard. 1990. "State and Foreign Capital in the East Asian NICs," in Frederic C. Deyo, ed. *The Political Economy of the New Asian Industrialism.* Ithaca, NY: Cornell University Press.

Cheng, Y. C., and T. Townsend. 2000. "Educational Change and Development in the Asia-Pacific Region: Trends and Issues," in Townsend and Cheng, eds. *Educational Change and Development in the Asia-Pacific Region: Challenges for the Future,* 317–44. Leiden: Swets and Zeitlinger Publisher.

Cheung Wai-lam. 2000. *Unemployment-Related Benefits Systems in Singapore*. Singapore: Research and Library Services Division, Legislative Council Secretariat.

Chiang, Tung-ling, and Shou-hsia Cheng. 1997. "The Effect of Universal Health Insurance on Health Care Utilization in Taiwan," *Journal of the American Medical Association* 278, 2 (July): 89–93.

Chirot, Daniel. 1978. "Social Change in Communist Romania," *Social Forces* 57, 2 (December): 457–99.

———. 1989. *The Origins of Backwardness in Eastern Europe: Economic and Politics from the Middle Ages until the Early Twentieth Century*. Berkeley: University of California Press.

Chiu, Shean-Bii. 2004. "Taiwan: Compulsory Occupational Pensions Still Dominate." Paper prepared for Conference on Pensions in Asia: Incentives, Compliance and Their Role in Retirement, Asian Development Bank Institute, Tokyo (February 23–24).

Choi, Minsik. 2006. "Threat Effects of Capital Mobility on Wage Bargaining," in Pranab Bardhan, Samuel Bowles, and Michael Wallerstein, eds. *Globalization and Egalitarian Distribution*. New York: Russell Sage Foundation; Princeton, NJ: Princeton University Press.

Chow, Peter C. Y. 2001. *Social Expenditure in Taiwan (China)*. Washington, DC: World Bank.

Chua Beng Huat. 1997. *Political Legitimacy and Housing: Stakeholding in Singapore*. New York: Routledge.

———. 2004. "Welfare Developmentalism in Singapore and Malaysia," unpublished manuscript. Department of Sociology, National University of Singapore.

Ciobanu, Monica. 2002. "Democratic Consolidation or One-Party Domination? Romania Post-1996: From Democratic Illusions to Democratic Survival." New York: Transregional Center for Democratic Studies, New School University.

Clark, Mary A. 2001. *Gradual Economic Reform in Latin America: The Costa Rican Experience*. Albany: State University of New York Press.

———. 2004. "Reinforcing a Public System: Health Sector Reform in Costa Rica," in Robert R. Kaufman and Joan M. Nelson, eds. *Crucial Needs, Weak Incentives: Social Sector Reform, Democratization, and Globalization in Latin America*. Washington, DC: Woodrow Wilson Center Press; Baltimore, MD: Johns Hopkins University Press.

Coady, David. 2003. "Alleviating Structural Poverty in Developing Countries: The Approach of Progresa in Mexico." Washington, DC: International Food Policy Research Institute, Food Consumption Division (February).

Coady, David, Margaret Grosh, and John Hoddinott. 2004. "Targeting Outcomes Redux," *World Bank Research Observer* 19, 1 (Spring): 61–85.

Cohen, Paul. 1989. "The Politics of Primary Health Care in Thailand, with Special Reference to Non-Governmental Organizations," in Paul Cohen, and John Purcal, eds. *The Political Economy of Primary Health Care in Southeast Asia*. Canberra: Australian Development Studies Network ASEAN Training Centre for Primary Health Care Development.

Collier, David. 1976. *Squatters and Oligarchs: Authoritarian Rule and Policy Change in Peru*. Baltimore, MD: Johns Hopkins University Press.

————, ed. 1979. *The New Authoritarianism in Latin America*. Princeton, NJ: Princeton University Press.

Collier, David, and Richard Messick. 1975. "Prerequisites versus Diffusion: Testing Alternative Explanations of Social Security Adoption," *American Political Science Review* 69, 4 (December): 1299–315.

Collier, Ruth, and David Collier. 1991. *Shaping the Political Arena: Critical Junctures, the Labor Movement, and Regime Dynamics in Latin America*. Princeton, NJ: Princeton University Press.

Cook, Linda J. 1993. *The Soviet Social Contract and Why It Failed: Welfare Policy and Workers' Politics from Brezhnev to Yeltsin*. Cambridge, MA: Harvard University Press.

————. 2007. *Postcommunist Welfare States: Reform Politics in Russia and Eastern Europe*. Ithaca, NY: Cornell University Press.

Cook, Linda J., and Mitchell A. Orenstein. 1999. "The Return of the Left and Its Impact on the Welfare State in Russia, Poland, and Hungary," in Linda J. Cook, Mitchell A. Orenstein, and Marilyn Rueschemeyer, eds. *Left Parties and Social Policy in Postcommunist Europe*. Boulder, CO: Westview Press.

Cooley, Thomas F., and Jorge Soares. 1999. "A Positive Theory of Social Security Based on Reputation," *Journal of Political Economy* 107, 1 (February): 135–60.

Coppedge, Michael. 1998. "The Dynamic Diversity of Latin American Party Systems," *Party Politics* 4, 4 (October): 547–68.

Cordova, Efren. 1972. "Labour Legislation and Latin American Development: A Preliminary Review," *International Labour Review* 106, 5 (November): 445–74.

Cornia, Giovanni Andrea. 2002. "Social Funds in Stabilization and Adjustment Programmes: A Critique." CHILD Working Paper no. 13/2002. Turin: Center for Household Income, Labour, and Demographic Economics, http:www.child -centre.it, accessed May 17, 2007.

Corrales, Javier. 2002. *Presidents without Parties: The Politics of Economic Reform in Argentina and Venezuela in the 1990s*. University Park: Pennsylvania State University Press.

————. 2004. "Multiple Preferences, Variable Strengths: The Politics of Education Reform in Argentina," in Robert R. Kaufman, and Joan M. Nelson, eds. *Crucial Needs, Weak Incentives: Social Sector Reform, Democratization, and Globalization in Latin America*. Washington, DC: Woodrow Wilson Center Press; Baltimore, MD: Johns Hopkins University Press.

Corsetti, G., P. Pesenti, and N. Roubini, 1998. "What Caused the Asian Currency and Financial Crisis? Part 1: A Microeconomic Overview," National Bureau of Economic Research Working Paper 6833. Cambridge, MA: National Bureau of Economic Research.

Cox, Gary. 1987. *The Efficient Secret: The Cabinet and the Development of Political Parties in Victorian England*. Cambridge: Cambridge University Press.

Cox, Gary, and Matthew McCubbins. 2001. "The Institutional Determinants of Economic Policy Outcomes," in Stephan Haggard and Matthew McCubbins, eds. *Presidents, Parliaments and Policy*. New York: Cambridge University Press.

Crepaz, Markus M. L., and Ann W. Moser. 2004. "The Impact of Collective and Competitive Veto Points on Public Expenditures in the Global Age," *Comparative Political Studies*, 37, 3 (April): 259–85.

Crouch, Harold. 1996. *Government and Politics in Malaysia*. Ithaca, NY: Cornell University Press.

Crowther, William E. 1988. *The Political Economy of Romanian Socialism*. New York: Praeger.

Cruz-Saco Oyague, Maria Amparo. 1998. "The Pension System Reform in Peru: Economic Rationale versus Political Will," in Maria Amparo Cruz-Saco Oyague, and Carmelo Mesa-Lago, eds. *Do Options Exist? The Reform of Pension and Health Care Systems in Latin America*. Pittsburgh, PA: University of Pittsburgh Press.

Cruz-Saco Oyague, Maria Amparo, and Carmelo Mesa-Lago, eds. 1998. *Do Options Exist? The Reform of Pension and Health Care Systems in Latin America*. Pittsburgh, PA: University of Pittsburgh Press.

Danguilan, Marilen. 1999. "Bullets and Bandages: Public Health as a Tool of Engagement in the Philippines," Takemi Program in International Health Research Paper No. 161. Cambridge: Harvard School of Public Health.

Deacon, Bob. 1983. *Social Policy and Socialism: The Struggle for Socialist Relations of Welfare*. London: Pluto Press.

———. 1992a. "East European Welfare: Past, Present, and Future in Comparative Context," in Bob Deacon, ed. *The New Eastern Europe: Social Policy Past, Present and Future*. London: Sage Publications.

———, ed. 1992b. *The New Eastern Europe: Social Policy Past, Present and Future*. London: Sage Publications.

———. 1997. With Michelle Hulse and Paul Stubbs. *Global Social Policy: International Organizations and the Future of Welfare*. London: Sage Publications.

———. 2000a. *Globalization and Social Policy*, UNRISD Occasional Paper 5. Geneva: United Nations Research Institute for Social Development.

———. 2000b. "Eastern European Welfare States: the Impact of the Politics of Globalisation," *Journal of European Social Policy* 10, 2 (May): 146–61.

Deacon, Bob, and Paul Stubbs. 2005. "The Making of Social Policy in South Eastern Europe: Theories, Methods, Politics," in Stein Kuhlne, ed. *Social Policy Development in South Eastern Europe: Outside Influence and Domestic Forces*. Bergen: Stein Rokkan Centre for Social Studies Report No. 2.

Deacon, Bob, and Anna Vidinova. 1992. "Social Policy in Bulgaria," in Bob Deacon, ed. *The New Eastern Europe: Social Policy Past, Present and Future*. London: Sage Publications.

De Ferranti, Guillermo, G. Perry, Francisco H. G. Ferreira, and Michael Walton. 2004. *Inequality in Latin America: Breaking with History?* Washington, DC: World Bank.

Deininger, Klaus, and Lynn Squire. 1996. "A New Data Set Measuring Income Inequality," *World Bank Economic Review* 10, 3: 565–591, http://siteresources.worldbank.org/INTRES/Resources/469232-1107449512766/648083-11081407 88422/A_New_Dataset_Measuring_Income_Inequality.zip, accessed May 27, 2007.

Desai, Raj M., Anders Olofsgård, and Tarik Yousef. 2006. "The Logic of Authoritarian Bargains." Washington, DC: Georgetown University, Edmund A. Walsh School of Foreign Service Working Paper, http://ssrn.com/abstract=896133, accessed June 1, 2007.

Deyo, Frederic. 1981. *Dependent Development and Industrial Order: An Asian Case Study*. New York: Praeger.

————. 1989. *Beneath the Miracle: Labor Subordination in the New Asian Industrialism.* Berkeley: University of California Press.

Diamond, Larry. 1999. *Developing Democracy: Toward Consolidation.* Baltimore, MD: Johns Hopkins University Press.

Diaz-Alejandro, Carlos F. 1965. "On the Import Intensity of Import Substitution," *Kyklos* 18, 3 (August): 495–511.

Diaz-Cayeros, Alberto, Beatriz Magaloni, and Federico Estévez 2006. "Vote-Buying, Poverty and Democracy: The Politics of Social Programs in Mexico, 1989–2006." Unpublished book ms. presented at Meeting of Political Economy of Public Expenditures (PEPE) and the Distributive Politics Working Groups, Stanford University, September 22–23, http://www.stanford.edu/~albertod/conference/papers, accessed May 30, 2007.

————. 2007. "Strategies of Vote Buying: Poverty, Democracy, and Social Transfers in Mexico." Unpublished ms., Stanford University, http://www.stanford.edu/~albertod/buyingvotes/buyingvotes.html.

Dios, Emmanuel de. 1998. "Philippine Economic Growth: Can It Last?" Unpublished manuscript. Manilla: University of the Philippines, School of Economics. http://www.ciaonet.org/book/ass01/ass01_b.html, accessed June 12, 2005.

Diokno, Benjamin E. 2003. "Decentralization in the Philippines After Ten Years: What Have We Learned? What Have I Learned?" Discussion Paper No. 0308. Manila: University of the Philippines, School of Economics (December).

Dion, Michelle. 2004. "Globalization, Political Institutions, and Social Spending Change in Middle Income Countries, 1980–99," paper presented at the Annual Meeting of the American Political Science Association, Chicago, September 1–5, http://www.prism.gatech.edu/%7Emd177/papers.html, accessed May 27, 2007.

Dixon, J., and H. S. Kim, eds. 1985. *Social Welfare in East Asia.* London: Croom Helm.

Dollar, David, and Art Kray. 2002. "Growth is Good for the Poor," *Journal of Economic Growth,* 7, 3 (September): 195–222.

Dominguez, Jorge, ed. 1997. *Technopols: Freeing Politics and Markets in Latin America in the 1990s.* University Park: Pennsylvania State University Press.

Donaldson, Dayl, Supasit Pannarunothai, and Viroj Tangcharoensathien. 1999. *Health Financing in Thailand: Technical Report.* Boston: Management Sciences for Health for the Asian Development Bank Health Management and Financing Study Project.

Dornbusch, Rudiger, and Sebastian Edwards, eds. 1991. *The Macroeconomics of Populism.* Chicago: University of Chicago Press.

Doronila, Amando. 1992. *The State, Economic Transformation, and Political Change in thePhilippines, 1946–1972.* Singapore: Oxford University Press.

————. 2001. *The Fall of Joseph Estrada: The Inside Story.* Pasig City, Philippines: Anvil Publishing.

Draibe, Sónia M. 2004. "Federal Leverage in a Decentralized System: Education Reform in Brazil," in Robert Kaufman and Joan M. Nelson, eds. *Crucial Needs, Weak Incentives: Social Sector Reform, Democratization, and Globalization in Latin America.* Washington, DC: Woodrow Wilson Center Press; Baltimore, MD: Johns Hopkins University Press.

Drazen, Allan. 2000. *Political Economy in Macroeconomics.* Princeton, NJ: Princeton University Press.

Drazen, Allan, and Vittorio Grilli. 1993. "The Benefit of Crisis for Economic Reforms," *American Economic Review* 83, 3 (June): 598–607.

Dreher, Axel, and Roland Vaubel. 2004. "The Causes and Consequences of IMF Conditionality," *Emerging Markets Finance and Trade* 40, 3 (May): 26–54.

Dreze, Jean, and Amartya Sen. 1989. *Hunger and Public Action*. Oxford: Oxford University Press.

Durán-Valverde, Fabio 2002. "Anti-Poverty Programmes in Costa Rica: The Non-Contributory Pension Scheme." Extension of Social Security Paper No. 8. Geneva: International Labor Office, Social Security Policy and Development Branch.

Easterly, William. 2001. *The Elusive Quest for Growth: Economists' Adventures and Misadventures in the Tropics*. Cambridge, MA: MIT Press.

Economic and Social Commission for Asia and the Pacific. 2001. *Strengthening Policies and Programmes on Social Safety Nets: Issues, Recommendations and Selected Studies*. Social Policy Paper No. 8. New York: United Nations.

Economic Commission for Latin America and the Caribbean (ECLAC). 1995. *Social Panorama of Latin America*. Santiago, Chile: Economic Commission for Latin America and the Caribbean.

———. 1998. *The Fiscal Covenant: Strengths, Weaknesses, Challenges*. Santiago, Chile: Economic Commission for Latin American and the Caribbean.

———. 2001. *Statistical Yearbook for Latin America and the Caribbean*. http://www.eclac.cl/cgi-in/getProd.asp?xml=/publicaciones/xml/1/9641/P9641.xml&xsl=/deype/tpl-i/p9f.xsl&base=/tpl-i/top-bottom.xsl, accessed May 27, 2007.

Edwards, Sebastian. 1995. *Crisis and Reform in Latin America: From Despair to Hope*. New York: Oxford University Press.

Edwards, Sebastian, and Nora Lustig. 1997. *Labor Markets in Latin America: Combining Social Protection with Market Flexibility*. Washington, DC: Brookings Institution Press.

EIU (Economic Intelligence Unit). 2001a. *Country Report Romania*. http://portal.eiu.com/index.asp?autologin=bulk, accessed through University of California, San Diego May 11, 2006.

———. 2001b. *Country Report Slovakia*. http://portal.eiu.com/index.asp?autologin=bulk, accessed through University of California, San Diego May 11, 2006.

Ekiert, Grzegorz. 1996. *The State Against Society*. Princeton, NJ: Princeton University Press.

Ekiert, Grzegorz, and Jan Kubik 1999. *Rebellious Civil Society: Popular Protest and Democratic Consolidation in Poland, 1989–1993*. Ann Arbor: University of Michigan Press.

Elkins, Zachary. 2000. "Gradations of Democracy? Empirical Tests of Alternative Conceptualizations," *American Journal of Political Science* 44, 2 (April): 293–300.

Elkins, Zachary, and Beth Simmons. 2005. "On Waves, Clusters, and Diffusion: A Conceptual Framework," *Annals of the American Academy of Political and Social Science* 598, 1 (March): 33–35.

Engerman, Stanley L., Elisa Mariscal, and Kenneth L. Sokoloff. 2000. "Schooling, Suffrage, and the Persistence of Inequality in the Americas, 1800–1945." Unpublished ms., University of California, Los Angeles and National Bureau of Economic Research.

Engerman, Stanley L., and Kenneth L. Sokoloff. 2000. "Institutions, Factor Endowments, and Paths of Development in the New World," *Journal of Economic Perspectives*, 14, 3 (Summer): 217–32.

———. 2002. "Factor Endowments, Inequality,, and Paths of Development among New World Economies," *Economia* 3, 1 (Fall): 41–109.

Esping-Andersen, Gøsta. 1990. *The Three Worlds of Welfare Capitalism*. Princeton, NJ: Princeton University Press.

———. ed. 1996. *Welfare States in Transition: National Adaptations in Global Economies*. London: Sage.

———. 1999. *Social Foundations of Postindustrial Economies*. New York: Oxford University Press.

Estevez-Abe, Margarita, Torben Iversen, and David Soskice. 2001. "Social Protection and the Formation of Skills: a Reintepretation of the Welfare State," in Peter Hall and David Soskice, eds. *Varieties of Capitalism: the Institutional Foundations of Comparative Advantage*. New York: Oxford University Press, 145–83.

European Bank for Reconstruction and Development. Various years. *Transition Report*. London: EBRD.

European Commission. 2003. *Joint Memorandum on Social Inclusion of the Czech Republic*. Brussels: European Commission.

European Observatory on Health Care Systems. 2000. *Health Care Systems in Transition: Romania*. Copenhagen: European Observatory on Health Care Systems.

Evans, Peter. 1979. *Dependent Development: The Alliance of Multinational, State and Local Capital in Brazil*. Princeton, NJ: Princeton University Press.

Ewig, Christina. 2004. "Piecemeal But Innovative: Health Sector Reform in Peru," in Robert R. Kaufman and Joan M. Nelson, eds. *Crucial Needs, Weak Incentives: Social Sector Reform, Democratization, and Globalization in Latin America*. Washington, DC: Woodrow Wilson Center Press; Baltimore, MD: Johns Hopkins University Press.

Falconi Palomino, José. 2003. "Social Programmes, Food Security and Poverty in Peru." Extension of Social Security Paper No. 14. Geneva: International Labor Office, Social Security Policy and Development Branch.

Fallenbuchl, Zbigniew M. 1991. "Employment Policies in Poland," in Jan Adam, ed. *Employment Policies in the Soviet Union and Eastern Europe*. London: Macmillan Press.

Fallon, Peter R., and Robert E. B. Lucas. 2002. "The Impact of Financial Crises on Labor Markets, Household Incomes, and Poverty: A Review of the Evidence," *World Bank Research Observer* 17, 1 (Spring): 21–45.

Faria, Vilmar E. 2003. "Reformas institucionales y coordinación gubernamental en la politica de protección social de Brasil." Santiago, Chile: Comisión Económica para America Latina (CEPAL) Division de Desarrollo Social, Serie Politicas Sociales, No. 64.

Fearon, James, and David Laitin. 2005. "Civil War Narratives." Unpublished manuscript. Stanford University, Department of Political Science.

Fei, John C. H., and Gustav Ranis. 1964. *Development of the Labor Surplus Economy: Theory and Practice*. Homewood, IL: Richard D. Irwin.

Fell, Dafydd. 2002. "Party Platform Change in Taiwan's 1990s Elections," *Issues and Studies* 38, 2 (June): 31–60.

Ferge, Zsuzsa. 1979. *A Society in the Making: Hungarian Social and Societal Policy 1945–1975*. White Plains: M.E. Sharpe, 1979.

———. 1991. "Recent Trends in Social Policy in Hungary," in Jan Adam, ed. *Economic Reforms and Welfare Systems in the USSR, Poland and Hungary*. New York: St. Martin's Press.

———. 1997. "The Changed Welfare Paradigm: The Individualization of the Social," *Social Policy and Administration* 31, 1 (March), 20–44.

———. 2001. "Disquieting Quiet in Hungarian Social Policy," *International Social Security Review* 54, 2–3 (April–September): 107–26.

Ferge, Zsuzsa, and Katalin Tausz. 2002. "Social Security in Hungary: A Balance Sheet after Twelve Years," *Social Policy and Administration* 36, 2 (April): 176–99.

Fernández, Raquel, and Dani Rodrik. 1991. "Resistance to Reform: Status Quo Bias in the Presence of Individual-Specific Uncertainty," *American Economic Review* 81, 5 (December): 1146–55.

Fields, Gary S. 1994. "Changing Labor Market Conditions and Economic Development in Hong Kong, the Republic of Korea, Singapore, and Taiwan, China," *World Bank Economic Review*, 8, 3 (September): 395–414.

———. 2004. "Dualism in the Labor Market: A Perspective on the Lewis Model after Half a Century," *Manchester School* 77, 6 (December): 724–35.

Figueiredo, A. C., and Fernando Limongi. 2000. "Presidential Power, Legislative Organization, and Party Behavior in the Legislature," *Comparative Politics* 32, 2 (January): 151–70.

Filgueira, Carlos, and Fernando Filgueira. 1997. "Taming Market Reform: The Politics of Social State Reform in Uruguay." Paper presented at Conference on "Social Policies for the Urban Poor in Latin America," Notre Dame, Kellogg Institute (September 12–14).

Filgueira, Fernando. 1995. "A Century of Social Welfare in Uruguay: Growth to the Limit of the Batllista Social State," Kellogg Institute Democracy and Social Policy Series, Working Paper #5 (Spring). Translated by Judy Lawton. Notre Dame, Kellogg Institute.

Filinson, Rachel, Darke Chmielewski, and Darek Niklas. 2004. "Health Care Reform and Older Adults: Notes from the Polish Experience," *Journal of Aging and Social Policy* 16, 1 (February): 69–88.

Filmer, Deon, and Lant Pritchett. 1999. "The Impact of Public Spending on Health: Does Money Matter?" *Social Science and Medicine* 49, 10 (November): 1309–23.

Fischer-Galati, Stephen, ed. 1981. *Eastern Europe in the 1980s*. Boulder, CO: Westview Press.

———. 1990. "The Impact of Modernization on the Educational System: A Comparative Survey," *East European Quarterly*, 24, 2 (June): 275–80.

———. 1998. "Romania under Communism," in Dinu C. Giurescu and Stephen Fischer-Galati, eds. *Romania: A Historical Perspective*. East European Monographs No. 457. New York: Columbia University Press.

Flakierski, Henryk. 1986. *Economic Reform and Income Distribution: A Case Study of Hungary and Poland*. Armonk NY: M. E. Sharpe.

———. 1991. "Social Policies in the 1980s in Poland: A Discussion of New Approaches," in Jan Adam, ed. *Economic Reforms and Welfare Systems in the USSR, Poland and Hungary*. New York: St. Martin's Press.

Fodor, Eva, Christy Glass, Janette Kawachi, and Livia Popescu. 2002. "Family Policies and Gender in Hungary, Poland and Romania," *Communist and Post-Communist Studies* 35, 4 (December): 475–90.

Forteza, Álvaro, and Martin Rama 1999. "Labor Market 'Rigidity' and the Success of Economic Reforms across More than One Hundred Countries," World Bank Policy Research Working Paper, No. 2521. Washington, DC: World Bank (November).

Franco, Álvaro, Carlos Álvarez-Dardet, and Maria Teresa Ruiz. 2004. "Effect of Democracy on Health: Ecological Study," *BMJ* 329 (18–25 December): 1421–23, http://bmj.com/cgi/content/full/329/7480/1421, accessed May 27, 2007.

Freeman, Richard. 1995. "Are Your Wages Set in Beijing?" *Journal of Economic Perspectives* 9, 3 (Summer): 15–32.

Frey, R. Scott, and Ali Al-Roumi. 1999. "Political Democracy and the Physical Quality of Life: The Cross-National Evidence," *Social Indicators Research* 47, 1 (May): 73–97.

Frieden, Jeffery A. 1992. *Debt, Development, and Democracy: Modern Political Economy and Latin America, 1965–1985.* Princeton, NJ: Princeton University Press.

Friedman, Benjamin. 2005. *The Moral Consequences of Economic Growth.* New York: Knopf.

Frye, Timothy. 2005. "Oligarchs and Markets: The Political Economy of Postcommunist Transformation." Unpublished ms. (January).

Fukuyama, Francis. 1995. *Trust: the Social Virtues and the Creation of Prosperity.* New York: Free Press.

Gaal, Peter. 2004. *Health Care Systems in Transition: Hungary.* Copenhagen: European Observatory on Health Systems and Policies.

Ganzeboom, Harry B. G., and Paul Nieuwbeerta. 1999. "Access to Education in Six Eastern European Countries Between 1940 and 1985. Results of a Cross-National Survey," *Communist and Post-Communist Studies* 32, 4 (December): 339–57.

Garrett, Geoffrey, 1995. "Capital Mobility, Trade and the Politics of Economic Policy," *International Organization* 49, 4 (Autumn): 657–88.

———. 1998. *Partisan Politics in the Global Economy.* Cambridge: Cambridge University Press.

———. 2001. "Globalization and Government Spending Around the World," *Studies in Comparative International Development* 35, 4 (Winter): 3–29.

Garrett, Geoffrey, and Deborah Mitchell. 1996. "Globalization and the Welfare State: Income Transfers in the Industrial Democracies, 1990–1996." Paper delivered at the annual meeting of the American Political Science Association, San Francisco (August 28–Sept. 1, 1996).

Gauri, Varun, and Peyvand Kaleghian. 2002. "Immunization in Developing Countries: Its Political and Organizational Determinants," Policy Research Working Paper No. 2769. Washington, DC: World Bank.

Gavin, Michael, and Roberto Perotti. 1997. "Fiscal Policy in Latin America," *NBER Macroeconomics Annual.* Cambridge, MA: MIT Press.

Geddes, Barbara. 1999. "What Do We Know About Democratization After Twenty Years?" *Annual Review of Political Science* 2 (June): 115–44.

———. 2003. *Paradigms and Sand Castles: Theory Building and Research Design in Comparative Politics.* Ann Arbor: University of Michigan Press.

George, Alexander L., and Andrew Bennett. 2005. *Case Studies and Theory Development in the Social Science*. Cambridge, MA: MIT Press.

Gerring, John. 2006. *Case Study Research: Principles and Practices*. New York: Cambridge University Press.

Gerring, John, Philip Bond, William T. Barndt, and Carola Moleno. 2005. "Democracy and Economic Growth: A Historical Perspective" *World Politics*, 57, 3 (April): 323–64.

Gerring, John, and Strom C. Thacker. 2002. "Social Democracy or Neoliberalism? A Global Test of Public Policies and Human Development." Paper prepared for the annual meeting of the American Political Science Association, Boston, August 29–September 1.

Gertler, Paul, and Orville Solon. 2002. "Who Benefits from Social Insurance? Evidence from the Philippines." Unpublished ms. Haas School of Business, University of California, Berkeley.

Ghobarah, Hazem Adam, Paul Huth, and Bruce Russett. 2004. "Comparative Public Health: The Political Economy of Human Misery and Well-Being," *International Studies Quarterly* 48, 1 (March): 73–94.

Gibson, Edward L. 1997. "The Populist Road to Market Reform: Policy and Electoral Coalitions in Mexico and Argentina," *World Politics* 49, 3 (April): 339 70.

Gilberg, Trond. 1975. *Modernization in Romania Since World War II*. New York: Praeger.

———. 1990. *Nationalism and Communism in Romania: The Rise and Fall of Ceauşescu's Personal Dictatorship*. Boulder, CO: Westview Press.

Gilbert, Neil. 2002. *Transformation of the Welfare State: The Silent Surrender of Public Responsibility*. New York: Oxford University Press.

Gilder, George. 1981. *Wealth and Poverty*. New York: Basic Books.

Giurescu, Dinu, and Stephen Fischer-Galati, eds. 1998. *Romania: a Historical Perspective*. East European Monographs No. 457. New York: Columbia University Press.

Glatzer, Miguel, and Dietrich Rueschemeyer, eds. 2005. *Globalization and the Future of the Welfare State*. Pittsburgh, PA: University of Pittsburgh Press.

Gleditsch, Kristian. 2002. *All Politics is Local: The Diffusion of Conflict, Integration, and Democratization*. Ann Arbor: University of Michigan Press.

Gleditsch, Kristian, and Michael Ward. 1997. "Double Take: A Reexamination of Democracy and Autocracy in Modern Politics," *Journal of Conflict Resolution* 41, 3 (June): 361–83.

Gokahle, Jaghdesh, and Kent Smetters. *Fiscal and Generational Imbalances: New Budget Measure for New Budget Priorities*. Washington, DC: American Enterprise Institute.

Gomez, E. T., and K. S. Jomo. 1997. *Malaysia's Political Economy: Politics, Patronage and Profits*. Cambridge: Cambridge University Press.

González, Marino J. 2001. "Reformas del sistema de salud en Venezuela (1987–1999): Balance y Perspectivas." Comisión Económica para America Latina (CEPAL), Serie Financiamiento del Desarrollo, No. 111. Santiago, Chile: CEPAL.

González-Rossetti, Alejandra. 2004. "Change Teams and Vested Interests: Social Security Health Reform in Mexico," in Robert R. Kaufman and Joan M. Nelson, eds. *Crucial Needs, Weak Incentives: Social Sector Reform, Democratization, and Glob-*

alization in Latin America. Washington, DC: Woodrow Wilson Center Press; Baltimore, MD: Johns Hopkins University Press.

Goodman, Roger, and Ito Peng. 1996. "The East Asian Welfare States: Peripatetic Learning, Adaptive Change, and Nation-Building," in Gøsta Esping-Andersen, ed. *Welfare States in Transition*. Thousand Oaks, CA: Sage.

Goodman, Roger, Gordon White, and Huck-Ju Kwon, eds. 1998. *The East Asian Welfare Model: Welfare Orientalism and the State*. London: Routledge.

Gopinathan, S. 1974. *Towards a National Education System 1946–1973*, Singapore: Singapore University Press.

———. 1980. "Moral Education in a Plural Society: A Singapore Case Study," *International Review of Education* 26, 2: 171–85.

———. 1991. "Education," in Ernst C. T. Chew and Edwin Lee, eds. *A History of Singapore*. Singapore: Oxford University Press.

Gough, Ian. 2001a. "Globalization and Regional Welfare Regimes: The East Asian Case," *Global Social Policy* 1, 2 (August): 163–89.

———. 2001b. "Social Welfare and Competitiveness," in Christopher Pierson and Francis G. Castles, eds. *The Welfare State: A Reader*. Cambridge: Polity Press.

Gough, Ian, and Geof Wood, eds. 2004. *Insecurity and Welfare Regimes in Asia, Africa, and Latin America: Social Policy in Development Contexts*. London: Cambridge University Press.

Gourevitch, Peter. 1986. *Politics in Hard Times: Comparative Responses to International Economic Crises*. Ithaca, NY: Cornell University Press.

Government of Malaysia, Economic Planning Unit. 2002. *Malaysia's Experience with Poverty Reduction*. Kuala Lumpur: Government of Malaysia.

Government of Poland. 1992. "Memorandum of the Government of Poland on Economic Policies," in International Monetary Fund, "Poland: Request for Stand-By Agreement, Letter of Intent," EBS/92/119 (December 22).

———. 1994. "Memorandum of the Government of Poland on Economic Policies," in International Monetary Fund, "Poland: Request for Stand-By Agreement," EBS/94/145 (July 15).

Graham, Carol. 1994. *Safety Nets, Politics and the Poor: Transition to Market Economies*. Washington, DC: Brookings Institution Press.

———. 1998. *Private Markets for Public Goods: Raising the Stakes in Economic Reform*. Washington, DC: Brookings Institution Press.

Grant, Nigel. 1969. *Society, Schools and Progress in Eastern Europe*. Oxford: Pergamon Press.

Green, David Jay, and J. Edgardo Campos. 2001. "Fiscal Lessons from the East Asian Financial Crisis," *Journal of Asian Economics* 12, 3 (Autumn): 309–29.

Greskovits, Béla 1998. *The Political Economy of Protest and Patience: East European and Latin American Transformations Compared*. Budapest: Central European University Press.

———. 2001. "Brothers-in-Arms or Rivals in Politics? Top Politicians and Top Policy Makers in the Hungarian Transformation," in János Kornai, Stephan Haggard, and Robert R. Kaufman, eds. *Reforming the State: Fiscal and Welfare Reform in Post-Socialist Countries*. New York: Cambridge University Press.

Griffith-Jones, Stephany. 1982. *The Role of Finance in the Transition to Socialism*. Lanham, MD: Rowman and Littlefield.

Grindle, Merilee S. 2004. "Interests, Institutions, and Reformers: The Politics of Education Decentralization in Mexico," in Robert R. Kaufman and Joan M. Nelson, eds. *Crucial Needs, Weak Incentives: Social Sector Reform, Democratization, and Globalization in Latin America.* Washington, DC: Woodrow Wilson Center Press; Baltimore, MD: Johns Hopkins University Press.

Grossman, Gene M., and Elhanan Helpman. 2001. *Special Interest Politics.* Cambridge, MA: MIT Press.

Grzymala-Busse, Anna. 2002. *Redeeming the Communist Past: The Regeneration of Communist Parties in East Central Europe.* New York: Cambridge University Press.

Haber, Stephen. 2005. "Development Strategy or Endogenous Process? The Industrialization of Latin America," unpublished ms., Department of Political Science, Stanford University (September).

Habermas, Jurgen. 1975. *Legitimation Crisis.* Boston: Beacon Press.

Habibi, Nader. 1994. "Budgetary Policy and Political Liberty: A Cross-Sectional Analysis," *World Development* 22, 4 (April): 579–86.

Hacker, Jacob. S. 2006. *The Great Risk Shift.* New York: Oxford University Press.

Haggard, Stephan. 1990. *Pathways from the Periphery: The Politics of Growth in the Newly Industrializing Countries.* Ithaca, NY: Cornell University Press.

———. 2000a. *The Political Economy of the Asian Financial Crisis.* Washington, DC: Institute for International Economics.

———. 2000b. "Interests, Institutions, and Policy Reform," in Anne Krueger, ed. *Economic Policy Reform: The Second Stage.* Chicago: University of Chicago Press.

———. 2005. "The Political Economy of the Asian Welfare State," in Richard Boyd and Tak-Wing Ngo, eds. *Asian States: Beyond the Developmental Perspective.* New York: Routledge.

Haggard, Stephan, and Robert R. Kaufman. 1992. "Introduction: Institutions and Economic Adjustment," in Haggard and Kaufman, eds. *The Politics of Economic Adjustment.* Princeton, NJ: Princeton University Press.

———. 1995. *The Political Economy of Democratic Transitions.* Princeton, NJ: Princeton University Press.

———. 2004. "Revising Social Contracts: Social Spending in Latin America, East Asia and the Former Socialist Countries, 1980–2000." Paper prepared for the International Studies Association Convention, Montreal (March 18–21).

Haggard, Stephan, Robert R. Kaufman, and Matthew Shugart. 2001. "Politics, Institutions, and Macroeconomic Adjustment: Hungarian Fiscal Policy Making in Comparative Perspective," in János Kornai, Stephan Haggard, and Robert R. Kaufman, eds. *Reforming the State: Fiscal and Welfare Reform in Post-Socialist Countries.* New York: Cambridge University Press.

Haggard, Stephan, and Matthew D. McCubbins, eds. 2001. *Presidents, Parliaments and Policy.* New York: Cambridge University Press.

Haggard, Stephan, and Steven B. Webb. 1993. "What Do We Know about the Political Economy of Economic Policy Reform," *World Bank Research Observer* 8, 2 (July): 143–68.

Hall, Peter A. 1986. *Governing the Economy: The Politics of State Intervention in England and France.* New York: Oxford University Press.

Hall, Peter, and David Soskice, eds. 2001. *Varieties of Capitalism: The Institutional Foundations of Comparative Advantage.* New York: Oxford University Press.

Ham, John C., Jan Svejnar, and Katherine Terrell. 1998. "Unemployment and the Social Safety Net during Transition to a Market Economy: Evidence from the Czech and Slovak Republics." *American Economic Review* 88, 5 (December): 1117–42.

Hammond, Thomas T. 1975. *The Anatomy of Communist Takeovers*. New Haven, CT: Yale University Press.

Hardy, Clarisa, ed. 2004. *Equidad y protección social: Desafíos de políticas sociales en America Latina*. Santiago: LOM Ediciones.

Hassan, Fareed M. A., and Kyle Peters, Jr. 1996. "The Structure of Incomes and Social Protection During the Transition: The Case of Bulgaria," *Europe-Asia Studies* 48, 4 (June): 629–46.

Hausner, Jerzy. 2001. "Security through Diversity: Conditions for Successful Reform of the Pension System in Poland," in Janos Kornai, Stephan Haggard, and Robert R. Kaufman, eds. *Reforming the State: Fiscal and Welfare Reform in Post-Socialist Countries*. New York: Cambridge University Press.

Heath, Roy E. 1981. "Education," in Stephen Fischer-Galati, ed. *Eastern Europe in the 1980s*. Boulder, CO: Westview Press.

Heaver, Richard. 2002. *Thailand's National Nutrition Program: Lessons in Management and Capacity Development*. Health, Nutrition and Population Discussion Paper. Washington, DC: World Bank.

Heckman, James J., and Carmen Pages. 2004. *Law and Employment: Lessons from Latin America and the Caribbean*. Chicago: University of Chicago Press.

Heimer, Franz-Wilhelm. 1975. "Education and Politics in Brazil," *Comparative Education Review* 19, 1 (February): 51–67.

Helpman, Elhanan. 2004. *The Mystery of Economic Growth*. Cambridge, MA: Belknap Press.

Hellman, Joel S. 1998. "Winners Take All: The Politics of Partial Reform in Postcommunist Transitions," *World Politics* 50, 2 (January): 203–34.

Henderson, Karen. 1994. "Divisive Political Agendas: the Case of Czechoslovakia," in Patrick Dunleavy and Jeffrey Stanyer, eds. *Contemporary Political Studies 1994: Proceedings of the Political Studies Association's 1994 Annual Conference*. Belfast: UK Political Studies Association.

Heng, Choon Leong, and Tan Siew Hoey. 1997. " Malaysia: Social Development, Poverty Reduction, and Economic Transformation," in Santosh Mehrotra and Richard Jolly, eds. *Development with a Human Face: Experiences in Social Achievement and Economic Growth*. New York: Oxford University Press.

Hewison, Kevin. 2003. "Crafting Thailand's New Social Contract," unpublished manuscript. Southeast Asia Research Centre, City University of Hong Kong.

Hicken, Allen. 2006. "Party Fabrication: Constitutional Reform and the Rise of Thai Rak Thai," *Journal of East Asian Studies* 6, 3 (September): 381–408.

Hicks, Alexander. 1999. *Social Democracy and Welfare Capitalism: A Century of Income Security Policies*. Ithaca, NY: Cornell University Press.

Hicks, Alexander M., and Duane H. Swank. 1992. Politics, Institutions, and Welfare Spending in Industrialized Democracies, 1960–82. *American Political Science Review*, 86, 3 (September): 658–74.

Hicks, Norman, and Quentin Wodon. 2000. "Economic Shocks, Safety-Nets, and Fiscal Constraints: Social Protection for the Poor in Latin America." Paper prepared for the XII Seminario Regional de Política Fiscal, Santiago, Chile (January).

Hirschman, Albert O. 1968. "The Political Economy of Import-Substituting Industrialization in Latin America," *Quarterly Journal of Economics*.82, 2 (February): 1–32.

Hirszowicz, Maria. 1986. *Coercion and Control in Communist Society: The Visible Hand of Bureaucracy*. Brighton: Wheatsheaf Books.

Hlavacka, Svätopluk, Róbert Wágner, and Annette Rieseberg 2004. *Health Care Systems in Transition: Slovakia*. Geneva: World Health Organization on behalf of the European Observatory on Health Systems and Policies.

Ho, Hing-Sho. 2005. "Taiwan's State and Social Movements under the DPP Government, 2000–2004," *Journal of East Asian Studies 5*, 3 (September–December): 401–26.

Hoffman, Barak. 2006. "Political Accountability at the Local Level in Tanzania." PhD dissertation, University of California, San Diego.

Holliday, Ian. 2000. "Productivist Welfare Capitalism: Social Policy in East Asia," *Political Studies 48*, 4 (September): 706–23.

Holliday, Ian, and Paul Wilding. 2004. *Welfare Capitalism in East Asia: Social Policy in the Tiger Economies*. New York: Palgrave MacMillan.

Holmes, Stephen, and Cass R. Sunstein.1999. *The Cost of Rights*. New York: W. W. Norton.

Hong, Per Heong. 2006. "Reframing the Development of Malaysian Healthcare Policy: From the Perspectives of Interest Groups and Institutionalism," paper presented at the Fifth Annual Malaysian Studies Conference, Universiti Putra Malaysia, Serdang, Selangor (August 8–10).

Hsiao, William C. 1995. "Medical Savings Accounts: Lessons from Singapore," *Health Affairs 14*, 2 (Summer): 260–67.

Hsiao, Hsin-Huang. 2001. "Taiwan's Social Welfare Movement Since the 1980s," in Christian Aspalter, ed. *Understanding Modern Taiwan: Essays in Economics, Politics and Social Policy*. London: Ashgate.

Huber, Evelyne. 1996. "Options for Social Policy in Latin America: Neoliberal versus Social Democratic Models," in Gøsta Esping-Andersen, ed. *Welfare States in Transition: National Adaptations in Global Economies*. London: Sage Publications.

———, ed. 2002. *Models of Capitalism: Lessons for Latin America*. College Station: Pennsylvania State University Press.

Huber, Evelyne, Thomas Mustillo, and John D. Stephens. 2004. "Determinants of Social Spending in Latin America." Paper prepared for the meeting of the Society for the Advancement of Socio-Economics, Washington, DC (July 8–11).

Huber, Evelyne, Francois Nielsen, Jenny Pribble, and John D. Stephens. 2004. "Social Spending and Inequality in Latin America and the Caribbean." Paper prepared for the meeting of the Society for the Advancement of Socio-Economics, Washington, DC (July 8–11).

Huber, Evelyne, and John D. Stephens. 2001. *Development and Crisis of the Welfare State: Parties and Policies in Global Markets*. Chicago: University of Chicago Press.

———. 2005. "State Economic and Social Policy in Global Capitalism" in Thomas Janoski, Robert Alford, Alexander M. Hicks, and Mildred Schwartz, eds. *A Handbook of Political Sociology: States, Civil Societies, and Globalization*. New York: Cambridge University Press.

Human Development Network and United Nations Development Program. 2000. *Philippine Human Development Report 2000*. Manila: Human Development Network and United Nations Development Program.

Huntington, Samuel. 1991. *The Third Wave: Democratization in the Late Twentieth Century.* Norman: University of Oklahoma Press.

Hutchcroft, Paul. 1998. *Booty Capitalism: The Politics of Banking in the Philippines.* Ithaca, NY: Cornell University Press.

———. 2003. "Paradoxes of Decentralization: The Political Dynamics behind the Passage of the 1991 Local Government Code of the Philippines," in Michael H. Nelson, ed. *The KPI Yearbook 2003.* Bangkok: King Prajadhipok's Institute.

Hwang, Gyu-Jin. 2006. *Pathways to State Welfare in Korea: Interests, Ideas, Institutions.* Aldershot: Ashgate Publishing.

Hwang, In-Won. 2003. *Personalized Politics: The Malaysian State under Mahathir.* Singapore: Institute of Southeast Asian Studies.

Iankova, Elena. 2002. *Eastern European Capitalism in the Making.* New York: Columbia University Press.

Inter-American Development Bank 2004. *Good Jobs Wanted: Labor Markets in Latin America.* Economic and Social Progress Report. Washington, DC: Inter-American Development Bank; Baltimore: Johns Hopkins University Press.

Inglot, Tomasz A. 1994. "The Communist Legacy and Post-Communist Politics of Welfare: The Origins, Evolution, and Transformation of Social Policy in Poland from the 1920s to 1993." PhD dissertation, University of Wisconsin.

———. 1995. "The Politics of Social Policy Reform in Post-Communist Poland: Government Responses to the Social Insurance Crisis During 1989–1993," *Communist and Post-Communist Studies* 28, 3 (September): 361–73.

———. 2003. "Historical Legacies, Institutions, and the Politics of Social Policy in Hungary and Poland, 1989–1999," in Grzegorz Ekiert and Stephen E. Hanson, eds. *Capitalism and Democracy in Central and Eastern Europe. Assessing the Legacy of Communist Rule.* Cambridge: Cambridge University Press.

International Labour Organization (ILO). 1998. *World Labour Report 1997–98.* Geneva: International Labour Organization.

International Labour Review. 1960. "Reports and Inquiries: Social Security Protection for Members of Farmers' Co-operatives in Eastern Europe," *International Labor Review* 81, 4 (April): 319–34.

International Monetary Fund (IMF). 2000. "Bulgaria: Selected Issues and Statistical Appendices," IMF Staff Country Report No. 00/54 (April). Washington, DC: International Monetary Fund.

———. *Government Finance Statistics Yearbook.* Washington, DC: International Monetary Fund. Various Issues.

———. *International Financial Statistics.* Washington, DC: International Monetary Fund. Various Issues.

International Social Survey Program (ISSP). 1996. "Role of Government III [Computer File]. Cologne, Germany: Zentralarchiv für empirische Sozialforschung (producer). Ann Arbor, MI. Inter-University Consortium for Political and Social Research (distributor), 1999.

Ishiyama, John. 1995. "Communist Parties in Transition: Structures, Leaders and Processes of Democratization in Eastern Europe," *Comparative Politics* 27, 2 (January): 147–66.

Iversen, Torben. 2001. "The Dynamics of Welfare State Expansion: Trade Openness, De-industrialization, and Partisan Politics," in Paul Pierson, ed. *The New Politics of the Welfare State.* New York: Oxford University Press.

———. 2005. *Capitalism, Democracy and Welfare*. New York: Cambridge University Press.

Iversen, Torben, and Thomas R. Cusack. 2000. "The Causes of Welfare State Expansion: Deindustrialization or Globalization?" *World Politics* 52, 3 (April): 313–49.

Iversen, Torben, and Anne Wren. 1998. "Equality, Employment, and Budgetary Restraint: The Trilemma of the Service Economy," *World Politics* 50, 4 (July): 507–46.

Jacoby, Wade. 2004. *The Enlargement of the European Union and NATO: Ordering from the Menu in Central Europe*. New York: Cambridge University Press.

Jervis, Robert. 1980. "The Impact of the Korean War on the Cold War," *Journal of Conflict Resolution* 24, 4 (December): 563–92.

Jesudason, James V. 1989. *Ethnicity and the Economy: The State, Chinese Business, and the Multinationals in Malaysia*. Singapore: Oxford University Press.

Jimenez, Ramon. T. 1993. "Philippines," in Stephen Deery and Richard Mitchell, eds. *Labour Law and Industrial Relations in Asia*. Melbourne: Longman Cheshire.

Johnson, Chalmers, ed. 1970. *Change in Communist Systems*. Stanford, CA: Stanford University Press.

Johnson, Simon, and Marzena Kowalska. 1994. "Poland: The Political Economy of Shock Therapy," in Stephan Haggard and Steven B. Webb, eds. *Voting for Reform: Democracy, Political Liberalization and Economic Adjustment*, 185–242. New York: Oxford University Press.

Jomo, K. S. 1986. *A Question of Class: Capital, the State, and Uneven Development in Malaysia*. Singapore: Oxford University Press.

———. 1994. *U-Turn? Malaysian Economic Development Policy after 1990*. Cairns, Australia: Centre for East and Southeast Asian Studies, James Cook University of North Queensland.

Jomo, K. S., and Lee Kwok Aun. 1999. "Social Consequences of the Economic Crisis." Unpublished ms. Bangkok: Thai Development Research Institute.

Kapstein, Ethan, and Branko Milanovic, eds. 2002. *When Markets Fail: Social Policy and Economic Reform*. New York: Russell Sage Foundation.

Karl, Terry Lynn. 1997. *The Paradox of Plenty: Oil Booms and Petro-States*. Berkeley and Los Angeles: University of California Press.

Karnow, Stanley. 1989. *In Our Image: America's Empire in the Philippines*. New York: Ballantine Books.

Kaser, Michael. 1976. *Health Care in the Soviet Union and Eastern Europe*. London: Westview Press.

Kato, Junko. 2003. *Regressive Taxation and the Welfare State: Path Dependence and Policy Diffusion*. New York: Cambridge University Press.

Katzenstein, Peter, ed. 1978. *Between Power and Plenty: Foreign Economic Policies of the Advanced Industrial States*. Madison: University of Wisconsin Press.

———. 1985. *Small States in World Markets: Industrial Policy in Europe*. Ithaca, NY: Cornell University Press.

Kaufman, Robert R. 1979. "Industrial Change and Authoritarian Rule in Latin America: A Concrete Review of the Bureaucratic-Authoritarian Model," in David Collier, ed. *The New Authoritarianism in Latin America*. Princeton, NJ: Princeton University Press.

Kaufman, Robert R., Carlos Bazdresch, and Blanca Heredia. 1994. "The Politics of the Economic Solidarity Pact in Mexico," in Stephan Haggard and Steven B. Webb, eds. *Voting for Reform*. New York: Oxford University Press.

Kaufman, Robert R., and Leo Zuckermann Behar. 1998. "Attitudes toward Economic Reform in Mexico: The Role of Political Orientations," *American Political Science Review* 92, 2 (June): 359–75.

Kaufman, Robert R., and Joan M. Nelson, eds. 2004. *Crucial Needs, Weak Incentives, The Politics of Health and Education Reform in Latin America*. Washington, DC: Woodrow Wilson Center Press; Baltimore: Johns Hopkins University Press.

Kaufman, Robert R., and Alex Segura-Ubiergo. 2001. "Globalization, Domestic Politics and Social Spending in Latin America: A Time-Series, Cross-Section Analysis 1973–1997," *World Politics* 53, 4 (July): 553–87.

Kay, Stephen J. 1999. "Unexpected Privatizations: Politics and Social Security Reform in the Southern Cone." *Comparative Politics* 31, 4 (July): 403–22.

———. 2000. "The Politics of Postponement: Political Incentives and the Sequencing of Social Security Reforms in Argentina and Uruguay." Paper presented at the Year 2000 International Research Conference on Social Security, September 25–27, Helsinki.

Keane, Michael P., and Eswar S. Prasad. 2002. "Inequality Transfers and Growth: New Evidence from the Economic Transition in Poland." Bonn: Institute for the Study of Labor Discussion, Paper No. 448 (April).

Kende, Pierre, and Zdenek Strmiska, eds. 1987. *Equality and Inequality in Eastern Europe*. Leamington Spa: Berg.

Kerkvliet, Benedict J. 1977. *The Huk Rebellion: A Study of Peasant Revolt in the Philippines*. Berkeley: University of California Press.

Kessler, Richard J. 1989. *Rebellion and Repression in the Philippines*. New Haven, CT: Yale University Press.

Kho Boo Teik. 1995. *Paradoxes of Mahathirism: An Intellectual Biography of Mahathir Mohamad*. Kuala Lumpur: Oxford University Press.

Kim, Byung-Kook. 2003. "The Politics of Chaebol Reform, 1980–1997," in Stephan Haggard, Wonhyuk Lim, and Euysung Kim, eds. *Economic Crisis and Corporate Restructuring in Korea*, 53–78. Cambridge: Cambridge University Press.

Kim, Byung-Kook, and Hyun-Chin Lim. 1999. "Labor Against Itself: A Fundamental but Contentious Labor Movement and Structural Dilemmas of State Monism," in Larry Diamond and Byung-Kook Kim, eds. *Consolidating Democracy in South Korea*, 111–38. Boulder, CO: Lynne Rienner.

Kim, So Young. 2007. "Openness, External Risk, and Volatility: Implications for the Compensation Hypothesis." *International Organization* 61, 1 (January): 181–216.

King, Gary, Robert O. Keohane, and Sidney Verba. 1994. *Designing Social Inquiry: Scientific Inference in Qualitative Research*. Princeton, NJ: Princeton University Press.

Kingstone, Peter R. 1999. *Crafting Coalitions for Reform: Business Preferences, Political Institutions, and Neoliberal Reform in Brazil*. University Park: Pennsylvania State University Press.

Kitschelt, Herbert. 1994. *The Transformation of European Social Democracy*. New York: Cambridge University Press.

————. 2001. "Partisan Competition and Welfare State Retrenchment: When Do Politicians Choose Unpopular Policies?" in Paul Pierson, ed. *The New Politics of the Welfare State*. New York: Oxford University Press.

Kitschelt, Herbert, Peter Lange, Gary Marks, and John D. Stephens, eds. 1999. *Continuity and Change in Contemporary Capitalism*. Cambridge: Cambridge University Press.

Kitschelt, Herbert, Zdenka Mansfeldova, Radoslaw Markowski, and Gabor Toka. 1999. *Post-Communist Party Systems. Competition, Representation and Inter-Party Cooperation*. New York: Cambridge University Press.

Kligman, Gail. 1998. *The Politics of Duplicity: Controlling Reproduction in Ceauşescu's Romania*. Berkeley: University of California Press.

Kohli, Atul. 2004. *State-Directed Development: Political Power and Industrialization in the Global Periphery*. New York: Cambridge University Press.

Kojima, Kiyoshi. 2000. "The 'Flying Geese' Model of Asian Economic Development: Origin, Theoretical Extensions, and Regional Policy Implications," *Journal of Asian Economics* 11, 9 (Autumn): 375–401.

Kolodko, Grzegorz W. 2000. *From Shock to Therapy: The Political Economy of Post-Socialist Transformation*. Oxford: Oxford University Press.

Koo, Hagen. 2001. *Korean Workers: The Culture and Politics of Class Formation*. Ithaca, NY: Cornell University Press.

Korea Labor Institute. 1998. *Korean Labor and Employment Laws*. Seoul: Korean Labor Institute.

Kornai, János. 1992. *The Socialist System: the Political Economy of Communism*. Princeton, NJ: Princeton University Press.

————. 2001. "The Borderline between the Spheres of Authority of the Citizen and the State: Recommendations for the Hungarian Health Reforms," in János Kornai, Stephan Haggard, and Robert R. Kaufman, eds. *Reforming the State: Fiscal and Welfare Reform in Post-Socialist Countries*, 181–209. New York: Cambridge University Press.

————. 2005. "The Great Transformation of Central Eastern Europe: Success and Disappointment." Presidential address, Fourteenth International Economic Association, World Congress, Marrakech, Morocco, http://www.colbud.hu/fellows/kornai.shtml.

Kornai, János, and Karen Eggleston. 2001. *Welfare, Choice and Solidarity in Transition: Reforming the Health Sector in Eastern Europe*. New York: Cambridge University Press.

Kornai, János, Stephan Haggard, and Robert R. Kaufman, eds. 2001. *Reforming the State: Fiscal and Welfare Reform in Post-Socialist Countries*. New York: Cambridge University Press.

Korpi, Walter. 1983. *The Democratic Class Struggle. Swedish Politics in a Comparative Perspective*. London: Routledge and Kegan Paul.

Kovács, János M. 2002. "Approaching the EU and Reaching the US? Rival Narratives on Transforming Welfare Regimes in East-Central Europe," *West European Politics* 25, 2 (April): 175–204.

Kraus, Michael. 2003. "The Czech Republic's First Decade," *Journal of Democracy* 14, 2 (April): 50–64.

Krause, Kevin Deegan. 2001. "Any Way You Slice It: The Politics of Partial Cleavages in Slovakia and the Czech Republic." Paper prepared at the American Political Science Association convention, San Francisco (August 30–September 2).

———. 2006. *Elected Affinities: Democracy and Party Competition in Slovakia and the Czech Republic*. Palo Alto, CA: Stanford University Press.

Krueger, Anne O. 1974. "The Political Economy of the Rent-Seeking Society," *American Economic Review*, 64, 3 (June): 291–303.

Krugman, Paul. 2003. "The Tax Cut Con," *New York Times Magazine*, September 14.

Ku, Yeun-wen. 1997. *Welfare Capitalism in Taiwan*. New York: St. Martin's Press.

———. 1998. "Who Will Benefit? The Planning of National Pension Insurance in Taiwan," *Public Administration and Policy* 7, 1 (March): 33–46.

———. 2002. "Towards a Taiwanese Welfare State: Demographic Change, Politics and Social Policy," in Christian Aspalter, ed. *Discovering the Welfare State in East Asia*. New York: Praeger.

Kubicek, Paul. 1999. "Organized Labor in Postcommunist States: Will the Western Sun Set on It, Too?" *Comparative Politics* 32, 1 (October): 83–102.

Kugler, Adriana D. 2004. "Determinants of Labor Demand in Colombia, 1976–1996," in James J. Heckman, and Carmen Pages, eds. *Law and Employment: Lessons from Latin America and the Caribbean*. Chicago: University of Chicago Press.

Kuhonta, Erik. 2003. "The Political Economy of Equitable Development in Thailand," *American Asian Review* 21, 4 (Winter): 69–108.

Kuhonta, Erik, and Alex Mubeti. 2007. "Thaksin's Pro-Poor Populist Programs: Rhetoric or Innovation?" Unpublished ms., Dept. of Political Science, McGill University.

Kurtz, Marcus J. 2004. "The Dilemmas of Democracy in an Open Economy: Lessons from Latin America" *World Politics*, 52, 2 (January): 262–302.

Kuruvilla, Sarosh. 1996. "Linkages between Industrialization Strategies and Industrial Relations/Human Resource Policies: Singapore, Malaysia, the Philippines and India," *Industrial and Labor Relations Review* 49, 4 (July): 635–57.

Kuruvilla, Sarosh, and Rodney Chua. 2000. "How Do Nations Increase Workforce Skills? Factors Influencing the Success of the Singapore Skills Development System," *Global Business Review*, 1,1 (February): 11–49.

Kuruvilla, Sarosh, Christopher L. Erickson, and Alvin Hwang. 2002. "An Assessment of the Singapore Skills Development System: Does it Constitute a Viable Model for Other Developing Countries?" *World Development* 30, 8 (August): 1461–76.

Kuwajima, Kyoki. 2003. "Health Sector Management and Governance in Thailand," in Shimomura Yasutami, ed. *The Role of Governance in Asia*. Singapore: Institute for Southeast Asian Studies.

Kwon, Huck-ju. 1998. "Democracy and the Politics of Social Welfare: a Comparative Analysis of Welfare Systems in East Asia," in R. Goodman, G. White, and H. J. Kwon, eds. *The East Asian Welfare Model: Welfare Orientalism and the State*. New York: Routledge.

———. 1999a. *The Welfare State in Korea: the Politics of Legitimation*. New York: St. Martin's Press.

———. 1999b. "Inadequate Policy or Operational Failure? The Potential Crisis of the Korean National Pension Program," *Social Policy & Administration* 33, 1 (March): 20–28.

Kwon, Hyeok Yong, and Jonas Pontusson. 2005. "The Rise and Fall of Government Partisanship: Dynamics of Social Spending in OECD Countries, 1962–2000." Unpublished manuscript, Department of Politics, Princeton University.

Kwon, Soonman. 2002. "Achieving Health Insurance for All: Lessons from the Republic of Korea," Extension of Social Security Paper No. 1. Geneva: International Labour Organization, Social Security and Development Branch.

———. 2003. "Pharmaceutical Reform and Physician Strikes in Korea: Separation of Drug Prescribing and Dispensing," *Social Science & Medicine* 57, 3 (August): 529–38.

Kwon, Soonman, and Michael Reich. 2005. "The Changing Process and Politics of Health Policy in Korea," *Journal of Health Politics, Policy and Law*, 30, 6 (December): 1003–25.

Labán, Raúl, and Federico Sturzenegger. 1994. "Distributional Conflict, Financial Adaptation and Delayed Stabilization," *Economics and Politics* 6, 3 (November): 257–76.

Lake, David A., and Matthew A. Baum. 2001. "The Invisible Hand of Democracy: Political Control and the Provision of Public Services," *Comparative Political Studies* 34, 6 (August): 587–621.

Lamberte, Mario B. 1986. "Social Adequacy and Economic Effects of Social Security: The Philippine Case," *ASEAN Economic Bulletin*, 3, 1 (July): 92–123.

Lampe, John R. 1986. *The Bulgarian Economy in the Twentieth Century*. London : Croom Helm.

Lane, David. 1982. *The End of Social Inequality? Class, Status and Power under State Socialism*. London: George Allen and Unwin.

Lane, Timothy, Atish Ghosh, Javier Hamann, Steven Phillips, Marianne Schulze-Ghattas, and Tsidi Tsikata. 1999. "IMF-Supported Programs in Indonesia, Korea, and Thailand: A Preliminary Assessment." Occasional Paper 178. Washington: International Monetary Fund.

Laquian, Aprodicio A., and Eleanor R. Laquian. 2002. *The Erap Tragedy: Tales from the Snake Pit*. Manila: Anvil.

Laursen, Thomas. 2001. "Pension System Viability and Reform Alternatives in the Czech Republic." International Monetary Fund Working Paper WP/00/16. Washington, DC: International Monetary Fund.

Lavigne, Marie. *The Economics of Transition: From Socialist to Market Economy*, 2nd ed. New York: St. Martin's Press.

Lee, Baldwin J., and Joseph S. Lee. 2006. "Taiwan," in William L. Keller, ed. *International Labor and Employment Laws*. Washington, DC: BNA Books.

Lee, H. K. 1999. "Globalization and the Emerging Welfare State: the Experience of South Korea," *International Journal of Social Welfare* 8, 1 (January): 23–37.

Levi, Margaret. 1988. *Of Rule and Revenue*. Berkeley: University of California Press.

Levitsky, Steven. 2001. "Organization and Labor-Based Party Adaptation: The Transformation of Argentine Peronism in Comparative Perspective," *World Politics* 54, 1 (October): 27–56.

Levitsky, Steven, and Lucan A. Way. 1998. "Between a Shock and a Hard Place: The Dynamics of Labor-Backed Adjustment in Poland and Argentina," *Comparative Politics* 30, 2 (January): 171–92.

Levitsky, Steven, and Lucan A. Way. 2002. "The Rise of Competitive Authoritiarianism," *Journal of Democracy* 13, 2 (April): 51–65.

Lewis, Arthur. 1954. "Economic Development with Unlimited Supplies of Labour." *Manchester School* 22 (May): 139–91.

Lim, Meng-Kin. 2004. "Shifting the Burden of Health Care Finance: a Case Study of Public-Private Partnership in Singapore," *Health Policy* 69, 1 (July): 83–92.

Lin, Ching-jiang. 1983. "The Republic of China (Taiwan)," in Thomas R. Murray and T. Neville Postlewaite, eds. *Schooling in East Asia: Forces of Change.* New York: Pergamon Press.

Lin, Kuo-min. 1997. "From Authoritarianism to Statism: The Politics of National Health Insurance." PhD dissertation, Yale University.

Lindbeck, Asar. 2005. "Sustainable Social Spending," CESifo Working Paper 1594 (November), http://www.cesifo-roup.de/portal/page?_pageid=36,34677&_dad =portal&_schema=PORTAL.

Lindert, Peter H. 1994. "The Rise of Social Spending, 1880–1930." *Explorations in Economic History* 31, 1 (January): 1–36.

———. 2004. *Growing Public: Social Spending and Economic Growth Since the Eighteenth Century.* Vol. 1, *The Story.* New York: Cambridge University Press.

Lindert, K., E. Skoufias, and J. Shapiro. 2006. "Redistributing Income to the Poor and the Rich: Public Transfers in Latin America and the Caribbean." World Bank Social Protection Discussion Paper No 0605. Washington, DC: World Bank.

Ling, Suet-ling, 1993. "Preferential Policies and Secondary School Attainment in Peninsular Malaysia," *Sociology of Education* 66, 4 (October): 245–61.

Linz, Juan J., and Alfred Stepan. 1996. *Problems of Democratic Transition and Consolidation: Southern Europe, South America, and Post-Communist Europe.* Baltimore, MD: Johns Hopkins University Press.

Linz, Juan. 2000. *Totalitarian and Authoritarian Regimes.* Boulder, CO: Lynne Riemer.

Lipsmeyer, Christine S. 2000. "Reading Between the Welfare Lines: Politics and Policy Structure in Post-Communist Europe," *Europe-Asia Studies* 52, 7 (November): 1191–211.

———. 2002. "Parties and Policy: Evaluating Economic and Partisan Influences on Welfare Spending During the European Post-Communist Transition," *British Journal of Political Studies* 32, 4 (October): 641–61.

———. 2003. "Welfare and the Discriminating Public: Evaluating Entitlement Attitudes in Post-Communist Europe," *Policy Studies Journal* 31, 4 (November): 545–64.

Liu, Tsai-Ching, Chin-Shyan Chen, and Li-Mei Chen. 2002. "The Impact of National Health Insurance on Neonatal Care Use and Childhood Vaccination in Taiwan," *Health Policy and Planning* 17, 4 (December): 384–92.

Lloyd-Sherlock, Peter, ed. 2000. *Healthcare Reform and Poverty in Latin America.* London: Institute of Latin American Studies.

———. 2004, "Ambitious Plans, Modest Outcomes: The Politics of Health Care Reform in Argentina," in Robert R. Kaufman and Joan M. Nelson, eds. *Crucial Needs, Weak Incentives: Social Sector Reform, Democratization, and Globalization in Latin America*, 93–124. Washington, DC: Woodrow Wilson Center Press; Baltimore, MD: Johns Hopkins University Press.

London, B., and B. A. Williams. 1990. "National Politics, International Dependency, and Basic Needs Provision: A Cross-national Analysis," *Social Forces* 69, 2 (December): 565–84.

Londoño, Juan Luis. 1995. "Poverty, Inequality and Human Capital Development in Latin America, 1950–2025," in Shahid Javed Burki, Sebastian Edwards, and Sri-Ram Ayer, eds. *Annual World Bank Conference on Development in Latin America and the Caribbea 1995: The Challenge of Reform.* Washington, DC: World Bank.

Lott, John R., Jr. 1999. "Public Schooling, Indoctrination and Totalitarianism," *Journal of Political Economy* 107, 6, pt. 2 (December): S127–S157.

Low, Linda, and T. C. Aw. 1997. *Housing a Healthy, Educated and Wealthy Nation through the CPF.* Singapore: Institute of Policy Studies.

Lowden, Pamela S. 2004. "Education Reform in Colombia: The Elusive Quest for Effectiveness," in Robert R. Kaufman and Joan M. Nelson, eds. *Crucial Needs, Weak Incentives: Social Sector Reform, Democratization, and Globalization in Latin America,* 350–75. Washington, DC: Woodrow Wilson Center Press; Baltimore, MD: Johns Hopkins University Press.

Lowenthal, Richard. 1976. "The Ruling Party in a Mature Society," in Mark G. Field, ed. *Social Consequences of Modernization in Communist Societies.* Baltimore, MD: Johns Hopkins University Press.

Lubyova, Martina, and Jan van Ours. 1997. "Unemployment Dynamics and the Restructuring of the Slovak Unemployment Benefit System," *European Economic Review* 41, 3–5 (April): 925–34.

Luna, Juan Pablo. 2006. "Frente Amplio and the Crafting of Social-Demcratic Alternatives in Uruguay." Unpublished ms. Puntificia Universidad Católica de Chile, Instituto de Ciencia Política.

Lustig, Nora, ed. 1995. *Coping with Austerity: Poverty and Inequality in Latin America,* Washington, DC: Brookings Institution.

MacIntyre, Andrew, ed. 1994. *Business and Government in Industrializing Asia.* Ithaca, NY: Cornell University Press.

———. 2003. *The Power of Institutions: Political Architecture and Governance.* Ithaca, NY: Cornell University Press.

Maddison, Angus. 2003. *The World Economy: Historical Statistics.* Paris: Organization for Economic Cooperation and Development.

Madrid, Raúl. 2003. *Retiring the State: The Politics of Pension Privatization in Latin America and Beyond.* Palo Alto, CA: Stanford University Press.

Magaloni, Beatriz. 2006. *Voting for Autocracy: Hegemonic Party Survival and its Demise in Mexico.* New York: Cambridge University Press.

Mahoney, James. 2001. *The Legacies of Liberalism: Path Dependence and Political Regimes in Central America.* Baltimore, MD: Johns Hopkins University Press.

———. 2003. "Strategies of Causal Assessment in Comparative Historical Analysis," in James Mahoney and Dietrich Rueschemeyer, eds. *Comparative Historical Analysis in the Social Sciences.* New York: Cambridge University Press.

Mahoney, James, and Dietrich Rueschemeyer, eds. 2003. *Comparative Historical Analysis in the Social Sciences.* New York: Cambridge University Press.

Mainwaring, Scott P. 1999. *Rethinking Party Systems in the Third Wave of Democratization: The Case of Brazil.* Palo Alto, CA: Stanford University Press.

Mainwaring, Scott, Daniel Brinks, and Aníbal Pérez-Liñán. 2001. "Classifying Political Regimes in Latin America, 1945–1999," *Studies in Comparative International Development* 36, 1 (Spring): 37–65.

Mainwaring, Scott, and Timothy R Scully. 1995. "Introduction: Party Systems in Latin America," in Mainwaring and Scully, eds. *Building Democratic Institutions: Party Systems in Latin America*. Palo Alto, CA: Stanford University Press.

Malloy, James M. 1979. *The Politics of Social Security in Brazil*. Pittsburgh, PA: University of Pittsburgh Press.

Maloney, William F. 2001. "Self-Employment and Labor Turnover in Developing Countries: Cross-Country Evidence" in Shanta Devarajan, F. Halsey Rogers, and Lyn Squire, eds. *World Bank Economists' Forum*. Washington, DC: World Bank.

Manasan, Rosario. 2000. "Basic Education: Improving Quality and Quantity," *PIDS Policy Notes* 2000–20 (December). Manila: Philippine Institute for Development Studies.

Manning, Nick. 2004. "Diversity and Change in Pre-Accession Central and Eastern Europe Since 1989," *Journal of European Social Policy* 14, 3 (August): 211–32.

Marée, Jörgen, and Peter P. Groenewegen. 1997. *Back to Bismarck: Eastern European Health Care Systems in Transition*. Aldershot: Avebury.

Mares, Isabela. 2001. "Firms and the Welfare State: When, Why and How Does Social Policy Matter to Employers," in Peter Hall and David Soskice, eds. *Varieties of Capitalism: The Institutional Foundations of Comparative Advantage*. New York: Oxford University Press.

———. 2004. *The Politics of Social Risk: Business and Welfare State Development*. New York: Cambridge University Press.

Marshal, Monty, and Keith Jaggers 2004. Polity IV Project. College Park MD: Center for International Development and Conflict Management, University of Maryland. http:?/www.cidem.umd.edu/polity/data (accessed May 27, 2007).

Marshall, T. H. 1965. *Class, Citizenship, and Social Development*. New York: Doubleday Anchor.

Márquez, Gustavo, and Clementina Acedo. 1994. "The Social Insurance Crisis in Venezuela," in Francisco E. Barreto de Oliveira, ed. *Social Security Systems in Latin America*. Washington, DC: Inter-American Development Bank.

Martz, John D. 1966. *Acción Democrática: Evolution of a Modern Political Party in Venezuela* Princeton, NJ: Princeton University Press.

McAdam, Doug, Sydney Tarrow, and Charles Tilly. 2001. *Dynamics of Contention*. New York: Cambridge University Press.

McCarthy, David, Olivia S. Mitchell and John Piggott. 2001. "Asset Rich and Cash Poor: Retirement Provision and Housing Policy in Singapore." Pension Research Council Working Paper 2001–10 (May). Philadelphia: Wharton School, University of Pennsylvania.

McCoy, Alfred. 1982. "The Social History of an Archipelago," in Alfred McCoy and Ed. C. de Jesus, eds. *Philippine Social History: Global Trade and Local Transformations*. Quezon City: Ateneo de Manila University Press.

McCubbins, Matthew D., Roger G. Noll, and Barry Weingast. 1989. "Structure and Process, Politics and Policy: Administrative Arrangements and the Political Control of Agencies," *Virginia Law Review* 75, 2 (March): 431–82.

McGinn, Noel F., et al. 1980. *Education and Development in Korea*. Studies in the Modernization of the Republic of Korea: 1945–1975. Cambridge, MA: Council on East Asian Studies, Harvard University, distributed by Harvard University Press.

McGuire, James W. 1999. "Labor Union Strength and Human Development in East Asia and Latin America," *Studies in Comparative International Development* 33, 4 (Winter): 3–34.

———. 2001a. "Social Policy and Mortality Decline in East Asia and Latin America," *World Development* 29, 10 (October): 1673–97.

———. 2001b. "Democracy, Social Policy, and Mortality Decline in Brazil." Paper presented at the Twenty-third International Congress of the Latin American Studies Association, Washington, DC (September 6–8).

———. 2002a. "Democracy, Social Provisioning, and Under-5 Mortality: A Cross-National Analysis." Paper presented at annual meeting of the American Political Science Association, Boston August 29–September 1.

———. 2002b. "Democracy, Social Policy and Mortality Decline in Thailand." Unpublished ms., Department of Political Science, Wesleyan University.

Medhi Krongkaew. 1982. "The Distribution of and Access to Basic Health Services in Thailand," in Peter Richards, ed. *Basic Needs and Government Policies in Thailand*. Singapore: Maruzen Asia.

Medici, André. 2004. "The Political Economy of Reform in Brazil's Civil Servant Pension Scheme," Sustainable Development Department. Washington, DC: Inter-American Development Bank.

Meerman, Jacob. 1979. "Public Services for Basic Needs in Malaysia," *World Development* 7, 6 (June): 615–634.

Melo, Marcus André. 2004. "The Politics of 'Hard-Wiring': Social Policy and the Transformation of Brazilian Federalism." Paper presented at the Latin American Studies Association meeting, Las Vegas (5–7 October).

Meltzer, A., and S. Richard. 1981. "A Rational Theory of the Size of Government," *Journal of Political Economy* 89, 5 (October): 914–27.

Menil, Georges de, and Eytan Sheshinski. 2002. "Romania's Pension Reform: From Crisis to Reform," in Martin Feldstein and Horst Siebert, eds. *Social Security Pension Reform in Europe*. Chicago: University of Chicago Press.

Mesa-Lago, Carmelo. 1978. *Social Security in Latin America: Pressure Groups, Stratification, and Inequality*. Pittsburgh, PA: University of Pittsburgh Press.

———. 1989. *Ascent to Bankruptcy: Financing Social Security in Latin America*. Pittsburgh, PA: University of Pittsburgh Press.

———. 2000. "Desarrollo social, reform del estado y de la seguridad social, al umbral del siglo XXI." Comisión Económica para América Latina (CEPAL), Division de Desarrollo Social, Serie Políticas Socials, No. 36. LC/L 1249-P.

———. 2004. "Las reformas de pensiones en América Latina y su impacto en los principios de la seguridad social." Comisión Económica para América Latina (CEPAL), Serie Financiamento de Desarrollo. Proyecto CEPAL/GTZ, "Desarrollo y equidad social en América Latina y el Caribe." No. 144. LC/L 2090-P.

———. 2005. "Evaluation of a Quarter Century of Structural Pension Reforms in Latin America," in Carlin A. Crabbe, ed. *A Quarter Century of Pension Reform in Latin America and the Caribbean: Lessons Learned and Next Steps*. Washington, DC: Inter-American Development Bank.

Mesa-Lago, Carmelo, and Mariela Arenas. 1998. "Social Security in Venezuela: Diagnosis and Reform," in Maria Ampara Cruz-Saco Oyague and Carmelo Mesa-Lago, eds. *Do Options Exist?: The Reform of Pension and Health Care Systems in Latin America*. Pittsburgh, PA: University of Pittsburgh Press.

Mieczkowski, Bogdan. 1978. "The Relationship between Changes in Consumption and Politics in Poland," *Soviet Studies* 30, 2 (April): 262–69.

Mihalyi, Peter. 2000. "Post-Socialist Health Systems in Transition: Czech Republic, Hungary and Poland." Budapest: Central European University Department of Economics, Working Paper, WP4/2000.

———. 2004. "HMO Experiment in Hungary: A Unique Road to Health Care Reform." Unpublished manuscript, Central European University, Department of Economics.

Milanovic, Branko. 1994. "Cash Social Transfers, Direct Taxes, and Income Distribution in Late Socialism," *Journal of Comparative Economics* 18, 2 (April): 175–97.

———. 1995. "Poverty, Inequality, and Social Policy in Transition Economies." World Bank Policy Research Working Paper No. 1530 (November). Washington, DC: World Bank.

———. 1998. *Income, Inequality and Poverty during the Transition from Planned to Market Economy*. Washington, DC: The World Bank.

Milesi-Ferretti, Gian Maria, Roberto Perotti, and Massimo Rostagno. 2002. "Electoral Systems and Public Spending," *Quarterly Journal of Economics* 117, 2 (May): 609–57.

Millard, Frances. 1992. "Social Policy in Poland," in Bob Deacon, ed. *The New Eastern Europe: Social Policy Past, Present and Future*. London: Sage Publications.

Mills, Anne. 1991. "Exempting the Poor: The Experience of Thailand." *Social Science and Medicine* 33, 11: 1241–52.

Minassian, Garabed. 1998. "The Road to Economic Disaster in Bulgaria," *Europe-Asia Studies* 50, 2 (March): 331–49.

Mingat, Alain. 1998. "The Strategy Used by High-Performing Asian Economies in Education: Some Lessons for Developing Countries," *World Development*, 26, 4 (April): 695–715.

Mishra, Ramesh. 1999. *Globalization and the Welfare State*. Northampton, MA: Edward Elgar Publishing.

Molinar Horcasitas, Juan, and Jeffrey A. Weldon 1994. "Electoral Determinants and Consequences of National Solidarity," in Wayne A. Cornelius, Ann L. Craig, and Jonathon Fox, eds. *Transforming State-Society Relations in Mexico: The National Solidarity Strategy*. La Jolla: Center for US-Mexican Studies.

Monaldi, Francisco, Rosa Amelia González-Pacheco, Richard Obuchi, and Michael Penfold. 2006. "Political Institutions, Policy Making Processes and Policy Outcomes in Venezuela," Latin American Research Network of the Inter-American Development Bank, Research Network Working Paper R-507 (January), http://idbdocs.iadb.org/wsdocs/getdocument.aspx?docnum=844402, accessed November 6, 2007.

Montero, Sary, and Manuel Barahona. 2003. "La Estrategia de lucha contra la pobreza en Costa Rica: Institucionalidad, finaciamento, políticas, programas. Comisión Económica para América Latina y el Caribe (CEPAL), División de Desarrollo Social, Serie Políticas Sociales, No.77. LC/L 2009-P.

Moon, Bruce E., and William J. Dixon. 1985. "Politics, the State, and Basic Human Needs: A Cross-National Study," *American Journal of Political Science*, 29, 4 (November): 661–94.

Moon, Chung-in, and Jae-jin Yang. 2002. "The Kim Dae Jung Government and Productive Welfare Initiative: Ideals and Reality," in Chung-in Moon and David Steinberg, eds. *Korea in Transition: Three Years under the Kim Dae Jung Government*. Seoul: Yonsei University Press.

Moon, Hyungpo. 2001. "The Korean Pension System: Present and Future," Korean Development Institute Working Paper 2001–1 (March). Seoul: Korea Development Institute.

Moore, David. 2005. "Slovakia's Tax and Welfare Reforms," International Monetary Fund Working Paper WP/05/133. Washington, DC: International Monetary Fund.

Morley, Samuel A. 1995. *Poverty and Inequality in Latin America: The Impact of Adjustment and Recovery in the 1980s,* Baltimore, MD: Johns Hopkins University Press.

Morley, Samuel A., and David Coady. 2003. *From Social Assistance to Social Development: Targeted Education Subsidies in Developing Countries.* Washington, DC: Center for Global Development, International Food Policy Research Institute (September).

Morrison, Christian. 1984. "Income Distribution in Eastern European and Western Countries," *Journal of Comparative Economics* 8, 2 (June): 121–38.

Mostajo, Rossana. 2000. "Gasto social y distribución del ingreso: Caracterización e impacto redistributivo en paises seleccionados de américa latina y el caribe," Comisión Económica para América Latina y el Caribe (CEPAL), Serie Reformas Economicas No. 69.

Müller, Katharina. 1999. *The Political Economy of Pension Reform in Central-Eastern Europe.* Northampton, MA: Edward Elgar.

———. 2002a. "Privatizing Old-Age Security: Latin America and Eastern Europe Compared." Research Report, Frankfurt Institute for Transformation Studies, Frankfurt.

———. 2002b. "Beyond Privatization: Pension Reform in the Czech Republic and Slovenia," *Journal of European Social Policy* 12, 4: 293–306.

Mulligan, Casey, Ricard Gil, and Xavier Sala-i-Martin. 2003. "Do Democracies Have Different Public Policies than Nondemocracies?" *Journal of Economic Perspectives*, 18, 1 (Winter): 51–74.

Murillo, Maria Victoria. 2000. "From Populism to Neoliberalism: Labor Unions and Market Reforms in Latin America," *World Politics* 52, 2 (January): 135–74.

———. 2001. *Labor Unions, Partisan Coalitions, and Market Reforms in Latin America.* New York: Cambridge University Press.

Murray, Charles. 1984. *Losing Ground: American Social Policy, 1950–1980.* New York: Basic Books.

Muscat, Robert J. 1994. *The Fifth Tiger: A Study of Thai Development Policy.* Armonk, NY: M. E. Sharpe.

Naim, Moisés. 1993. *Paper Tigers and Minotaurs: The Politics of Venezuela's Economic Reforms.* Washington, DC: Carnegie Endowment for International Peace.

———. 1995. "Latin America: the Second Stage of Reform," in Larry Diamond and Mark Plattner, eds. *Economic Reform and Democracy.* Baltimore: Johns Hopkins University Press.

Nelson, Daniel N. 1988. *Romanian Politics in the Ceauşeşcu Era.* New York: Gordon and Breach Science Publishers.

———. 1995. *After Authoritarianism: Democracy or Disorder?* Westport, CT: Greenwood Press.

Nelson, Joan M. 1990. "Introduction," in Joan Nelson, ed. *Economic Crisis and Policy Choice.* Princeton, NJ: Princeton University Press.

———. 1992. "Poverty, Equity and the Politics of Adjustment," in Stephan Haggard and Robert Kaufman, eds. *The Politics of Adjustment: International Constraints, Distributive Conflicts and the State.* Princeton, NJ: Princeton University Press.

———. 1998. "The Political Economy of Colombia's Health Reforms of 1993." Paper presented at the Inter-American Development Bank/International Development Research Centre Research Program on Processes of Economic Reform in Education and Health: Design, Implementation, and Interest Groups (June 26).

———. 2001. "The Politics of Pension and Health-Care Reform in Hungary and Poland," in János Kornai, Stephan Haggard, and Robert R. Kaufman, eds. *Reforming the State: Fiscal and Welfare Reform in Post-Socialist Countries.* New York: Cambridge University Press.

———. 2004. The Politics of Health Sector Reform: Cross-National Comparisons," in Robert R. Kaufman and Joan M. Nelson, eds. *Crucial Needs, Weak Incentives: Social Sector Reform, Democratization, and Globalization in Latin America.* Washington, DC: Woodrow Wilson Center Press; Baltimore, MD: Johns Hopkins University Press.

———. 2005 "External Models, International Influence, and the Politics of Social Sector Reforms, in Kurt Weyland, ed. *Learning from Foreign Models in Latin American Policy Reforms.* Washington, DC: Woodrow Wilson Center Press; Baltimore: Johns Hopkins University Press.

Nelson, Michael. 2001. "Thailand: Problems with Decentralization?" in Michael Nelson, ed. *Thailand's New Politics.* KPI Yearbook 2001. Bangkok: King Prajadhipok's Institute.

Nicolov, Boyko, et al. 2004. "Understanding Reform: A Country Study for Bulgaria." Global Development Network Southeast Europe (GDN-SEE). Sofia: Centre for Economic and Strategic Research.

Niwat Kanjanaphoomin. 2004. "Pension Fund, Provident Fund and Social Security System in Thailand." Paper presented at conference on Pensions in Asia: Incentives, Compliance and Their Role in Retirement, Hitotsubashi University, February 23–24.

Noble, Lela Garner. 1986. "Politics in the Marcos Era," in John Bresnan, ed. *Crisis in the Philippines: The Marcos Era and Beyond.* Princeton, NJ: Princeton University Press.

Noncheva, Teodora. 1999. *Social Policy Aspects of Bulgaria's EU Accession.* Sofia: Center for the Study of Democracy.

Nooruddin, Irfan, and Joel W. Simmons. 2006a. "Openness and the Political Economy of Government Spending." Paper presented at the annual meeting of the International Studies Association, San Diego, March 22.

———. 2006b. "The Politics of Hard Choices: IMF Programs and Government Spending," *International Organization*, 60, 4 (October): 1001–33.

Nussbaum, Martha, and Amartya Sen, eds. 1993. *The Quality of Life*. New York: Oxford University Press.

O'Connnor, James. 1973. *The Fiscal Crisis of the State*. New York: St. Martin's Press.

O'Donnell, Guillermo A. 1971. *Modernization and Bureaucratic-Authoritarianism: Studies in South American Politics*, Institute of International Studies Politics of Modernization Series, no. 9. Berkeley: University of California.

OECD (Organization for Economic Cooperation and Development). 2004. *Economic Survey of Poland, 2004*. Paris: OECD.

———. 2005. *Economic Survey of Hungary, 2005*. Paris: OECD.

Olson, Mancur. 1982. *The Rise and Decline of Nations: Economic Growth, Stagflation, and Social Rigidities*. New Haven, CT: Yale University Press.

O'Neil, Shannon. 2006. "Un-Privatizing Pensions? The Dynamic Policy Effects of Social Security Reform in the Short, Medium and Long Term." paper presented at the American Political Science Association Conference, Philadelphia, PA, August 31st–September 3rd.

Orenstein, Mitchell A. 2000. "How Politics and Institutions Affect Pension Reform in Three Postcommunist Countries." World Bank Policy Research Working Paper No. 2310. Washington, DC: World Bank.

———. 2001. *Out of the Red: Building Capitalism and Democracy in Postcommunist Europe*. Ann Arbor: University of Michigan Press.

———. 2006. *Transnational Politics and the New Pension Reforms*. Unpublished ms., Syracuse University, Department of Political Science.

Orenstein, Mitchell A., and Martine R. Haas. 2003. "Globalization and the Development of Welfare States in Postcommunist Europe," paper presented at the annual meeting of the American Political Science Association, Philadelphia (August 28–31).

Orenstein, Mitchell A., and Erika Wilkens. 2001. "Central and East European Labor Market Institutions in Comparative Perspective." Paper presented at the annual meeting of the American Political Science Association, San Francisco (August 29–September 2).

Ortega, Daniel, and Michael Penfold-Becerra. 2006. "Does Clientelism Work: Electoral Returns of Public and Excludable Goods in Chavez's Misiones Programs in Venezuela." Unpublished paper, Instituto de Estudios Superiores de Administración, Caracas, Venezuela.

Ost, David. 2000. "Illusory Corporatism in Eastern Europe: Neoliberal Tripartism and Postcommunist Identities," *Politics and Society* 28, 4 (December): 503–30.

Ovseiko, Pavel. 2002. "Challenge for Effective Health Sector Governance in Hungary: Co-Operation between the Medical Profession and Government." Open Society Institute: Center for Policy Studies, International Policy Fellowships, Public Health Working Paper No. 2002–02, http://www.policy.hu/ovseiko, accessed November 6, 2007.

Paes de Barros, Ricardo, and Carlos Henrique Corseuil, 2004. "The Impact of Regulation on Brazilian Labor Market Performance," in James J. Heckman and Carmen

Pages, eds. *Law and Employment: Lessons from Latin America and the Caribbean.* Chicago: University of Chicago Press.

Palacios, Robert, and Montserrat Pallares-Miralles. 2000. International Patterns of Pension Provision. Social Protection Discussion Paper, no. 9 (April). Washington, DC: World Bank.

Pampel, Fred C., and John B. Williamson. 1989. *Age, Class, Politics and the Welfare State.* New York: Cambridge University Press.

Papadópoulos, Jorge. 1998. "The Pension System in Uruguay: A Delayed Reform," in Maria Amparo Cruz-Saco Oyague and Carmelo Mesa-Lago, eds. *Do Options Exist?: The Reform of Pension and Health Care Systems in Latin America.* Pittsburgh, PA: University of Pittsburgh Press.

Pârvulescu, Sorana. 2004. "2004 Romanian Elections: Test Case for a True Romanian Democracy," *Romanian Journal of Political Science* 4, 2 (Winter): 7–28.

Pastor, Manuel, Jr., and Carol Wise. 1999. "The Politics of Second-Generation Reform," *Journal of Democracy* 10, 3 (July): 3–48.

———. 2004, "Picking Up the Pieces: Comparing the Social Impacts of Financial Crisis in Mexico and Argentina." Paper presented at the meetings of the International Studies Association, Montreal, March 17–21.

Pasuk Phongpaichit and Chris Baker. 2003. *Thaksin: the Business of Politics in Thailand.* Chiang Mai: Silkworm Books.

Pauly, Mark V. 2001. "Medical Savings Accounts in Singapore: What Can We Know?" *Journal of Health Politics, Policy and Law* 26, 4 (August): 727–31.

Pawadee, T. 1986. "Social Security for the Thai People," *ASEAN Economic Bulletin,* 3,1 (July): 145–56.

Pazitny, Peter, and Rudolf Zajac. 2005. "Health Care Reform in Slovak Republic." Policy Brief no. 9 William Davidson Institute, University of Michigan, http://wdi.umich.edu/Publications/PolicyBriefs/, accessed May 2, 2006.

Penfold-Becerra, Michael. 2004. "Electoral Dynamics and Decentralization in Venezuela," in Alfred Montero and David Samuels, eds. *Decentralization and Democracy in Latin America.* Notre Dame, IN: University of Notre Dame Press.

———. 2005. "Social Funds, Clientelism and Redistribution: Chavez's 'Misiones' Programs in Comparative Perspective." Caracas, Venezuela: Instituto de Estudios Superiores de Administracion (IESA) (November).

Persson, Torsten, and Guido Tabellini. 1999. "The Size and Scope of Government: Comparative Politics with Rational Politicians," *European Economic Review,* 43, 4–6 (April): 699–735.

———. 2000. *Political Economics: Explaining Economic Policy.* Cambridge, MA: MIT Press.

———. 2003. *The Economic Effects of Constitutions.* Cambridge, MA: MIT Press

Pierson, Paul. 1994. *Dismantling the Welfare State? Reagan, Thatcher and the Politics of Retrenchment.* New York: Cambridge University Press.

———. 1996. "The New Politics of the Welfare State," *World Politics* 48, 2 (January): 143–79.

———. 2000. "Increasing Returns, Path Dependence, and the Study of Politics," *American Political Science Review* 94, 2 (June): 251–67.

———. 2001a. "Coping with Permanent Austerity," in Paul Pierson, ed. *The New Politics of the Welfare State.* New York: Oxford University Press.

———. ed. 2001b. *The New Politics of the Welfare State*. New York: Oxford University Press.

———. 2004. *Politics in Time: History, Institutions, and Social Analysis*. Princeton, NJ: Princeton University Press.

Pineda, Virginia S. 2001. "Impact of the East Asian Financial Crisis on Social Services Financing and Delivery," in Mario B. Lamberte et al., eds. *Economic Crisis-Once More*. Makati City: Philippine Institute for Development Studies.

Pinheiro, Vinícius C. 2005. "The Politics of Pension Reform in Brazil," in Caroline A. Crabbe, ed. *A Quarter Century of Pension Reform in Latin America and the Caribbean: Lessons Learned and Next Steps*. Washington, DC: Inter-American Development Bank.

Pong, Suet-ling. 1993. "Preferential Policies and Secondary School Attainment in Peninsular Malaysia," *Sociology of Education* 66, 4 (October): 245–61.

Pontusson, Jonas. 2005. *Inequality and Prosperity: Social Europe vs. Liberal America*. Ithaca, NY: Cornell University Press.

Porket, J. L. 1979. "Old-Age Pension Schemes in the Soviet Union and Eastern Europe," *Social Policy and Administration* 13, 1 (Spring): 22–37.

———. 1982. "Retired Workers under Soviet-type Socialism," *Social Policy and Administration* 16, 3 (Autumn): 253–69.

Potůček, Martin. 2001. "Czech Social Reform after 1989: Concepts and Reality," *International Social Security Review* 54, 2 and 3 (April and September): 81–106.

———. 2004. "Accession and Social Policy: the Case of the Czech Republic," *Journal of European Social Policy* 14, 3 (August): 253–66.

Powell, John Duncan 1971. *The Political Mobilization of the Venezuelan Peasant*. Cambridge, MA: Harvard University Press.

Poznanski, Kazimierz Z. 1997. *Poland's Protracted Transition: Institutional Change and Economic Growth. 1970–1994*. New York: Cambridge University Press.

Pravda, Alex, and Blair Ruble, eds. 1986. *Trade Unions in Communist States*. Boston: Allen and Unwin.

Preker, Alexander S., and Richard G. A. Feachem. 1994. "Policy Design and Implementation. Health and Health Care," in *Labor Market and Social Policy in Central and Eastern Europe: The Transition and Beyond*. New York: Oxford University Press.

Pritchett, Lant. 2001. "Where Has All the Education Gone?" *World Bank Economic Review* 15, 3: 367–391.

———. 2004. "Does Learning to Add Up Add Up? The Returns to Schooling in Aggregate Data," Bureau for Research in Economic Analysis and Development (BREAD) Working Paper No. 53. Cambridge, MA: BREAD.

Prud'homme, Remy. 1995. "On the Dangers of Decentralization," *World Bank Research Observer* 10, 2 (August): 201–20.

Przeworski, Adam. 1985. *Capitalism and Social Democracy*. New York: Cambridge University Press.

———. 1991. *Democracy and the Market: Political and Economic Reforms in Latin America and Eastern Europe*. Cambridge: Cambridge University Press.

———. 2003. *States and Markets: A Primer in Political Economy*. New York: Cambridge University Press.

———. 2004. "Institutions Matter?" *Government and Opposition* 39, 2 (Spring): 527–40.

Przeworski, Adam, Michael A. Alvarez, Jose Antonio Cheibub, and Fernando Limongi. 2000. *Democracy and Development: Political Institutions and Well-Being in the World, 1950–1990.* New York: Cambridge University Press.

Public Opinion Research Center (CBOS). 2002. "The Economic Implications of the Access to the European Union: The Opinions of Respondents From Selected Candidate Countries." *Public Opinion Research Report* No. 10 (January), www.cbos.com.pl, accessed May 2, 2006.

Putzel, James. 1992. *A Captive Land: the Politics of Agrarian Reform in the Philippines.* New York: Monthly Review Press.

Raczynski, Dagmar. 2000. "Overcoming Poverty in Chile," in Joseph S. Tulchin and Allison M. Garland, eds. *Social Development in Latin America.* Boulder, CO: Lynne Reiner.

Ramesh, M. 2000. With Mukul G. Asher. *Welfare Capitalism in Southeast Asia: Social Security, Health and Education Policies.* New York: St. Martin's Press.

———. 2003. "Health Policy in the Asian NIEs," *Social Policy and Administration,* 37, 4 (August): 361–75.

———. 2004. *Social Policy in East and South East Asia: Education, Health, Housing and Income Maintenance.* New York: Routledge Curzon.

———. 2007. "Reasserting the Role of the State in the Healthcare Sector: Lessons from Asia." Paper presented at the conference on The Role of the State in Public Service Delivery, Lee Kuan Yew School of Public Policy, National University of Singapore, September 27–28.

Ramesh, M., and Ian Holliday. 2001. "The Health Care Miracle in East and Southeast Asia: Activist State Provision in Hong Kong, Malaysia and Singapore," *Journal of Social Policy* 30, 4 (October): 637–51.

Ramírez, Patricia. 2004. "A Sweeping Health Reform: The Quest for Unification, Coverage, and Efficiency in Colombia," in Robert R. Kaufman and Joan M. Nelson, eds. *Crucial Needs, Weak Incentives: Social Sector Reform, Democratization, and Globalization in Latin America.* Washington, DC: Woodrow Wilson Center Press; Baltimore, MD: Johns Hopkins University Press.

Ramos, Elias T. 1990. *Dualistic Unionism and Industrial Relations.* Quezon City, Philippines: New Day.

Ravallion, Martin. 2000. "Are the Poor Protected From Budget Cuts? Theory and Evidence for Argentina." World Bank Policy Research Working Paper No. 2391. Washington, DC: World Bank.

Reinecke, Gerhard. 1993. "Social Security in Thailand: Political Decisions and Distributional Impact," *Crossroads* 8, 1: 78–115.

Remmer, Karen L. 1989. *Military Rule in Latin America.* Boston: Unwin Hyman.

———. 2002. "The Politics of Economic Policy and Performance in Latin America," *Journal of Public Policy* 22, 1 (January–April): 29–59.

Republic of China. *Taiwan Statistical Data Book.* Taipei: Council for Economic Planning and Development. Various Issues.

Republic of the Philippines. *Philippine Statistical Yearbook.* Manila: National Economic and Development Authority. Various Issues.

Reyes, Celia M. 2002. *The Poverty Fight: Have We Made an Impact?* PIDS Discussion Paper Series No. 2002–20. Manila: Philippine Institute of Development Studies.

Riedinger, Jeffrey M. 1995. *Agrarian Reform in the Philippines: Democratic Transitions and Redistributive Reform*. Palo Alto, CA: Stanford University Press.

Rigger, Shelley. 2001. *From Opposition to Power: Taiwan's Democratic Progressive Party*. Boulder, CO: Lynne Rienner.

Ritchie, Bryan K. 2001. "The Political Economy of Technical Intellectual Capital Formation in Southeast Asia." PhD dissertation, Emory University.

———. 2005. "Progress through Setback or Mired in Mediocrity? Crisis and Institutional Change in Southeast Asia," *Journal of East Asian Studies*, 5, 2 (May–August): 273–314.

Roberts, Kenneth. 1995. "Neoliberalism and the Transformation of Populism in Latin America: The Peruvian Case," *World Politics* 48, 1 (October): 82–126.

———. 2006. "Changing Course: Parties, Populism, and Political Representation in Latin America's Neoliberal Era." Unpublished ms., Cornell University, Department of Government.

Roberts, Kenneth, and Moisés Arce. 1998. "Neoliberalism and Lower Class Voting Behavior in Peru," *Comparative Political Studies* 31, 2 (April): 217–46.

Roberts, Kevin. 1977. "Voting Over Income Tax Schedules," *Journal of Public Economics* 8, 3 (December): 329–40.

Rock, David. 1985. *Argentina, 1516–1982: From Spanish Colonization to the Falklands War*. Berkeley: University of California Press.

Rodan, Garry. 1989. *The Political Economy of Singapore's Industrialization: National State and International Capital*. New York: Palgrave Macmillan.

Rodrik, Dani. 1994. "The Rush to Free Trade in the Developing World: Why So Late? Why Now? Will It Last?" in Stephan Haggard and Steven B. Webb, eds. *Voting for Reform: Democracy, Political Liberalization, and Economic Adjustment*. New York: Oxford University Press.

———. 1996. "Understanding Economic Policy Reform," *Journal of Economic Literature* 34 (March): 9–41.

———. 1997. *Has Globalization Gone Too Far?* Washington, DC: Institute for International Economics.

———. 1998. "Why Do More Open Economies Have Bigger Governments?" *Journal of Political Economy* 106, 5 (October): 997–1032.

———. 2003. "Growth Strategies." Unpublished ms., Kennedy School of Government, Harvard Univeristy.

Roeder, Philip. 2001. "Ethnolinguistic Fractionalization (ELF) Indices, 1961 and 1985," February 16, http//:weber.ucsd.edu\~proeder\elf.htm, accessed data May 27, 2007.

Roemer, Milton. 1991. *National Health Systems of the World*. Vol. 1, *The Countries*. New York: Oxford University Press.

Rojas, Armando León. N.d. "Pensiones: La revolución debe continuar," http://www.ucla.edu.ve/dac/investigaci%C3%B3n/compendium7/Pensiones.htm.

Roland, Gerard. 2000. *Transition and Economics: Politics, Markets, and Firms*, Cambridge, MA: MIT Press.

Romer, Thomas.1975. "Individual Welfare, Majority Voting, and the Properties of a Linear Income Tax," *Journal of Public Economics* 4, 1 (February): 163–85.

Ronnas, Per. 1989. "Turning the Romanian Peasant into a New Socialist Man: An Assessment of Rural Development Policy in Romania," *Soviet Studies* 41, 4 (October): 543–59.

Rosenberg, Mark B. 1979. "Social Security Policymaking in Costa Rica: A Research Report," *Latin American Research Review* 14, 1: 116–33.

Ross, Michael. 1999. "The Political Economy of the Resource Curse," *World Politics* 51, 2 (January): 297–322.

———. 2005. "Is Democracy Good for the Poor?" Unpublished ms, Department. of Political Science University of California, Los Angeles.

Rothschild, Joseph. 1975. *East Central Europe between the Two World Wars.* Seattle: University of Washington Press.

———. 1989. *Return to Diversity: A Political History of East Central Europe Since World War II.* New York: Oxford University Press.

Roubini, Nouriel. 1991. "Economic and Political Determinants of Budget Deficits in Developing Countries," *Journal of International Money and Finance* 10, 1 (March): S49–S72.

Roubini, Nouriel, and Jeffrey D. Sachs. 1989. "Political and Economic Determinants of the Budget Deficits in the Industrial Democracies," *European Economic Review* 33, 5 (May): 903–38.

Rudra, Nita. 2002. "Globalization and the Decline of the Welfare State in Less-Developed Countries," *International Organization* 56, 2 (Spring): 411–45.

———. 2007. "Welfare States in Developing Countries: Unique or Universal?" *Journal of Politics* 69, 2 (May) 378–96.

Rudra, Nita, and Stephan Haggard. 2005. "Globalization, Democracy, and Effective Social Spending in the Developing World," *Comparative Political Studies* 38, 9 (November): 1–35.

Rueschemeyer, Dietrich, Evelyne Huber Stephens, and John Stephens. 1992. *Capitalist Development and Democracy.* Chicago: University of Chicago Press.

Ruggie, John Gerard. 1982. "International Regimes, Transactions, and Change: Embedded Liberalism in the Postwar Economic Order," *International Organization,* 36, 2 (Spring): 379–415.

Saavedra, Jaime, and Maximo Torero. 2004. "Labor Market Reform and Their Impact over Formal Labor Demand and Job Market Turnover: The Case of Peru," in James J. Heckman and Carmen Pages, eds. *Law and Employment: Lessons from Latin America and the Caribbean.* Chicago: University of Chicago Press.

Schamis, Hector E. 1999. "Distributional Coalitions and the Politics of Economic Reform in Latin America," *World Politics* 51, 2 (January): 236–68.

Scharpf, Fritz W., and Vivien A. Schmidt, eds. 2000. *Welfare and Work in the Open Economy.* 2 vols. London: Oxford: Oxford University Press.

Scheuer, Markus, and Robert J. Gitter. 2001. "The Rise in Czech Unemployment, 1998–2000," *Monthly Labor Review* 124, 5 (May), http://www.bls.gov/opub/mlr/2001/05/intlrpt.htm, accessed May 7, 2006.

Schneider, Ben. 2004. *Business, Politics and the State in Twentieth Century Latin America.* New York: Cambridge University Press.

Schonfeld, Andrew. 1965. *Modern Capitalism: The Changing Balance of Public and Private Power.* New York: Oxford University Press.

Schöpflin, George 1993. *Politics in Eastern Europe, 1945–1992*. Oxford: Blackwell.

Schwarzer, Helmut, and Ana Carolina Querino. 2002. "Non-Contributory Pensions in Brazil: The Impact on Poverty Reduction." Extension of Social Security Paper No. 11. Social Security Policy and Development Branch, International Labour Office.

Segura-Ubiergo, Alex. 2007. *The Political Economy of the Welfare State in Latin America: Globalization, Democracy, and Development*. New York: Cambridge University Press.

Sen, Amartya. 1984. *Resources, Values and Development*, Oxford: Blackwell.

———. 1999. *Development as Freedom*. London: Oxford University Press.

Seth, Michael J. 2002. *Education Fever: Society, Politics and the Pursuit of Schooling in South Korea*. Honolulu: University of Hawai'i Press and Center for Korean Studies, University of Hawai'i.

Seton-Watson, Hugh. 1956. *The East European Revolution*. New York: Praeger.

Shafir, Michael. 1985. *Romania, Politics, Economics, and Society: Political Stagnation and Simulated Change*. Boulder, CO: Lynne Rienner Publishers.

Shandra, John M., Jenna Nobles, Bruce London, and John B. Williamson. 2004. "Dependency, Democracy, and Infant Mortality," *Social Science and Medicine* 59, 2 (July): 321–33.

Sharpe, Leslie, and S. Gopinathan. 2002. "After Effectiveness: New Directions in the Singapore School System?" *Journal of Education Policy* 17, 2 (April): 151–66.

Shin, D. G. 1989. "Political Democracy and the Quality of Citizens' Lives: A Crossnational Study," *Journal of Developing Societies* 5: 30–41.

Shirk, Susan. 1993. *The Political Logic of Economic Reform in China*. Berkeley: University of California Press.

Shlapentokh, Vladimir. 2001. *A Normal Totalitarian Society: How the Soviet Union Functioned and How It Collapsed*. Armonk, NY: M. E. Sharpe.

Shopov, Georgi. 1993. "Unemployment, Poverty, Social Security: the Bulgarian Experience," Sofia: Center for the Study of Democracy, (June).

———. 2002. *The Social Dialogue in Bulgaria*. Sofia: Human Resource Development Center.

Shopov, Georgi, Teodora Noncheva, and Borislav Tafradjiyski. 2005. *The Pension Reform in Bulgaria: Bridging Social Policy Research and Policy Making*. Sofia: Club Economika 2000.

Shugart, Matthew. 1992. *Presidents and Assemblies: Constitutional Design and Electoral Dynamics*. New York: Cambridge University Press.

———. 2006. "Comparative Electoral Systems Research: The Maturation of a Field and New Challenges Ahead," in Michael Gallagher and Paul Mitchell, eds. *The Politics of Electoral Systems*. New York: Oxford University Press.

Sidel, John. 1999. *Capital, Coercion, and Crime: Bossism in the Philippines*. Palo Alto, CA: Stanford University Press.

Sikkink, Kathryn. 1991. *Ideas and Institutions: Developmentalism in Brazil and Argentina*. Ithaca, NY: Cornell University Press.

Silliman, G. Sidney, and Lela Garner Noble, eds. 1998. *Organizing for Democracy: NGOs, Civil Society, and the Philippine State*. Honolulu: University of Hawai'i Press.

Simonovits, András. 2002. "Hungarian Pension System: The Permanent Reform." Institute of Economics, Hungarian Academy of Sciences (February 25).

Simons, Thomas W. 1991. *Eastern Europe in the Postwar World*. 2nd ed. New York: St. Martin's Press.

Singh, Anoop, Agnès Belaisch, Charles Collyns, Paula De Masi, Reva Krieger, Guy Meredith, and Robert Rennhack. 2005. "Stabilization and Reform in Latin America: A Macroeconomic Perspective on the Experience Since the Early 1990s." Washington, DC: International Monetary Fund Occasional Paper No. 238, http://www.imf.org/external/pubs/ft/op/238/index.htm, accessed May 27, 2007.

Sipos, Sandor. 1994. "Income Transfers: Family Support and Poverty Relief," in Nicholas Barr, ed. *Labor Market and Social Policy in Central and Eastern Europe: The Transition and Beyond*. New York: Oxford University Press.

Siripen Supakankunti. 1997. Untitled manuscript. Takemi Program in International Health, Harvard School of Public Health, http://www.hsph.harvard.edu/takemi/RP131.pdf.

———. 2000. "Future Prospects of Voluntary Health Insurance in Thailand," *Health Policy and Planning* 15, 1 (March): 85–94.

Sitek, Michael. 2000. "Formal and Informal Institutions in the Transformation of the Polish Health Care System," in Slawomir Kapralski and Susan C. Pearce, eds. *Reformulations; Markets, Policies, and Identities in Central and Eastern Europe*, 135–57. Warsaw: IFiS Publishers.

———. 2005. "Policy Process of Health Care Regulation in Poland: Ideas, Interests and Institutions." Warsaw: Institute of Philosophy and Sociology of the Polish Academy of Science (April).

Skilling, Gordon. 1976. *Czechoslovakia's Interrupted Revolution*. Princeton, NJ: Princeton University Press.

Skocpol, Theda. 2001. *The Missing Middle: Working Families and the Future of American Social Policy*. New York: W. W. Norton.

Smith, Anthony. 1981. *The Pattern of Imperialism: The United States, Great Britain and the Late-Industrializing World since 1815*. New York: Cambridge University Press.

Smith, Michael. 2007. *Hard Times in the Land of Plenty*. Ithaca, NY: Cornell University Press.

Snodgrass, Donald R. 1980. *Inequality and Economic Development in Malaysia*. New York: Oxford University Press.

Snyder, James M., Jr., and Irene Yackovlev. 2000. "Political and Economic Determinants of Government Spending on Social Protection Programs." Unpublished ms., Department of Political Science, Massachusetts Institute of Technology (April).

Son, Annette Hye Kyung. 2001. "Taiwan's Path to National Health Insurance (1950–1995)," *International Journal of Social Welfare* 10, 1 (January): 45–53.

Song, Ho Keun. 2003. "The Birth of a Welfare State in Korea: The Unfinished Symphony of Democratization and Globalization," *Journal of East Asian Studies* 3, 3 (September): 405–32.

Sotiropoulos, Dimitri A., Ileana Neamtu, and Maya Stoyanova. 2003. "The Trajectory of Post-Communist Welfare State Development: The Cases of Bulgaria and Romania," *Social Policy and Administration* 37, 6 (December): 656–73.

Spalding, Rose J. 1980. "Welfare Policymaking: Theoretical Implications of a Mexican Case Study," *Comparative Politics* 12, 4 (July): 419–38.

Spulber, Nicolas. 1957. *The Economics of Communist Eastern Europe*. Cambridge, MA: Technology Press of the Massachusetts Institute of Technology: New York: John Wiley.

Stallings, Barbara. 1990. "Politics and Economic Crisis: A Comparative Study of Chile, Peru, and Colombia," in Joan Nelson, ed. *Economic Crisis and Policy Choice: The Politics of Adjustment in the Third World*. Princeton, NJ: Princeton University Press.

Stallings, Barbara, and Wilson Peres. 2000. *Growth, Employment and Equity: The Impact of the Economic Reforms on Latin America*. Washington, DC: Brookings Institution.

Standing, Guy. 1996. "Social Protection in Central and Eastern Europe: A Tale of Slipping Anchors and Torn Safety Nets," in Gøsta Esping-Andersen, ed. *Welfare States in Transition: National Adaptations in Global Economies*. Thousand Oaks, CA: Sage.

Stark, David, and László Bruszt. 1998. *Postsocialist Pathways: Transforming Politics and Property in East Central Europe*. New York: Cambridge University Press.

Starner, Frances Lucille. 1961. *Magsaysay and the Philippine Peasantry: The Agrarian Impact on Philippine Politics, 1953–1956*. Berkeley: University of California Press.

Stasavage, David. 2005. "Democracy and Primary Education in Africa." *American Journal of Political Science* 49, 2 (April): 343–58.

Steinmo, Sven. 1993. *Taxation and Democracy: Swedish, British and American Approaches to Finance the Modern State*. New Haven, CT: Yale University Press.

Stepan, Alfred. 1971. *The Military in Politics: Changing Patterns in Brazil*. New Haven, CT: Yale University Press.

Stephens, John. 1986. *The Transition from Capitalism to Socialism*. Urbana: University of Illinois Press.

Stephens, John, Evelyne Huber, and Leonard Ray. 1999. "The Welfare State in Hard Times," in Herbert Kitschelt, Peter Lange, Gary Marks, and John D. Stephens, eds. *Continuity and Change in Contemporary Capitalism*. Cambridge: Cambridge University Press.

Stevens, John N. 1985. *Czechoslovakia at the Crossroads: The Economic Dilemmas of Communism in Postwar Czechoslovakia*. New York: Columbia University Press.

Stiglitz, Joseph E. 2002. *Globalization and its Discontents*. New York: W. W. Norton.

Stokes, Susan C. 2001. *Mandates and Democracy: Neoliberalism by Surprise in Latin America*. Cambridge: Cambridge University Press.

Stone, Randall. 2002. *Lending Credibility: The International Monetary Fund and the Post-Communist Transition*. Princeton, NJ: Princeton University Press.

Stubbs, Richard. 1989. *Hearts and Minds in Guerilla Warfare: The Malayan Emergency 1948–1960*. New York: Oxford University Press.

Sukanya Nitungkorn. 1988. "The Problems of Secondary Education Expansion in Thailand," *Southeast Asian Studies* 26, 1 (June): 24–42.

Supasit Pannarunothai, Direk Patmasiriwat, and Samrit Srithamrongsawat. 2004. "Universal Health Coverage in Thailand: Ideas for Reform and Policy Struggling," *Health Policy* 68, 1 (April): 17–30.

Supasit Pannarunothai, Samrit Srithamrongsawat, Manit Kongpan, and Patchanee Thumvanna. 2000. "Financing Reforms for the Thai Health Card Scheme," *Health Policy and Planning* 15, 3 (September): 303–11.

Surdej, Aleksander. 2004. "The Judiciary and the Development of Employment Regulations in Poland." Paper presented at the Second Pan-European Conference of the Standing Group on EU Politics, Bologna, June 24–26.

Svorenova, Maria, and Alexandra Pretasova. 2005. "Social Protection Expenditure and Performance Review: Slovak Republic." Budapest: International Labour Office, Subregional Office for Central and Eastern Europe.

Swank, Duane. 1998. "Funding the Welfare State: Globalization and the Taxation of Business in Advanced Market Economies," *Political Studies* 46, 4 (September): 671–92.

———. 2002. *Global Capital, Political Institutions, and Policy Change in Developed Welfare States.* New York: Cambridge University Press.

Swenson, Peter A. *Capitalists against Markets: The Making of Labor Markets and Welfare States in the United States and Sweden.* New York: Oxford University Press.

Szalai, Julia, and Eva Orosz, 1992. "Social Policy in Hungary," in Bob Deacon, ed. *The New Eastern Europe: Social Policy Past, Present and Future.* London: Sage Publications.

Szelényi, Iván. 1983. *Urban Inequalities under State Socialism.* New York: Oxford University Press.

Szikra, Dorottya. 2005. "Hungarian Family and Child Support in the Light of its Historical Development." Paper presented at Conference on Fighting Poverty and Reforming Social Security: What Can Post-Soviet States Learn from the New Democracies of Central Europe? Woodrow Wilson International Center for Scholars, Washington, DC, June 10.

Szurek, Jean-Charles. 1987. "Family Farms in Polish Agricultural Policy: 1945–1985," *East European Politics and Societies* 1, 2 (March): 225–54.

Tafradjiyski, Borislav, Pobeda Loukanova, George Shopov, and Dochka Staykova. 2002. "The Pension Reform in Bulgaria: Two Years After the Start." Paper presented at the International Workshop on Population, Labor Market, Pension and Quality of Life in Transitional Countries, Kunitachi, Tokyo (February 23).

Tan, Jee-Peng, and Alain Mingat. 1992. *Education in Asia: A Comparative Study of Cost and Financing.* Washington, DC: World Bank.

Tan, Peng Boo. 1997. "Human Resource Development for Continued Economic Growth: The Singapore Experience." Paper presented at the ILO Workshop on Employers' Organizations in Asia-Pacific in the Twenty-First Century Turin, Italy, May 5–13.

Tang, Kwong-Leung. 2000. *Social Welfare Development in East Asia.* New York: Palgrave.

Tanzi, Vito, and Ludger Schucknecht. 2000. *Public Spending in the 20th Century: A Global Perspective.* New York: Cambridge University Press.

Taylor, Lance. 1990. "Real and Money Wages, Output and Inflation in the Semi-Industrialized World," *Economica,* n.s., 57, 227 (August): 329–53.

Teichova, Alice. 1988. *The Czechoslovak Economy, 1918–1980.* London: Routledge.

Tendler, Judith. 2000. "Safety Nets and Social Delivery: What Are Social Funds Really Telling Us?" in Joseph S. Tulchin and Allison M. Garland, eds. *Social Development in Latin America.* Boulder, CO: Lynne Reiner.

Terrell, Katherine, and Vit Sorm. 1999. "Labor Market Policies and Unemployment in the Czech Republic," *Journal of Comparative Economics* 27, 1 (March): 33–60.

Thelen, Kathy. 2004. *How Institutions Evolve: The Political Economy of Skills in Germany, Britain, the United States and Japan*. New York: Cambridge University Press.

Thillainathan, R. 2004. "Malaysia: Pension and Financial Market Reforms and Key Issues on Governance." Paper presented at for International Conference on Pensions in Asia: Incentives, Compliance and Their Role in Retirement, Hitotsubashi University, Tokyo, Japan (23–24 February).

Thomas, Vinod, Yan Wang, and Xibo Fan. 2001. "Measuring Education Inequality: Gini Coefficients of Education for 140 Countries, 1960–2000," World Bank Policy Research Working Papers 2525. Washington, DC: World Bank.

———. 2003. "Measuring Education Inequality: Gini Coefficients of Education for 140 Countries, 1960–2000," *Journal of Educational Planning and Administration*, 17, 1 (January): 5–33.

Tökes, Rudolf. 1996. *Hungary's Negotiated Revolution*. Cambridge: Cambridge University Press.

Tomes, Igor. 1991. "Social Reform: A Cornerstone in Czechoslavakia's New Economic Structure," *International Labour Review* 130, 2: 191–98.

Tomka, Béla. 2004. *Welfare in East and West: Hungarian Social Security Policy in an International Comparison 1918–1990*. Berlin: Akademie Verlag.

———. 2005. "Politics of Institutionalized Volatility: Some Lessons From East Central European Welfare Reforms." Presented at Conference on Fighting Poverty and Reforming Social Security: What Can Post-Soviet States Learn from the New Democracies of Central Europe? Woodrow Wilson International Center for Scholars, Washington, DC (June 10).

Tornell, Aaron, and Philip R. Lane. 1999. "The Voracity Effect," *American Economic Review* 89, 1 (March): 22–46.

Towse, Adrian, Anne Mills, and Viroj Tangcharoensathien. 2004. "Learning From Thailand's Health Reforms." *BMJ* 328, 10 (January): 103–5.

Tragakes, Ellie, ed. 2003. *Health Care Systems in Transition: Bulgaria*. Copenhagen: European Observatory on Health Care Systems.

Tremewan, Christopher. 1994. *The Political Economy of Social Control in Singapore*. New York: Palgrave Macmillan.

Troxel, Luan. 1995. "Bulgaria," in Zoltan Barany and Ivan Volgyes, eds. *The Legacy of Communism in Eastern Europe*. Baltimore, MD: Johns Hopkins University Press.

Tsebelis, George. 2002. *Veto Players: How Political Institutions Work*. Princeton, NJ: Princeton University Press.

Turnock, David. 1986. *The Romanian Economy in the Twentieth Century*. London: Croom Helm.

United Nations. 2001. *World Population Prospects: The 2000 Revision*. New York: Population Division, Department of Economic and Social Affairs.

United Nations Economic Commission for Europe. 1967. *Incomes in Postwar Europe: A Study of Policies, Growth and Distribution*. Geneva: Economic Commission for Europe.

United Nations Educational, Cultural and Scientific Organization (UNESCO). 2000. *Education for All: The Year 2000 Assessment Thailand Country Report*, http://www2.unesco.org/wef/countryreports/thailand/contents.html.

————. 2002. World Education Institute Programme, "Estimates and Projections of Adult Illiteracy for Population aged 15–24 years old," http://www.uis.unesco.org /ev .php?URL_ID=5294&URL_DO=DC>http://www.uis.unesco.org/ev.php?URL_ID =5294&URL_DO=DC, accessed September 28, 2006.

United States Census Bureau. *International Data Base*, http://www.census.gov/ipc/ www/idbnew.html, accessed May 27, 2007.

University of Texas Inequality Project. 2006. "Estimated Household Inequality Data Set" and "UTIP-UNIDO Data Set," http://utip.gov.utexas.edu/data.html, accessed May 27, 2007.

Valenzuela, Arturo. 1978. *The Breakdown of Democratic Regimes: Chile.* Baltimore, MD: Johns Hopkins University Press.

Valev, Neven. 2004. "No Pain, No Gain: Market Reform, Unemployment and Politics in Bulgaria," *Journal of Comparative Economics* 32, 3 (September): 409–25.

Vanhuysse, Pieter. 2006. *Divide and Pacify: Strategic Social Policies and Political Protests in Post-Communist Democracies.* Budapest: Central European University Press.

Vasile, Valentina, and Akira Uegaki. 2003. "Romanian Pension Reform in Comparative Persepctive Part I: The Reform of the Pension System in Romania: Expectations and Reality," Paper prepared for the PIE International Workshop on Pension Reform in Transition Economies, Hitotsubashi University (February 22).

Vasile, Valentina, and Gheorge Zaman. 2005. "Romania's Pension System Between Present Restrictions and Future Exigencies." Romanian Academy, Institute of National Economy PIE, Discussion Paper Series (March).

Večernik, Jiři. 1991. "Earnings Distribution in Czechoslovakia: Intertemporal Changes and International Comparison," *European Sociological Review* 7, 3 (December): 237–52.

————. 2004. "Czech Social Reform / Non-Reform: Routes, Actors and Problems." William Davidson Institute Working Paper No. 651, University of Michigan, http:// wdi.umich.edu/Publications/WorkingPapers/WP601to700, accessed May 2, 2006.

Verma, A., T. A. Kochan, and R. D. Lansbury 1995. *Employment Relations in the Growing Asian Economies*, New York: Routledge.

Villegas, Bernardo. 1987. "The Philippines in 1986: Democratic Reconstruction in the Post-Marcos Era," *Asian Survey* 27, 2 (February): 194–205.

Vinocur, Pablo, and Leopoldo Halperin. 2004. "Pobreza y políticas sociales en Argentina de los años noventa." CEPAL, Division de Desarrollo Social, Serie politicas socials, No. 85. LC/L 12107-P.

Voravidh, Charonenloet. 2000. "Industrialization and Labour Fragmentation in Thailand," in Kwong-Leung Tang, ed. *Social Development in Asia*, 99–125. Dordrecht: Kluwer Academic Publishers.

————. 2002. "Thailand and Industrial Restructuring: Government Policies and the Labor Situation since 1997," *Journal of Comparative Asian Development* 1, 2 (Fall): 245–61.

Viroj Tangcharoensathien, Anuwat Supachutikul, Jongkol Lertiendumrong. 1999. "The Social Security Scheme in Thailand: What Lessons Can Be Drawn?" *Social Science and Medicine* 48, 7 (April): 913–23.

Vreeland, James Raymond. 2003. *The IMF and Economic Development*. New York: Cambridge University Press.

Wade. Robert. 1990. *Governing the Market: Economic Theory and the Role of Government in East Asian Industrialization*. Princeton, NJ: Princeton University Press.

Wagener, Hans-Jürgen. 2002. "The Welfare State in Transition Economies and Accession to the EU," *West European Politics* 25, 2 (April): 152–74.

Wagstaff, Adam. 2005. "Health Systems in East Asia: What Can Developing Countries Learn from Japan and the Asian Tigers," World Bank Policy Research Working Paper No. 3790 (December). Washington, DC: World Bank.

Wallerstein, Michael, and Karl Ove Moene. 2003. "Earnings Inequality and Welfare Spending: A Disaggregated Analysis," *World Politics* 55, 4 (July): 485–516.

Wang, Bee-Lan Chan. 1987. "Educational Reforms for National Integration: The West Malaysian Experience," *Comparative Education Review*, 22, 3 (October): 464–79.

Warr, Peter, ed. 1994. *The Thai Economy in Transition*. New York: Cambridge University Press.

Warr, Peter, and Isra Sarntisart. 2004. *Poverty Targeting in Thailand*. Tokyo: Asian Development Bank Institute.

Watts, Ronald L. 1999. *Comparing Federal Systems*. Montreal: McGill-Queen's University Press.

Weede, Erik. 1993. "The Impact of Democracy or Repressiveness on the Quality of Life, Income Distribution, and Economic Growth Rates," *International Sociology* 8:177–95.

Weyland, Kurt. 1996. *Democracy without Equity: The Failure of Reform in Brazil*. Pittsburgh, PA: University of Pittsburgh Press.

———. 1998. "Swallowing the Bitter Pill: Sources of Popular Support for Neoliberal Reform in Latin America," *Comparative Political Studies* 31, 5 (October): 539–68.

———. 2002. *The Politics of Market Reform in Fragile Democracies: Argentina, Brazil, Peru, and Venezuela*. Princeton, NJ: Princeton University Press.

———, ed. 2004. *Learning from Foreign Models in Latin American Policy Reform*. Washington, DC: Woodrow Wilson Center; Baltimore, MD: Johns Hopkins University Press.

White, Stephen. 1986. "Economic Performance and Communist Legitimacy," *World Politics* 38, 3 (April): 462–82.

Wibbels, Erik. 2005. *Federalism and the Market: Intergovernmental Conflict and Economic Reform in the Developing World*. New York: Cambridge University Press.

———. 2006. "Dependency Revisited: International Markets, Business Cycles, and Social Spending in the Developing World," *International Organization* 60, 2 (Spring): 433–68.

Wibbels, Erik, and Moisés Arce. 2003. "Globalization, Taxation, and Burden-Shifting in Latin America." *International Organization* 57, 1 (Winter): 111–36.

Wickrama, K.A.S., and C. S. Mulford. 1996. "Political Democracy, Economic Development, Disarticulation, and Social Well-being in Developing Countries," *Sociological Quarterly* 37, 3 (June): 375–90.

Wilensky, Harold. 1975. *The Welfare State and Equality*. Berkeley: University of California Press.

William Davidson Institute. 1998. "Searching for Optimal Unemployment Policies" in *Transition: The Newsletter About Reforming Economies* 9, 6 (December), http:// siteresources.worldbank.org/INTTRANSITION/Newsletters/20561449/ novdec98.pdf, accessed May 2, 2006.

Williams, Mark Erik. 2002. "Market Reforms, Technocrats and Institutional Innovation," *World Development* 30, 3 (March): 394–412.

Williamson, John, ed. 1990. *Latin American Adjustment: How Much Has Happened?* Washington, DC: Institute for International Economics.

Williamson, John, and Stephan Haggard. 1994. "The Political Conditions for Economic Reform," in John Williamson, ed. *The Political Economy of Policy Reform.* Washington, DC: Institute for International Economics.

Williamson, John B. 1987. "Social Security and Physical Quality of Life in Developing Countries: A Cross-National Analysis," *Social Indicators Research*, 19, 2 (May): 205–27.

Witte, Johanna. 2000. "Education in Thailand after the Crisis: A Balancing Act Between Globalization and National Self-contemplation," *International Journal of Educational Development* 20, 3 (May): 223–45.

Wolchik, Sharon L. 1983. "Regional Inequalities in Czechoslovakia," in Daniel N. Nelson, ed. *Communism and the Politics of Inequalities*, 249–70. Lexington, MA: D.C. Heath and Company.

Wong, Joseph. 2003. "Resisting Reform: The Politics of Health Care in Democratizing Taiwan," *American Asian Review* 21, 2 (Summer): 25–56.

———. 2004. *Healthy Democracies: Welfare Politics in Taiwan and South Korea.* Ithaca, NY: Cornell University Press.

Wong, Soon Teck. 1993. "Education and Human Resource Development," in Linda Low et al., eds. *Challenge and Response: Thirty Years of the Economic Development Board.* Singapore: Times Academic Press.

World Bank. 1993. *The East Asian Miracle.* New York: Oxford University Press.

———. 1994a. *Philippines: Devolution and Health Services, Managing Risks and Opportunities.* Report No. 12343-PH. Washington, DC: World Bank.

———. 1994b. *Averting the Old Age Crisis.* New York: Oxford University Press.

———. 1995. *World Development Report: Workers in an Integrating World.* Washington, DC: World Bank.

———. 1998. *Philippines Social Expenditure Priorities.* Report No. 18562-PH. Washington, DC: World Bank.

———. 1999. *East Asia: Road to Recovery.* Washington, DC: World Bank.

———. 2000. *World Development Report: Attacking Poverty.* New York: Oxford University Press.

———. 2002a. *Thailand: Country Development Partnership: Social Protection.* Report No. 24378. Washington, DC: World Bank.

———. 2002b. *Romania: Local Social Services Delivery Study.* Vol. 1, *Summary Report.* Report No. 23492-RO. Washington, DC: World Bank.

———. 2002c. *Romania: Local Social Services Delivery Study.* Vol. 2, *Main Report.* Report No. 23492-RO. Washington, DC: World Bank.

———. 2003. *Global Development Finance.* Washington, DC: World Bank.

———. 2004a. *World Development Indicators.* Washington, DC: World Bank.

————. 2004b. *World Development Report: Making Services Work for the Poor*. New York: Oxford University Press.

World Bank. 2005. "Database of Political Institutions," http://econ.worldbank .org/WBSITE/EXTERNAL/EXTDEC/EXTRESEARCH/0,,contentMDK:20649465~ pagePK:64214825~piPK:64214943~theSitePK:469382,00.html, accessed May 27, 2007.

————. 2006. Fiscal Decentralization Indicators, http://www1.worldbank.org/ publicsector/decentralization/fiscalindicators.html, accessed November 13, 2006.

————. 2007. "World Development Indicators." Washington, DC: World Bank, http://devdata.worldbank.org/dataonline, accessed June 5, 2007.

World Bank Thailand Office. 1999a. *Thailand Social Monitor 1: Challenge for Social Reform*, (January). Bangkok.

————. 1999b. *Thailand Social Monitor 2: Coping with the Crisis in Education and Health*, (July). Bangkok.

World Health Organization (WHO). *The World Health Report: Report of the Director-General*. Geneva: World Health Organization. Various Issues.

————. 2007. Countries: National Health Accounts, http//www.who.int/countries, accessed November 7, 2007.

Wurfel, David. 1959. "Trade Union Development and Labor Relations Policy in the Philippines," *Industrial and Labor Relations Review* 12, 4 (July): 582–608.

Yager, Joseph A. 1988. *Transforming Agriculture in Taiwan: The Experience of the Joint Commission on Rural Reconstruction*. Ithaca, NY: Cornell University Press.

Yang, Bong-min. 2001. "Health Insurance and the Growth of the Private Health Sector in the Republic of Korea." Washington, DC: World Bank Institute.

Yang, Jae-jin. 2000. "The 1999 Pension Reform and a New Social Contract in South Korea." PhD dissertation, Rutgers University.

————. 2006. "Corporate Unionism and Labor Market Flexibility in South Korea," *Journal of East Asian Studies* 6, 2 (May–August): 205–32.

Yoo, Kil-Sang, Jaeho Keum, Jai-Joon Hur, Byung Hee Lee, Jiyuen Chang. 2002. "Labor Market Trends and the Employment Insurance System in Korea," in Kil-Sang Yoo and Jiyuen Chang, eds. *Active Labor Market Policies and Unemployment Insurance in Selected Countries*. Seoul: Korea Labor Institute.

Young, F. W. 1990. "Do Some Authoritarian Governments Foster Physical Quality of Life?" *Social Indicators Research* 22, 4 (June): 367–84.

Zweifel, Thomas D., and Patricio Navia. 2000. "Democracy, Dictatorship and Infant Mortality," *Journal of Democracy* 11, 2 (April): 99–114.

Index

Abdul-Rahman, Saaidah, 255
Abueva, Ramon, 120
Acción Democrática (Democratic Action Party, Venezuela) (AD), 50, 93, 94, 272, 303
Acción Popular (Peru), 111
Acemoglu, Daron, studies coauthored with Simon Johnson, and James A. Robinson by, 6
Adam, Jan, 70, 71, 148, 156, 159
Adserá, Alícia, study coauthored with Carles Boix by, 64
Afonso, António, study coauthored with Christiane Nickel and Philipp Rother by, 305
Akcja Wyborcza Solidarność (Solidarity Electoral Action, Poland) (AWS), 314
Alesina, Alberto, study coauthored with Edward L. Glaeser by, 39; study coauthored with Edward Glaeser and Bruce Sacerdote by, 38
Alessandri, Arturo, 48
Alfonsín, Raúl, 277
Aliança Renovadora Nacional (National Renewal Alliance Party, Brazil) (ARENA), 101, 102
Alianza Popular Revolucionaria Americana (American Popular Revolutionary Alliance, Peru) (APRA), 49, 96, 106, 111, 113, 115, 267, 268
Allende, Salvador, 50, 60, 90–91, 100, 107
Alonso, Guillermo V., 109
Ames, Barry, 84, 281
Amsden, Alice, 69
Antall, József, 316
Aquino, Corazon, 123, 235–36, 237–39, 242, 261
Argentina, 95, 96, 109, 110, 277–81; Administración Nacional de Seguro de Salud (National Administration for Healthcare) (ANSAL), 280; authoritarianism in, 74, 81, 86, 109; Communist parties in, 95; Convertibility Law of, 277; democracy in, 74, 77, 81, 85, 262, 263; economic crisis in, 20; economic growth in, 187; economy of, 192, 262, 264, 265, 269, 276–81, 283, 289, 291, 299; education in, 110, 169, 170, 271, 280, 281, 299, 300; fiscal constraints in, 192, 277; franchise in, 111, 112; health-care spending in, 212, 213, 387; health insurance in, 96, 109; health system in, 32, 33, 96, 168, 169, 279–81, 291, 299, 300; import-substitution industrialization in, 62, 95, 278; labor in, 48, 95, 189, 190, 217, 278–81; left (political) in, 303; military in, 48, 95, 109–10; and partisanship, 361; pensions in, 30, 31, 110, 209, 277–79, 299, 300; policy and political realignments in, 48, 60; policy developments in 1945–80 period in, 79, 80–86, 89, 95–96, 107, 109–10; policy developments in 1980–2005 period in, 277–81, 299, 300; political parties in, 303; populism in, 195–96; poverty in, 280–81; protectionism in, 63; semidemocracy in, 48, 74, 81, 85, 95; social insurance in, 95, 140; social-security spending in, 29; technocrats in, 278, 279; Trabajar program in, 280; unions in, 95, 96, 199, 278–80, 361; urban sector in, 95; welfare reform in, 219
Arretche, Marta, 284, 285
Arvone, Robert R, 98
Asher, Mukul, 243, 244; study coauthored with Amarendu Nandy by, 245
Asian financial crisis of 1997–98, 11, 20, 224, 228, 236, 242, 248–56
Aspalter, Christian, 227–28, 231
Atinc, Tamar Manuelyan, 249
Atkinson, Anthony, study coauthored with John Micklewright by, 161
authoritarianism: in Argentina, 74, 81, 86, 109; in Brazil, 74, 77, 81, 86; in Chile, 74, 81, 87; coding of, 73; in Colombia, 74, 81, 87, 105; competitive vs. hard, 76, 79; in East Asia, 10, 16, 52, 56, 57, 75, 115–17, 129, 142, 354, 357; in Eastern Europe, 16, 56–58, 76, 143, 175; effects of, 15–16; in Korea, 52,